ELEVENTH EDITION

CONGRESS
RECONSIDERED

SAGE was founded in 1965 by Sara Miller McCune to support the dissemination of usable knowledge by publishing innovative and high-quality research and teaching content. Today, we publish over 900 journals, including those of more than 400 learned societies, more than 800 new books per year, and a growing range of library products including archives, data, case studies, reports, and video. SAGE remains majority-owned by our founder, and after Sara's lifetime will become owned by a charitable trust that secures our continued independence.

Los Angeles | London | New Delhi | Singapore | Washington DC | Melbourne

ELEVENTH EDITION

CONGRESS
RECONSIDERED

Lawrence C. Dodd
University of Florida

Bruce I. Oppenheimer
Vanderbilt University

EDITORS

FOR INFORMATION:

CQ Press
An Imprint of SAGE Publications, Inc.
2455 Teller Road
Thousand Oaks, California 91320
E-mail: order@sagepub.com

SAGE Publications Ltd.
1 Oliver's Yard
55 City Road
London, EC1Y 1SP
United Kingdom

SAGE Publications India Pvt. Ltd.
B 1/I 1 Mohan Cooperative Industrial Area
Mathura Road, New Delhi 110 044
India

SAGE Publications Asia-Pacific Pte. Ltd.
3 Church Street
#10-04 Samsung Hub
Singapore 049483

Senior Acquisitions Editor: Michael Kerns
Developmental Editor: Nancy Matuszak
Editorial Assistant: Zachary Hoskins
Production Editor: David C. Felts
Copy Editor: Jared Leighton
Typesetter: Hurix Systems Pvt. Ltd.
Proofreaders: Christine Dahlin, Bonnie Moore
Indexer: Beth Nauman-Montana
Cover Designer: Anupama Krishnan
Marketing Manager: Amy Whitaker

Copyright © 2017 by CQ Press, an Imprint of SAGE Publications, Inc. CQ Press is a registered trademark of Congressional Quarterly Inc.

All rights reserved. No part of this book may be reproduced or utilized in any form or by any means, electronic or mechanical, including photocopying, recording, or by any information storage and retrieval system, without permission in writing from the publisher.

Printed in the United States of America

Library of Congress Cataloging-in-Publication Data

Names: Dodd, Lawrence C., 1946– editor. | Oppenheimer, Bruce Ian. editor.

Title: Congress reconsidered / edited by Lawrence C. Dodd, University of Florida ; Bruce I. Oppenheimer, Vanderbilt University.

Description: Eleventh edition. | Thousand Oaks, California : CQ Press, 2017. | Includes bibliographical references and index.

Identifiers: LCCN 2016029296 | ISBN 978-1-5063-2878-2 (pbk. : alk. paper)

Subjects: LCSH: United States. Congress.

Classification: LCC JK1021 .C558 2017 | DDC 328.73—dc23 LC record available at https://lccn.loc.gov/2016029296

This book is printed on acid-free paper.

16 17 18 19 20 10 9 8 7 6 5 4 3 2 1

Contents

✧ ✧ ✧

Tables and Figures   vii
Preface   xiii
Contributors   xix

Part I Patterns and Dynamics of Congressional Change   1

1. The New World of U.S. Senators   1
   Barbara Sinclair

2. Lending and Reclaiming Power: Majority Leadership in the House Since the 1950s   29
   John H. Aldrich and David W. Rohde

Part II Elections, Constituencies, and Representation   61

3. Voters, Candidates, and Issues in Congressional Elections   61
   Robert S. Erikson and Gerald C. Wright

4. Partisanship, Money, and Competition: Elections and the Transformation of Congress Since the 1970s   89
   Gary C. Jacobson

5. Constituency Representation in Congress: In General and in Periods of Higher and Lower Partisan Polarization   119
   Soren Jordan, Kim Quaile Hill, and Patricia A. Hurley

6. Black–Latino Relations in Congress: Examining Inter–Minority Group Relations in Institutional Context   139
   Rodney E. Hero and Robert R. Preuhs

Part III Parties and the Politics of Polarization   163

7. The Dynamics of Party Government in Congress   163
   Steven S. Smith and Gerald Gamm

8. Legislating in Polarized Times   189
   Sarah Binder

9. Moderate Polarization and Policy Productivity in Congress: From Harding to Obama   207
Lawrence C. Dodd and Scot Schraufnagel

10. An Examination of Congressional Efforts to Repeal the Affordable Care Act   237
Jordan Ragusa

Part IV   Legislators, Committees, and the Policy Process   259

11. Legislative Effectiveness and Problem Solving in the U.S. House of Representatives   259
Craig Volden and Alan E. Wiseman

12. The Endurance of Nonpartisanship in House Appropriations   285
Peter C. Hanson

13. Filibusters and Majority Rule in the Modern Senate   311
Gregory Koger

14. ANWR and CAFE: Frustrating Energy Production and Conservation Initiatives in Congress Over Three Decades   331
Bruce I. Oppenheimer

Part V   Congress and Public Policy in a Separation-of-Powers System   357

15. The Balance of Power Between the Congress and the President: Issues and Dilemmas   357
Joseph Cooper

16. Is Advice and Consent Broken? The Contentious Politics of Confirming Federal Judges and Justices   399
Sarah Binder and Forrest Maltzman

17. Congress, Public Opinion, and the Political Costs of Waging War   421
Douglas L. Kriner

18. Congress in the Age of Trump: The 2016 National Elections and Their Aftermath   451
Lawrence C. Dodd and Bruce I. Oppenheimer

Suggested Readings   479
Index   499

Tables and Figures

✧ ✧ ✧

Tables

1-1	Increase in Filibusters and Cloture Votes, 1951–2014	8
1-2	Increasing Frequency of Extended-Debate–Related Problems on Major Measures	11
1-3	Where Major Measures Failed	23
3-1	Regression of 2014 Democratic House Vote on 2012–2013 Incumbent Roll Call Ideology, 2012 District Presidential Vote, and 2014 Candidate Spending	77
3-2	Voters' Perceptions of the Ideology of Their Representative	81
4-1	Candidate Effects in U.S. House Elections, 1972–2014 (by Decade)	109
6-1	Shared Salience and Congruence on Votes on NAACP and NHLA Scorecards, 105th–108th and 113th Congresses	143
6-2	Predicted Effects of Black and Latino Representation and Population on NAACP and NHLA Scorecards	149
6-3	Summary of Expected Intergroup Relationships	156
9-1	The Bivariate Relationship Between Moderate Polarization and Policy Productivity	214
9-2	Variables Associated With Topical Legislation Passed: Congress as the Unit of Analysis, 67th Through 113th Congresses	222
9-3	Variables Associated With Topical Legislation Passed: *Congressional Digest* Articles as the Unit of Analysis, 1921–2014	223
9-4a	Polarization, Government Type, and the Proportional Productivity of Depolarized Congresses, 1921–2015	227

viii Tables and Figures

9-4b	Polarization, Government Type, and the Proportional Productivity of Polarized Congresses, 1921–2015	227
10-1	Full and Partial ACA Repeal Votes in the 112th and 113th Congresses	245
10-2	Predicting ACA Repeal Votes and Bill Sponsorship	251
11-1	Tests of Temporal-Effects Hypotheses	267
11-2	Tests of Expertise Hypotheses	271
12-1	Closed Rule and Party Polarization Correlation Matrix	295
12-2	Amendments Filed and Allowed to FY 2010 Appropriations Bills	297
12-3	Legislative History of FY 2015 Appropriations Bills	303
17-1	Costly Congressional Criticism and Change in Support for the Afghan War	439
18-1	Victory Margins of Presidential and Senate Candidates by State	459
18-2	Results of Toss-Up Senate Contests, 2004-2016	460
18-3	Results of Toss-Up House Contests, 2008-2016	461
18-4	Distribution of House Seats by Region and Party	467
18-5	Distribution of Senate Seats by Region and Party	468

Figures

3-1	Democratic House Seats and Vote Share, 1946–2014	63
3-2	Partisanship and House Seat Shares, 1946–2014	64
3-3	The Decreased Incumbency Advantage in the House, 2000 and 2014	72
3-4	Representatives' Roll Call Ideology, 2013–2014, by District Presidential Vote in 2014	78
3-5	Ideology and the House Vote, 2014	80
4-1	Ideology and Party Identification of Voters, 1972–2012	91
4-2	Party Loyalty and Ticket Splitting, 1952–2012	92
4-3	Ticket Splitting by Republican Presidential Voters in the Southern Congressional Elections, 1952–2012	93

4-4	Correlations Between District-Level Presidential and House Vote, 1952–2014	94
4-5	Correlations Between District-Level Presidential and Senate Vote, 1952–2014	95
4-6	The Polarization of U.S. House Constituencies, 1952–2014	96
4-7	The Polarization of U.S. Senate Constituencies, 1952–2014	96
4-8	Ideological Divergence of Electoral Constituencies of Parties in the House and Senate, 1972–2012	97
4-9	Average Campaign Spending in House Elections, 1972–2014	98
4-10	Campaign Spending by Incumbents and Challengers in Close and Not-Close Races, 1972–2010	99
4-11	House and Senate Members' Contributions to Other Candidates' Campaigns, 1990–2012	101
4-12	House and Senate Members' Contributions to Congressional Campaign Committees, 1990–2012	101
4-13	Party Spending in House and Senate Elections, 1990–2014	102
4-14	Independent Spending in House and Senate Races, 1978–2014	104
4-15	Competitive States and Districts, Measured by the Adjusted Presidential Vote, 1972–2012	106
4-16	The Competitiveness of House Elections, 1972–2014	107
4-17	Winning Against the Partisan Grain, 1972–2014	110
5-1	Models of Representation Predicted to Arise Under Varying Conditions of Party Polarization and Issue Complexity	123
5-2	Polarization by Chamber	129
5-3	House Opposition by Issue and Decade	133
6-1	Vote Counts for NAACP and NHLA Scorecards, by Topic	142
6-2	Mean NAACP and NHLA U.S. House of Representatives Scorecard Ratings, by Party and Black and Latino Representative	146

6-3	Estimated Coefficients (90% and 95% CIs) for Pooled Models of NAACP and NHLA Support Scores for Democratic Members of Congress	151
7-1	House Seats, by Party, 1877–2014	168
7-2	Senate Seats, by Party, 1877–2014	168
7-3	House Liberal-to-Conservative Scores, Party Medians, 1877–2014	169
7-4	Senate Liberal-to-Conservative Scores, Party Medians, 1877–2014	170
7-5	Appropriations for Senate Party Offices, 1946–2015 (in Millions of Dollars)	182
8-1a	Total Number of Legislative Issues on the Agenda, 1947–2014	195
8-1b	Number of Salient Legislative Issues on the Agenda, 1947–2014	196
8-2	Frequency of Legislative Deadlock, 1947–2014	197
8-3	Number of Conference Reports Considered in Both Chambers, 1947–2014	200
9-1	Percentage of Topical Legislation Passed, by Congress, 67th Through 113th	212
9-2	Polarization by Congress: Two-Chamber Average	213
11-1	Theoretical Expectations	265
11-2	Average Legislative Effectiveness Scores, by Seniority and Status	266
11-3	Average Legislative Effectiveness Scores, by Expertise in Role	269
11-4	Average Legislative Effectiveness Scores, by Expertise in Role, by Party	279
12-1	Majority and Minority Support for Appropriations Bills: U.S. House of Representatives, 1979–2014	291
12-2	Proportion of Minority Party Voting Yes: U.S. House of Representatives, 1979–2014	292
12-3	Open Rules for Legislation: U.S. House of Representatives, 104th–113th Congresses, 1995–2014	294

12-4	Roll Call Votes on Amendments to Appropriations Legislation: U.S. House of Representatives, 1981–2012	296
12-5	Permitted Amendments to Appropriations Bills: U.S. House of Representatives, 2009	298
12-6	Debate on Appropriations Bills: U.S. House of Representatives, 1995–2014	300
13-1	Percentage of Votes Held Tuesday Through Thursday, 1933–2013	315
13-2	Filibusters and Cloture Votes in the Senate, 1917–2015	316
13-3	Party Unity in the Senate, 1961–2014	318
13-4	Cloture Votes on Nominations, 2001–2014	324
16-1	Confirmation Rates for Judicial Nominations, 1947–2014	403
16-2	Length of Confirmation Process for Successful Judicial Nominees, 1947–2014	404
16-3	Confirmation Rates by Circuit, 1993–2012	405
16-4	Senators' Votes for Confirmed Nominees, 2013–2014	416
17-1	Effect of Congressional Position Taking on Support for Withdrawal Within One Year	429
17-2	Public Support for the War in Afghanistan, 2001–2010	433
17-3	Congressional War Cues Reported on the *NBC Nightly News* or in the *New York Times*	435
17-4	Congressional Rhetoric and Support for the Afghan War	436
17-5	American Casualties in Afghanistan, 2006–2010	438
18-1	Women House Members, 1982-2016	462
18-2	Women Senators, 1982-2016	463
18-3	States with Senators of Opposite Parties after Presidential Elections, 1980-2016	466

Preface

✧ ✧ ✧

In writing prefaces for the previous ten editions of *Congress Reconsidered*, several objectives have been common to most, if not all, of them. We have emphasized the continuing change of political institutions in response to internal demands and external conditions; stressed how much our contributors are responsible for the quality and the long-term success of the book; outlined how we've organized the chapters in each edition and the coverage the essays provide; and acknowledged a personal and professional debt to colleagues, friends, and family who continue to be supportive of our endeavors. We are most pleased to have the opportunity to do all of those things again. But first, let us make a new observation or two.

We recently realized that *Congress Reconsidered* has been in print long enough that the youngest users of the first edition, undergraduates in Congress classes in 1977, are now approaching or are already in their early sixties. Through its many editions, the book has been used by a diverse array of generations, including baby boomers, Gen X, Gen Y, and Millennials and by undergraduates, graduate students, teachers, and researchers. A book that we thought would only have a single edition, assuming that we were fortunate enough to get it published, has now endured for eleven editions and more than four decades.

Some things have persisted. We planned the book to be accessible to a range of potential users and to provide both an up-to-date perspective and a historical context. And our contributors in each edition have stretched across scholarly generations as well. A couple of the contributors to the eleventh edition, Dave Rohde and Joe Cooper, have been generous enough to have written articles in every edition. Yet this edition, like the others, also includes junior scholars and other first-time contributors. Yes, we were once among the younger contributors, as well.

Like previous editions, about two-thirds of the chapters are entirely new to this edition, and the other third are significant revisions of material from the past edition. This is decidedly *not* a barely touched rehash of the previous edition. With the exception of a couple of chapters in the initial edition, which were reprints of previously published scholarship, our authors have always written the articles specifically for *Congress Reconsidered*. One more consistency is the Capitol on the cover (the case for all but the first edition). This time, it is appropriately camouflaged with scaffolding while under repair, perhaps symbolically suggesting the institution it houses needs repair as well.

To those who ask us why we are reconsidering Congress yet again, we offer a couple of explanations. The first is that the institution continues to evolve.

As graduate students, we were trained to believe that the "modern Congress" of the post–World War II era was stable and unchanging. Our year as congressional fellows led us to question the wisdom of that axiom. And subsequently, we realized that change was not episodic, but it was instead ongoing. Second, the loyal users of the book have come to expect up-to-date perspectives, data, and analysis from leading congressional scholars. Thankfully, there has continued to be an audience for the book. Each time we prepare a new edition, we are sensitized to how much Congress changes. This is especially true as we look back to the first edition, when the focus was on the decentralizing effects of subcommittee government, the weakening of committee chairs, the then new budget process, and a House and Senate in which Democratic majorities seemed permanent.

Even since the tenth edition, a number of major changes have occurred. The schism within the Republican Party in both chambers has deepened, with a small faction of extreme conservatives able to hamstring the party leadership, resulting in the rare mid-Congress resignation of a Speaker and uncertainty in finding someone willing to take the once-prized position. In the Senate, Democrats in the 113th Congress used a parliamentary maneuver to lower the cloture requirements on nominations, except those of Supreme Court justices, from three-fifths of the membership to a simple majority. It remains unclear whether a Republican majority will adhere to this parliamentary precedent or whether there will be further inroads made in the application of cloture. And most measures of legislative productivity continue to decline in an era of polarized parties and divided party government.

The quality of *Congress Reconsidered* has been maintained by the outstanding group of contributors to each volume and never more so than this year, which includes both a continuing array of established contributors and also participation by seven authors new to the volume: Rodney Hero, Kim Quaile Hill, Patricia Hurley, Soren Jordan, Robert Preuhs, Jordan Ragusa, and Peter Hanson. All have provided first-rate chapters that are both cutting edge in terms of timeliness, substance, and centrality to the study of Congress and in terms of accessibility to the book's readership. In addition, the contributors throughout the eleven editions have been unfailingly cooperative, especially when it has come to meeting both reasonable and unreasonable deadlines and doing last-minute updates as events warrant. The book has provided us an opportunity to interact on a regular basis with professional colleagues who are not just excellent scholars but are also among the nicest people that one can find in academia. Accordingly, it saddened us greatly to learn that our friend and congressional studies colleague, Barbara Sinclair, passed away in March. We knew Barbara for around forty years, and her Senate chapter in this edition will be her tenth contribution to *Congress Reconsidered*. Barbara always delivered her chapter early. So we weren't surprised when she sent it to us in December. We are most pleased and feel very fortunate to have her chapter lead off this volume. Barbara also managed to complete a fifth edition to her outstanding book, *Unorthodox Lawmaking*. She was a consummate professional, a mentor to new generations of women in the profession, and a dear person.

As noted above, Part I of the book, "Patterns and Dynamics of Congressional Change," opens with Barbara Sinclair's essay on the Senate and contains a companion overview chapter on the House by John Aldrich and David Rohde. Combined, they highlight contemporary patterns of institutional change in Congress. Sinclair charts the Senate's post–World War II transformation from a courtly "gentleman's club" into today's chamber of partisan warriors. Aldrich and Rohde document the ways that polarization in the House of Representatives from the 1980s onward initially gave rise to strong majority party leadership, only to foster conditions in recent years that upend leaders' effectiveness.

Part II, "Elections, Constituencies, and Representation," deals with electoral strategies, campaign finance, voter decision making, and constituent representation. Robert Erikson and Gerald Wright open by demonstrating that elections matter in contemporary America, with House and Senate electorates choosing representatives who faithfully represent their ideological orientations. Gary Jacobson argues that these ideological outcomes owe not just to the actions of voters but to the coevolution of a range of factors, including the strategic calculations of candidates and parties and the nation's campaign finance system, which together foster polarized ideological representation. Soren Jordan, Kim Hill, and Patricia Hurley caution scholars and citizens alike to remember that not all policy conflicts fit a left–right ideological continuum so that legislators may engage in different kinds of constituent representation as they confront different types of policy issues, even when polarized ideological conflict predominates. Finally, Rodney Hero and Robert Preuhs demonstrate that African American and Latino legislators cooperate with one another in Congress, uniting to pursue policies that aid both African American and Latino constituencies, despite opposing one another at local and state levels in conflicts over scarce policy resources. Hero and Preuhs remind us that patterns of group representation can differ greatly within our federal system, as the focus shifts from subnational to national policy making.

The four chapters that compose Part III, "Parties and the Politics of Polarization," provide historical perspective on the evolution of parties in Congress and examine the effect that party polarization has on congressional policy making. Steve Smith and Gerald Gamm open the section by contrasting the development of House and Senate party leadership from the nineteenth century to the present era of polarized politics. Sarah Binder presents a newly updated version of the empirical analysis presented in her 2003 book, *Stalemate*. In doing so, she highlights the continuing difficulties that polarized politics introduces into contemporary policy making, reviews theoretical perspectives that help explain the ongoing stalemate, and assesses conditions that could limit or magnify the policy-making difficulties confronting Congress. Lawrence Dodd and Scot Schraufnagel document the extent to which moderate polarization has aided policy productivity across the forty-seven Congresses since 1921, whereas both low and high polarization undermined it. They also highlight the distinctive role that quasi-divided governments have played in magnifying deadlock in the current polarized era. Finally, Jordan Ragusa looks beyond issues of policy productivity and examines the extent to which polarized partisanship can foster efforts to repeal policy, as documented by his analysis of the postenactment struggle over the Affordable Care Act.

Part IV, "Legislators, Committees, and the Policy Process," focuses on the role that members of Congress, the standing committees, institutional procedures, and historical context play in policy making. Craig Volden and Alan Wiseman open with a study of legislators' effectiveness as lawmakers, showing that the expertise and political acumen of committee and subcommittee chairs aids the enactment of legislation, rather than it coming solely as a result of the "must-pass" nature of legislation. Peter Hanson looks at policy making in the House Appropriations Committee from 1979 to 2014 and finds that institutionalized norms and decision contexts also matter, with the HAC maintaining comparable levels of productivity in key policy areas despite the less experienced committee leadership generated by the Republican revolution. Gregory Koger traces the development of the most famous institutional procedure in Congress, the Senate filibuster; assesses its contemporary role in policy making; highlights recent developments designed to moderate its use; and considers the possibility that the Senate could end it. Finally, Bruce Oppenheimer examines energy policy making over the past thirty years, focused on CAFE and ANWR. He highlights the difficulties posed for both conservative and liberal policy agendas by the move from committee to party government; the proliferation of filibuster threats; undermined efforts at compromises; and the prevalence of narrow, unstable party majorities.

Part V, "Congress and Public Policy in a Separation-of-Powers System," concludes the book by pointing to the ways in which Congress and its policy actions are shaped by the American constitutional system. Joseph Cooper provides a rich historical perspective on the evolving roles of Congress, with special attention to the ongoing influence Madisonian institutional arrangements have on the operation of Congress; the emergence of a powerful presidency contending with Congress for policy dominance; and the vital influence citizens have on Congress through their general assessments of it and vote choices in congressional elections. Sarah Binder and Forrest Maltzman focus on the Senate's responsibility to provide advice and consent on presidential nomination of federal judges and justices. They argue that the extreme partisan and ideological conflict in national politics is crippling the Senate's capacity to adequately fulfill this role. Douglas Kriner examines the ways in which Congress asserts influence on war making. He concludes that Congress's capacity to constrain presidents today comes more through political than constitutional means, with its members most effective when they use public debate to challenge presidential action and rally the public against him. Finally, we conclude the book with an assessment of the ways in which the 2016 House and Senate elections, together with the election of the new president, are likely to shape the ongoing evolution of Congress and its role in American politics.

The folks at CQ Press and more recently at Sage have once again made producing another edition of *Congress Reconsidered* a joy. How many other publishers could allow us to write a postelection chapter (which we complete before the Thanksgiving turkey goes in the oven) and manage to have books available before the ball drops at Times Square to ring in the New Year. For this edition, we are especially appreciative of the work by Michael Kerns, Nancy Matuszak, Zachary Hoskins, David Felts, Anupama Krishnan, and Jared Leighton, as well as the opportunity to continue our long-term working relationship with Charisse Kiino.

We also want to acknowledge professional colleagues at our respective institutions who contribute directly and indirectly in providing supportive intellectual environments in which we are able to prosper. Larry continues to appreciate the opportunity the University of Florida has given him to participate in building a major doctoral program in political science, deep in the wintertime warmth of the American South, and to benefit from the vibrant intellectual and scholarly milieu provided by department colleagues and graduate students. Yet he also acknowledges that none of this would "work" were it not for joys and diversions provided by his family: Leslie, Cris, Meredith, Andy, and Puk. Bruce is most appreciative of the support of the Department of Political Science at Vanderbilt and his many fine colleagues who provide intellectual stimulation, especially the ever-growing core of colleagues among the American politics faculty at Vanderbilt: Larry Bartels, Josh Clinton, John Geer, Marc Hetherington, Cindy Kam, Dave Lewis, Efren Perez, Ed Rubin, Alan Wiseman, and Hye Young You. Plus, his daughter, Anne, of whom he is justly proud, continues to be a delight, even now as she begins her own career after graduating from college.

Of course, this preface would not be complete if we did not mention the debt we have to one another. We've been friends and professional colleagues since meeting as APSA Congressional Fellows in 1974–1975. As we have noted in the prefaces to previous editions, we are not two peas in the same pod. Outside of our interests in Congress and politics and sharing the same general partisan predispositions, we have different tastes and preferences. Larry still loves country music, even if he two-steps a little slower these days, and Bruce still prefers watching baseball and basketball. Yet we've remained friends for more than four decades. Part of the reason is that we nicely compensate for each other's shortcomings. (Those are too numerous to list here.) A kinder way of putting it is that we bring different strengths to the ongoing project that has been *Congress Reconsidered*. In addition, we treat our differences with tolerance and good humor. Larry knows that Carrie Underwood is married to some hockey player, and Bruce knows that Mike Fisher is married to some country singer. We just don't ask each other to name them. Producing a new edition of *Congress Reconsidered* every four years is an important link in our long friendship. It also gives us reason for hope and optimism about the future of Congress, even when it is under strain. After all, if we've gotten along as well as we have, maybe there's still hope for Democrats and Republicans in Congress.

Contributors

✧ ✧ ✧

About the Editors

Lawrence C. Dodd holds the Manning J. Dauer Eminent Scholar Chair in Political Science at the University of Florida. His books include *Coalitions in Parliamentary Government* (1976), *Congress and the Administrative State* (coauthored with Richard Schott, 1979), *The Dynamics of American Politics* (coedited with Cal Jillson, 1994), *Learning Democracy* (coauthored with Leslie E. Anderson, 2005), and *Thinking About Congress* (2012). His articles have appeared in the *American Political Science Review*, *Journal of Politics*, *Polity*, *Journal of Democracy*, and elsewhere. Dodd has served as a congressional fellow, Hoover national fellow, and Woodrow Wilson Center fellow; president of the Southern and Southwestern Political Science Associations; and chair of the APSA's Legislative Studies Section.

Bruce I. Oppenheimer is professor of political science at Vanderbilt University and director of the Center for the Study of Democratic Institutions. He has been a Brookings fellow in Governmental Studies (1970–1971) and an APSA congressional fellow (1974–1975). He is author of *Oil and the Congressional Process: The Limits of Symbolic Politics* (1974). His book *Sizing Up the Senate: The Unequal Consequences of Equal Representation* (1999), cowritten with Frances Lee, was awarded the Lyndon Baines Johnson Foundation's D. B. Hardeman Prize for the best book on Congress. He is also the editor of *U.S. Senate Exceptionalism* (2002) and the author of numerous articles. His recent research focuses on Congress and energy policy and on variation in competition in open-seat House primaries.

About the Contributors

John H. Aldrich earned his PhD at the University of Rochester. He is Pfizer-Pratt University Professor of Political Science, Duke University. He specializes in American and comparative politics and behavior, formal theory, and methodology. Books he has authored or coauthored include *Why Parties*, *Before the Convention*, *Linear Probability, Logit and Probit Models*, *Interdisciplinarity*, and a series of books on elections, the most recent of which is *Change and Continuity in the 2012 Elections*. His articles have appeared in the *American Political Science Review*, *American Journal of Political Science*, *Journal of Politics*, *Public Choice*, and other journals and edited volumes. He has served as coeditor of the *American*

Journal of Political Science. He is past president of the Southern Political Science Association, the Midwest Political Science Association, and the American Political Science Association. He has been a Guggenheim fellow and is a fellow of the American Academy of Arts and Sciences. He is finishing a book (with John Griffin) on the history of Southern politics since Andrew Jackson.

Sarah Binder is a professor of political science at George Washington University and a senior fellow at the Brookings Institution. She has written *Minority Rights, Majority Rule: Partisanship and the Development of Congress* (1997) and *Stalemate: Causes and Consequences of Legislative Gridlock* (2003) and has coauthored *Politics or Principle? Filibustering in the United States Senate* (1997) and *Advice and Dissent: The Struggle to Shape the Federal Judiciary* (2009). Her work has also appeared in the *American Political Science Review* and elsewhere. She was elected to the American Academy of Arts and Sciences in 2015.

Joseph Cooper is an Academy Professor of Political Science at Johns Hopkins University (retired). He is the author of *The Origins of the Standing Committees in the House of Representatives* (1970), *Congress and Its Committees* (1988), and *The Previous Question: Its Status as a Precedent for Cloture* (1962), as well as several edited works, including *The House at Work* (1981) and *Congress and the Decline of Public Trust* (1999). His work has appeared in articles in the *American Political Science Review*, *Journal of Politics*, *Political Science Quarterly*, *Legislative Studies Quarterly*, and *Congress and the Presidency*. He has served as provost at Johns Hopkins, dean of social sciences at Rice University, and staff director of the U.S. House Commission on Administrative Review (Obey Commission).

Robert S. Erikson is professor of political science at Columbia University. He has coauthored *The Timeline of Presidential Elections* (2012), *The Macro Polity* (2002), *Statehouse Democracy* (1994), and numerous journal articles. He has coauthored nine editions of *American Public Opinion*. Erikson is past editor of the *American Journal of Political Science* and *Political Analysis*.

Gerald Gamm is professor of political science and history at the University of Rochester. He is the author of *The Making of New Deal Democrats: Voting Behavior and Realignment in Boston, 1920–1940* (1989), *Urban Exodus: Why the Jews Left Boston and the Catholics Stayed* (1999), and a forthcoming book with Steven S. Smith on the rise of party leadership in the U.S. Senate. His current research is on Congress, state legislatures, and state party platforms.

Peter C. Hanson is an assistant professor of political science at Grinnell College and the author of *Too Weak to Govern: Majority Party Power and Appropriations in the U.S. Senate* (Cambridge University Press, 2014). He studies the U.S. Congress and is a specialist on the politics of the federal budget. His studies of appropriations have been published by *Political Research Quarterly* and the Brookings Institution. He has been interviewed for PBS *NewsHour*, Colorado Public Radio, the BBC, *Roll Call*, and other media outlets. His work has been featured in the *New York Times*. Hanson received his PhD from the University of California, Berkeley, in 2010 and his AB from Harvard University in 1995. From 1996 to 2002, he served on the staff of Senate Democratic leader Tom Daschle, D-S.Dak. His areas of focus were appropriations and environmental policy.

Rodney E. Hero is the Haas Chair in Diversity & Democracy and professor in the Department of Political Science at the University of California, Berkeley. His research focuses on American politics and democracy, with special attention to Latino politics, racial and ethnic politics, state and urban politics, and federalism. His books include *Latinos and the U.S. Political System: Two-Tiered Pluralism*, which received the American Political Science Association's 1993 Ralph J. Bunche Award; *Faces of Inequality: Social Diversity in American Politics*, which received the APSA's Woodrow Wilson Award in 1999; and *Racial Diversity and Social Capital: Equality and Community in America* (2007). His coauthored books include *Black–Latino Relations in U.S. National Politics*, with Robert Preuhs. Hero has served as president of the American Political Science Association (2014–2015), president of the Midwest Political Science Association (2007–2008), and president of the Western Political Science Association (1999–2000). He previously held faculty positions as Packey J. Dee Professor of American Democracy in the Department of Political Science at the University of Notre Dame (2000–2010) and at the University of Colorado at Boulder (1989–2000).

Kim Quaile Hill is the Cullen-McFadden Professor of Political Science and a Presidential Professor of Teaching Excellence at Texas A&M University. He is the author, coauthor, or editor of numerous scholarly articles, books of original research, and textbooks. His most recent publication is *Representation in Congress: A Unified Theory* (Cambridge University Press, 2015), which is coauthored with Soren Jordan and Patricia A. Hurley. Professor Hill has also served as the editor of the *American Journal of Political Science* and the president of the Southern Political Science Association.

Patricia A. Hurley is a professor of political science and an associate dean in the College of Liberal Arts at Texas A&M University. Her research articles have appeared in the *American Journal of Political Science*, the *Journal of Politics*, *Legislative Studies Quarterly*, and the *American Politics Quarterly* among others. Her most recent publication is *Representation in Congress: A Unified Theory* (Cambridge University Press, 2015), which is coauthored with Kim Quaile Hill and Soren Jordan.

Gary C. Jacobson is Distinguished Professor of Political Science Emeritus at the University of California, San Diego, where he taught from 1979 to 2016. He received his AB from Stanford in 1966 and his PhD from Yale in 1972. He specializes in the study of U.S. elections, parties, interest groups, public opinion, and Congress. He is the author of *Money in Congressional Elections*, *The Politics of Congressional Elections*, and *The Electoral Origins of Divided Government* and coauthor of *Strategy and Choice in Congressional Elections* and *The Logic of American Politics*, as well as more than one hundred research articles. His most recent book is *A Divider, Not a Uniter: George W. Bush and the American People*.

Soren Jordan is an assistant professor in the Department of Political Science at Auburn University. Before assuming that position, he held a postdoctoral research appointment in the Department of Political Science at Texas A&M University. His research has appeared in *The Forum* while his most recent publication is *Representation in Congress: A Unified Theory* (Cambridge University Press, 2015), which is coauthored with Kim Quaile Hill and Patricia A. Hurley.

Gregory Koger is an associate professor of political science at the University of Miami. Koger specializes in legislative politics and political parties. After earning his BA at Willamette University, Koger worked as a legislative assistant in the U.S. House, then earned his PhD from UCLA in 2002. Gregory Koger is the author of *Filibustering: A Political History of Obstruction in the House and Senate* (University of Chicago Press, 2010). *Filibustering* was awarded the 2011 Fenno Prize for the best book on legislative studies. Koger's research on filibustering and the Senate has led to interviews with the *Washington Post* and *Fresh Air With Terry Gross* and testimony before the Senate Rules Committee. Koger has also published research articles on parties, lobbying, and Congress in the *American Journal of Political Science*, the *Journal of Politics*, *Legislative Studies Quarterly*, *American Political Research*, the *British Journal of Political Science*, *PS: Political Science and Politics*, and the *Journal of Theoretical Politics*.

Douglas L. Kriner is associate professor of political science at Boston University. He has written four books, including, most recently, *Investigating the President: Congressional Checks on Presidential Power* (with Eric Schickler) and *The Particularistic President: Executive Branch Politics and Political Inequality* (with Andrew Reeves), which received the 2016 Richard E. Neustadt Award for the best book on the American presidency. *After the Rubicon: Congress, Presidents, and the Politics of Waging War* also received the Lyndon Baines Johnson Foundation's D. B. Hardeman Award for the best book on Congress. His work has also appeared in the *American Political Science Review*, *American Journal of Political Science*, and *Journal of Politics*, among other outlets.

Forrest Maltzman is professor of political science and provost at George Washington University. The institutions of American national government are the focus of his teaching and research. His most recent work focuses on the interplay between the judicial and legislative branches. He is the author of *Competing Principals* (1997) and the coauthor of *The Constrained Court: Law, Politics, and the Decisions Justices Make* (2011), *Advice and Dissent: The Struggle to Shape the Federal Judiciary* (2009), and *The Collegial Game: Building the Law on the U.S. Supreme Court* (2000). His work has also appeared in the *American Political Science Review*, *American Journal of Political Science*, and elsewhere.

Robert R. Preuhs is associate professor of political science at Metropolitan State University of Denver. His scholarly interests revolve around the issues of representation, racial and ethnic politics, state politics, and public policy. Preuhs's research in these areas has appeared in leading scholarly outlets, such as the *American Journal of Political Science* and the *Journal of Politics*, among others. Preuhs is also the coauthor of *Black–Latino Relations in U.S. National Politics* (2013), which was the recipient of the Best Book Award from the Latino Caucus of the American Political Science Association.

Jordan Ragusa is assistant professor of political science at the College of Charleston. He received his PhD from the University of Florida in 2011. His research focuses on congressional organization, political parties, polarization, and roll call behavior. His chapter in this volume is part of a book project that examines when and why Congress repeals landmark laws. His scholarly work also includes research on presidential and congressional elections, political behavior, and political economy.

David W. Rohde is the Ernestine Friedl Professor of Political Science at Duke University and director of the Political Institutions and Public Choice Program. He has researched various aspects of American national politics, including the Congress, the presidency, the Supreme Court, and presidential and congressional elections. He has served as editor of the *American Journal of Political Science* (1988–1990) and chair of the Legislative Studies Section of the American Political Science Association (1991–1993). In 2000, he was elected to membership in the American Academy of Arts and Sciences. Rohde is the author of *Parties and Leaders in the Postreform House* (University of Chicago Press, 1991) and coauthor of a series of books on every national election since 1980, the most recent of which is *Change and Continuity in the 2012 and 2014 Elections* (CQ Press, 2016). In 2010, he received the Samuel Eldersveld Career Achievement Award from the Political Organizations and Parties Section of the American Political Science Association.

Scot Schraufnagel is the chair of the Department of Political Science at Northern Illinois University. He studies Congress, political parties, and elections worldwide. He has a broad interest in institutional effectiveness and policy making, with a particular academic focus on promoting a civil, representative, and effective legislative process in the United States. His research has appeared in the *American Journal of Political Science*, *Publius: The Journal of Federalism*, *American Politics Research*, and other notable outlets. His book, *Third Party Blues: The Truth and Consequences of Two-Party Dominance*, explores the role minor parties can theoretically and empirically play promoting legislative innovation.

Barbara Sinclair was professor emeritus (formerly the Marvin Hoffenberg Professor) at UCLA. She specialized in American politics and primarily research on the U.S. Congress. Her publications include articles in the *American Political Science Review*, the *American Journal of Political Science*, the *Journal of Politics*, and *Legislative Studies Quarterly* and the following books: *Congressional Realignment* (1982),

Majority Leadership in the U.S. House (1983), *The Transformation of the U.S. Senate* (1989), *Legislators, Leaders, and Lawmaking: The U.S. House of Representatives in the Postreform Era* (1995), *Party Wars: Polarization and the Politics of National Policy Making* (2006), and *Unorthodox Lawmaking: New Legislative Processes in the U.S. Congress* (1997, 2000, 2007, 2012, 2016). She was an American Political Science Association congressional fellow in the office of the House majority leader in 1978–1979 and a participant observer in the office of the Speaker in 1987–1988. She testified before the Senate Committee on Rules and Administration on the filibuster in July 2010.

Steven S. Smith is the Kate M. Gregg Distinguished Professor of Social Sciences, professor of political science, and the director of the Weidenbaum Center on the Economy, Government, and Public Policy at Washington University. He is the director of the American Panel Survey (TAPS). He has authored or coauthored several books on congressional politics, including *The Senate Syndrome*; coauthored a book on the formation of the Russian State Duma; coauthored *The American Congress* (now in its ninth edition); and coedited a volume on American politics. He has served as a congressional fellow of the American Political Science Association and was a senior fellow at the Brookings Institution. He served as the chair of the Legislative Studies Section of the American Political Science Association.

Craig Volden is associate dean for academic affairs and professor of public policy and politics at the Frank Batten School of Leadership and Public Policy at the University of Virginia. His research focuses on the politics of policy making, with an emphasis on issues in legislative politics and in federalism. He is codirector of the Legislative Effectiveness Project (www.thelawmakers.org). He has contributed articles to the *American Political Science Review*, *American Journal of Political Science*, *Journal of Politics*, and *Legislative Studies Quarterly*, and is coauthor of *Legislative Effectiveness in the United States Congress: The Lawmakers* (2014).

Alan E. Wiseman is a professor of political science and law (by courtesy) at Vanderbilt University. He has research and teaching interests in American political institutions and positive political economy, focusing on legislative and electoral politics, regulation, bureaucratic policy making, and business–government relations. His is the coauthor (with Craig Volden) of *Legislative Effectiveness in the United States Congress: The Lawmakers* (Cambridge University Press, 2014), which won the 2015 Gladys M. Kammerer Award for the best book on U.S. national policy, as well as the 2015 Richard F. Fenno Jr. Prize for the best book in legislative studies. He is currently the codirector (along with Craig Volden) of the Legislative Effectiveness Project (www.thelawmakers.org). His research has also been published in numerous journals, such as the *American Political Science Review*, *American Journal of Political Science*, the *Journal of Politics*, and *Legislative Studies Quarterly*.

Gerald C. Wright is professor of political science and chair of the Department of Political Science at Indiana University and formerly director of the political science program at the National Science Foundation. He is the author of *Electoral Choice in America* (1974), coeditor of *Congress and Policy Change* (1986), and coauthor of *Statehouse Democracy: Public Opinion and Policy in the American States* (1993) and *Keeping the Republic: Power and Citizenship in American Politics* (4th ed., 2009). He is working on a comparative analysis of policy representation in the states and Congress, as well as a project examining inequality of representation of the rich and the poor.

Part I
Patterns and Dynamics of Congressional Change

1. The New World of U.S. Senators

Barbara Sinclair

The U.S. Senate has the most permissive rules of any legislature in the world, but the extent to which senators make full use of their prerogatives under the rules has varied over time. In the clubby, inward-looking Senate of the 1950s, senators were highly constrained in the use of their prerogatives. By the 1970s, as the Senate became more outward looking, individuals and small groups of senators routinely employed extended debate and the amending process for their own individual purposes. In the contemporary Senate, increasingly cohesive party contingents aggressively exploit Senate rules to pursue partisan advantage. The majority party leadership has responded to the minority's aggressive use of Senate prerogatives with hardball procedural ploys, and a procedural arms race has ensued. Intense partisan polarization, when combined with nonmajoritarian rules, greatly alters how the Senate functions and leaves the chamber in continual danger of policy gridlock.

- A courtly older gentleman—probably a conservative Southern Democrat, perhaps even white haired and clad in a white linen suit—working in committee behind closed doors
- A policy entrepreneur—Democrat or Republican, liberal or conservative—pursuing his cause singly or with a few allies on the Senate floor, aggressively using nongermane amendments and extended debate as his weapons
- A partisan warrior, acting as a member of a party team, dueling with his opposing-party counterparts in the public arena and on the floor, using all of the procedural and PR tools available

These three images capture the differences among the Senates of the 1950s, the 1970s, and the 1990s and beyond. To be sure, they are simplifications, and some elements of the 1950s Senate and many of the 1970s Senate persist. Yet the Senate of the early twenty-first century is very different from the 1950s Senate, which fictional and some journalistic accounts still often depict as current, and it is appreciably different from the 1970s Senate.

The U.S. Senate has the most permissive rules of any legislature in the world.[1] Extended debate allows senators to hold the floor as long as they wish, unless cloture is invoked, and that requires a supermajority of sixty votes. The Senate's amending rules enable senators to offer any—and as many—amendments as they please to almost any bill, and those amendments need not even be germane. The extent to which senators make full use of their prerogatives under the rules has varied over time. The Senate of the early twenty-first century is characterized by increasingly cohesive party contingents that aggressively exploit Senate rules to pursue partisan advantage but also by the persistence of the Senate individualism that developed in the 1960s and 1970s.

In this chapter, I briefly examine how and why the Senate changed from the 1950s to the present. I then analyze the impacts of intensified partisanship and of continuing individualism on how the contemporary Senate functions and on legislative outcomes.

Development of the Individualist, Partisan Senate

The Senate of the 1950s was a clubby, inward-looking body governed by constraining norms; influence was relatively unequally distributed and centered in strong committees and their senior leaders, who were most often conservatives, frequently Southern Democrats.[2] The typical senator of the 1950s was a specialist who concentrated on the issues that came before his committees. His legislative activities were largely confined to the committee room; he was seldom active on the Senate floor, was highly restrained in his exercise of the prerogatives the Senate rules gave him, and made little use of the national media.

The Senate's institutional structure and the political environment rewarded such behavior.[3] The lack of staff made it hard for new senators to participate intelligently right away, so serving an apprenticeship helped prevent a new member from making a fool of himself early in his career. Meager staff resources also made specialization the only really feasible course for attaining influence. Restraint in exploiting extended debate was encouraged by the absence of the time pressure that would later make extended debate such a formidable weapon; when floor time is plentiful, the leverage senators derive from extended debate is much less.[4] Furthermore, the dominant Southern Democrats had a strong constituency-based interest in restricting and thus protecting the filibuster for their one big issue: opposition to civil rights.

The majority of senators, especially the Southern Democrats, faced no imminent reelection peril so long as they were free to reflect their constituents' views in their votes and capable of providing the projects their constituents desired. The system of reciprocity, which dictated that senators do constituency-related favors for one another whenever possible, served them well. The seniority system, bolstered by norms of apprenticeship, specialization, and intercommittee reciprocity, assured members of considerable independent influence in their area of jurisdiction if they stayed in the Senate long enough, and it did not make that influence dependent on their voting behavior. For the moderate-to-conservative Senate membership, the parochial and limited legislation that such a system produced was quite satisfactory. The Senate of the 1950s was an institution well designed for its generally conservative and electorally secure members to further their goals.

Membership turnover and a transformation of the political environment altered the costs and benefits of such behavior and induced members to change the institution; over time, norms, practices, and rules were altered.[5] The 1958 elections brought into the Senate a big class of new senators with different policy goals and reelection needs. Mostly northern Democrats, they were activist liberals, and most had been elected in highly competitive contests, in many cases defeating incumbents. Both their policy goals and their reelection needs dictated a more activist style; these senators simply could not afford to wait to make their mark. Subsequent elections brought in more and more such members.

In the 1960s, the political environment began a transformation. A host of new issues rose to prominence—first, civil rights, then, environmental issues and consumer rights; the war in Vietnam and the questions about American foreign and defense policy that it raised; women's rights and women's liberation; the rights of other ethnic groups, especially Latinos and Native Americans; the rights of the poor and disabled; and, by the early 1970s, gay rights. These were issues that engaged, often intensely, many ordinary citizens, and politics became more highly charged. The interest group community exploded in size and became more diverse; many of the social movements of the 1960s spawned or already had interest groups. A hoard of environmental groups, consumer groups, women's groups, and other liberal social welfare and civil rights groups joined the Washington political community and made it more diverse. Then, in response to some of these groups' policy successes—for example, on environmental legislation—the business community mobilized. In the 1970s, many more businesses established a permanent presence in Washington, and specialized trade associations proliferated. The media, especially television, became a much bigger player in politics.

This new environment offered tempting new opportunities to senators.[6] The myriad interest groups needed champions and spokesmen, and the media needed credible sources to represent issue positions and provide commentary. Because of the prestige and small size of the Senate, senators fit the bill. The opportunity for senators to become significant players on a broader stage, with possible policy, power, reelection, or higher-office payoffs, was there, but to take advantage of the opportunity, senators needed to change their behavior and their institution.

From the mid-1960s through the mid-1970s, senators did just that. They increased the number of positions on good committees and the number of subcommittee leadership positions and distributed them much more broadly. Staff was greatly expanded and made available to junior, as well as senior, senators. Senators were consequently able to involve themselves in a much broader range of issues, and they did so. Senators also became much more active on the Senate floor, offering more amendments to a wider range of bills. Senators exploited extended debate to a much greater extent, and the frequency of filibusters shot up.[7] The media became an increasingly important arena for participation and a significant resource for senators in the pursuit of their policy, power, and reelection goals.

By the mid-1970s, the individualist Senate had emerged. The Senate had become a body in which every member, regardless of seniority, considered himself entitled to participate on any issue that interested him for either constituency or policy reasons. Senators took for granted that they—and their colleagues—would regularly exploit the powers that the Senate rules gave them. Senators became more outwardly directed, focusing on their links with interest groups, policy communities, and the media more than on their ties to one another.

The 1980 elections made Ronald Reagan president and, to almost everyone's surprise, brought a Republican majority to the Senate. As president, Reagan was more conservative and confrontational than his Republican predecessors of the post–World War II era, and his election signaled an intensification of ideological conflict that increasingly fell along partisan lines.

Realignment in the South, the Proposition 13 tax-cutting fever, the rise of the Christian right, and the increasing prominence of supply-side economics were changing the political parties. In 1961, not a single senator from the eleven states of the old Confederacy was a Republican; by 1973, seven were, and by 1980, the number had risen to ten. In 2015, the number stood at nineteen, or 86 percent of the senators from the once solidly Democratic old South. As conservative Southern Democrats were replaced by even more conservative Southern Republicans, the congressional Democratic Party became more homogeneously liberal and the Republican Party more conservative. Outside the South as well, Republican candidates and activists were becoming more ideologically conservative.

Voting on the Senate floor became increasingly partisan. In the late 1960s and early 1970s, a majority of Democrats opposed a majority of Republicans on only about a third of Senate roll call votes. By the 1990s, between half and two-thirds of roll calls were such party votes, and that has continued; the average over the Congresses from 2003 through 2014 is 63 percent. The frequency with which senators voted with their partisan colleagues on party votes increased significantly as well. By the 1990s, a typical party vote saw well over 80 percent of Democrats voting together on one side and well over 80 percent of Republicans on the other. In the 113th Congress (2013–2014), majorities of Democrats and Republicans opposed each other on 68 percent of the Senate's recorded votes, and 97 percent of Democrats opposed 89 percent of Republicans on a typical party vote.[8]

Partisan polarization has made participation through their party more attractive to senators than it was when the parties were more heterogeneous and the ideological distance between them less. Recent Senate party leaders have sought to provide more channels for members to participate in and through the party.[9] Increasingly, senators of the same party are acting as a party team and are exploiting Senate prerogatives to gain partisan advantage.

Over this same period, the Senate membership has become more diverse. Although most senators are still white men, the 113th Congress included twenty women—an all-time high—two African Americans, three Latinos (all Cuban Americans), and one Asian American. By contrast, in the Eighty-fifth Congress (1957–1958), every senator was white, and only one was female. The greater diversity influences how the Senate operates, but its impact is much less than those of individualism and intense partisanship.

The Legislative Process in the Contemporary Senate

What effect has the combination of individualism and partisanship had on the legislative process in the Senate? Individualism changed the way Senate committees work and altered even more floor-related legislative routines, complicating the Senate majority leader's job of floor scheduling and coordination. Intensified partisanship exacerbated the problems the majority leader faces in keeping the Senate functioning as a legislative body.

Senate Committees and the Prefloor Process

Senators hold multiple committee assignments and usually lead at least one subcommittee, often more. In the 112th Congress, senators averaged 4 committee assignments and 8.4 subcommittee assignments each; members of the majority party averaged 1.7 chairmanships.[10] Thus, senators are stretched very thin; they treat their committees not as work groups in which to participate regularly but as arenas in which they pick and choose whether to participate depending upon their interest in the subject being considered. Senators rely heavily on staff for committee work. Committee decisions on many issues are made by the "interesteds," who make up considerably less than the full committee membership.[11] A major tax bill will elicit active participation from all the members of the relevant committee; a rewrite of copyright law, important but narrower and more technical legislation, may be left to a handful of senators.

Because of senators' workloads and the large number of subcommittees, subcommittees are usually "starring" vehicles for their chairs. The chairs can use their subcommittees to publicize problems and policy solutions, to cater to allied interest groups, to promote themselves, or to do all three. Under most circumstances, other senators, even the chair of the full committee, are too busy to interfere.

The marking up of bills most frequently takes place in full committee.[12] Senators on the subcommittee do not have time to go through two markups, and they know that any interested committee member not on the subcommittee would insist on having a say at the full committee level.

Even in this period of heightened partisanship, Senate committees not infrequently work in a bipartisan fashion. Bill sponsors know that their legislation's chances of surviving the Senate floor are much better if it has broad support. Committee chairs usually try to negotiate the *chairman's mark*, the legislative language from which the committee will work, with their minority party counterpart and other interested committee members. In 2011, for example, Tom Harkin, chair of the Committee on Health, Education, Labor and Pensions (HELP), and Mike Enzi, the committee's ranking member, worked together to draft a bill reauthorizing the No Child Left Behind Education Act that garnered bipartisan support in the committee. Similarly, in 2015, Lamar Alexander, R-Tenn., HELP committee chair, and Patty Murray, D-Wash., ranking minority member, negotiated a compromise reform of the program that passed the committee unanimously. Conflict within committees is also sometimes dampened down by senators' tendency to postpone contentious issues until floor debate. When negotiating and marking up the bill reauthorizing farm programs in 2007, the Agriculture Committee agreed to put off amendments for stricter crop payment limits; highly controversial, that issue would be fought out on the floor again in any case. To report legislation in a timely manner and to maintain its bipartisan style of internal decision making, the Appropriations Committee regularly agreed to withhold divisive, policy-related amendments until the floor.

Committee decision making must be sensitive to the policy preferences of interested senators who are not members of the committee. Because any senator can cause problems for legislation on the floor and may, in fact, be able to block it from getting to the floor, committee proponents of particular legislation have considerable incentive to try to anticipate other senators' views and bargain with those with intense preferences before the committee reports the bill. Senate committees are perforce highly permeable.

Senate committee decision making is, nevertheless, more likely to be partisan than it used to be. In the Congresses of the 1960s and 1970s, the Senate committee process was partisan on less than one in ten major measures; that increased to about one in seven in the 1980s.[13] In the Congresses of the 1990s and 2000s (103rd–110th), the Senate committee process was partisan on about a quarter of the major measures considered, and the figure rose to almost 40 percent in the 111th Congress, but it declined in the two subsequent Congresses to an average of 15 percent.[14]

Still, Senate committee decision making has been considerably more partisan since the mid-1990s than it was before. The figures for partisanship in committee decision making are not higher, in part, because frequently now, committees are bypassed on the most partisan issues (as discussed later). Despite incentives in Senate procedures to avoid narrow supportive majorities, partisan polarization has made finding compromises acceptable to both political parties much more difficult. With the intensification of partisanship, majority party committee contingents have also become increasingly responsive to their party leader and their party colleagues. Majority leaders now often involve themselves in the substance of legislation in committee, as well as after a bill has been reported. The then majority leader Bill Frist, R-Tenn., was a major participant in negotiating the substance of the bill adding a prescription drug benefit to Medicare in 2003. The lobbying and ethics reform bill that the Senate debated in early 2007 was the result of negotiations between majority leader Harry Reid, D-Nev., and minority leader Mitch McConnell, R-Ky.; it never went through committee. And after the HELP and Finance Committees reported very different health care reform bills in the summer and fall of 2009, Reid played a central role in putting together the bill that went to the floor and was passed by the chamber right before Christmas, on December 24, 2009. The 2015 budget deal—to relax for two years the draconian spending cuts dictated by the 2011 deal and to suspend the debt ceiling until after the 2016 elections—was crafted by the top-four party leaders and the White House.

Majority Leadership and the Senate Floor

In the contemporary Senate, floor scheduling is, of necessity, an exercise in broad and, in the end, bipartisan accommodation.[15] Although he is not the Senate's presiding officer and lacks many of the powers the House Speaker commands, the Senate majority leader is as close to a central leader as the chamber has, and he is charged with scheduling legislation for floor consideration. To bring legislation to the floor, the majority leader uses his right of first recognition, a prerogative the leader has had under Senate precedent since the 1930s. The majority leader can move that a bill be taken off of the calendar and considered, but the motion to proceed is a debatable motion—and thus subject to filibuster. Or he can ask for unanimous consent that the bill be taken off of the calendar and considered, a request that can be blocked by any senator's objection. Clearly, any senator can cause problems for the majority leader.

How Senators Cause Trouble: The Strategic Use of Senate Rules

Understanding the problems of legislative scheduling in the Senate and the routines that have developed requires a look at the strategic use of Senate rules by the individualistic and now also highly partisan Senate membership.

The filibuster—the use of extended debate to prevent a vote on a motion or measure unless a supermajority (now usually sixty) can be mustered—is certainly the best-known strategic use of Senate rules. With the development of the individualist Senate, the use of extended debate—and of cloture to try to cut it off—increased enormously (see Table 1-1). To be sure, the data must be regarded with some caution.[16] Exactly when lengthy debate becomes a filibuster is, in part, a matter of judgment. Furthermore, as I discuss later, filibusters have changed their form, and threats to filibuster have become much more frequent than actual talkathons. As a consequence, cloture is sometimes sought before a filibuster manifests itself on the floor. Nevertheless, experts and participants agree that the frequency of obstructionism has increased. In the 1950s, filibusters were rare; they increased during the 1960s and again during the 1970s. By the late 1980s and the 1990s, they had become routine. Cloture votes have increased in tandem, and more than one cloture vote per issue is now the norm.

Table 1-1 Increase in Filibusters and Cloture Votes, 1951–2014

Years	Congress	Filibusters per Congress	Cloture Votes per Congress	Successful Cloture Votes per Congress
1951–1960	82nd–86th	1.0	0.4	0.0
1961–1970	87th–91st	4.6	5.2	0.8
1971–1980	92nd–96th	11.0	22.0	9.0
1981–1986	97th–99th	17.0	23.0	10.0
1987–1992	100th–102nd	27.0	39.0	15.0
1993–2006	103rd–109th	30.0	53.0	21.0
2007–2014*	110th–113th	55.0	91.0	55.0

* Filibusters and cloture votes on nominations after the rules change on November 21, 2013, reducing number required for cloture to a simple majority are not counted.

Sources: Data for 82nd–102nd Congresses: Congressional Research Service, comp., "A Look at the Senate Filibuster," in Democratic Studies Group Special Report, June 13, 1994, Appendix B; Norman Ornstein, Thomas Mann, and Michael Malbin, *Vital Statistics on Congress 1993–1994* (Washington, DC: CQ Press, 1994), 162. Data for 103rd Congress: Richard S. Beth, "Cloture in the Senate, 103d Congress," memorandum, Congressional Research Service, June 23, 1995. Data for 104th–108th Congresses: *CQ Almanac* for the years 1995–2007 (Washington, DC: CQ Press); 108th–114th Congresses, CQ online, library.cqpress.com/cqweekly.

As filibusters became more frequent, the character of the filibusterers and of the targeted legislation broadened. By the 1970s, liberals and conservatives frequently used this weapon, and senators used it on all sorts of legislation, parochial as well as momentous. For example, as Congress was rushing to adjourn in October 1992, Sen. Alfonse D'Amato, R-N.Y., held the floor for fifteen hours and fifteen minutes to protest the removal of a provision that he said could have restored jobs at a New York typewriter plant from an urban-aid tax bill.[17]

Senators use actual or threatened filibusters for a variety of purposes. Their aim may be to kill legislation, but it may also be to extract substantive concessions on a bill. Sometimes, senators' use of extended debate is a form of position taking; senators may know that they cannot kill or weaken the legislation but may want to make a strong statement about their position and the intensity of their feelings about it. Targeting one measure to extract concessions on another, sometimes known as "hostage taking," has become an increasingly frequent use of extended debate.

Nominations, as well as legislation, can be filibustered. In the late 1990s, Republicans killed a number of President Bill Clinton's judicial nominations by refusing to report them from committee. Democrats, lacking a Senate majority during most of the early 2000s and thus unable to prevent nominees they considered too extreme from being reported out, blocked a number of President

George W. Bush's judicial nominations on the floor. Republicans failed to get the requisite sixty votes to cut off debate and bring to a vote the nomination of Miguel Estrada to the Court of Appeals for the District of Columbia; after the seventh unsuccessful cloture vote, Estrada withdrew. President Barack Obama's judicial and many of his executive-branch nominees have routinely faced extended-debate-related problems.

Senators now often block nominees they do not oppose to gain a bargaining chip for use with the administration. In February 2010, Richard Shelby, R-Ala., placed a hold on more than seventy Obama nominees; Shelby demanded funding for the KC-135 Air Force tanker fleet, a project that could generate thousands of jobs in Alabama, and the restoration of a funding cut from the budget for the FBI's Terrorist Explosive Device Analytical Center, also located in Alabama. After intense media attention and widespread criticism, Shelby lifted his holds on most of the nominees, claiming he had accomplished his purpose: "to get the White House's attention."[18] Frustrated by the Federal Emergency Management Agency's treatment of a couple who were his constituents, Sen. Mark Pryor, D-Ark., in October 2011, placed holds on all Treasury Department nominees. Only after FEMA had reached an agreement with the couple over mistakenly awarded disaster relief funds did Pryor release his hold. Note that in this case, it was a member of the president's party who held up the nominations. "Hostage taking," as a strategy, is not limited to the president's opponents.

The offering of many, not necessarily germane, amendments on the floor is a signature characteristic of the individualist Senate. When major bills are considered, dozens of amendments are routinely offered. Budget resolutions frequently see more than forty amendments offered and pushed to a recorded vote; on the FY2010 budget resolution, there were thirty-eight roll call votes on amendments. The 2009 economic stimulus bill and the 2010 financial services reform bill (Dodd-Frank) were also subject to amending marathons, with twenty-six amendment-related roll calls on the former, twenty-eight on the latter, and many more amendments disposed of without roll calls. During floor consideration of the Department of Defense authorization bill in late 2011, 104 amendments were pending simultaneously; that is, they had been offered and had to be disposed of before the bill could come to a passage vote.[19]

Most amendments are germane, and the sponsor's aim is to influence the substance of the bill. But individual senators do use nongermane amendments to pursue their personal agendas and to bring to the floor issues that the leadership might like to avoid. Among the amendments offered to a 2007 bill on student loans were ones repealing the alternative minimum tax, barring the Federal Communications Commission from reinstating the Fairness Doctrine, requiring voters in federal elections to present photo identification, and expressing the sense of the Senate that detainees at Guantanamo Bay, including senior members of al Qaeda, should not be transferred to the United States.[20]

With the growth of partisan polarization, the minorities making use of Senate prerogatives are more often organized, partisan ones. The ideological polarization that coincides with the partisan polarization means that Democrats and Republicans have very different and often conflicting notions of what constitutes good public policy. Consequently, the minority party in the Senate has strong incentives to use its prerogatives to stymie the majority, and the minority's efforts to do so have only intensified in recent congresses (as discussed later).

In the 1990s, exploiting Senate prerogatives to attempt to seize control of the agenda from the majority party became a key minority party strategy. The lack of a germaneness requirement for amendments to most bills severely weakens the majority party's ability to control the floor agenda. If the majority leader refuses to bring a bill to the floor, its supporters can offer it as an amendment to most legislation that the leader does bring to the floor. The majority leader can make a motion to table the amendment, which is nondebatable. That does, however, require his members to vote on the issue, albeit in a procedural guise, and the leader may want to avoid that. Furthermore, even after the minority's amendment has been tabled, the minority can continue to offer other amendments, including even individual parts of the original amendment, and can block a vote on the underlying bill that the majority party wants to pass. The leader can, of course, file a cloture petition and try to shut off debate, but he needs sixty votes to do so.

The minority party can use this strategy to bring its agenda to the floor, and if the strategy is accompanied by a sophisticated public relations campaign (which the Senate parties are increasingly capable of orchestrating), it can draw favorable publicity and sometimes pressure enough majority party members into supporting the bill to pass it. In 1996, Senate Democrats used this strategy to enact a minimum wage increase. In 2001, campaign finance legislation passed the Senate before the Democrats took control of the chamber. John McCain, R-Ariz., and the Democrats had threatened to use the add-it-as-an-amendment-to-everything strategy, which would have wreaked havoc with the consideration of President Bush's program. Furthermore, Republicans knew that the cost of trying to stop campaign finance from being considered would be terrible publicity, so the Senate Republican leadership capitulated and agreed to bring it to the floor.

The majority's limited agenda control can also create problems for legislation the majority wants and has the votes to pass. The minority can sometimes come up with "killer" amendments that result in the defeat of a bill that otherwise would command a majority. In the 111th Congress, conservative Republicans offered an amendment to the District of Columbia Voting Rights Act that would have repealed the District's strict gun control provisions; although the amendment's passage did not prevent the bill, which Republicans strongly opposed, from passing the Senate, it killed the bill in the House.

Getting Legislation to the Senate Floor

Given the extent to which senators, as individuals and as party teams, now exploit their prerogatives, how does the Senate manage to legislate at all? As shown in Table 1-2, major legislation is now very frequently subject to some sort of extended-debate–related problem, discernible from the public record.[21] Since the early 1990s, about half of the major legislation that was vulnerable to a filibuster actually encountered some sort of filibuster-related problem, and in the period 2007 to 2014, that rose to about 70 percent. If measures protected by rules from filibusters (budget resolution and reconciliation bills) are included, the proportion decreases only marginally.

The Senate has long done most of its work through unanimous consent agreements (UCAs). By unanimous consent, senators agree to bring a bill to the floor, perhaps to place some limits on the amendments that may be offered or on the length of debate on specific amendments and then maybe to set a time for the final vote.[22] Some UCAs are highly elaborate and govern the entire floor consideration of a bill, but a series of partial agreements is more frequent than a single comprehensive one. As a highly knowledgeable participant explained, "Usually you have a UCA only to bring something to the floor, and then maybe you have another one that will deal with a couple of important amendments, and then perhaps a little later, one that will start limiting amendments to some extent, and then perhaps one that specifies when a vote will take place. So it's done through a series of steps, each of which sort of leaves less and less leeway."

Ordinarily, Senate floor consideration of legislation begins with the majority leader asking and receiving unanimous consent to take a bill off the calendar

Table 1-2 Increasing Frequency of Extended-Debate–Related Problems on Major Measures

Years*	Measures Affected (in Percentages)[a]
1960s	8
1970s–1980s	27
1990s–mid-2000s	51
2007–2008	70
2009–2010	72
2011–2012	59
2013–2014	68

*Congresses included: 1960s: 87, 89, 91; 1970s–1980s: 94, 95, 97, 100, 101; 1990s–mid-2000s: 103, 104, 105, 107, 108, 109

[a] Figures represent percentage of "filibusterable" major measures that were subject to extended-debate–related problems.

Source: Author's calculations.

and proceed to consider it. This seemingly simple and easy process for getting legislation to the floor has been preceded by an elaborate consultation process to ensure that unanimous consent is forthcoming. The party leaders oversee the negotiation of unanimous consent agreements. The majority and minority party secretaries of the Senate now are the most important staffers involved; they serve as clearinghouses and points of continuous contact between the parties and often do much of the negotiating.

When the majority leader, after consultation with the relevant committee chair, decides that he wants to schedule a bill, the process begins. To ensure that there will be no objections to the consent request on the floor, it must be cleared with the minority leader, committee leaders, other senators who have expressed an interest in the bill, and, in effect, every senator on both sides of the aisle. The party secretaries keep the list of those senators who have requested that they be consulted before the bill is scheduled. If a fellow party member has expressed opposition to the bill being brought to the floor, negotiations may be necessary to take care of his or her concerns. When the leaders reach a tentative agreement, both parties put out a recorded message on their telephone hotline and also send an e-mail to all Senate offices. The message lays out the terms of the agreement and asks senators who have objections to call their leader within a specified period of time. If there are objections, they have to be taken care of. When every senator is prepared to assent to the unanimous consent agreement, the majority leader takes it to the floor and makes the request.

When a senator informs his leader, directly or through the party secretary, that he wishes to be consulted before a measure is scheduled, the senator may only want to be sure that he or she is not otherwise committed, is prepared for floor debate, or is ready to offer an amendment. Often, however, such a notification is a *hold*. "A hold," as a knowledgeable participant explained, "is a letter to your leader telling him which of the many powers that you have as a senator you intend to use on a given issue." Most holds, then, are threats to object to a unanimous consent agreement, and in a body that conducts most of its business through UCAs, that is, in effect, as a leadership staffer said, "a threat to filibuster."

The party secretaries confer every morning and tell each other what new holds there are on legislation or nominations. They do not reveal the names of the members who have placed the holds, so holds can be secret. The Senate has made a number of attempts to mandate disclosure, but none have been particularly effective. Of course, holds are often invitations to negotiate, and those, of necessity, have to be made public. "There's no point in taking a hostage, if you're not going to write a ransom note," a knowledgeable participant explained.

Visible filibusters, then, are just the tip of the iceberg. The Senate's permissive rules have much more effect on the legislative process through filibuster threats than through actual filibusters (see Table 1-2; remember that holds and filibuster threats, as well as actual filibusters, are reflected in the figures). "Classic" filibusters, with the Senate in session all night, senators sleeping on cots off the Senate floor, and filibusterers making interminable speeches, no longer occur. Occasionally, the majority leader will force senators opposing a matter to take to the floor. The judicial nomination of Miguel Estrada was debated for almost one hundred hours over the course of a month before the majority leader filed a cloture petition, and during that period, the Senate did little else.[23] However, once the first cloture vote failed, Majority Leader Frist went on to other business (though there were more cloture votes). Most of the time, the majority leader does not force such a prolonged showdown.

Since holds are nowhere mentioned in the Senate rules, why do Senate leaders condone and, in fact, maintain the hold system? "It's to the majority leader's advantage to have holds because it gives him information," a knowledgeable observer explained. "He's always trying to negotiate unanimous consent agreements, and he needs to know if there are pockets of problems, and holds do that." An expert concluded succinctly, "The only way you could get rid of holds would be to change the rules of the Senate drastically."

Critics often argue that leaders should be tougher and call members' bluffs more often. The threat to filibuster supposedly inherent in holds would, in many cases, prove to be empty rhetoric if put to the test, such critics claim. In fact, holds are not automatic vetoes. A hold cannot kill must-pass legislation, such as appropriations bills. A hold "doesn't mean the legislation won't come to the floor," a former majority leader explained. "Leaders are always bringing up legislation that has a hold on it; they do it all the time. But you know what you're getting into, that somebody is likely to obstruct, that you're going to have to jump through a lot of procedural hoops." Although holds are certainly not absolute, the time pressure under which the Senate operates gives them considerable power. Frist could let the Estrada nomination dominate floor business in February 2003 because it was early in the first year of a Congress, and not much legislation was ready for floor consideration. By March, that situation had changed. If Republicans had forced Democrats to continue, it would have been at the expense of President Bush's initiatives. As a staffer explained, "Holds are effective because the majority leader has a finite amount of time. If there are going to be cloture votes and the like, it can take days to ram something through this place. You can't do it on every bill. You can only do it on a selected few bills." Senators, most of whom have legislation they want considered on the floor, as well as many other demands on their time, want floor time used productively, and the majority leader needs to use the time efficiently if he is to pass as much of the party agenda as possible. In making a choice of which bills to bring to the floor, the majority leader must consider how much time a bill will take, as well as the likelihood of successful passage.

As a result, senators who want their bills to receive floor consideration are under tremendous pressure to negotiate with those who have holds on them. "Things that aren't a top priority for the majority leader, he wants you to work it out," a senior staffer explained. "If you go to him and say you want something brought to the floor, he'll say, 'You work it out. You find out who has holds on it. You work out whatever problems they have, and I'll schedule it when you've worked it out.'" In fall 2007, Sen. Tom Coburn, R-Okla., placed a hold on a bill providing suicide prevention services to veterans because he opposed a section instructing the Veterans Affairs Department to track the veterans helped; Coburn claimed that that might prevent those veterans from being able to buy handguns.[24] Although no one else opposed the bill, the sponsors were forced to remove the provision in order to move the bill. In the 109th Congress, Frist never scheduled a major telecommunications bill because there was a Democratic hold on it, and the committee chair was unable to assure Frist that he had sixty votes. Thus, a measure often must command a substantial majority simply to get to the floor. When time is especially tight—before a recess and at the end of a session—a single objection can kill legislation. In the lame-duck (postelection) session of the 113th Congress, a bill extending a number of broadly supported tax breaks died; an unnamed Republican senator had put a hold on the bill, and although that was not the only problem, it contributed to the bill's demise. Sen. Coburn, a prolific employer of holds, stopped another broadly supported bill, the Terrorism Risk Insurance Act (TRIA), in the same lame-duck session. Although the bill had passed both houses, and a compromise between the chambers had been worked out, Majority Leader Reid did not bring the bill to the floor; time was simply too limited so long as there were objections. "Coburn's holding everything up," said Senator Chuck Schumer, D-N.Y., who had brokered the deal with Financial Services chairman Jeb Hensarling, R-Tex. "He won't let us do anything. Coburn is holding it all up."

Majority and Minority Cooperation and Conflict

Keeping the Senate functioning as a legislature requires broad accommodation; it dictates satisfying every senator to some extent. A reasonably cohesive majority party can run the House of Representatives without consulting the minority. The Senate only runs smoothly when the majority leader and the minority leader cooperate—and not always then. The party leaders or their top aides consult on a daily basis. "The two leaders talk extensively to each other during the day," a knowledgeable participant explained. "You see it during votes. We'll have two or three votes a day at least, usually, and that's one of the times when they confer. But they have to talk to each other; if they don't, that's when things break down." A telephone hotline connects the leaders' offices directly to facilitate quick communication.[25] The leaders often work together to get unanimous consent agreements and to get essential legislative business done.

Yet the Senate leaders are party leaders, elected by their party members in the chamber, and those members expect them to pursue partisan advantage. With the increase in partisan polarization, the often narrow margins, and the shifts in partisan control of the chamber, senators' expectations that their leader promote their collective partisan interests have intensified. With the changes in the character of politics and the role of the media in political life, those expectations have also changed in form. Over the second half of the twentieth century, the role of the media in American politics increased enormously. National politics has come to be played out on the public stage much more than formerly, often with audience reactions determining who wins and who loses. In the 1990s, policy battles increasingly came to be fought out in public through public relations, or PR, wars.[26] Whether in the majority or in the minority, senators now expect their party leader to promote their collective partisan interests through message strategies directed at the public, as well as by internal procedural and legislative strategies.

These expectations create a dilemma for the leaders, especially for the majority leader. Majority party senators expect their leader to promote the party agenda by passing legislation and publicizing party positions and successes. They also expect him to keep off the floor the other party's agenda, which often consists of issues on which the minority party and a significant segment of the public agree, thus putting some members of the majority party in a tough position. And all senators expect their leaders to keep the Senate functioning. Yet in the Senate, unlike the House, a majority is not sufficient to act. To keep the Senate functioning requires supermajorities, and that almost always requires the majority leader to accommodate the minority to some extent.

The Sixty-Vote Senate and the Procedural Arms Race

The conundrum of leading a nonmajoritarian chamber in a partisan age has only become knottier in recent years. The minority party increasingly perceives obstructionism as its best strategy for furthering its policy and political objectives. Given the ideological divide between the parties, a bill that both consider better than the status quo of no new legislation often does not exist, especially on the most salient issues of the day. And even on nonideological issues, the minority may benefit from making the majority look incapable of governing.[27] Majority leaders have responded to minority obstructionism with hardball procedural ploys, and a procedural arms race has ensued.[28] As Chuck Schumer, third ranking in the Democratic leadership, summed up the situation in 2011,

> You are frustrated because you feel the tree is filled all the time and you cannot make amendments. But we are frustrated because the 60-vote rule—which has always been used here—is now used routinely, which never has been done before. . . . [D]istrict court judges . . . Routine appointees—assistant secretaries of this, deputy secretaries of that—60 votes. . . .
>
> In the past, the motion to proceed was not routinely blocked. And almost every single bill . . . on minor bills—we had a filibuster on technical corrections to the Transportation bill, where 287 was written down by mistake instead of 387. It was filibustered—60 votes. So our defense is to fill the tree.[29]

On major legislation, majority leaders now are central to the policy process.[30] Not infrequently, they bypass committee and bring legislation directly to the floor. In the Congresses of the 1960s through the 1980s for which data are available, the committee was bypassed in the Senate on 7 percent of major measures; for the 103rd through 110th Congresses, the average increased to 26 percent; in the period 2009 through 2014, it was 52 percent. Usually, though not always, committee leaders are involved in the process and have, in fact, drafted the bill. But the majority leader's strategy dictates going directly to the floor rather than allowing the committee to mark up and report the bill. Thus, in 2013, the Federal Aviation Administration (FAA) began furloughing air traffic controllers to meet the spending cuts required by legislation Congress had passed earlier. Fearing an outcry from passengers, who, after all, are constituents, members quickly passed a bill allowing the FAA to transfer money to prevent the furloughs. To do so quickly, committees were bypassed in both chambers. Later the same year, Majority Leader Harry Reid, D-Nev., brought to the floor a bill establishing a uniform national system for collecting sales taxes on online purchases. He bypassed the Finance Committee because its chair, Max Baucus of Montana, opposed the bill. Montana does not have a sales tax, and he feared the bill would hurt his state's businesses.

The minority's strategy in recent years entails filibustering, not just the bill but the motion to proceed to consider the bill. If successful, this prevents the bill from ever being formally considered on the floor, and even if not, it eats up time. By the 112th Congress (2011–2012), votes on motions to proceed had become commonplace. In that Congress, there were forty-two roll calls on thirty-four different measures—on motions to proceed or, more frequently, on imposing cloture on the motion to proceed offered by the majority leadership, eight of which failed. In 2013–2014, there were thirty-six such roll calls on twenty-nine different measures; eleven failed.

Increasingly, then, all Senate decisions require sixty votes. When in the minority, Republican leader Mitch McConnell argued that this is a long-established Senate tradition. In fact, that is not the case, but a cohesive minority of more than forty senators can force the majority to get sixty votes to act.

Starting in the early 1990s—when Minority Leader Bob Dole used the filibuster against President Bill Clinton's agenda, blocking some items and forcing substantive concessions on others—and ratcheting up ever since, minorities have forced majorities to get supermajorities to act. Democrats frequently used extended debate to obstruct when they were in the minority during the George W. Bush administration, and minority Republicans ratcheted up the employment of obstructionist strategies still more after they lost their majority in the 2006 elections, as Table 1-2 shows. By refusing to agree to bring up by unanimous consent and then voting against cloture on the motion to proceed, minority Democrats in the 109th Congress (2005–2006) blocked several Republican attempts to repeal the estate tax and refused Republicans an up-or-down vote on a constitutional amendment banning gay marriage. They killed legislation on abortion notification by refusing to allow the bill to go to conference and killed drilling in the

Arctic National Wildlife Refuge (ANWR) by blocking a vote on the conference report that contained the provision. Some legislation on the Republican Party agenda did pass: a bill on class action lawsuits and one overhauling bankruptcy laws. Democrats had blocked both in the previous Congress, and Republicans had been forced to make substantial compromises to get the sixty votes necessary for passage. On legislation altering offshore drilling policy, House Republicans were forced to swallow a weak Senate bill to get any legislation at all. Minority Democrats also used the Senate's permissive amending rules to force votes on issues, such as the minimum wage, that they wanted to highlight.

In the 110th Congress, Republicans, newly but barely in the minority, made even greater use of obstructionist strategies. The number of filibusters, defined as matters on which cloture was attempted, jumped to fifty-four in the 110th and the number of cloture votes to 112, an all-time record. Bills allowing the government to negotiate drug prices with pharmaceutical companies for Medicare patients, making union organizing easier, and giving the District of Columbia a vote in the House of Representatives—all Democratic Party priorities—were blocked from floor consideration when Republicans refused to allow votes on the motions to proceed. Resolutions expressing opposition to the "surge" in Iraq were also blocked from an up-or-down vote, as were various other anti-Iraq provisions. The price of an up-or-down vote on a bill raising the minimum wage was the attachment to it of large tax breaks for small business. Republicans allowed legislation implementing the 9/11 Commission's recommendations to go to conference only after Democrats agreed to a UCA guaranteeing that the provision allowing collective bargaining for Transportation Security Agency screeners would be dropped.

Political circumstances—a new president who had run on an ambitious agenda and a Congress in which the same party had big majorities in both chambers—were much more conducive to major legislative accomplishments in 2009 to 2010. And in fact, the 111th Congress was extraordinarily productive, perhaps the most productive Congress since the Great Society Congresses of the mid-1960s. A massive stimulus bill, health care reform that went a long way toward providing universal coverage, and major financial services regulation reform (Dodd-Frank) are best known, but other significant legislation enacted included the Lilly Ledbetter Fair Pay Act, a major change in the student loan program to free up more money for loans, food safety and child nutrition bills, a credit card regulation bill, legislation to allow the FDA to regulate tobacco, an expansion of the hate crimes covered by federal law, and repeal of "Don't Ask, Don't Tell." The Senate also ratified the New Strategic Arms Reduction Treaty (START).

Yet despite the favorable conditions, passing this legislation was often extraordinarily difficult, and the problem was most often the Senate. Over the course of the Congress, Senate Democrats numbered between fifty-eight and sixty, a huge majority by recent standards. But Republicans decided even before the Congress began that their best strategy was all-out opposition. Most Republicans sincerely opposed the Democratic agenda on policy grounds, and they were confident that Republican activists would reward them for refusing to compromise.

They believed that, in any case, if Obama's policies appeared to work, Obama and the Democrats would get the credit, even if the Republicans had participated in passing it. The Republican strategy meant that Senate Democrats would have to amass sixty votes for essentially everything except measures, primarily budget resolutions and reconciliation bills, protected from filibusters by Senate rules.

Getting to sixty was often difficult and required painful concessions; furthermore, even when sixty votes were in hand, the process could be excruciatingly slow. To pass the stimulus bill early in 2009, Majority Leader Harry Reid needed the votes of at least two Republicans. The price for the three votes he got was a significant cut in the size of the stimulus, with considerable aid to the states being deleted. (One of the Republicans, Arlen Specter, quickly discovered that his vote for the stimulus had so enraged the Republican base in his home state of Pennsylvania that he would lose in the 2010 primary. He switched to the Democratic Party and, with the seating of Al Franken once the Minnesota recount was decided, gave the Democrats a Senate majority of sixty.)

The cloture process is time consuming and cumbersome. Any senator may circulate a cloture petition. When the senator has gathered sixteen signatures, the petition is filed; after a one-day layover, the Senate votes. Even after a successful cloture vote, debate does not necessarily end immediately. Senate Rule 22, the cloture rule, places a cap of thirty hours on consideration after the cloture vote, and opponents can insist on the time. The thirty hours does include time spent on quorum calls and voting, as well as on debate. The rule also requires that amendments considered after cloture must be germane.

If opponents are determined, supporters may need to impose cloture at more than one stage in a bill's progress through the chamber. Thus, extended debate can occur on the motion to proceed to consider the measure, on specific amendments, on the measure itself, on the motion related to going to conference, and on the conference report. No single measure has ever been subject to filibusters at all of these stages, but it is not uncommon for cloture to be sought at several stages. To pass the tobacco regulation bill in 2009, supporters had to win cloture votes on the motion to proceed; on the Dodd amendment in the nature of a substitute, which was the committee bill; and on passage. The process took two weeks of Senate floor time.

Because filibuster threats, in their various forms, have become so routine, sixty-vote requirements for passage of legislation are now sometimes written into unanimous consent agreements. The majority agrees because it saves time; the minority may extract substantive concessions or, for a variety of possible reasons, may not want to go through the time-consuming cloture process either. And if cloture is invoked, the minority may not insist on using the thirty hours. Yet a minority intent on making its opposition dramatically evident, perhaps to convince its activist base it fought to the bitter end, can stretch the process out for days.

The health care reform bill's passage in the Senate in 2009 illustrated how excruciatingly difficult the process can be when the minority insists on using all of its prerogatives.[31] At 7 a.m. on Christmas Eve morning, the bill passed the Senate on a straight party-line vote of 60–39. The Senate had debated the bill for twenty-five days, without breaks for weekends, since early December; not only did Democrats have to win five cloture votes, Republicans forced thirty hours of debate after each, only relenting on the last so that senators could beat a major snowstorm out of Washington on Christmas Eve. Provisions that a large majority of the Democratic membership strongly supported had to be dropped to get the requisite sixty votes. This case vividly illustrates why the "make them filibuster" strategy cannot be routinely employed.

The majority party and its agent, the majority leader, are not without weapons to combat obstructionist strategies. The majority leader's right of first recognition allows him to use a tactic called *filling the amendment tree*—that is, offering amendments in all of the parliamentarily permissible slots, thus preventing other senators from offering their amendments, and then usually filing for cloture. Although no complete list of all of the instances when majority leaders have used this parliamentary tactic is available (identifying them is not easy), experts agree that the practice has increased in recent years.[32] Majority Leader Frist appears to have done so on initial consideration of legislation six times in 2005–2006; Reid did it nine times in 2007–2008 and even more frequently in 2009–2010. Minority Leader McConnell has claimed that Reid filled the tree forty-three times in the 2007–2010 period.[33]

Reid's big majority in the 111th Congress made filling the amendment tree an often successful tactic. For example, Reid used it in December 2009 on the health care bill; after the bill had been on the floor for a number of days, and he had cobbled together a compromise that all sixty Democratic senators could support, Reid offered that compromise as a manager's amendment, filled the amendment tree, and then immediately filed for cloture. These moves meant that no further amendments would be in order until Reid's were disposed of, and if cloture were invoked, he could run out the clock—that is, prevent his amendments from coming to a vote until the postcloture time had expired so no other amendments could be offered. The majority leader can sometimes use the explicit or implicit threat to fill the tree as a bargaining tool to get the minority to agree to unanimous consent agreements, placing some limits on the amendment process. In fact, UCAs specifying that certain amendments require sixty votes to pass have become relatively common in recent years. In the 109th Congress, six amendments were subject to a sixty-vote requirement in UCAs; this shot up to thirty-three in the 110th Congress. Minority party members agree to such UCAs because the UCA gives them an up-or-down vote on their amendment, and in most cases, they know their amendment would, in any case, fail to get a simple majority. The sponsors' primary motive may well be to publicize their own proposals or to force their opponents to cast a difficult-to-explain vote.

Threatening to fill the amendment tree may induce the minority to bargain; actually doing so may block amendments altogether. But its limitation as a strategy, in either case, is that unless the majority leader can muster sixty votes (or at least persuade the minority he can do so), he cannot bring the bill at issue to a passage vote. In the late 1990s, Majority Leader Trent Lott used the tactic a number of times, but because Democrats maintained high cohesion on cloture votes, it usually just led to gridlock. In eight of the fifteen times it was employed by Frist and Reid in the 109th and 110th Congresses, the majority leader either had to pull the bill off the floor or withdraw his amendments so as to allow other senators to offer theirs. The minority party complains bitterly when the tactic is used. However, when the majority party is required to get a supermajority to pass almost everything, then, once the sixty votes are in hand, the majority leader has every incentive to fill the tree and cut off amendments.

In the 112th and 113th Congresses, with the Democratic majority severely reduced, the dilemmas inherent in leading a nonmajoritarian chamber in a hyperpartisan environment became even more marked. Reid could use strategies like filling the tree to protect his members from having to take politically perilous votes. He could actually pass legislation only with minority party acquiescence, which was often not forthcoming. With the House controlled by Republicans, Reid knew that major Democratic Party agenda items had little chance of becoming law. Thus, he had little incentive to allow Republicans to offer nongermane amendments, which were often aimed at embarrassing Democrats and furthering the Republican agenda. Over the course of his eight years as majority leader, Reid filled the tree ninety-five times, according to the Congressional Research Service.[34] In 2014, he allowed votes on only fifteen amendments.

Even bills with bipartisan support were often caught in the procedural morass. In the spring and summer of 2011, the Senate spent many days considering a small-business research bill and an Economic Development Administration reauthorization, both noncontroversial bills, but was never able to get to a passage vote on either. Numerous amendments were debated, but reaching a UCA to end debate proved to be impossible, and cloture votes failed.

The Republican minority complained bitterly about Reid's aggressive filling of the tree to prevent GOP amendments. If the electorate gave them a Senate majority in the 2014 elections, he would eschew the tactic, Republican leader Mitch McConnell promised, and return to an open amendment process. Republicans did, in fact, win a majority in 2014, and Mitch McConnell became majority leader. In his first year as majority leader, McConnell did allow more votes on amendments; there were 145 amendment votes during the first seven months of 2015.[35] (Obviously, this is a much greater number than the fifteen Reid allowed in 2014, when he had largely given up on passing legislation. It is a less stark contrast with the ninety-nine such votes Reid allowed in the first seven months of 2013.)

McConnell found, however, that he too sometimes had to fill the amendment tree if he wished to bring legislation to a passage vote. He did so twelve times in his first eleven months as leader, including on the Keystone XL Pipeline bill, on a highway bill, and on trade legislation.

Democrats did not obstruct legislation across the board, as Republicans had; with a fellow partisan in the White House, both policy and political motives dictated some cooperation. Furthermore, some of the legislation McConnell sought to pass in the early months of his tenure were bills that Democrats had unsuccessfully tried to pass in the previous Congress, such as an antiterrorism insurance bill. When, however, McConnell tried to pass legislation Democrats opposed, they made full use of their Senate prerogatives to block action. Thus, early in 2015, the House sent the Senate an appropriations bill funding the Department of Homeland Security (DHS) with a provision defunding the Obama administration's immigration plan. Democrats filibustered the motion to proceed and, despite six cloture votes intended to embarrass them, refused to give in. To avoid leaving the DHS without funds, McConnell was forced to pass a clean bill—that is, one without the immigration provision. Democrats blocked an up-or-down vote on the Iran Nuclear Agreement Disapproval Resolution, thus killing it. They refused to allow the Senate to consider appropriations bills until a bipartisan agreement was reached on spending increases for domestic discretionary programs. Through October 22, 2015, the Senate voted on cloture fifty-six times; on twenty-six of these votes, cloture was invoked, often after multiple unsuccessful cloture votes and most often after Democrats gained concessions. In sum, the Senate continues to frequently suffer from gridlock. Reconciliation bills—ones making changes in law in accordance with instructions in the budget resolution—are not subject to filibuster. Consequently, the temptation for the majority party to accomplish its policy goals through the budget process is strong. The big tax cuts that President Bush requested in 2001 and 2003 were enacted through reconciliation bills whose passage only required a simple majority. In 2010, after the Senate Democrats lost their sixty-vote majority, they knew they would not be able to pass a health care reform bill making the necessary compromises with the House version through the normal process. The House agreed to pass the Senate bill, and the "fixes" to the Senate version on which the House insisted were included in a reconciliation bill. Democrats were also able to include a major revision of the student loan program in the reconciliation bill. Senate rules—most importantly, the Byrd rule barring extraneous matters in reconciliation bills—restrict the use of this strategy. (The student loan provisions met the Byrd rule test because they saved money.) The Byrd rule can only be waived by a three-fifths supermajority. In 2015, Republicans hoped to repeal "Obamacare" through the reconciliation process, but the Byrd rule proved to be a major impediment.

With limited exceptions, as long as the minority can command forty-one votes, it can prevent the majority from acting. Only damage to the minority party's reputation or to the reelection chances of its members acts as a constraint.

Nominations have been a particular source of conflict in recent years. Both parties have used the filibuster to deny confirmation to nominees of presidents of the other party. In 2005, after Democrats had blocked a number of Bush judicial nominees, Majority Leader Frist threatened to change the rules for presidential nominations through a highly controversial procedure that required only a simple majority. This "nuclear option" would have entailed the Senate's presiding officer ruling—against established Senate precedents—that cutting off debate on nominations only requires a simple majority. Democrats would, of course, have appealed the ruling, but only a simple majority is required to uphold a ruling of the chair. A deal put together by seven Democrats and seven Republicans averted the move.[36] In the 111th Congress, the first of the Obama presidency, the Democrats' majority was wide enough that Majority Leader Reid could usually impose cloture if he was willing to take the time to do so, but because of time constraints, the backlog of unconfirmed nominees reached unprecedented levels. With the size of their majority reduced after the 2010 elections, Senate Democrats had even more difficulty confirming nominations, and junior members began to press their leaders to institute filibuster reform.

Under a threat from Democrats of "going nuclear," Republicans agreed to reduce the amount of debate time allowed after cloture on many nominees. The standing order, a Senate rules change valid for only the current Congress, was reached in 2013, at the beginning of the 113th Congress. The rules change did not, however, reduce the votes needed to invoke cloture, and Republicans, with forty-five members, often refused Democrats an up-or-down vote on President Obama's nominees. Frustrated by the minority's blocking of nominees for secretary of labor, head of the Consumer Finance Protection Bureau (CFPB), administrator of the Environmental Protection Agency, and twelve other executive-branch nominees who, Majority Leader Harry Reid claimed, had been waiting about 260 days for confirmation votes, Reid threatened the nuclear option again; McConnell had not lived up to his promise to limit delays, Reid argued. Again, a deal was reached for an up-or-down vote on seven of the nominees.

In fall 2013, Republicans blocked votes on three nominees to the U.S. Court of Appeals for the D.C. Circuit. Although it is considered the second-most-important federal court after the Supreme Court because of the significance of the cases it hears, Republicans argued it did not need a full complement of judges. Democrats responded that Republicans were just trying to maintain a Republican majority on the court. On November 21, 2013, after Republicans had, on October 31, again prevented cloture on one of the nominees, Reid pulled the trigger on the nuclear option. He moved to reconsider one of the nominations and then raised a point of order that, for non–Supreme Court nominations, only a simple majority was required to invoke cloture. In conformity with then current precedent, the presiding officer ruled that sixty votes were required. Reid appealed the ruling of the chair to the entire Senate, which voted by a simple majority in Reid's favor. Thus, until it is changed again, which could be done in the same way, invoking cloture on all nominees, except Supreme Court Justices, requires a simple majority. The rules change allowed Democrats to confirm many more nominees than previously. From the date of the rules change through the end of the 113th Congress, just a little over a year, the Senate confirmed ninety-six judges and about three hundred executive-branch nominees.

Despite their outrage at the use of the nuclear option, Republicans did not change the rule when they won control of the Senate. They did, however, drastically slow down the confirmation of Obama nominees. As Senate majority leader, Mitch McConnell has honored the holds of fellow Republicans. He has also refused to bring most judicial nominations to the floor for a vote.[37] Thus, the battle over the confirmation of presidential nominees continues.

Individualism, Partisanship, and Legislative Outcomes

How does the combination of individualism and intense partisanship that characterizes the contemporary Senate affect legislative outcomes? As shown in Table 1-3, the likelihood of a major measure becoming law is less in recent Congresses than in earlier ones. In the Congresses since the early 1990s, during which half or more of the major legislation was subject to some sort of filibuster problem, 43 percent of the major measures failed enactment. By contrast, in the earlier Congresses, characterized by less filibuster activity, 28 percent of the major measures failed. Of course, there are many steps in the legislative process, and these figures, by themselves, do not prove that the Senate is responsible for the increase in legislative failures. However, as also shown in Table 1-3, in the more recent Congresses, legislation was much more likely to pass the House but fail in the Senate than the reverse; in the earlier Congresses, the difference was not very great.

Does the increasing frequency with which measures encounter extended-debate–related problems in the Senate explain this pattern? Filibuster problems do, in fact, depress a measure's chances of surviving the legislative process. In Congresses between the 1960s and 2010, 28 percent of major measures that did not encounter such a problem, either because senators chose not to use their prerogatives or because the measure enjoyed statutory protection, failed to be enacted; 42 percent of those that did experience a filibuster problem failed to become law.[38]

Table 1-3 Where Major Measures Failed

	Failed Measures	
What Happened?	87th–101st Congresses	103rd–113th Congresses
Passed by neither House nor Senate	40%	26%
Passed by House but not by Senate	19%	49%
Passed by Senate but not by House	13%	6%
Passed by House and Senate	28%	19%
Total number of failed measures	112 (of 405 measures)	233 (of 537 measures)
Percentage of total measures that failed	27.7	43.4

Source: Author's calculations.

Inasmuch as filibusters and filibuster threats are by no means always intended to kill legislation, these figures suggest a considerable effect.

Thus, the combination of individualism and intense partisanship that characterizes the contemporary Senate does depress the likelihood of bills successfully surviving the legislative process. Yet given the Senate rules and the ways that senators currently exploit them, it is perhaps more surprising that the Senate manages to legislate at all. The Senate does pass legislation, both must-pass measures, such as appropriations legislation, and other major bills. To be sure, some measures—budget resolutions and reconciliation bills, most importantly—are protected from filibusters and nongermane amendments by law; that has been vital to the passage of some of the most important legislation of the last decade.[39] But considerable legislation without such protection gets through the Senate as well.

Dodging Legislative Breakdown?

Clearly, the Senate could not function if senators maximally exploited their prerogatives—if, for example, every senator objected to every unanimous consent agreement on any matter that he or she did not completely support. What, then, has kept senators, as individuals and as party teams, from pushing their prerogatives over the limit and miring the Senate in total gridlock? And is true legislative breakdown now an imminent danger?

Asked that question, senators, staff members, and informed observers uniformly respond that almost all senators want to "get something done" and are aware that many senators exploiting their prerogatives to the limit would make that impossible. As one knowledgeable insider phrased it, "I like to think of the Senate as a bunch of armed nuclear nations. Each senator knows he can blow the place up. But most of them came here to do something, and if he does blow things up, if he does use his powers that way, then he won't be able to do anything." Using one's prerogatives aggressively entails concrete short-run costs, most also argued. "If you do object [to a unanimous consent request], it's going to hurt someone and maybe more than one person," a senior staffer explained. "So the next time you want something, it may very well happen to you."

Similar considerations have tended to restrain senators as party teams and have especially restrained their leaders. The leaders are very much aware that as much as senators want to gain partisan advantage on the big issues, they also want, for both reelection and policy reasons, to pass bills. As the earlier discussion of the interactions between the party leaders indicated, the leaders are instrumental in maintaining the cooperation necessary to keep the Senate functioning. They do so by working together closely, by adeptly employing both procedural and peer pressure to encourage the recalcitrant to deal, and by accommodating, to some extent, all senators with problems.[40] Although the procedural resources and the favors the leaders command are fairly meager, they do have one persuasive argument for inducing cooperation. As a knowledgeable insider put it, senators "can use the powers they have to create chaos and confusion on the floor, in which case senators don't have a life, where the floor debate goes on to all hours without any knowledge of when anything will happen, or they can defer to their leaders to create a structure with some predictability, and then they do have a life. And that's the bargain they have made." Leaders are not shy about using senators' desire for predictability and time off to pressure them. As a Capitol Hill reporter stated, "Vows to cancel a recess, hold a session late into the night or meet through the weekend have in recent years become standard parts of a Senate Majority Leader's repertoire."[41]

Leaders also need to concern themselves with guarding the party's reputation within the chamber and with the public. The minority party's influence within the chamber depends on its being able to block cloture when a party effort is made to do so, and that has tended to require using obstructionism selectively. The minority has to avoid being perceived as obstructionist on legislation popular with the public.

In its everyday functioning, the contemporary Senate exhibits a peculiar combination of conflict and cooperation, of aggressive exploitation of rules and accommodation. The hottest partisan legislative battles are studded with unanimous consent agreements. Thus, the Senate will agree by unanimous consent on a time to begin consideration of a motion to proceed that everyone knows the minority will block. And the more intense the partisan fight, the more frequently the majority and minority leaders confer. On bills not at the center of partisan conflict, senators routinely cooperate across the partisan divide. As a senior aide expressed the consensus, "If you really want to move stuff, if it's not a big partisan matter, a big ideological issue, and you really want to move it, then you really have to be bipartisan. You've got to work out the difficulties, and you've got to work across the aisle." Bipartisanship is especially important on legislation of secondary importance because the majority leader requires that the problems be resolved before he attempts to bring those bills to the floor. Senators, as individuals, do put holds on one another's bills, but they also often attempt to accommodate one another on an individual basis in ways that extend far beyond what occurs in the House. A staffer explained such responsiveness not by norms of civility and reciprocity but by the facts of life in the contemporary Senate. It is "because they need to accommodate you to move something," the aide continued. "They want to get something done. They want to get legislation, and to do that, you have to take care of people's problems."

Thus, senators' acute awareness of the weapons all senators command can work to produce cooperation and some restraint. Yet in an era of intensified partisanship, combined with the continuing individualism that has characterized the Senate since the 1970s, the Senate legislative process is fragile. Senate party leaders are under considerable pressure from their members to pursue partisan advantage aggressively, and partisan battles aimed at electoral gain are zero sum. Most of the time, the Senate has managed to maintain the minimum restraint and cooperation necessary to avoid total gridlock, yet the chamber regularly seems to teeter on the precipice of legislative breakdown.

In the last few years, Senate functioning has become increasingly problematic. The minority party seems to perceive less danger to its reputation in almost constant obstructionism, perhaps because attentive citizens are themselves so split along coinciding ideological and partisan lines. The majority has become increasingly frustrated and has sometimes acted in ways that have exacerbated partisan rancor. Whether this Senate can continue to dodge legislative breakdown is an open question.

Notes

The definitive work on the Senate in the 1950s is Donald Matthews's *U.S. Senators and Their World* (New York: Vintage Books, 1960). The title of this chapter is intended as a tribute to Don and his classic. All unattributed quotations in the main text of the chapter are from interviews conducted by the author.

1. Barbara Sinclair, *Unorthodox Lawmaking* (Washington, DC: CQ Press, 1997; 2nd ed., 2000; 3rd ed., 2007; 4th ed., 2011); Sarah Binder and Steven S. Smith, *Politics or Principle? Filibustering in the United States Senate* (Washington, DC: Brookings Institution Press, 1997).
2. Donald R. Matthews, *U.S. Senators and Their World* (Chapel Hill: University of North Carolina Press, 1960).
3. Barbara Sinclair, *The Transformation of the U.S. Senate* (Baltimore: Johns Hopkins University Press, 1989); Ralph Huitt, "The Internal Distribution of Influence: The Senate," in *The Congress and America's Future*, ed. David Truman (New York: Prentice Hall, 1965).
4. Bruce Oppenheimer, "Changing Time Constraints on Congress: Historical Perspectives on the Use of Cloture," in *Congress Reconsidered*, 3rd ed., ed. Lawrence C. Dodd and Bruce I. Oppenheimer (Washington, DC: CQ Press, 1985); Gregory Koger, *Filibustering: A Political History of Obstruction in the House and Senate* (Chicago: University of Chicago Press, 2010).
5. Sinclair, *Transformation;* Michael Foley, *The New Senate* (New Haven: Yale University Press, 1980); David Rohde, Norman Ornstein, and Robert Peabody, "Political Change and Legislative Norms in the U.S. Senate, 1957–1974," in *Studies of Congress*, ed. Glenn Parker (Washington, DC: CQ Press, 1985).
6. See also Burdett Loomis, *The New American Politician* (New York: Basic Books, 1988).
7. Binder and Smith, *Politics or Principle?*
8. *CQ Weekly*, January 16, 2012, 117. Party support score figures are adjusted for absences.
9. Patrick J. Sellers, "Winning Media Coverage in the U.S. Congress," in *U.S. Senate Exceptionalism*, ed. Bruce Oppenheimer (Columbus: The Ohio State University Press, 2002); Donald Baumer, "Senate Democratic Leadership in the 100th Congress," in *The Atomistic Congress*, ed. Ronald Peters and Allen Herzke (Armonk, NY: M. E. Sharpe, 1992); Steven S. Smith, "Forces of Change in Senate Party Leadership and Organization," in *Congress Reconsidered*, 5th ed., ed. Lawrence C. Dodd and Bruce I. Oppenheimer (Washington, DC: CQ Press, 1993); Mary Jacoby, "Waiting in Wings, a Kinder, Gentler Lott?" *Roll Call*, March 9, 1995, 22.
10. Computed from committee and subcommittee lists on Senate committee Web sites, accessed through www.senate.gov.

11. Richard Hall, *Participation in Congress* (New Haven: Yale University Press, 1996).
12. Christopher J. Deering and Steven S. Smith, *Committees in Congress* (Washington, DC: CQ Press, 1997).
13. Major measures are defined as those measures in lists of major legislation published in *CQ Almanacs* and the *CQ Weekly*, plus those measures on which key votes occurred, again according to *Congressional Quarterly*.
14. Sinclair, *Unorthodox Lawmaking*, 4th ed., 8–9, 43–44.
15. Roger H. Davidson, "Senate Leaders: Janitors for an Untidy Chamber?" in *Congress Reconsidered*, 3rd ed., ed. Lawrence C. Dodd and Bruce I. Oppenheimer (Washington, DC: CQ Press, 1985); Sinclair, *Transformation*; Smith, "Forces of Change."
16. See Richard Beth, "What We Don't Know about Filibusters," paper presented at the annual meeting of the Western Political Science Association, Portland, OR, March 15–18, 1995; also Sinclair, *Unorthodox Lawmaking*, 1st ed., 47–49; Koger, *Filibustering*. Sources for the data are given in the note to Table 1-1. The House Democratic Study Group publication relies on data supplied by Congressional Research Service experts; these experts' judgments about what constitutes a filibuster are not limited to instances in which cloture was sought. For the 103rd through the 110th Congresses, instances in which cloture was sought are used as the basis of the filibuster estimate. One can argue that this overestimates because in some cases, cloture was sought for reasons other than a fear of extended debate (for example, as a test vote or to impose germaneness). However, one can also argue that it underestimates because those cases in which cloture was not sought—perhaps because it was known to be out of reach—are not counted. For an estimate based on a different methodology, see Table 1-2.
17. Phil Kuntz, "Drawn-Out Denouement Mirrors Character of 102nd Congress," *CQ Weekly Report*, October 10, 1992, 3128.
18. *Washington Post*, February 8, 2010.
19. *Congressional Record*, December 1, 2011, S8114–37.
20. *CQ Weekly*, July 23, 2007, 2208–11.
21. Holds and threats to filibuster, as well as actual extended-debate-related delay on the floor, were coded as filibuster problems (see below). The definition of major legislation used here—those measures in lists of major legislation published in *CQ Almanacs* and the *CQ Weekly*, plus those measures on which key votes occurred, again according to *Congressional Quarterly*—yields forty to sixty measures per Congress. Thus, although truly minor legislation is excluded, the listing is not restricted to only the most contentious and highly salient issues.
22. C. Lawrence Evans and Walter Oleszek, "The Procedural Context of Senate Deliberation," in *Esteemed Colleagues: Civility and Deliberation in the U.S. Senate*, ed. Burdett Loomis (Washington, DC: Brookings Institution Press, 2000).
23. *Congressional Record*, March 6, 2003, S3216.
24. *CQ Weekly*, October 29, 2007, 3179.
25. Tom Daschle, *Like No Other Time* (New York: Crown, 2003), 208.
26. See Sellers, "Winning Media Coverage"; Barbara Sinclair, "The Plot Thickens: Congress and the President," in *Great Theatre: The American Congress in Action*, ed. Herbert Weisberg and Samuel Patterson (Cambridge, UK: Cambridge University Press, 1998); C. Lawrence Evans and Walter Oleszek, "Message Politics and Agenda Control in the U.S. Senate," in *The Contentious Senate*, ed. Colton C. Campbell and Nicol C. Rae (Lanham, MD: Rowman and Littlefield, 2001).

27. Francis Lee, *Beyond Ideology: Politics, Principles and Partisanship in the U.S. Senate* (Chicago: University of Chicago Press, 2009).
28. Steven Smith, *The Senate Syndrome* (Norman: University of Oklahoma Press, 2014).
29. *Congressional Record*, October 6, 2011, S6319.
30. Smith, *Senate Syndrome*.
31. Sinclair, *Unorthodox Lawmaking*, 4th ed., Chapter 8.
32. Richard Beth, Valerie Heitshusen, Bill Heniff, and Elizabeth Rybicki, "Leadership Tools for Managing the U.S. Senate," paper presented at the annual meeting of the American Political Science Association, Toronto, Canada, September 1–4, 2009.
33. *Congressional Record*, December 18, 2010, S10664.
34. Manu Raju, "McConnell Employs Reid's Hardball Tactic," *Politico*, July 30, 2015, http://www.politico.com/story/2015/07/mitch-mcconnell-harry-reid-hardball-tactic-120801.
35. *CQ Weekly*, July 27, 2015, 7.
36. Sarah A. Binder, Anthony Madonna, and Steven S. Smith, "Going Nuclear, Senate Style," *Perspectives on Politics* 5 (2007): 729–40.
37. Seung Min Kim and Burgess Everett, "Angry GOP Senate Freezes Out Obama Nominees," Politico, October 14, 2015, http://www.politico.com/story/2015/10/gop-senate-barack-obama-cotton-214700.
38. Based on selected Congresses, 87th–111th. Measures that did not get far enough to encounter the prospect of a filibuster problem are coded as missing data on the filibuster variable.
39. See the case studies of the 1993, 1995, and 1997 reconciliation (that is, budget) bills in Sinclair, *Unorthodox Lawmaking*, 2nd ed.
40. Barbara Sinclair, "The Senate Leadership Dilemma: Passing Bills and Pursuing Partisan Advantage in a Non-Majoritarian Chamber," in *The Contentious Senate*, ed. Colton C. Campbell and Nicol C. Rae (Lanham, MD: Rowman and Littlefield, 2001).
41. *Roll Call*, July 25, 2007.

2. Lending and Reclaiming Power
Majority Leadership in the House Since the 1950s

John H. Aldrich and David W. Rohde

For nearly half a century, the House of Representatives has been characterized by almost constant change in its institutional rules—that is, how it governs itself. In this chapter, we will outline the broad contours of those changes, focusing particularly on the shifting balance of power between the majority party leadership and the committee system. In this account, we will offer an explanation of the ebb and flow of that balance. Key to this ebb and flow has been the set of elections that have brought sometimes similar, sometimes different kinds of members to serve. Two of the most consequential changes in this regard have been (1) the breakup of the "solid, lily-white" Democratic Party in the South, the existence of which caused considerable strains within the majority Democratic Party from the 1950s into the 1970s, and, related to this, (2) the rise of partisan polarization in the 1980s and beyond, in which the two parties in the House have been increasingly divergent from each other in terms of policy preferences and, for much of the period, increasingly homogeneous internally. The now majority Republican Party has seen increasing internal strains in the last few Congresses, however. We use these developments and the theory we call conditional party government to explain the changes in the way the House is structured and thus how the majority party is (or is not) empowered to achieve its aims.

For decades, from the 1920s through the 1960s, the House was relatively unchanging in terms of its internal rules that defined how its powers would be allocated.[1] The majority party and its leadership had relatively limited powers while the standing committees and their chairs were relatively more powerful. These committee powers were, in turn, mostly allocated to individual members via seniority. This pattern of House rules began to come under strain in the late 1950s and led to changes that began, in the 1970s, to give greater powers to the two parties in the House and especially to the majority party leadership. From the 1980s and into the twenty-first century, partisan polarization increased. That is, the differences in how Republicans voted, compared to Democrats, increased, with fewer and fewer crossing party lines to support policies favored by the other party. These differences have greatly shaped how the Congress has gone about its business, the kinds of controversies in it, and the policies they have—and have not—enacted. The following sections trace these changes from the 1950s to the present and offer an explanation as to why these changes have occurred and with what consequences. We move rapidly through the earlier decades, placing closer attention on the events that have shaken the House during the speakerships of John Boehner and the current Speaker, Paul Ryan—that is, to the House under

Republican leadership since the elections of 2010 brought them back to power. We begin with a consideration of the baseline from which change occurred: the House in the mid-1950s.

The Era of Committee Government in the House

The midterm elections for the Eighty-fourth Congress (1955–1957) were both conventional and yet proved to be surprising. In 1952, the Republican Party won the presidency and small majorities in both chambers of Congress, including a scant four-seat majority in the House. The 1954 midterm elections were typical of most midterms, with the incumbent party losing votes and seats, and with such a close balance of seats, it also lost its majorities.[2] In the House, the Democrats picked up nineteen seats, a genuine but not unusually large victory. Their fourteen-seat majority must have felt vulnerable, especially in light of what was correctly expected to be a landslide reelection for President Dwight Eisenhower. The Democrats turned out to be able to hold their House majority that year, even picking up two seats. The surprise emanating from that election was that they would continue to hold that majority for forty years, from 1955 to 1995, by far the longest such reign in U.S. history.

The Democratic majority was possible, in part, because it contained great ideological diversity, pairing mostly liberal northern Democrats with mostly conservative Southern Democrats. This coalition of seemingly odd bedfellows was, in turn, possible to some degree because of the way the House worked in this period.[3] From about 1920 until the 1970s, the House operated under a set of rules that allocated power by virtually fixed standards.[4] Committees had established policy jurisdictions and great control over policy making (or blocking) in those areas. Once a member of the House received a seat on a committee, he or she held rights to keep that seat as long as desired. Chairs were given potentially dictatorial powers over their committee's operation, and the majority party awarded chairmanships to the most senior member of the majority party on the committee, simply by virtue of seniority. These features decentralized powers greatly.[5] The result was that the Speaker of the House (Sam Rayburn, D–Tex.) worked with the committee chairs to determine how the Democrats would use their majority in the House in 1954 and onward, through the end of his speakership (1961) and into the reform era we discuss in the next section.

This allocation of powers in the House (making up the so-called "textbook Congress"[6]) had the odd feature of giving these powers predominantly to Southern Democrats. That happened because there was no Republican Party in most of the South, and virtually no Southern Democrats faced challenges to reelection.[7] Once they won their seat, it was theirs until they chose to give it up or, very rarely, lost in a primary. Thus, in time, Southern Democrats became the most senior members of the Democratic Party and hence held most committee chairs in the House. This would not be a problem on its own but would become so when two other features held. First, Southern Democrats in the 1950s were only a minority of the Democrats in the House. Second, what they wanted was different from what their northern partisan peers wanted to achieve, and these policy differences proved to grow larger and deeper over time. The rules allocated power on the basis of fixed standards such as seniority for reasons that went back through decades, and the rules would continue to allocate power to a Southern conservative minority unless the House and the majority party changed them, but as we will see, that took decades to effect.

Perhaps the most important political event in 1954 was the issuance of the opinion of the Supreme Court in the case *Brown v. Board*. They ruled that the separate educational facilities at the heart of Jim Crow laws in the South were inherently unequal and had to change. The following year, the modern civil rights movement began in Montgomery, Alabama. These events, as one of their effects, raised the salience of the division between the two wings of the congressional Democratic Party.

The 1958 midterm elections were even more favorable than those of 1954 to the Democrats, adding a substantial forty-nine seats to their then current majority. Virtually all of these seats went to Northern Democrats. The Democrats thus held a commanding majority in the House (and Senate), and Northern Democrats held a majority within their party. Southern Democrats, however, still held power under the rules of the textbook Congress. Southern Democrats therefore could simply block any initiatives they chose, and they chose to block anything related to increasing civil rights for African Americans, among other issues. The result was conflict within the majority party that extended for nearly two decades, as the party and the House struggled to choose a set of rules—an institutional structure—to reflect these new realities. While the 1958 elections were critical in introducing the struggle, it would not be until the 1970s that significant changes were made.[8]

After the 1958 elections, a set of liberal, Northern Democrats formed the Democratic Study Group (DSG) to try to counteract the effects of the conservative, Southern Democrats. In 1961, Rayburn and newly elected president John F. Kennedy succeeded in expanding the number of members of the Rules Committee to at least modestly dilute the powerful grip of the Southern Democrats and especially its chair, Howard Smith, D-Va.

The elevation of Lyndon Johnson to president in the wake of Kennedy's assassination and the Republicans' nomination of Sen. Barry Goldwater, R-Ariz., to face Johnson in 1964 led to a Democratic landslide. They held 295 seats in the House (just over a two-thirds majority) and sixty-eight in the Senate (enough, if unified, to invoke cloture, ending any Republican attempt at a filibuster). The resulting Great Society Congress was one of the most active ever, passing the Voting Rights Act of 1965 and much other liberal legislation under the umbrellas of the Great Society and the war on poverty amid continuing support for the war in Vietnam. Conservative Southerners generally held the opposite preferences, except for support for the war, but when public opinion turned increasingly against the war, opposition to it was led by liberal Democrats and resisted most fiercely by Southern Democrats. As the Great Society Congress opened, DSG-led Democrats reformed the House rules, two of these reforms further modifying the hold of the Rules Committee.[9]

Perhaps because of such large majorities, pushing for additional reforms might have seemed less important than passing legislation. The following congressional elections of 1966 and 1968 reduced the size of the Democratic majority of the Great Society Congress and saw Republican Richard M. Nixon elected president in 1968. The DSG revitalized its efforts for reform, which led to a new era, one that we call the *reform era* in the House. The Voting Rights Act of 1965 marked the end of the Jim Crow South and began to reshape fundamentally party and electoral politics in that region. Of course, these changes, which undermined one-party control there, were resisted. The development of the Republican Party into a fully competitive party was slow and did not really take root in the South until the Reagan administration in the 1980s and did not fully mature until 1994, when Republicans first won a majority of the Southern delegation on their way to winning their first congressional majority in forty years.

The Reform Era in the House

By the 1970s, Northern Democrats were finally able to change the party's rules allocating power to committee chairs. This process began in 1971 with an initial reform of the inviolability of the seniority selection system, continued in 1972 with the "subcommittee bill of rights," and culminated in 1975 with the Democrats stripping three Southern Democrats of their chairmanships, in violation of seniority.[10] There followed a series of reform efforts in both parties (but especially in the majority Democratic Party) to weaken the old structure of Congress and to place more powers in the hands of the leadership in the majority party. While Thomas P. "Tip" O'Neill, D-Mass., Speaker from 1977 to his retirement in 1987, was considered particularly adept at working with President Ronald Reagan "across the aisle," his successor, James Wright, D-Tex., aroused considerably greater partisan conflict in the House.

Southern Democrats not only saw their power in the chamber eroding in the early 1970s but also saw their electoral safety diminishing. As noted earlier, most Southern Democrats faced little or no reelection challenge in the 1950s. That began to change slowly in the wake of the passage of the Civil Rights Act in 1964 and especially of the passage of the Voting Rights Act in 1965, which enabled heretofore excluded African Americans to register and vote in the South.[11] In the 1970s, Southern Democrats increasingly voted against their northern partisan peers on the floor of Congress, and when they did, the result was a roll call vote that formed what was known as a *conservative coalition*.[12] While this strategy of siding with conservative Republicans emerged as early as 1937, it became increasingly common in the early to mid-1970s, becoming nearly as frequent as a party vote,[13] amounting to close to one-third of roll call votes on occasion.[14]

This behavior is at least consistent with Southern Democrats trying to forestall the development of a Republican challenger in their districts. Starting in the late 1970s and continuing into the 1980s, however, the Republican Party was finally able to get sufficiently organized in the South to mount opposition for a majority of congressional seats. In the 1978 congressional elections, Democrats, who held 90 percent of the available seats in the South in the 1950s, won "only" 69 percent of the seats. And whereas three-quarters of Democratic victories were noncompetitive in the 1950s, only one-third were in 1978.[15] Longtime incumbents might survive such challenges, but over time, conservative Southern Republicans won more and more seats while Southern Democrats in less conservative districts (made more liberal by the ability of African Americans to vote) became more moderate. Indeed, districts with near or actual African American majorities elected members who voted as liberally as their Northern counterparts.

Southern Democrats were thus either replaced by conservative Republicans or began to vote as (or were replaced with) more moderate Democrats, depending on the composition of their district. The decline of conservative voting among these Southern Democrats contributed heavily to the growing partisan polarization of the House.[16] By the time Wright became Speaker in 1987, he presided over a House in which Democrats increasingly voted alike and voted differently from Republicans, who also voted similarly to one another. That is to say that at least in terms of roll call voting on the floor of Congress, each party was increasingly homogeneous, and even more evidently, the two parties became very different in roll call voting behavior from each other and became so over an increasingly broad array of issues. The emergence of partisan polarization enabled reformers to centralize majority party power more fully into the hands of the leaders of that party. This was starting to take effect in the 1970s, but the increased centralization of power into the party leadership really took off during Wright's speakership.

Progress toward stronger party leadership slowed as the Wright era ended in 1989. Speaker Tom Foley, D-Wash., who served from 1989 until his electoral defeat in 1994, proved to be a relatively weak Speaker. He failed, in particular, to respond effectively to such excesses as the House post office and banking scandals. Centralization of power began to accelerate again with the 1994 elections in which Republicans won a majority of seats in the South and a majority in the House overall, ending the forty-year reign of the Democrats and making Newt Gingrich, R-Ga., Speaker. From the Gingrich through the Hastert, Pelosi, Boehner, and now Ryan speakerships, not only has power been centralized in the party leadership far more than during the "textbook Congress" era, but the two parties have also been locked in close competition for winning House majorities in elections. In the following section, we outline a way to think about the nature of the reform process from the 1950s to the present and, even more, about how these reforms have helped shape House politics and policy making.

Conditional Party Government

The long period of the "textbook Congress" and its seeming inability to be reformed allowed many scholars and observers to assume this constancy was permanent. As we have seen already and will in more detail in the rest of this chapter, that permanence was illusory. Change seems a better description. And perhaps that should not be surprising in a House that, except for the sparse provisions in the Constitution, writes and enacts its own rules, by simple majority vote, at the beginning of every Congress.[17] Since about the 1890s, the major question is how much power will be centralized into the hands of the leadership of the majority party and how much will decentralized, as in the "textbook Congress" days when power was distributed among the various committees.[18] The authors have developed an explanation we call *conditional party government* to help us understand power and its allocation. There are three parts of the account. The third step—the ultimate outcome of this process—is to understand how the House and the parties within it allocate their powers and, in particular, when they will grant their leaders more rather than less power.

The first step in this explanation is to understand just what it is that the individual legislators are seeking to accomplish. What are their goals? Many find that a great deal can be explained by simply assuming that every member's only goal is ensuring reelection, and it is certainly the case that reelection dominates much congressional activity.[19] Like others, we find that exclusive a focus insufficient to understand all congressional behavior.[20] We believe that members of Congress share, in varying degrees, four goals: reelection, making good public policy, seeking individual power in the chamber, and having their party hold a majority in the chamber. To be sure, reelection is important for achieving all of the other goals, but it is hard to see how we can make sense of all of what legislators do if we do not imagine they also care about policy making and about power, both personal and partisan.

We call the explanation conditional party government because we believe that members distribute power as they do only under certain conditions. The second step, therefore, is to define those conditions. Party members will want to give more power to the party leadership when there is greater consensus in the party about what to do with those powers and when it is more important that the leadership have the tools to achieve those goals. This situation occurs when it is the case that the opposition wants something very different. That is, the more homogeneous preferences are within each party, and the more heterogeneity there is between the two parties, the more power members will give (more accurately, will lend) their leadership. The conditions, when applied to policy, are almost exactly the definition of partisan polarization. Thus, the growth in partisan polarization, from a low point in the 1950s, 1960s, and 1970s to increasingly highly partisan Congresses in the last thirty years, is an indication that the condition for conditional party government has become more fully realized. We therefore should expect changes in House and party rules that centralize power in leadership hands.

The growing degree of partisan polarization in the 1980s fits smoothly with increased centralization of power in the hands of the majority party and its leadership. The transition in leadership from O'Neill to Wright gave an opportunity for acting on that centralization. As Wright did so, he attracted the ire of the minority party and especially its more junior—and increasingly often Southern—Republican members, such as Newt Gingrich, R-Ga.

Of course, even if there is a great divide between the two parties, there still may be and generally are tensions within one or both parties.[21] When this erupts, as it appears to have done in recent Congresses and especially in the Republican Party, we would expect that party's representatives to pull power back away from its leadership, at least in terms and on issues that shape the internal party divide. Conditional party government thus provides a simple basis for understanding changes that have come about in the House, especially since WWII, the period covered in this chapter.

From Speaker Wright to Speaker Gingrich: The End of Continuous Democratic Rule

From 1987 to 1994, the Democrats continued their long run in power, with very little change in the number of seats they controlled. Indeed, the 1992 congressional elections returned them to the same point as in 1987. Thus, the big change in the House was the continual increase in partisan polarization on the floor and, of course, the election of the new Speaker, one who had long been more sharp edged in his partisanship than O'Neill.[22] As noted earlier, Wright used the Speaker's newly acquired powers more fully than his predecessor. In part, this was to achieve policy victories. Upon his election as Speaker, Wright announced a program of ten bills he wanted to see pass the House, and all did, with nine of ten becoming law (including one over a presidential veto). Of course, these particular bills were announced as goals of the new Speaker only after the election and with an eye toward what was possible to achieve. As the theory leads us to expect, they reflected the use of special rules—in particular, ones that restricted the ability of the minority party to offer amendments.[23] While his program mostly passed into law, the House quickly became mired in less policy-relevant controversies for the next several Congresses.

While we noted that the Democrats held a fairly consistent majority in this period (varying over the One Hundredth through 103rd Congresses, from 58 percent to 62 percent and back to 58 percent), there was an erosion of their electoral appeal, even if it did not reveal itself in seat losses. Thus, for example, the percentage of the two-party vote received by the Democrats declined from 1986 to 1992, from 54 percent to 53 percent to 52 percent to 50 percent, even though the percentage of seats those votes won for the Democrats changed little.[24] Perhaps illustrative of the reasons for a general loss of support was a scandal discovered in 1991 involving misuse of funds in the congressional post office, leading to a guilty plea to charges of mail fraud by one of the most powerful figures in Washington, Dan Rostenkowski, D-Ill., chair of the House Ways and Means Committee, and damaging the reputations of numerous others.

Earlier and more importantly, Speaker Wright was forced to resign. He came under investigation by the House Ethics Committee in 1988 for misuse of funds received as royalties and speaking fees for a book he had written. The charges were filed by Gingrich and undermined Wright's effectiveness. These events led him to resign in 1989, once his successor was selected.

Gingrich, as a key leader of younger Republican members, differed in his orientation toward his party's minority status. Many longtime Republicans had become used to perpetual minority status (even in the face of landslide victories for their presidential candidates) and developed ways of eking out small victories from the majority party. Gingrich sought to win a majority for the Republicans, and to that end, he and others were active in helping recruit and support potentially winning candidates. In the wake of these scandals that occurred under the Democratic watch, Gingrich embarked on an ambitious such campaign for 1994, hoping (he asserted) to make real inroads into the Democratic majority. To that end, he and other Republican leaders formulated a ten-point program dubbed the "Contract With America."[25] The Contract was created in advance of the 1994 campaign and was designed to create a national platform for incumbents and challengers alike in the party. Republican candidates gathered with incumbents in Washington in September for a "signing" ceremony and photo opportunity but were left free to run on the platform as a whole or any portion of it, as fit their needs best. This legislative campaign document was combined with recruitment and support programs in an unusually large number of districts. Even the day before the election, Gingrich admitted to expecting to be in the minority in the 104th Congress. However, the Republicans ended up winning a massive fifty-four-seat majority with 52 percent of the vote, a gain of nearly 7 percent over 1992.

The 1994 elections brought a dramatic change in the makeup of the Republican Party in the House.[26] In 1993, at the opening of the 103rd Congress, the Republicans had advanced to holding about 31 percent of the Southern seats in the House. In 1995, this percentage swelled to 53 percent, and thus, the Republicans, for the first time since the end of Reconstruction, were the majority party in the South. Leadership in Congress generally changed dramatically as a result of 1994 (Speaker Foley was defeated for reelection, for example), often changing the generation of the leaders. The House Republican leadership change was particularly dramatic, as Gingrich assumed the leadership of the House Republicans and thus the speakership; Dick Armey, R-Tex., was chosen majority party leader; and Tom DeLay, R-Tex., became majority whip. Thus, the top party leadership was entirely Southern, another first, with Bob Livingston, R-La., chairing Appropriations and Bill Archer, R-Tex., chairing Ways and Means, adding to the newfound Southern accent at the center of the Republican House delegation and its leadership.

Speaker Gingrich announced the leadership selection of three major committee chairs in violation of seniority: Livingston as chair of Appropriations; Thomas Biley, R-Va., as chair of Energy; and Henry Hyde, R-Ill., as chair of Judiciary.[27] Other substantial changes were in store, such as a general weakening of the independent powers of committee chairs, increasing party leadership oversight of committees, changing the committee assignment process, and adopting term limits (six years for committee chairs, eight for the Speaker). A number of newly elected Republicans received unusually plum committee appointments. The leadership, in practice, also employed control over the Rules Committee.

Giving leadership more control over Rules had been a major step in centralizing power in the Democratic majority. By following suit when they were the majority party, Republicans were also able to use influence over Rules to help achieve their goals. At one point that included more open rules for amendments, but (as discussed later) that proved unworkable, and they used restrictive rules more commonly. The party leadership also sought to shape the content of bills, such as by bypassing committees entirely on occasion and using party leadership influence in Appropriations to include substantive legislation rather than sending it to the authorizing committee with appropriate jurisdiction.[28]

This substantial centralization of power in the party leadership was meant, in large part, to facilitate the ability of the new Republican majority to act on its more nearly consensual policy preferences, a consequence of the combination of overall partisan polarization; the special features of 1994, including the use of the "Contract With America"; and simply being forty years out of power. Given the size and unexpected nature of their victory, Gingrich also felt that he owed a significant part of majority status and thus his speakership to the newly elected representatives, and they, in turn, could reasonably conclude that they owed their victories, in part, to the efforts of Gingrich and other party leaders and perhaps to the Contract as well. Gingrich made passage of the Contract a first order of business, seeking (successfully) to resolve all ten programs within the first one hundred days of the 104th Congress. Once passed in the House, many were changed substantially in the Senate (also with a new Republican majority), and few became law. Along the way to initial House passage of the bill concerning unfunded mandates, the amending rule was open, and the Democrats offered thirty-seven amendments that led to roll call votes (including in this number two of them proposed by an independent member of Congress, Bernie Sanders, I-Vt.). None passed, but the delay reduced Republican enthusiasm for the return to permitting the opposition wide access to the floor for amending.

Gingrich and the Republicans ruled the House and even national politics for some time. At one point, in 1995, President Clinton felt compelled to say in a press conference, "I am relevant. The Constitution gives me relevance. A president, especially an activist president has relevance."[29] Even so and as they found with the Contract, the House Republicans had more difficulties fulfilling their ambitions when other branches of government were involved. The two most important examples are the showdowns with the president over the budget for 1996, which led to (partial) government shutdowns in 1995 and again in 1996, and the impeachment of the president, tried in the Senate. With respect to the budget impasse and shutdowns and contrary to at least some expectations among Republicans in the House leadership, 46 percent of the public blamed Republicans while 27 percent blamed the Clinton administration.[30]

The 1998 congressional elections were held just before impeachment reached the House floor. In every midterm election of the century except 1934, when the Democratic New Deal majority was still emerging, the party of the incumbent president lost seats. In 1998, the Democrats reversed that and actually won four seats, yielding a narrow five-vote majority for the Republicans. Recriminations were loud, including concern that Gingrich and the Republicans had failed to make the campaign sufficiently nationalized over policy.[31] Livingston announced on Friday, November 6, that he would challenge Gingrich as Speaker. Gingrich, however, announced later that day that he would resign as Speaker and as a member of Congress.[32]

House Republicans voted articles of impeachment against President Clinton on December 19, 1998, over his handling of the Monica Lewinsky affair, by close but also nearly perfect party-line votes for perjury (228–206) and obstruction of justice (221–212). The Senate voted against conviction in both cases, and as before, Clinton's poll standings increased. During the House debate, Livingston announced he would not run for Speaker but would resign his seat over a recently disclosed extramarital affair. Thus, only four years into their majority, two of the key Republican leaders felt compelled to leave their posts, and the Gingrich era ended but not the Republican majority.

Speaker Hastert, 1999–2007

Dennis Hastert, R-Ill., became the new Speaker in 1999. Never as acerbically partisan as some, his acceptance speech called for a tamping down of partisanship. He also called for a return to "regular order," meaning that he would seek to return to the rules and practices of earlier years. As it happened, he did not. First, the 2000 election was a virtual tie in many ways. George W. Bush won the presidency with a half-million fewer votes than Al Gore. The Democrats won just enough seats to create an exact 50–50 tie in the Senate, making the Democrats the majority party until the end of the Clinton–Gore term and then making the Republicans the majority party when the new vice president, Dick Cheney, would cast the tie-breaking vote, rather than Gore. That changed again when Jim Jeffords, R-Vt., declared himself an independent in June, caucusing with the Democrats and thus giving them a 51–49 edge. In Hastert's House, the national vote divided 47.6 percent to 47.1 percent for the Republicans, but they lost two seats and thus held only a seven-seat majority.

Any thought of returning to regular order ended when the Republicans' term limits of six years for committee chairs came due in 2000. In an atmosphere in which pressures were pushing in both directions, Hastert decided to enforce the new rules and require chairs to step down at the end of six years. In addition, the new chair of Ways and Means, Bill Thomas, R-Calif., was chosen in violation of seniority and chosen because of his partisan approach.[33]

Hastert also lent his name to the so-called "Hastert rule," in which the party would not allow legislation to reach the floor without the support of at least a majority in the majority party. While this may sound tepid in today's climate, it was a dramatic extension of majority party power. It was not a *rule* in the sense of being adopted formally into the Republican Conference rules.[34] It did, however, set an informal expectation that the party would seek (and often achieve) an at least majority-level consensus before acting. As we will see, the events leading up to Speaker Boehner's resignation in 2015 flowed, in part, from failure to meet this level of aspiration on legislation important to Republicans.

The Appropriations Committee also continued to be a place where Republicans would focus on legislating. In 2000, Hastert and the GOP selected C. W. Bill Young, R-Fla., as chair. Young, despite his initial promises to work in the spirit of "bipartisanship, collegiality, and consensus-building,"[35] demonstrated from the start that he was a committed conservative who would work with the Speaker and the leadership on appropriations legislation. Under Hastert, GOP appointments to Appropriations continued to increase the ideological polarization within the committee, which extended the reversal of the committee's special role in bipartisanship in the "textbook Congress" era.[36] One result was that in all of the years in which Hastert was Speaker, appropriations were made only under continuing resolutions. "Regular order" passage of appropriations by ordinary legislation proved impossible, even though there were some years (2003–2007, plus the part of 2001–2003 that Republicans ruled the Senate) in which Hastert was Speaker during unified Republican control of the government. Of course, unlike Gingrich, Hastert served under a Republican president, a president who served during 9/11 and the wars that followed. No matter who would have been Speaker, he would have been less a national leader than circumstances gave Gingrich the opportunity to be.

The Democrats Return to the Majority With the First Female Speaker, Nancy Pelosi, 2007–2011

The wars in Afghanistan and Iraq reduced support for President Bush and Republicans generally. These concerns, Bush's handling of Hurricane Katrina (which hit the United States in August 2005), and an economic slowdown (setting the stage for the bursting of the "housing bubble" and then the Great Recession that began the next year and exploded during the 2008 campaign) hit home in the 2006 midterm congressional elections. The Democrats gained 5 percent more votes nationally than two years earlier and won thirty-one new House seats, giving them a fifteen-seat majority. When then Democratic Party leader Richard Gephardt, D-Mo., retired at the end of the 108th Congress (ending in 2005), Democrats selected Nancy Pelosi, D-Calif., as party leader. This was the first time in U.S. history that a congressional party was led by a female. Thus, her leading the party to majority status in 2006 meant that she became the first female Speaker of the House in 2007.

The return to majority status and selection of a new Speaker provided another opportunity for the House or the Democratic majority party to reduce the centralization of power in the party leadership and seek a more bipartisan approach. This path was plausible given a very narrow Senate majority and, of course, a Republican president. Pelosi did oversee reducing some degree of centralization of powers. For example, when they took over, the Democrats reverted to their previous selection system for committee chairs, presuming that the most senior member got the first shot but requiring a secret-ballot vote to confirm each one. They also kept some of the rules that the Republicans had added, including term limits on chairs, at least temporarily.[37] By this point, the committee chairs (who had been ranking minority members before the new Congress) were, in many cases, part and parcel of Pelosi's leadership team, perhaps especially David Obey, D-Wis., on Appropriations.

There was one prominent exception. John Dingell, D-Mich., who had been originally elected to the House in 1955, was known as a moderately liberal to progressive politician and had served as the senior Democrat on the Energy and Commerce Committee for many, many years.[38] He was, however, a thorn in Pelosi's side and very public hard feelings—and disruption of legislation—erupted. After the 2008 elections, Henry Waxman, D-Calif., challenged Dingell for committee chair and, with Pelosi's support, defeated him.

The majority party's efforts to control the agenda and the divisive partisan conflict over those efforts persisted during the two Democratic Congresses from 2007 to 2011. From the time she took the top post, Speaker Pelosi was willing to continue, even extend, the use of special rules to that end.[39] The return to majority status gave the Democrats the chance to appoint five new members to the Rules Committee. During the textbook Congress days, this was a particularly important committee and assignment so it went to more senior members. By the 110th Congress, it had become an arm of the leadership rather than an autonomous source of power. One way to see that was that four of the five assignments went to newly elected Democrats.

In 2008, the huge economic crisis now known as the Great Recession happened during the electoral campaign itself. This fact cemented Barack Obama's hold on the presidential race and improved the chances of Democrats throughout the nation. He thus became president with a solid House majority, with Democrats gaining twenty-one seats to reach a thirty-nine-seat majority in the House, and they held (for a short time) a bare filibuster-proof majority of sixty in the Senate. With unified control and an economic crisis to deal with, the 111th Congress was the most productive of major legislation since the Great Society Congress of 1965 to 1967, with major legislation directed toward the Great Recession and many other issues, including Obama's signature health care bill, the Affordable Care Act (popularly called "Obamacare").

This run of legislation would wane with the end, first, of the filibuster-proof Senate. A Republican, Scott Brown, R-Mass., replaced the longtime liberal leader of the party, Sen. Ted Kennedy, D-Mass., in a surprise showing in a special election called upon Kennedy's death. Even more importantly, the economic recovery legislation and others contributed to increased deficits, at least in the short term, if not the long term, which was more debatable. The Affordable Care Act became a symbol to some of the alleged ever-growing powers of the federal government. Out of questioning the size of government and the national debt and deficit grew a firestorm of protest that began to solidify in what became known as the Tea Party.[40]

John Boehner and the Challenges of Leadership

In November of 2010—in the wake of a slow economic recovery, an unhappy electorate, and the focusing of responsibility on the Democrats due to unified control of government—the Republicans achieved a major triumph in the midterm elections. They gained sixty-three House seats, regaining control and achieving their largest majority since the 1946 elections, and they gained six Senate seats (although they fell short of a majority in that chamber). Many of the new GOP representatives were identified with the Tea Party movement and held strongly conservative policy positions.

This result exacerbated the partisan polarization of the House. A measure of candidate ideology developed by Adam Bonica shows that while Republican members who returned to the House after the election were very conservative, the newly elected representatives were even more so. "An amazing 77% of the newly arriving Republicans, including dozens of Tea Party–backed Republicans, are to the right of the typical Republican in the previous Congress—and many are to the right of *almost all* continuing Republicans."[41] This was a continuation and acceleration of a trend for the GOP. Analysis by Edward G. Carmines (using a different ideology measure than Bonica's) shows that in each of the five Congresses before the 2010 elections, newly elected Republicans were more conservative, on average, than those Republicans who returned from the previous Congress. This was the opposite of the pattern for Democrats. In that party, in every Congress, newly elected members were more moderate on average than those Democrats who were reelected.[42] As we will see, these developments had significant implications for the Republicans' party leadership.

The 112th Congress (2011–2013)

In January of 2011, in the heady days after their landslide victory, John Boehner was elected Speaker by a unanimous vote of the Republican majority. This apparent consensus did not, however, indicate universal satisfaction among Republicans with their new leader. During the 2010 campaign, there had been plenty of negative opinions expressed about Boehner and much of the rest of the party leadership, especially among candidates and activists identified with the Tea Party movement. But those elements of the party were not inclined to begin Republican majority control with a sure-to-fail challenge to Boehner.

The new Speaker had often complained about the way the Democrats ran the chamber, especially their centralization of control over the agenda at the top and their restriction of the amendment process on the House floor. And he had promised that when his party took control, they would "run a more open House, governed by 'regular order,'" with a greater reliance on committees.[43] Of course, as we noted earlier, previous Speakers had promised a return to regular order and enhanced committee responsibility, so many observers were skeptical about the prospects for change. Early in the new Congress, when initially considering the continuing-appropriations bill to provide government funding for the rest of the fiscal year, the GOP leadership permitted more than one hundred amendments to be voted on, many of them offered by conservatives from their own party. This experience pleased Republican members and enabled Boehner to hold together virtually his entire coalition. On February 19, only three GOP members voted against the passage of the resolution, along with every House Democrat. But not surprisingly, the Democratic Senate refused to accept the GOP proposal, beginning a series of fiscal conflicts that would dominate the next two years. The negotiations on the appropriations continued for the next two-and-a-half months.

Shortly before time ran out in early April, Boehner concluded an agreement with Senate majority leader Harry Reid that provided for $39 billion in cuts. President Obama praised the compromise, but not all House Republicans were pleased. On final passage of the bill, fifty-nine of the most conservative Republican representatives defected and voted "nay," along with a majority of Democrats. This outcome contained the seeds of problems to come, as budget and spending issues were to remain central for the rest of the 112th Congress and beyond.

The day after the adoption of the continuing-appropriations resolution, the House took up the fiscal year 2012 budget resolution. Authored by Budget Committee chair Paul Ryan of Wisconsin, the ten-year plan called for massive spending cuts, the repeal of most of "Obamacare," and the replacement of Medicare as it was originally structured.[44] This plan was appealing to conservatives, and it was adopted with the parties nearly unanimously opposed to one another. The next major fiscal issue was an administration request for Congress to raise the debt ceiling by August to avoid a default on the nation's debts. Negotiations between the president and Boehner ensued, with the Republican leader pressing for major spending cuts commensurate with the increase in the debt ceiling. Twice during the summer, the two leaders were on the verge of a large agreement that included significant changes to both entitlements and discretionary spending and alterations in the tax code. However, because of pressure from conservatives opposed to tax increases, Boehner refused to agree.

Instead of concluding a "grand bargain," the principal actors agreed to a debt ceiling increase and the creation of a "supercommittee" drawn from both chambers that was charged with finding ways to cut the deficit by at least $1.2 trillion via spending cuts or revenue increases. November 23 was set as the deadline. If they failed, substantial automatic cuts would be imposed on both defense and domestic spending. On the day before that date, the committee indicated that it could not come to an agreement. Republicans would not entertain any tax increases, and Democrats refused to agree to a plan that involved only spending cuts. As a result, the automatic cuts (called *sequestration*) took effect. The session ended with little accomplished and intensified bad feelings between the parties in Congress and in the public toward Congress.

The 2012 session began with a positive result: a bipartisan vote in the House on February 17 to extend a temporary reduction in the Social Security payroll tax. But the seeds of future discontent were apparent when 38 percent of House Republicans voted against the deal because the costs of the extension were not offset by reductions in spending. The rest of the year's congressional activity mainly revolved around efforts to deal with a "fiscal cliff," which involved the scheduled expiration of the 2001 and 2003 George W. Bush tax cuts at the end of the year, coupled with the imposition of the sequestration spending cuts. Many observers feared that the combination would push the country back into recession, undermining the economic recovery.

The conflict over what to do ran right up to the brink, as had become commonplace. Many conservative Republicans were shocked by their party's unsuccessful effort to win the presidency, and there were widespread sentiments that it was due to their failure to field a "real conservative" as an opponent for Obama. Boehner, however, recognized the reality of continued Democratic control of both the presidency and the Senate, and he sought to negotiate the best deal he could. Shortly after the election, he offered $800 billion in additional tax revenue as part of a package to avoid the fiscal cliff. And in mid-December, he went further in private negotiations, proposing the inclusion of higher tax rates on those with high incomes. However, the proposal leaked, and Boehner backed off.[45] Instead, he sought to bring up a bill to extend the tax rates on incomes under $1 million. But the Democrats would not agree, and Boehner couldn't round up enough votes from his own party to pass the plan. As a result, he withdrew from negotiations, indicating that a solution was up to the Senate and the White House.

The further negotiations, mainly between Vice President Joe Biden and Senate minority leader Mitch McConnell of Kentucky, yielded an even worse result for the Republicans. It included permitting taxes to increase on those with incomes over $400,000 and no compensatory spending cuts. Rather than seek to block the plan (and go over the fiscal cliff, damaging his party's reputation), Boehner permitted a House vote. The bill passed on January 1 due to heavy support from Democrats, but almost two-thirds of Republicans voted against it, including Majority Leader Eric Cantor of Virginia and Majority Whip Kevin McCarthy of California.[46] The cliff was avoided, but many conservatives were angry at the Speaker for failing to achieve the policy outcomes they wanted.

The 113th Congress (2013–2015)

The conservative anger was given concrete manifestation just two days after the fiscal-cliff bill passed, when the House voted on the election of the Speaker for the new Congress. In addition to objections about the resolution of that dispute, they resented Boehner's efforts in December to strengthen his control over the GOP Steering Committee (which makes committee assignments and chooses their chairs) and to punish four rebellious conservatives by removing them from the choice committees they served on.[47] Allies of the targeted members organized an attempted coup against Boehner. Since election of the Speaker requires an absolute majority of the members voting and since all of the Democratic members would normally vote for their own candidate, the conservatives reasoned that if enough of their group would withhold their votes from Boehner, he could be blocked from election on the first ballot. If that occurred, a more conservative alternative might emerge. Sources indicate that the rebels agreed that they would go ahead if twenty-five members committed to vote for someone other than Boehner and that the threshold was reached, but then, one member changed his or her mind.[48] On the actual vote, ten GOP members voted present or for an alternative candidate.

The dissidents made clear that their ire was directed at their leaders' failure to meet their expectations. Tim Huelskamp of Kansas called the debt ceiling deal a "massive disaster" and said the passage of the continuing-appropriations resolution "confirmed Republicans were unwilling to cut spending."[49] Boehner's opponents hoped that their actions would pressure him to change his strategy. One of them, Paul Broun of Georgia, indicated that "Mr. Boehner has promised us as a Republican Conference that he was going to act in a different way toward the president."[50] But such conservative hopes were quickly dashed.

At the end of 2012, House leaders refused to take up a Senate-passed bill providing disaster aid to victims of "superstorm" Sandy, which had ravaged the east coast in the fall. GOP leaders brought up legislation to deal with the issue, but conservatives attempted to require that the money allocated to aid be offset by across-the-board cuts in other discretionary spending. When this effort failed, the bill passed with only one negative vote from Democrats, but Republicans opposed it, 49–179. The result violated the "Hastert rule" that we described earlier. That had also been true of the fiscal-cliff bill, and that was one feature that had angered its opponents.

Then, six weeks later, the House considered the Violence Against Women Act, which reauthorized a law from 1994 designed to fight domestic violence, sexual assault, and stalking. While there was widespread bipartisan support for renewal of the original provisions, partisan conflict resulted when Senate Democrats (with the support of twenty-three Republican senators) added provisions designed to aid domestic-violence victims who were gay or lesbian, illegal immigrants, or American Indians. The public pressure from Senate passage induced the House leadership to bring the bill to the floor. After the Republicans failed to secure adoption of a narrower alternative bill, the House passed the Senate version with unanimous Democratic support but only 39 percent of GOP members. This was another violation of the Hastert rule.

The most intense intraparty conflict for the majority in 2013 again revolved around government funding. An omnibus appropriations bill passed in March had extended funding through the end of the fiscal year (September 30). But as that deadline approached, appropriations for the new fiscal year had not been completed. Moreover, the nation's borrowing had again reached the debt ceiling, so that matter also needed to be addressed. Yet the central sticking point regarding these issues turned out not to be either spending or debt levels but "Obamacare." The House GOP had engineered dozens of floor votes on the repeal of the medical plan over the previous three years, without avail due to Democratic control of the Senate. Now, a group of the most conservative members argued that their party could compel the president and the Senate to accept repeal by withholding appropriations and an increase in the debt ceiling, threatening a government shutdown and debt default. Part of their reason for pushing the matter then was the fear that public acceptance of the program would grow with the passage of time so that it would be harder to secure repeal later.

Conservative members in both chambers rallied their colleagues to sign letters to the party leaders demanding that no continuing-appropriations bill be adopted that did not include a complete defunding of Obamacare. Outside of the Congress, conservative advocacy groups ran negative ads against Republican members who were opposed to or reluctant about the strategy.[51] Supporters of the strategy were unconcerned about opposition from business leaders and about poll data that indicated that most of the public would blame the GOP for a shutdown.[52] Their plan was to take the issue to the people and persuade them. One of them, Rep. Thomas Graves of Georgia, said, "There's going to be a strong argument from the American people saying, 'This is the path forward,' putting pressure on the Senate to adopt it as we passed it in the House."[53] Then, on September 20, ten days before appropriations expired, the House passed a continuing resolution blocking funding for the implementation of the health law and extending appropriations until December 15. That bill and subsequent efforts to achieve the same result were blocked by the Senate. Time ran out, and parts of the government shut down. On October 10, Boehner and other GOP leaders met with the president but without agreement. The Speaker then sought to secure agreement from members of his party for two different alternative bills, but there was not sufficient support for either of them.

At that point, bargaining shifted to the Senate. The respective party leaders came to an agreement on a continuing resolution without provisions to repeal or delay Obamacare, which passed with the support of 60 percent of GOP senators. With the debt ceiling deadline only hours away, Boehner capitulated and permitted a vote on the Senate bill that extended appropriations until January and suspended the debt ceiling until February. Democrats voted for it unanimously, but Republicans were against, 87–144. Yet another major bill passed over the objections of a majority of Republican representatives.

In the wake of the shutdown, Republicans in and out of Congress believed that their party has lost badly in the confrontation. A CNN/ORC poll after the government reopened indicated that over 80 percent of respondents thought the shutdown was a bad idea. Half of those polled said the Republicans were mainly responsible, compared to one-third who blamed the president. Moreover, 75 percent of those surveyed said that most Republican members of Congress did not deserve reelection, versus 54 percent who said that about congressional Democrats.[54] With little inclination to face another confrontation, Republicans and Democrats produced a compromise budget agreement for the rest of fiscal year 2014 and for fiscal year 2015, negotiated by Paul Ryan and his Senate counterpart, Budget Committee chair Patty Murray of Washington. While both sides made compromises, and passage was bipartisan, the agreement was more accepted by Democrats than the GOP. More than a fourth of Republican representatives voted no.[55]

The compromise and follow-up actions settled some matters for the time being, but it left the debt ceiling to be dealt with again by February 2014. Under pressure from conservatives, Boehner and Senator McConnell argued that any debt ceiling increase must be matched with spending cuts of at least an equal amount. Conservative interest groups like Heritage Action and the Club for Growth also demanded a plan to balance the budget within ten years.[56] Democrats, however, contended this was inappropriate because the increase would cover government commitments from the past, not the future. Boehner also sought alternative conditions that could be imposed, but he was unable to marshal enough GOP votes to adopt them. He told reporters, "When you don't have 218 votes, you have nothing."[57] In the face of another threat of a government default, Boehner permitted a vote on an extension of the debt ceiling until March 15, 2015, without any conditions (a so-called "clean" bill). It passed with the support of only twenty-eight Republicans (including the top three leaders), versus 199 who voted against. One of those nay votes was from Budget chairman Ryan.

The actions on appropriations and the debt ceiling largely took care of intraparty conflict on those matters for most of the rest of the year. However, continued discontent within the GOP's base in the electorate was visible, especially in June of 2014 when the party's majority leader, Eric Cantor of Virginia, was shockingly defeated in his primary by an unknown college professor who was identified with the Tea Party and the Club for Growth. The winner, David Brat, had promised to fight for "real, conservative, free-market change" and had campaigned against the House leadership's decisions, particularly the budget deal passed in December.[58] Establishment Republicans saw this as a clear message. Former Virginia GOP Representative Thomas Davis said, "When Eric Cantor, a conservative and member of the leadership, is too moderate, it sends a chilling effect to other Republicans and makes it that much harder to cross over and work together."[59]

Cantor announced that he would resign from the House, and the Republican Conference moved quickly to promote the majority whip, Kevin McCarthy, to the majority leader post. The vote for McCarthy was overwhelming, but the seeds of future problems were visible despite his promises to take a more open and conservative approach to running the chamber. Members of the core group of very conservative representatives who were central to the government shutdown backed an alternative to McCarthy and expressed dissatisfaction with his election, as did voices of conservative activists outside of Congress.[60]

After this, legislative time was short before the House recessed for the upcoming elections. Unwilling to risk a major confrontation at that point, Congress adopted a continuing-appropriations bill to carry them through until a postelection legislative session. Then, due to GOP gains in the elections and the expectation of a stronger strategic position in the new Congress, the House Republicans compromised with the Democrats on an omnibus appropriations bill to cover most discretionary spending for the rest of the fiscal year, although sixty-seven Republicans voted against the bill.

2015: Another Coup Attempt and the Creation of the Freedom Caucus

The 2014 elections gave the GOP their largest majority in the House since the Great Depression and strengthened the numbers of the party's very conservative wing. They also brought Republican control of the Senate. Not surprisingly, the conservative wing expected that their party's gains should translate into the adoption of the policies they preferred. Many of them, however, continued to believe that the results they wanted would not be achieved under the current leadership. They felt betrayed by Boehner's unwillingness to be responsive to their demands to force another shutdown by using the omnibus appropriations bill the previous month to block funding to enforce the president's executive order offering temporary legal status to illegal immigrants.[61] The distrust of Boehner by conservatives within the House was reinforced by anger against him from outside. For example, more than two dozen conservative activists and pundits signed an open letter that called on House Republicans to "fire" the Speaker, saying that his service in the office had been "nothing short of a disaster."[62]

The dissatisfied conservative members knew that they commanded far too few votes to elect an alternative candidate against Boehner, but they hoped that if they could deny him a majority on the first ballot he might withdraw, or another option might emerge. When the vote was taken, they fell short, but twenty-four GOP members voted for someone other than Boehner, more than twice as many as had opposed him two years earlier. The top opponent was Daniel Webster of Florida, with twelve votes; the other dozen were scattered among eight other candidates.

Boehner, in his speech to the House after his reelection, urged his colleagues to set aside their differences and prove that they could get things done.[63] However, those sentiments didn't prevent him from taking action against those who opposed him, including removing Daniel Webster from his position on the House Rules Committee the same day. This retaliation further angered the rebels and set the stage for their decision to form a new organization within the GOP Conference to pursue their goals. The new group was announced on January 26 and was dubbed the House Freedom Caucus (HFC).[64]

While only three of the nine founding members had defected from Boehner on the vote for Speaker, all were advocates of a confrontational stance against the president and the Democrats. They decided to make membership by invitation only and to keep the roster secret (although many of the members have been publicly identified). Within a week, the group indicated that it had about thirty members.[65]

Public statements from the group indicated that they would take positions on legislation when there was consensus among the membership and that they hoped to be able to avoid confrontations with the leadership, to avoid (according to one of them, John Fleming of Louisiana) being "destructive." "Destructive would be taking down bills, voting against rules. We can do that, but that's not really our goal. Our goal is to say you know, we are 30–40 strong, work with us." But they made clear that they expected concrete accomplishments. Raul Labrador of Idaho (another founder) said that there were two reasons to force fights with the Democrats in the current Congress. "The first reason is for messaging. But I think we have to do it for more than just messaging. You can actually pass things when you have a Republican House and a Republican Senate." They also indicated that they would press the leadership for major gains. As Jim Jordan of Ohio, the HFC chairman, said, "We accomplish in proportion to what we attempt." However, the caucus members were not only concerned about policy but also process within the House. "More amendments, more participation from the members—that may be where you see the biggest push out of us in the first year," said Mick Mulvaney of South Carolina.[66]

The first confrontation within the GOP after the caucus was created occurred over the Homeland Security funding bill. The compromise on appropriations in December funded all of the government for the rest of the fiscal year except that department, which was given appropriations only until February 27. Conservatives demanded that exception because Homeland Security included funding related to immigration, and they wanted to use that bill as a vehicle to reverse the president's executive orders on that subject. The initial bill to fund Homeland Security that passed the House in the new Congress included provisions that would have blocked the executive orders. Obama said that he would veto that bill, and Democrats in the Senate blocked taking up the bill three times, calling for the passage of a "clean bill" without the immigration provisions. Senator McConnell (who had promised at the beginning of the Congress that there would be no more government shutdowns) said that the Senate would not go forward with the House-passed bill and asked that the House offer a different plan. Boehner, however, reflected conservative pressure and told reporters, "It's time for the Senate to do their work."[67]

On the last day of funding for the department, the Senate passed a clean bill for a full year of funding. Worried that his members would not support a yearlong appropriation, Boehner brought to the House a proposal for a twenty-day extension. However, the move failed when fifty-two GOP conservatives (including almost all of the Freedom Caucus) and every Democrat voted no. Later in the day, the leadership brought up a one-week extension of funding. It passed, but sixty members, almost all conservatives, were opposed.[68] The Freedom Caucus members preferred to let a shutdown occur. The extra week did not alter the situation, and on March 3, the Senate and House adopted a bill to fund the department for the rest of the year. Seventy-five Republicans joined the Democrats in support, and 167 GOP members were against. The anger of conservatives at the leadership was intense (although many more mainstream Republican members just voiced relief). Rep. Mick Mulvaney, an HFC founder, termed the outcome "an unmitigated loss for conservatives," and another conservative, Tim Huelskamp of Kansas, said Boehner had "just caved in" and that his strategy had failed.[69]

The Fall of Speaker Boehner

Over the next few months, the Freedom Caucus was a source of conflict with the leadership and other mainstream members on a number of issues. They temporarily succeeded in blocking renewal of the Export–Import Bank, and many of the members (but not all) were against trade promotion (or "fast-track") authority for the president. When the special rule to permit floor consideration of a bill granting fast-track authority was considered on June 11, thirty-four Republicans (most of them HFC members) voted no. The rule passed by only five votes. The party leadership viewed opposition on the procedural vote adopting the special rule to be unacceptable, and they took action against the rebels. Three HFC members were removed from the party's whip team, and Mark Meadows of North Carolina, one of the HFC founders, was stripped of his subcommittee chairmanship on the Oversight and Government Reform Committee by its chairman, Jason Chaffetz of Utah.[70]

Freedom Caucus members were angry about the retaliation. Chairman Jordan said, "What they did to [Meadows] was exactly wrong. . . . And there are a number of us who are fed up with it."[71] Subsequently, Boehner said that he "absolutely" supported Chaffetz's action, and "when it comes to procedural votes in the House, the majority has to stick together." But Raul Labrador contended that the reason for the retaliations was that the leadership was afraid. "They want to break our backs because they're afraid that that number is just going to continue to grow." And just a week after Meadows lost his position, Chaffetz reversed his decision and reinstated him. In addition, another planned retaliation—the removal of HFC member Ken Buck of Colorado as president of the freshman class—was shelved after opposition was expressed by many freshman members. These actions were seen by many observers as evidence of the strength of the HFC and the weakness of the leadership.[72]

Mark Meadows's strength was manifested in his July 28 introduction of a resolution on the House floor calling for the removal of Boehner as Speaker. At the time, most observers thought the move had no practical consequences. A few voices outside of Congress, like FreedomWorks (a Tea Party group), endorsed the idea, but most members, including many conservatives, were critical. For example, Tom McClintock of California (an HFC member) called it "about the dumbest idea I've seen here."[73] Indeed, the reactions of his colleagues led Meadows to resign from the board of the Freedom Caucus. But in the weeks after the introduction, conservatives pressed the leadership on their priorities (such as blocking the nuclear agreement with Iran, restricting spending, and ending government funding for Planned Parenthood), and they were far from satisfied. As a result, some came to see the resolution in a more positive light, with one HFC member calling it a "sword of Damocles" hanging over Boehner that might induce him to change direction.[74]

In early September, with the end of the fiscal year (and therefore, the end of all appropriations) looming at the end of the month, the legislative focus again became the potential for a government shutdown. Given the short time, attention was on a continuing resolution to extend the time for negotiations on a deal to cover the entire next fiscal year. On the resolution, the HFC was adamant. The caucus took a formal position (that required the agreement of at least 80 percent of its members) that they would not vote for any continuing resolution that did not defund Planned Parenthood.[75] This left the leadership with a choice between acceding to the HFC and accepting a likely shutdown or seeking Democratic support to pass the continuing resolution.

On September 10, HFC chairman Jordan admitted that the GOP had been blamed for the 2013 shutdown, but he contended that this time, the result did not have to be the same, if the leadership adopted the right tactics. He said, "We just need to make the case in a compelling repetitive way, over and over again, so the American people clearly understand what is at stake here."[76] Recognizing that the Senate was unlikely to adopt defunding and that, in any event, the president would probably veto a bill containing it, the GOP leadership sought an alternative strategy. On September 24, with less than a week to go, they adopted the idea of seeking defunding in a separate action using a procedure called reconciliation, which could not be filibustered by Senate Democrats. They planned to explain their strategy to the members the next morning at a closed meeting of the Republican Conference.[77]

When the conference meeting convened, however, the appropriations fight was overshadowed by an announcement: Boehner said he would resign as Speaker and from the House the following month. Members of the HFC claimed credit for forcing Boehner out. They argued that if a vote were taken on the resolution to vacate the Speaker's position, Boehner would not have had sufficient votes to survive without turning to the Democrats for support. Huelskamp of Kansas indicated that Boehner quit because of conservative pressure. "There's no question in my mind," he said. "He didn't have the votes to keep the job." And the Speaker's own statements seemed to generally reflect the same view. He cited "this turmoil that's been churning for a couple of months" and a concern that the "prolonged leadership turmoil would do irreparable harm to the institution."[78]

A New Speaker Is Chosen . . . Eventually

The obvious candidate to succeed Boehner was Majority Leader McCarthy. Most observers thought the choice was a foregone conclusion, although a couple of other minor candidates (including Daniel Webster) had also announced. But the Freedom Caucus persisted in their interest in changing party rules and the powers of the leadership. As part of that effort, they sought commitments on rules changes before the conference vote on their party's candidate, and they submitted an extensive questionnaire regarding rules to the candidates. The changes they were seeking included more influence for the HFC and other rank-and-file members on the party's Steering Committee (which selects committee chairs and assigns members to committees), more access to the floor for amendments they favored, and protection from leadership retaliation.[79]

At a forum the conservatives held for Speaker candidates two days before the scheduled vote, McCarthy indicated a favorable attitude toward changing representation on the Steering Committee and supported a more inclusive process, but that was not sufficient for the HFC. They voted to support Webster for Speaker. Convinced that he would probably not have a sure majority when the full House voted, McCarthy withdrew from the race. This left the situation in chaos, and the conference postponed the vote on their choice.

Over the next two weeks, the action revolved around whether Paul Ryan could now be persuaded to run. He had persistently asserted that he did not want the job, but he was the consensus candidate of virtually all members outside of the conservative wing, and the pressure on him to accept was intense. The conservatives, on the other hand, were skeptical, and they had conditions for accepting a Ryan speakership similar to those they voiced in discussions about McCarthy's bid. Then, on October 20, Ryan publicly indicated that he was willing to serve in principle, but he too had conditions. He wanted indications that all segments of the party were united behind him, that the party would adopt a more positive stance on policy, that House rules would be revised to make members more effective (including revision of the motion to vacate the Speaker's position), and that he would be able to spend adequate time with his family.[80] Members of the HFC initially expressed some skepticism about Ryan's terms, but the following day, the group met with Ryan, and afterward, they announced that more than two-thirds of the members indicated they would support his bid. Ryan had indicated support for revising the Steering Committee and had pledged not to bring up an immigration bill without the support of a majority of the conference. Apparently, no other commitments were made regarding rules changes from either side.[81] The next day, in a letter to all House Republicans, Ryan announced that he was "ready and eager to be our speaker." On October 29, the House elected him to the post.

In the last two months of 2015, Ryan and his team grappled with the competing interests that led to the change in party leadership. He demonstrated a commitment to a more open process during the consideration of the highway bill by permitting more than 120 amendments. And the bill passed the House with only sixty-five negative votes, although all of those came from (mostly conservative) Republicans. Less than two weeks later, on the other hand, House leaders announced that they would bring up a bill to revise the rules of the refugee program for those coming from Iraq and Syria. The bill had received no committee consideration, and no amendments would be permitted.[82]

The Speaker formed a task force to recommend changes to the Steering Committee and an advisory group that included both HFC members and moderates. On November 18, he announced the plan to reconfigure the Steering Committee until the next Congress. The six major committee chairmen would be removed and replaced by six temporary "at-large" members elected from the Republican Conference. By the end of the year, those six would be replaced by six additional elected regional representatives, added to the thirteen who already served.[83] (When the election was held, HFC member Huelskamp was one of the chosen; however, two members of the moderate Tuesday Group were also picked.)

Closing out the year, Congress dealt again with funding the government. On December 15, Congress and the president reached a compromise agreement on a $1.1 trillion spending bill. The package contained some wins for the GOP, including making some tax breaks permanent. However, there were also losses in the final bill. These included the addition of more than $60 billion in spending and the removal of many policy riders the Republicans wanted. HFC conservatives were unhappy, and most voted against the final bill, but they did not put most of the blame on Ryan.

The Republican Majority and Conditional Party Government

We can now turn to a consideration of what conclusions we can draw from the Boehner speakership and its aftermath regarding the theoretical issues addressed by the theory of conditional party government (CPG). In our view, the major implications of the theory are supported. The central prediction of CPG theory is that a homogeneous majority party that has sharp policy differences with the minority party will be willing to delegate strong powers to its leadership in hopes of advancing the party members' goals. As we outlined earlier, that prediction is strongly supported by the patterns of behavior of majorities from the 1970s through the Pelosi speakership. If that is true, then we should also expect that in instances where one or both of the theory's conditions are undermined, the willingness of some significant portion of the members to delegate should also be undermined. That is exactly what we observed during Boehner's years in the top job and in the transition to Speaker Ryan.

The members of the Freedom Caucus and their allies had preferences that were different in important ways from their GOP colleagues. They did not believe that Boehner and his leadership team shared their views on what should be done, and they did not trust those leaders to act as faithful agents for the party in executing their jobs. Thus, we would expect them to seek to reduce the powers of their leaders and restrict the exercise of the powers the leaders retained. That is what the HFC tried to do, and those efforts are persisting in 2016. We would not, however, expect that the members around the median of the Republican Conference would also favor such restrictions, and that too seems to be the case. Indeed, a number of mainline and moderate Republican representatives have argued against going too far with reducing leadership power.[84]

But even though the predictions of CPG theory appear to be supported again in the Boehner era, events in that period have offered new insights about the theory and its application. First, we have observed, for the first time, significant differences in the patterns of change of the two conditions of CPG theory. That is, in previous periods, the homogeneity of the parties and the divergence between them both generally increased and did so in tandem. From 2010 through 2015, however, the influx of Tea Party–linked Republicans continued to increase interparty divergence while the majority party became more *heterogeneous*. Furthermore, the heterogeneity increased toward the extreme of the party rather than toward the median of the chamber, which is unusual. In this instance, the influence of increased heterogeneity seems to have trumped the continued divergence in influencing the behavior of the members in undermining leadership authority. It does not seem, however, that this is a necessary consequence of the theory, and so, which condition has the dominant effect when they are pushing in opposite directions with respect to the allocation of powers may be idiosyncratic.

A second insight is that the degree of homogeneity or heterogeneity that influences the behavior of the actors need not be solely a matter of preferences about policy outcomes. It seems that both the HFC and the mainstream GOP members would have preferred that Obamacare be repealed and that Planned Parenthood be defunded. What they disagreed about were the strategies that should be pursued to accomplish those ends and about what might be called the "state of the world." By that term, we mean disagreements about what would be the likely outcomes that flowed from the choice of a given strategy. Freedom Caucus Republicans believed that shutdowns or debt defaults could give them leverage over the administration and Senate Democrats, perhaps causing them to capitulate and accept the policies the right wanted. The GOP leadership, on the other hand, believed that those same strategy choices would lead to their party being blamed and its brand being damaged, potentially threatening the party's majority status. In past Congresses, the majority leadership and their members were usually on the same page with regard to strategy and expectations about them.[85] But as we have seen, these differences were frequent and consequential from 2011 through 2015.

How will these issues regarding heterogeneity within the Republican Conference play out under Speaker Ryan? Initially, his handling of the final negotiations and aftermath on the budget deal with the Democrats gained much praise from many actors in the process.[86] Shortly thereafter, however, attention focused on the initial steps to draft the budget for the next fiscal year. Immediately after Boehner announced his decision to quit, analysts wondered if his successor would inevitably face the same problems,[87] and early in 2016, events indicated that the concerns were valid. Members of the conservative wing openly criticized Ryan's management of the final 2015 deal. Rep. Paul Gosar of Arizona said, for example, that Ryan had "folded like a cheap suit" by supporting the omnibus appropriations bill.[88] And regarding the new budget, many of them sought to pressure Ryan to go back on the previous deal's commitment to increase spending.[89]

Ryan's biggest challenge will be to persuade conservatives to trust him sufficiently to give him leeway to make strategic decisions for the party. This will be difficult given the past friction with leadership and the low esteem for party leaders among rank-and-file GOP voters.[90] John Boehner once said, "A leader without followers is just a guy out for a walk." Paul Ryan is likely to lead. Whether enough members will follow is a different matter.

Notes

1. We want to express our appreciation to Connor Phillips of Duke University for his excellent work as our research assistant in pulling together substantial amounts of information about the House Freedom Caucus.
2. Since 1900, the president's party has gained seats in only three midterm elections (1934, 1998, and 2002). Senate seat losses are less systematic; they have occurred well over half the time.
3. In parallel fashion, it worked that way in some degree because of the diversity of opinion in both parties.
4. The Republicans were the majority party in the country from 1896 until about 1932. They had split in 1912 over the presidency, enabling Woodrow Wilson to win two terms and bring congressional majorities with him. The Republicans reasserted their majority in the post–WWI period.
5. Decentralization was intended, as this system emerged in the wake of the 1910 "revolt" against the then centralized powers of the Speaker, "Czar" Joseph Cannon, R-Ill. See Joseph Cooper and David W. Brady, "Institutional Context and Leadership Style: The House From Cannon to Rayburn," *American Political Science Review* 75 (1981): 411–25.
6. Kenneth A. Shepsle, "The Changing Textbook Congress," in *Can the Government Govern?* ed. John E. Chubb and Paul E. Peterson (Washington, DC: Brookings Institution, 1989), 238–66.
7. In 1954, for example, the former states of the Confederacy held 106 seats, divided between ninety-eight Democrats and eight Republicans. Democrats were unopposed in sixty-seven, and Republicans won less than one vote in five in eighteen more, making a full 80 percent of those seats uncompetitive wins by Democrats.
8. See David W. Rohde, *Parties and Leaders in the Postreform House* (Chicago: University of Chicago Press, 1991) and Edward G. Carmines and James A. Stimson, *Issue Evolution: Race and the Transformation of American Politics* (Princeton, NJ: Princeton University Press, 1989), who place their respective arguments as starting as a result of the 1958 elections. This was, in part, because outside of the Great Society Congress of 1965 to 1967, Northern Democrats were a majority in their party but not on the floor, and they could not convince any others to join their reform efforts. Why would Republicans, say, empower their liberal opponents to be more effective in legislating, especially if they imagined that they would be a minority for the foreseeable future? And why should Southern Democrats vote to reduce the powers they currently held?
9. Bruce I. Oppenheimer, "The Rules Committee: New Arm of Leadership in a Decentralized House," in *Congress Reconsidered*, ed. Lawrence C. Dodd and Bruce I. Oppenheimer (New York: Praeger Publishers, 1977), 96–116.

10. See Rohde, *Parties and Leaders*, and Steven H. Haeberle, "The Institutionalization of the Subcommittee in the United States House of Representatives," *Journal of Politics* 40 (1978): 1054–65.
11. The Civil Rights Act passed, in part, in commemoration of the assassinated president, John F. Kennedy. The Republican presidential nominee, Sen. Barry Goldwater, R-Ariz., voted against it, with the result that he carried five Southern states for the first time since Reconstruction by a Republican (and no other state except his home state). That election gave the Northern Democrats a large majority in each chamber and enabled passage of the Voting Rights Act, although the congressional Democrats chose to use their huge majorities to pass this and other Great Society legislation but not to change the rules of the House.
12. A *conservative coalition* vote was one in which a majority of Northern Democrats voted one way, and a majority of Republicans and of Southern Democrats voted the other way.
13. A *party vote* is one in which a majority of Democrats vote one way, and a majority of Republicans vote the other way.
14. See John H. Aldrich and John Griffin, *Why Parties Matter: Political Competition and Democracy in the American South, 1832–2012* (forthcoming, University of Chicago Press).
15. Here, we are using the definition of the South employed by *Congressional Quarterly* and used by most scholars of Congress, which adds Kentucky and Oklahoma to the states of the former Confederacy.
16. There were similar, if less severe, changes in the Republican Party as "Rockefeller Republicans" in the northeastern and Great Lakes states, liberal on social issues but conservative on economic issues, began to lose in the late 1960s and early 1970s, which also made the Republicans less diverse. We focus here on the Democrats because they held the majority in the House throughout the relevant period.
17. One of the sparse set of Constitutional provisions is that the House writes its own rules anew every two years. The Senate is very different in this regard, as it has standing rules that continue across Congresses because it considers itself a chamber that is in session continuously. The result is that it is very difficult and unusual for the Senate to change its rules, even on seemingly minor matters.
18. Either way, the majority party in the House will hold power, as has been true since the speakership of Thomas B. Reed, R-Maine, and the adoption of "Reed's rules" in 1890, which made the House a majoritarian institution. The majority party could, in principle, give that up, but a majority giving up its powers voluntarily is extremely unlikely.
19. The classic statement is David R. Mayhew, *Congress: The Electoral Connection* (New Haven, CT: Yale University Press, 1974).
20. We draw heavily from Richard F. Fenno, *Congressmen in Committees* (New York: Little, Brown, 1973), but add valuing having one's party hold majority status in the chamber—a variable that seemed irrelevant in 1973, as the Democrats seemed in nearly permanent majority.
21. That is to say that the two parts of the condition are independent, and one (e.g., internal party agreement), the other (disagreement between the two parties), both, or neither of the two parts may hold at any given time.
22. It is important to note that the Senate, which had a Republican majority since the election of 1980, had returned to Democratic control in 1986, when that class of 1980 stood for reelection. The president, no longer fresh from a historic landslide reelection victory, was just beginning to face the Iran–contra scandal that helped erode his popular support.

23. Special rules are resolutions from the Rules Committee that accompany most major bills and that specify the terms for consideration of that bill, such as length of time for debate, what amendments may be considered, and whether exceptions to the standing rules of the House are made during consideration.
24. It is important to point out that the percentage of votes received by the Republicans is not the remainder of 100 minus the Democratic vote percentage. For example, the Republicans received about 45 percent of the vote in 1992 while the Democrats received 50 percent, with the rest going to various third-party and independent candidates.
25. See, for example, James G. Gimpel, *Legislating the Revolution: The Contract With America in Its First 100 Days* (New York: Allyn & Bacon, 1996).
26. The data here are discussed in detail in John H. Aldrich, "Political Parties in a Critical Era," *American Politics Quarterly* 27 (1999): 9–32.
27. These paragraphs are drawn heavily from John H. Aldrich and David W. Rohde, "The Republican Revolution and the House Appropriations Committee," *Journal of Politics* 62 (2000): 1–33.
28. Such legislating is done by adding as so-called "riders" with special rules to circumvent the prohibition of Appropriations bills being used for authorizing legislation.
29. "Clinton: 'The President Is Relevant,'" *Time*, April 18, 1995, http://content.time.com/time/nation/article/0,8599,3632,00.html.
30. The figures are from a *Washington Post*/ABC News poll in November 1995. See comparison at http://www.people-press.org/2013/09/23/blame-for-both-sides-as-possible-government-shutdown-approaches.
31. This position is thus a reversal from the unusually nationalized "Contract" election of 1994, the last midterm, and in sharp contrast to the favorite aphorism of Tip O'Neill that "all politics is local."
32. Guy Gugliotta and Juliet Eilperin, "Gingrich Steps Down in Face of Rebellion," *Washington Post*, November 7, 1998, http://www.washingtonpost.com/wp-srv/politics/govt/leadership/stories/gingrich110798.htm.
33. Thomas worked closely with Majority Leader Tom DeLay, R-Tex., to bring partisan legislation to the floor (often relying on restrictive rules to do so) and frequently denied the minority party time to review legislation, let alone offer alternative proposals. When the Democrats protested their inability to review a pension reform bill in 2003, Thomas even called the Capitol Police, only apologizing for his behavior after being pressured by the Speaker, Dennis Hastert, D-Ill.
34. The organizational name for all Republican members of the House is the Republican *Conference*, whereas Democrats refer to theirs as the Democratic *Caucus*.
35. Carl Hulse, "New Panel Chairman, Ways of Old Pragmatist," *New York Times*, November 28, 1998, http://www.nytimes.com/1998/11/28/us/in-new-panel-chairman-ways-of-old-pragmatist.html?pagewanted=all&src=pm.
36. Fenno, *Congressmen in Committees*. This and the preceding paragraphs are developed further in John H. Aldrich, Brittany N. Perry, and David W. Rohde, "Richard Fenno's Theory of Congressional Committees and the Partisan Polarization of the House, in *Congress Reconsidered*, 10th ed., ed. Lawrence C. Dodd and Bruce I. Oppenheimer (Washington, DC: CQ Press, 2013), 193–220.
37. Most observers considered this move by Speaker Nancy Pelosi to be a warning to committee chairs that they should be responsive to the party leadership. Two years later, Pelosi permitted the limits to be repealed.

38. He first won a special election to the House to replace his deceased father in 1955 and served until the 2014 elections. (That is, he served in Congress for sixty years, retiring in 2015.) He was succeeded by his wife.
39. See John H. Aldrich and David W. Rohde, "Congressional Committees in a Continuing Partisan Era," in *Congress Reconsidered*, 9th ed., ed. Lawrence C. Dodd and Bruce I. Oppenheimer (Washington, DC: CQ Press, 2009), 236.
40. It was so named for the common use of the Boston Tea Party, a symbol of American colonies' protest against the overreaching British crown and government.
41. Theda Skocpol and Vanessa Williamson, *The Tea Party and the Remaking of Republican Conservatism* (New York: Oxford University Press, 2012), 170.
42. Edward G. Carmines, "Review Symposium: Class Politics, American Style," *Perspectives on Politics* 9 (2011): 645–47.
43. Major Garrett and Susan David, "The GOP Blueprint," *National Journal*, November 6, 2010, 22.
44. For more details on the developments described in this and the next few paragraphs, see Lawrence C. Dodd and Bruce I. Oppenheimer, "The House in a Time of Crisis: Economic Turmoil and Partisan Upheaval," in *Congress Reconsidered*, 10th ed., ed. Lawrence C. Dodd and Bruce I. Oppenheimer (Washington, DC: CQ Press, 2013), 48–52.
45. Jonathan Strong, "Speak Softly or Carry a Big Stick," *CQ Weekly*, January 14, 2013, 63.
46. Interestingly, one of those voting for the bill was Budget Committee chairman Ryan.
47. See Strong, 63.
48. Ibid., 63–64.
49. Ibid., 64.
50. Ibid.
51. Sheryl Gay Stolberg and Mike McIntire, "A Federal Budget Crisis Months in the Planning," *New York Times*, October 5, 2013, http://www.nytimes.com/2013/10/06/us/a-federal-budget-crisis-months-in-the-planning.html.
52. Daniel Newhauser and Emily Ethridge, "Shutdown Showdown," *CQ Weekly*, September 23, 2013, 1550–54.
53. Ibid., 1552.
54. Paul Steinhauser, "CNN Poll: 75% Say Most Republicans in Congress Don't Deserve Reelection," CNN, October 21, 2013, http://www.cnn.com/2013/10/21/politics/cnn-poll-shutdown-re-election.
55. In the Senate, on the other hand, 80 percent of Republicans were opposed.
56. Michael Needham, Tony Perkins, and Chris Chocola, "Why Debt Limit Must Be Used to Force a Balanced Budget," *Politico*, January 15, 2013, http://www.politico.com/story/2013/01/why-the-debt-limit-must-be-used-to-force-a-balanced-budget-086244.
57. Susan Davis, "House Approves 'Clean' Debt Ceiling Extension," *USA Today*, February 11, 2014, http://www.usatoday.com/story/news/politics/2014/02/11/debt-ceiling-republicans-boehner/5390293.
58. Susan Davis and Catalina Camia, "GOP Leader Eric Cantor Loses in Shock Tea Party Upset," *USA Today*, June 11, 2014, http://www.usatoday.com/story/news/politics/elections/2014/06/10/eric-cantor-majority-leader-defeated/10304543.
59. Jonathan Martin, "Eric Cantor Defeated by David Brat, Tea Party Challenger, in G.O.P. Primary Upset," *New York Times*, June 10, 2014, http://www.nytimes.com/2014/06/11/us/politics/eric-cantor-loses-gop-primary.html.
60. Paul Kane and Ed O'Keefe, "House Republicans Elect Kevin McCarthy as Majority Leader, Steve Scalise as Majority Whip," *Washington Post*, June 19, 2014,

https://www.washingtonpost.com/politics/house-republicans-elect-kevin-mccarthy-as-majority-leader-steve-scalise-as-majority-whip/2014/06/19/212a6a24-f7d0-11e3-8aa9-dad2ec039789_story.html.
61. Jeremy W. Peters, "Boehner Fends Off Dissent as G.O.P. Takes the Reins," *New York Times*, January 6, 2015, http://www.nytimes.com/2015/01/07/us/congress-returns-boehner.html.
62. Ashley Parker, "Boehner Facing Dissent and Defections in Vote to Remain Speaker of House," *New York Times*, January 5, 2015, http://www.nytimes.com/2015/01/06/us/politics/boehner-facing-dissent-and-defections-in-vote-to-remain-speaker-of-house.html.
63. Peters, op cit.
64. Lauren French, "9 Republicans Launch House Freedom Caucus," *Politico*, January 26, 2015, http://www.politico.com/story/2015/01/house-freedom-caucus-conservative-legislation-114593.
65. As of October 1, 2015, forty-one members were identified, although two of them had resigned by November.
66. The quotations in this paragraph were taken from Katy O'Donnell, "The Right Recalibrates," *Roll Call*, March 2, 2015, pp. 15, 17, 17, and 19, respectively.
67. Sean Sullivan and Ed O'Keefe, "Top Republicans Disagree on How to Fund Department of Homeland Security," *Washington Post*, February 11, 2015, https://www.washingtonpost.com/politics/top-republicans-disagree-on-how-to-fund-homeland-security-department/2015/02/11/e462af82-b13f-11e4-886b-c22184f27c35_story.html.
68. Ashley Parker, "House Passes One-Week Funding Extension for Homeland Security," *New York Times*, February 27, 2015, http://www.nytimes.com/2015/02/28/us/senate-house-homeland-security.html.
69. Ashley Parker, "House Approves Homeland Security Budget, Without Strings," *New York Times*, March 3, 2015, http://www.nytimes.com/2015/03/04/us/house-homeland-security.html.
70. The three taken off the whip team were Cynthia Lummis of Wyoming, Trent Franks of Arizona, and Steve Pearce of New Mexico.
71. Scott Wong, "Punished GOP Lawmaker Stirs New Talk of Boehner Rebellion," *The Hill*, June 22, 2015, http://thehill.com/homenews/house/245764-punished-gop-lawmaker-stirs-new-talk-of-boehner-rebellion.
72. Scott Wong, "GOP Leaders Retreat in Fight With Rebels," *The Hill*, June 25, 2015, http://thehill.com/homenews/house/246207-gop-leaders-retreat-in-fight-with-rebels.
73. Sean Wong and Cristina Marcos, "Attempt to Oust Speaker Goes Belly Up," *The Hill*, July 30, 2015, 1.
74. Mike DeBonis, "Meet the Donald Trump of the House of Representatives," *Washington Post*, September 7, 2015, https://www.washingtonpost.com/politics/meet-the-donald-trump-of-the-house-of-representatives/2015/09/07/bfd3c854-53f6-11e5-8c19-0b6825aa4a3a_story.html.
75. The animus against Planned Parenthood resulted from the revelation in July of two videos surreptitiously recorded by antiabortion activists that purported to show that officials of Planned Parenthood were discussing the sale of fetal tissue for medical research. See Jackie Calmes, "With 2 Videos, Activist Ignites Abortion Issue," *New York Times*, July 22, 2015, A1.

76. Bob Cusack, "Conservative Lawmaker Insists GOP Can Win Shutdown Fight," *The Hill*, September 10, 2015, http://thehill.com/homenews/house/253326-conservative-lawmaker-insists-gop-can-win-shutdown-fight.
77. Rebecca Shabad, Peter Sullivan, and Bernie Becker, "Boehner, GOP, Settle on Strategy to Prevent Oct. 1 Shutdown," *The Hill*, September 24, 2015, http://thehill.com/policy/finance/254886-boehner-gop-settle-on-strategy-to-prevent-oct-1-shutdown.
78. These quotations are taken from Matt Fuller, "Conservatives Take Credit for Boehner Resignation," *Roll Call*, September 25, 2015, http://www.rollcall.com/news/home/conservatives-take-credit-boehner-resignation.
79. Matt Fuller, "HFC Looks for Leverage in Speaker's Race," *Roll Call*, October 7 2015, http://www.rollcall.com/news/home/can-rule-changes-solve-mccarthys-math-problem.
80. Matt Fuller, "Paul Ryan Sets Conditions for Speaker Bid," *Roll Call*, October 20, 2015, http://www.rollcall.com/news/home/paul-ryan-speaker-run; Scott Wong, "Ryan Tells GOP He'll Run for Speaker—With Conditions," *The Hill*, October 20, 2015, http://thehill.com/homenews/house/257548-ryan-tells-gop-hell-run-for-speaker-with-conditions.
81. Matt Fuller and Emma Dumain, "Paul Ryan Clears Biggest Hurdle to Speaker Bid," *Roll Call*, October 21, 2015, http://www.rollcall.com/news/home/freedom-caucus-stops-short-ryan-endorsement.
82. Dana Milbank, "Paul Ryan Quickly Restores the House's Regular Disorder," *Washington Post*, November 18, 2015, https://www.washingtonpost.com/opinions/paul-ryan-abandons-his-promise/2015/11/18/2512fdc6-8e3e-11e5-baf4-bdf37355da0c_story.html.
83. Emma Dumain, "House GOP Steering Proposal Could Deliver Results—Or Not," *Roll Call*, November 18, 2015, http://www.rollcall.com/news/home/paul-ryan-steering-committee-proposal-vote.
84. Indeed, some even argued for further strengthening of leadership power. For example, the moderate Tuesday Group supported the idea of expelling from the conference GOP members who voted against the party's Speaker nominee on the floor. See Kate Ackley, Eliza Newlin Carney, and Shawn Zeller, "Trapped in a Bad Marriage," *CQ Weekly*, October 5, 2015, 20.
85. Although in the 1995–1996 government shutdowns, the GOP experienced problems similar to those of the Boehner years, which included a division among the Republican leaders over the correct path.
86. Emma Dumain, "Ryan Gets High Marks for First Big Showdown," *Roll Call*, December 17, 2015, 1.
87. Carl Hulse, "Next Speaker Will Face the Same Difficulties With Conservatives," *New York Times*, September 25, 2015, http://www.nytimes.com/2015/09/26/us/next-speaker-will-face-the-same-difficulties-with-conservatives.html.
88. Jennifer Steinhauer, "Ryan's Budget Strategy Runs Afoul of Conservative Colleagues' Hard Line," *New York Times*, February 11, 2016, A17.
89. Ibid.
90. A Pew Center poll in 2015 showed that only 68 percent of Republican identifiers approved of their own party. This was a decline of 18 percentage points in a year. See Ackley, Carney, and Zeller, "Trapped in a Bad Marriage," 19.

Part II
Elections, Constituencies, and Representation

3. Voters, Candidates, and Issues in Congressional Elections

Robert S. Erikson and Gerald C. Wright

This chapter offers an overview of congressional elections. The chapter discusses the nature of the national outcome in terms of both the vote for the House of Representatives and the distribution of seats. Then, it discusses outcomes of individual House races and shows the declining impact of factors such as incumbency, candidate spending, and candidate ideology and the greater centrality of partisanship in House elections. Emphasis is given to issues of representation—do the voters get representatives who share their views? Although the chapter emphasizes the House of Representatives, Senate elections are also discussed.

Elections for the U.S. House of Representatives fascinate observers of American politics almost as much as do presidential elections. Unlike Senate elections, which come at staggered six-year intervals, House elections provide a regular biennial measure of the national electoral pulse. Interest in House elections centers on the partisan balance of seats and the electorate's collective motivations that underlie this verdict.

Another source of fascination with House elections is their large number. Every two years, the composition of the new U.S. House is the result of 435 separate contests for 435 separate seats. In part, these outcomes are determined by national electoral forces. But also, to a large extent, they are determined by the candidates in these contests and the conduct of their individual campaigns.

In this chapter, first, we examine the national forces in House elections and their influence on the partisan division of votes and seats. Next, we look at the role of candidates and parties in individual House contests. Finally, we compare elections for the House with elections for the Senate.

The National Verdict in House Elections

The founders designed the House of Representatives to be the popular branch of government. Elections for the House were expected to reflect the ebb and flow of public preferences. And even though the Senate has also become responsive to public opinion, analysts and journalists continue to watch House elections for what they say about what the public wants and the future directions of U.S. public policy.

For a long time, the question of the House of Representatives' partisan makeup was framed as interest in the precise size of the Democrats' majority. For forty years—from the elections of 1954 to 1994—the Democrats controlled the House. The long-held assumption of Democratic dominance in the House came to a screeching halt when the 1994 election gave the Republicans the majority, surprising virtually all observers. In the five elections from 1996 through 2004, the Republicans retained their newly won control, albeit by narrow margins. Then, in 2006, the Democrats won back their House majority. As in 1994, this transfer of power surprised most observers, up until the eve of the election. In 2008, the Democrats consolidated their majority, only to see the Republicans roar back to power in 2010 and then build on this in 2014, achieving their largest share of House seats since 1928.

Since World War II, the party division of House seats varied from 67 percent Democratic and 33 percent Republican (after the 1964 election) to 57 percent Republican and 43 percent Democratic (following the 2014 election). In terms of the number of seats, this is a range of 105 seats (out of 435) between each party's high and low watermarks. As Figure 3-1 shows, the partisan seat division follows closely (but imprecisely) from the national vote division. On average, the party that gains seats gains seven new seats (about 1.5 percent of the total) for each added percentage point of the major-party vote. This ratio of seat percentage gained or lost per vote percentage gained (1.5) is called the swing ratio.

The exact swing ratio varies from one election to the next, dependent on several factors. These include where the votes are won and lost, as well as the level of competitiveness of the seats. For example, if one party gains most of its votes where the other party previously won by a large margin, its added votes may not result in additional seats. If the party gains the same number of votes where the opposition party barely squeaked by in the last election, it gains many more seats for the same number of votes.[1]

The earlier forty-year Democratic run of party control was based on a stable but small Democratic majority of the congressional vote. In the twenty House elections between 1954 and 1992, the national division of the major-party vote varied only within the narrow range from 51 to 59 percent Democratic. Thus, a swing of only eight votes in one hundred separated the strongest Republican electoral tide from the largest Democratic tide. Even when the electoral landscape changed so dramatically in the Republicans' favor with the 1994 Republican landslide, the swing was due to a small minority of voters. Between 1992 and 1994, the national major-party vote shifted only six percentage points. During the 1994 to 2004 era of Republican control, the national vote for Congress hovered close to the 50–50 range. The Democratic resurgence in 2006 was accomplished with a swing of only four percentage points in the national vote. Even the 2010

Figure 3-1 Democratic House Seats and Vote Share, 1946–2014

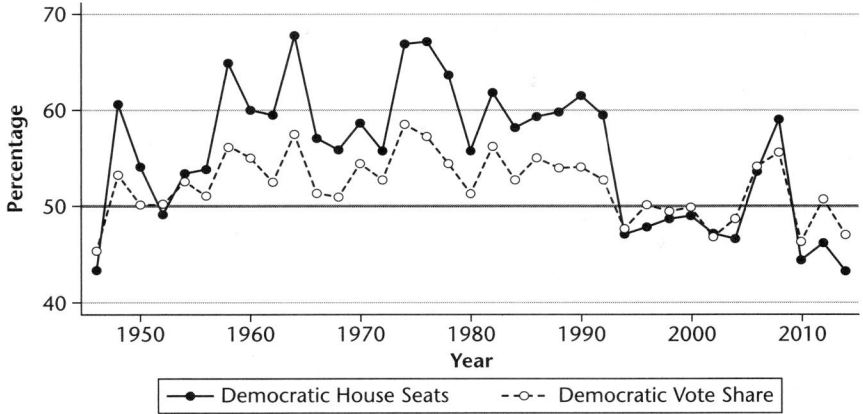

Source: Compiled by authors.

Republican triumph involved a swing of only nine percentage points. The 2008 to 2010 surge was as if one out of six Democratic voters from 2008 switched to vote Republican in 2010.

To summarize, changes in the party composition of congressional seats typically are a function of a small fraction of the electorate switching from one party to the other with its congressional vote. We next discuss the causes of these small changes in the partisan tide. Relevant explanatory variables include the electorate's party identification, the electorate's ideological mood, and reactions to the current presidential administration's performance, particularly on the economy.

The Partisan Base of the Congressional Vote

Most voters in the United States identify with one of the two dominant political parties—the Republicans or the Democrats. This identification provides voters with a standing decision to vote for their favored party—unless the information from the current campaign gives reason to temporarily defect with their vote. Most votes are partisan votes (Republicans voting Republican and Democrats voting Democratic), and voters rarely change their partisanship. This provides a certain stability to the national congressional vote over time. The national division of party identification—sometimes called *macropartisanship*—is not a constant; however, small changes in macropartisanship imply small changes in the electorate's collective standing decision, and these carry electoral consequences. Macrolevel changes in partisanship typically represent shifting evaluations of the parties' relative competence in governing, including economic performance.

The national verdict in House elections closely follows the national division of party identification. Most Democrats vote Democratic; most Republicans vote Republican; and independents usually split about 50–50. The outcome of this process is the *normal vote*.[2] Figure 3-2 illustrates tracking macropartisanship and the House seat division over time.[3]

Now, we gain some understanding of how the Democrats were able to control the House of Representatives for forty years. The Democrats were the dominant party in terms of party identification; thus, more people voted Democratic than Republican. The Democrats' loss of their competitive advantage in partisanship in the late 1980s and early 1990s eventually caught up to them in 1994, with the Republicans' takeover.

The one-time Democratic advantage was not all due to a dominant Democratic position in party identification. Democrats in Congress were helped by their collective incumbency advantage (discussed later). With most incumbents being Democrats and most incumbents seeking reelection, the Democrats were able to keep their congressional majority beyond the point where they held a dominant plurality in terms of party identification. Also, being out of power caused disillusionment among Republican House members and their earlier retirement. This too advantaged the majority Democrats.

These processes worked in reverse when the Republicans gained power in 1994. Most incumbents were Republicans, and Democrats retired early, allowing further Republican opportunities. When the Democrats reclaimed majority status in 2006, their incumbency advantage was insufficient to overcome the 2010 Republican wave. By 2014, the Republicans' increased hold on the House resulted in some commentators predicting Republican control of the House through the

Figure 3-2 Partisanship and House Seat Shares, 1946–2014

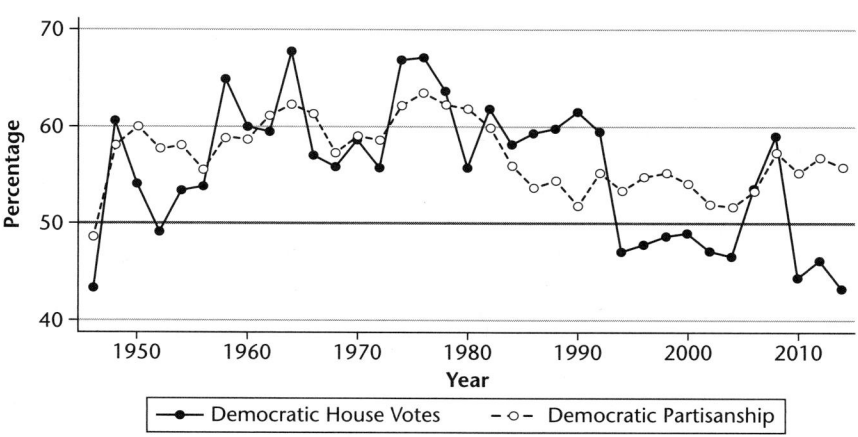

Source: Compiled by the authors.

2016 elections, even in the face of a Democratic presidential win,[4] and probably through the 2020 redistricting.[5] A good part of the expectation for continuing Republican control of the House is the party's electoral *structural advantage*, which we discuss next.

The translation of partisan votes into seats in the legislature is not automatically fair. Almost always, the party that wins the most votes nationwide wins a greater proportion of seats than its proportion of the votes. This is understandable, as the dominant party typically wins a plurality of the vote in a greater proportion of districts than its proportion of votes. A party's share of seats is also affected by gerrymandering—natural or man made. Man-made gerrymandering occurs when the party controlling the districting draws district lines for partisan advantage, which usually involves packing the opposition party's voters in very safe or one-sided districts, where their votes go wasted. The districts of the 2012 to 2020 period were drawn by state legislatures following the 2010 Census, and since these were legislatures elected in 2010, a Republican year, most were drawn to aid Republicans.

But beyond purposeful partisan gerrymandering, Democrats have a *structural* problem in the form of a natural gerrymander that is generated by the geographic location of the two major parties' supporters. Democrats tend to cluster in densely populated urban areas; Republicans are spread out in the suburbs and rural areas and are not so geographically concentrated. In many places, it is simply not possible to draw district lines that treat the parties fairly.[6] Court mandates to create majority-minority districts (that is, where a majority of voters are of a racial minority) adds a further constraint.

One can see the Republican advantage in districting from Figure 3-3, which reveals the partisan division of districts in voting for president. In 2012, there were far more very safe districts for Obama than for Romney, his Republican opponent. A vivid illustration of the Republican bias is that in 2012, Romney actually "won" more congressional districts than Obama, even as he lost the popular vote, 52–48. It follows that this partisan bias extends to elections for the House of Representatives so that the Democrats need somewhat more than 50 percent of the vote in order to win the most House seats. Thus, the Democrats face an uphill battle to regaining the House majority. As we said above, the translation of votes to legislative seats is not always fair.

Policy Mood

Partisanship is not the only force that shapes long-term voting patterns. In addition, the national verdict depends on the nation's collective preference for more liberalism or more conservatism in its national policies—the nation's policy (or ideological) *mood*. James Stimson has measured the nation's policy mood on an annual basis as a sophisticated composite of available public opinion polls.[7] The national electoral verdict for the House—like elections for the presidency and for the Senate—is significantly related to the nation's ideological mood. When the public is "in the mood" for more government activism from Congress, it votes more Democratic. The most liberal mood, according to Stimson's index, was in the early 1960s, which was also a time of Democratic congressional dominance. The most conservative times were around 1952, at the start of Stimson's series, and around 1980, when Reagan was elected president with the help of considerable Republican strength in Congress.[8] Both macropartisanship and mood help to explain the Democratic resurgence in the 2006 election and the Republican rebound in 2010. The 2006 electorate was both more Democratic and more liberal (in terms of Stimson's mood measure) than it had been in over a decade. But by 2010, the conservative trajectory resumed, signaling increased resistance to government programs.

Presidential Election Years

In presidential years, the short-term forces of the presidential election and the House elections run in the same partisan direction, so the party that performs better than the normal vote for president will also perform better than normal for Congress. In part, this results from people voting for president and Congress being influenced by the same national issues; in part, it results from people voting for Congress based on their vote for president. Whatever the cause, the phenomenon is known as the coattail effect, as if an extraordinary number of candidates of the winning presidential party are swept into office on the president's coattails.

Democratic coattails were at their strongest in 1964, when Lyndon Johnson's landslide victory created an overwhelming 295–140 Democratic majority. Republican coattails were particularly strong in 1980, when Ronald Reagan won the presidency. In some elections, presidential coattails appear to be virtually nonexistent. For instance, Clinton's reelection in 1996 carried so few Democratic House candidates to victory that the Democrats were unable to regain control of Congress.

The size of the coattail effect is decidedly irregular. One statistical estimate for post–World War II elections puts it at about +.40 congressional votes nationally for every percentage of the vote gained by the party at the presidential level.[9] Put another way, every ten votes gained by a presidential candidate also adds about four votes for her congressional running mates.

Midterm Years

At the moment when Barack Obama won the presidency in 2008, it was possible to make a safe prediction about the congressional election of 2010: The Republicans would gain strength in House elections. While it may have surprised some that the Republicans regained the House majority in 2010, it was no surprise that they gained seats over their allotment from the 2008 election. If one regularity has governed House elections throughout history, it has been the phenomenon of midterm loss—that the party controlling the presidency suffers a net loss of seats in Congress in the election following the presidential contest. Through 1994, only once in the twentieth century (1934) did the presidential party gain seats at midterm.

In 1998, the midterm rule broke down, as the Democrats gained congressional seats while in control of the presidency, even as President Clinton was undergoing a highly unpopular impeachment. It happened again in 2002, when the Republicans gained seats as the presidential party, with President George W. Bush still enjoying the fruits of his post-9/11 popularity. Some congressional observers now see the rule of midterm loss as nothing more than an obsolete statistical oddity. But this would be a mistake. The presidential party lost congressional seats in a string of sixteen consecutive midterm elections (1938–1994), as well as in the three most recent midterm elections. This is a regularity too strong to dismiss. It requires explanation.

The two leading explanations for midterm loss are *withdrawn coattails* and *ideological balancing*. The former explanation ties the presidential party's midterm loss to the loss of presidential coattails. The latter explanation ties it to an electoral tendency toward ideological balancing of the presidency and Congress.

The withdrawn-coattails argument goes as follows: In presidential years, the congressional vote for the president's party is inflated by presidential coattails. At the next midterm, the congressional vote reverts to its normal-vote outcome. The result is an electoral decline for the president's party.

This withdrawn-coattails thesis appears plausible, looking over the fourteen midterm elections from 1946 through 1998.[10] On average, the presidential party suffered a decline of 1 percent of the seats for every percentage of the vote gained in the prior presidential election. In other words, the larger the coattails that are withdrawn, the greater the decline in seats. The withdrawn-coattails thesis has a special appeal to explain the violation of the midterm loss rule in 1998. Clinton had virtually no coattails in 1996; therefore, with no coattails to withdraw in 1998, the Democratic congressional vote did not decline.

While the withdrawn-coattails argument explains midterm loss in terms of the circumstances in the prior election, the ideological-balancing thesis explains the loss in terms of the circumstances at midterm itself. By this theory, the electorate votes against the president's party at midterm as an ideological hedge. Moderate voters, seeing themselves ideologically between the Democratic and Republican positions, have some incentive to balance the president's ideology with a congressional vote for the "out" party. The process encourages divided government, with one party controlling the presidency and the other at least one house of Congress.[11]

Like withdrawn coattails, the balancing thesis has its plausibility. On average, over the eighteen midterm elections from 1942 to 2010 (equally divided between Republican and Democratic presidencies), each party enjoyed about twenty-eight more House seats when it did *not* control the presidency. In other words, the way for a party to achieve the highest level of success at midterm is to lose the prior presidential election. Balancing theory has its special appeal to explain the violation of the midterm-loss rule in 1998. In 1996, with party control of the House at stake, a potent partisan argument of the congressional campaign was that moderate voters should vote Republican for Congress to block Clinton, who everybody knew was about to be reelected. The 1996 result was no coattails and balancing in anticipation of Clinton's election. With balancing in advance (and no coattails to withdraw), the 1998 election became the exception to the rule of midterm loss for the presidential party.[12]

Neither coattails, nor balancing, of course, can explain the Republican gains of 2002. The 2002 exception may have been due to the huge boost in Bush's popularity following the attacks of 9/11 as well as the Democrats' inability to mount an effective campaign. Moreover, Republicans gained from redistricting following the 2000 Census.[13]

Electoral Change as a Search for Policy Direction

Every two years, the electorate collectively chooses a new Congress, with a new partisan makeup. Does Congress's party composition reflect the electorate's policy preferences? The popular view, often propounded by pundits at election time, is that partisan tides reflect the electorate's changing ideological mood—as if Democratic gains signify a demand for more liberalism and Republican gains a demand for more conservatism. For example, the major Democratic gains associated with Johnson's landslide victory in 1964 were interpreted at the time as a mandate for a new liberal policy agenda. A conservative mood switch is identified with Reagan's surprise win in 1980 and the accompanying Republican gains in Congress. More recently, the Republican takeover of Congress in 2010 was widely proclaimed by the victors and the media to indicate a sharp rejection of the liberalism of President Obama and his signature legislation, the Affordable Care Act. Congress responded with legislation that matched the purported public cries for change, which included at least sixty votes in the Republican-controlled House to repeal the ACA.

While many things influence the ups and downs of partisan fortunes in Congress, such as scandals and the economy, the electorate's collective preference for more liberalism or more conservatism is an important part of the mix. Actually, the electorate *was* relatively liberal at the time of the Great Society and conservative when the Reagan revolution began; similarly, it *was* liberal when it elected Clinton with a Democratic Congress in 1992 but conservative in 1994. And the electorate was in a conservative mood in 2002 (when Bush's Republicans scored a rare presidential-party gain) and then liberal again in 2006, when the Democrats regained control, but decidedly less so by 2010. The electorate chooses the partisan makeup of the Congress (House and Senate) based, *in part*, on its preferred degree of policy liberalism, adjusting also for the expected ideological pressure from the occupant of the White House.

The Role of Candidates in House Contests

Voters in congressional elections vote not only on the basis of national issues and the parties' policy positions but also on the basis of what they learn about their local candidates. At first glance, it would seem that voters generally have insufficient information about the candidates to vote on anything more than a partisan basis. Consider some evidence from surveys: Only about one-half of voters can name their U.S. representative, and slightly fewer claim to have "read or heard" something about him or her. The content of this information is generally vague ("He is a good man," or, "She knows the job"), and it rarely touches on policy issues or roll call voting. Only on the generous test of recognition of the representative's name does the electorate score well. More than 90 percent claim to recognize their representative's name when supplied with it. Candidates for open seats are even less visible than incumbent candidates. Challengers trying to defeat incumbent representatives are the least visible of all. Typically, only about 20 percent of the voting electorate can recall the challenger's name or anything else about this person. Only about half will claim to recognize the challenger's name when supplied with it.[14]

Although voters generally are not well informed about their local House candidates, it does not follow that the candidates have little impact on election outcomes. Movement by relatively few voters in a constituency can create a major surge for or against a candidate. This movement, the *personal vote*, results from the constituency's reaction to the specific candidates, as opposed to the *partisan vote*, which results from the constituency's partisanship. From the 1960s until recently, the personal vote had been almost as important as the partisan vote in deciding elections. However, with today's intense partisan polarization, the candidates themselves have declined in importance in congressional elections. Increasingly, voters rely on the party affiliation of candidates as the most relevant cue when voting in congressional elections.

The Success of House Incumbents

One prominent fact about House elections has been the success rate of incumbents. Averaged over many election years, over 95 percent of incumbent candidates have been reelected. Nevertheless, even taking into account surge elections such as 1994, 2006, 2010, and 2014, over 90 percent of incumbent candidates return to Congress. Why do incumbents do so well at the ballot box? Several factors contribute to their electoral success.

District Partisanship

When we ask why incumbents generally win reelection, the most obvious explanation is district partisanship. Most districts are either one-party Republican or one-party Democratic (as measured in Figure 3-3 by the presidential vote). Most House seats, therefore, are nearly guaranteed for the candidate of the locally favored party.

We see the importance of district partisanship from the following statistics. The 2012 presidential election provides a benchmark for partisan competitiveness. We can set a strict definition of a very competitive district (in terms of underlying partisanship) as one where neither presidential candidate received more than 53 percent of the major-party vote in 2012. Of the 435 districts in place for the 2012 election, only fifty-four (or 12 percent) had met this standard of closeness in their presidential voting. The strong pro-Republican partisan tide of 2014 can be seen in the outcomes of the competitive districts: The GOP won forty-three, or 80 percent, of those contests. In the other 88 percent of districts where the Romney–Obama vote diverged by at least three percentage points from 50–50 and therefore could be considered at least reasonably safe for the dominant party, 97 percent of those seats were won by the dominant party in 2014. Thus, only within a quite a narrow window, encompassing just a fraction of the districts, are House elections usually "in play."

Electoral Selection

One simple but sometimes overlooked reason incumbents win is that (in competitive districts) incumbency status must be earned at the ballot box. Apart from district partisanship and partisan trends, elections are won on the basis of which party can field the stronger candidate. Strong candidates tend to win and retain their strength in subsequent contests as incumbents. They survive until they falter or lose to even stronger candidates. Retirement of a successful incumbent starts the process again.

Weak Challengers

Incumbents augment their electoral success from their ability to draw weak challengers. Candidates and their supporters behave strategically, so they are reluctant to expend funds and political reputations against formidable foes.[15] Strong challengers conserve their political resources and tend to run when they can win, either because the incumbent is vulnerable, the national short-term forces favor the party, or they have a shot at an open seat.

The tendency for potential challengers to behave strategically can be seen in the pattern of challenger quality facing incumbents in safe and competitive districts. Incumbents with safe districts are the least likely to face experienced challengers. Experienced and otherwise attractive candidates are scared off by strong incumbents. In their place, we find weak challengers who hand even larger victories to the incumbent.

Strategic Retirement

One reason why incumbents rarely lose is the process of *strategic retirements*. When incumbents are threatened by an imminent loss, they generally announce their retirement rather than face the verdict from the voters. On average, incumbents retire with about the same frequency as their objective probability of defeat. For instance, representatives facing a 60 percent chance of losing will retire about 60 percent of the time.

The Incumbency Advantage

Finally, there is the incumbency advantage—the electoral benefits that accrue to the incumbent by virtue of being the incumbent. More precisely, there are opportunities that incumbents have to strengthen their electoral position by virtue of their serving in the House. Most members exploit these resources, although some more energetically than others.

Several means can be used to measure the incumbency advantage. Arguably the most intuitive is the sophomore surge, or the percentage of the vote that candidates gain between their first election (as a nonincumbent) and their first reelection attempt (as an incumbent). Averaged across elections and adjusted for the national partisan trend, the sophomore surge is a simple and accurate way to measure the typical vote share gained from incumbency. The value of incumbency has changed markedly. The sophomore surge ran only about two percentage points in the 1950s, when partisanship was the dominant consideration in congressional elections. By the 1970s, the sophomore surge had reached about seven percentage points, where it remained into the twenty-first century.[16]

In very recent years, the incumbency advantage has declined again.[17] By 2014, it was back to the minimal 2 percent level of the 1950s! Claims about how candidates increase their electoral safety once they win office no longer seem quite so applicable. What happened?

To illustrate the change, Figure 3-3 graphs the relationship between the House district vote in 2000 and 2012 as percentage Democratic (on the vertical axis) and the share of the major-party vote for the winning Democratic presidential candidate in the same district (on the horizontal axis). The Democratic vote in 2000 and 2012 is a good measure of a constituency's partisan and ideological leanings.

The devaluation of incumbency as an electoral asset is illustrated in the comparison of how incumbents fared in 2000 and 2014. In the top figure, we see incumbents running better than their presidential candidates, especially in competitive districts (those near where Democratic nominee Al Gore got 50 percent of the vote). Democratic incumbents above the line did better than Gore, whereas Republicans below the line beat the eventual Republican winner, George W. Bush, in their districts. The correlation between the House and presidential vote in 2000 was .79—a strong effect for partisanship but still leaving plenty of room for the personal vote, much of which appears here to be incumbency.

Continued party polarization has increased the centrality of party labels and consequently diminished the impact of the incumbents' personal vote. We see

Figure 3-3 The Decreased Incumbency Advantage in the House, 2000 and 2014

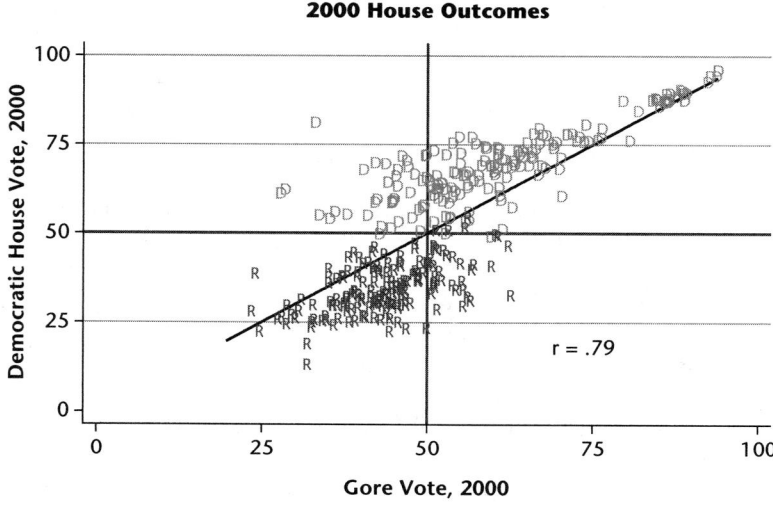

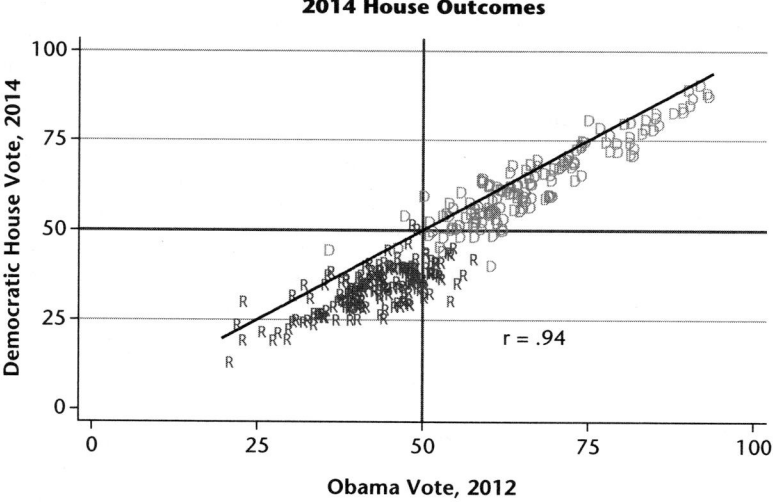

Source: Compiled by authors.

Note: Ds above the diagonal line indicate that the district House vote for the Democratic candidate exceeded the Democratic vote for president. Ds below the diagonal line indicate that the district House vote for the Democratic candidate ran behind the Democratic vote for president. Outcomes above the horizontal line, at 50 percent, indicate a Democratic victory; dots below this line indicate a Republican victory.

this clearly in the lower panel of Figure 3-3, where House vote outcomes adhere much more closely to district partisanship. Notice how closely the outcomes are packed to the line of district partisanship. This is summarized in the very strong House–presidential vote correlation of 0.94.

The growth in the incumbency advantage in the 1960s and the recent decline can be explained. The increase from the 1950s was a result of weakening party ties and the growth of independent voters, culminating in a period centered in the 1970s known for its "decline of parties."[18] The result was that other forces (e.g., incumbency) could have greater sway. A second trend was that members of Congress increasingly turned their offices into reelection machines.[19] In the mid-1960s, Congress changed its rules to bestow on its members several increases in the resources of office, or *perks*. These perks included free mailing privileges (the frank), increased travel allowances to visit their districts and build district favor, and increased staff to handle constituents' growing concerns with the federal bureaucracy.[20] The result was that incumbents were well thought of by their constituents and often for reasons that had nothing to do with policy-making or partisan considerations at all.

The current decline in the incumbency advantage—and the Congress members' personal vote in general—is the resurgence of parties in the form of today's polarized congressional parties. Nationally, the parties have become more combative, making every battle take on importance beyond the issue at hand, and at the same time, the parties have become more ideologically distinct from each other and more internally homogeneous.[21] Today, unlike the 1960s or 1970s, the party labels tell voters a great deal about what a candidate stands for on a broad array of social and economic issues. As a result, voters are giving more weight to party labels (and the issue positions they represent) and less attention to other candidate differences. This is reinforced as the increased partisan hostility evident in Congress[22] is reflected in greater partisan intensity and identifications in the mass public.[23] In an age of partisan warfare, fewer voters can see past party lines to appreciate the traditional perks and the personal vote incumbents try to build with their districts.

Referring back to Figure 3-3, one can see these changes at work. In both the 2000 and 2014 elections, those from clearly safe districts earned about the vote margin as expected by their districts' partisanship (presidential vote). The changes in incumbency are evident in the competitive districts. Notice that in the 2000 election (like those going back to the 1970s), the incumbents in competitive districts and adverse districts ran clearly ahead of the presidential vote (Democrats above the diagonal line, Republicans below it). By 2014, however, this pattern is barely detectable; all of the incumbents bunch closer to the line of district partisanship than in earlier elections. This is another illustration of the greater role of party and the diminished impact of incumbency that has transpired in this era of extreme party polarization.

The Incumbency Advantage as an Investment

Because incumbents almost always win, it might seem that incumbents can ignore constituency concerns. This may seem particularly true today, with the general decline of the candidates' personal vote. But this impression would be quite mistaken. Even though representatives know that they are unlikely to lose the next election, they also understand that their chances are roughly one in three that they will eventually lose. After all, roughly one in three got to Congress in the first place by defeating a sitting incumbent.[24]

House members, we have argued, do not get their incumbency advantage automatically; they must earn it by hard work. Part of the work is constituent service and bringing home the pork, in the form of government construction projects, local government contracts, and the like. But there is also an important policy component to the incumbent's investment. One way representatives earn the incumbency advantage is by representing their districts' policy interests. Often, these interests can be expressed as a summary ideological preference. As we shall see in the next section, representatives protect their seats by representing the policy interests of their constituencies.[25]

Candidates, Issues, and the Vote

In this section, we explore how House members hold onto their seats by offering ideological representation. The process works as follows: Voters select, in part, based on which candidate and party is closest to their own views, and this gives the candidates an incentive to move to the constituency's center—toward the position of the district's median voter.[26] This does not mean that all members would be moderates since there is a huge variation in the ideological leanings of districts and hence the ideological and policy preferences of median voters in the districts. The strength of this incentive is proportional to the attentiveness of the electorate and the extent to which the contest is close due to nonideological factors.

If ideological proximity were all the voters cared about, candidates would always converge toward the center of their district because to do otherwise would be to lose. But in reality, voters are only partially attentive and responsive to ideological appeals, thus limiting candidates' electoral gains from moderation. In addition, candidates have to be increasingly concerned about keeping their primary electorates and donors happy, and these groups pull candidates toward their parties' ideological extremes.[27] As a result, candidates do not converge at the center. Instead, they strike a balance between the general electoral security gained from adopting the position of the constituency's median voter on the one hand and the more extreme ideological position of their primary electorates and activist supporters on the other.[28]

While candidates have some motivation to move toward the center, they rarely move so far that the views of the Democratic and Republican candidates converge. While some Republican candidates in the nation are to the left of some Democrats, it is rare to find a Republican candidate on the left of the Democratic opponent within the same district. Indeed, among the many studies comparing congressional candidates in the same district, it is almost always the case that the Democratic candidate is the more liberal candidate, and the Republican is the more conservative candidate. (Presumably, the district's median voter is in between.) The candidates' party affiliations clearly provide voters the basis of ideological choice.

Figure 3-4 depicts the relationship between constituency opinion, represented by the 2012 Obama vote, and the ideological record of House incumbents in the 113th Congress (2013–2014). We measure congressional ideology using voting records as the weighted average (over the two years of the 113th Congress) of the first and second dimension DW-NOMINATE scores, developed by political scientists Keith Poole and Howard Rosenthal. Scores on the second dimension are weighted only .35 times the weight of scores on the dominant first dimension.[29]

The most obvious feature of the graph is that Congress is divided between liberal Democrats and conservative Republicans. (Vertically, Democrats are positioned in the bottom half of the graph, indicating liberalism; Republicans are positioned in the top half as conservatives.) This ideological division is, of course, indication of the increasing polarization of Congress in recent years. Not only are Democratic and Republican House members ideologically distinct, but Democratic and Republican House members also represent different constituencies. Not surprisingly, Democrats represent Democratic (and liberal) districts, and Republicans represent Republican (and conservative) districts. The battleground is the set of somewhat moderate and competitive districts in the middle, which sometimes elect Republicans and sometimes Democrats.

Clearly, districts tend to vote for Congress consistent with their partisanship and ideology, electing the most ideologically appropriate candidate. As we will see, besides using partisanship, constituencies also sort candidates into winners and losers, in part, based on the candidates' personal ideologies. This also affects the contours of the graph in Figure 3-4. Figure 3-4 focuses only on incumbents, but it shows that within each party's congressional delegation, ideological positions respond to district ideology. While very Democratic (liberal) and Republican (conservative) districts have predictably liberal and conservative representation respectively, the winning candidates (incumbents) in competitive districts tend to be more moderate than their counterparts in more solidly one-party districts. In part, this is due to the electorate's selection. In competitive districts, ideologically extreme candidates tend to fail, leaving relative moderates as the incumbents. Additionally, competitive (moderate) districts motivate incumbents toward the center, consistent with their motivation to be more ideologically appealing than their opponents. And finally, competitive districts may draw more moderate incumbents simply because the centrism of these districts draws candidates with more centrist views.

In summary, Figure 3-4 shows that much of the ideological variation within parties is a function of constituency. The more liberal and Democratic the district (as measured by the 2012 Obama vote), the more liberal are the two parties' candidates. This congressional responsiveness to constituency preferences indicates that candidates *believe* that constituencies vote on the basis of ideological proximity to the candidates as well as the ideological identities of their parties. Next, we examine the evidence regarding whether this belief is correct.

While we do not have a measure of challengers' ideological position, we can test for the effect of the incumbent's roll call ideology on the vote. We examine the effect of incumbent ideology (measured as conservatism) on the Democratic vote while controlling for district presidential voting and the candidates' relative spending. We present regression equations for incumbent candidates in 2014 separately for Democrat-held and Republican-held seats. Since our hypothesis is that moderation (conservatism) wins votes for Democrats, and moderation (liberalism) wins votes for Republicans, we expect the signs of the ideology variables to be positive.

The equations are shown in Table 3-1. We can visualize the estimated effects of incumbent ideology the following way. The coefficients are 2.75 for Democrats and 6.36 for Republicans, for an average of about 4.6. Based on the 4.6 average, members of Congress typically gain almost half (0.46) of a percentage point of the vote for every tenth of a point of movement toward moderation on the ideology index. For instance, a rare moderate at 0 in the middle of the scale on our ideology scale would gain about 3.5 percentage points beyond what would be obtained if the member mimicked their party's extreme members out at the +0.75 or −0.75 range on the scale.[30]

The estimated effects of incumbent ideology in Table 3-1 are smaller than for previous election years. The coefficients are about half of what they had been in previous decades. For Democratic incumbents, the 2014 coefficient does not even achieve statistical significance. As party affiliation increasingly determines congressional behavior, incumbent ideology becomes a less valuable cue to voters. And with voters discounting ideological distinctions within a party, congressional candidates have less electoral incentive to depart from their party's orthodox position.[31]

Nonetheless, ideological distinctions within the party still matter, just less than they had before. Figure 3-5 shows how districts shape the ideology of their representatives. It displays the relationship between the congressional vote in the subsequent 2014 election and 2012 presidential voting (the marker for district partisanship) for incumbents with distinctive ideological positions. Within each party, we separate out the most moderate from the most extreme.

For Republicans, we separate out the most conservative incumbents, who are at least one standard deviation (for the Republican party) more conservative than

Table 3-1 Regression of 2014 Democratic House Vote on 2012–2013 Incumbent Roll Call Ideology, 2012 District Presidential Vote, and 2014 Candidate Spending

	Regression Coefficient	T-Ratio	Standardized Coefficient
Republican Incumbents			
Incumbent ideology (conservatism)	6.36	2.9	0.178
Percentage for Obama, 2012	0.547	10.1	0.646
Log Democrat spending minus log Republican spending	1.08	5.8	0.337
Constant	10.26	3.0	
Adjusted R^2 = .561; N = 145			
Democratic Incumbents			
Incumbent ideology (conservatism)	2.75	1.1	0.060
Percentage for Obama, 2012	0.841	14.6	0.840
Log Democrat spending minus log Republican spending	0.906	3.5	0.168
Constant	7.53	2.5	
Adjusted R^2 = .813; N = 117			

Source: Compiled by authors.

Note: Candidate ideology scores are the weighted average of the first and second dimension DW-NOMINATE scores for the 113th Congress, where the second dimension is weighted .35 times the first dimension. The Obama vote is his percentage of the two-party vote in each House district. Candidate spending is measured in units of thousands of dollars as log of dollars spent minus 5,000. Only contested elections are included.

their party's mean (*C*s in the top panel), from the moderates, at least one standard deviation more liberal than the Republican mean, in the more liberal half (*M*s in the top panel). Two things should be noted. First, all of the safe seats are represented by conservatives, with the moderates mostly representing competitive seats where the Obama vote was about 50–50 or less. This is evidence that politicians moderate according to electoral need. Second, while the conservatives ran about five percentage points ahead of Obama in their districts, the moderates generally led the 2012 Obama vote by over 10 percent. In a party that has become markedly more conservative over the years,[32] it is clear that moderation has a nontrivial electoral payoff.

For Democrats, we find the mirror image pattern, although not quite as distinct. We separate out the most liberal incumbents, those at least one standard deviation more liberal than the Democratic mean (*L*s in the bottom

Figure 3-4 Representatives' Roll Call Ideology, 2013–2014, by District Presidential Vote in 2014

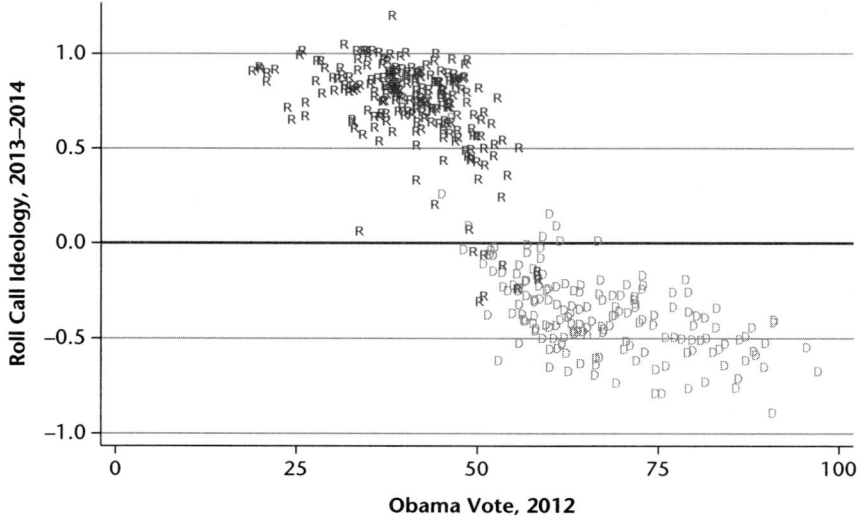

Source: Poole-Rosenthal DW-NOMINATE Data. http://voteview.com/dwnomin.htm.

Note: Roll call ideology is weighted average of DW-NOMINATE scores (conservatism) on the first and second dimension, where second dimension scores are weighted .35 times first dimension scores.

panel), from the moderates, voting at least one standard deviation more conservative than the Democratic mean. True to form, we observe that the liberals tend to represent the more pro-Obama districts, and these outcomes are closely aligned with district partisanship. Moderates, compared to liberals, ran ahead of Obama—but just barely so. What we do see is greater variance in outcomes; some did better, and some did worse, and six lost their seats in spite of their moderate voting. In 2014, numerous moderate Democrats who had previously survived in their competitive or even Republican districts finally succumbed to the Republican tide, falling to the vigorous campaigns of Republican challengers.

Congressional Elections and Representation

The political parties and the candidates provide the mechanism by which constituencies can electorally determine the policy positions of their representatives in Congress. First, consider the role of political parties. Democratic and Republican candidates for Congress are sufficiently divergent from one another on the liberal–conservative spectrum to provide their constituencies with a clear choice. Liberal districts generally vote Democratic and elect liberals, whereas conservative districts generally vote Republican and elect conservatives.

Second, not only the parties' general reputations but also the precise ideological positions of the candidates matter. Candidates for Congress often deviate from their party's ideological orthodoxy. By moving toward a more moderate position, one that is closer to a constituency's prevailing views, the candidate may enhance his or her electoral chances and, by doing so, enhance the representation of constituency views.

As we saw in Figure 3-4, the net result is a clear pattern whereby the most liberal districts elect the most liberal members, and the most conservative districts elect the most conservative members. Representatives' ideological positions and constituency ideology (proxied by the presidential vote) correlate at a substantial +0.86. Very liberal districts almost always elect Democrats; very conservative districts almost always elect Republicans. In the battleground districts in the middle, candidate ideology can be the decisive factor.

Interestingly, while we observe evidence of considerable representation, we cannot be sure about the prevalence of a residual ideological bias. We compare ideology scores of congressional candidates on the one hand with the presidential voting of constituencies on the other. While both may reflect ideological positioning, they are not calibrated on a common scale. It could be the case, for instance, that members of Congress are systematically more liberal (or systematically more conservative) than their constituencies despite the evidence of district-level representation.

Similarly, we can ask whether the House, as a whole, is too liberal, too conservative, or just right in terms of the net taste of the American electorate. A Congress that is off-center from the people ideologically would be a Congress out of equilibrium. To restore equilibrium, either Congress would realize its mistake and change its policy making, or the people would realize their mistake and vote in a more ideologically compatible Congress. Another possibility would be a system in equilibrium due to forces beyond public opinion. For instance, the persistent influence of money on politics could permanently skew congressional policy making away from the trajectory preferred by public opinion.

One way to estimate the ideological match between Congress and the public is to compare voters' ideological ratings of their recently elected representative with their personal ideological preferences. Relevant data from several elections, available from the National Election Studies and Cooperative Congressional Election Study (CCES), are displayed in Table 3-2. Over several Congresses, similar percentages of voters see their recently elected member as more liberal than themselves as see their member as more conservative. But the pattern is not completely symmetrical. For most years, more voters see their representative as more liberal than themselves than more conservative. In 2014, however, following the Republican surge, slightly more saw their member to their right than left. Complicating

Figure 3-5 Ideology and the House Vote, 2014

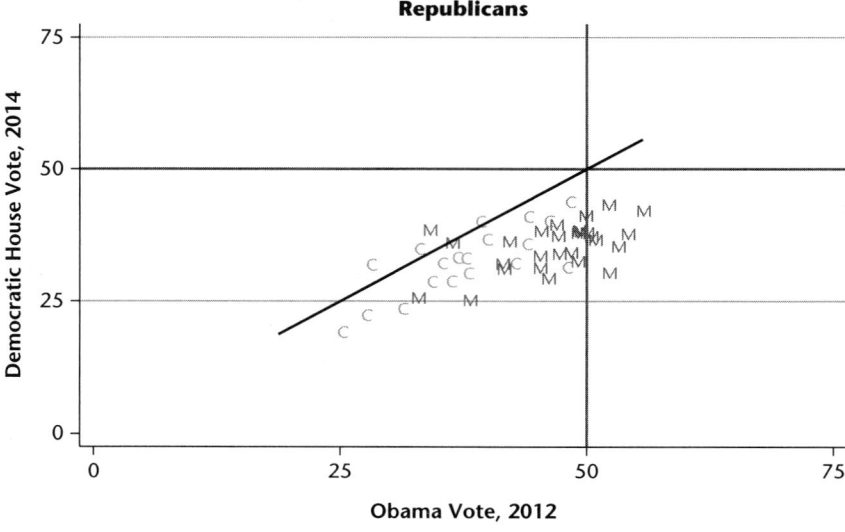

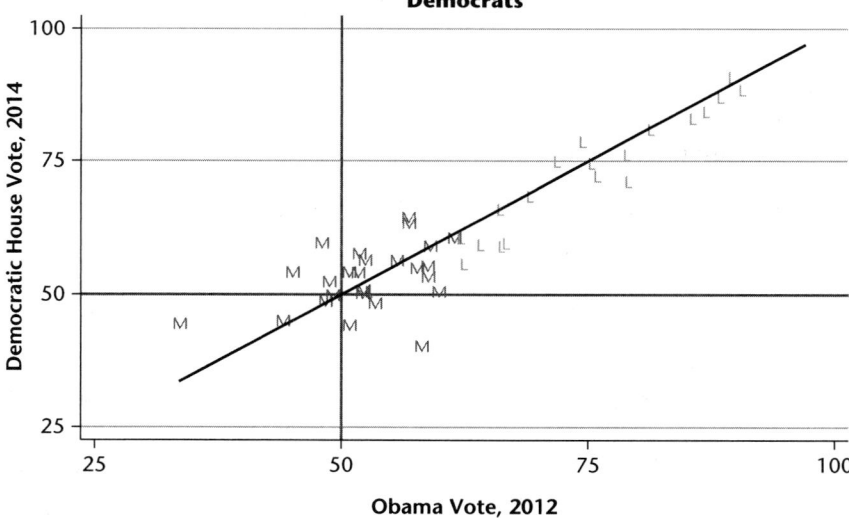

Source: Compiled by the authors.

Note: C denotes conservative Republican, M denotes both moderate Democrats and moderate Republicans, and L denotes liberal Democrats. The diagonal line indicates where equal vote percentages for the Democratic House candidate in 2014 and Obama in 2012 would be plotted. The horizontal indicates 50 percent of the House vote. Districts above the line were won by the Democrat in 2014, and those below it were won by the Republican. Liberal Democrats are more than one standard deviation more liberal than the Democratic mean. Conservative Republicans are more than one standard deviation more conservative than the Republican mean. Moderates are more than one standard deviation more moderate than their party's ideological mean.

Table 3-2 Voters' Perceptions of the Ideology of Their Representative

Percentage who see their representative as...	1990	1994	1998	2002	2006	2010	2012	2014
More conservative than themselves	37	34	36	39	49	33	38	39
Similar to themselves	21	26	20	16	5	24	25	24
More liberal than themselves	42	41	43	45	46	43	38	37

Source: 1990–2002: NES survey data. 2006–2012: CCES Survey data. Based solely on respondents who rate themselves and their newly elected member of Congress on the same ideological scale. Proportion in the middle category (giving themselves and the representative the same rating) for 2006 is not comparable to the other because of differences in the ratings scales used: 1–100 in 2006 and 1–7 in other years.

the picture, the many survey respondents who fail to rate their member of Congress tend toward liberal views. In large part, it is because conservatives are more able to articulate their ideological beliefs that survey-based perceptions of Congress tend to see the membership as more liberal than conservative.[33]

House–Senate Differences in Representation

The framers of the Constitution intended the Senate to be an elite chamber, isolated from the popular demands on the House. Regardless of how well or poorly this intention has been realized, there are fundamental constitutional differences between the two chambers. The most remarkable difference has been eliminated. Before 1913 and ratification of the Seventeenth Amendment, state legislatures selected their state's senators. Today, voters elect their senators directly. Because senators have six-year terms, they are relatively free from the never-ending campaigns carried on by representatives. And for the most part, the constituencies senators represent are larger and much more diverse than those of representatives.

Election Results and the Senate

In terms of national election results, the party composition of the Senate reflects the same forces that determine the party composition of the House. The division between Democrats and Republicans in the Senate is influenced by presidential coattails in presidential years and the bounce to the out party at midterm. The Senate's partisan division responds more sluggishly to national trends, however, because only one-third of the senators are up for reelection in any election year.

As a general rule, Senate elections are more competitive than House elections. Senate races with no incumbent are almost always sharply contested by both parties, and an incumbent senator who seeks reelection has a considerably greater chance of defeat than does an incumbent representative who seeks reelection. Incumbent senators are reelected at a rate of about 78 percent, in comparison to 95 percent for incumbent representatives. One reason that Senate races are more closely contested is that the statewide Senate constituencies are less dominated by one political party than the smaller House districts. Another major factor is that Senate races attract strong challengers. A senator is far more likely than a representative to face a politically seasoned and well-financed opponent. Historically, senators have been unable to obtain the strong incumbency advantage that representatives have enjoyed, averaging no better than a few percentage points as their average sophomore surge. (Evidently, senatorial challengers find it easier to generate visibility for their campaigns than do challengers to incumbent representatives.) Senators perform well electorally, compared with nonincumbent candidates of their party, partly because they had to be good candidates to be elected the first time, and increasingly, states' voting has been shaped by sharpened partisanship—widely discussed in term of "red" and "blue" states.

Although reelection to the Senate is more difficult than reelection to the House, senators need to run only once every six years. The appropriate comparison of electoral security is a comparison of survival rates over the same period of time. Measured over six years, representatives seeking reelection have a survival rate of approximately 78 percent—about the same as the reelection rate for senators.[34] Therefore, the six-year term for senators almost exactly offsets the greater reelection rates of the House. Senators run less often but at higher risk. The long-run survival rates for the two chambers would appear to be roughly equal.

Is the Senate any less responsive to popular opinion than the House? Six-year terms would seem to provide senators with ample freedom from electoral concerns, except for the final run up to election. Moreover, when senators decide to be attentive to their electorates, their diverse constituencies make full representation difficult.

As are representatives, senators are sensitive to constituency opinion, with each party's most conservative senators found in conservative states and most liberal members found in liberal states. In terms of partisan politics, the states are competitive enough that each party has a chance at a Senate seat. As a result, many states send both a Republican and a Democrat to the Senate, a pattern that baffles some observers. In a pattern similar to that of the House, senators from states in which the other party dominates often are ideologically atypical for their party.[35]

State Populations and the Senate

Although states vary considerably in population, each has two senators. California's 34 million people get the same number of senators as Alaska's 600,000. To some extent, this constitutionally designed malapportionment favors political conservatism.[36] Small, politically conservative states enjoy an extra margin of representation in the Senate.

During the Reagan years, when the Republicans enjoyed a six-year Senate majority, the Senate was the more conservative chamber. One is tempted to attribute this senatorial conservatism to the Senate's overrepresentation of small states. However, in the immediate aftermath of the Republican takeover of both houses of Congress in 1994, the Senate was the more moderate of the two chambers. The greater responsiveness of the House to national forces in that year brought in a crew of conservative freshmen legislators who, coupled with vigorous conservative leadership, put the House distinctly in the lead of the Republican revolution launched by the 1994 election. Two decades later, the Republicans in the House remain distinctly more conservative than their Senate counterparts. This is likely due to the Republican structural advantage in House elections discussed earlier. Senators with the more diverse states have tended to be less steadfast in their conservatism than Republicans in the House. Later, in 2006, when the Democrats decisively regained the House, the Senate went Democratic only 50–48, with the Democrats holding majority status only with the help of two independent senators. Again, the people's House responded to changing voter sentiment faster than the Senate. The 2010 election provides the final illustration of this principle. The Democrats held onto the Senate, despite the Republican wave that swept away so many House members up for reelection.

The Six-Year Term

Because the next election for representatives is never more than two years away, electoral considerations are always important for members of the House. For senators, the six-year term can provide some leeway. Voters—so it sometimes seems—are electorally myopic, forgetting what senators do early in their terms and remembering only what they do close to the election.

Whether or not this view of the electorate is valid, there is a good deal of evidence that senatorial roll call voting responds to the six-year cycle.[37] In the year or two before they must run again, incumbents edge away from their party's extreme. Democrats inch in a conservative direction, and Republicans slip a bit to the left. The purpose, in each instance, is to appeal to moderate voters.

Because senators moderate their ideological positions as reelection approaches, they presumably have good reason to do so: Senators must believe that moderation enhances their chances of electoral success. Earlier, we saw evidence that representatives with moderate ideological positions are more likely to be reelected. Is the same true for senators?

Candidates' policy positions affect their election chances. For the Senate, candidates do better if they avoid their party's ideological extremes. Gerald Wright and Michael Berkman estimated the effect of candidates' issue positions by comparing different pairings of ideological positions while statistically controlling for the effects of several constituency characteristics and attitudes.[38] They estimated that whether a Senate candidate represents the party's moderate wing or more extremist wing creates a difference ranging from five to eight percentage points. This effect is similar to that observed for House elections at the time. The evidence suggests that the same electoral connection leading to representation exists in the Senate as in the House, with the added twists of the larger, more heterogeneous constituencies and the latitude of the six-year Senate term.

Conclusion

Along with presidential elections, congressional elections provide citizens with their main opportunity to influence the direction of national policy. When elections bring about significant changes in the party composition of Congress, we can be fairly confident of two things. The first is that the new Congress will have a different ideological cast. Democratic and Republican candidates for the House and Senate stand for quite different things. Therefore, electing more Democrats or more Republicans increases the likelihood of policy movement in the ideological direction of the advantaged party. Ironically, the second is that such changes do not always stem from the electorate's desire for new policy directions. The Republican takeover in 1994 did coincide with an increase in conservative Republican sentiments in the mass electorate. Other, less substantial changes, however, have stemmed from factors such as presidential coattails or the usual slump the presidential party experiences at midterm.

We see the electorate's influence on policy direction most clearly in the relationship between constituencies and their elected representatives. In terms of ideological direction, individual House and Senate members respond to their constituencies. In turn, ideological direction matters when constituencies decide which candidates they will elect and which they will not.

The average voter knows little about his or her representative and only a bit more about his or her senators. House challengers are almost invisible, and only a portion of the electorate has even a modest amount of information about senatorial challengers. Nevertheless, the electorates that candidates and parties face are smart and discerning, and they reward faithful representation. Candidates, generally desirous of attaining and staying in office, heed their electorate's wishes and work to give them what they want. Elections bring about much higher levels of policy representation than most observers would expect based on the low levels of citizen awareness.

Notes

1. The swing ratio is inversely related to the size of the incumbency advantage, discussed later. The more incumbents can protect themselves with a strong incumbency advantage, the less the seat swing depends on the national division of the vote. The classic discussion of this point is David Mayhew, "Congressional Elections: The Case of the Vanishing Marginals," *Polity* 6 (1973): 295–318.
2. At one time, the normal vote was thought of as essentially constant 53–47 or 54–46 Democratic advantage. On the origin of the normal vote concept, see Philip E. Converse, "The Concept of the Normal Vote," in *Elections and the Political Order*, ed.

Angus Campbell, Philip E. Converse, Warren E. Miller, and Donald E. Stokes (New York: Wiley, 1966), 9–39.
3. Macropartisanship is measured here as the Democratic percentage of Republican and Democratic identifiers in the third quarter of the election year. The correlation between macropartisanship and the vote is +.65.
4. See, for example, Gerald F. Seib, "Why the GOP Majority is Safe in 2016," *Washington Wire*, June 9, 2015, http://blogs.wsj.com/washwire/2015/06/09/why-the-republicans-house-majority-is-safe-in-2016.
5. Gary C. Jacobson, "Obama and Nationalized Electoral Politics in the 2014 Midterm," *Political Science Quarterly* 130, no. 1 (2015): 1–25.
6. Robert S. Erikson, "Malapportionment, Gerrymandering, and Party Fortunes in Congressional Elections," *American Political Science Review* 66 (1972): 1234–45; Jowei Chen and Jonathan Rodden, "Unintentional Gerrymandering: Political Geography and Electoral Bias in Legislatures," *Quarterly Journal of Political Science* 8 (2013): 239–69. By *fairly* here, we simply mean districts in which the size of partisan majorities of the two parties mirror one another—that is, so one party is not "wasting" votes by having overwhelming majorities compared to the other party.
7. James A. Stimson, *Public Opinion in America*, 2nd ed. (Boulder, CO: Westview, 1999).
8. See Stimson, *Public Opinion in America*; Robert S. Erikson, Michael B. MacKuen, and James A. Stimson, *The Macro Polity* (New York: Cambridge University Press, 2002). The electorate's mood is not the same as its macropartisanship, and the two should not be confused with each other. In fact, if anything, the sign of the correlation, over time, between mood and macropartisanship is negative rather than positive. (When Democratic identification is high, policy preferences trend conservative.) In part, mood is driven by the nation's economy—inflation worries trigger desires for conservatism or less government, and unemployment worries stimulate demand for liberalism or more government. Mood is also a function of past policies. For instance, when a pent-up demand for more liberalism goes unmet, the electorate gets even more liberal; as the government produces the more liberal policies in response, the demand eases, and the public becomes more conservative.
9. Robert S. Erikson, "Congressional Elections in Presidential Years: Presidential Coattails and Strategic Voting," *Legislative Studies Quarterly* 41 (2016): 551–74.
10. Angus Campbell, "Surge and Decline: A Study of Electoral Change," in *Elections and the Political Order*, 40–62. See also James A. Campbell, "The Presidential Surge and Its Midterm Decline in Congressional Elections," *Journal of Politics* 53 (1991): 477–87.
11. Alberto Alesina and Howard Rosenthal, *Partisan Politics, Divided Government, and the Economy* (New York: Cambridge University Press, 1995); Morris Fiorina, *Divided Government* (New York: Allyn and Bacon, 1995); Joseph Bafumi, Robert S. Erikson, and Christopher Wlezien, "Balancing, Generic Polls, and Midterm Congressional Elections," *Journal of Politics* (2010): 705–19.
12. Congressional balancing can occur in presidential election years, as well as midterms, when the outcome is a landslide that is anticipated in advance. An argument can be made that in the landslides of 1956, 1972, 1984, and 1996, presidential coattails appeared weak because they were offset by ideological balancing against the presidential party. Balancing may have been the cause of the largest congressional surge of a presidential party in the twentieth century. In 1948, President Truman's Democratic Party gained over eighty seats in the House, in part, perhaps, because people were voting Democratic to defeat "President" Dewey. (Almost all observers in 1948 anticipated

that Dewey would defeat Truman.) Truman's campaign against the "do-nothing" Republican Congress was surprisingly effective. Note, however, that the emphasis of his message was "vote for me to stop the congressional Republicans," not "vote Democratic for Congress." The 1948 example suggests that votes for president can be affected by the anticipated party control of Congress, as well as the reverse. For more on balancing, see Erikson, "Congressional Elections"; Bafumi, Erikson, and Wlezien, "Balancing."

13. In terms of the two-party vote, the 2002 Republican gain was 2.6 percentage points, which is sizable as congressional vote shifts go. Some of this gain, however, was due to the Democrats contesting fewer seats than usual. With the shifting district lines, one can measure the 2000 to 2002 shift as the change in the mean deviation of the House vote in *contested* seats relative to the 2000 presidential vote in the new (2002–2010) and old (1992–2000) districts. By this measure, the Republicans gained only about 1 percent of the vote. The Republicans gained more seats than usual from a one-percentage-point vote gain. This was partially due to population movement so that Republican states gained more seats with the 2000 Census. Republicans also controlled more state legislatures than did the Democrats, giving them a political advantage when carving up the new congressional districts. On the partisan impact of congressional redistricting, see Gary W. Cox and Jonathan N. Katz, *Eldridge Gerry's Salamander: The Electoral Consequences of the Reapportionment Revolution* (Cambridge, UK: Cambridge University Press, 2002).

14. The limits to the public's knowledge of congressional candidates have been known for some time. See Donald E. Stokes and Warren E. Miller, "Party Government and the Salience of Congress," in *Elections and the Political Order*, 194–211; Thomas E. Mann, *Unsafe at Any Margin: Interpreting Congressional Elections* (Washington, DC: American Enterprise Institute, 1978). For more recent developments regarding voter information, see Michael X. Delli Carpini and Scott Keeter, *What Americans Know About Politics and Why It Matters* (New Haven, CT: Yale University Press, 1996); Cheryl Boudreau and Arthur Lupia, "Political Knowledge," in *Handbook of Experimental Political Science*, ed. James Druckman, Donald P. Green, James H. Kuklinski, and Arthur Lupia (New York: Cambridge University Press, 2013), 171–86.

15. Gary C. Jacobson and Samuel Kernell, *Strategy and Choice in Congressional Elections*, 2nd ed. (New Haven, CT: Yale University Press, 1983).

16. Stephen D. Levitt and Catherine D. Wolfram, "Decomposing the Sources of the Incumbency Advantage in the U.S. House," *Legislative Studies Quarterly* 22 (1997): 45–60; John R. Alford and David W. Brady, "Personal and Partisan Advantage in U.S. Congressional Elections," in *Congress Reconsidered*, 5th ed., ed. Lawrence C. Dodd and Bruce I. Oppenheimer (Washington, DC: CQ Press, 1993); Andrew Gelman and Gary King, "Measuring the Incumbency Advantage Without Bias," *American Journal of Political Science* 34 (1990): 1142–64; Robert S. Erikson and Rocio Titiunik, "Using Regression Discontinuity to Uncover the Incumbency Advantage," *Quantitative Journal of Political Science* 10 (2015): 101–19.

17. Robert S. Erikson, "The Congressional Incumbency Advantage Over Sixty Years: Measurement, Trends and Implications," in *Governing in a Polarized Age: Elections, Parties, and Political Representation in America*, ed. Alan S. Gerber and Eric Schickler (Cambridge, UK: Cambridge University Press, in press); Jacobson, "Obama and Nationalized Electoral Politics."

18. Martin P. Wattenberg, *The Decline of American Political Parties, 1952–1992* (Cambridge, MA: Harvard University Press, 1994).
19. David Mayhew, *Congress: The Electoral Connection* (New Haven, CT: Yale University Press, 1974).
20. Morris Fiorina, *Congress: Keystone of the Washington Establishment*, 2nd ed. (New Haven, CT: Yale University Press, 1989).
21. Nolan M. McCarty, Keith T. Poole, and Howard Rosenthal, *Polarized America: The Dance of Ideology and Unequal Riches* (Cambridge, MA: MIT Press, 2006).
22. Frances E. Lee, *Beyond Ideology: Politics, Principles, and Partisanship in the U.S. Senate* (Chicago: University of Chicago Press, 2009); Sean Theriault, "Polarization We Can Live With. Partisan Warfare Is the Problem," *Washington Post*, January 10, 2014, https://www.washingtonpost.com/news/monkey-cage/wp/2014/01/10/polarization-we-can-live-with-partisan-warfare-is-the-problem.
23. Lilliana Mason, "'I Disrespectfully Agree': The Differential Effects of Partisan Sorting on Social and Issue Polarization," *American Journal of Political Science* 59 (2015): 128–45.
24. Robert S. Erikson, "Is There Such a Thing as a Safe Seat?" *Polity* 9 (1976): 623–32.
25. Because of the incumbency advantage, the winning party in a "landslide" election can protect its lead over subsequent elections. Democratic surges sent waves of freshman Democrats to Congress in 1964 and 1974 (plus other years), who were then able to stay in office after their initial Democratic tide receded, thanks to the incumbency advantage. The Republican surge of 1994 had a similar effect, as their newfound incumbency advantage insulated new Republican House members from defeat in subsequent elections. For more on incumbency, the swing ratios, and party strength in Congress, see Cox and Katz, *Eldridge Gerry's Salamander*.
26. Anthony Downs, *An Economic Theory of Democracy* (New York: Harper and Row, 1957). Chapter 8 is the classic source on ideological moderation.
27. David W. Brady, Hahrie Han, and Jeremy C. Pope, "Primary Elections and Candidate Ideology: Out of Step With the Primary Electorate?" *Legislative Studies Quarterly* 32 (2007): 79–106.
28. Gerald C. Wright, "Policy Voting in the U.S. Senate: Who Is Represented?" *Legislative Studies Quarterly* 14 (1989): 465–86.
29. DW-NOMINATE scores are normally reported only for the dominant first dimension, which is highly correlated with the member's party affiliation. The evidence shows that voters also incorporate the second dimension into their ideological judgments, although with lesser weight than they give the first dimension. Our choice of weighing the two dimensions by a weight of 100:35 (roughly 3:1) is a defensible choice, if unavoidably arbitrary. On DW-NOMINATE scores, see Keith T. Poole and Howard Rosenthal, *Ideology and Congress: A Political-Economic History of Roll Call Voting*, 2nd ed. (New Brunswick, NJ: Transaction Publishers, 2007).
30. For more on candidate ideology and election outcomes, see our contributions to previous editions of *Congress Reconsidered*. See also Robert S. Erikson, "The Electoral Impact of Congressional Roll Call Voting," *American Political Science Review* 65 (1971): 1018–32; Gerald C. Wright, "Candidates' Policy Positions and Voting in U.S. House Elections," *Legislative Studies Quarterly* 3 (1978): 445–64; Robert S. Erikson and Gerald C. Wright, "Policy Representation of Constituency Interests," *Political Behavior* 1 (Summer 1980): 91–106; Robert S. Erikson and Gerald C. Wright, "Representation of Constituency Ideology in Congress," in *Continuity and*

Change in Congressional Elections, ed. David Brady and John Cogan (Stanford, CA: Stanford University Press, 2000), chap. 8. For discussions by other authors, see Stephen Ansolabehere, James M. Snyder Jr., and Charles Stewart II, "Candidate Positioning in U.S. House Elections," *American Journal of Political Science* 45 (2001): 136–59; Brandice Canes-Wrone, David W. Brady, and John F. Cogan, "Out of Step, Out of Office: Electoral Accountability and House Members' Voting," *American Political Science Review* 96 (2002): 127–40; Stephen Ansolabehere and Phil Jones, "Constituents, Policy Preferences and Approval of Their Members of Congress," *American Journal of Political Science* 54 (2010): 583–97; Danielle A. Joesten and Walter J. Stone, "Reassessing Proximity Voting: Expertise, Party, and Choice in Congressional Elections," *Journal of Politics* 76 (2014): 740–53. Anthony D. Hall provides a novel illustration of the importance of candidate ideology in general elections. (See Anthony D. Hall, "What Happens When Extremists Win Primaries?" *American Political Science Review* 109 [2015]: 18–42.) Hall finds that when the winner of a close primary election is the more moderate candidate, the candidate performs much better in the general election.

31. For years when data on challenger positions are available, statistical analysis suggests that challenger ideology has only a negligible effect on the vote. Candidate ideology evidently matters most when candidates transform into incumbents. This is consistent with evidence from voter surveys, which consistently show that challengers are considerably less visible to voters than are incumbents. See our analysis of earlier congressional elections in the third through ninth editions of *Congress Reconsidered*, ed. Lawrence C. Dodd and Bruce I. Oppenheimer (Washington, DC: CQ Press, 1989, 1993, 1997, 2001, 2005, 2009).

32. Thomas E. Mann and Norman J. Ornstein, *It's Even Worse Than It Looks: How the American Constitutional System Collided With the New Politics of Extremism* (New York: Basic Books, 2012).

33. For an interesting graphic depiction of representation, see Joseph Bafumi and Michael C. Herron, "Leapfrog Representation and Extremism: A Study of American Voters and Their Members in Congress," *American Political Science Review* 104 (2010): 619–22.

34. Amihai Glazer and Bernard Grofman, "Two Plus Two Plus Two Equals Six: Tenure of Office of Senators and Representatives, 1953–1983," *Legislative Studies Quarterly* 12 (1987): 555–63.

35. Robert S. Erikson, "Roll Calls, Reputations, and Representation in the U.S. Senate," *Legislative Studies Quarterly* 15 (1990): 623–42.

36. Robert S. Erikson, Gerald C. Wright, and John P. McIver, *Statehouse Democracy: Public Opinion and Policy in the American States* (New York: Cambridge University Press, 1993), chap. 2. For a detailed examination of asymmetries of state size and senatorial representation, see Frances E. Lee and Bruce I. Oppenheimer, *Sizing Up the Senate: The Unequal Consequences of Equal Representation* (Chicago: University of Chicago Press, 1999).

37. Richard F. Fenno Jr., *The United States Senate: A Bicameral Perspective* (Washington, DC: American Enterprise Institute, 1982); Martin Thomas, "Electoral Proximity and Senatorial Roll Call Voting," *American Journal of Political Science* 29 (1984): 96–111; Gerald C. Wright, "Representation and the Electoral Cycle in the U.S. Senate," paper delivered at the annual meeting of the Midwest Political Science Association, Chicago, April 15–17, 1993.

38. Gerald C. Wright and Michael B. Berkman, "Candidates and Policy in U.S. Senatorial Elections," *American Political Science Review* 80 (1986): 576–90.

4. Partisanship, Money, and Competition
Elections and the Transformation of Congress Since the 1970s

Gary C. Jacobson

The House and Senate are dramatically more partisan, contentious, centralized, and divided ideologically now than they were back in the 1970s. This chapter shows that these transformations are tightly linked to complementary developments in electoral politics at all levels, including changes in the electorate, the activities of party and nonparty campaign organizations, and campaign finance rules and practices. It concludes that electoral and congressional politics have coevolved over the past four decades in ways that have contributed powerfully to the polarized national politics of today. Congress's current propensity for partisan conflict and stalemate, firmly rooted in electoral politics, is thus likely to persist.

The 114th Congress that convened in January 2015 included a handful of members who knew firsthand what it had been like to serve on Capitol Hill in the 1970s.[1] If any of these veterans thought to compare life in Congress then and now, the contrast had to be jarring. In the 1970s, party conflict was muted. Ideological differences between the congressional parties and party-line voting on roll call votes were at historically low levels.[2] Republicans and Democrats battled it out rhetorically on the floor but crafted legislation together in committees and subcommittees. These subunits enjoyed considerable autonomy in their assigned domains, and lawmaking was relatively decentralized. Party leaders acted as brokers, deal makers, and coordinators, exerting party discipline, if at all, with a light touch.

The legislative process generally followed predictable routines. The minority party usually abjured disruption—Senate filibusters were becoming more common but were far less frequent than today[3]—and participated importantly, if not equally, in lawmaking and oversight. And that minority was invariably Republican; Democrats had been in control of both chambers since 1955, and few observers expected them to lose their hegemony anytime soon. Congress regularly tangled with the president—whether Republican or Democrat—but the conflicts were as much institutional as partisan, and party differences in support for the president's legislative proposals were comparatively modest.[4] Friendships crossed the aisles, with partisan political disputes routinely set aside in convivial after-hours socializing.

Readers of the other essays in this volume or with even a passing awareness of contemporary national politics know that life on the Hill is now radically different. Bitter partisan conflict is the normal state of affairs. Ideological divisions between the congressional parties are now the widest ever recorded. Party unity on divisive roll call votes and partisan differences in support for the president's agenda are at their highest level since measurements began in the 1950s. Party leaders dominate policy making at the behest of their caucuses, especially in the House; committees are ignored or circumvented if deemed insufficiently responsive to the majority party. The House minority can forget about participating in anything significant, except on the infrequent occasions when the majority fragments and decisions cannot be postponed, as with budget enactments necessary to keep the government functioning. Senate minorities participate by engaging in obstruction, easy to do under that chamber's rules; filibusters or their threat assure that any controversial measure not specially exempted from filibustering requires sixty votes to pass. Every significant action is taken with an eye to the next election, for neither party has a lock on majority status in either chamber. (Since 1992, the House has changed party control three times; in the Senate, it has changed control five times.) In the unending struggle for control, mutual hostility has become personal, as well as partisan, and cross-party socializing has become rare.[5]

A transformation this profound has naturally attracted a great deal of scrutiny from scholars and journalists hoping to understand and explain it.[6] It is axiomatic among students of Congress that congressional life is shaped fundamentally by electoral politics,[7] and so, the electoral domain is an obvious place to look for insights into what has occurred. In this essay, I examine the major trends in congressional election politics that have paralleled the growth in partisan acrimony and ideological polarization in Congress over the past four decades. The evidence suggests that developments on the Hill and developments in electoral politics have shared a powerful reciprocal relationship; virulent partisan conflict in Washington has sturdy electoral roots and thus is unlikely to fade anytime soon.

The Fundamental Trend: Partisan Realignment

The widening partisan divisions in Congress and many of the related trends in electoral politics I examine here are a direct consequence of a gradual but thorough ideological realignment of the Republican and Democratic parties. The realignment was driven by elite and popular reactions to political changes initiated in the 1960s and early 1970s. Chief among them was the civil rights revolution, crowned by the Voting Rights Act of 1965, which brought Southern blacks into the electorate as Democrats while moving conservative whites to abandon their ancestral allegiance to the Democratic Party in favor of the ideologically and racially more compatible Republicans. The rise of social issues—led by abortion, after its legalization in *Roe v. Wade*, but including other women's rights and gay rights—augmented this shift, as the Republican Party adopted the conservative positions on these issues favored by the evangelical Christians who populate Southern electorates. This provoked a smaller countermovement among socially liberal and moderate Republicans elsewhere, particularly in the Northeast, who no longer found themselves at home in the reconstituted Republican Party and gradually adopted a Democratic identity.

These changes were key components of a broader process of ideological sorting that has left partisans on opposite sides of a diverse and growing range of issues. As a result, the mass bases of the two parties have grown increasingly distinct in their political values and ideological preferences. Ordinary Americans have not, to be sure, become as starkly divided by party and ideology as their leaders, but the more active they are in politics, the more faithfully their divisions have come to echo those within the political class.[8]

Figure 4-1 documents the growing ideological divergence of partisans in the electorate since the 1970s (with highs and lows labeled).[9] The Republican Party has always attracted the larger share of conservatives, and the Democratic Party has attracted the larger share of liberals but with far greater consistency now than earlier. In 1972, self-identified liberals and conservatives identified with the "appropriate" party 71 percent of the time; in 2012, they did so 90 percent of the time. The electorate's increasing partisan coherence is also evident in the growing links between partisanship and opinions on issues ranging from abortion to race to the proper role of government to global warming.[10]

Figure 4-1 Ideology and Party Identification of Voters, 1972–2012

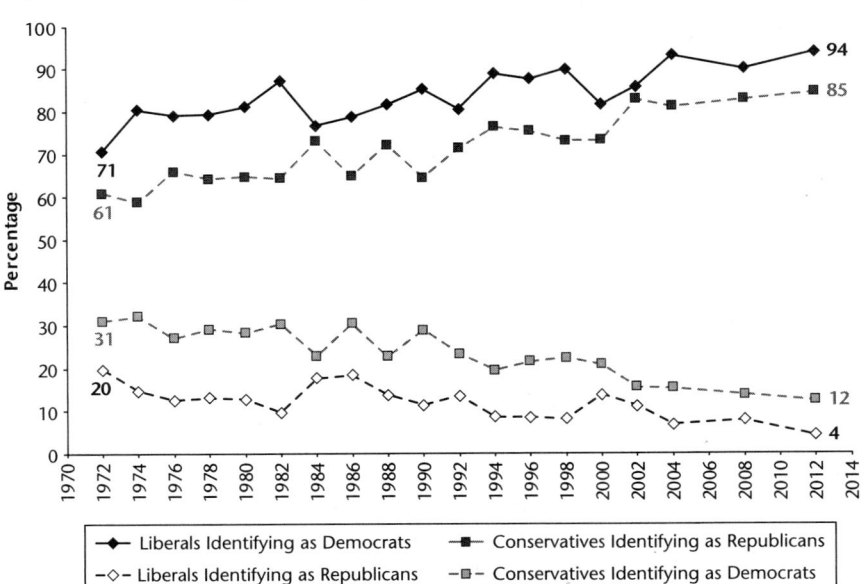

Source: American National Election Studies cumulative data file; 2012 data are from the face-to-face component.

Trends in Individual Voting Behavior

The growth in partisan ideological coherence led to more consistent party-line voting. Party identification has always been the most important shaper of voting in House and Senate elections. Its impact weakened during the 1950s and 1960s, however, and reached a low point in the 1970s. As voters subsequently brought their partisan identities, ideological self-locations, and issues preferences into closer alignment, this trend was reversed, and in recent elections, the proportion of self-identified partisans voting for their party's candidates has matched the high levels of the 1950s. (See Figure 4-2; high and low points are labeled.) Over this entire period, the proportion of voters who identify themselves as independents and who say they lean toward neither party has remained small, between 5 and 10 percent, and they split their vote fairly evenly between the parties.[11] Thus, to an increasing degree, members of Congress owe their victories to loyal partisans rather than crossover voters from the other party.

Party loyalty has also increased in presidential elections since the 1970s, and thus, *ticket splitting*—voting for the House or Senate candidate of one party and for the presidential candidate of the other—has declined as well (dashed lines

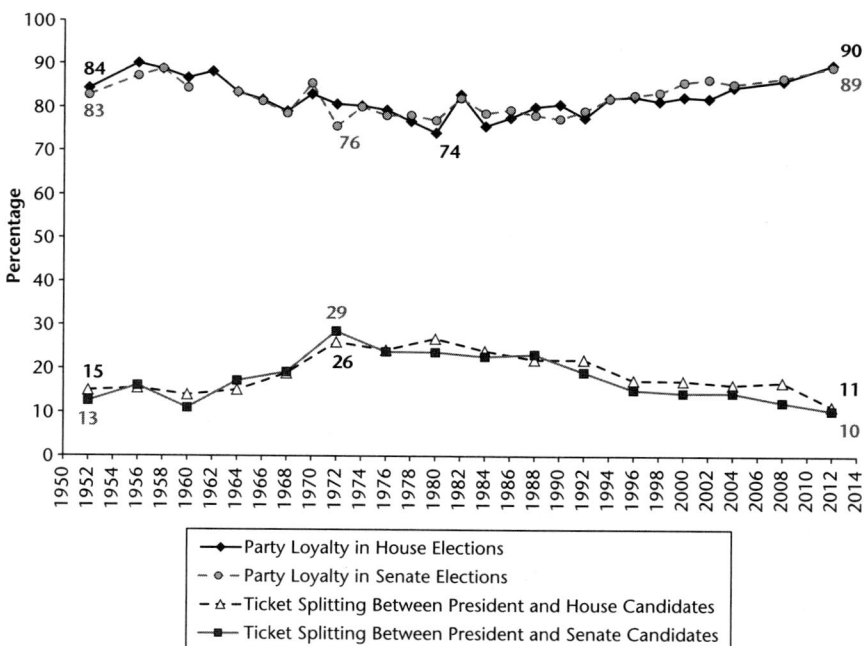

Figure 4-2 Party Loyalty and Ticket Splitting, 1952–2012

Source: American National Election Studies cumulative data file; 2012 data are from the face-to-face component.

in Figure 4-2). The Southern realignment produced an especially pronounced drop in ticket splitting in that region. As recently as the 1980s, many conservative Southerners voted for Republican presidential candidates while retaining their Democratic habits in congressional elections. As Figure 4-3 indicates, this is no longer the case; the great majority now vote for Republican congressional candidates when they vote for Republican presidential candidates, and ticket splitting is no more common now in the South than it is elsewhere.

The presidential connection has also grown stronger in midterm congressional election voting even though presidential candidates are not on the ballot. The proportion of midterm voters whose congressional votes were consistent with their evaluation of the president's performance—for the presidential party's candidate if they approve, for the other party's candidate if they disapprove—has risen steeply since the 1970s, from below 60 percent in 1974 to 85 percent in 2014.[12] This trend is a product of widening partisan differences in presidential approval, as well as increasing party loyalty.[13] A growing share of midterm voters also say that their vote for Congress represents an endorsement or repudiation of the president; Jimmy Carter mattered to only 37 percent of voters in 1978, whereas, in 2010, an average of 56 percent of voters said Barack Obama was a factor in their decision, the highest for the entire period.[14]

Figure 4-3 Ticket Splitting by Republican Presidential Voters in the Southern Congressional Elections, 1952–2012

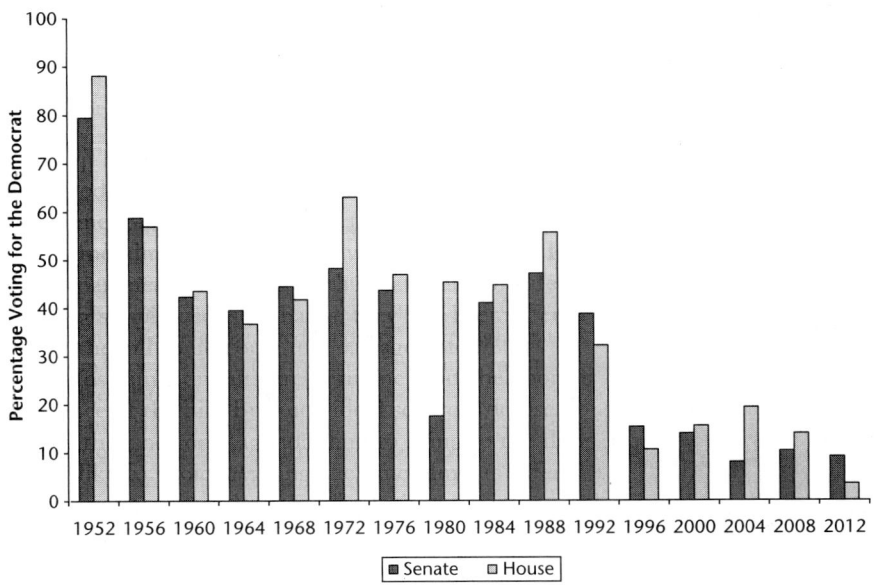

Source: American National Election Studies cumulative data file; 2012 data are from the face-to-face component.

Aggregate Effects

These trends in individual voting behavior are echoed when the votes are aggregated to the state and district levels, leaving the congressional parties with increasingly divergent local electoral coalitions. As Figures 4-4 and 4-5 show, the correlations between major-party presidential vote share and the House and Senate vote shares at the state and district levels declined sharply between the 1950s and the 1970s (the midterm correlation is with the presidential vote in the state or district two years earlier); indeed, the Senate correlations were actually negative for 1966, 1972, and 1974, although the relationships were far from statistically significant. Since then, the connection between presidential and congressional voting has grown much stronger (although the trend is more erratic for the Senate because of the revolving subsets of thirty-three or thirty-four states having Senate contests in any year). One important consequence is that split verdicts—district or state majorities for presidents of one party, congressional candidates of the other—have become increasingly rare. In 1972, for example, 44 percent of House districts and 50 percent of the states delivered split verdicts; in 2012, the respective percentages were 6 percent and 18 percent.[15]

Greater partisan consistency in individual voting and aggregate election results has had the important effect of reducing the proportion of voters shared by the president and members of Congress from the opposition party. For example, when Ronald Reagan took office in 1981, he faced a Congress in which 34 percent

Figure 4-4 Correlations Between District-Level Presidential and House Vote, 1952–2014

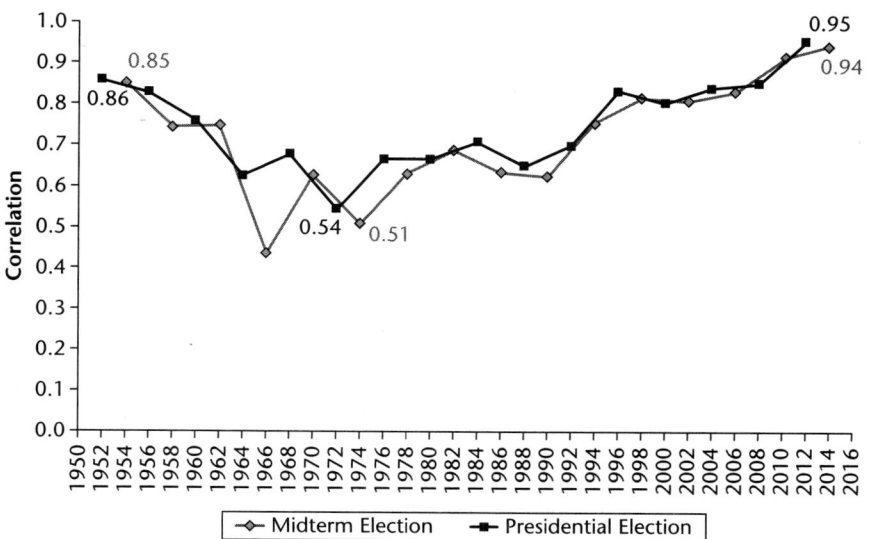

Source: Compiled by author.

Figure 4-5 Correlations Between District-Level Presidential and Senate Vote, 1952–2014

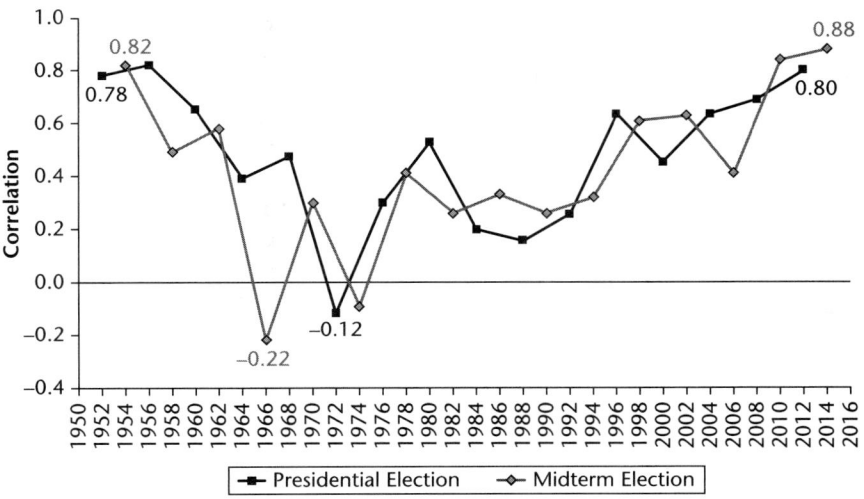

Source: Compiled by author.

of House Democrats' voters and 37 percent of Senate Democrats' voters had also voted for him. When Barack Obama began his second term in 2013, he shared only 17 percent of the House Republicans' voters and only 9 percent of the Senate Republicans' voters. With fewer of their own voters favoring the president, opposition party senators and representatives have less reason to support his initiatives, and fewer do so. Meanwhile, the president's own partisans have become much more supportive of his proposals. Thus, in the Ninety-seventh Congress (1981–1982), partisan difference in support for Reagan's initiatives was comparatively narrow, with House Republicans voting his way 67 percent of the time and House Democrats voting his way 34 percent of the time. In the 113th Congress (2013–2014), in contrast, House Democrats supported Obama 82 percent of the time, and House Republicans supported Obama only 9 percent of the time (the comparable figures for the Senate were 76 percent and 33 percent in the Ninety-seventh Congress and 94 percent and 16 percent in the 113th Congress).[16]

The stronger linkages between presidential and congressional election results have given the congressional parties increasingly divergent constituencies, as is evident from Figures 4-6 and 4-7. Figure 4-6 displays the average difference in the share of major-party presidential votes between House districts won by Democrats and those won by Republicans in elections since 1952. Back in the early 1970s, the difference was relatively small, on the order of seven or eight percentage points. Since then, the gap has more than tripled, with most of the increase occurring in the past two decades. In 2014, Obama's (2012) share of the vote in House districts won by Democrats (67 percent) was, on average,

Figure 4-6 The Polarization of U.S. House Constituencies, 1952–2014

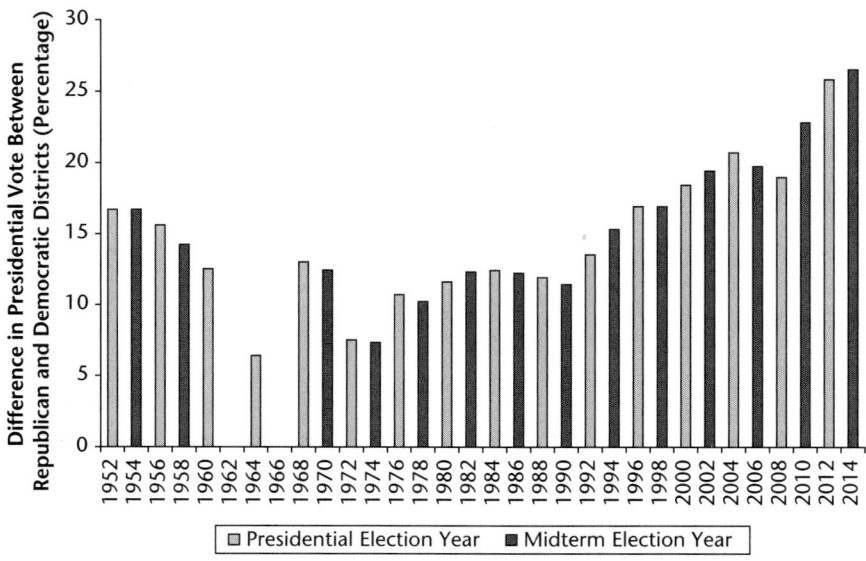

Source: Compiled by author.

Figure 4-7 The Polarization of U.S. Senate Constituencies, 1952–2014

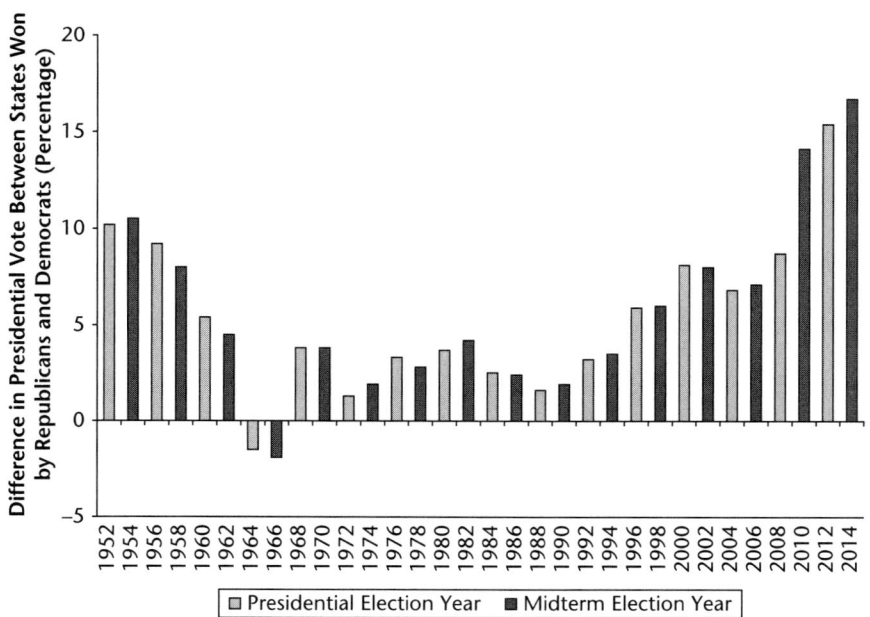

Source: Compiled by author.

twenty-six percentage points higher than in districts won by Republicans (41 percent). Thus, the House party coalitions now represent constituencies that are far more dissimilar, politically, than they were in the 1970s. A similar trend appears in comparable data on Senate elections (Figure 4-7). States tend to be more heterogeneous, politically and otherwise, than congressional districts, so the difference in the presidential vote between states won by Senate Democrats and Republicans is smaller. Nonetheless, we see a notable increase in this gap since the 1970s, most of it occurring in the past two decades.

Finally, survey data confirm that the congressional parties represent increasingly distinctive sets of voters. Those voters who supported each party's winning congressional candidates compose the congressional parties' respective electoral constituencies. Differences in the ideological makeup of electoral constituencies can be measured by subtracting the mean self-placement on the seven-point NES ideological scale (see footnote 9) of respondents who voted for one party's winning candidates from the mean self-placement of those who voted for the other party's winning candidates. Figure 4-8 displays the growth in the ideological distance between parties' electoral constituencies in the House and Senate since 1972. In the 1970s, ideological differences were modest, about 0.5 points on the seven-point scale. By 2012, the gaps had more than tripled for both chambers.[17]

Figure 4-8 Ideological Divergence of Electoral Constituencies of Parties in the House and Senate, 1972–2012

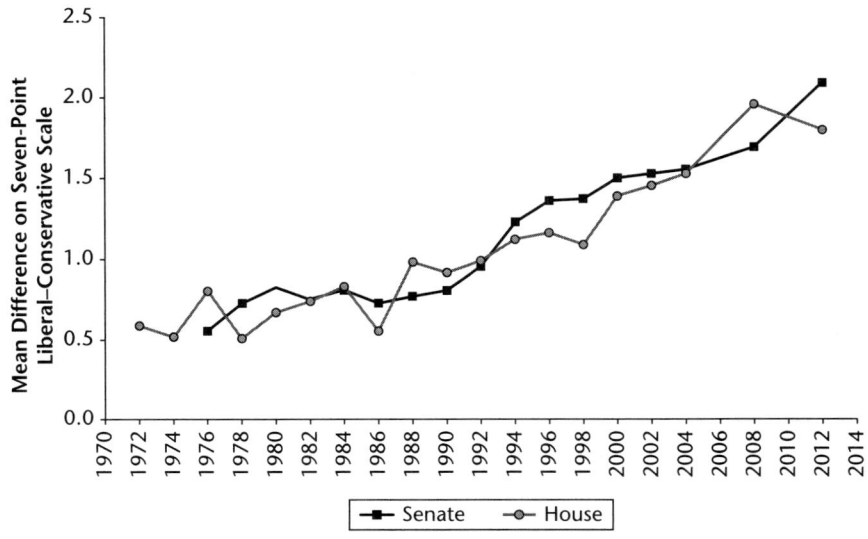

Source: Compiled by author from American National Election Studies data; 2012 data are from the face-to-face component.

The Evolution of Congressional Campaigns

Congressional campaigns have evolved in ways that have both reflected and enhanced the growing partisan coherence and ideological polarization of Congress and the congressional electorate. The most consequential changes have occurred in the financial domain. Not only have candidates spent increasing sums trying to win elections but so have parties and, most recently, their allies in nonparty organizations. The end result is that most potentially competitive races—those in which both candidates are considered to have some real prospect of winning—are now bitterly contested and attract a lavish investment of campaign money on both sides, a considerable portion of which is not controlled by the candidates.

The growth in campaign spending by general-election candidates for the House since 1972 (adjusted for inflation, 2014 = 1.00) is displayed in Figure 4-9. House candidates' average spending, in real dollars, increased by 450 percent between 1972 and 2010 before tapering off a bit since then; it has exceeded $1 million in the five most recent elections. Spending by Senate candidates has increased even more (though more erratically because of variations in the set of states with Senate elections in any given year), growing by an average of 11 percent from election to election. In 1972, the average Senate candidate spent about $2.1 million; the average peaked at $9.6 million in 2012, before falling to $7.8 million in 2014.

Figure 4-9 Average Campaign Spending in House Elections, 1972–2014

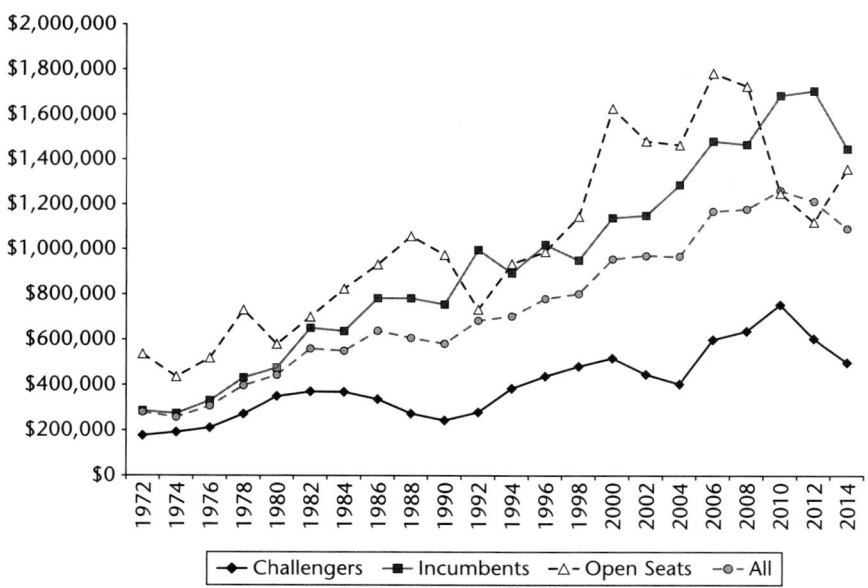

Source: Campaign Finance Institute, "House Campaign Expenditures," at http://www.cfinst.org/data.aspx, accessed August 10, 2015.

The growth in campaign spending by incumbents (and candidates for open seats) has outpaced that of challengers. In the 1970s, incumbents spent, on average, about 1.5 times as much as their challengers; in the most recent decade, they spent 2.5 times as much. However, much of this change resulted from increased spending by incumbents in safe districts. Figure 4-10, which distinguishes close races (defined as those in which the challenger won at least 45 percent of the major-party vote) from the rest, shows that the incumbent's average spending advantage over the challenger has widened more in uncompetitive than in competitive races, reflecting a growing concentration of financial resources in the campaigns of the most promising challengers. The typical competitive challenger remains at a financial disadvantage but currently raises enough money to mount a full-scale campaign ($1 million is sufficient at present in most districts), and because challengers reap greater marginal returns (in vote shares) than do incumbents on the dollars they do spend, the overall increase in campaign spending has not made it any harder for them to defeat incumbents.[18]

Unless they supply it themselves,[19] the money candidates spend on their campaigns must be raised from private individuals and political action committees (PACs) under restrictions imposed by federal law. The Federal Election

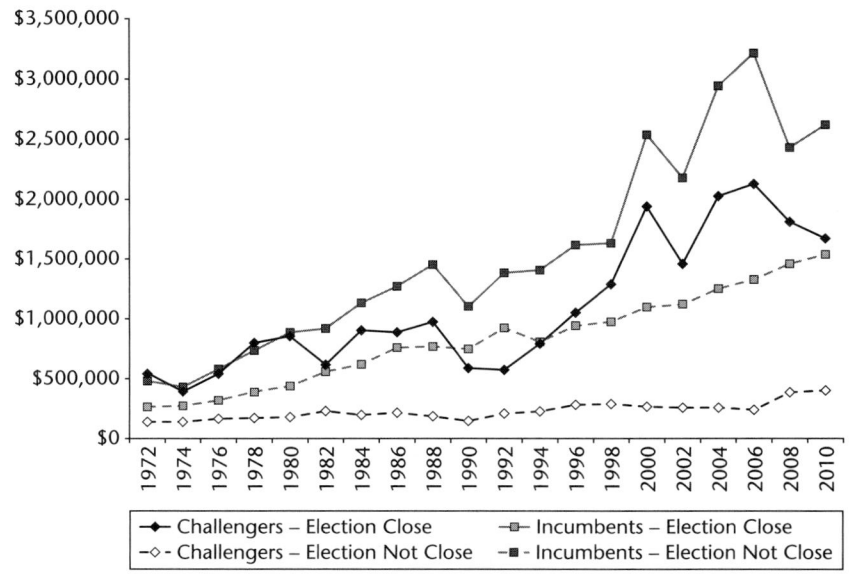

Figure 4-10 Campaign Spending by Incumbents and Challengers in Close and Not-Close Races, 1972–2010

Source: Compiled by author from Federal Election Commission Data.

Campaign Act of 1974 (FECA) limited individual donations to a maximum of $1,000 and PAC donations to a maximum of $5,000 per candidate per campaign. The limits were not adjusted for inflation until 2002, when the individual ceiling was raised to $2,000 and indexed to inflation for subsequent elections (for 2016, the limit was $2,700, the equivalent of $559 in 1974 dollars); the PAC limit was left unchanged and was not indexed. Because the limits apply separately to primary and general-election campaigns, the effective contribution ceilings are twice the designated maximums. Still, no single contribution accounts for more than a tiny fraction of what it now takes to finance a full-scale campaign. To achieve the more than twenty-fold increase in nominal campaign spending observed in House and Senate races between 1972 and 2014, candidates have thus had to multiply vastly the number of contributions they receive. This has become a particularly acute problem for Senate candidates, whose campaigns can run into tens of millions of dollars that must be raised under the same contribution limits that apply to House candidates. Fund-raising has thus become an endless, time-consuming, and, to most candidates, thoroughly unpleasant necessity. To the degree that donors are strong partisans—as most are[20]—it also discourages departures from partisan orthodoxy.

The growth in congressional campaign spending reflects both supply and demand, although the former is more determinative because the demand for campaign funds—driven by competitive pressures to make full use of the expanding menu of advertising venues and technologies for identifying and mobilizing supporters—appears to be virtually unlimited.[21] The supply has been augmented partly by growing prosperity and thus discretionary income among the affluent citizens responsible for most contributions,[22] but its main stimulus has been the escalating struggle for control of Congress in a highly polarized political environment. Higher stakes and inflamed partisan passions generate more contributions as well as more assiduous work to attract them.

The Growing Importance of Party Money

The widening partisan divide and its effects on the House and Senate's internal operations have raised the value of majority status, giving members an enlarged stake in their party's collective electoral performance. Congressional leaders have become increasingly insistent and successful in persuading their party's secure incumbents to raise money to pass along to their parties' House and Senate campaign committees—the so-called Hill committees[23]—and to their needier candidates. Members can do so by transferring funds contributed to their own campaigns or raised through their personal PACs (the so-called *leadership PACs*) to other candidates' campaigns and to their party's campaign committee. The growing prevalence of these practices is evident in Figure 4-11, which displays the inflation-adjusted growth in member-to-member contributions over the past two decades, and Figure 4-12, which does the same for member-to-party contributions. These intraparty transfers amounted to $162 million in 2012, up from $10 million in 1990. About 75 percent of the member-to-member contributions

Partisanship, Money, and Competition   101

Figure 4-11 House and Senate Members' Contributions to Other Candidates' Campaigns, 1990–2012

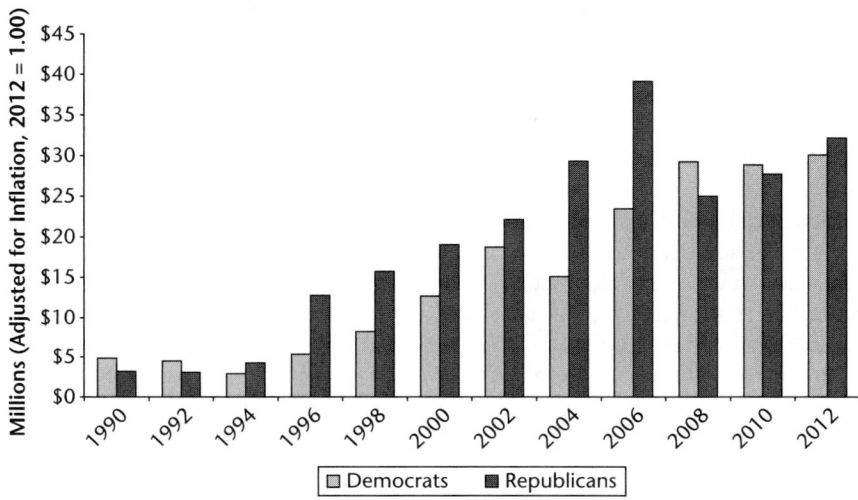

Source: Center for Responsive Politics, "Spreading the Wealth," at https://www.opensecrets.org/bigpicture/wealth.php?cycle=2012, accessed August 7, 2015.

Figure 4-12 House and Senate Members' Contributions to Congressional Campaign Committees, 1990–2012

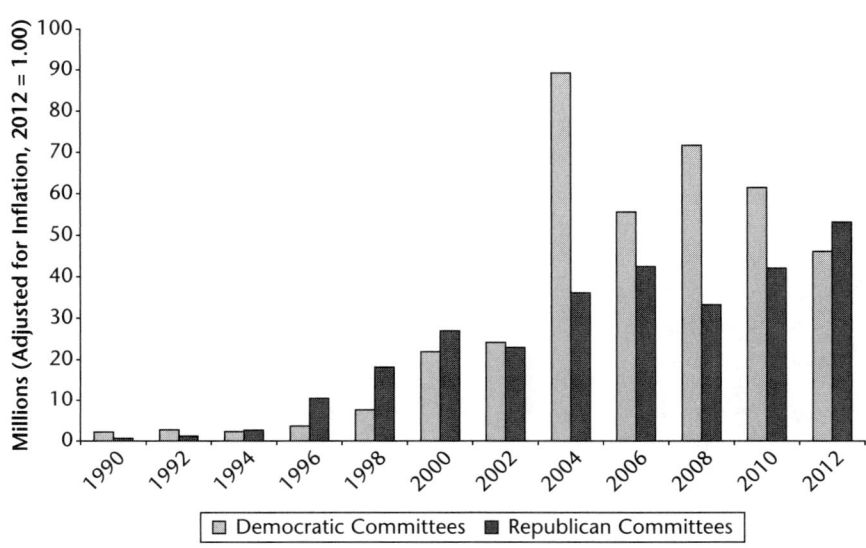

Source: Center for Responsive Politics, "Spreading the Wealth," at https://www.opensecrets.org/bigpicture/wealth.php?cycle=2012, accessed August 7, 2015.

come from leadership PACs, reflecting their primary purpose of cultivating colleagues in pursuit of leadership positions;[24] leadership PACs account for only 6 percent of the member-to-party contributions. The Hill committees still raise most of their funds from individuals and regular PACs, but contributions from members and leadership PACs have accounted for as much as 25 percent of a committee's receipts in recent years.[25]

How have the parties used this money? The FECA allows only a small share of it to go directly to candidates for their campaigns; party committees are subject to the PAC limit of $5,000 for House candidates, $46,800 (in 2016) for Senate candidates. The FECA does, however, allow the parties to spend additional sums in coordination with their candidates' campaigns that are subject to higher limits, indexed to inflation, and some party assistance does take this form. For 2016, parties were allowed to spend up to $48,000 for House candidates and between $96,000 and $2,847,100 for Senate candidates, depending on a state's population.[26]

Prior to the enactment of the Bipartisan Campaign Reform Act of 2002 (BCRA), the Hill committees had exploited a loophole in the FECA allowing them to spend unlimited sums for their candidates, raised in unlimited amounts from any source, in conjunction with state parties, under the transparent fiction that the spending was exclusively for "party building" and "voter mobilization."

Figure 4-13 Party Spending in House and Senate Elections, 1990–2014

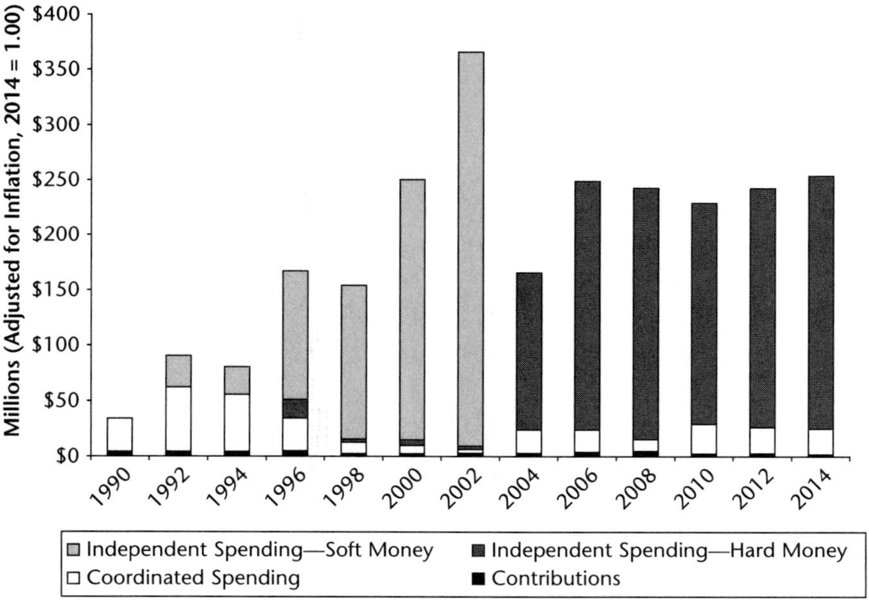

□ Independent Spending—Soft Money   ■ Independent Spending—Hard Money
□ Coordinated Spending   ■ Contributions

Source: Compiled by author from Federal Election Commission Data.

When BCRA closed this so-called *soft-money* spigot, the parties responded by ramping up their take of *hard money*, funds raised under the FECA's contribution limits.[27] The parties took to using first the soft and then the hard money for independent campaigns supporting their candidates—independent because they are not supposed to be coordinated in any way with the candidates' own campaigns. This option was encouraged by a 1996 Supreme Court decision rejecting any limits on independent party spending on First Amendment grounds[28] and a 2003 decision striking down a provision in BCRA compelling parties to choose between making coordinated and independent expenditures.[29]

Independent spending is now the dominant form of party involvement in campaign finance, accounting for about 90 percent of the parties' campaign investments (Figure 4-13). The formal "independence" requirement forbids collusion between the parties and candidates, but campaign professionals working for both have little difficulty tacitly coordinating their campaign work and messages, if they so desire, simply by keeping an eye on what the other is doing and adopting a complementary strategy.

Nonparty Independent Spending

Parties have no monopoly on independent spending; independent campaigns conducted by PACs and other organizations have been a part of the process since the 1970s (Figure 4-14). That part was small until quite recently but has suddenly become huge. In 2006 and 2008, independent-spending totals were at $39 million and $44 million, respectively, nearly double those of the highest earlier years. This was only a prelude to the next three cycles, during which the totals skyrocketed to reach more than $500 million in 2014, more than twice as much as spent independently by party committees. Again, Supreme Court decisions spurred this trend. Prior to the enactment of BCRA, the Court had ruled that the First Amendment protects the right to conduct unrestricted so-called voter education or issue advocacy campaigns, even if clearly intended to influence voters (by, for example, tendentious comparisons of candidates' issue positions), as long as terms such as "vote for," "elect," "vote against," "defeat," and "reject" are not used.[30] In 2007, the Court blocked BCRA's attempt to limit the effect of these campaigns through a ban on mentioning candidates' names in them during a fixed preelection period (thirty days for primaries and sixty days for general elections).[31] Then, in 2010, the Court decided, in *Citizens United v. Federal Election Commission*, that any limit at all on any independent campaigning by any person or entity violated the First Amendment.[32]

The largest independent campaigns are now conducted by so-called super PACs, also referred to as 527 and 501(c) organizations (after the provisions in the tax code applying to them), created solely for this purpose. Although their campaign ads must still refrain from specifically advocating a vote for or against a candidate, avoiding the Court's forbidden "magic words" does not prevent the production of ads that are indistinguishable from ordinary campaign ads.[33] Nearly

Figure 4-14 Independent Spending in House and Senate Races, 1978–2014

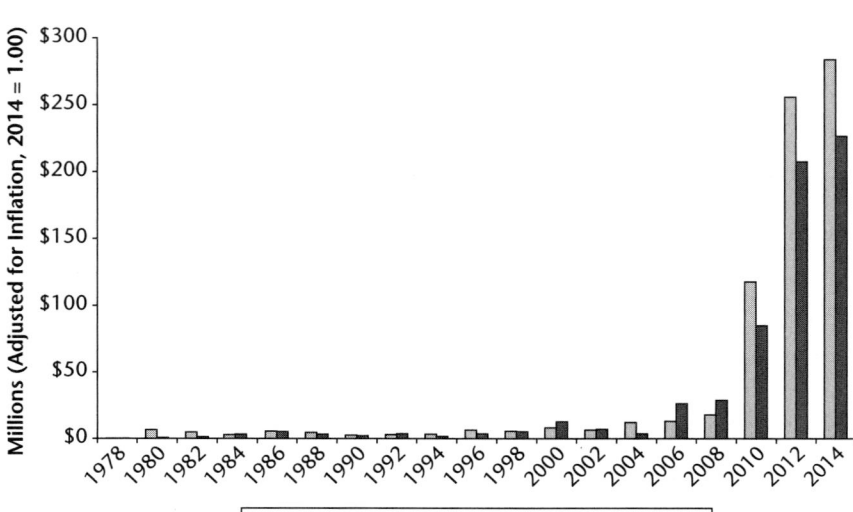

Source: Campaign Finance Institute, "Non-Party Independent Expenditures in House and Senate Elections, 1978–2014," at http://www.cfinst.org/data.aspx, accessed August 7, 2015.

all of these groups strongly favor one party's candidates over the other and, at least in general elections, act as the parties' auxiliaries. For example, on the Republican side, in 2010, the top three independent spenders were the U.S. Chamber of Commerce; the American Action Network, whose board is composed largely of current or former Republican elected officials; and American Crossroads, organized by veteran Republican operatives Karl Rove and Ed Gillespie. Most of the independent spending for Democrats was by labor unions.

In addition to inspiring the creation of super PACs, the Court's 2010 *Citizens United* decision freed corporations and unions to finance campaigns from their treasuries, assuring the continued growth of outside spending in future elections.[34] Groups incorporated as 501(c) organizations, such as the Chamber of Commerce and the American Action Network, are not even required to disclose their donors. As the law now stands, it is possible not only for any individual or organization to spend without limit on campaigns to sway congressional electorates but to do so anonymously.

Although nearly all of the major independent-spending groups are manifestly partisan, some represent their party's ideological extremes and back likeminded candidates in primary elections, including those challenging incumbents they deem overly moderate, even over the objection of the party's congressional leaders. For example, outside money helped several far-right Tea Party favorites win nominations over establishment Republicans in 2010 and 2012, albeit with mixed consequences for the Republican cause.[35] To the extent that they can credibly threaten the reelection of members who deviate from partisan or ideological orthodoxy, such groups discourage bipartisan cooperation and reinforce partisan polarization in Congress.

Like parties, independent groups concentrate their efforts in the most competitive general-election contests, and their level participation can rival that of the parties and even the candidates themselves. Analyzing data available through November 7, 2014, for the forty-six closest House contests (defined as those lost by incumbents or in which the winner received less than 55 percent of the vote), the Campaign Finance Institute found that the average Democrat was supported by $4.1 million and the average Republican was supported by $3.7 million in campaign expenditures from all sources. Democrats received a larger share via donations directly to their campaigns (51 percent, compared with 37 percent for Republicans). Independent party spending accounted for fairly similar shares both parties' candidates (32 percent for Democrats, 36 percent for Republicans), but nonparty independent spending was a larger part of the Republican effort (27 percent, compared to 17 percent for Democrats).[36] Outside spending played an even more conspicuous role in several high-profile Senate contests. A remarkable 73 percent of $83.1 million spent in the 2014 Iowa contest between Democrat Bruce Braley and Republican Joni Ernst was not legally under the candidates' control; in five other Senate contests, outside spending accounted for more than half of the total. In all, independent spending accounted for 58 percent of the astonishing $667 million spent in the nine 2014 Senate races rated "toss-ups" by the *Cook Political Report*.[37]

Independent spending by outside groups is, for the most part, driven by the same partisan and ideological goals that animate the parties. The prize is control of Congress, and fierce competition in the absence of accountability encourages unrestrained attacks on targeted candidates. Accuracy is not a priority; as one early pioneer of independent campaigning conceded, "A group like ours could lie through its teeth and the candidate it helps stays clean."[38] If not necessarily trafficking in blatant lies, independent campaigns, including those mounted by the parties, frequently push the outer boundaries of deceptive negative campaigning.[39] Scorched-earth campaigns are better suited to mobilizing the party's base than to reaching out to independents or across party lines and thus promote, as well as exploit, partisan voting habits.

In sum, then, the financing of campaigns has evolved ways that both reflect and reinforce the widening partisan and ideological divisions observable in Congress and in the electorate. The endless quest for resources contributes importantly to keeping Congress in a permanent campaign mode in which every action is taken with an eye to its effect on party prospects in the next election. That so much of the money is provided by people and groups with strong partisan and ideological commitments discourages cross-party cooperation and compromise. The threat of primary challenges generously financed by ideologues—and the reality that primary voters tend to be more extreme than other partisans[40]—has the same effect.

Money and Competition

The campaign finance system, as it now operates, produces highly competitive campaigns wherever the outcome is plausibly in doubt. Party committees and their allies are increasingly willing to put up venture capital, and it has become rare for either party to lose seats it might conceivably have won for lack of sufficient investment. This development has offset another trend that might otherwise have dampened competition for congressional seats. Gauged by presidential voting, the proportion of competitive states and districts has been shrinking. Figure 4-15 displays the share of districts and states in which the presidential vote fell within two points and within five points of the national vote in elections since 1972. By either standard, the number of more closely balanced House and Senate constituencies has decreased substantially.

Deliberate gerrymandering is commonly blamed for the House trend, but the evidence in Figure 4-15 suggests the blame is largely misplaced. The trend for states, whose boundaries have, of course, not changed, parallels the downward trend for districts. Moreover, most of the district-level change occurred between rather than in the (redistricting) years ending in "2"; depending on the measure examined, between 64 and 90 percent of the falloff in the number of closely

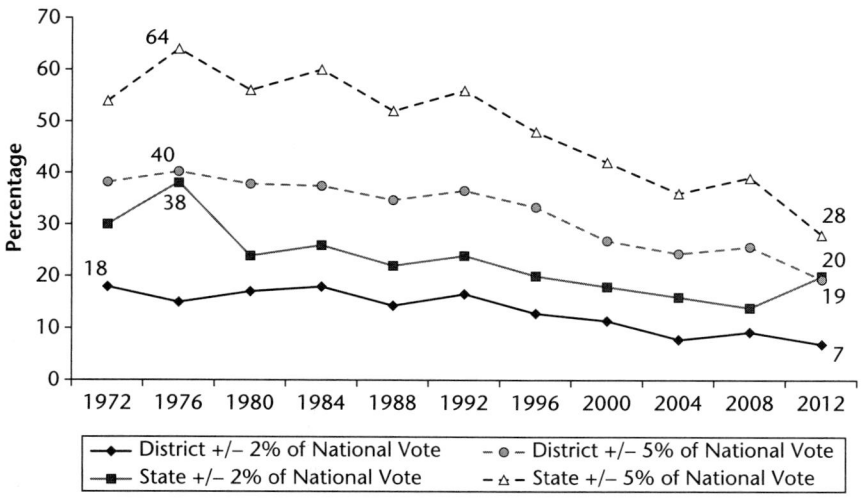

Figure 4-15 Competitive States and Districts, Measured by the Adjusted Presidential Vote, 1972–2012

Source: Compiled by author.

balanced districts since the 1970s resulted from changes in presidential voting patterns within established districts rather than changes in district boundaries.[41]

Although fewer states and districts now have a close partisan balance, competition for seats remains vigorous whenever conditions are conducive to competition. Figure 4-16 displays three measures of competitiveness in House elections during the past four decades: total turnover of seats, the number of incumbents defeated, and the number of seats won with less than 55 percent of the major-party vote.[42] Competitiveness has varied a great deal from election to election over this period but shows no sustained trend. Low turnover in the late 1980s and again from 1998 to 2004 provoked much hand-wringing about the supposed disappearance of electoral competition, but the large swings in electoral fortunes that followed these periods of electoral stasis point to the real source of low turnover: the absence of a significant national partisan tide. In years when voter sentiment has turned clearly against a party, its rival has exploited the opportunity by recruiting and financing superior candidates, expanding the competitive range, and producing the dramatic shifts in partisan fortunes observed in 1994, from 2006 to 2008, and in 2010. More generally, the change in a party's share of seats is strongly and directly responsive to changes in its share of votes, and this relationship has not changed over the four decades.[43] The same analysis applies to

Figure 4-16 The Competitiveness of House Elections, 1972–2014

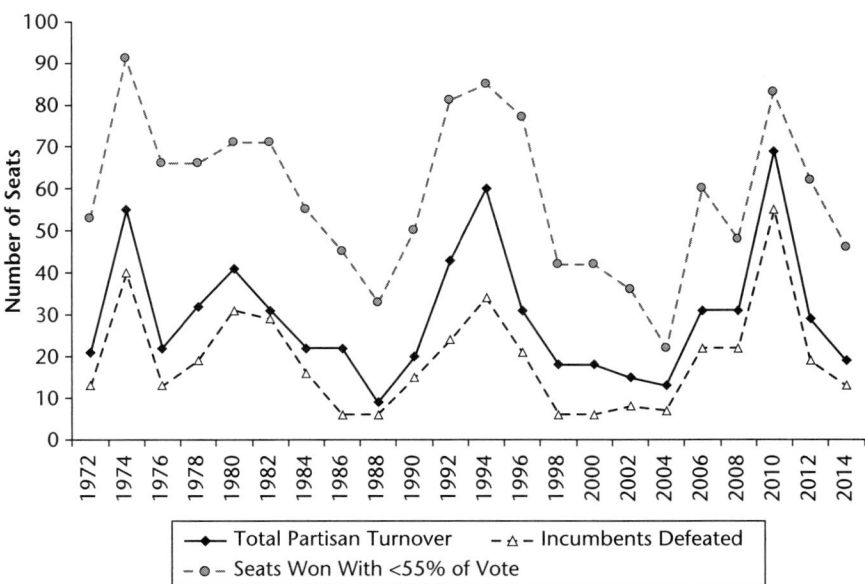

Source: 1972–2012 data from Norman J. Ornstein, Thomas E. Mann, and Michael J. Malbin, *Vital Statistics on Congress 2014* (Washington, DC: Brookings Institution, 2014); 2012, 2014 data compiled by author.

Senate elections, although, as usual, with the greater idiosyncrasy generated by the cyclical pattern of Senate contests. (Witness the Republicans' nine-seat gain in 2014.)

There is no evidence, then, of any general decline in competition for congressional seats. Were it not for the expanded financial efforts of party committees and their allies, however, the growth in party loyalty and the decline in the number of states and districts with a close partisan balance would most probably have reduced the number of competitive races. Abundant financial resources have given the parties leeway to invest in longer shots, some of which have paid off. In technical terms, party officials now worry less about wasting money on false positives (mistakenly investing in unwinnable races) and so can avoid false negatives (wrongly ignoring candidates capable of winning). One result is that the attrition in the number of states and districts with a close partisan balance has not allowed incumbents to rest any easier.

Candidate-Centered Elections?

Historically, congressional elections have always been shaped by some mix of candidate- and party-centered forces, but the relative importance of these components has varied. Following World War II, the balance shifted toward candidate-centered electoral politics, a trend that peaked in the 1970s. Since then, however, the changes in electoral behavior examined in this chapter have shifted the balance back toward a more party-centered electoral process. The candidate component remains central, to be sure—even the parties' independent campaigns focus primarily on promoting or trashing individual candidates—but the personal vote is a much smaller electoral factor now than it was in the 1970s and 1980s.[44]

This is evident in the diminishing electoral effects of incumbency status and challenger quality, documented in Table 4-1. The first two rows display estimates of two standard measures of the incumbency advantage, the *slurge*, an average of the sophomore surge and retirement slumps, and the Gelman-King index, for each of the past four decades plus the first two elections in this one.[45] Both measures had registered a sharp increase in the incumbency advantage during the mid-1960s that was sustained through the 1980s. Since then, the incumbency advantage has declined noticeably by either measure, and in this decade, it has fallen to levels last seen in the 1950s.[46] The third and fourth rows estimate the Gelman-King index for incumbents with and without high-spending challengers (defined, for this analysis, as those spending at least $500,000 in inflation-adjusted dollars on their campaigns). The incumbency advantage has always been inversely related to the challenger's level of spending,[47] and in most decades, incumbents facing challengers spending in excess of $500,000 have typically enjoyed about the same, relatively modest vote advantage—a reminder that incumbents thrive by discouraging serious opposition.[48] The vote advantage of incumbents who avoided well-financed challenges, however, has dropped

Table 4-1 Candidate Effects in U.S. House Elections, 1972–2014 (by Decade)

	1970s	1980s	1990s	2000s	2012–2014
Incumbency Advantage					
"Slurge"	8.0	8.8	6.3	5.9	3.0
Gelman-King index	8.1	10.6	8.8	6.9	3.8
High-spending challenger	−0.7	3.5	4.1	2.9	3.0
Low-spending challenger	9.4	11.9	10.5	8.3	4.0
Challenger Quality Effect					
No controls	8.5	7.4	8.6	8.8	8.1
Controls, except spending	4.0	3.6	2.6	1.6	0.7
Controls, including spending	1.8	1.7	0.8	0.7	0.3

Note: Entries are estimated differences in vote share for candidates in each category. Computation of coefficients is defined in footnotes 45 (incumbency advantage) and 50 (quality effect). High-spending challengers are defined as those spending $500,000 or more in 2014 dollars; the rest are considered low spending.

sharply in recent elections, a direct result of the increase in party-line voting documented in Figure 4-2; fewer partisan voters now defect to incumbents of the rival party even when their own party's challenger languishes in underfinanced obscurity.

High-quality challengers, defined as those who have previously held elective public office,[49] do just as well as ever, with their vote typically running more than eight percentage points higher than that of inexperienced challengers (fifth row of Table 4-1). But because such challengers are more likely to take the field when national and local conditions are particularly conducive to success, measuring the independent effect of candidate quality on the vote requires taking such conditions into account. When this is done, the estimated effect of quality is lower and, more to the point, has clearly declined across the last four decades.[50] When campaign spending is also taken into account (high-quality challengers raise and spend more money than the others), the estimated effect of elective-office experience per se is even smaller and has become almost negligible. Again, the electoral importance of a candidate characteristic has decreased as party loyalty among voters has grown.

The diminishing impact of the personal vote has made it increasingly difficult for candidates to win elections against a district's partisan grain. The evidence is in Figure 4-17. For this analysis, a district's partisan leanings are defined by the current or, for midterms, most recent presidential vote. Districts in which the presidential vote is at least two percentage points greater than the national average are considered leaning toward the president's party; districts in which the presidential vote is at least two percentage points lower than that average are considered leaning toward the other party; the rest are considered neutral.

Figure 4-17 Winning Against the Partisan Grain, 1972–2014

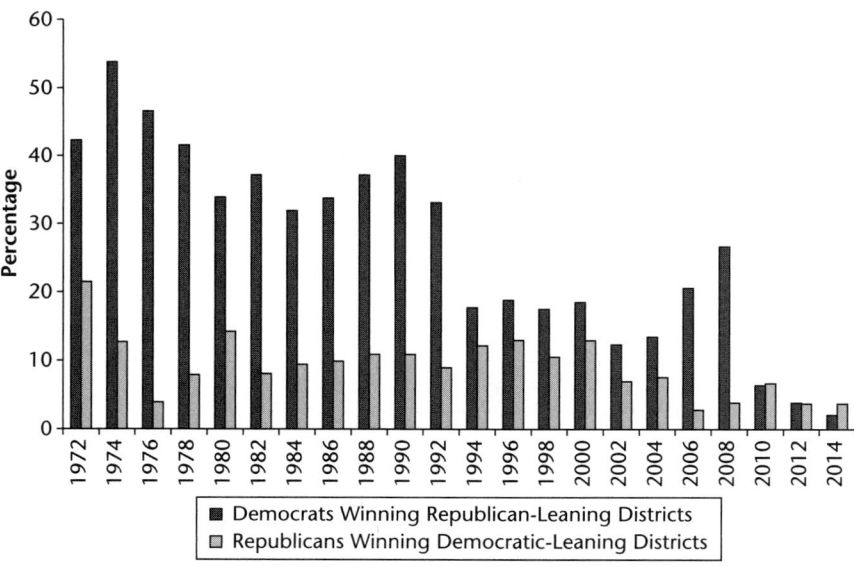

Source: Compiled by author.

The proportion of House seats held by candidates of the "wrong" party has obviously declined, most notably among Democrats. Note the large drop between 1992 and 1994; the Republicans' historic victory in 1994 derived mainly from district electorates voting for Congress as they had, for years, been voting for president, especially in the South. Note also that the gains Democrats achieved in 2006 and 2008 left them defending a surfeit of Republican-leaning seats (fifty-eight by this measure), leaving them vulnerable to a contrary national tide in 2010; two-thirds of the Republican pickups in 2010 occurred in such districts.[51] The 2012 and 2014 elections, held in districts newly drawn after the 2010 census, continued the downward trend in victories against the partisan grain; after 2014, only twelve members (seven Republicans and five Democrats) represented districts leaning toward the other party.

These data point to another important consequence of the increase in partisan electoral coherence: It has benefited Republicans more than Democrats. Republicans have enjoyed a structural advantage over the entire postwar period because their regular voters are distributed more efficiently across House districts than are regular Democratic voters. The Democrats' problem is that their core supporters tend to be concentrated in urban districts with lopsided Democratic majorities, giving them a larger share of "wasted" votes compared to Republicans, whose voters, spread more evenly across suburban and rural areas, typically deliver narrower victories. Thus, after the 2012 election, which Obama won by a margin of nearly 5 million votes, there were 180 districts where Obama ran at least two points ahead of his national average but 226 districts in which he ran at least two points behind. (The remaining twenty-nine districts were within two points of the national average.) Thus, at present, Republicans can achieve a majority by winning only seats in Republican-leaning territory, whereas Democrats would have to win at least eleven Republican-leaning seats even if they won all of the Democratic-leaning and balanced districts in order to reach 218. The Republicans' structural advantage, which applies to states as well as districts, is nothing new,[52] but it has grown more significant because of the trends in voting behavior documented in this chapter. The more partisan electoral context means that Democrats now face a steeper uphill battle in pursuit of congressional majorities. The 2006 and 2008 elections proved that, with a strong wind at their back, they can succeed, but 2010 showed how ephemeral that success could be, depending, as it did, on holding onto Republican-leaning territory, where the party's president, policies, and national image could become a liability.

The 114th Congress (2015–2016) contained the smallest proportion of members representing districts leaning toward the other party on record, 3 percent, down from the high of 37 percent in the Ninety-fourth Congress (1975–1976). Such members are, of electoral necessity, more moderate than their colleagues, so their disappearance automatically increases ideological polarization in Congress.[53] The concentration of Democratic losses in 2010 in Republican-leaning districts, for example, left the 112th Congress even more polarized than its record-setting predecessor. Ninety-two percent of the seats Republicans took from Democrats had been represented by members whose roll call votes put them to the right of their party's median member, and the further to the right, the greater the toll; thirty-two of the forty-seven most moderate Democrats (defined as those whose DW-NOMINATE scores were greater than -.2) were replaced by Republicans. The mean DW-NOMINATE score for all Democrats in the 111th House was -.36; the departing Democrats averaged -.20 on the scale, leaving the remaining Democrats with a mean of -.41. Two-thirds of the newly elected Republicans represent Republican-leaning districts and were under no pressure to moderate—quite the opposite, given the demonstrated clout of the party's resolutely conservative Tea Party wing. Insofar as voters were expressing a desire for more moderate national policies in 2010, as rational-balancing theories of midterm voting behavior posit,[54] they did so by voting out the moderates and replacing most of them with extremists. Those Republicans who replaced Democrats in 2010 were ideologically indistinguishable from other House Republicans; the average DW-NOMINATE scores for both groups were virtually identical and the most conservative on record. The next two Congresses were the most ideologically polarized since the Civil War, with a seemingly intractable partisan stalemate on the Hill as the unsurprising result.

Conclusion

The partisan disputes over taxes, spending, and deficits that brought the U.S. government to the brink of paper insolvency in the summer of 2011 unified the public on one thing at least: disdain for Congress. Public comments on the process were scathing, with "ridiculous," "disgusting," and "stupid" topping the list of one-word descriptions reported in the July 28–31 Pew survey.[55] Over the next several months, disapproval of Congress's performance exceeded 80 percent in every survey that asked about it, and the sentiment was thoroughly bipartisan.[56] This is no anomaly, for Americans always say they detest the kind of partisan bickering epitomized by the budget showdown.[57] Since then, gridlock has largely prevailed, and disapproval of Congress has remained extraordinarily high, averaging 79 percent from 2012 through mid-2016.[58] The irony is that the divisive politics and partisan gridlock voters almost universally condemn is the product of their own electoral choices and the winners' fidelity to their electoral bases.

The congressional parties did not polarize in a vacuum. The data examined here reveal a robust connection between electoral processes and the widening partisan divide on the Hill. Ordinary Democrats and Republicans have grown increasingly distant from one another in ideology and policy preferences. The links between partisanship and voting have strengthened. The president has become a more compelling—and more partisan—focal point for congressional electorates. At the aggregate level, vote differences between the states and districts won by Republicans and Democrats have widened, leaving the congressional parties with increasingly homogeneous and dissimilar electoral constituencies. The campaign finance system has evolved in ways that intensify partisan competition in elections and discourage compromise in Washington. As career strategies, political independence and moderation have lost efficacy both at home and on the Hill. In short, electoral and congressional politics have coevolved over the past four decades in ways that have contributed powerfully to the polarized national politics of today. The profound and widely lamented changes in life on the Hill since the 1970s rest on solid electoral ground and thus are likely to endure until that ground begins to erode.

Notes

1. Four representatives and eight senators had begun their congressional service prior to 1980 (including three senators who had served in the House in the 1970s).
2. As measured by Keith Poole and Howard Rosenthal's DW-NOMINATE scores, http://voteview.com/political_polarization_2014.htm, accessed August 10, 2015.
3. Barbara Sinclair, *Unorthodox Lawmaking: New Legislative Processes in the U.S. Congress*, 3rd ed. (Washington, DC: CQ Press, 2007), 110.
4. Gary C. Jacobson and Jamie L. Carson, *The Politics of Congressional Elections*, 9th ed. (Lanham, MD: Rowman & Littlefield, 2015), Figures 7-6, 7-7, and 7-8.
5. Marc J. Hetherington and Thomas J. Rudolph, *Why Washington Won't Work: Polarization, Political Trust, and the Governing Crisis* (Chicago: University of Chicago Press,

2015); Frances E. Lee, *Beyond Ideology: Politics, Principles, and Partisanship in the U.S. Senate* (Chicago: University of Chicago Press, 2009).
6. The most thorough and readable account of these developments and their myriad causes is Barbara Sinclair's *Party Wars: Polarization and the Politics of National Policy Making* (Norman: University of Oklahoma Press, 2006).
7. The classic statement is in David R. Mayhew, *Congress: The Electoral Connection* (New Haven, CT: Yale University Press, 1974).
8. Matthew Levendusky, *The Partisan Sort: How Liberals Became Democrats and Conservatives Became Republicans* (Chicago: University of Chicago Press, 2009); Alan I. Abramowitz, *The Disappearing Center: Engaged Citizens, Polarization, and American Democracy* (New Haven, CT: Yale University Press, 2010).
9. Ideology is respondents' self-location on a seven-point scale: extremely liberal, liberal, slightly liberal, moderate, slightly conservative, conservative, and extremely conservative. The proportion of voters calling themselves liberals or conservatives has grown over time; typically, about 80 percent of voters can place themselves on the scale, and about 70 percent of those voters place themselves either to the left or right of center.
10. Gary C. Jacobson, *A Divider, Not a Uniter: George W. Bush and the American People*, 2nd ed. (New York: Longman, 2011), 26, 275; Abramowitz, *Disappearing Center*, 43–47; Joseph Bafumi and Robert Y. Shapiro, "A New Partisan Voter," *Journal of Politics* 71 (2009): 1–24.
11. People initially call themselves independents but then admit to leaning toward a party vote about as consistently for that party's candidates as people who initially call themselves Democrats or Republicans but do not identify strongly with their chosen party. Thus, partisan leaners are appropriately treated as closet partisans.
12. Gary C. Jacobson, "Presidents, Partisans, and Polarized Politics," in *Can We Talk? The Rise of Rude, Nasty, Stubborn Politics*, ed. Daniel M. Shea and Morris P. Fiorina (New York: Pearson, 2013), Figures 10 and 11. The 2014 figure is from Stephen Ansolabehere, *Cooperative Congressional Election Study, 2014: Common Content* [Computer file] (Cambridge, MA: Harvard University, 2015), http://cces.gov.harvard.edu.
13. Jacobson, *Divider*, 6.
14. The figure for 2014 was 48 percent. Data are from Pew, Gallup, CNN, CBS News/*New York Times*, NBC News/*Wall Street Journal*, Ap-GFK, and ABC News/*Washington Post* polls.
15. Jacobson and Carson, *Congressional Elections*, Figures 6-3 and 6-15.
16. Ibid., Figures 7-8 and 7-9. Based on data generously supplied by George C. Edwards III.
17. Realignment in the South explains only part of this change, since the gap between Republican and Democratic constituencies outside the South also grew (from 0.7 to 1.8 points in the House and from 0.6 to 2.0 in the Senate).
18. Jacobson and Carson, *Congressional Elections*, chap. 3.
19. The typical candidate does supply a significant portion of money spent by his or her campaign. On average, in elections from 1992 through 2014, candidate contributions and loans accounted for 11 percent of the money raised by Senate candidates and 6 percent of that raised by House candidates; for House challengers, the average is 18 percent. See Campaign Finance Institute, "Campaign Funding Sources for House and Senate Candidates, 1984–2014," http://www.cfinst.org/data.aspx, accessed August 11, 2015.

20. Jonathan Wand, "The Allocation of Campaign Contributions by Interest Groups and the Rise of Elite Polarization," manuscript, Stanford University, n.d., http://wand.stanford.edu/research/mixedmotives.pdf, accessed November 14, 2011; Adam Bonica, "Ideology and Interests in the Political Marketplace," *American Journal of Political Science* 47, no. 2 (2013): 294–311; Peter Francia, Paul S. Herrnson, John C. Greene, Lynda Powell, and Clyde Wilcox, *The Financiers of Congressional Elections: Investors, Ideologues, and Intimates* (New York: Columbia University Press, 2003).
21. Candidates and their supporters—or more precisely, their teams of consultants and pollsters—seem to be able to find a way to spend every dollar they can get their hands on. What could otherwise explain the $110 million spent pursuing Alaska's 506,000 registered voters during the 2014 Senate contest between Mike Begich and Dan Sullivan?
22. Clyde Wilcox, "Contributing as Political Participation," in *A User's Guide to Campaign Finance Reform*, ed. Gerald C. Lubenow (Lanham, MD: Rowman & Littlefield, 2001), 116–20.
23. The Hill committees are, in the House, the National Republican Congressional Committee and the Democratic Congressional Campaign Committee and, in the Senate, the National Republican Senatorial Committee and the Democratic Senatorial Campaign Committee.
24. Marian Currinder, *Money in the House: Campaign Funds and Congressional Party Politics* (Boulder, CO: Westview Press, 2009); Eric S. Heberlig and Bruce A. Larson, *Congressional Parties, Institutional Ambition, and the Financing of Majority Control* (Ann Arbor: University of Michigan Press, 2012).
25. Gary C. Jacobson, "A Collective Dilemma Solved: The Distribution of Party Campaign Resources in the 2006 and 2008 Congressional Elections," *Election Law Journal* 9, no. 4 (2010): 386.
26. In states with a single House district, the Senate limit of $96,000 applies. The national parties can also act as agents of state parties, which are allowed to spend as much as the national parties on coordinated campaigns for congressional candidates, effectively doubling these limits.
27. The limits are $25,000 from individuals and $15,000 from PACs.
28. Colorado Republican Federal Campaign Committee v. Federal Election Commission, 518 U.S. 604 (1996).
29. McConnell v. Federal Election Commission, 540 U.S. 93 (2003).
30. Jonathan D. Salant, "GOP Bumps Up Against Court Precedent in Trying to Block AFL-CIO," *CQ Weekly Report* 54 (1996): 996–97.
31. Federal Election Commission v. Wisconsin Right to Life, Inc., 551 U.S. 449 (2007).
32. Citizens United v. Federal Election Commission, 558 U.S. 310 (2010).
33. One study found that fewer than 10 percent of *candidates'* broadcast ads used any of the words deemed by the Court to be out of bounds for issue advocacy campaigns. See Brennan Center for Justice, "Straight Talk on Campaign Finance: Separating Fact from Fiction," Paper No. 5, n.d., http://www.brennancenter.org/sites/default/files/legacy/d/paper5.pdf, accessed July 2, 2007.
34. Eric S. Heberlig and Bruce A. Larson, "U.S. House Incumbent Fundraising and Spending in a Post–*Citizens United* and Post–*McCutcheon* World," *Political Science Quarterly* 129 (2014–2015): 613–41.
35. In 2010, Tea Party candidates won in Florida, Kentucky, Pennsylvania, and Wisconsin but cost Republicans almost certain victories in the Delaware and Nevada Senate races

and probably in Colorado as well; see Gary C. Jacobson, "The Republican Resurgence in 2010," *Political Science Quarterly* 126 (2011): 39. Tea Party favorites also cost Republicans winnable Senate seats in Indiana and Missouri in 2012; see Gary C. Jacobson, "How the Economy and Partisanship Shaped the 2012 Presidential and Congressional Elections," *Political Science Quarterly* 128 (2013): 1–38. In 2014, establishment Republican operatives and donors made a concerted and successful effort to prevent the nomination of extreme ideologues in winnable states and thus were able to take full advantage of the favorable partisan landscape that year; see Gary C. Jacobson, "Obama and Nationalized Electoral Politics in the 2014 Midterm," *Political Science Quarterly* 130 (2015): 1–25.

36. Campaign Finance Institute, "Whose Voices Were Loudest?" November 7, 2014, http://www.cfinst.org/Press/PReleases/14-11-07/Parties_and_Candidates_Outspent_Non-Party_Groups_in_Almost_Every_Close_House_Race_in_2014_Non-party_Groups_Were_More_Important_in_the_Senate.aspx.
37. Jacobson, "Electoral Politics in 2014," 13.
38. Myra MacPherson, "The New Right Brigade," *Washington Post*, August 10, 1980, F1.
39. Greg Sargent, "Rove, Chamber Ads Widely Debunked as False or Misleading," *Washington Post*, October 13, 2010, at http://voices.washingtonpost.com/plumline/2010/10/rove_chamber_ads_widely_debunk.html; Jacobson and Carson, *Politics of Congressional Elections*, 79.
40. Gary C. Jacobson, "The Electoral Origins of Polarized Politics: Evidence From the 2010 Cooperative Congressional Election Study," *American Behavioral Scientist* 56 (2012): 1612–30.
41. Gary C. Jacobson, "Competition in U.S. Congressional Elections," in *The Marketplace of Democracy: Electoral Competition and American Politics*, ed. Michael P. McDonald and John Samples (Washington, DC: Brookings Institution Press, 2006), 26–52.
42. The three measures are highly correlated with each other and with related measures, such as net partisan change, *Congressional Quarterly's* preelection ratings of district competitiveness, and (negatively) the proportion of uncontested seats.
43. Regressing changes in the percentage of seats won by the Democratic Party on changes in the percentage of votes its candidates won nationally from 1972 through 2014 produces the following equation: Seat Swing = $-.23(.51) + 1.40 \times$ Vote Swing$(.14)$, adjusted $R^2 = .83$, $N = 22$. Standard errors are in parentheses. An interaction term testing for change over time in this relationship was small and statistically insignificant ($p = .52$).
44. The term is from Bruce E. Cain, John A. Ferejohn, and Morris P. Fiorina, "The Constituency Service Basis of the Personal Vote for U.S. Representatives and British Members of Parliament," *American Political Science Review* 78 (1984): 110–25.
45. The *slurge* is the average of the sophomore surge (the average gain in vote share won by candidates running as incumbents for the first time compared to their vote share in their initial election) and the retirement slump (the average drop in the party's vote from the previous election when the incumbent departs and the seat becomes open). See Albert D. Cover and David R. Mayhew, "Congressional Dynamics and the Decline of Competitive Congressional Elections," in *Congress Reconsidered*, 2nd ed., ed. Lawrence C. Dodd and Bruce I. Oppenheimer (Washington, DC: CQ Press, 1981), 70; Robert S. Erikson, "Malapportionment, Gerrymandering, and Party Fortunes in Congressional Elections," *American Political Science Review* 66 (1972): 1240;

David W. Brady, Brian Gaines, and Douglas Rivers, "The Incumbency Advantage in the House and Senate: A Comparative Institutional Analysis" (unpublished manuscript, 1994).

The Gelman-King index is computed by regressing the Democrats' share of the two-party vote on the Democrats' vote in the previous election, the party holding the seat, and incumbency (which takes a value of 1 if the Democratic candidate is an incumbent, −1 if the Republican is an incumbent, and 0 if the seat is open). The coefficient on the incumbency variable estimates the value (in percentage of votes) of incumbency for each election year. Analysis is confined to districts that were not redrawn between elections. See Andrew Gelman and Gary King, "Measuring Incumbency Without Bias," *American Journal of Political Science* 34 (1990): 1142–64. In combining the data by decade, I added a measure of the average interelection vote swing to account for national trends. Decades are defined by redistricting cycles; the 1970s include 1972 to 1980, for example.

46. Detailed evidence for a decline in the incumbency advantage is in Gary C. Jacobson, "It's Nothing Personal: The Decline of the Incumbency Advantage in U.S. House Elections," *Journal of Politics* 77 (2015): 861–73.
47. Gary C. Jacobson, "The Variability and Contingency of the Incumbency Advantage in U.S. House Elections," paper presented at the Conference on the Incumbency Advantage, Texas A&M University, College Station, Texas, September 21–22, 2007.
48. Jacobson and Carson, *Politics of Congressional Elections*.
49. For a justification of this measure, see Gary C. Jacobson and Samuel Kernell, *Strategy and Choice in Congressional Elections*, 2nd ed. (New Haven, CT: Yale University Press, 1983), 30–31.
50. The coefficient is estimated by regressing the challenger's vote on the quality measure (1 if the challenger has held elective office, 0 otherwise), the incumbent's vote in the previous election, the national swing in the average vote for the challenger's party in the election year, and the presidential vote for the challenger's party in the district in the current or (for midterms) previous presidential election.
51. Jacobson, "Republican Resurgence," 27–52.
52. Jacobson and Carson, *Politics of Congressional Elections*, Figure 2-3. Republicans' structural advantage in Senate elections is a consequence of their disproportionate share of voters in the less populous states.
53. Richard Fleisher and Jon R. Bond, "The Shrinking Middle in the U.S. Congress," *British Journal of Political Science* 34 (2004): 429–51; Sarah H. Binder, *Stalemate: Causes and Consequences of Legislative Gridlock* (Washington, DC: Brookings Institution Press, 2003), 64–67.
54. Albert Alesina and Howard Rosenthal, "Partisan Cycles in Congressional Elections and the Macroeconomy," *American Political Science Review* 83 (1989): 373–98; Joseph Bafumi, Robert S. Erikson, and Christopher Wlezien, "Balancing, Generic Polls and Midterm Congressional Elections," *Journal of Politics* 72 (2010): 705–19.
55. Results reported at http://people-press.org/files/legacy-questionnaires/08-1-11%20Topline%20For%20Release.pdf, accessed November 11, 2011.
56. The question was asked in seventeen surveys between August and November 2011; see "Congress—Job Rating," at http://www.pollingreport.com/CongJob.htm, accessed November 14, 2011; Frank Newport, "Congress' Job Approval Entrenched at Record

Low of 13%," Gallup, November 14, 2011, http://www.gallup.com/poll/150728/ Congress-Job-Approval-Entrenched-Record-Low.aspx.
57. John R. Hibbing and Elizabeth Theiss-Morse, *Congress as Public Enemy: Public Attitudes Toward American Political Institutions* (New York: Cambridge University Press, 1995), 16–20.
58. Approval averaged only 15 percent over this period; data are from http://www.pollingreport.com/CongJob.htm, accessed July 18, 2016.

5. Constituency Representation in Congress
In General and in Periods of Higher and Lower Partisan Polarization

Soren Jordan, Kim Quaile Hill, and Patricia A. Hurley

Political scientists have produced abundant research on how members of the U.S. Congress represent the preferences and interests of their constituents. Yet there is no agreement in that research on how one might best summarize the character of representation empirically or judge its quality normatively. We argue this situation arises because the bulk of research has failed to take account of fundamental insights from early empirical work on this topic. In this essay, we summarize a systematic theory of representation from our earlier research that helps resolve this intellectual impasse. Our party polarization and issue complexity theory accounts well for the different forms (or models) that representation might take that were anticipated by early research and thus provides a good overall characterization of constituency representation. Yet it can also account for other important aspects of congressional behavior. Some of the most prominent concerns about such behavior have been with the effects of the increased ideological polarization of the two major parties of the last few decades. As we explain in detail in this essay, our theory can account for two important such effects: how constituency representation has both changed in some respects and stayed the same in others as the major parties became more polarized ideologically.

The principal normative purpose of a democratic government is to ensure the preferences of the general public are represented in government policy. How well that expectation is realized in national politics in the United States is, in good part, dependent on how members of Congress represent the geographic constituencies that elected them. Despite a huge body of research on representation in Congress, however, with new studies of the topic published in major scholarly journals and books every year, there is no consensus among political scientists about whether constituency representation is generally good or poor, whether some constituents are better represented than others, or about the varied ways members of Congress might represent the preferences and interests of their constituents.

This essay offers answers to the preceding questions by explicating the research in our book *Representation in Congress: A Unified Theory*.[1] In the latter research, we took account of the different assumptions in past scholarship on the character of representation and how it should be examined, and we adopted those assumptions that appeared to be most promising. Then, we crafted a systematic theory of constituency representation that makes a priori predictions about the different ways members of Congress offer representation to their constituencies and that indicates which constituents, if any, are best represented on different kinds of policy issues. We offered considerable evidence for the latter predictions, and this *empirical* work suggests answers to various *normative* questions about the quality of representation. In this essay, we also extend the work in our book through an original investigation of whether patterns of representation today, in an era of very high party polarization, are different from past periods of lower polarization and more bipartisan congressional policy making.

Classic and Contemporary Research on Constituency Representation in Congress

A lack of consensus in the research literature about the character of representation exists, in good part, because the bulk of existing scholarship fails to take account of fundamental assumptions about representation from the earliest scientific research on that topic and especially the seminal publication on the subject by Warren Miller and Donald Stokes in 1963.[2]

Miller and Stokes, like virtually all the scholars writing in the same period, assumed there was no single, overall way to characterize how members of Congress represented the policy preferences of their constituents in voting on legislative proposals. Instead, members might effectively provide different kinds of representation on different issues. In the language of this early research, which is still used in congressional politics textbooks, if not much contemporary basic science research, different "models" of representation were thought to arise on different policy issues. On issues that especially divided the two major parties in the general public and in Congress (and which, thus, demonstrated high party *polarization*), Miller and Stokes hypothesized that members would represent the preferences of their copartisan constituents instead of the preferences of the average constituent or the median voter—providing, then, what has been labeled *responsible-party* representation.

On issues for which a member's constituents of both parties share a common preference, the member was hypothesized to vote for the constituency-wide preference—either because he or she shared the same view and was demonstrating *belief-sharing* representation or because the member felt compelled to follow constituency preferences as an *instructed delegate*.

Miller and Stokes also anticipated that on some issues, the elite and the general-public members of both parties might be internally divided on the best policy course *or* that the party elites might be divided while constituencies would not have a clear policy preference. On the latter sorts of issues, members would not face a clear policy "signal" from either their national party or their constituency and would have to make policy decisions based on their own judgment, thus providing *trustee* representation.

Miller and Stokes and other scholars writing at the same time offered suggestive evidence for the appearance of these different models of representation on different issues. Yet despite their research being conceptually and methodologically innovative for its time, it was not sufficiently rigorous to confirm that such patterns generally arise *or* to develop a theory to account for when and why they arise.

Only rarely has later scholarship taken account of these alternative models of representation. Instead, the vast majority of research after Miller and Stokes has attempted to assess what might be called the most common or "average" form of representation occurring at any one time. To do so, such research typically calculates averaged constituency preferences (on some scale, from being highly liberal to highly conservative) across a wide range of issues. Then, legislators' policy decisions on roll call votes are also averaged across many issues, and legislators' averaged policy positions are compared with their constituencies' averaged positions to assess how closely the two match.[3]

Research like that described above attempts to create a parsimonious, summary estimate of representation. Yet such research has foundered as a basis for constructing systematic theory for at least two reasons. First, it aggregates across too many different forms of representation that are operating simultaneously, as Miller and Stokes hypothesized to be the case and as our research to be discussed here confirms. Because delegate, belief-sharing, responsible-party, and trustee representation are all occurring simultaneously, even if some are more numerous than others, an average across all of them cannot portray any of the single models well. Thus, such an averaged mode of analysis offers a distorted *empirical* characterization of issue representation. Because it does not seek evidence for the alternative models of representation, it also cannot inform us about when and why the different models arise.

The fact that different models of representation arise simultaneously for different policy issues means that different constituency groups are being favored on different issues, *and* for some models, there is no literal representation of constituency preferences. Thus, *normative* assessments of the quality of representation—whether it is good or poor, for example—based on an averaged characterization that ignores the existence of the different models must also be biased or incomplete.

Second, because different studies attempting to assess average representation use different combinations of policy issues to estimate average constituency preferences and legislator roll call vote positions, the findings of those studies can differ for these research design considerations alone. Any single study might offer only a distinctive, distorted characterization of representation. Thus, the comparability of different studies can be compromised, and the findings of research across different ones cannot cumulate to a valid overall depiction of even the average character or process of representation.

In light of the preceding discussion, a fundamental goal for research on representation should be to develop rigorous evidence that either confirms or disconfirms the expectation that different models of representation arise on different policy issues. Research of the latter sort should also lead to an understanding of the conditions under which—or one might say the reasons why—different models arise on different issues, if they do. And such an understanding should ideally accumulate into a systematic theory of representation.

But even brief consideration of the alternative models suggests a second puzzle: Does the prevalence of the different models change under conditions of higher or lower polarization between the two major parties? As is widely known, the major parties have advocated especially different ideological preferences on very many issues since the late 1990s. Thus, the parties are said to be highly *polarized* because they are highly unified internally but also widely separated from each other in their ideological stances. Yet such polarization is unusual in the post–World War II era. Perhaps, then, responsible-party representation predominates today, and belief-sharing, delegate, and trustee representation have largely disappeared. Conversely, the latter models of representation might have been more common in periods of lower polarization and partisan representation less common. To complicate the preceding concerns and to heighten their importance, several recent studies provide evidence that members of Congress are today much more ideologically extreme than their constituencies and argue that constituency representation might be entirely compromised for that reason, although the accuracy and meaning of such evidence has been challenged.[4]

In sum, two important puzzles have not been addressed by contemporary scholarship. First, do the alternative models of representation commonly arise, and if they do arise, under what conditions? And second, does the prevalence of the alternative models rise or fall with varying levels of polarization? Because contemporary scholarship has not addressed the first of these questions, it also cannot provide an answer to the second one. Yet our recent research, reported in detail in our book *Representation in Congress: A Unified Theory* provides a systematic theory to solve the first of these puzzles. That theory also logically implies how one can address the second puzzle, as we do here.

The Party Polarization and Issue Complexity Theory of Constituency Representation

A scientific theory is a leap of intellectual faith. One creates a theory based on consideration of past research and intuition about how a comprehensive explanation for some phenomenon, like constituency representation, arises and the forms it might take. Such a theory might be simple or complex, and it might seem compellingly commonsensical or radically nonsensical. Yet one must marshal sufficient empirical evidence for any such theory to convince other scholars that it is meritorious.

The construction of theory can also be deliberate or remarkably casual, and one can cite examples of both sorts in every science. Perhaps because it is a young discipline, political science has many so-called theories that are casually—or one could say poorly—developed and stated. We have sought to be highly deliberate and "transparent" in the creation of our theory, and the full exposition of the theory in *Representation in Congress* explains, in detail, the assumptions on which it is based, the key concepts for (or attributes of) the policy issues it includes, and the predictions based on those assumptions and attributes. The full theory includes lengthy discussions of those several parts. Here, we only summarize the ones that are especially fundamental for understanding the theory.

Constituency Representation in Congress   123

The theory assumes, first, that different models of representation can arise simultaneously on different policy issues. That is, members of Congress will be voting on different bills in ways that indicate they are providing different forms of representation at the same time. The type of representation they provide on each issue—that is, the model of representation indicated by their roll call voting—will also be shaped by two factors. One factor is how easy or difficult particular policy issues are for the general public to understand and, thus, whether constituencies demonstrate discoverable, relatively liberal or conservative policy positions that might guide legislator behavior. The second factor is how polarized the parties in Congress have themselves been, in liberal versus conservative positions, on the issues. When the national parties have distinctive positions on issues, they also send signals that might affect legislators' roll call voting. Thus, we have named this the *party polarization and issue complexity theory* based on the importance of these critical determinants of when different models of representation arise. We also assume that specific issues can evolve over time in terms of which model of representation they evoke, as abortion, civil rights, and social welfare policy (as but three good examples) have been demonstrated to evolve in past scholarship.[5] Such *issue evolution* comes about when the complexity of an issue for public understanding or the parties' relative positions on it change notably.

Principally based on the preceding assumptions, our theory predicts that five different models of representation exist in congressional roll call voting, with different models applying to different types of policy. Figure 5-1 presents a depiction of how the two primary attributes of policy issues discussed above relate to the appearance of these five models. We also explain, in modest detail, how these attributes are expected to generate each particular model.

Figure 5-1 Models of Representation Predicted to Arise Under Varying Conditions of Party Polarization and Issue Complexity

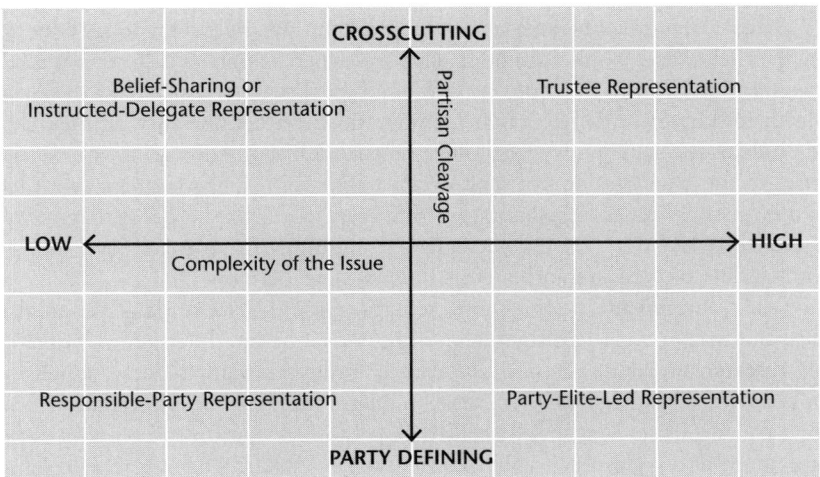

The theory predicts that *responsible-party* representation will arise on policy issues that are easy for the public to understand—thus, on which legislative constituencies can easily form identifiable preferences—*and* on which the two major parties have well-established polarized positions among both their elite and general-public members. The theory anticipates, further, that incumbent legislators will respond more to the preferences of their constituency copartisans than to those of the full constituency on such issues but also that the policy preferences of legislators themselves and those of their constituency copartisans mutually influence and reinforce each other. As we state in our book, "Partisan constituents expect the continuation of the policies on such issues, and elected members of the party reinforce such expectations through continued emphasis of the party's commitment to such policies."[6] Observe, too, that incumbent legislators share the preferences of the bulk of their fellow partisans in Congress, as well as of their constituency copartisans, on such issues. Thus, one might say they are encouraged to sustain their commitment to specific policies on such issues by a signal from their colleagues in Congress and one from their copartisan constituents.

In an especially notable contrast, as depicted in Figure 5-1, the theory anticipates that *trustee* representation will arise on policy issues that are difficult for the public to understand (and thus, on which it is difficult for constituencies to reach a consensus preference either among the full constituency or in its Democratic or Republican subsets) *and* on which the parties in Congress are themselves internally divided. On such issues, members of Congress have no signal from either their fellow partisans in Congress or from their full or copartisan constituencies for what position they should adopt. They then have the necessity—or the luxury—of adopting policy positions based on their own judgments. A good deal of research has uncovered instances of such trustee representation where legislators make policy decisions on personal grounds, such as their religious preferences or personal experiences or on beliefs about what policy is in the best interest of the nation.[7]

Belief-sharing or *instructed-delegate* representation arise when policy issues are easy for the general public to understand and when members of both parties, in the general public and in Congress, might adopt the same position on the issues. Indeed, the theory anticipates that Democratic and Republican constituents will widely share the same policy preference on such issues. And because the national parties in the Congress do not send distinct signals to their members about how to vote on such issues, legislators are free to respond to the constituency-wide preference (which also means they are responding to their mass copartisans in their districts, as well as to other constituents there).

Belief-sharing and delegate representation, then, share some common attributes. But they are distinguished in an important way that draws upon ideas from early research on representation *and* that is highly relevant to some contemporary behavior of members of Congress. Scholarly students of representation in the 1950s and 1960s were especially sensitive to the fact that on some policy issues, there might be a widespread policy consensus in a constituency that the legislator for the district disagreed with but felt compelled to follow. Lewis Anthony Dexter observed, after interviews with members of Congress in the 1950s, that many of them understood that their constituents held strong preferences on some policy issues that they themselves disagreed with, and "when the chips are down . . . they will vote against their convictions and for their constituents' preferences."[8] Many other scholars offer evidence for such *delegate* representation, where the legislator bows to a widespread preference in the constituency he or she does not share.

Belief-sharing issues, in contrast, are ones where the member of Congress personally shares the consensus policy position in the district. In his classic study of U.S. senators, Donald R. Matthews refers to this as a "natural harmony between the views of the senator and his constituents."[9] In such cases, members of Congress are expected to vote in response to the widely shared position among their constituents, but they are not compelled to do so against their own preferences, as in the case of delegate representation.

One broad category of belief-sharing policy issues might be casually called "apple pie and motherhood" ones. Bills before Congress that would provide new material benefits to members of the armed forces, veterans, or their families are good examples from that category. Yet at times, major foreign-policy issues, as well as ones on many other topics, have engendered widespread public consensus, as well as consensus among both Democrats and Republicans in Congress and thus have induced belief-sharing representation. As one example, in recent election campaigns, many Democratic and Republican members of Congress have aggressively promoted the facts that they are gun owners, hunters, and perhaps even members of the National Rifle Association, and for these reasons, they are opposed to new laws that would regulate gun ownership. Most of these legislators represent congressional districts or states where gun ownership is common and where many constituents share the legislator's views.[10] Such members of Congress are actively promoting the fact that they share their constituents' policy views on this topic and thus are exhibiting behavior compatible with the belief-sharing model.[11]

Our theory also identifies a final model of representation, which we label the *elite-led model*, that has not been discussed in earlier research on representation but that is compatible with much of what we know about party-elite behavior in Congress. The theory predicts that this model will arise on policy issues that are difficult for the general public to understand and thus take clear positions, but on which the party elites in Congress are highly polarized. The theory also predicts that on such issues, the only representational "linkage" will be from the preferences of members of Congress to those of their constituency copartisans. Issues like this doubtless arise from time to time, and it is widely recognized that members of Congress and party leaders attempt to "lobby" their constituents to adopt the policy preference of the party elite. Some of these efforts succeed, and thus, the linkage from incumbent legislators' preferences to those of their mass copartisans will eventually be observed. But many efforts of this sort have also failed.

Evidence in Support of the Party Polarization and Issue Complexity Theory

The value of a scientific theory is best illustrated in the degree to which it predicts successfully the phenomena it is intended to explain. To satisfy the latter criterion, we mounted a large number of tests of the predictions from the theory about *when* alternative models of representation should arise and for some of the underlying details about *why* they arise under those circumstances. The most rigorous and complete evidence comes from investigation of ten policy cases, drawn from the late 1950s to the early 2000s. Complete tests of the expectations for when specific models of representation occur require data that are very difficult to acquire, thus limiting the number of cases we could subject to complete analysis. Yet the findings of these analyses provide strong support for the theory.

As examples, analyses of data on abortion policy in the early 2000s and on social welfare policy in the late 1950s and early 2000s confirmed our prediction that responsible-party representation would arise because all three of these cases demonstrated high party polarization and were easy for the general public to understand. Comparably, civil rights policy in the late 1950s, military spending policy in the early 1980s, and social welfare policy in the late 1970s all demonstrated belief-sharing representation, as was predicted, because they were easy for the public to understand, and both parties in Congress took generally the same political position on them, *or* they were sufficiently divided that members could defer to their constituents' preferences in light of the weak "signal" from their fellow partisans in Congress. Finally—and again, as predicted based on their attributes on measures of issue easiness and of party polarization—abortion policy in the late 1970s and foreign policy in the late 1950s demonstrated trustee representation.[12]

In addition to the comprehensive theory tests summarized above, we assembled data to test more limited implications of the theory for a number of other policy issues, including AIDS funding in the late 1990s (a responsible-party issue), defense spending in the late 2000s (a belief-sharing issue), gun control in the early 1990s (a weakly belief-sharing issue at this time), prayer in school in the late 1990s (a party-elite-led issue), support for the Strategic Defense Initiative in the late 1990s (a trustee issue), and support for the Violence Against Women Act in the late 2000s (a belief-sharing issue). All of these tests also produce evidence in support of the theory.

Indeed, some of the latter tests provide especially valuable information. The tests for the ten policy cases that we examined more intensively confirm predictions from the theory about *when* different models of representation arise (evidence for so-called causal effects). But some of the less comprehensive tests provide evidence for *why* different models arise in particular circumstances (evidence for so-called causal processes).

Polarization in American Politics and in Congress and Its Implications for Constituency Representation

The preceding sections of this essay indicate that our theory provides a good explanation for the patterns of representation provided by members of the Congress to their constituents. That is, the theory provides a good explanation for representation, as we will say, *at any one time*. Yet the theory can also help explain how patterns of representation will change as party polarization varies from relatively low to relatively high.

News accounts, as well as many scholarly works, often suggest that the rise of high party polarization in contemporary times has carried all arenas of policy in its wake so that all policy issues have become polarized into conservative-versus-liberal questions. Additionally, given how dominant polarization seems to be in contemporary politics, it may be difficult to imagine how the policy views of the Democratic and Republican members of Congress might be expressed in other ways. But high party polarization has not always been the norm in American politics. And we first illustrate the different political climates of periods of high and low polarization with two sets of quotations taken from leading candidates in United States presidential elections placed fifty years apart.

In the first set of quotations—both from the first presidential debate in 1960—the Republican, Richard M. Nixon, and the eventually victorious Democrat, John F. Kennedy, almost compete to take moderate stands on a variety of important societal issues. Now considered to be an almost impossible goal, Senator Kennedy tries to convey an ambition to expand social programs without spending undue amounts of federal money:

> There have been statements made that the Democratic platform would cost a good deal of money and that I am in favor of unbalancing the budget. That is wholly wrong, wholly in error . . . my view is that you can do these programs—and they should be carefully drawn—within a balanced budget if our economy is moving ahead.

Concurrently, Vice President Nixon attempts to justify a pro-government stance that would interfere in local and state issues like education, even extending a willingness to pledge federal money for local salaries:

> Now, why should there be any question about the federal government aiding teachers' salaries? Why did Senator Kennedy take that position then? Why do I take it now? We both took it then, and I take it now, for this reason: we want higher teachers' salaries. We need higher teachers' salaries.

Vice President Nixon makes special note of his agreeing with Senator Kennedy's roll call votes on using federal monies to raise teachers' salaries. In turn, Senator

Kennedy makes a special effort to pair his commitment to new government spending and programs with a balanced federal budget. Both of the latter two policy positions—federal (rather than local) spending on education and a balanced federal budget—would be described today as *extreme* and thus *polarizing* political issues, belonging to the Democratic and Republican parties, respectively. Yet in 1960, both candidates staked moderate positions on these two policies that bridged the party aisle.

Contrast those positions with ones offered by presidential candidates in 2016. Donald Trump, the Republican front-runner at the time of the writing of this chapter, launched his Republican presidential bid not with a bipartisan commitment to education spending but with a unilateral promise to "build a great wall" separating the United States from its southern neighbor, Mexico.

> I will build a great wall—and nobody builds walls better than me, believe me—and I'll build them very inexpensively. I will build a great, great wall on our southern border, and I will make Mexico pay for that wall. Mark my words.

Even absent the flamboyant rhetoric on his wall-building prowess, a campaign promise for a physical wall illustrates a severe shift toward more ideological policy. And compare this statement with one by Democratic presidential candidate Senator Bernie Sanders, who has made a variety of campaign promises reminiscent of ones he gave in a *Washington Post* interview in 2009, promising to work toward a single-payer health care system.

> If the goal of health care reform is to provide comprehensive, universal health care in a cost-effective way, the only honest approach is a single-payer approach.

Regardless of the eventual winner of the presidential election, neither of the preceding two proposals is likely to be enacted into law after the 2016 election unless one political party wins control of both the presidency and the full Congress. But these divergent promises indicate especially clearly the shift in ideology that has occurred over time—not just among the politicians who offer policy proposals but in the constituents who demand them and who vote in the primary elections for candidates who make them. And while we have used examples of moderate and polarized policy positions from presidential candidates because of their prominence, virtually every Democrat or Republican running for election to Congress today could be quoted for extreme—and therefore polarizing—ideological positions.

The puzzle this presents to contemporary *legislators* is how to represent constituency interests as the positions of the two major parties in Congress have grown more extreme *and* as the preferences of their respective Democratic or Republican constituents have also grown more extreme compared to the full constituency. The puzzle this presents to *scholars* is how a theory of representation can predict the character of representation that we should observe under conditions of higher or lower party polarization. The party polarization and issue complexity theory is uniquely advantaged to address the latter puzzle.

Polarization, Lawmaking, and Representation in Congress

To illustrate how our theory can help account for the character of representation under varying conditions of polarization, it is first useful to summarize how party polarization has varied across time. Such variations are well documented, and they indicate that the parties themselves have changed dramatically over time. The two major American parties were principally ideological and competing—that is, highly polarized—through much of the nineteenth century. Then, they entered a period of ideological overlap as a result of the failed laissez-faire governmental stance toward business that led to the Great Depression, the short-term decline of the Republican Party in the 1930s, and the dominance of the Democratic Party, which led the country out of the Great Depression and through World War II and the early postwar period.[13]

Figure 5-2 further offers a graphic representation of polarization in the U.S. Senate and the House from 1947 to 2012, for what might be called the modern Congress. The measures here are based on ratings of how liberal or conservative the roll call voting of each party was in a given chamber and year from the Americans for Democratic Action (ADA) lobby group, adjusted so as to be comparable over time.[14] The numbers on the y-axis of the figure indicate the absolute value of the difference between the means of the adjusted ADA ratings of each party in each house of Congress. Thus, higher scores indicate greater polarization in each chamber. As one example, Figure 5-2 shows that the measure of polarization for both chambers is in the range of seventy to seventy-five in the late 2000s. A score of one hundred would indicate that the roll call voting of the two parties was exactly opposite from each

Figure 5-2 Polarization by Chamber

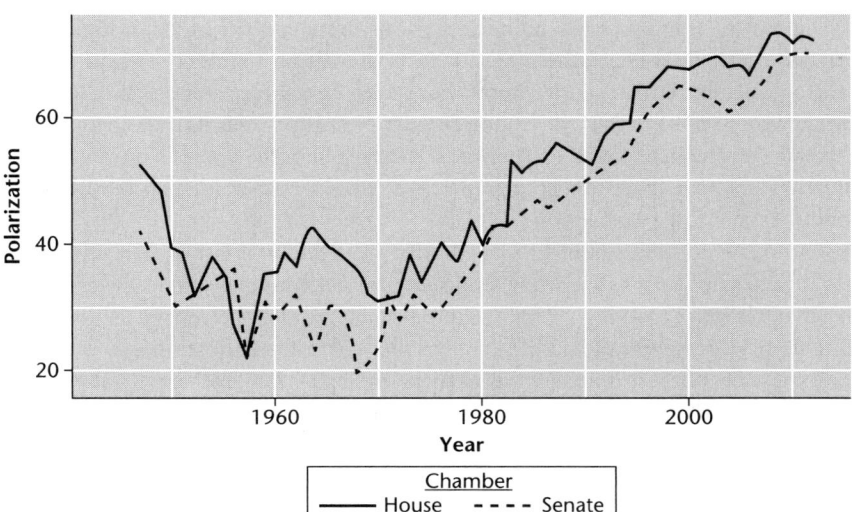

Source: See endnote 14.

other in liberal versus conservative ideology. Scores in the mid-seventies, then, mean that overall roll call voting is very highly, if not exactly, opposite for the two parties.

Figure 5-2 also indicates that the parties were relatively less polarized in the period of the late 1950s and into the early 1970s. Indeed, polarization scores in the range of twenty to thirty in both chambers of Congress in the 1960s indicate that roll call voting was very much bipartisan. Polarization began to rise in the measures in Figure 5-2 in the late 1970s. The data in Figure 5-2, as well as other commonly used measures of polarization, also indicate that the parties became especially polarized in the late 1990s and continue to be so today. That is, their ideological centers of gravity are widely separated, and most members of each party are close to their respective centers in roll call voting.

The causes of the recent upsurge in polarization have been the subject of considerable investigation, but their effects are less well understood. Research by Soren Jordan and Barbara Sinclair, however, finds that polarization influences the lawmaking process in the House of Representatives in an intuitively logical way. In the circumstance of high polarization, the majority party especially controls the rulemaking and roll-call-voting processes to ensure it gets legislation adopted that is compatible with its ideological center of gravity, thus leading to more ideologically extreme policy.[15] As the parties become more polarized, the work of lawmaking also deviates from the classic textbook congressional process where, when bills appear on the floor, there is ample time for debate and amendments by members of both parties. Instead, under high polarization, much more of the lawmaking process occurs in the majority-party-dominated committees and particularly the committees with disproportionate influence over the rules. And the minority party has few opportunities to influence proposed legislation once it gets to the floor of the House.

If lawmaking becomes more ideologically extreme in periods of high polarization, then members of the majority party are voting together for bills that are ideologically extreme. And we know from even casual observation of day-to-day congressional politics that the minority party typically wages its own ideologically extreme counterefforts, even if they must mostly fail in the face of a unified majority. But how does the "landscape" of representation differ in such periods from that in eras of low polarization?

Our previous research did not confront the latter question. Yet our theory has logical implications for what representation should look like in different eras of polarization. These logical implications arise because the theory distinguishes models of representation with regard to the role of polarization on *individual* policy issues. That is, it recognizes that the major parties are highly polarized on responsible-party and elite-led issues but not on belief-sharing, delegate, or trustee ones. The complete elaboration of the theory also implies that in a period of high polarization, the full agenda of Congress must be especially heavily populated with responsible-party issues and less heavily populated with belief-sharing issues than in a period of low polarization. And the fact that the aggregate measure of polarization in Figure 5-2 rises to a high level in contemporary times is independent confirmation of this logical implication of the theory.

While the theory itself does not explicitly address the following point, it is our intuition that issues that evoke belief-sharing, delegate, and trustee representation are likely to occur across all levels of polarization. The theory anticipates that issues that are easy for the public to understand and that crosscut the usual lines of party cleavage will evoke belief-sharing or delegate representation. Comparably, it anticipates that issues that cut across the lines of party cleavage and that are difficult to understand will lead to trustee representation. Our prior research uncovered issues of all of these types, even during the current period of high polarization, and we suspect they are likely to arise in notable numbers in any period.

In summary, the logic of our theory, our additional intuitions, and the general evidence in Figure 5-2 indicate that in any period, we should observe a diverse political agenda composed of issues that evoke all of the various models of representation. What should especially change as the parties polarize is the relative number of issues that fall into categories that can be broadly described as party defining or crosscutting.

But we can make a stronger case for the preceding argument based purely on theory, intuition, and very general evidence. To do so, we have assembled new empirical evidence about how representation on a subset of individual issues varied across time as polarization in Congress rose from the low period in the 1960s to the high period today. Recall that earlier we cited research on issue evolution, where the operating model of representation on a particular issue changed over time. The existing research on that topic assumes that the specific issues it considers—and the most important research of this sort has examined abortion, civil rights, and social welfare policy—have evolved in this way for idiosyncratic reasons. But the logic of our theory and the numerical implications of steeply rising or falling polarization imply that there are systematic processes at work that shape the model of representation on a host of issues simultaneously. We provide novel evidence on these systematic processes. This evidence also complements the preceding argument about how the theory logically anticipates patterns of representation under different levels of polarization.

To provide evidence on how party polarization changed on specific policy issues over time, we searched the Policy Tracker research tool in the *CQ Almanac* online edition.[16] The Policy Tracker provides all of the stories written by *Congressional Quarterly* reporters over almost seventy years about debates in Congress on a long list of specific policy issues. For this analysis, we collected information from this source on party polarization on roll call votes on three issues that have evoked responsible-party representation in contemporary times—abortion, climate change, and gun control policy—as well as four that were demonstrated in our previous research to evoke belief-sharing representation—military appropriations, the regulation of lurid acts and pornography, veteran affairs, and social welfare for women.

For each of the preceding seven issues, we identified a sample of roll call votes from Policy Tracker stories from the 1960s through the first decade of the present century and grouped these roll call votes by decade. We then generated a measure of the polarization of the roll call votes on each issue in the House of Representatives in each decade, which we call a measure of *opposition*. If approximately equal proportions of both parties vote in the same direction, this measure would tend toward zero. If the two parties vote in large numbers in opposite directions, the measure would tend toward a large positive number, with a maximum value of two. Thus, larger scores on this measure indicate more party polarization on a given issue.

We present the opposition scores on these policy issues as an illustrative but not definitive characterization of how party polarization on them evolved as the aggregate policy agenda became increasingly polarized. Recall, however, the intuitions from our theory that we offered earlier that all of the models of representation will always appear regardless of the level of polarization while the balance among those models will shift toward responsible-party issues with increasing aggregate polarization. If those intuitions and the circumstances under which the theory anticipates individual models of representation will arise are both correct, then we should see evidence in the opposition scores for all of them.

Figure 5-3 presents the opposition scores from the 1960s through the 2000s for the seven issues, and the issue-specific patterns there conform to all of our expectations. The three issues that have recently been responsible-party ones demonstrate remarkable increases in polarization in roll call votes over the period of increasing aggregate polarization. That is, the evidence in Figure 5-3 indicates that those issues only modestly divided the parties during the period of low polarization of the 1960s and 1970s. But those issues evolved to where they now reflect very high partisan divisions.[17]

In contrast, the four issues that our prior research found to reflect considerable bipartisan consensus and usually belief-sharing representation were not remarkably changed from that characterization as aggregate polarization rose. Perhaps, not surprisingly, concern in Congress with pornography, veteran affairs, and aid for women demonstrate low party polarization through the entire time series in Figure 5-3. Yet polarization on the often contentious subject of military appropriations has not risen to particularly high levels. Recent polarization scores in the range of fifty to sixty for that issue indicate that the modal roll call vote had substantial majority support from both parties in Congress.

In sum, the evidence in Figure 5-3 suggests that increasing aggregate polarization largely came about by dramatically enhancing the longtime, if incomplete, tendency for Democrats to vote relatively liberally and Republicans to vote relatively conservatively on a range of specific issues. Yet Figure 5-3 also confirms our earlier conclusion that crosscutting policy issues, many of which will demonstrate belief-sharing representation, also arise under all levels of polarization. Thus, the original evidence in Figure 5-3 supports and amplifies our earlier conclusions about how the landscape of representation will both, in part, stay the same and, in part, vary as levels of aggregate party polarization change.

Figure 5-3 House Opposition by Issue and Decade

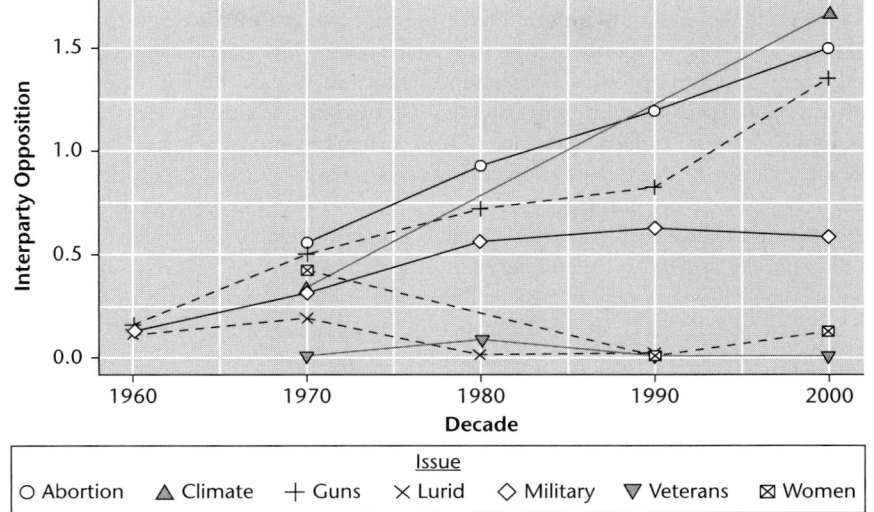

Source: Calculated by authors.

Conclusion

Previous research on congressional politics has not produced a systematic explanation of how members of that body represent the preferences and interests of their constituents. For that reason, such research cannot explain whether constituencies are well or poorly represented, whether they are represented well under some conditions and not others, or whether representation will take different forms on different issues. We built upon the voluminous body of prior research, however, and crafted a theory that accounts systematically for how representation occurs. We adopted the *models of representation* typology from early research, which anticipated that belief-sharing, delegate, responsible-party, and trustee models would arise on different individual issues but which itself could not predict when and why those different models would arise in particular instances. Our *party polarization and issue complexity theory* offers explanations for both when and why these models individually arise. For that reason, it can be labeled a *unified theory* in that it accounts for all of the alternative models of representation conventionally identified in scientific research.

One could also conclude that the different models of representation arise as members of Congress make rational decisions about how to vote on proposed legislation. And some of their decisions and the conditions under which they arise produce representation that we believe would be widely endorsed. When constituencies at large and legislators themselves share policy preferences, the *belief-sharing* model will arise. At least in many instances when constituencies have very strong and widely held preferences that legislators do not share, they will bow to those constituency preferences and provide *delegate* representation.

When members of Congress have no clear policy "instructions" from their national party or their constituency, they make policy decisions based on their own judgment and thus provide *trustee* representation. Given the conditions under which such representation generally arises, however, it is difficult to be critical of such behavior. Indeed, Americans have often accepted that they must defer to the wisdom of their elected representatives on some issues, especially ones of this sort.[18] Finally, when legislators, their copartisans in the Congress, and their copartisans in their constituencies all share a preference on some policy issue, they will generally vote with that preference and provide *responsible-party* representation. Some observers may be especially uneasy about the normative implications of such representation, but we address those concerns momentarily.

We have also presented new evidence for how our theory helps anticipate patterns of representation under varying levels of party polarization. That evidence indicates the kinds of specific policy issues, especially in terms of which model of representation they conventionally evoke, that contribute to aggregate polarization and the kinds that do not. In general, issues that were at least moderately responsible-party ones before the dramatic increase in overall polarization of recent decades were ones where the legislators of the two major parties diverged even more dramatically over time. This phenomenon is compatible with other accounts of change in Congress in this period. But our evidence also demonstrates—and likely uniquely—that issues which conventionally induce belief-sharing, delegate, or trustee representation do not contribute to aggregate polarization. Further, the landscape of polarization continues to be populated with issues of the latter three types even in the current period of high polarization.

Finally, we return to an early observation in this chapter: that many political scientists and doubtless many members of the general public fear that high party polarization today is eroding the quality of congressional representation. Those fears, we argue, are not always based on a full consideration of the factual character of representation. We suspect that most of this concern is about the fact that responsible-party issues—for which legislators' constituency copartisans get the best representation—are especially numerous today. Yet a series of additional observations might mitigate some of that concern.

Consider that a notable majority of Americans today claim a psychological preference for one of the two major parties. Gallup Poll data from early 2016 indicate that almost 90 percent of Americans identify either as strong partisans of one or the other major party, weak partisans of one of them, or as independents who lean to one of the parties (and who tend typically to vote like weak partisans).[19] That is, most Americans especially identify with the major policy positions their preferred party distinctively holds, which would be, of course, on responsible-party issues. Thus, such individuals who are represented in Congress by legislators of their preferred party get good representation on the issues they evidently care especially about.

Further, the most politically attentive members of the general public also tend to be the most partisan. These individuals also especially benefit (through policy representation) from being copartisans of their member in Congress. Moreover, these individuals are strongly predisposed to reject policy compromise for partisan victory.[20] Instead, they prefer their member to hold out for stronger policy positions that better reflect the preferences of the party. Even if the average member of the public were to reject the partisanship of Congress, it would be rational for legislators to maintain high levels of partisanship if the most attentive voters preferred this strategy. And we reiterate, our theory predicts unique benefits for these copartisan identifiers as more issues become party defining.

If there is reason to be concerned about high party polarization today, in our view, it is because neither party has been able to gain full control of the presidency and Congress long enough to translate its policy agenda into law. A policy achievement of that sort would provide a clear basis for public assessment, in subsequent elections, of that agenda and of its alternatives. In the current state of what has been called policy gridlock, however, where no party can succeed with its agenda, partisans of all stripes have reason to be discontented, although not necessarily with the representation they get from their own members of Congress.

Notes

1. Kim Quaile Hill, Soren Jordan, and Patricia A. Hurley, *Representation in Congress: A Unified Theory* (New York: Cambridge University Press, 2015).
2. Warren E. Miller and Donald E. Stokes, "Constituency Representation in Congress," *American Political Science Review* 57 (1963): 45–56.
3. A variety of other scholars have proposed that different policy issues might stimulate different patterns of lawmaking and perhaps representation. The most noted of such works are Aage R. Clausen, *How Congressmen Decide: A Policy Focus* (New York: St. Martin's Press, 1973), and John S. Lapinski, *The Substance of Representation: Congress, American Political Development, and Lawmaking* (Princeton, NJ: Princeton University Press, 2013). But such work has not attracted much attention from other scholars, perhaps because it has not produced systematic theory based on the assumption that different policy issues evoke different kinds of representation.
4. Evidence that members of Congress and the political elite generally are more ideologically extreme than the constituencies of members and the general public predates the current period of high party polarization, as demonstrated in Christopher H. Achen, "Measuring Representation," *American Journal of Political Science* 22 (1978): 475–510, and in Herbert McClosky, Paul J. Hoffman, and Rosemary O'Hara, "Issue Conflict and Consensus Among Party Leaders and Followers," *American Political Science Review* 54 (1960): 406–27. Recent research like that of Joseph Bafumi and Michael C. Herron, "Leapfrog Representation and Extremism: A Study of American Voters and Their Members in Congress," *American Political Science Review* 104 (2010): 519–42, provides contemporary evidence for how members of Congress are more ideologically extreme than their constituencies. However, Robert S. Erikson and Gerald C. Wright, "Voters, Candidates, and Issues in Congressional Elections," in *Congress Reconsidered*, 8th ed., ed. Lawrence C. Dodd and Bruce I. Oppenheimer (Washington, DC: CQ

Press, 2005), 97–98, provide evidence from public survey data that suggests this is not necessarily the case. Further, a number of studies, such as that of James Adams, Benjamin G. Bishin, and Jay K. Dow, "Representation in Congressional Campaigns: Evidence for Discounting/Directional Voting in U.S. Senate Elections," *Journal of Politics* 66 (2004): 348–73, indicate voters generally prefer election candidates who are more ideologically extreme than they are.

5. On the evolution of abortion policy in terms relevant to which model of representation was operating for it at different historical times, see Greg D. Adams, "Abortion: Evidence of an Issue Evolution," *American Journal of Political Science* 41 (1997): 718–37. For the evolution of civil rights policy, see Edward G. Carmines and James A. Stimson, *Issue Evolution: Race and the Transformation of American Politics* (Princeton, NJ: Princeton University Press, 1989). For social welfare policy, see Patricia A. Hurley and Kim Quaile Hill, "Beyond the Demand-Input Model: A Theory of Representational Linkages," *Journal of Politics* 65 (2003): 304–26.

6. Hill, Jordan, and Hurley, *Representation in Congress*, 43–44.

7. For recent evidence that legislators' personal values can lead to trustee roll call voting see, Barry C. Burden, *Personal Roots of Representation* (Princeton, NJ: Princeton University Press, 2007), and Elizabeth Anne Oldmixon, *Uncompromising Positions: God, Sex, and the U.S. House of Representatives* (Washington, DC: Georgetown University Press, 2005). For recent evidence for trustee roll call voting in the interest of good public policy, see Edward L. Lascher Jr., Steven Kelman, and Thomas J. Kane, "Policy Views, Constituency Pressure, and Congressional Action on Flag Burning," *Public Choice* 76 (1993): 79–102, and John A. Hird, "The Political Economy of Pork: Project Selection at the U.S. Army Corps of Engineers," *American Political Science Review* 85 (1991): 429–56.

8. Lewis Anthony Dexter, "The Representative and His District," *Human Organization* 16, no. 1 (1957): 2–13.

9. Donald R. Matthews, *U.S. Senators and Their World* (Chapel Hill: University of North Carolina Press, 1960), 231, note 26. Matthews recognizes that this harmony may not extend to positions on all policy issues, but he argues it is associated with especially important political values and preferences in senators' home states.

10. The contrast between what we have called apple pie and motherhood issues and gun control suggests another reason why systematic theory is valuable. Apple pie issues produce comparable belief-sharing representation *across* legislative constituencies. But gun control likely produces belief-sharing representation in some constituencies and responsible-party representation in others. A conventional empirical analysis of representation might discover instances of the former sort, but a nuanced theory of representation would help one uncover both sorts.

11. Richard F. Fenno Jr., *Home Style: House Members in Their Districts* (Boston: Little, Brown, 1978), 59, refers to such behavior as an attempt by a legislator to earn the trust of his or her constituents by demonstrating that, "You can trust me because we are like one another." Thus, shared political values anticipated by the belief-sharing model of representation can be a foundation for trust between constituents and legislators.

12. Two other policy cases—campaign finance reform in the late 1990s and gun control policy in the 2000s—did not have sufficiently clear combinations of issue easiness and party polarization scores to make confident predictions for the model of representation they should reflect. In addition, we were unable to discover cases of delegate or party-led representation for which data to test our predictions were available.

13. For more detailed evidence on the evolution of polarization in Congress, see Richard Fleisher and John R. Bond, "The Shrinking Middle in the US Congress," *British Journal of Political Science* 34 (2004): 429–51; Soren Jordan, Clayton McLaughlin Webb, and B. Dan Wood, "The President, Polarization, and the Party Platforms, 1944–2012," *The Forum* 12 (2013): 169–89; B. Dan Wood and Soren Jordan, "Electoral Polarization: Definition, Measurement, and Evaluation," paper delivered at the American Political Science Association Annual Meeting, Seattle, September 4–6, 2011.
14. The original polarization scores for the House and the Senate come from Tim Groseclose, Steven D. Levitt, and James M. Snyder Jr., "Comparing Interest Group Scores Across Time and Chambers: Adjusted ADA Scores for the U.S. Congress," *American Political Science Review* 93 (1999): 33–50. The time series was updated to 2007 by Sarah Anderson and Philip Habel, "Revisiting Adjusted ADA Scores for the U.S. Congress, 1947–2007," *Political Analysis* 17 (2009): 83–88, and to 2012 by Soren Jordan.
15. Soren Jordan, "Polarization and Lawmaking Over Time: A Detailed Test of Conditional Party Government," paper delivered at the Conference on Parties and Polarization in American Government, College Station, TX, April 23–24, 2014; Barbara Sinclair, *Unorthodox Lawmaking: New Legislative Procedures in the U.S. Congress* (Washington, DC: CQ Press, 2000).
16. The *CQ Almanac* online Policy Tracker is available at http://library.cqpress.com/cqalmanac/toc.php?mode=cqalmanac-policy.
17. Comparable analyses for the Senate, not reported for limitations of space, indicate over-time patterns of representation compatible with those for the House.
18. Thomas E. Cronin, *Direct Democracy: The Politics of Initiative, Referendum, and Recall* (Cambridge, MA: Harvard University Press, 1989), 1–9.
19. These data were retrieved from http://www.gallup.com/poll/15370/party-affiliation.aspx on March 14, 2016.
20. Laurel Harbridge and Neil Malhotra, "Electoral Incentives and Partisan Conflict in Congress: Evidence From Survey Experiments," *American Journal of Political Science* 55 (2011): 494–510.

6. Black–Latino Relations in Congress
Examining Inter–Minority Group Relations in Institutional Context

Rodney E. Hero and Robert R. Preuhs

This essay expands on previous studies of relations between Blacks and Latinos, as they exist in the U.S. Congress. We explore whether different and perhaps more cooperative relationships are formed between these groups in national politics, as juxtaposed to local politics. We first consider votes identified as important to Black and Latino interests by two prominent minority advocacy groups, the National Association for the Advancement of Colored People (NAACP) and the National Hispanic Leadership Agenda (NHLA); we then examine the level of support that minority and other members of Congress (MCs) give to the NAACP and NHLA positions on the scorecards of important votes. These analyses reveal a striking departure from the findings on Black–Latino relations indicated in research focused on urban government and other political activities. Rather than conflict, which is basically absent, the two minority advocacy groups and—importantly here—Black and Latino MCs primarily engage in "independent" or cooperative behavior. Politics at the national level—and specifically in the nation's premier legislative body—indeed differs from other venues. Our theory and findings thus underscore the relevance of institutional context, and further, this has implications for contemporary and future minority intergroup relations.

Virtually all of the research on relations between Black and Latino political groups in the United States has focused on local and urban, rather than national, governmental institutions. This research finds that *conflict* rather than *cooperation* characterizes Black–Latino relations, so that a "rainbow coalition" of Blacks and Latinos is more a hope than a reality in American politics.[1] The major explanation for this conflict is the frequent zero-sum competition between Black and Latino groups over scarce resources that exist for minority groups at the local, urban, and even state level, such as jobs, political offices, and governmental services. Reflecting the tenor of the local and urban literature on Black–Latino relations, Claudine Gay's 2006 study concludes that "idealized notions of 'natural' intergroup comity and mutual support collapse when confronted by a finite number of public and (low-skilled) private sector jobs; by the lack of educational resources to meet the needs of black children and Spanish-speaking Latino children; by a shortage of adequate and affordable housing; and by the desire among both groups for descriptive political representation on neighborhood councils, on school boards, and in municipal government."[2]

Nevertheless, the concentration of research on relations between Black and Latino political groups at the local or subnational levels, we will argue, creates a distorted picture of the potential for cooperation among Blacks and Latinos within the nation at large and particularly within its major representative institution, the U.S. Congress. While Black and Latino groups may often be pitted against one another in subnational politics, the nature of public policy at the national level more often emphasizes general concerns about equality, group inclusion, and equitable distribution of broad policy benefits that can unite Black and Latino groups. These concerns, moreover, characterize many of the most visible and important policies of the national government—ranging from civil rights, affirmative action, welfare, and Medicaid to macroeconomics, banking, finance, and immigration. If, as prominent political scientist Theodore Lowi has argued, "policy (frequently) shapes politics," then the factors that shape policy at the national level may well create a different kind of politics than the factors shaping policy at the subnational level.[3]

Our goal in this essay is to expand the study of Black–Latino relations to the American Congress. We seek to determine whether different and perhaps more cooperative relationships, in fact, exist between these groups in national politics, as juxtaposed to localized politics. We begin by examining the votes identified as important to Black and Latino interests by two prominent minority advocacy groups, the National Association for the Advancement of Colored People (NAACP) and the National Hispanic Leadership Agenda (NHLA). These votes serve as the basis for evaluating the degree to which advocacy groups demonstrate cooperative, conflictual, or independent behavior as they attempt to influence Congress. We then turn to evidence on the level of support that members of Congress (MCs) give to the NAACP and NHLA positions on the scorecards' important votes. Both analyses reveal a striking departure from the findings of the local and urban literature. Instead of conflict, which is basically absent, the two minority advocacy groups—and importantly, Black and Latino MCs—tend to primarily engage in independent or cooperative behavior. Politics at the national level indeed differs from local- or urban-level politics, with important implications for contemporary and future minority intergroup relations.

Inter–Minority Group Relations and Institutional Context

The political context in which Black and Latino groups and their respective descriptive representatives act may be significantly different in national institutions, providing compelling reasons to examine Congress further. *Politics* differs across levels in a federal system, and *the nature of Black–Latino relations* could be expected to differ as well. Along with institutional factors, the particular nature of the *minority* groups, especially their situation or place within the American social and racial hierarchy, requires attention as well, similar to what Gay described (earlier) and as others have articulated with the concept of *two-tiered pluralism*.[4]

This leads us to consider evidence beyond what has been examined previously to further (re)assess our claims regarding these assertions.[5]

Our contention is that in the national decision-making arena, policies more often have an ideological dimension and are facilitated by the role of the party (here, belonging to the same [Democratic] party) in congressional policy making. This ideology is oriented toward civil rights and substantive equality and is more strongly manifest through national policies and institutions. When issues are (substantially) salient for each group's interests, they overlap or, at least, do not directly conflict; thus, *non*conflict is more prevalent. Yet the degree to which issues are (highly) salient for *both* groups is modest. Furthermore, an array of related evidence—including Black and Latino advocacy groups' amicus brief filings on Supreme Court cases, along with evidence presented later—all demonstrates that independence or nonconflict dominate.[6] Conflict, however, was almost completely absent.

Minority Interest Groups: Salience and Congruence on Congressional Votes

Few studies have considered issues of Black–Latino relations in national-level institutions, such as Congress.[7] Yet some recent studies of congressional voting and advocacy group behavior, as well as interactions with the Supreme Court, suggest that rather than conflict suggested by local-level studies, nonconflict (or independence) and cooperation are more prevalent at the national level.[8] Politics differs across levels, and thus, we should be cautious about extending findings from one level to another. Herein lies the justification for closely examining Black–Latino relations in Congress, as well as the benefits of expanding the time frame beyond that examined in previous research to include the last decade, a period which witnessed strong growth in the minority (particularly Latino) population.

At the heart of our evaluation of the degree of Black–Latino relations in the congressional context are congressional scorecard ratings for members of the U.S. House of Representatives from two prominent Latino and Black advocacy groups, the National Hispanic Leadership Agenda and the National Association for the Advancement of Colored People, respectively. Congressional scorecard ratings evaluate members of Congress based on the positions they take on key votes in Congress that the advocacy groups identified as being important to their group's membership and constituencies. Each MC receives a rating based on the percentage of votes that aligned with the position of the advocacy group. A zero rating on the NHLA scorecard, for instance, indicates that the MC voted against the NHLA's positions on all identified votes, whereas a 100 percent rating would indicate complete support of NHLA positions; the same interpretation applies for NAACP scorecard ratings.

In subsequent sections, we use the NHLA and NAACP scorecards to gauge the degree of cooperation or conflict among Black and Latino MCs as they consider the other group's interests in formal roll call voting decisions, but these ratings also indicate the nature of Black and Latino advocacy group relations. We thus begin by looking at the types of votes in the scorecards and the degree to which each group identified the same votes (shared *salience*) and took the same position on those votes (*congruence*). A lack of salience suggests independence among the groups, whereas congruence suggests at least a degree of cooperative behavior in the interests they seek to represent.

The NAACP scorecards provide measures of MC support from the 104th through the 113th Congresses (1995–2014), reflecting twenty years of this Black advocacy group's preferences over specific sets of votes. The NHLA produced scorecards from the 105th through the 108th (1997–2004) and, after a hiatus, for the 113th (2013–2014). Figure 6-1 presents the distribution of votes included in all of these scorecards, broken down by the issues the votes addressed and whether only the NAACP, the NHLA, or both groups included the vote in their scorecard. The scorecards varied in terms of policy emphasis, as Figure 6-1 demonstrates, and cover an array of issues, from civil rights to education to immigration and even international relations. While the more numerous Congresses covered by the NAACP led to more overall votes, the key point from Figure 6-1 is

Figure 6-1 Vote Counts for NAACP and NHLA Scorecards, by Topic

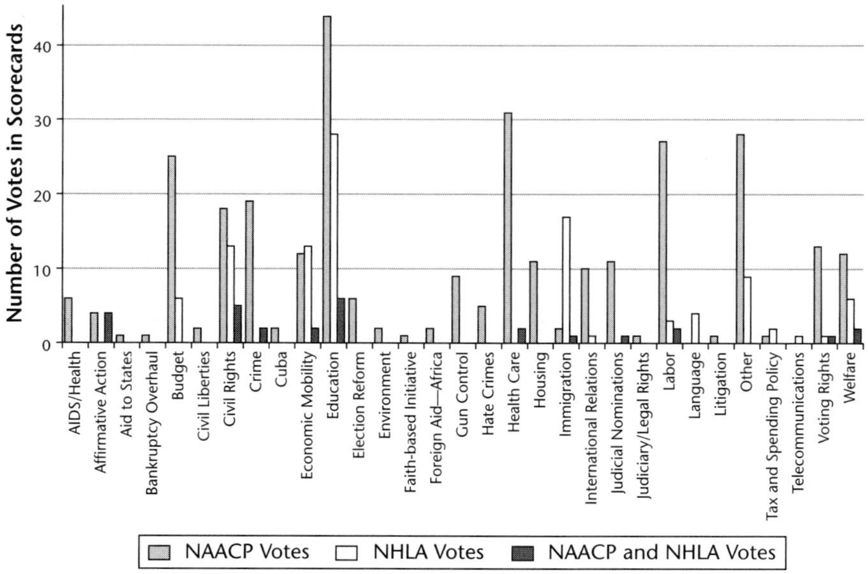

Note: NAACP = National Association for the Advancement of Colored People. NHLA = National Hispanic Leadership Agenda. Counts of votes identified on NAACP and NHLA scorecards are presented. "NAACP and NHLA Votes" are votes included in both groups' scorecards. Categories are mutually exclusive. For the NAACP, counts are based on scorecards from the 104th to the 113th Congresses. For the NHLA, counts are based on scorecards from the 105th to 108th and the 113th Congresses.

that very few votes were identified by *both* groups (about 8.5 percent during the Congresses with ratings from both groups). Thus, while both groups often emphasized broadly similar *issues*, they seldom identified the same *votes* as salient to their group's interests.

This point is yet more apparent in Table 6-1, which presents the total vote counts for each advocacy group by whether each identified the vote alone or if the vote shared salience (both groups identified the vote as important to include in the scorecard), by Congress. It also presents the percentage of these shared-salience votes, where the same position was taken (yea or nay) by both groups. The statistics in Table 6-1 reflect the general lack of overlap (or common salience) in votes seen in Figure 6-1, but there is some variation, with more shared salience in the 105th through the 107th Congresses, which then began tapering in the 108th Congress, where only three votes were included in both scorecards. In the 113th, *only one* was included in both groups' scorecards. At the same time and importantly, the data reveal a complete absence of conflict. On each and every roll call vote in the House of Representatives that both the NHLA and NAACP identified as salient, they never took opposing positions; for salient votes, congruence occurred 100 percent of the time. In short, a vast majority of votes (about 90 percent overall) included

Table 6-1 Shared Salience and Congruence on Votes on NAACP and NHLA Scorecards, 105th–108th and 113th Congresses

Congress	NAACP Votes	NHLA Votes	Shared Salience (Votes Identified by Both Groups)	Congruence (Percentage of Shared Salience Votes With the Same Outcome Preferred)
105th (1997–1998)	23	33	7	100%
106th (1999–2000)	30	36	6	100%
107th (2001–2002)	50	34	12	100%
108th (2003–2004)	63	24	3	100%
113th (2013–2014)	14	6	1	100%
Total	180	133	29	100%

Note: NAACP = National Association for the Advancement of Colored People. NHLA = National Hispanic Leadership Agenda. Since shared salience and congruence can only be determined for Congresses with both groups' scorecards, we omit the counts of votes for the 109th through the 112th Congresses.

in both roll calls were distinct between the NHLA and NAACP scorecards. But when Black and Latino advocacy groups concurred and identified the same significant votes, they always agreed. For these two major minority advocacy groups, though mostly viewing and assessing issues independently, there was no sign of conflict and a modicum of cooperation—behaviors that diverge from the local-level studies, which have suggested conflict between Blacks and Latinos.

A second point regarding the votes included in the NHLA and NAACP scorecards is that issues important to these advocacy groups varied over time and often reflected a changing congressional and national policy agenda. For instance, in the 113th Congress (2013–2014), five of the seven votes included in the NHLA scorecard related to immigration (none of which were included in the NAACP scorecard). NHLA scorecards from the 105th to 108th Congresses focused more on education issues (almost 27 percent of all votes) and civil rights (about 14 percent) and less on immigration (about 10 percent). The NAACP's scorecards varied by Congress as well. In the 113th Congress, the most frequent votes concerned labor and welfare issues (about 21 percent each), but in the midst of votes dealing with the economic recovery and the Obama administration's health care reforms in the 111th Congress, labor and health care topped the list, with about 15 percent of scorecard votes each. And the NAACP also included the DREAM Act, which was intended to provide some relief from deportation for children of undocumented immigrants, as a salient vote in their 111th Congress scorecard.

In sum, scorecards provide a basis for observing minority advocacy groups' salient issues and concerns, as well as the degree to which those issues are shared between Black and Latino groups. In this sense, there was a great deal of independence, with some interspersed overlap in salience. No conflict is observed—and again, this is fundamentally different than the pattern observed at the local level. More importantly for present purposes, scorecards can also be used to measure the degree to which MCs support Black and Latino interests, and that is the focus of the subsequent analysis.

Black and Latino House Members' Voting on the Minority Interest Group Scorecards

NAACP and NHLA scorecards indicated an absence of conflict between Black and Latino advocacy groups. Does the same hold for Black and Latino members of Congress? Employing NAACP and NHLA scorecard ratings of members of Congress to gauge the level of mutual support, we first describe and discuss the general voting patterns of minority—Black and Latino—members, as well as of nonminority Democrats and Republicans. Recall that for the 104th and then for the 109th through 112th Congresses, we have data for NAACP scorecards but not for NHLA scorecards. Additionally, the analyses of voting patterns of minority descriptive representatives (Black and Latino members) are necessarily confined to the House of Representatives because there were very few Black or Latino members of the U.S. Senate during the period analyzed. Our second step in analyzing MCs' voting behavior controls for a variety of additional factors related to the MC's legislative district and constituency, thus providing a more rigorous test of whether Black–Latino conflict emerges in Congress.

Comparing Means of NAACP and NHLA Scores: A General Analysis

To begin, Figure 6-2 presents data on the average ratings on NAACP and NHLA scorecards of MCs, categorized by their party affiliation and racial or ethnic group background. Recall that ratings potentially range from 0 to 100, and the average for each group indicates the general level of support for Black and Latino interests, respectively, across the groups we examine. As would be expected, this initial evidence demonstrates that Black Democrats rated very highly on the NAACP scorecard (see top chart of Figure 6-2), with the average support score ranging from 88.9 per Figure 6-2 percent in the 104th Congress (the only time the average was below 90 percent) to 98.6 percent in the 105th. In all but one Congress, Black Democrats had the highest average support score for NAACP positions. Moreover, Black Democrats also consistently displayed high NHLA ratings, including the highest average ratings on NHLA scorecards in the 105th, 108th, and 113th Congresses. Along with high scores on the NHLA ratings, Latino Democratic MCs generally rated quite high on the NAACP indicator (with one exception, the 104th Congress), and in one instance (the 107th Congress), Latinos actually rated slightly higher than Black Democrats on this measure (refer to the bottom chart of Figure 6-2). Latino Democrats maintained higher NAACP ratings than White Democrats, though not always by a large amount, averaging 6.7 points higher across the ten Congresses (104th to 113th). Overall, there is some amount of preliminary evidence that Latino and Black Democrats are more supportive of both Black and Latino interests than are other Democrats. We can interpret this, albeit cautiously, as a heightened level of cooperation across groups, especially when compared to their partisan counterparts.

Another point in Figure 6-2 is notable. Though few in number, Latino Republican MCs rate higher than White Republicans on the NHLA scorecards. The former average over nineteen points higher than the latter over the five Congresses (105th to 108th, and 113th), and Latino Republicans also had higher NAACP support scores than White Republicans in seven of the ten Congresses examined. Hence, while Latino Republicans have much lower ratings than Latino Democrats and are broadly similar to White Republicans overall, they nonetheless initially appear to have somewhat higher scores on "Latino-salient" issues than do White Republicans.

The basic and consistent pattern that Black and Latino Democratic lawmakers tend to support their own groups' interests highly, as well as the interests of the other minority group, and to a greater extent than do other lawmakers underscores the general orientation of nonconflict (and perhaps implicit cooperation) in the

Figure 6-2 Mean NAACP and NHLA U.S. House of Representatives Scorecard Ratings, by Party and Black and Latino Representative

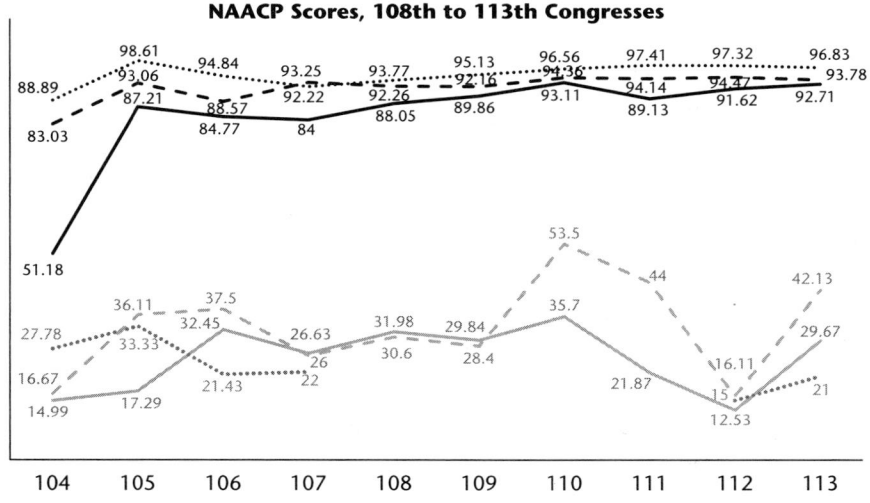

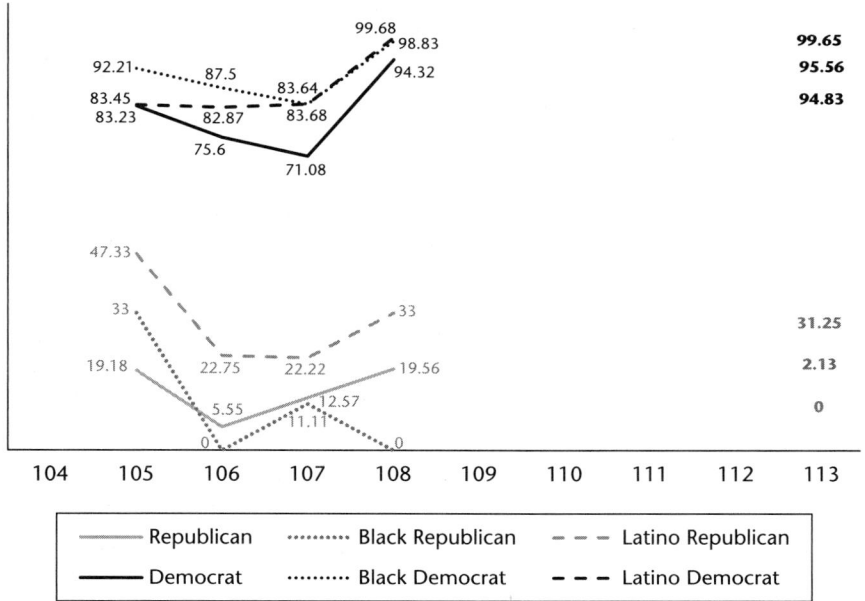

realm of congressional voting. Conflict does not seem to be present, as would be indicated by lower average scores, for instance, for Black Democrats on NHLA positions relative to other Democrats. Clearly, party matters, and it is obviously a source of cross-group support, as is the racial or ethnic background of the MC. However, other factors that likely affect the degree of congressional support for minority issues need to be accounted for before we can be certain that Black–Latino conflict is limited to decisions to support Black or Latino interests in Congress. Do these patterns of heightened cross-group support still hold when other factors, especially political party affiliation but also the nature of the MC's constituency, are considered?

Controlling for Other Factors in MC Support: Multivariate Analysis

While there seems to be a high degree of compatibility with Black or Latino interests and broader "liberal" policy orientation, as we just saw, there are differences between NHLA and NAACP scorecard ratings of House members, which can be leveraged to examine the nature of intergroup relations and voting behavior more precisely. A good deal of research relevant to such concerns has addressed the extent of influence of Black and Latino members of Congress on policy, assessing issues of both *descriptive* and *substantive* representation.[9] These studies consider whether minority members actually vote differently than others and thus whether descriptive representation (Black MCs representing Black constituencies, for instance) really matters. There have also been parallel studies focused on *state* legislatures.[10] Political party (and/or ideology) is clearly the most important factor, yet Black and Latino MCs also tend to be stronger advocates for their coracial or coethnic group constituents than others (as we have seen in our first set of analyses).

To this point, however, we know little of Black and Latino legislative voting patterns *on issues of concern to each other* and thus the effect of descriptive representation on cooperation or conflict in the congressional arena.[11] It is thus essential to not only consider the degree to which members of Congress vote on issues identified by minority advocacy groups but also to consider other factors that might explain those voting patterns. We start by acknowledging that the MCs' party is the most important factor in cross-group support. Throughout the Congresses for which we have data, Democrats are universally more supportive of NHLA and NAACP votes than Republicans. This partisan divide complicates a more systematic analysis since very few minority MCs are Republicans, nor are Republicans generally elected from districts with large minority populations (the types of districts most likely to elect minority descriptive representatives). There are simply too few comparable cases from which to draw conclusions that distinguish between the effects of party, the racial or ethnic background of the MC, and the characteristics of the district's population. To overcome this empirical reality, we stipulate that party affiliation is a factor, which comports with previous research.[12] And we thus focus only on Democrats in assessing how Black and Latino MCs and their districts' characteristics affect support for Latino and Black issues. This allows us to control for party, as the sample is solely of Democrats, and then determine what additional factors affect cross-group support.

The literature suggests that a number of other factors may also affect MCs' voting decisions generally and should be considered in assessing dispositions toward the agendas of Black and Latino national advocacy groups. Black and Latino representatives are each included as separate variables to evaluate the degree to which descriptive representation's influence, relative to White MCs, remains after controlling for an array of district-level characteristics that have been shown to affect or are plausibly related to support for minority advocacy group interests.[13] Since officeholders likely respond to constituency pressures, the models account for the proportion of the population that is Latino, Black, and Asian, as well as the proportion of foreign-born people in each district. If racial backlash influences legislative voting behavior or if there is an increased propensity to oppose minority interests as minority population size increases, higher levels of minority population size would be negatively associated with NAACP and/or NHLA scores.[14] Conversely, minority population size may increase representative support for minority issues, as MCs presumably respond to the interests of their minority constituents.[15]

In addition to the racial and ethnic background of the constituents, we also take account of various general demographic factors shown to influence the voting behavior of MCs.[16] These include the proportion of the district's population with a college degree (education), living in an urban area, and living below the poverty line. Also included are the percentage of the district who voted for the Democratic presidential candidate in the previous election and separate variables for each Congress (omitting the earliest available for each scorecard) to account for differences in overall support for each group's interests across Congresses. Since there are relatively few Black and Latino MCs, even in the House of Representatives, we combine all of the Congresses for which we have data into one sample, although the sample size does vary since NAACP and NHLA scorecards cover different congressional timespans.[17] There will thus be two models—one examining NAACP scores and the other examining NHLA scores—for Democratic House members.

Beyond providing better evidence as to the effect of descriptive representation on cross-group support and the proportion of Latinos and Blacks in the district, the multivariate models help in determining the extent to which Black–Latino cooperation, independence, or conflict exists in congressional voting patterns. Table 6-2 lays out a set of expectations for each of the types of behavior (cooperation, conflict, or independence) for each set of scorecards (NAACP and NHLA) and whether that is exerted through descriptive representation (Black or Latino MCs) and/or through constituency pressures (Black or Latino *population size*).

Based on the direction of the effect (positive or negative) for each variable, the models characterize the way cross-group support plays out in Congress (if it exists) since different types of intergroup relations result in diverging patterns of effects.

For instance, if Black and Latino MCs tend to support each other's positions—indicating compatibility and at a higher degree than with Whites—the effects for the descriptive representative variables should be positive and significant across both scorecards. If Black and Latino descriptive representation only matters regarding support for their (own) respective group's policy positions, and compatibility across groups is not evident in descriptive representation, then we should see a pattern of Black MCs having significantly higher support only on NAACP issues and Latino MCs doing the same for NHLA models. This would suggest not outright cooperation but independence, related to the unique effects of descriptive representation. While the average scores suggest that both groups tend to be more supportive of minority advocacy group positions than Whites (as we saw in Figure 6-1), it is possible that Black MCs' support for NHLA positions and Latino MCs' support for NAACP positions are lower than White support for each after controlling for district and party effects. This competition hypothesis can also be tested: If the Black representative effects are positive in the NAACP models but negative in the NHLA models and/or if Latino representative effects are positive in the NHLA models but negative for NAACP models, then conflict would be indicated.

We can further address the cooperation, conflict, or independence hypotheses at the congressional-district level by examining the differences in the sign of the

Table 6-2 Predicted Effects of Black and Latino Representation and Population on NAACP and NHLA Scorecards

Variable	Cooperation/Compatibility		Tacit Noncooperation/Independence		Conflict	
	NAACP scorecard	NHLA scorecard	NAACP scorecard	NHLA scorecard	NAACP scorecard	NHLA scorecard
Representation						
Black Representative	Positive	Positive	Positive	No effect	Positive	Negative
Latino Representative	Positive	Positive	No effect	Positive	Negative	Positive
Population						
Proportion Black	Positive	Positive	Positive	No effect	Positive	Negative
Proportion Latino	Positive	Positive	No effect	Positive	Negative	Positive

Note: Cell entries report the direction of the expected effect. No effect indicates there is an expected null relationship.

relationships for the racial and ethnic minority constituency size variables and comparing those to the effects of descriptive representation. Following the line of reasoning in the discussion earlier and presented in the bottom half of Table 6-2, if larger Latino populations are positively associated with support for NHLA positions but negatively associated with support for NAACP positions and if Black population size is positively associated with support for NAACP positions but negatively associated with support for NHLA positions, competition, channeled through constituency factors, is suggested. If both Latino and Black population variables are positively associated with NAACP *and* NHLA scores, then there is evidence of not only substantive representation but cross-group support arising from responsiveness to districts' racial and ethnic characteristics. Finally, noncooperation or independence would be suggested if positive effects for the population variables are present in only their respective group's scorecard and are not significantly (and not negatively) related in the other group's model. In short, by controlling for districts' racial and ethnic characteristics and comparing results across NAACP and NHLA scorecards, we can determine the form and degree of Black–Latino relations in Congress.

Beyond addressing the primary concern of Black–Latino relations, the additional variables included in the model help to determine how well each of these general explanations performs when examining the specific votes identified by Black or Latino groups. While extensive research exists on broader measures of MCs' voting behavior, testing the effect of socioeconomic variables on minority-specific scorecards is less common. Doing so should provide additional insight into how minority interests diverge from or coincide with what we know about congressional behavior in general.

The results of the two models are presented graphically in Figure 6-3, which is based on an OLS regression analysis.[18] The independent (or explanatory) variables included in the models are listed on the left. The estimated effect of each variable is plotted within the body of the figure, with a diamond relative to the zero line. Effects that fall to the right of the zero line are positive while effects to the left are negative. The short horizontal lines by the diamonds are confidence intervals, which reflect the uncertainty in our estimates. (When the intervals are shorter, we are more certain of our estimates.) If the confidence intervals cross the zero line, there is too much uncertainty in the estimate to describe it as either a positive or negative effect. Black diamonds (and lines) are the effects on the NAACP ratings while gray diamonds (and lines) correspond to the effects on NHLA scorecard ratings.

It is also important to note that the effects of the Black and Latino representative variables are reported *relative to White (Democrat) representatives* (which is the reason a White representative variable is not included). For instance, the positive effects for Black representatives on both the NAACP and NHLA scorecards simply mean that Blacks are more supportive of both groups' interests than are White Democrats. No effect, which is denoted by horizontal confidence intervals that cross the zero line, for either type of MC means that they are no more supportive than White Democrats. So what drives support for minority advocacy group positions among Democratic members of Congress?

Figure 6-3 Estimated Coefficients (90% and 95% CIs) for Pooled Models of NAACP and NHLA Support Scores for Democratic Members of Congress

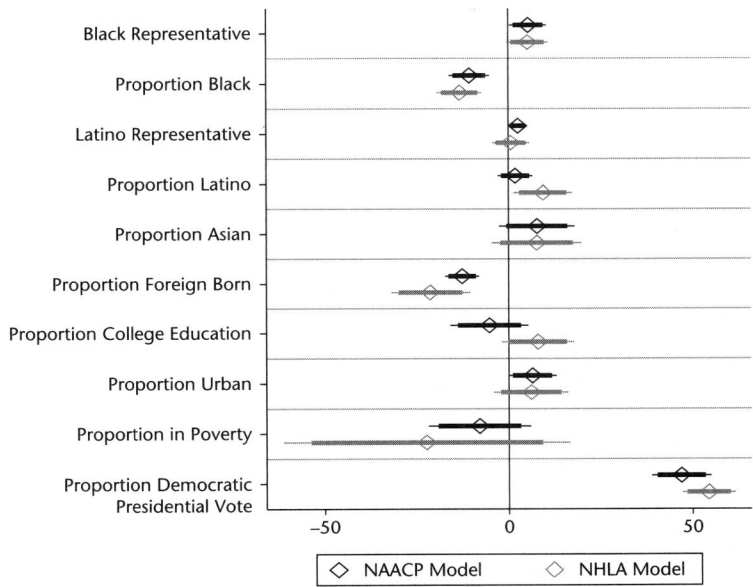

Note: The figure reports the coefficient estimate (diamond) for each variable from the OLS regression models based on pooled data for the available Congresses. Standard errors were adjusted for clustering by Congress. The 90% (thick lines) and 95% (thin lines) confidence intervals are also reported. Dummy variables for each Congress were included in the model but not reported here. For NAACP scores, data cover the 104th to the 113th Congresses (N = 2048; R^2 = .62). For NHLA scores, data cover the 105th through the 108th and the 113th Congresses (N = 1021; R^2 = .51).

The results generally support the contention that the voting behavior of minority descriptive representatives manifests cross-groups support or, at minimum, does not indicate any conflict. Comparing the results in Figure 6-3 with the expectations presented in Table 6-2 regarding NAACP scorecards, we find that Latino MCs tend to support NAACP positions at a higher rate than White Democrats, averaging 2.6 percent higher on the scorecards. Black MCs tend to have higher NHLA ratings than White Democrats, with about 5.3 percent higher ratings on average. The heightened support by the "other" groups' descriptive representatives suggests not only independence—or even partisan orientations, as the sample is limited to Democrats—but Black–Latino cooperation through descriptive representation. An interesting exception is that Latino representatives seem not to be different than White representatives in terms of support for NHLA (or Latino) interests. The effect is positive, but the level of uncertainty means we cannot conclude that Latino Democrats are clearly distinct from White Democrats. Nevertheless, the major concern here is with Black or Latino cross-group support, and there is enough consistency with the expectations to conclude that descriptive representatives are a source of Black–Latino cooperation.

The results presented in Figure 6-3 also do not indicate a pattern of clear intergroup conflict associated with constituency characteristics. The effect for Latino population size is positive for the NAACP support scores, but the level of uncertainty indicates that Latino population size lacks a clear effect in either direction. The negative effect from the size of the black population on NHLA scorecards suggests some backlash linked to Latino issues emerging from districts having larger Black populations. However, the negative effect for the Black population variable in the NAACP model implies that this may be part of a more general backlash against minority interests, as opposed to Black constituencies being less supportive of Latino issues, as well as Black issues. Moreover, the sizes of the effects across models are statistically *in*distinguishable, further indicating a more general rather than specific backlash related to social and demographic change. A similar phenomenon is suggested by the impact of the size of the foreign-born population, with a negative effect estimated for both scorecard models, and this compares to some recent research demonstrating that immigration plays an important role in party orientations among the masses.[19]

Overall, then, the analysis of congressional voting behavior on issues identified as important by prominent Black and Latino advocacy groups, covering a wide span of time, indicates very little, if any, evidence of (direct) conflict in congressional voting between Black and Latino interests and representatives. Political party affiliation clearly plays a strong role, but in addition, Black and Latino Democratic representatives tend to support the other groups' interests through higher levels of scorecard ratings than do other, White Democrats. Moreover, the racial and ethnic composition of the district, though a factor, does not seem to exert influence consistent with minority intergroup conflict. Scorecard ratings of MCs are dampened by increasing Black populations, whereas support for Latino interests increases as Latino population increases. In sum, the voting patterns of Black and Latino representatives suggest that nonconflict and independence—and perhaps some (implicit) cooperation—are the norm regarding policy concerns of the other group.

A final point regarding the analysis should be recognized. Apart from the strong influence of the districts' presidential preference, which shows that districts with more Democratic supporters tend to be represented by MCs with stronger support levels for NAACP and NHLA issues, very few of the "standard" explanations of congressional voting seem applicable to minority group concerns. Districts' levels of education, urban population, and poverty are all *un*related to NAACP and NHLA scorecard ratings in general. This underscores the unique nature of minority politics, which is evident (even) in processes and voting patterns in this important national policy-making institution, the U.S. House of Representatives.

Independence and Cooperation in National Institutions

While emerging narratives of Black–Latino intergroup relations suggest that conflict is common, much of this research focuses on subnational politics and, typically, zero-sum contexts where competition over political representation and economic opportunities occurs. However, in the realm of national institutions, such as Congress, where ideology (and political party) plays a larger role, and interests are more likely to either coincide, or *non*-zero-sum policies are more probable, Black–Latino independence and cooperation are manifest.

Why is there an apparent lack of minority intergroup conflict at the national level, as we have shown in the preceding sections? Our explanation, which we now more fully elaborate, is that the federal system creates distinct institutional contexts and policy authority that also shape the politics that emerge at different levels of government and, in turn, (minority) intergroup relations. Ideologically based policies are more prominent in Congress than, say, city council decisions, and the shared ideology of the minority groups tends to mitigate potential conflict. Furthermore, the role of political parties in Congress clearly plays a role that helps foster ideologically based coalitional activity. The clear distinction in levels of support for NHLA and NAACP positions between Democrats and Republicans underscores the importance of parties in government to understanding Black–Latino political relationships. Interests also play a role, and when interests overlap in the national context, we would expect compatibility; when they do not, independence or noncooperation is likely to emerge, on the assumption that there is an underlying shared ideology. And it is not uncommon that one group views an issue as important while the other group does not; that lack of shared salience is important to note, as is the high policy congruence when there *is* a shared sense of salience. Inter–minority group collaboration *does* emerge in Congress and seemingly rather more frequently and broadly so than in other venues or access points of American governance.

The geographic arena (the *sphere* or *scope*) of authority or decision making, a consequence of the American federalism framework, itself shapes policy, as was argued by Madison (*The Federalist* No. 10) and has been rearticulated by various contemporary scholars.[20] Hence, decision making in Congress is rather different in its breadth and would be expected to have different dynamics and implications than those of local- or state-level legislatures and governments. Furthermore, policy shapes the nature of politics (sometimes as much as the reverse), as is also widely agreed upon.[21] It thus stands to reason that geographic breadth and the policies at stake would also shape intergroup relations and politics. Because the types of policy responsibilities of the national government are unique, we might also expect inter–minority group relations to diverge from what has been found in local or subnational contexts.

Two-Tiered Pluralism as Manifested in National Politics

While the policies considered at the national level differ due to the federal structure of American political institutions, a second element distinct to minority politics interacts with this reality that likely constrains conflict at the national level. Pluralism, a commonly used framework, interprets American politics as grounded in numerous groups advocating on behalf of their members in a system where there is roughly equal resource footing across interest and advocacy groups and multiple "access points" through which influence can be pursued.[22] It contends that groups form coalitions as they seek to advance and/or compete with other groups over policies and benefits in the political system. The political system is subsequently responsive to various groups at various times, and responsiveness to citizen preferences is based on the ability of individuals with shared concerns to form effective advocacy groups and, in turn, group coalitions. Inter–minority group relations would, by implication, seem to be partly a matter of cooperating when policy preferences are shared across their constituencies, though competing when preferences are not shared.

Yet pluralism often does not adequately recognize that racial and ethnic minorities commonly face socioeconomic impediments, political-resource constraints, and racialized politics, all of which cast doubt on the basic assumption of an "equal playing field." Group-based politics for racial and ethnic minority groups may, in general, be better understood as *two tiered*, with minority groups facing a different set of political and socioeconomic challenges as they engage in politics from the second tier. *Both* Blacks and Latinos are largely in the "second tier" of politics due to their (shared and lower) socioeconomic status, combined with a racialized status.[23] This injects a "horizontal" dimension and some degree of commonality to Black–Latino relations, as both seek not only group-specific interests (as presumed by pluralism) but also share a common ideology of equality and gaining equal access to political, economic, and social institutions due to their second-tier status.

Second-tier status means that disadvantaged minority groups quite often seek similar policy goals; however, when they do not, at the national level, they are less likely to face situations where their interests collide, which would undermine the broader ideological grounding for their coalition. The consequences of the policy advocated by one minority group may not be perceived to have the same effect on the other, as it does on largely White "first-tier" interests or in the zero-sum policies often prevalent at the local level. Policy advocacy at the national level by one second-tier group can simultaneously be perceived as competition with groups in the first tier but not competition among groups that share second-tier status. In short, two-tiered pluralism, along with the geography of politics and policy authority associated with federalism, may interact and affect the likelihood that different Black–Latino relations emerge at different levels of government.

Minority Intergroup Relations in the Context of Federalism

Tendencies in the Patterns of Interests and Ideology Across Levels

To further consider inter–minority group relations at the national level and to offer explanations of those relations, we describe some general tendencies in intergroup relations associated with the salience of issues and (if salient) how relations are affected by the intersection of groups' ideologies and interests. That conflict is not the predominant mode of Black–Latino relations at the national level and that the degree of conflict could vary according to geographic scope and (related) policy type also suggest that the nature of Black–Latino relations do not only have the commonly assumed conflict *or* cooperation forms. We could see less conflict (than often found in urban-level studies), in part, because there might be lower levels of salience attached to and less direct overlap between competing material interests in the broader national-level policy arena. Minority groups and their (interest group) advocates might be more able to pursue their own group's goals while relatively seldom reacting strongly (negatively or positively) to other groups' policy positions. And policies that do overlap will also be less conflictual, for several interrelated reasons, including that they do not entail zero-sum circumstances and are moderated by ideological convergence. This is the key interaction between two-tiered pluralism and policies often considered at the national level—a higher likelihood of *non*-zero-sum policies and concurrent ideological orientations—that produces less conflict. These points are summarized in Table 6-3.

Inter–minority group relations and potential coalitions may be more or less similar based on their convergence or divergence of interests and ideology.[24] We suggest these are important and (also) vary according to the levels or arenas of government and lay out some of the potential outcomes. Interests are often understood in terms of whether policies are viewed as more or less win/lose or zero sum by groups affected by the issues. It can be the case that interests may not clash (or cause conflict) because one or the other (or both) of the groups does not see certain issues as particularly salient or as a high priority; when that occurs, the likelihood of conflict diminishes, and we suggest this tends to happen more often at the national rather than the local level. Ideology pertains to whether groups share similar basic egalitarian, civil rights, social justice, or socioeconomic values. Our assumption is that Black and Latino representatives indeed share those beliefs strongly and consistently; that is linked to their strong tendency to identify with one party (as Democrats) but also seems to go beyond just party.[25]

Following the implications of the two dimensions of ideology and interests (and also recognizing that in actual practice, interest and ideology may blur or be otherwise ambiguous to some extent), four broad relational possibilities can be identified (refer to Table 6-3). Echoing arguments made throughout this essay, we label these four types of relations as cooperation, conflict, independence, and negotiation. When there is a convergence or agreement between groups on *both*

Table 6-3 Summary of Expected Intergroup Relationships

Ideology and Interests*		Expected Intergroup Relations	Relative Frequency of Conditions (Low to High) in Local and National Institutions
Shared ideology High	Shared interests High	No conflict (cooperation or comity)	LOCAL Low
	(less often zero sum)		NATIONAL Moderate
Shared ideology Modest to high	Shared interests Low to modest	Little or no conflict Independence (possibly negotiation)**	LOCAL Moderate
			NATIONAL High
Shared ideology Low	Shared interests Low	Conflict	LOCAL High
	(more often zero sum)		NATIONAL Low

* Interests are (also) very much affected by the authority for different policies, and types of policy authority and policy types are different at the national level versus the local level.
** It is possible for independence and negotiation to lead to similar empirical observations, and thus, we include both types of relations and observations in the same cells.

ideology and interests, *cooperation* would be expected. Conversely, *conflict* would be highest when there are differences or disagreements in terms of both ideology and interest (more zero-sum policies). We would expect that interest divergence is more common than ideological divergence between Blacks and Latinos because to a considerable degree, there is general consensus around concerns and support for civil rights, equality—both racial/ethnic and economic—and related values. How those values actually apply across groups in particular policies and circumstances—that is, where interests come in—can be a source of tension. But the broad ideological agreement presumably tempers the tension and may even help channel it away from overtly conflicting outcomes.

Apart from the circumstances we identify regarding conflict and cooperation, other types of relations are murkier. However, where there is basic agreement on ideology but a difference of interests, *independence* may be possible,[26] particularly on issues that are not equally or highly salient to both groups. Thus, groups may not be in direct conflict and may simply be independent or "go their own way" under such conditions. Ongoing discussion seeking to establish mutually acceptable policies is likely. This may lead to a type of "distributive" politics where the substantive differences are not fully resolved and to policy positions where "there's a little something for everyone." Symbolic or recognition politics may also take place. Lastly, *negotiation* possibly occurs where there is ideological disagreement, and interest concerns are not clearly at stake or diverge. Again, the assumption is that there are relatively few instances of ideological divergence because minority advocacy groups most often (though not always) share broader purposive goals. Latinos and Blacks have been seen as parts of liberal coalitions in urban politics and, similarly, as being in Democratic and liberal coalitions in state politics.[27] Furthermore, both groups strongly support Democratic candidates in congressional and presidential elections (with a few notable exceptions), and both groups are also liberal on economic policy. We expect these tendencies would be clearer and stronger in national politics than in local politics.[28] Thus, closer attention is given here to independence than cases of ideological divergence. Overall, the extensive evidence presented in the various analyses above has, we think, generally affirmed our central theoretical arguments.

Conclusion

Growing racial and ethnic diversity in the United States is well known. Most Americans witness this in their communities, in their states, and at the national level. For Latinos and African Americans, diversity has recently been accompanied by a growing tension at the local level—a relationship documented in studies of urban politics and in various public opinion research. However, as we have shown, conflictual relationships in the congressional arena—at least in both scorecard votes selected by advocacy groups *and* the roll call voting patterns of Black and Latino MCs (on those scorecards)—are strikingly absent. Shared ideology and partisanship, the policies considered at the national level, and likely other factors lead to more independence and cooperation than at the local level.

The United States has evolved from a largely "bifurcated" racial context that varied by region (Black–White politics in the Southern states and Northern industrial states; and Latino–White politics in much of the Southwest and West) to a more heterogeneous context across the country. The demographic composition of Congress echoes, though does not entirely reflect, these population trends. While below parity in both chambers, African Americans are closer than Latinos in the House with 10.1 percent of the 435 seats. Combined, Latinos and African American legislators now account for just under 20 percent of the U.S. House membership and over a third of the Democratic Caucus. Thus, understanding the nature of relations between Black and Latino interests and representation in Congress takes on greater importance than any time in history. Our results suggest that multiracial coalitions are evident between minority MCs, unlike the conflict observed at local levels that is often attributed to the tensions of a diversifying context. Conflict is part of the congressional process and is growing by several measures. Yet Black–Latino relations in this arena over the last twenty years or more depart from this trend and contrast starkly with what has been found regarding Black–Latino relations in other places in the political system.

Whether and, if so, how much this ultimately mitigates the racial and related socioeconomic inequalities that have long persisted in American politics is highly debatable. Nonetheless, having a better sense of the limitations of and some possibilities for inter–minority group relations and how the potential for coalitions is conditioned by the context of American institutions is worth pursuing. That is especially so for the U.S. Congress, given its fundamentally important place in the American polity.

Notes

1. For a discussion of conflict, see Claudine Gay, "Seeing Difference: The Effect of Economic Disparity on Black Attitudes Toward Latinos," *American Journal of Political Science* 50, no. 4 (2006): 982–97; Karen M. Kaufman, "Cracks in the Rainbow: Group Commonality as a Basis for Latino and African-American Political Coalitions," *Political Research Quarterly* 56, no. 2 (2003): 199–210; Nicolas C. Vaca, *The Presumed Alliance: The Unspoken Conflict Between Latinos and What It Means for America* (New York: Ray, 2004).
2. Gay, "Seeing Difference." For more studies echoing this general finding, see Michael Jones-Correa, "Commonalities, Competition and Linked Fate," in *Just Neighbors?: Research on African American and Latino Relations in the United States*, ed. Edward Telles, Mark Q. Sawyer, and Gaspar Rivera-Salgado (New York: Russell Sage, 2011), 63–95; Paula D. McClain, Niambi M. Carter, Victoria M. DeFrancesco Soto, Monique L. Lyle, Jeffrey D. Grynaviski, C. Shayla Nunnally, Thomas J. Scotto, J. Alan Kendrick, Gerald F. Lackey, and Kendra Davenport Cotton, "Racial Distancing in a Southern City: Latino Immigrants' Views of Black Americans," *Journal of Politics* 68 (2006): 571–84; William E. Nelson Jr. and Jessica Lavariega Monforti, eds. *Black and Latino/a Politics: Issues in Political Development in the United States* (Miami: Barnhardt & Ashe Publishing, 2005); Edward Telles, Mark Q. Sawyer, and Gaspar Rivera-Salgado, eds., *Just Neighbors?: Research on African American and Latino Relations in the United States* (New York: Russell Sage, 2011).
3. Theodore J. Lowi, "American Business, Public Policy, Case-Studies, and Political Theory," *World Politics* 16, no. 4 (1964): 677–715.
4. For an explanation of two-tiered pluralism, see Rodney E. Hero, *Latinos and the U.S. Political System: Two-Tiered Pluralism* (Philadelphia: Temple University Press, 1992).
5. This article builds on previous work regarding Black–Latino relations, in particular Rodney E. Hero and Robert R. Preuhs, *Black–Latino Relations in U.S. National Politics: Beyond Conflict and Cooperation* (New York: Cambridge University Press, 2013). Also see Rodney E. Hero and Robert R. Preuhs, "Beyond (the Scope of) Conflict: National Black and Latino Advocacy Group Relations in the Congressional and Legal Arenas," *Perspectives on Politics* 7, no. 3 (2009): 501–17; Rodney E. Hero and Robert R. Preuhs, "Black–Latino Political Relationships: Policy Voting in the U.S. House of Representatives," *American Politics Research* 38, no. 3 (2010): 531–62; Robert R. Preuhs and Rodney E. Hero, "A Different Kind of Representation: Black and Latino Descriptive Representation and the Role of Ideological Cuing," *Political Research Quarterly* 64, no. 1 (2011): 157–71.
6. Hero and Preuhs, *Black–Latino Relations*. See also Hero and Preuhs, "Beyond (the Scope of) Conflict"; Hero and Preuhs, "Black–Latino Political Relationships."
7. For partial exceptions, see Dianne M. Pinderhughes, "Black Interest Groups and the 1982 Extension of the Voting Rights Act," in *Blacks and the American Political System*, ed. Huey L. Perry and Wayne Parent (Gainesville: University Press of Florida, 1995), 203–24; John D. Skrentny, *The Minority Rights Revolution* (Cambridge, MA: Belknap

Press of Harvard University Press, 2002). See also our own work, Hero and Preuhs, *Black–Latino Relations in U.S. National Politics*.
8. See footnote 5 for a list of studies finding nonconflict as a norm.
9. Studies identifying the unique effects of descriptive representation include Charles Cameron, David Epstein, and Sharyn O'Halloran, "Do Majority-Minority Districts Maximize Substantive Black Representation in Congress?" *American Political Science Review* 90 (1996): 794–812; David T. Canon, *Race, Redistricting, and Representation* (Chicago: University of Chicago Press, 1999); Jason Casellas, "Latino Representation in Congress: To What Extent Are Latinos Substantively Represented?" in *Latino Politics: Identity, Mobilization and Representation*, ed. Rodolfo Espino, David L. Leal, and Kenneth J. Meier (Charlottesville: University of Virginia Press, 2007), 219–31; Rodolfo Espino, "Is There a Latino Dimension to Voting in Congress?" in *Latino Politics: Identity, Mobilization and Representation*, ed. Rodolfo Espino, David L. Leal, and Kenneth J. Meier (Charlottesville: University of Virginia Press, 2007), 197–218; Richard Fleisher, "Explaining the Change in Roll-Call Voting Behavior of Southern Democrats," *Journal of Politics* 55 (1993): 327–41; Christian Grose, "Disentangling Constituency and Legislator Effects in Legislative Representation," *Social Science Quarterly* 86 (2005): 427–43; Rodney E. Hero and Caroline J. Tolbert, "Latinos and Substantive Representation in the U.S. House of Representatives: Direct, Indirect or Nonexistent?" *American Journal of Political Science* 39 (1995): 640–52; M. V. Hood III and Irvin L. Morris, "Boll Weevils and Roll-Call Voting: A Study in Time and Space," *Legislative Studies Quarterly* 23 (1998): 245–69; Vincent Hutchings, "Issue Salience and Support for Civil Rights Legislation Among Southern Democrats," *Legislative Studies Quarterly* 23 (1998): 521–44; David Lublin, *The Paradox of Representation: Racial Gerrymandering and Minority Interests in Congress* (Princeton, NJ: Princeton University Press, 1997); L. Marvin Overby and Kenneth M. Cosgrove, "Unintended Consequences? Racial Redistricting and the Representation of Minority Interests," *Journal of Politics* 58 (1996): 540–50; Christine LeVeaux Sharpe and James C. Garand, "Race, Roll Calls, and Redistricting: The Impact of Race-Based Redistricting on Congressional Roll Call," *Political Research Quarterly* 54 (2001): 31–51; Susan Welch and John R. Hibbing, "Hispanic Representation in the U.S. Congress," *Social Science Quarterly* 65 (1984): 328–35; Kenny J. Whitby, *The Color of Representation* (Ann Arbor: University of Michigan Press, 1997); Kenny J. Whitby and George A. Krause, "Race, Issue Heterogeneity and Public Policy: The Republican Revolution in the 104th U.S. Congress and the Representation of African-American Policy Interests," *British Journal of Political Science* 31 (2001): 555–72.
10. For evidence of the effect of descriptive representation at the state level, see Kathleen A. Bratton and Kerry L. Haynie, "Agenda Setting and Legislative Success in State Legislatures: The Effects of Gender and Race," *Journal of Politics* 61 (1999): 658–79; Kerry L. Haynie, *African American Legislators in the American States* (New York: Columbia University Press, 2001); Eric Juenke and Robert R. Preuhs, "Irreplaceable Legislators? Rethinking Minority Representatives in the New Century," *American Journal of Political Science* 56 (2012): 705–16; Chris T. Owens, "Black Substantive Representation in State Legislatures from 1971–1999," *Social Science Quarterly* 84 (2005): 779–91; Robert R. Preuhs, "Descriptive Representation, Legislative Leadership, and Direct Democracy: Latino Influence on English Only Laws in the States, 1984–2002," *State Politics and Policy Quarterly* 5 (2005): 203–24; Robert R. Preuhs, "The Conditional Effects of Minority Descriptive Representation: Black Legislators

and Policy Influence in the American States," *Journal of Politics* 63 (2006): 585–99; Robert R. Preuhs, "Descriptive Representation as a Mechanism to Mitigate Policy Backlash: Latino Incorporation and Welfare Policy in the American States," *Political Research Quarterly* 60 (2007): 277–92; Robert R. Preuhs and Eric Gonzalez Juenke, "Latino U.S. State Legislators in the 1990s: Majority-Minority Districts, Minority Incorporation, and Institutional Position," *State Politics and Policy Quarterly* 11 (2011): 48–75.

11. Moreover, the studies typically rely on measures of general ideology, which may obfuscate the particular issues of greater importance to minority advocacy groups (and, by implication, minority constituencies). See Canon, *Race, Redistricting, and Representation*, 290–91, for criticisms of these. For exceptions, see Andy Baker and Corey Cook, "Representing Black Interests and Promoting Black Culture: The Importance of African American Descriptive Representation in the U.S. House," *Du Bois Review* 2, no. 2 (2005): 1–20; Hero and Tolbert, "Latinos and Substantive Representation."

12. Scholars often need to combine Congresses to estimate effects of small groups on voting behavior. Examples of studies that take this approach to understanding the effects of descriptive representation are Hero and Tolbert, "Latinos and Substantive Representation"; Grose, "Disentangling Constituency"; Lublin, *Paradox of Representation*.

13. See footnote 12 for a set of studies highlighting these additional variables.

14. For some evidence suggesting this negative relationship, see Matthew C. Fellowes and Gretchen Rowe, "Politics and the New American Welfare States," *American Journal of Political Science* 48 (2004): 362–73; Michael W. Giles and Arthur Evans, "The Power Approach to Intergroup Hostility," *Journal of Conflict Resolution* 30 (1986): 469–86. And for a discussion of how representation mitigates backlash, see Preuhs, "Descriptive Representation as a Mechanism."

15. For evidence of positive responsiveness to minority population size, see Baker and Cook, "Representing Black Interests"; Grose, "Disentangling Constituency"; Hero and Tolbert, "Latinos and Substantive Representation"; Lublin, *Paradox of Representation*.

16. Specifically, we refer to the following to justify the included variables. For evidence of positive responsiveness to minority population size, see Baker and Cook, "Representing Black Interests"; Grose, "Disentangling Constituency"; Lublin, *Paradox of Representation*. But also see studies referenced in footnote 10 for a more comprehensive listing of previous studies and the controls utilized.

17. The regression analysis is based on the following model: Level of Support (NHLA or NAACP) = $\alpha + \beta_1$(Black Representative) + β_2(Latino Representative) + β_3(Proportion Black) + β_4(Proportion Latino) + β_5(Proportion Asian) + β_6(Proportion Foreign Born) + β_7(Education) + β_8(Urban) + β_9(Poverty) + β_{11}(Percent Democratic) + β_n(Congress) + error.

18. Data for the demographic characteristics were obtained from the 1990 and 2010 U.S. Censuses.

19. For an excellent presentation of how immigration affects political orientations, see Zoltan Hajnal and Michael U. Rivera, "Immigration, Latinos, and White Partisan Politics: The New Democratic Defection," *American Journal of Political Science* 58 (2014): 773–89.

20. Paul Peterson, *City Limits* (Chicago: University of Chicago Press, 1981).

21. Lowi, "American Business."

22. A major source for a discussion of pluralism is Robert A. Dahl, *Who Governs?* (New Haven, CT: Yale University Press, 1961). For other studies that recognize pluralism but highlight significant divergences in the reality of politics, see Hero, *Latinos and the U.S. Political System*; Martin Gilens and Benjamin I. Page, "Testing Theories of American Politics: Elites, Interest Groups, and Average Citizens," *Perspectives on Politics* 12 (2014): 564–81.
23. Hero, *Latinos and the U.S. Political System*.
24. For example, see Stokely Carmichael and Charles V. Hamilton, *Black Power: The Politics of Liberation in America* (New York: Vintage Books, 1967); Raphael J. Sonenshein, *Politics in Black and White: Race and Power in Los Angeles* (Princeton, NJ: Princeton University Press, 1993).
25. For a discussion of how a different approach to representation is taken by minority lawmakers, see Chapter 6 of Hero and Preuhs, *Black–Latino Relations*.
26. For evidence of how different policy issues affect conflict at the local level, see Paula D. McClain, "The Changing Dynamics of Urban Politics: Black and Hispanic Municipal Employment—Is There Competition?" *Journal of Politics* 55 (1993): 399–414; Rene R. Rocha, "Cooperation and Conflict in Multiracial School Districts," in *Latino Politics: Identity, Mobilization and Representation*, ed. Rodolfo Espino, David L. Leal, and Kenneth J. Meier (Charlottesville: University of Virginia Press, 2007), 161–76.
27. For urban-level coalitions, see Rufus P. Browning, Dale Rogers Marshall, and David H. Tabb, *Protest Is Not Enough: The Struggle of Blacks and Hispanics for Equality in Urban Politics* (Berkeley: University of California Press, 1984). The inclusion in state-level party coalitions has been shown by Preuhs, "Conditional Effects"; Juenke and Preuhs, "Irreplaceable Legislators?"; Preuhs, "Descriptive Representation as a Mechanism."
28. Jessica Trounstine, "Representation and Accountability in Cities," *Annual Review of Political Science* 13 (2010): 407–24.

Part III
Parties and the Politics of Polarization

7. The Dynamics of Party Government in Congress

Steven S. Smith and Gerald Gamm

What is the nature of party leadership, and how does it differ between the House and the Senate? Standard accounts of congressional leadership emphasize that strong leaders emerge only when their followers are cohesive and when divisions between the parties are sharp. This essay examines existing theories and suggests some new perspectives on congressional leadership. Drawing on both historical and contemporary examples— ranging from Joe Cannon and Nelson Aldrich to Paul Ryan and Mitch McConnell— the essay highlights the importance of distinguishing between the policy and electoral goals of congressional parties. It also emphasizes the effect of long-standing differences between leadership in the House and in the Senate that are rooted in the institutional contexts of the two chambers.

After several years of trying to lead his party conference, House Speaker John Boehner, R-Ohio, unexpectedly announced in September 2015 that he would resign from the speakership—in the middle of the 114th Congress. He was facing an open revolt among the most conservative Republicans, who insisted that the House refuse to approve spending bills until the Senate and President Barack Obama agreed to defund Planned Parenthood, which provides abortion services for women. Failing to pass the bills by October 1 would have forced many government departments to shut down, an outcome that Boehner sought to avoid. The last government shutdown, in 2013, when spending bills were held hostage to defunding the Affordable Care Act (Obamacare), was blamed on Republicans, and the Speaker did not want a repeat of that situation. As weeks passed, members of the conservative Freedom Caucus intensified their rhetoric, and eventually, Boehner threw in the towel.

Legislators and outside observers differ about what caused Boehner to quit. Tensions were building among congressional Republicans about how to use their majority party status in the House as leverage to gain policy concessions from the Senate and the Democratic president. At least a few dozen House Republicans insisted that their party use its majority in the chamber to refuse to pass bills to fund the federal government unless concessions were forthcoming. Most of them were associated with the Tea Party movement and were recently elected to the House, promising an end to compromise on key issues such as abortion and Obamacare. Boehner and the Republican leadership did not seem to disapprove of the conservatives' policy objectives on Planned Parenthood or Obamacare, but in 2015, they clearly believed that the party's reputation would suffer a serious blow if another shutdown occurred. At a minimum, the contending voices among House Republicans disagreed about how to balance the party's electoral and policy goals. When Speaker Boehner, as the majority party's top leader, could not find a formula to balance these goals that was acceptable to major factions in the party, he gave up and hoped that his successor, Paul Ryan, R-Wis., could do better.

In the Senate, Majority Leader Mitch McConnell, R-Ky., struggled to deal with rebellious party colleagues, too, but he did not experience the severe problems that Boehner faced in 2015. In 2013, Senator Ted Cruz, R-Tex., had urged his colleagues to hold up appropriations bills in an effort to kill Obamacare and was blamed for encouraging his House colleagues to engage in brinksmanship with the Democrats. Nevertheless, McConnell had little trouble persuading his party colleagues that delaying action on spending bills was bad politics. For McConnell and most Senate Republicans, the risk of being blamed by the public for another government shutdown and then losing several Republicans seats and the Senate's Republican majority in the 2016 elections was a real possibility and the greater concern.

The challenges facing Boehner and McConnell reflected similar needs to balance electoral and policy goals but were shaped by the different contexts provided by the two chambers. In the House, the Speaker and his party could act decisively to pass legislation but only if the party was cohesive enough to muster majorities without relying on minority party votes. In 2015, Boehner led a party that was remarkably cohesive on major issues, but serious disagreements about legislative strategy limited his options. In the Senate, where the minority party can obstruct legislation, the majority party may not be able to pass legislation in the form it wants even if it is cohesive. McConnell and most other Senate Republicans had accepted that they could not pass the controversial legislation that House conservatives backed and chose to survive the appropriations process with minimal damage to their party's reputation.

Our purpose in this chapter is to provide a framework for understanding how congressional parties and their leaders behave. Our perspective is simple: Congressional parties and their leaders seek to achieve their collective electoral and policy goals in a competitive political environment that shapes their strategies. The key features of the environment are competition with the other party for control of the House and Senate, the degree of partisan polarization, and the rules of governing the policy-making institutions. We argue that the intensity of partisan warfare and the power of central party leaders are stronger when the rules allow a cohesive majority to adopt the rules and pass legislation, when party control over the policy-making institutions is in doubt, and when the parties are sharply polarized.

Party Dynamics in the House and Senate

Congress is two legislative bodies that share the power to legislate. Each chamber has a committee system and rules that govern how legislation is considered and passed. Within each chamber, two parties, a majority and a minority party, organize themselves, elect their own leaders, and arrange for the appointment of members to committees. In the House, the majority party's leader is elected Speaker, who enjoys considerable power over the floor agenda. In the other body, the vice president serves as president of the Senate, a position that has not been assigned much power because the vice president cannot be held accountable to the majority and may not be of the same party as the Senate majority. Instead, the majority leader heads the majority in the Senate.

The congressional parties exist to meet the electoral and policy needs of their members. Legislators would like to be in the majority party, a status that gives them access to chairmanships, additional staff, and, through their party, more control of the legislative agenda. A well-organized, well-staffed, and well-led party may more effectively compete to gain and maintain majority party status. Legislators also have policy goals, some of which reflect the expectations of their constituencies. The more party members share important policy goals, the more willing they are to collaborate and empower effective leaders to pursue common ends.

These observations imply three propositions about the distribution of power in the House and Senate and the associated behavior of the parties and their leaders.

First, *uncertainty about future control of each house or a sudden shift in control motivates legislators to expand the organizational capacity of their parties*. That is, as interparty competition for the House and Senate intensifies, the parties seek to improve their competitiveness, which they do by empowering leaders, elaborating the party organization, enlarging party staffs, expanding public relations efforts, exploiting opportunities to score political points against the other party, and behaving in a more disciplined way.

If party control over a chamber remains uncertain for long, a party's efforts are likely to take lasting organizational form and soon be matched by the other party. Once greater organizational capacity—leadership positions, party committees and task forces, and staffs—is acquired, it tends to be replicated or expanded from Congress to Congress. In this way, party organization tends to grow with time and seldom shrinks.

The subtext is that party size matters.[1] A large majority party need not be very concerned about losing its majority status in the next election and has the freedom to allow some of its members to vote against the party to keep themselves elected. When the parties are more evenly matched, the majority party may struggle to balance its interest in disciplined voting to win legislative battles with the desire to allow its members to vote as their individual electoral needs dictate. This requires careful calculation and coordination and may require that wavering legislators be persuaded to vote with the party, which places important strategic choices in the hands of party leaders.

Second, *polarized parties delegate power to their leaders to improve their capability in the legislative process*. That is, as each party's members become more alike in their policy views and more different than the other party, members of a party become more willing to license their central leaders to aggressively pursue the party's legislative goals. In turn, more aggressive leaders create more disciplined parties. This is known as the "conditional party government" thesis.[2] It implies that agreement on policy goals makes it easier for a party to act in a coordinated way. Internally fragmented parties have trouble supporting strong leaders, as do parties where many members share policy goals with those across the aisle.

Legislators' policy preferences are largely a product of who elects them to Congress.[3] When the electoral bases of the two parties are not too different, their members tend to have similar or overlapping policy preferences; cross-party coalitions working in committee and on the floor can pass legislation; and party leaders tend to have a secondary, service-oriented role in the process. When the electoral bases of the two parties are very different, legislators tend to be quite polarized by party and are more eager to have their party leaders aggressively pursue their party goals. Responsibility for legislating tends to move from committees to party leaders, who can better coordinate party strategy.

Third, *the House majority party is capable of more fully centralizing power than the Senate majority party.* The House majority party can create both party and chamber rules to empower its top leader. The House adopts its rules anew in each Congress, which gives the majority party the opportunity to change the rules. From time to time, the majority party enhances or reduces the power of its top leader, the Speaker. These rules concern many features of House procedure, including the referral of legislation to committee, the timing of floor votes, and naming members of conference committees. A majority of the House also can approve special rules to govern action on individual bills, including suspending or supplanting most standing rules, limiting debate, and preventing amendments. The House also has a motion on the previous question: If a simple majority approves the motion, debate on the matter at hand is closed, and a vote on the issue takes place. In this way, as long as the majority party leadership can muster a majority, it freely controls the floor agenda.

Moreover, both House parties have shown a willingness to adopt internal party rules that give their top leaders extra influence. The top leader of both parties has a special role in making committee assignments and organizing party offices. He or she also names the members of the Rules Committee, which writes the special rules governing floor debate and amendments.

In the Senate, the minority party stands in the way of giving the majority leader substantial control over the chamber's agenda. While there are important exceptions, changes in the rules can be filibustered by the minority, which means that efforts to enhance the majority leader's powers are seldom adopted. Most legislation can be blocked by filibusters, too, which forces the majority to find a three-fifths majority (sixty votes) to invoke cloture and get a vote on a bill. The majority party might give its leader more power over internal party matters, but majority party senators know that most cohesive minority parties can block their legislative proposals anyway.

Institutional rules do not change frequently, but when the rules do change, it can make a significant difference. The 1974 Budget Act set up important procedures that allow a simple majority to pass budget measures in both chambers. The process encourages House and Senate majority parties to incorporate favored legislation in budget measures. In 2013, Senate Democrats forced a change in the interpretation of the cloture rule that allowed a simple majority of senators to close debate and get a vote on presidential nominations, with the exception of Supreme Court nominations. Otherwise, the House is majoritarian, which gives the majority party an opportunity to move at will, as long as it is sufficiently disciplined, whereas the Senate minority usually is in a position to block nonbudget legislation.

The overall picture is that both intense interparty competition and polarized parties encourage a party-oriented legislative process in which party leaders play a central role in devising party strategy that guides most legislative activity. Leaders become fully engaged in setting agendas, building floor majorities, and writing the details of major bills. Intense interparty competition tends to come periodically, sometimes for short periods and sometimes for long periods, but the improvements in organizational capacity that it spurs tend to be retained once made. Polarized parties come and go, at least over the long term, so the central role of party leaders may wax and wane, too. Because of differences in institutional rules, this pattern fits the House better than the Senate, but even in the Senate, there is considerable variation in the role of parties and their leaders.

In the sections that follow, we illustrate these themes by examining House and Senate party leadership in two eras—the years just before and after 1900 and, in our own time, the 1990s and early twenty-first century. Both were eras of party polarization, though, in both eras, the Republican Party grew more factionalized over time. In the earlier period, it was once frequently claimed, the Senate's majority leadership looked similar to the House leadership in its ability to control the chamber. But looks prove deceiving. The "centralized" power of Senate leaders a century ago was grounded in few formal institutions; it could not be transferred, and it could not be reliably employed, even by its most powerful practitioners. We argue, in fact, that the century-long effort to equate the Senate's "Aldrichism" with "czar rule" in the House reflects a misunderstanding of Senate leadership in that era. In the 1990s, 2000s, and 2010s, strong majority party leadership did not emerge at all in the Senate. Meanwhile, in the House, the two parties have allowed strong central leaders to emerge. But in both eras, strong House leaders were followed by weaker leaders, reflecting the countervailing electoral interests of individual legislators and the people responsible for coordinating party action.

1890 to 1910

After many years when the parties had nearly equal strength, Republicans gained sizable House and Senate majorities in 1894 and controlled Congress for the next sixteen years. The 1894 elections occurred in a deep economic depression while Democratic president Grover Cleveland was in the White House. The Democratic majority of 1893 to 1895 lost 127 House seats, and the Republicans started a period of reasonably safe control of the House, which they did not give up until 1910 (Figure 7-1). The Senate also became majority Republican in 1895, and they enjoyed an advantage that ranged from four to thirty-two seats over the Democrats until 1913 (Figure 7-2). Republicans easily won the presidency in four consecutive elections.

168 Part III Parties and the Politics of Polarization

Figure 7-1 House Seats, by Party, 1877–2014

Source: Compiled by authors.

Figure 7-2 Senate Seats, by Party, 1877–2014

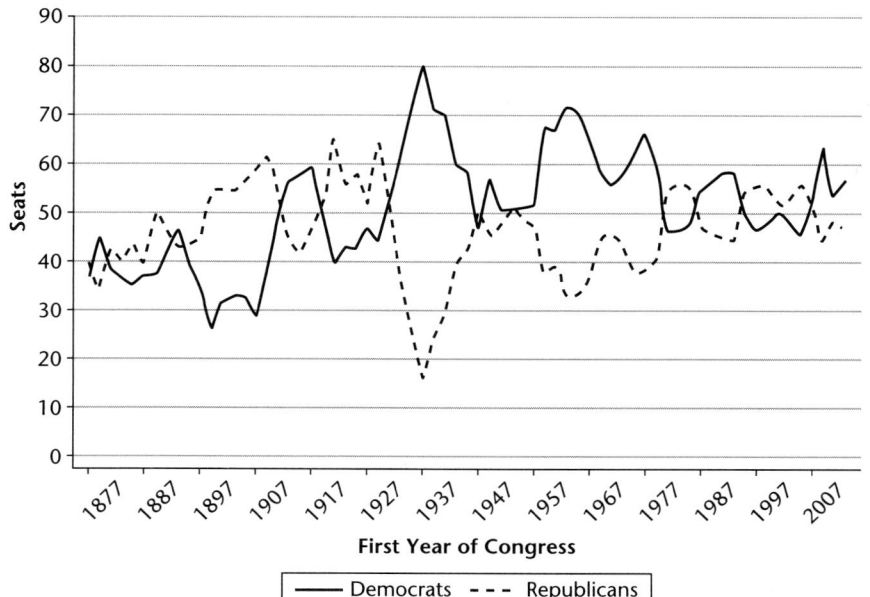

Source: Compiled by authors.

While this was a fairly long period with little serious competition between the parties for majority control of the House and Senate, it was a period of sharply polarized parties. Figures 7-3 and 7-4 display one component of polarization: interparty difference in the roll call voting record of the House and Senate. The figures are based on statistical estimates of the liberal-to-conservative positions of legislators.[4] In the figure, we plot the two parties' median scores. Throughout the late-nineteenth century and through the 1910s, the parties were very different in both chambers.

The period from 1890 to 1910 produced the strongest party leaders in the history of the House of Representatives. A comparable group existed in the Senate in that era, although it lacked the tools to exercise firm control. In both bodies, scholars have argued in the past, sharp party polarization, rooted in divided electoral constituencies, created centralized policy-making processes. For the House, the argument is strongly supported by the evidence, but for the Senate, the story is more complicated.

The House of Speakers Thomas Brackett Reed and Joseph Cannon

House Republicans enjoyed the leadership of two aggressive Speakers—Thomas Brackett Reed, R-Maine, and Joseph Cannon, R-Ill.—when they found themselves in the majority during most of the 1890 to 1910 period.[5] Reed and Cannon

Figure 7-3 House Liberal-to-Conservative Scores, Party Medians, 1877–2014

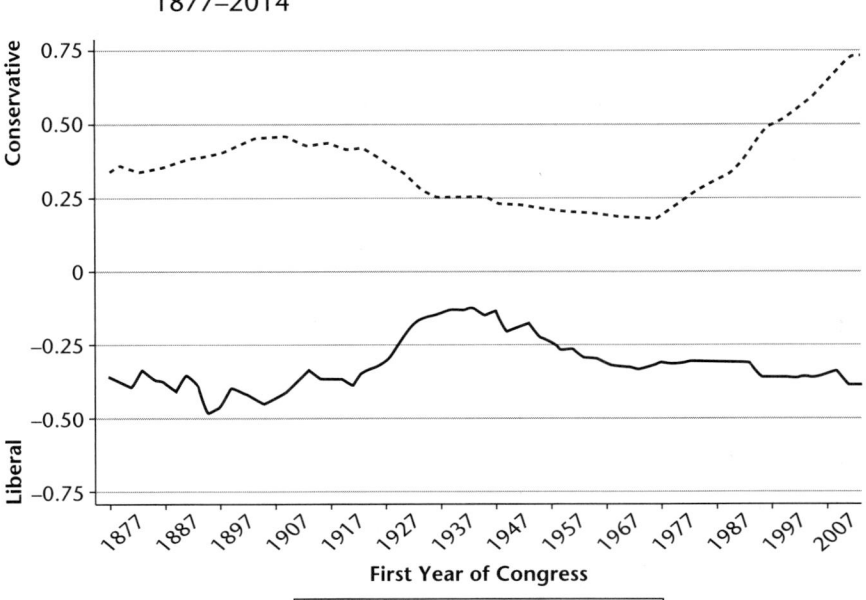

Source: Common Space DW-NOMINATE scores, voteview.com.

Figure 7-4 Senate Liberal-to-Conservative Scores, Party Medians, 1877–2014

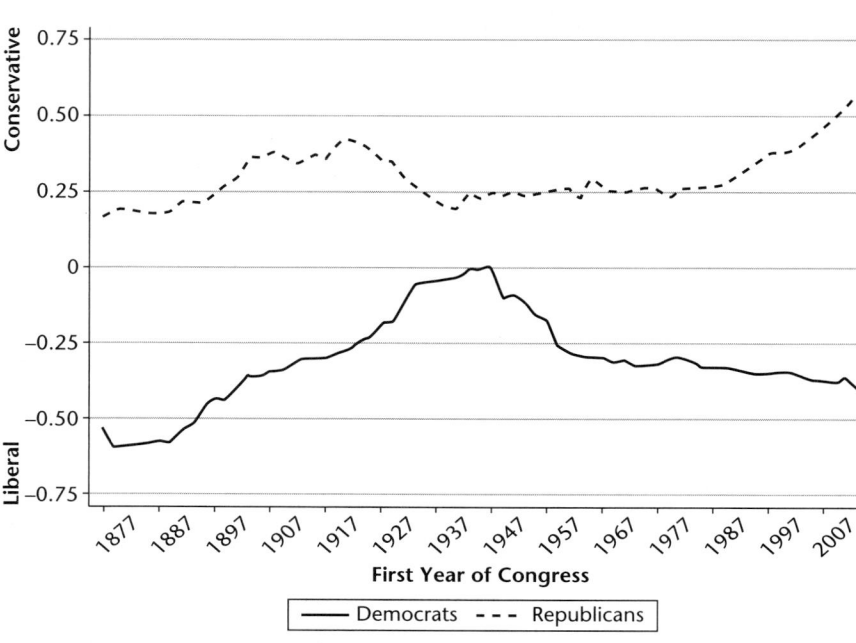

Source: Common Space DW-NOMINATE scores, voteview.com.

inherited substantial powers and, in Reed's case, substantially increased the powers of the office. The Speaker in this era appointed all members to standing committees and chairmanships and chaired the Committee on Rules, which wrote the resolutions that brought major legislation to the floor. During floor sessions, the Speaker exercised discretion over the recognition of members to make motions, including motions to bring up legislation. And the Republicans gave their leader a special tool in that a vote of the party caucus would bind all party members to support the party's policy position. These tools gave the Speaker important formal controls over the flow of legislation and a set of rewards and sanctions with which to influence the behavior of legislators. Reed and Cannon were known as "czars" of the House.

The evidence is generally consistent with the thesis that polarized parties centralize power in their top leaders. But as the political scientist Eric Schickler observes, a qualification of the thesis is required, inasmuch as the thesis does not explain the adoption of the Reed rules in 1890.[6] Speaker Reed and his fellow Republicans put in place landmark rules that undercut minority party obstructionism. The parties had distinct policy preferences but were not yet as polarized as they were soon to become (see Figure 7-2).[7] Even the Republicans had noteworthy internal divisions on important issues, such as currency and tariffs.

A reasonable hypothesis is that the relative sizes of the two parties played a critical role in the adoption of the Reed rules in 1890. The House parties were nearly equal in size in 1890—156 Democrats and 173 Republicans—and the margin had been narrow for some time. This meant that the absence of a few majority party members would be a serious problem for their party. By refusing to answer quorum calls and offering dilatory motions, the minority could prevent the House from conducting business. The *Reed rules*, as they came to be known, gave the Speaker the power to count members as present if they were in the chamber but not answering to a roll call, reduced the quorum in the Committee of the Whole from a majority of the House to one hundred members, and allowed the Speaker to ignore dilatory motions. Speaker Reed skillfully exploited a partisan debate over contested elections, as well as an upcoming bill that would provide for federal supervision of elections in the South, to increase his party's marginal control over the House.[8] He did so not by proposing rules changes in the usual way—offering a resolution at the start of a new Congress—but by making rulings from the chair at opportune moments and asking his fellow Republicans to back him up.

Oddly, immediately after the Democrats gained a majority in the 1890 elections, they dropped the Reed rules.[9] In spite of their interest in preventing minority obstruction, they felt obliged to follow through on campaign promises to restore "democratic" procedures to the House. To be sure, the Democrats were not a unified party and so may not have tolerated a powerful Speaker, as the conditional party thesis suggests, but it does appear that electoral motivations rather than policy considerations led to this precipitous action. Over the next few years, as the Republicans proved obstructionist, the Democrats reestablished some of the Reed rules, often with prodding from Reed himself and other minority Republicans.

Thus, when the Republicans regained a House majority in 1895, their Speaker enjoyed procedural advantages that were not the product of a newly cohesive majority in a polarized House. Rather, they were inherited from previous majorities that were concerned about reelection and party reputation, and they also may have reflected concerns about the functionality of the House on the part of members on both sides of the aisle. It is fair to say that Speaker Cannon soon came to use the procedural tools on behalf of a cohesive party in a polarized House, but the tools were the product of a mix of political considerations.

The House parties were sparse organizations during this period. In most Congresses, there was not much need for party organization. Republicans had a secure majority and relied on a small campaign committee to assist their candidates with publications and a little money. Even top leaders operated with little staff and largely relied on the official officers of the House to get assistance with their formal responsibilities.

The era of the czars came to an end when divisions within the House Republican party led to a revolt against Speaker Cannon in 1909 to 1910. The increasing dispersion that Figure 7-3 depicts during the late 1890s and 1900s gives a hint of what took place. Progressive Republicans from the Midwest and West became unhappy with the policy direction of the eastern establishment of their party, and they resented the strong-arm tactics that Cannon used to try to keep them in line. Moreover, the addition of Progressives to the House Democratic caucus began to reduce the distance between the parties.

Progressive Republicans joined with Democrats to impose new rules that reduced the Speaker's control over the flow of legislation to the floor. In 1909, the consent calendar was created, and a procedure allowing committees to call up bills every Wednesday was established. More important, in 1910, the coalition pushed through rules that prevented the Speaker from sitting on the Rules Committee and provided for its election by the House. When the Democrats took over majority control in 1911, they amended the House rules to provide for the election of all standing committees, an innovation that House Republicans also embraced.

During most of the rest of the twentieth century—until the 1970s, when Democrats began instituting a series of reforms—the Speaker was less powerful, and bargaining became the modus operandi of the majority party leadership. In fact, during the middle decades of the century, a conservative coalition of minority Republicans and Southern Democrats held sway on many issues. Party polarization declined, and both parties became more diverse. Legislative initiative slipped from central party leaders and shifted to committees and their chairs. Many bills were passed with cross-party coalitions, often with little trace of influence by party leaders.

The Senate of Nelson W. Aldrich and William Boyd Allison

During the 1890 to 1910 era, Republican leadership in the Senate was centered in a handful of men: Nelson Aldrich, R-R.I.; William Allison, R-Iowa; Orville Platt, R-Conn.; and John Spooner, R-Wis. A few others—such as Eugene Hale, R-Maine; Henry Cabot Lodge, R-Mass.; and James McMillan, R-Mich.—were considered insiders, too. The group functioned as an interlocking directorate of Republican committee and party leaders. With no powerful presiding officer, the Senate parties looked to other means to facilitate collective action.[10] In the 1890s, Aldrich and his comrades assumed personal responsibility for leading the Republican cause.

Aldrich, in part because of his leading role on the Finance Committee and in part because of his personality and political connections, helped lead the group. Allison chaired the Appropriations Committee and, beginning in 1897, the Republican caucus. From 1892 onward, the group dominated the Committee on Committees, which made committee assignments for the party, and the Steering Committee, which set a legislative agenda for the party.

The Senate's "Aldrichism" was often equated with the House's "Cannonism" by progressive politicians and journalists in those years and by scholars in the century since then. On the surface, the Aldrich-Allison team appears to be the Senate counterpart of the House czars. In fact, though, Aldrichism represented much less centralization and control than Cannonism. Unlike Reed and Cannon, Aldrich possessed no special procedural tools or party office. His leadership was exercised jointly with other senators and, given their positions as committee chairs, reflected the decentralized nature of the Senate. On his own and even in cooperation with the others, Aldrich showed considerably less ability than the House Speakers of the period to push party legislation through the chamber. Allison, who chaired both the Republican caucus and the Republican Steering Committee in these years, possessed even less effective power than Aldrich.

Why did the Senate Republican majority fail to develop a formal leader comparable to the House Speaker? The primary reason appears to be the inherited institutional context of the post–Civil War Senate. The essential features of that context were the absence of a presiding officer empowered to act in the interest of the majority party and the absence of a limit on debate and amendments. Unlike the House, the majority party in the Senate does not empower the presiding officer of the Senate. The Constitution provides that the vice president serve as president of the Senate, and nineteenth-century vice presidents generally served faithfully as presiding officers. But vice presidents need not be of the same party as the Senate majority, and, even when they were, they were not beholden to senators.

Senate presidents pro tempore, who were elected in the absence of the vice president, also proved feeble vessels for majority leadership. Nineteenth-century senators believed that the term of a president pro tempore ended abruptly upon the return of the vice president, and they also believed that the Senate lacked the constitutional authority to remove a president pro tempore from office under any other circumstance, including a shift in majority control. Although the Senate experimented occasionally with the assignment of some powers to its presiding officer, it emerged from the nineteenth century with a presiding officer with very little authority, even over routine floor proceedings.[11] The Senate, therefore, lacked a formal leader who could combine the powers of the presiding officer with the influence of a party leader, as did the Speaker of the House.

Furthermore, unlike the House, where cohesive majorities could impose rules changes, the Senate majority confronted a filibuster of any change in rules that might put a minority at a disadvantage. Until 1917, the Senate had no process for limiting debate as long as senators sought recognition to speak.[12] The immediate consequence was that Senate majority parties that might have wanted to enhance the formal power of their leadership did not have the ability to do so. Any enhancement of the influence of majority party leadership in the Senate would be limited to innovations within the parties' internal caucuses—proceedings invisible in the official Senate record. The Senate floor, unlike the House floor, was an inhospitable place for establishing majority party prerogatives.

Still, even informal leaders did not emerge until relatively late in the period of partisan polarization in the Senate. The most important innovation—the emergence of an elected floor leader—did not occur for Republicans until after Aldrich, Allison, and most of their allies had died or retired. Floor leadership was a Democratic invention, made when they were in the minority and dating to 1890. Republicans did not adopt this model until 1913. Yet Aldrich clearly stood at the center of a powerful group of senators. Their leadership was grounded, first, in their control of Senate committees and, second, in the establishment of a regular steering committee in 1892 to 1893.

Accumulated seniority allowed members of the Aldrich-Allison faction to gain positions of potential influence just as they gained additional cohesiveness.[13] In 1893, Allison was named chairman of both the Republican Committee on Committees and the newly strengthened Republican Steering Committee, and both were peopled by his allies. By virtue of his seniority, Allison became caucus chairman in 1897 and retained the chairmanship of the Republican Steering Committee, the party's agenda-setting group. Aldrich and Hale, both named to the Republican Steering Committee in 1893, kept this assignment continuously until they left the Senate in 1911—and Allison chaired the Steering Committee until his death in 1908. To the chairmanship of the Committee on Committees, Allison appointed McMillan in 1897, Aldrich in 1899, Platt in 1901, and Hale in 1903, 1905, and 1907. Meanwhile, Allison continued to chair the Appropriations Committee, as he had done for many years when the Republicans were in the majority. Aldrich chaired the Rules Committee in 1897, then became Finance Committee chairman two years later. No new rules facilitated this accumulation of power in a few senators' hands. The coordinative role of Allison and Aldrich was facilitated by the seniority rule, which governed committee chairmanships, as well as the caucus chairmanship, and gave them their committee and party positions.

The only significant structural change in this era by the majority party was the establishment of a permanent Republican Steering Committee in the winter of 1892–1893. Members of the caucus created the steering committee to pursue policy and electoral goals, but it was an election crisis that was the immediate cause of this institutional innovation. Republicans, who had controlled the Senate for a decade, realized in November 1892 that their majority was in serious jeopardy. State elections throughout the country portended an imminent transfer of control to the Democrats. Rather than acquiesce in the result, the Republican caucus established a steering committee, charging it to seek ways to influence the votes being cast for U.S. senators in state legislatures where the outcome was in doubt.

Once established, steering committees proved to be durable institutions for both Senate parties. Through the 1890s and the first decade of the new century, the steering committees set policy agendas and shaped legislation. Although the Senate party caucuses had often formed committees in the past, the earlier committees had been ad hoc, single-purpose creations, which reported quickly and then dissolved. The new steering committees assumed permanence, and Allison and Aldrich understood the importance of these institutions in coordinating decision making in the Senate. The Aldrich-Allison team asserted itself at a time when intraparty decision making was shifting decisively from the caucus to the steering committee. But the creation of the steering committee had little to do with the centralization of power in the hands of Aldrich and Allison and much more to do with the intense partisan competition for control of the Senate.[14]

Control over the machinery of the majority party did not translate into control over the Senate as directly or fully for party leaders as it did for the Speaker of the House. In part, the reason was factionalism with the Republican majority party: the presence of Populists in the Senate from 1897 to 1900 and the rise of progressives in the following decade. But the Republican establishment did not demonstrate the degree of control over committees and policy outcomes that the Speaker of the House did. An example is the action taken on an important tariff bill in 1897. At the height of Aldrich's and Allison's power, Republican committee members refused to support the party line and forced significant policy concessions before the bill could be reported from Aldrich's committee. In 1905, another Republican president's top priority, railroad regulation, was thwarted by Republican committee members until Democrats provided the votes required to report the bill to the floor. And then a Democrat had to be called on to manage it.[15]

Moreover, majority party leaders' control over the Senate floor agenda was far less perfect than the Speaker's control of the House agenda. In early 1900, for example, Republicans committed themselves to the passage of a gold standard bill. On this issue, Aldrich was the bill manager. In a story titled "Mr. Aldrich's Clever Move," the *Washington Post* reported how Aldrich took advantage of a nearly empty Senate chamber to secure unanimous consent to have the bill considered to the exclusion of all other business until it came to a vote eight days later. "The agreement was secured by Senator Aldrich yesterday afternoon," the *Post* stated, "when there were only eighteen Senators in the chamber, and when Senator Chandler, who is in charge of the Quay case; Senator Pettigrew, who is a persistent opponent of the administration's policy in the Philippines; and Senator Jones, the Democratic leader, were all absent."[16] That Aldrich's leadership was best exercised when others had left the chamber suggests the limits to his power.

When the Senate entered the final days of consideration of the gold standard bill, the *Post* reported that the chamber's remaining order of business remained unsettled. "After that measure is disposed of there will be a contest for precedence in the interest of several measures. These include the bills for providing forms of government for Hawaii and Puerto Rico, the Nicaragua canal bill, and the resolution for the seating of Senator [Matthew] Quay," according to the *Post*. "Which of these will take precedence remains to be determined. Just now there is some sharp sparring for first place."[17] In 1899 to 1900, the sparring took place directly among majority party bill managers. The *Post*, which thoroughly covered Aldrich's management of the gold standard bill, makes it clear that no individual senator coordinated the chamber's agenda. The paper described the chaos, noting that "as soon as the Senate had disposed of the financial bill yesterday, Senator [Shelby] Cullom and Senator [William] Chandler sought recognition, the former to press the Hawaiian bill and the latter to suggest consideration of the Quay case."[18]

Additional examples illustrate the limitations of Aldrichism. In 1903, a statehood bill and a banking bill, the latter sponsored by Aldrich, died under filibuster and threatened filibuster, respectively. In 1907, a filibuster killed a bill long championed by the Republicans to increase subsidies for American merchant shipping. Democrats, who viewed subsidies for shipping as a gift to the steel industry, easily prevented a vote on the measure. In both years, a determined minority was able to thwart the legislative plans of the Aldrich-Allison team and a Republican president.[19]

Even successful attacks on the institutional bases of power of the Aldrich-Allison group were possible. In 1899, junior and western senators combined to force the adoption of a rule that gave seven committees authority to report appropriations (spending) bills for programs under their jurisdiction. The new rule substantially reduced the jurisdictional reach of Allison's Committee on Appropriations. Both Aldrich and Allison opposed the new rule (as did Democratic leader Arthur Pue Gorman of Maryland), yet many members of the majority party supported the effort to decentralize control over the initiation of spending bills.[20]

Thus, the control of the chamber's proceedings by the Aldrich-Allison team was measurably weaker than the control over the proceedings of the House by the Speaker, even when bills of great importance to the faction were involved. In the Senate, control over the party's own committee contingents was weaker. Stealth was sometimes required to get a major bill to the floor. Disputes among the majority party's bill managers over the floor agenda often were not resolved by party leaders. Aldrichism was not Cannonism.[21]

Less complete centralization of leadership functions within the majority party is part of the reason for the differences between the two chambers at the turn of the twentieth century but so is the fact that intraparty centralization did not extend to firm control of the chamber in the case of the Senate. No Senate presiding officer was empowered to enforce an agenda that party leaders set. Floor debate and amendments could not be limited, a situation that continued to generate bargaining power for committee members. And single senators could object to bill managers' requests for unanimous consent to consider legislation or limit debate, which continued to give every senator a source of leverage. In such a setting, alienating a colleague by imposing penalties on him for noncompliant behavior entailed risks of its own.

In 1913, two years after Aldrich retired, the Democrats gained a Senate majority for the first time since 1895. Having regarded their caucus chairman as their floor leader since 1890, the Senate Democrats established the position of majority leader when they elected John Kern of Indiana as their new caucus chairman. They used their caucus to impose discipline on votes important to the new Democratic president, Woodrow Wilson. Republicans, now in the minority, adopted the Democratic model and created the position of elected floor leadership in 1913. When the Republicans regained a Senate majority in 1919, the party represented great regional diversity and lacked a strongly motivated caucus chairman and floor leader. But as the Democrats had done, the Republican Senate caucus now relied on an elected leader to help keep order on the floor and manage the caucus's affairs. Senate leaders, however, generally deferred to committee chairs on policy matters.

1995 to 2016

The party polarization in the years surrounding the turn of the twenty-first century has been similar to the polarization of the late 1890s. Since the early 1990s, in both the House and the Senate, the two parties have diverged widely in their policy views. Fewer legislators have joined with legislators of the other party to form cross-party coalitions on important issues, as was common in the mid-twentieth century; party-based coalitions and party-line voting have been the norm in recent Congresses. We would expect to see the emergence of very assertive party leaders in the House and Senate, and we have.

The earlier era and the current period exhibit one critical difference. As Figures 7-1 and 7-2 show, the parties over the last three decades have experienced an exceptionally long period of tight competition for control of Congress and the presidency. After decades of Democratic dominance, the Senate became majority Republican as Republican Ronald Reagan won the White House in 1980. Majority control of the Senate has been contested ever since. Democrats held on to their House majority until the 1994 elections, but the House has been hotly contested since then. Party control of the House, Senate, and presidency has changed hands several times during the past three decades, and divided party control of the three institutions has been common.

This long period of intense interparty competition stands in sharp contrast to the period of Republican dominance at the turn of the twentieth century. While the 1896 elections inaugurated a fourteen-year period of unified Republican control of the House, Senate, and presidency, the current era has been characterized by divided government, hotly contested elections, and frequent changes in control of each branch of government.

This difference in interparty competitiveness is likely to have intensified partisanship beyond the effects of having polarized policy views. Within each party, concern about winning elections provides a stronger motivation to have party strategy carefully managed by central party leaders. Those leaders appear to behave in a more partisan manner. The need for party discipline to counter the other party's tactics is greater, making the parties appear even more polarized. The gamesmanship and emphasis on messaging politics increases tensions across party lines and reduces tolerance for those few legislators who are willing to work to build bipartisan coalitions.

The House of Speakers Newt Gingrich, Dennis Hastert, Nancy Pelosi, John Boehner, and Paul Ryan

When the House Republicans gained a majority of seats in the 1994 elections, they inherited a decision-making process that already was more centralized than the committee-centered process that had characterized Congress for most of the twentieth century. Since the 1970s, the Democratic majority had steadily centralized more agenda-setting responsibility in the speakership. Speakers Thomas P. "Tip" O'Neill, D-Mass. (1977–1987), Jim Wright, D-Tex. (1987–1989), and Thomas S. Foley, D-Wash. (1989–1995) possessed stronger formal powers than their immediate predecessors. Those powers gave the Democratic Speakers greater influence over committee assignments, bill referral, and the Rules Committee.[22] Speaker Wright, a Democrat, used these powers to push a legislative agenda more vigorously than any Speaker had done in many decades, at a time when an opposition party president was in the White House. His effort was brought to an end when he resigned from the House after the House Committee on Standards of Official Conduct charged him with several violations of ethics rules.

Oddly, from the point of view of the party polarization thesis, Democrats, as the House majority, enhanced the formal powers of their central party leader at the lowest point in party polarization in the history of the two parties—in the early 1970s (see Figure 7-3). Sharp intraparty factionalism, more than interparty differences, stimulated liberals to strengthen their central party leader and weaken the powers of full committee chairs, many of whom were conservatives. The Speaker at the time, Carl Albert, D-Okla., neither sought nor fully exploited those powers. Only later did Democratic Speakers begin to draw on them, particularly control of the Rules Committee, and interparty competition clearly stimulated that new aggressiveness. These developments led observers to refer to the *postreform House* of the 1970s, 1980s, and 1990s, which was much more party oriented and less committee oriented than the House of the mid-twentieth century.[23]

The centralization of the House initiated by Democrats ratcheted up with the Republican majority elected in the 1994 elections. With his assumption of the Speaker's chair in January 1995, Newt Gingrich, R-Ga., quickly became the most assertive Speaker since Cannon. Gingrich had taken the lead in recruiting Republican candidates, in fund-raising for Republicans, and in developing the "Contract With America," the Republicans' ten-point policy platform for the 1994 campaign. Gingrich handpicked full committee chairs, who were later endorsed by the party conference, and even picked several subcommittee chairs, who were then appointed by committee chairs. He exercised great influence over all important committee assignments and even reviewed the appointments of top committee staff. He directed the content and timing of committee actions on legislation, limited conference committee delegations to a few top committee leaders, and was intrusive in conference negotiations on major bills. Standing at the head of a unified party in a polarized House, Gingrich, by his behavior, seemed to confirm the conditional party government thesis.[24]

Gingrich's speakership ended in political disaster. The seeds of the disaster were planted early, when, in 1995, Gingrich led House Republicans in holding spending bills hostage to force President Clinton's approval of their budget plan. Clinton won the showdown, persuading most Americans that the congressional Republicans were responsible for shutting down many federal agencies when spending authority expired. In the aftermath of the crisis, Gingrich became less aggressive and reduced his public visibility, a strategy that brought criticism from his colleagues. Adding to his troubles was an ethics investigation into the financing of a college course he taught and the campaign fund-raising conducted by organizations he created. By the summer of 1997, he was considered so ineffective that several Republican leaders discussed replacing him as Speaker.

Gingrich never regained his aggressiveness in confronting a Democratic president who he helped to make more popular. The last straw came at the end of 1998, when Republicans lost seats in the House. In modern American history, no party had lost seats in the midterm elections of an opposition president's second term in office. Gingrich's greatest strength, election strategy, seemed to have faded. Gingrich was immediately challenged for reelection to the speakership by a party colleague who complained that Gingrich had failed to give voters a reason to vote Republican. Other Republicans seemed to agree, and during a turbulent time when the House Republicans were preparing to impeach the president, Gingrich chose to retire.[25]

Gingrich's successor, Dennis Hastert, R-Ill., initially seemed to be a very different leader. Not only did he follow through on his promises to allow committee chairs more independence and to act with the advice of a much wider range of Republicans, but he proved to be nearly invisible in the media. The Republicans' agenda was very small in 1999 because Speaker Hastert preferred to slow action on taxes and other legislation to avoid conflict with an opposition party president whose poll ratings remained very high. Remarkably, this shifting of gears in House Republican leadership occurred without a measurable change in party polarization. The policy differences between the two parties did not change greatly with the 1998 elections, and yet, the context in which Hastert operated in 1999 to 2000—the failed speakership of Gingrich, a popular opposition president, and a concern about the next elections—dictated a less aggressive and centralized approach to policy making in the House.

Once the Republican president George W. Bush was elected in 2000, the House Republican leadership reverted to the form predicted by the thesis. Hastert and his second-in-command, Majority Leader Tom DeLay, R-Tex., coordinated agendas with the White House, set strategy on measures important to the new administration, insisted on timely committee action, and proved quite willing to twist arms. In fact, at least as much as Gingrich, Hastert and DeLay soon centralized decision making and pressured members to support the party line.

Hastert gave up the top Republican leadership post after the Republicans lost their House majority in the 2006 elections. As had been the case with Gingrich, electoral failure—in this case, failure readily attributed to an unpopular president—meant that the House Republicans would be looking for a new direction, and the incumbent leader sensed the party's desire for a change in leadership.

Explaining the 1998 and 2006 changes in House Republican leadership requires moving beyond policy—and party polarization—to electoral concerns. In both cases, public displeasure with the performance of the Republicans, as expressed in election outcomes, generated disagreements among Republicans about how to respond.[26] In each case, a new leader seemed to be demanded by some partisans, and the new leader promised to work with all party members to address their concerns.[27] Electoral circumstances, not a realignment of legislators' policy preferences, stimulated a change in leadership.

After the 2006 elections, with the parties remaining as polarized as they had been under Republican majorities, Speaker Nancy Pelosi, D-Calif., proved to be an assertive leader. As they promised, Pelosi and Majority Leader Steny Hoyer of Maryland consulted regularly on the schedule with committee leaders and depended more on committees to write the details of major legislation than had Hastert and DeLay. They also made certain that all factions of the party had a voice on matters that affected their interests. This hybrid approach was a continuation of Pelosi's approach as minority leader: to recognize the expertise of colleagues, to keep the disparate factions of her party working together by bringing committee leaders into discussions with interested party members, and to protect the party's image.

As a result of the Republican takeover of the House following the 2010 elections, Pelosi served only two Congresses as Speaker and was replaced by John Boehner, who had been the Republican minority leader since Hastert retired at the end of 2006. Boehner benefited from a new and large majority eager to change the direction of public policy. Boehner, who had served as the lead Republican on the House Committee on Education and the Workforce, promised to give committee leaders more leeway, offer the minority more opportunities to offer floor amendments, and, at the same time, champion the aggressive policy agenda of party conservatives. Nevertheless, the Speaker directed the timing of committee action on major measures, and he quickly tightened special rules to limit the ability of Democrats to offer amendments that would divide Republicans or force some Republicans to cast difficult votes. Indeed, to a much greater degree than Speakers of the mid-twentieth century, Boehner directly negotiated the details of major legislation with party factions, the White House, and the Senate. Boehner, like Pelosi before him, circumvented conference committees, traditionally dominated by committee members, to facilitate quick action on some particularly important but politically sensitive bills.

Divided party control of the institutions of government created a difficult strategic context for Boehner. In 2011, Boehner struggled to negotiate with President Barack Obama, a Democrat, and Harry Reid, the Senate Democratic leader, while retaining the support of his Republican colleagues in the House. It is notable that Boehner, rather than a committee chair, led key negotiations and sometimes did so in private with President Obama; his direct leadership reflected the extraordinary level of centralization in the House Republican caucus in this era. But Boehner could not dictate his party's bargaining stance. Differences between Boehner and party conservatives—especially junior Republicans associated with the Tea Party movement—about where and when to compromise with the Democrats proved controversial and constrained Boehner's ability to negotiate on the central issue of fiscal policy.

Polarized parties, nearly continuous concern about the next elections, divided party control, and the majoritarian nature of the House thrust party leaders into their roles as chief negotiators. This role, dictated by party interest, also brought an end to the Boehner speakership. Differences over policy and electoral priorities came to a head for Boehner in 2015, when the most conservative Republicans, organized as the Freedom Caucus, refused to support the bills required to fund federal departments unless the legislation stripped funding for Planned Parenthood. Boehner thought that was a losing strategy, the Senate would not support the defunding provision, President Obama would veto the bill if the provision was included, and the Republicans would be blamed for shutting down government agencies. With the conservatives refusing to back down and threatening to force him from the speakership, Boehner resigned.

Boehner was replaced by Paul Ryan. Ryan, then the chair of the Committee on Ways and Means, his party's vice presidential candidate in 2012, and a former chair of the Budget Committee, managed to finish action on essential legislation in 2015. He took the speakership promising a more collaborative process in setting party strategy in the future, which the conservatives read as a commitment to give them more influence in setting party strategy. At this writing, in mid-2016, it is not clear that Ryan can create consensus within his party conference on budget and spending targets, given sharp disagreement over tactics and strategy.

The Boehner experience illustrates how even deep partisan polarization does not make life easy for the leader of the majority party. Differences over legislative strategy—in this case, differences about how a party should use their majority status in the House—can become troublesome when the alternatives are thought to have serious electoral implications for the party and its members. Boehner struggled with these differences throughout his service as Speaker, and Ryan has not proven yet that he can manage these intraparty issues more effectively.

The Senate of Majority Leaders Bob Dole, Trent Lott, Bill Frist, Harry Reid, and Mitch McConnell

The Senate, as much as the House, has experienced a long period of intense competition for majority control and sharply polarized parties. Nevertheless, *centralization* is not a term that any modern senator would apply to his or her institution. Party leaders are fully engaged in policy making and often pursue inventive parliamentary tactics, but bargaining, not command, has remained the modus operandi of both parties' floor leaders. The contrast with the House could not be sharper.

By the late 1980s, both Senate parties had rejuvenated their party conferences and created leadership offices, party committees, and task forces that performed a variety of functions. These forms of party activity and organization had atrophied by the middle of the twentieth century, as committee chairs had come to shape the chamber's business alongside floor leaders who were coordinating party affairs. Republicans started regular luncheon meetings in the late 1950s; Democrats did so in 1987. Beginning in the 1980s, each party's leader occasionally appointed task forces to help formulate a party strategy on important issues. In 1989, Democratic majority leader George Mitchell of Maine reinvigorated the party's Policy Committee, which for the first time had a cochair who controlled a sizable staff that provided a wide range of services for senators, including research and graphics services. The Policy Committee, led by Sen. Tom Daschle, D-S.Dak., developed and approved an annual legislative agenda. Still, only in exceptional cases did party leaders assume primary responsibility for developing and promoting specific legislation, deferring instead to committees.

As the partisan fight for control of Congress intensified, Senate parties acquired larger staffs in leadership offices, hired more public relations specialists, expanded campaign committee staffs, and invested in a wide range of communications technologies. Modern messaging politics involves a public relations effort on every major piece of legislation, a considerable volume of legislation that is pushed to the floor for public relations purposes, and central efforts to coordinate daily themes for party members to emphasize in their dealings with the media and public.

Much of this effort is supported with appropriations funding. Figure 7-5 shows that appropriations for party offices in the Senate grew at a phenomenal rate between the early 1980s and 2009, when continuing appropriations and spending limited further growth. The pattern for the House is very similar (not shown), although the House totals are larger, reaching over $22 million in recent years.

Figure 7-5 Appropriations for Senate Party Offices, 1946–2015 (in Millions of Dollars)

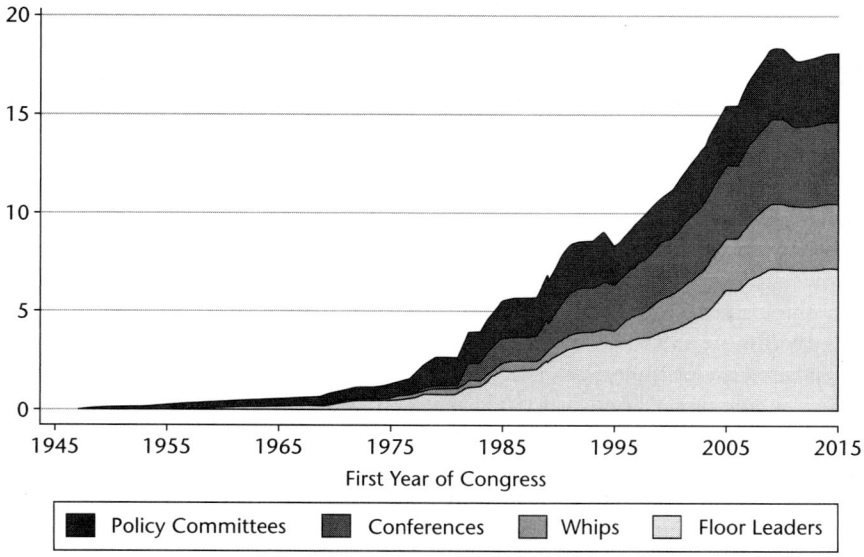

Source: Legislative Branch Appropriations bills.

While the Senate figures are shown here, the pattern of spending by House parties is very similar (data not shown). In the House, the Speaker, as a constitutional officer, receives funding beyond the sums that are given equally to the two parties, which gives an advantage to the majority party in that chamber. In both chambers, the parties have jointly added to their organizational capacity, which has given party leaders the resources to become more important to the pursuit of both electoral and policy goals, largely at the expense of committees and their chairs.

Developments since the 1994 elections are particularly important for understanding today's Senate. Republicans gained new majorities in the Senate, as well as the House, in the 1994 elections, but the decision-making process in the Senate remained less centralized than in the House.[28] Unlike the House Republicans, who radically changed party processes after becoming a majority in the 1994 elections, Senate Republicans changed little in intraparty decision-making processes after they gained a majority in the same elections. The Senate Republicans had been led by Bob Dole, R-Kans., for ten years by that time, and Dole continued to rely on weekly meetings, sessions with committee chairs, and occasional task forces, as he had done before.

Trent Lott, R-Miss., who took over when Dole became the Republican nominee for president in 1996, took Dole's approach a step farther. In what one Republican senator called *participatory management*, Lott appointed a diverse set of senators to serve in leadership posts and participate in weekly leadership meetings. He also appointed task forces in major policy areas, which would help set the party's agenda but would leave the writing of legislation to committees, several of which were chaired by party moderates. The facilitation of intraparty communication, bargaining, broad participation, and consensus building—not centralization of power—was the purpose.[29]

In late 2002, a videotape of Trent Lott saying that "we wouldn't have had all these problems over all these years" if Strom Thurmond's segregationist bid for the presidency in 1948 had been successful was shown in the national media. Lott apologized, but the media soon disclosed that he had made similar remarks earlier in his career. In spite of his best efforts, Lott failed to persuade his colleagues to give him a second chance. After Lott bowed out as leader, Sen. Bill Frist, R-Tenn., who was far more soft-spoken than Lott but perhaps a more effective spokesman, was elected to replace him. The party image, more than its legislative agenda, appeared to propel Frist to the top post.

When he became majority leader in 2006, Harry Reid, D-Nev., was expected by many observers to continue the soft-spoken and cooperative leadership style he had shown as minority leader, reaching across party lines to avoid filibusters and find common ground on some legislation. In fact, although the parties appeared to be as polarized as ever, Reid initially insisted on a more streamlined party organization, discontinued some of the party task forces, and worked more directly with members of standing committees.

The sharp policy differences between the two parties soon left Reid frustrated. The record of legislative achievement of the 110th and 112th Congresses

(2007–2008, 2011–2012) was limited, primarily because of the small Democratic majorities and the Republican minority's success in preventing action on many Democratic bills. Partisanship boiled over in sharp rhetoric on the Senate floor on many occasions, and both parties intensified their public relations efforts. Reid created a public relations effort, located in a "war room," run by senators and staff to publicize the party's positions and cast blame on the Republicans.

The 111th Congress (2009–2010) stands in sharp contrast to the 110th and 112th. With the Senate Democratic conference reaching fifty-nine members following the 2008 elections and then sixty after the seating of Senator Al Franken, D-Minn., in July 2009, Democrats were able to invoke cloture on a range of prominent measures, many of which remain controversial. With the Democrats also controlling the House and the White House, they passed Obamacare, a major economic stimulus package, Wall Street reform, equal-pay legislation, repeal of "Don't Ask, Don't Tell," and other measures.

The Senate has been infected, in the view of many senators and outside observers, by a partisan syndrome. Each party is quick to fully exploit its parliamentary prerogatives; the minority blocks action by refusing unanimous consent to take up legislation and opposing cloture motions, and the majority responds by attempting to limit the minority's opportunities to obstruct or amend legislation. The result is that the Senate frequently reaches points of legislative deadlock, which are circumvented only by getting cloture, setting aside legislation, or accepting lowest-common-denominator legislation, often in the form of short-term authorizations and appropriations that leaves most senators unhappy with the outcome. In the 1993 through 1998 period, about half of all major legislation was subject to filibusters or threatened filibusters, many times the rate that was typical of previous decades. The pace accelerated into the new century, when nearly all major bills were affected by a filibuster or cloture.[30] In the 107th Congress (2001–2002), sixty-one cloture votes were taken; in the 111th (2009–2010), ninety-one cloture votes were taken. Plainly, party size, along with party polarization, shapes outcomes.

Consequently, majority party leadership in the 2010s has been forced to adjust its strategy to respond to and anticipate minority moves. The process seems to intensify partisanship, as party members support their leaders' responses to the "unfair" tactics of the other side. Unfortunately for the majority party, as long as the minority is reasonably cohesive, as it is in a highly polarized Senate, the majority cannot readily translate its own cohesiveness into significant policy accomplishments. The majority can only hope that its dedicated floor leader can improve efficiency and persuade the public of its program.

After the Republicans won a Senate majority in the 2014 elections, new majority leader Mitch McConnell promised to return the Senate to "regular order," by which he meant more debate, more amendments, more negotiation, and less filibustering. This would be a process less centered in the party leaders, moving key negotiations back to committee rooms, and involving more senators. But the return to "regular order" never occurred, and in mid-2016, the Senate continues to be characterized by a pattern of minority obstruction and majority retaliation.

In the eyes of many senators, these developments have altered the nature of their institution. Rather than being the legislative chamber that operated informally and readily accommodated individual legislators' desire to debate and offer amendments, the Senate of the early twenty-first century has been bogged down by exploitation of formal rules and precedents and insistence on the protection of the minority's full range of parliamentary rights. The Senate party leaders are central to this process, but the majority leader—unlike his counterpart in the House, the Speaker—cannot expect to win very often in this context.

Conclusion

The comparison of patterns of party leadership at the turns of the twentieth and twenty-first centuries confirms three related propositions about the sources of centralization in Congress:

- Tightly contested battles for control of each chamber motivate legislators to expand the organizational capacity of their parties.
- Polarized parties—parties with high levels of internal cohesion, with sharp differences between the two parties—delegate power to their leaders to improve their capability in the legislative process.
- The House majority party is capable of more fully centralizing power than the Senate majority party.

In the House, where inherited rules allow a determined majority to gain action on its policy agenda, party polarization appears to stimulate the centralization of majority party leadership. Polarization was intense at the turn of the twentieth and twenty-first centuries, and in both cases, House Republicans allowed a strong central leader to emerge and direct the decision-making process. However, even in the House, electoral circumstances that evolved in the 1990s—and perhaps also the factionalism characterizing the majority party in the mid-2010s—can lead to a change in leadership and a significant diminution in the centralization of decision making.

The fairly tight correspondence between polarization and centralization of the House was not duplicated in the Senate. The Senate majority party centralization in the late nineteenth century was delayed and not as complete, and centralization has not appeared in the contemporary Senate. Ironically, truly polarized Senate parties—including a cohesive minority party—may be less conducive to majority party centralization and success than somewhat less polarized parties that make support for the majority's program by some minority members feasible. Cross-party coalitions are more important to the Senate than the House for shepherding legislation through a thicket of potential filibusters, nongermane amendments, and other parliamentary maneuvers.

For centralization to occur in a chamber, many stars need to align. We contend that centralization emerges when the parties are polarized, the parties are engaged in an intense battle over control of Congress, and the institutional context permits control of legislative outcomes by a centralized majority party. Even in the House, electoral circumstances and factional fights over strategy can limit the central leader's effectiveness. And in the Senate, inherited rules limit the degree to which the chamber's decision-making process can ever be centralized in the majority party leadership.

Notes

1. On the effects of party size, see the studies discussed in Sarah Binder, "Parties and Institutional Choice Revisited," *Legislative Studies Quarterly*, 31 (2006): 513–36.
2. David W. Rohde, *Parties and Leaders in the Postreform House* (Chicago: University of Chicago Press, 1991); John Aldrich and David W. Rohde, "The Transition to Republican Rule in the House: Implications for Theories of Congressional Politics," *Political Science Quarterly* 112 (1997–1998): 541–67; John Aldrich and David W. Rohde, "The Consequences of Party Organization in the House: The Role of the Majority and Minority Parties in Conditional Party Government," in *Polarized Politics: The President and the Congress in a Partisan Era*, ed. Jon Bond and Richard Fleisher (Washington, DC: CQ Press, 2000); John Aldrich and David W. Rohde, "The Logic of Conditional Party Government: Revisiting the Electoral Connection," in *Congress Reconsidered*, 7th ed., ed. Lawrence C. Dodd and Bruce I. Oppenheimer (Washington, DC: CQ Press, 2001).
3. Joseph Cooper and David W. Brady, "Institutional Context and Leadership Style: The House from Cannon to Rayburn," *American Political Science Review* 75 (1981): 411–25. The thesis has been extended to the Senate; see David W. Brady, Richard Brody, and David Epstein, "Heterogeneous Parties and Political Organization: The U.S. Senate, 1880–1920," *Legislative Studies Quarterly* 14 (1989): 205–23; David W. Brady and David Epstein, "Intraparty Preferences, Heterogeneity, and the Origins of the Modern Congress: Progressive Reformers in the House and Senate, 1890–1920," *Journal of Law, Economics, and Organization* 13 (1997): 26–49.
4. DW-NOMINATE scores, a measure of legislators' placement on the liberal–conservative scale, are used. The authors thank Keith Poole for their use. For an excellent discussion of party polarization, see Keith Poole and Howard Rosenthal, *Congress: A Political-Economic History of Roll Call Voting* (New York: Oxford University Press, 1997), 80–85.
5. On the Speakers of this era, see David W. Brady, *Congressional Voting in a Partisan Era: A Study of the McKinley Houses* (Lawrence: University of Kansas Press, 1973); David W. Brady, Joseph Cooper, and Patricia Hurley, "The Decline of Party in the U.S. House of Representatives, 1887–1968," *Legislative Studies Quarterly* 4 (1979): 381–407; George Brown, *The Leadership of Congress* (Indianapolis: Bobbs-Merrill, 1922); Chang-Wei Chiu, *The Speaker of the House of Representatives Since 1896* (New York: Columbia University Press, 1928); Paul DeWitt Hasbrouk, *Party Government in the House of Representatives* (New York: Macmillan, 1927); Cooper and Brady, "Institutional Context and Leadership Style"; Ronald M. Peters Jr., *The American Speakership: The Office in Historical Perspective*, 2nd ed. (Baltimore: Johns Hopkins University

Press, 1997); Roger H. Davidson, Susan Webb Hammond, and Raymond W. Smock, eds., *Masters of the House: Congressional Leadership Over Two Centuries* (Boulder, CO: Westview Press, 1998); Randall Strahan, *Leading Representatives: The Agency of Leaders in the Politics of the U.S. House* (Baltimore: Johns Hopkins University Press, 2007).

6. See Eric Schickler, *Disjointed Pluralism: Institutional Innovation and the Development of the U.S. Congress* (Princeton, NJ: Princeton University Press, 2001), chap. 2. Sundquist emphasizes the factionalism within the Republican Party prior to the realignment of 1896. See James L. Sundquist, *Dynamics of the Party System: Alignment and Realignment of Political Parties in the United States* (Washington, DC: Brookings Institution Press, 1983).
7. For a different perspective and different account of party polarization in the House of the Fifty-first Congress (1889–1891), see Cooper and Brady, "Institutional Context and Leadership Style."
8. Richard M. Valelly, "The Reed Rules and Republican Party Building: A New Look," *Studies in American Political Development* 23 (2009): 115–42.
9. Schickler, *Disjointed Pluralism*.
10. Gerald Gamm and Steven S. Smith, "Last Among Equals: The Senate's Presiding Officer," in *Esteemed Colleagues: Civility and Deliberation in the U.S. Senate*, ed. Burdett A. Loomis (Washington, DC: Brookings Institution Press, 2000).
11. Ibid.
12. On the history of filibusters and filibuster reform, see Franklin Burdette, *Filibustering in the Senate* (Princeton, NJ: Princeton University Press, 1940); Sarah Binder and Steven S. Smith, *Politics or Principle? Filibustering in the United States Senate* (Washington, DC: Brookings Institution Press, 1997); Gregory J. Wawro and Eric Schickler, *Filibuster: Obstruction and Lawmaking in the U.S. Senate* (Princeton, NJ: Princeton University Press, 2006); Gregory Koger, *Filibustering: A Political History of Obstruction in the House and Senate* (Chicago: University of Chicago Press, 2010).
13. Our emphasis is different from that of Brady, Brody, and Epstein, "Heterogeneous Parties and Political Organization," 211–13, who emphasize the committee seniority of northeastern Republicans. What seems more critical is that members of the Aldrich-Allison faction enjoyed such seniority that they held both top party and top committee posts.
14. Gerald Gamm and Steven S. Smith, "Senate Party Leadership in the 1890s," paper presented at the annual meeting of the Midwest Political Science Association, Chicago, April 2000.
15. See Brown, *Leadership of Congress*, 102, 134–35; DeAlva Stanwood Alexander, *History and Procedure of the House of Representatives* (Boston: Houghton Mifflin, 1916), 6–7.
16. "Mr. Aldrich's Clever Move," *Washington Post*, February 7, 1900, 4.
17. "Vote on Finance Bill," *Washington Post*, February 12, 1900, 3.
18. "Hawaiian Bill Taken Up," *Washington Post*, February 16, 1900.
19. Burdette, *Filibustering in the Senate*, 69–80.
20. Eric Schickler and John Sides, "Intergenerational Warfare: The Senate Decentralizes Appropriations," *Legislative Studies Quarterly* 25 (2000): 551–75.
21. Thus, we would qualify the assertion of Brady, Brody, and Epstein in "Heterogeneous Parties and Political Organization," who argue that "in 1900, the U.S. Senate was, in fact, hierarchical, centralized, and heavily partisan. The top leadership controlled committee assignments, set the agenda, and had sanctions to help them enforce party discipline on the floor" (209).

22. Rohde, *Parties and Leaders*.
23. Roger Davidson, *The Postreform Congress* (New York: St. Martin's, 1992); Rohde, *Parties and Leaders*.
24. Aldrich and Rohde, "Transition to Republican Rule"; Barbara Sinclair, *Unorthodox Lawmaking: New Legislative Processes in the U.S. Congress*, 4th ed. (Washington, DC: CQ Press, 2012), 175–216.
25. Bruce Alpert, "Grab for Top House Job Comes After Plan to Quit," *New Orleans Times-Picayune*, November 15, 1998, A18.
26. Richard E. Cohen and David Baumann, "After the Riot," *National Journal*, November 14, 1998, 2700.
27. Mary Agnes Carey, "New Strategy, Old Disputes," *CQ Weekly*, January 22, 1999; Karen Foerstel, "Parties Set Ambitious Agendas in the Shadow of Old Grudges," *CQ Weekly*, January 2, 1999. On the ten-point plan, see Andrew Taylor, "Issues Held Hostage in War Between Action, Gridlock," *CQ Weekly*, February 26, 2000, 394–399.
28. On Senate party activity, see Donald Baumer, "Senate Democratic Leadership in the 101st Congress," paper presented at the annual meeting of the American Political Science Association, San Francisco, September 1990; Samuel Patterson and Thomas Little, "The Organizational Life of Congressional Parties," paper presented at the annual meeting of the Midwest Political Science Association, Chicago, April 1992; Steven S. Smith, "Forces of Change in Senate Party Leadership and Organization," in *Congress Reconsidered*, 5th ed., ed. Lawrence C. Dodd and Bruce I. Oppenheimer (Washington, DC: CQ Press, 1993), 259–90.
29. Donna Cassata, "Lott's Task: Balance the Demands of His Chamber and His Party," *CQ Weekly Report*, March 8, 1997.
30. Steven S. Smith, *The Senate Syndrome: The Evolution of Procedural Warfare in the Modern U.S. Senate* (Norman: University of Oklahoma Press, 2014). See also Barbara Sinclair, "Hostile Partners: The President, Congress, and Lawmaking in the Partisan 1990s," in *Polarized Politics: The President and the Congress in a Partisan Era*, ed. Jon Bond and Richard Fleisher (Washington, DC: CQ Press, 2000), 145.

8. Legislating in Polarized Times

Sarah Binder

Is the U.S. Congress dysfunctional? The American public thinks so: In the winter of 2016, just 16 percent strongly approved of Congress.[1] Still, legislative scholars disagree about the severity of Congress's legislative challenges. Is legislative deadlock a sign that Congress can no longer identify and resolve major public problems? Or are Congress's difficulties temporary and correctable? In this chapter, I review competing perspectives on the dynamics of lawmaking and present evidence from the last half century to help us assess Congress's legislative performance. I argue that despite some recent progress in addressing big issues of the day, Congress still struggles to legislate in a polarized era. Whether or when Congress will recoup its legislative prowess in the coming years remains in question.

> Most of the imbalances I have analyzed . . . have *not* been major, permanent, systemic problems. More precisely, at least during recent generations, many alleged problems have proven to be nonexistent, short-term, limited, tolerable, or correctable.
>
> —David Mayhew[2]

> We hope that Mayhew is right and that this difficult patch will prove to be routine, short term and self-correcting . . . But we doubt it. These are perilous times and the political responses to them are qualitatively different from what we have seen before.
>
> —Thomas Mann and Norman Ornstein[3]

Is the contemporary U.S. Congress dysfunctional? The American public thinks so: Just 16 percent approved strongly of Congress in January of 2016.[4] Still, episodes of legislative deadlock—including a federal government shutdown in 2013 and near defaults on the nation's debt—fuel debate about whether and why Congress has lost its ability to identify and solve major public problems. Echoing the electorate's dismal view of its national legislature, Thomas Mann and Norman Ornstein offer the toughest critique: They argue that transformation of the Republican Party into an "insurgent outlier" has paralyzed our governing institutions.[5] David Mayhew, in contrast, urges caution: Antimajoritarian biases in American politics, he suggests, are rarely permanent. In short, Mayhew argues that our political system is self-correcting; Mann and Ornstein suggest instead that the Republican Party has forced Congress off its rails.

No one can say today, of course, whether Congress's current legislative difficulties are permanent. So we cannot now fully resolve the debate between Mayhew and his critics. However, Congress's loss of public legitimacy requires that we investigate the dynamics that drive congressional lawmaking and evaluate Congress's recent legislative performance. In this chapter, I review debates about the causes of legislative deadlock and draw on recent research to put contemporary stalemate into historical perspective over the past half century. I find that even when Congress and the president manage to reach agreement on the big issues of the day, intense partisanship and electoral competition continue to undermine Congress's capacity to solve public problems. Indeed, the 113th Congress (2013–2014) was the most deadlocked Congress over the postwar period. Whether and how well our political system can or will self-correct in the coming years remains an open question.

Theoretical Approaches to the Study of Lawmaking

The study of congressional lawmaking is deeply rooted within political science. The origins of the political science discipline lie partially in the study of American national institutions—their legal structures, institutional details, and broader function or performance in the American political system. Attention to Congress's lawmaking performance would not have been considered unusual to any of the discipline's first political scientists. Before the American Political Science Association was launched in 1906, Frank Goodnow and other Columbia University professors contemplated creating an American Society for the Study of Comparative Legislation.[6] Today, we might view the early work as descriptive and normative. Still, such studies sought to bring social science to bear on questions about politics and policy—to create "a practical role for social science." Those scholars naturally turned to analyses of the separation of powers, asking whether congressional, presidential, and administrative bodies were sufficiently accountable to the broader needs of the country. Woodrow Wilson's *Congressional Government* fits this vein perfectly—decrying Congress's domineering committees that he claimed thwarted the interests of the majority party and the president.[7]

Political science's early focus on the study of laws and institutions took a backseat by midcentury, turning instead to new questions and measures introduced by the behavioral revolution. Drawing from the fields of psychology and sociology, political scientists came to consider individuals, their roles, and their behaviors as central building blocks in the study of politics. Political action, in turn, stemmed from the aggregation of individual behavior. Viewing the political world as a place in which individuals followed roles and rules and learned by socialization, political scientists evinced relatively little interest in institutions at midcentury. As Kenneth Shepsle has observed, institutions were "empty shells to be filled by individual roles, statuses and values . . . There was no need to study institutions; they were epiphenomenal."[8] Some legislative scholars remained dedicated to the study of institutions in this period. Nelson Polsby's 1968 work on the institutionalization of the U.S. House and Joseph Cooper's 1970 work on the origins of the committee system come to mind. But Shepsle's comment captures the broader behavioral focus of the era.

Legislative scholars returned to the study of institutions with the adoption of economic modes of analysis in political science in the 1970s. Instead of seeing institutions as unimportant in the building of theory, scholars now considered the analytical relevance of actors' policy preferences and the structure and procedures of the legislative game. Influence conferred by rules and organization empowered certain individuals in the pursuit of their preferences. Legislative scholars applied economic models to a wide set of applications within the study of Congress, including the organization of its committees, bargaining and coalition building, and relations with the executive.[9] The flowering of legislative research was impressive and offered bedrock contributions to our understanding of legislative strategy and choice. Still, the analytical focus remained at the micro level. Theory was tuned to explain how rationally motivated individuals pursued their goals and how institutional features served to enhance or constrain purposive behavior.

Despite legislative scholars' return to the study of institutions, *macropolitics* received little attention in this era. If *micropolitics* emphasizes the individual as the critical analytical unit, macropolitics focuses on outputs—policy outcomes, lawmaking, and systemic performance (electoral, constitutional, or institutional). To be sure, legislative scholars never completely turned a blind eye to the study of congressional performance: Decades ago, scholars including Lawrence Chamberlain and James Sundquist evaluated patterns in legislative outputs, with an eye to both the impact of divided party government (Sundquist) and the relative balance of power between Congress and the president (Chamberlain).[10] Still, there was little attention to the development of macrolevel theory during this period. We gained detailed analyses of legislative performance in different eras but were left with little in the way of generalizable explanations. Nor did other scholars take up these works to test their implications in other periods or contexts. Microlevel analyses—first advanced by sociological perspectives in the 1950s and 1960s and then followed by economics-based theory in the 1970s and 1980s—dominated legislative studies.

Publication of David Mayhew's *Divided We Govern* in 1991 marks the origins of the contemporary study of legislative performance.[11] Mayhew brought systematic, quantitative evidence to bear in testing claims about the impact of divided party control on the production of landmark laws. To be sure, *Divided We Govern* came on the heels of a series of works by presidential and legislative scholars perplexed and frustrated by the frequent periods of divided party government that prevailed after World War II. Between 1897 and 1954, divided party control of government occurred 14 percent of the time; between 1955 and 1990, it occurred two-thirds of the time. And as V. O. Key observed in the 1960s, "Common partisan control of executive and legislature does not assure energetic government, but division of party control precludes it."[12] Decades later, scholars (including most prominently James Sundquist) were still calling for a new theory of coalitional government to explain how Congress and the president could secure major policy change in the presence of divided government.[13]

In *Divided We Govern*, Mayhew returns us to these pursuits by asking a simple and accessible question about Congress's performance in the postwar era: "Were many important laws passed?"[14] Mayhew's empirical goal is to set up a test of the effect of divided party control on the level of lawmaking. To do so, he identified landmark laws in a two-stage process that combined contemporary judgments about the significance of Congress's work each session with policy specialists' retrospective judgments about the importance of legislation. Based on these data, Mayhew generated a comprehensive list of landmark laws enacted in each Congress between 1947 and 1990 and subsequently updated online through 2014. Mayhew then tested whether the presence of divided government reduced the number of major laws enacted each Congress.

Mayhew concluded in *Divided We Govern* that it matters little whether a single party controls both the White House and Congress: Not much more gets done than under divided party control. Mayhew absolved divided government as a cause of legislative inaction and then attempted to disentangle several other primary influences on Congress's performance. Some of those forces—including legislators' electoral incentives—point toward constancy in the record of lawmaking. But other forces, Mayhew demonstrates, appear to be important alternative sources of variation in explaining congressional productivity, including shifting public moods or tastes for activist government, presidents' electoral cycles, and issue coalitions that cut across the left–right divide.

Mayhew's counterintuitive finding spawned theoretical and methodological debate about how best to explain and measure variation in Congress's legislative performance over the postwar period. One prominent theoretical response to Mayhew's work was Keith Krehbiel's *Pivotal Politics*.[15] Krehbiel's work was not strictly a challenge to Mayhew's argument because neither study placed much analytical weight on the impact of political parties on legislative outcomes in Congress. Instead, Krehbiel introduced a new theoretical framework for conceptualizing the conditions that foster lawmaking. Krehbiel's key contribution was the concept of legislative *pivots* engaged in a *pivotal politics* game—institutional actors endowed with key procedural rights within a stylized legislative game.

Krehbiel's central insight is that constitutional and extraconstitutional institutional rules create *pivotal* players on whom collective choice depends. In the congressional context, the collective choice at stake is the formulation of public law. Focusing on the presidential veto and the Senate filibuster, Krehbiel argues that the cloture and veto pivots are the critical actors for determining whether or not changes to the policy status quo will be adopted. Any existing policy that is located between these pivots (the *gridlock interval*) cannot be changed, assuming that legislative politics follows along a single dimension and that lawmakers' votes reflect their sincere preferences over policy. In other words, legislative stalemate can occur even in the presence of a congressional majority that favors a policy change.

The pivotal politics theory has important implications for understanding the conditions under which Congress and the president will be able to agree to major policy change. First, policy outcomes are consistent with the views of the supermajority pivots of the legislature. With a conservative president and a conservative majority, any effort to move policy substantially to the right would be blocked by a liberal filibuster pivot; right-of-center status quos would also remain unchanged, since a conservative president would veto any movement left of the policy, and the veto would be sustained by the veto pivot. Not surprisingly, the conditions that make policy ripe for change include elections that change the alignment of preferences of the pivotal players and major exogenous shocks that might alter the location of the policy status quo, such as leaving the status quo outside the existing gridlock interval. In other words, exogenous shocks—such as the terrorist attacks of September 11, 2001—can leave existing policy untenable to large congressional majorities.

Second, the pivotal politics model precludes an analytical role for political parties. Legislators in the basic model are individual utility maximizers rather than partisans seeking collective electoral or policy goals for the party. Parties are mere aggregations of individuals rather than pivotal actors endowed with formal blocking rights. One of the model's nice features is that it helps to explain why unified party control often fails to produce major policy change. Failure to secure the support of the filibuster pivot has hamstrung many a majority party, including Democrats under President Bill Clinton in 1993, when he sought a large stimulus bill, and Republicans under President George W. Bush in 2005, when he pushed to privatize Social Security. *Pivotal Politics* also helps to explain the challenges faced by President Barack Obama's Democratic majority in 2010 after the loss of its filibuster-proof Senate majority—requiring compromise with the Republicans, for example, in crafting the landmark Dodd-Frank Act that revamped the financial regulatory system.

The model also suggests that legislative gridlock would occur in periods of divided government—for instance, with a Democratic-controlled Congress and a Republican in the White House. In this scenario, a liberal congressional majority's effort to move centrally located policy to the left would be thwarted by a right-side filibuster pivot, as well as a right-side presidential veto. The veto pivot, whose vote would be necessary to override the president's veto, is also unlikely to prefer the liberal majority's bill proposal to the status quo. In short, policy gridlock ensues. Given the implication of the pivotal politics model that gridlock can occur under both unified and divided government, the model provides the theoretical basis for Mayhew's null effect for divided government. The broader implication of these nonpartisan models is that policy change is likely only in the context of large, bipartisan coalitions, particularly when existing policy is rather extreme. Moreover, as Krehbiel argues, the model helps to account for other empirical regularities identified by Mayhew, including the "honeymoon" effect, in which new presidents secure major policy change. The pivotal politics model suggests that gridlock would indeed be broken if a new president pushes major change when he inherits extreme status quo policies that are out of step with the views of new congressional majorities and the president.

In the nearly two decades since the publication of *Pivotal Politics*, other legislative scholars have challenged Mayhew and Krehbiel's nonpartisan accounts by building theory that expects party influence over the shape of policy outcomes. In my own work on gridlock, I suggest that both interbranch and intrabranch conflict—coupled with the ideological distribution of the two major parties—shape the prospects for major legislative change.[16] First, I show that the degree of partisan polarization matters, as ideologically distant parties make harder the crafting of large bipartisan majorities necessary for durable policy change. Second, I capture the impact of intrabranch conflict, showing that deadlock stems, in part, from bicameral differences in House- and Senate-favored policy outcomes. In other words, both intrabranch and interchamber conflict complicate lawmakers' capacity to resolve pressing public problems.

Measuring Congressional Performance

Competing theories of legislative politics generate expectations about the conditions under which Congress should be highly productive or mired in stalemate. To weigh the strength of these explanations, we need a robust measure of Congress's legislative performance over time. Legislative scholars disagree about how to measure Congress's tendency to legislate or deadlock. Mayhew's approach of counting landmark laws provides a numerator: a count of the major laws enacted by Congress and the president each Congress, as judged by both contemporary journalists and historical observers. Others have built on Mayhew's counting of laws in different ways, distinguishing, for example, different types of laws or degrees of public salience.

Judging Congress by how many laws it enacts is problematic. The measure provides an excellent sense of Congress's legislative accomplishments. But it can't capture legislative failure. Moreover, changes in procedural practices—for instance, the increase in omnibus legislating beginning in the 1980s that led party leaders to aggregate small bills into mammoth legislative packages—complicate comparisons of laws over time. One key alternative to simple counts appears in my book, *Stalemate*: a measure of legislative deadlock that isolates the set of salient issues on the nation's agenda and then determines the legislative fate of those issues in each Congress. The result is a ratio of failed measures to all issues on the agenda each Congress. My sense is that this measure of gridlock captures variation in Congress's performance, largely because it meets key benchmarks we might impose to judge a measure's construct validity. The measure identifies Lyndon Johnson's Great Society Congress as the most productive of the postwar period and determines that the 2013 to 2014 Obama Congress (in which Republicans drove the government to shut down and nearly defaulted on the nation's debt) was the most deadlocked. Such assessments comport with historical and contemporary coverage of Congress's postwar performance.

Legislating in Polarized Times   195

As I explained in detail in *Stalemate*, I devised a method for identifying every policy issue on the legislative agenda, based on the issues discussed in the unsigned editorials in the *New York Times*. Using the level of *Times* attention to an issue in any given Congress as an indicator of issue salience, I identified for each Congress between the Eightieth (1947–1948) and the 106th (1999–2000) the most salient issues on the legislative agenda. (As shown in Figures 8-1a and 8-1b, these data are now updated through the 113th Congress, 2013–2014). I then turned to news coverage and congressional documents to determine whether or not Congress and the president took legislative action in that Congress to address each salient issue. The measurement strategy produced a denominator of every major legislative issue raised by elite observers of Capitol Hill and a numerator that captured Congress's record in acting on those issues. The resulting gridlock score captures the percentage of agenda items left in limbo at the close of each Congress.

Figures 8-1a and 8-1b display the size of the policy agenda, updated through 2014, coupled with the number of failed legislative issues in each Congress.[17] Looking first at the smoothed trend line in the overall number of legislative issues mentioned each Congress in the *Times* editorials, the size of the overall agenda

Figure 8-1a   Total Number of Legislative Issues on the Agenda, 1947–2014

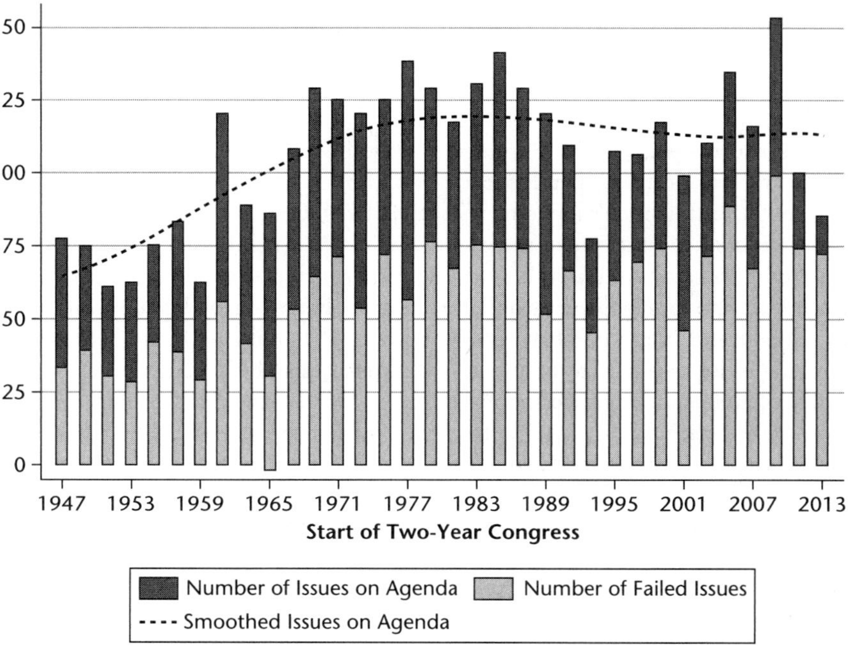

■ Number of Issues on Agenda   □ Number of Failed Issues
---- Smoothed Issues on Agenda

Source: Compiled by author.

Figure 8-1b Number of Salient Legislative Issues on the Agenda, 1947–2014

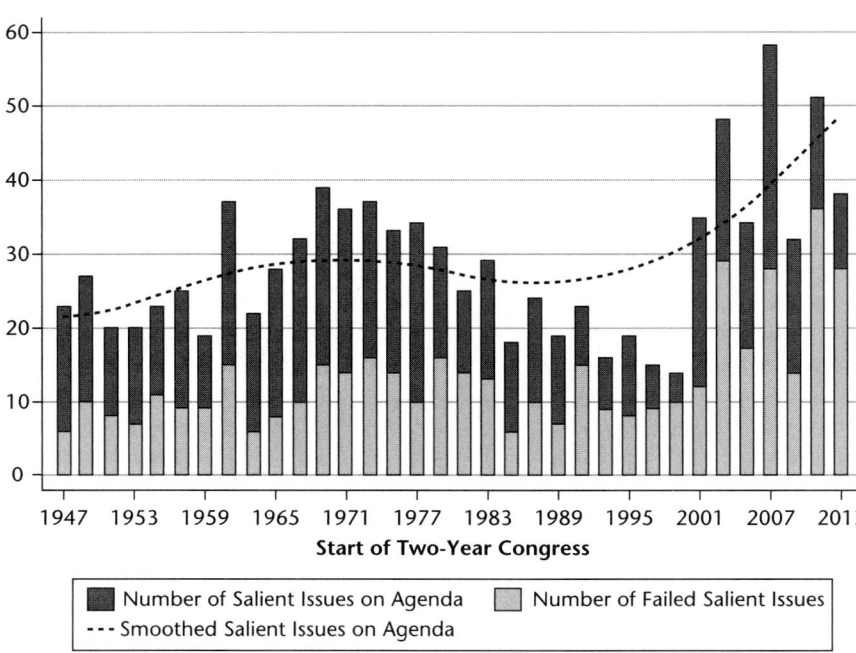

Source: Compiled by author.

increases as expected with the return of large liberal majorities during the mid-1960s and stays at this expanded level through the advent of the civil rights, environmental, and women's movements of the 1970s. Only in recent years do we see a slight increase in the size of the agenda, no doubt reflecting both later efforts to renew the spate of landmark laws of the earlier, activist period and newer issues brought to the fore by the war on terror, global climate change, and so on.

The trend in the number of salient issues in the bottom figure is more eye-catching. The overall size of the agenda increases only incrementally over the most recent decade, but the number of salient issues rises markedly in the most recent Congresses. It is possible that the recent rise in deadlock has helped to fuel expansion of the agenda: Big issues remain unsolved and thus recur on the nation's agenda in the following years. Failure to address reform of immigration law, entitlement programs, and the tax code, for example, likely helped to increase the number of salient issues on the agenda in recent years. Moreover, a spate of new issues in the past decade likely caught the attention of the *Times'* editorial writers, including homeland security, global warming, cyber security, U.S. wars in Iraq and Afghanistan, the onset of financial crisis, and the worst economy since the Great Depression.

Figure 8-2 Frequency of Legislative Deadlock, 1947–2014

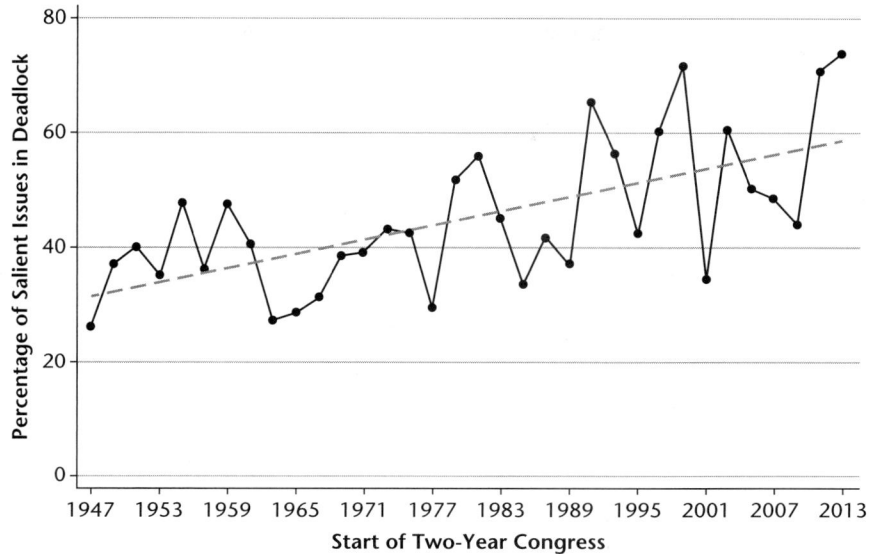

Source: Compiled by author.

Figure 8-2 shows the level of legislative deadlock on salient issues in each Congress between 1947 and 2014. Five features of the data stand out. First, the frequency of deadlock shows a secular increase over time. Perceptions that Congress (2013–2014) struggles more today than it did decades ago hit the mark. Second, the direst claims about recent Congresses are true. By this measure, the 113th Congress appears to be the "worst Congress ever"—at least since the series begins after the end of World War II. In fairness, the title should be shared with the last Congress of the Clinton administration in 1999 to 2000 and with the dismal 112th Congress (2011–2012). In all three Congresses, lawmakers and the president deadlocked on almost three-quarters of the most salient issues on the agenda. No surprise that public approval of the 113th Congress nearly fell off the charts, bottoming out at 7 percent when legislative stalemate closed down nonessential parts of the federal government for three weeks.

Third, caution is still in order in comparing recent Congresses. Some of the issues considered "successfully" addressed in recent Congresses might never have been deemed acceptable outcomes previously. For example, Congress and the president traditionally fund federal highway construction for multiyear periods. Following the expiration of highway programs in 2009, however, Congress and the president passed over thirty short-term extensions until the parties finally agreed to a fully funded, multiyear bill late in 2015. Two-week extensions seem like obvious failed efforts to reauthorize highway spending.

But what about the multiyear highway bill adopted in 2012, an agreement that funded only a third of a traditional six-year bill? I code the highway bill as a success, even though the two-year bill failed to ensure the solvency of highway trust funds after two years. Lawmakers did not resolve the financial impasse until late in the fall of 2015, when legislators raided the capital surplus of the Federal Reserve to replenish the highway trust fund.[18] Similarly, the challenge of raising the government's debt ceiling in the summer of 2011 was resolved, in part, by creating a special committee to generate over a trillion dollars in federal savings. I score the 2011 deficit reduction package a legislative success, even though the "supercommittee" that resulted from the budget deal folded in deadlock. Even recent peak levels of deadlock likely underestimate Congress's legislative difficulties.

Fourth, although President Obama's first Congress (the 111th in 2009 and 2010) was relatively productive compared to Congress's performances over the past decade (with the exception of the 9/11 Congress), the 111th Congress fell far shy of the records of the Great Society Congresses. Granted, the 111th Congress was nearly thirty points more productive than the Congresses that followed. But even the widely heralded 111th Congress left a lengthy list of major issues in limbo, including proposals to address secondary education, campaign finance, global warming, immigration, and gun control. Even with control of the White House and large Democratic majorities—and for a period of time, a filibuster-proof Senate majority—Democrats struggled to surmount significant barriers to major policy change.

Finally, a brief look at the 107th Congress's performance in the wake of the attacks of September 11, 2001, is instructive. Overall, the 107th Congress (with unified Republican control of both branches for just a few months early in 2001) was fairly productive, leaving just a third of the policy agenda in 2001 and 2002 in stalemate. But lawmakers' capacity to make deals was directly shaped by the events of 9/11. Eight of the thirty-five salient issues on the agenda in that Congress rose directly from the attacks of September 11. And on those eight issues, Congress and the president mustered a perfect record: They enacted the Patriot Act, wrote the Authorization for the Use of Military Force, addressed the needs of 9/11 victims, and more. Even on less salient issues stemming from September 11, congressional deadlock was extraordinarily rare, with just a single issue left in legislative limbo. Still, a cooperative spirit and unity of purpose did not extend to the rest of the policy agenda. If we exclude the issues related to the terrorist attacks, Congress and the president deadlocked on just under half of salient policy issues. Congress appears to have retained the capacity to act swiftly when some crises occur, also evidenced by Congress's 2008 bailout of Wall Street after the Federal Reserve and Treasury allowed Lehman Brothers to go under. However, as we might expect, legislative unity dissipates when Congress turns its attention back to the regular policy agenda. Moreover, not every crisis spurs action. Despite overwhelming majorities in favor of tougher restrictions on gun purchases after the killing of school children in Newtown, Connecticut, in 2012, Congress deadlocked and failed to act.

Why and When Do Lawmakers Deadlock?

Armed with a measure to systematically capture the degree of legislative deadlock over time, I return to the motivating question for this chapter: Is Congress dysfunctional? In *Stalemate*, I used the measure of the frequency of legislative gridlock to test alternative institutional and electoral explanations for variation in congressional stalemate. Unlike Mayhew's findings in *Divided We Govern* (but similar to his findings in his more recent work, *Partisan Balance*), my original study showed that unified party control of Congress and the White House significantly reduced the frequency of deadlock. In contrast, split party control of Congress and the White House empowers the opposition party to block policy measures that they oppose, generating higher levels of stalemate in periods of party control.

Importantly, *Stalemate* showed that party control alone was insufficient to explain variation in Congress's performance. Two additional forces shape Congress's likelihood of solving public problems. First, I showed that a shrinking political center drives up the frequency of stalemate.[19] The emergence of polarized political parties—even before the Bush and Obama presidencies—complicated the challenge of building coalitions capable of overcoming the veto points institutionalized on Capitol Hill. Second, I showed that bicameral policy differences interfere with the crafting of policy coalitions, even in periods of unified party control.[20] Although electoral and policy differences between the branches tend to garner the most attention in Washington, bicameral policy differences seemed to complicate lawmakers' capacity to find common ground across the chambers. The results of the 2010 and 2012 congressional elections—delivering control of the House to Republicans while keeping the Senate in Democratic hands—make plain the barriers imposed by intrabranch conflict.

How does this model hold up when we incorporate the records of the Congresses between 2001 and 2014? By updating the measures to capture legislative moderation, bicameral differences, and divided government between 1947 and 2014, I can re-estimate the analysis from *Stalemate* to examine the impact of interbranch and intrabranch conflict on Congress's legislative performance. Once again, partisan polarization appears to drive the incidence of legislative deadlock. Declining moderation—controlling for party control and bicameral conflict—leads to significantly more frequent bouts of deadlock. With moderation at barely a tenth of its postwar high, nearly 75 percent of salient issues were mired in deadlock in 2013 and 2014.

Interestingly, according to the model's results, party control and House–Senate differences no longer lead to disproportionately higher levels of deadlock once I control for the degree of chamber moderation. That said, my measure of bicameral differences is arguably a new victim of rising levels of polarization.

Figure 8-3 Number of Conference Reports Considered in Both Chambers, 1947–2014

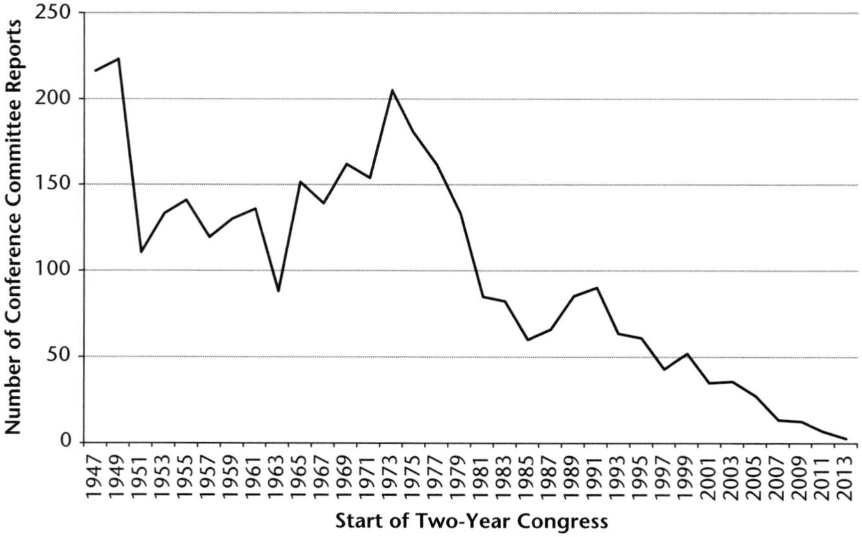

Source: See the "Bills Through Conference" section of annual final editions of House Calendars. Calendars for the 104th to the 113th Congresses are available online at https://www.gpo.gov/fdsys/browse/collection.action?collectionCode=CCAL&browsePath=112&isCollapsed=true&leafLevelBrowse=false&ycord=123, accessed February 15, 2016.

As shown in Figure 8-3, Congress no longer goes to conference to resolve bicameral disagreements. The sharp decline in conferencing partially reflects the overall decline in major lawmaking in Congress. But it also reflects party leaders' proclivity for negotiating deals behind closed doors rather than in the more open forum of a conference committee.[21] Whatever the reason, the measure no longer offers a robust way to capture the degree of bicameral conflict. In short, the model likely underestimates the impact of bicameral disagreement on Congress's ability to solve problems. After all, we know that the two chambers have taken markedly different approaches to numerous salient issues in recent years, including climate change, reform of the immigration laws, and repeal of Obamacare and Dodd-Frank. Regardless, the analysis reinforces the impact of rising polarization in American politics: Congress struggles to legislate when the two major parties pursue strongly divergent agendas.

What broader conclusions can we draw from this analysis? First, the results confirm scholars' findings about the impact of polarized parties on Congress's ability to legislate. That said, because we typically use lawmakers' floor voting records, it is difficult to disentangle the extent to which partisan polarization captures ideological differences across lawmakers' or members' partisan "team play" behavior. As Frances Lee shows using other vote-based data, a good portion of the party polarization we see in floor voting likely reflects a dose of both.[22] Here, I avoid treading into methodological and theoretical debates about distinguishing between partisan behavior and policy preferences. Regardless of whether we deem polarization a function of ideological differences, strategic disagreement by partisans seeking electoral advantage, or a mix of the two, the results are clear: When ideological or electoral incentives yield intensely partisan behavior, lawmakers struggle to find broadly palatable solutions to the range of problems they face.[23] Counter to the expectations of the American Political Science Association's *Towards a More Responsible Party System*, loyal, cohesive parties undermine rather than facilitate problem solving in Congress.

Second, results remain suggestive of the impact of bicameral differences on the difficulty of legislating. Even after controlling for the level of polarization and party control of the two branches, policy differences between the two chambers matter to Congress's ability to legislate over most of the postwar period. As the House and Senate react differently to bicameral policy compromises—regardless of whether party control is unified or split between the chambers—legislative deadlock likely grows.

Third, the effect of party control appears attenuated. *Stalemate* identified an independent effect of party control on legislative performance: The frequency of deadlock was higher in periods of divided, rather than unified, party control. In his recent work, Mayhew also identifies a party effect: Unified party control increases the chances that presidential proposals will be enacted.[24] To be sure, unified Democratic control of government after the election of 2008—coupled with a short-lived filibuster-proof Senate majority—yielded major legislative dividends in 2009 and 2010: Congress and the president overhauled federal health care programs, reformed the financial regulatory system, advanced major arms control, and dumped the military's "Don't Ask, Don't Tell" policy, among other accomplishments. Still, the analysis reported here suggests that divided party government today has only a limited impact on lawmakers' capacity to govern.

Why do we observe high levels of deadlock regardless of party control? This question would not puzzle Keith Krehbiel, whose pivotal politics model explored earlier suggests that policy change is a function of the location of the status quo and the preferences of supermajority pivots on the left and right of the median voter. Given the implicit threat of a filibuster and thus the inevitable need for a supermajority coalition in the Senate, in equilibrium, party control of a chamber should not matter to the frequency of legislative agreement. Of course, if the median (in recent years, a member of the majority party) and the filibuster pivot are relatively close to each other along the left–right policy dimension, then we should rarely expect filibusters to derail Senate bills; the median can easily accommodate the demands of the filibustering senator by amending the measure. That perhaps is why David Mayhew recently finds little systematic or sustained evidence of an antimajoritarian Senate. However, once the median and the filibuster pivot begin to diverge markedly as the parties polarize, the sixtieth senator's policy demands might be harder for the majority to accommodate, thus increasing the frequency of both filibusters and legislative deadlock.

I suspect that the recent, rising proclivity of opposition party senators to insist on sixty votes for adoption of most amendments and measures has undermined the legislative power of majority parties in periods of unified party control.[25] For example, increased minority party exploitation of its parliamentary rights would help to explain the litany of legislative measures left in limbo after Democrats lost their filibuster-proof majority in the winter of 2010, as well as the heavy load of measures left undone at the close of the Republican-led 108th Congress (2003–2004). As electoral incentives increase for the minority party to play a more confrontational role in the Senate and as the costs of filibustering decline, unified party control might prove a less powerful tool for driving the legislative process.

Discussion and Conclusions

The middle of the road is a dangerous place to be. Still, my analysis suggests that there is a good deal of truth both to Mayhew's sanguine view looking forward in American politics and to Mann and Ornstein's more dire analysis of the current state of Congress and its legislative capacity. In many ways, Congress's recent legislative performance fits the well-established pattern from *Stalemate*: When elections yield more polarized and partisan parties and chambers, bargaining is more difficult and compromise more frequently out of reach. To the extent that recent Congresses fit the broader pattern established in the postwar period, we might be on safe ground concurring with Mayhew that the recent "imbalances" during the Obama administration are not likely to be "permanent, systemic problems." That is an empirical judgment that can only be confirmed in the future.

Still, five reservations temper that conclusion. First, levels of legislative deadlock have steadily risen over the past half-century. Stalemate, at times, now reaches across three-quarters of the salient issues on Washington's agenda. Granted, legislators differ over what issues and conditions constitute "problems."[26] That might increasingly be so as the parties polarize; lawmakers today even disagree about basic facts. For example, many Republican lawmakers disbelieve scientific evidence of global climate change. Still, the absolute level of deadlock is remarkable. Moreover, pushing issues off to the future sometimes makes problems worse. Inaction on climate change, for example, makes future remediation more difficult and costly. Faced with deadlock over long-term solutions, lawmakers often patch differences with temporary measures when they run up against a deadline to act. The frequency of legislative solutions that "kick the can" down the road exasperates congressional critics and illustrates Congress's exceedingly low legislative capacity in recent years.

Second, even when Congress and the president muster agreement on a policy solution, such agreements sometimes create new problems. For example, some economists argued that fiscal-policy brinkmanship in the summer of 2011 over raising the nation's borrowing limit harmed the economy and set back the economic recovery.[27] Moreover, fiscal headwinds created by the Budget Control Act of 2011 are often noted as a key cause of the nation's sluggish recovery from the Great Recession.[28] If both congressional inaction and action make problems worse, then it is unclear how quickly the political system will rebound from its partisan impasse. No doubt, the system is corrigible. But it might take a long time to correct itself.

Third, it is not clear whether current levels of partisanship will subside soon. Partisan polarization appears to be on the verge of passing historical levels in the Senate and has surpassed House records stemming from the turn of the last century. In addition, many argue that such polarization is "asymmetric": Republicans (particularly in the House) have moved farther to the right than Democrats have moved to the left. One might wonder whether the asymmetric pattern stems, in part, from Republicans' minority status: Having lost the White House in 2008, the GOP was unleashed to shoot for the moon, promising conservatives that they would oppose Democrats' initiatives in Washington. So long as some degree of polarization is driven by sheer partisan team play, in which the opposition party is more likely to object to proposals endorsed by the president, then extreme levels of partisanship will continue to lead to unprecedented levels of deadlock. Whether the House and Senate wings of the Republican Party can self-correct and how long it would take remain to be seen. The success of the House Freedom Caucus in driving John Boehner, R-Ohio, from the speakership in the fall of 2015 is hardly a good sign of self-correction.

Fourth, if we move beyond legislative productivity as the benchmark for judging congressional performance, the assessment is still grim. Congress, in recent years, has struggled to fund federal programs on time and to conduct effective oversight of the executive branch, while the Senate has often been wrapped in partisan knots over the confirmation of presidential appointees. Indeed, it has been more than a decade since Congress last deliberated over and passed the full slate of spending bills to fund federal programs.[29] At its most extreme level of dysfunction, the federal government shut down and nearly defaulted on its obligations in the fall of 2013, when Republicans held government funding and the nation's debt ceiling hostage to their demand to defund the Affordable Care Act. Partisanship also pervades congressional oversight, to the extent that Congress conducts any at all.[30] And partisan and institutional obstacles in the confirmation process have left dozens of federal judgeships vacant in recent years, raising doubts about the judiciary's ability to dispense justice in a timely manner.[31] Across a broad spectrum of Congress's responsibilities, we see very low institutional capacity—no doubt putting Congress's powers vis-à-vis the other branches at risk.

Fifth, changes in the structure of electoral competition in recent decades likely alter lawmakers' calculations about coming to the bargaining table. As Frances Lee observes, margins of party control in the House and Senate since 1980 have been half the size (on average) of margins between 1933 and the 1980s.[32] Presidential elections have also been close, with the last landslide Electoral College win in 1984. High party competition for control of Congress and the White

House appears to affect party politics in Congress. Fierce electoral competition brings control of national institutions within reach for both parties, limiting lawmakers' incentives to compromise with the other party. Why settle on half a loaf of policy, when a full loaf can be delivered to the party base upon winning unified party control? As Morris Fiorina notes, "With majority status that much more valuable, and minority status that much more intolerable, the parties are less able to afford a hiatus between elections in which governing takes precedence over electioneering."[33] Congress's legislative capacity seems to be a victim of increased party competition in a period of polarized elites.

Ultimately, Mayhew may well be correct that our political system will weather this rough patch with little harm done. Even so, we are left, in the meantime, with a national legislature plagued by low legislative capacity. Half measures, second bests, and just-in-time legislating are a new norm, as electoral, partisan, and institutional barriers often limit Congress's capacity for more than lowest-common-denominator deals. Even if lawmakers ultimately find a way to get their institution back on track, Congress's recent difficulties have been costly—both to the fiscal health of the country and to its citizens' trust in government. The economy will likely regain its footing. Regenerating public support for Congress will be harder.

Notes

1. See "Congress and the Public," Gallup.com, http://www.gallup.com/poll/1600/Congress-Public.aspx?utm_source=genericbutton&utm_medium=organic&utm_campaign=sharing, accessed February 4, 2016.
2. David R. Mayhew, *Partisan Balance: Why Political Parties Don't Kill the U.S. Constitutional System* (Princeton, NJ: Princeton University Press, 2011), 190.
3. Thomas E. Mann and Norman J. Ornstein, *It's Even Worse Than It Looks: How the American Constitutional System Collided With the New Politics of Extremism* (New York: Basic Books, 2012), 111.
4. See "Congress and the Public."
5. See Mann and Ornstein, *It's Even Worse*, xiv.
6. See John Gunnell, "The Founding of the American Political Science Association: Discipline, Profession, Political Theory, and Politics," *American Political Science Review* 100 (2006): 479–86.
7. See Woodrow Wilson, *Congressional Government: A Study in American Politics* (New York: Houghton Mifflin, 1885).
8. See Kenneth Shepsle, "Studying Institutions: Some Lessons From the Rational Choice Approach," *Journal of Theoretical Politics* 1 (1989): 133.
9. See, among others, Keith Krehbiel, *Information and Legislative Organization* (Ann Arbor: University of Michigan Press, 1988); David P. Baron and John Ferejohn, "Bargaining in Legislatures," *American Political Science Review* 83 (1989): 1181–1206; John Ferejohn and Charles Shipan, "Congressional Influence on Administrative Agencies: A Case Study of Telecommunications Policy," in *Congress Reconsidered*, 4th ed., ed. Lawrence C. Dodd and Bruce Oppenheimer (Washington, DC: CQ Press, 1989), 393–410.

10. See Lawrence Chamberlain, *The President, Congress, and Legislation* (New York: Columbia University Press, 1946), and James L. Sundquist, *Politics and Policy: The Eisenhower, Kennedy, and Johnson Years* (Washington, DC: Brookings Institution Press, 1968).
11. David R. Mayhew, *Divided We Govern: Party Control, Lawmaking, and Investigations, 1946–1990* (New Haven, CT: Yale University Press, 1991); David R. Mayhew, *Divided We Govern: Party Control, Lawmaking, and Investigations, 1946–2002*, 2nd ed. (New Haven, CT: Yale University Press, 2005).
12. See V. O. Key Jr., *Politics, Parties, and Pressure Groups*, 5th ed. (New York: Thomas Y. Crowell Company, 1964), 688.
13. See James L. Sundquist, "Needed: A Political Theory for the New Era of Coalition Government in the United States," *Political Science Quarterly* 103 (1988–1989): 613–35.
14. Mayhew, *Divided We Govern*, 2nd ed., 36.
15. See Keith Krehbiel, *Pivotal Politics: A Theory of U.S. Lawmaking* (Chicago: University of Chicago Press, 1998). For a similar approach, see David Brady and Craig Volden, *Revolving Gridlock: Politics and Policy From Carter to Clinton* (Boulder, CO: Westview Press, 1998).
16. See Sarah A. Binder, "Dynamics of Legislative Gridlock, 1947–2000," *American Political Science Review* 93 (1999): 519–33, and Sarah A. Binder, *Stalemate: Causes and Consequences of Legislative Gridlock* (Washington, DC: Brookings Institution Press, 2003).
17. I discuss the methodological challenges of updating the data set in the appendix (pp. 20–22) to Sarah A. Binder, "Polarized We Govern," *Governance Studies Strengthening American Democracy Series*, no. 86, May 2014, http://www.brookings.edu/research/papers/2014/05/27-polarized-we-govern-congress-legislative-gridlock-polarized-binder.
18. Gabe Rubin, "Fed Is a 'Piggy Bank' for Highway Bill," Morning Consult, December 2, 2015, http://morningconsult.com/2015/12/fed-is-a-piggy-bank-for-highway-bill.
19. To capture legislative moderation, I built a measure of the size of the political center based on voting scores generated by Keith Poole and Howard Rosenthal's NOMINATE system. As detailed in *Stalemate*, I determined the number of "moderate" legislators in each chamber of each Congress and divided the percentage of moderates by the ideological distance between the two chamber parties. I then averaged both chambers' moderation to create a single moderation score for each Congress. I define "moderate" as a legislator whose first dimension DW-NOMINATE ideological score places him or her closer to the ideological median of the chamber than to his or her own party's median. Dividing by party distance helps to distinguish Congresses both by the size and relative location of the political center. For instance, a Congress with a small political center but ideologically proximate parties would score stronger on the "moderation" scale than a congress with a small political center and ideologically distant parties.
20. To capture the policy distance between the two chambers, I identified all conference reports considered by both the House and Senate in each Congress and determined the percentage of each chamber that voted in support of each report. To measure bicameral policy distance, I calculated the difference in chamber support for each report and generated a mean disagreement score for each Congress. I code conference reports approved by voice vote as 100 percent approval. The measure varied from a low of just 2 percent in the early 1950s to a high of over 10 percent in the mid-1990s.
21. The willingness to filibuster the Senate motions needed to go to conference also hamstrings the use of conference proceedings to resolve differences.

22. See Frances E. Lee, *Beyond Ideology: Politics, Principles, and Partisanship in the U.S. Senate* (Chicago: University of Chicago Press, 2009), and Frances E. Lee, "How Party Polarization Affects Governance," *Annual Review of Political Science* 18 (2015): 261–82.
23. On strategic disagreement as a cause of deadlock, see John Gilmour, *Strategic Disagreement: Stalemate in American Politics* (Pittsburgh: University of Pittsburgh Press, 1995).
24. Mayhew, *Partisan Balance*, 78.
25. See Steven S. Smith, *The Senate Syndrome: The Evolution of Procedural Warfare in the Modern U.S. Senate* (Norman: University of Oklahoma Press, 2014).
26. David R. Mayhew, "Congress as Problem Solver," in *Promoting the General Welfare: New Perspectives on Government Performance*, ed. Alan S. Gerber and Eric M. Patashnik (Washington, DC: Brookings Institution Press, 2006), 219–36.
27. Betsy Stevenson and Justin Wolfers, "Debt-Ceiling Déjà Vu Could Sink Economy," *Bloomberg View*, May 28, 2012, http://www.bloomberg.com/news/2012-05-28/debt-ceiling-deja-vu-could-sink-economy.html (accessed February 14, 2016).
28. Ben Bernanke, "The Federal Reserve: Looking Back, Looking Forward." Speech delivered at the annual meeting of the American Economic Association, Philadelphia, January 3, 2014.
29. Jessica Tollestrup, "Duration of Continuing Resolutions in Recent Years," Congressional Research Service, April 28 (RL32614).
30. Mann and Ornstein, *It's Worse Than It Looks*.
31. See Sarah A. Binder and Forrest Maltzman, *Advice and Dissent* (Washington, DC: Brookings Institution Press, 2009).
32. See Frances E. Lee, "Presidents and Party Teams: Debt Limits and Executive Oversight, 2001-2013," *Presidential Studies Quarterly* 43 (2013): 775–91.
33. Morris Fiorina, "Parties as Problem Solvers," in *Promoting the General Welfare*, ed. Eric M. Patashnik and Alan Gerber (Washington, DC: Brookings Institution Press, 2006).

9. Moderate Polarization and Policy Productivity in Congress
From Harding to Obama
Lawrence C. Dodd and Scot Schraufnagel

This essay explores the role that party polarization plays in fostering or inhibiting policy productivity in Congress. It argues that too much polarized conflict between congressional parties generates stalemate—but so does too little conflict. It is amid moderate party conflict that Congress tends to enact laws on controversial policy topics of the time. Moreover, both pure divided government and united party government prove productive in moderately polarized Congresses, though in different ways. In contrast, quasi-divided governments prove unproductive across levels of polarization. These arguments are supported by data on policy productivity derived from the Congressional Digest. *The statistical analysis covers forty-seven Congresses and includes examination of the effect that various other factors have in shaping policy productivity, including the role of severe economic crisis.*

Early in the post–World War II era, as President Harry Truman's legislative agenda lay in tatters despite united party government, scholars blamed weak, depolarized political parties for the deadlock on Capitol Hill. So much division over policy appeared to exist within the parties, and so little policy difference existed between them, that *united party government* almost seemed a meaningless term. Each party's members hesitated to invest strong powers in their leaders, lest they lead in the wrong direction on controversial policies, splitting the party. No other organized structure existed in Congress that could fashion an activist agenda across policy areas and work for its enactment. As a result, few innovative policies could make it through the complex legislative maze and across the two chambers to become law. Depolarized politics appeared to ensure sustained policy deadlock.

Hampered by weak and depolarized congressional parties, the nation appeared to need responsible-party government, in which the parties stood for different ideological agendas and members of Congress were loyal to their party. Then, a majority party could assert control of committee policy making and act to ensure policy productivity, particularly amid united party government headed by a like-minded president. Or so the argument went.[1] The thrust of this argument was to predict a negative relationship between party *depolarization* and policy productivity in Congress.

In the contemporary period of polarized politics, by contrast, congressional observers are not so sure about the advantages of responsible-party government and party polarization.[2] So much policy unity has existed within the parties, and so much ideological difference has existed between them, that partisan warfare seems the daily agenda on Capitol Hill. The vast majority of each party's members are party loyalists committed to their party's ideological agenda, with few in either the House or Senate willing to push for cross-party cooperation and compromise on topical legislation. Yet without compromise, it is exceedingly difficult to construct majorities large enough to overcome the procedural obstacles that proliferate in Congress.[3] Cross-party policy stalemate—and even cross-chamber stalemate—thus has become the norm.[4] The thrust of this argument is to predict a negative relationship between party *polarization* and policy productivity.

Watching the problematic policy performance of the contemporary polarized Congress and also recalling the deadlock of the depolarized era, one confronts a confounding question: How is it that Congress gained its reputation as one of the world's greatest lawmaking legislatures? If both depolarization and polarization tend toward policy gridlock, how has Congress generated such an impressive historical record of policy activism? The answer lies, we will argue, in recognizing the curvilinear relationship that exists between party system polarization and policy productivity in Congress: Too little party polarization, as well as too much, undermines policy productivity. In contrast, moderate party polarization can facilitate it.

We begin the essay by elaborating our *moderation thesis*. We then turn to testing how well it accounts for productivity by Congress in the ninety-four years from the presidency of Warren Harding through the first three Congresses of President Barack Obama. In doing so, we will pay particular attention to the ways in which other factors—such as economic crisis, presidential honeymoons, and divided government—may aid, complicate, or limit the ability of moderation to foster policy productivity.

The Moderation Thesis and Policy Productivity

The capacity of Congress to generate extensive policy productivity is aided, we will argue, by the capacity of the nation's electoral and institutional politics to foster moderate levels of conflict between its two congressional parties. In presenting our moderation thesis, we see party polarization as ranging across a continuum from low polarization on the left end to high on the right side. By definition, Congresses that fall toward the low, or depolarized, end of the continuum are characterized by extensive intraparty differences over policy, combined with higher levels of interparty similarity. With great divisions within parties and limited differences between them, depolarized political parties can have limited capacity to structure policy conflict and push alternative policy agendas forward, much as James MacGregor Burns and E. E. Schattschneider argued was the case in the early postwar era.[5] As a result, innovative policy productivity in depolarized Congresses should be low, and congressional committees should foster incremental policy making even under united party government.[6]

By contrast, Congresses that fall toward the high, polarized end of the continuum, on the right, are characterized by low intraparty differences over policy, combined with little interparty overlap in policy preferences. The great distance between polarized parties, combined with the high cohesion of their members, provides little room for compromise between the parties, much as Sarah Binder argued was the case in the late 1990s and early 2000s.[7] As a result, policy productivity in polarized Congresses also tends to be low, with this tendency reinforced by the obstructionist complexities of a bicameral legislature. This can be true even with a president of the same party as the majority in Congress, as in the mid-2000s, during the presidency of George W. Bush.

Moderate party polarization falls in the middle of the continuum—with moderate levels of agreement within the parties over policy and moderate levels of policy difference between them. In such conditions, (a) parties can etch out ideological positions across policy domains that are sufficiently distinct to structure an informative and coherent debate about new alternative policy directions, and yet (b) the membership of each party can be sufficiently heterogeneous and moderate in ideological orientation as to allow for cross-party persuasion and compromise. Moderate polarization can thus make possible the flexible and bipartisan crafting of majority coalitions across a range of policy areas, as argued by Joseph Cooper in 1970,[8] while the bipartisan quality of such coalitions can limit excessive minority party obstructionism. Moderate polarization thus should foster policy productivity.

The remainder of this essay explores the value of our moderate-polarization thesis. To be clear, we expect policy productivity to peak as Congress approximates moderate polarization at the center of our left–right continuum and decrease as Congress moves toward either low or high polarization, *ceteris paribus*. Of course, circumstances such as unified or divided government, presidential honeymoons, or a president's skillful leadership may complicate the relationship between polarization and productivity. Similarly, as illustrated by the Great Depression of the 1930s, extensive breakdown in the national and international economy can foster distinctive electoral pressures and generate unique moments of congressional activism, as witnessed in President Franklin Roosevelt's Seventy-third New Deal Congress. In contemporary times, the new, activist, and highly productive united party government of President Barack Obama's 111th Congress (2009–2010) was likewise elected in the first presidential election year following the coming of the Great Recession. One thus may need to be alert to and control for any distinctive level of productivity associated with economic crises.

The Measurement Strategies and Initial Findings

To test the moderation thesis, our central research strategy is to look at the quantitative relationship between moderate polarization and policy productivity.[9] To do so, we need statistical data for a number of comparable Congresses that chart their variation in policy productivity and party system polarization.

Measuring Policy Productivity

The most difficult issue that we have faced is finding data that allow us to assess the productivity of postwar Congresses, including recent Congresses through the 113th, while also including a number of Congresses from the decades prior to the World War II era. Including a broad array of Congresses helps ensure both that our Congresses range broadly across depolarized and polarized periods and that our findings reflect broad historical tendencies, rather than being unique to a specific time period. In the absence of estimates of contemporary policy productivity that include recent Congresses, as well as those prior to the postwar era, we have created our own measure of productivity by turning to the policy coverage provided by the *Congressional Digest*.[10]

The *Digest* has provided extensive coverage of policy debates in Congress every year since 1921, seeking to identify and discuss what it refers to as "controversial" policy topics in each Congress. The *Digest* has a reputation for providing nonpartisan policy analysis and doing so in a professional manner. It publishes informed analysis and contrasting points of view about each policy and refrains from partisan or policy endorsements. Its identification of major controversial legislation thus appears balanced and neutral in character, focused on a broad range of issues salient across parties. Using the *Digest* to identify the major policy struggles of each Congress allows us to examine how productive Congresses were, from the standpoint of the policy controversies of their time. At issue is not whether Congress produced historic, landmark legislation that analysts decades down the line would see as a defining long-term contribution to the nation. Our concern, rather, is to determine the extent to which a Congress responded to the pressing topics of their day, as identified by the *Digest* during that Congress, through the subsequent enactment of legislation.

Using the *Congressional Digest* to determine the pressing policy topics of a Congress allows us to extend the analysis of policy productivity across the quarter-century prior to the end of World War II while also including all postwar Congresses up to the 113th Congress. The forty-seven Congresses, which include all Congresses from 1921 through 2014, came after implementation of woman suffrage, after implementation of an elective Senate, and following adoption of the cloture rule in the Senate. The Congresses are thus reasonably comparable. At the same time, the resulting data set contains a large number of depolarized, moderately polarized, and polarized Congresses. There is thus considerable variation in the polarized nature of the Congresses, aiding our examination of the extent to which polarization shapes policy productivity. Finally, the size and format of the *Digest* are virtually unchanged across these Congresses. During each, it has published a discrete number of articles on the controversial policies of that Congress, with each Issue focused on a specific policy topic and including statements by supporters and opponents. The existence of statements for and against each policy allows us to use the articles to certify the "demand for controversial legislation," Congress by Congress, thereby addressing the denominator issue that Morris Fiorina and Sarah Binder have introduced into the study of policy productivity.[11]

To estimate the number of controversial policy topics that confronted a Congress, we count the number of policy areas that received issue-length coverage by the *Congressional Digest*. To estimate the productivity of a Congress, we first determined the number of these controversial policy areas discussed in the *Digest* and then the percentage of these policies in which legislation was subsequently passed during that Congress and signed by the president or passed into law over his veto, using the *U.S. Statutes at Large* to make this determination. This percentage score will serve as our Congress-by-Congress estimate of policy productivity on *topical legislation*—that is, on legislation that was seen by a major nonpartisan publication covering policy developments on Capitol Hill as sufficiently important to merit contemporary coverage. In this percentage score, the denominator certifies the number of areas in which highly salient and contested demand for legislation existed in a Congress, as reported by the *Digest*. The numerator indicates the number of these topical areas in which legislation was subsequently enacted, with Congress supplying legislation to meet demand.

Figure 9-1 presents the percentage of *Digest* article topics that were addressed by the extant Congress through the enactment of new public laws, from the start of Warren Harding's presidency in 1921, the Sixty-seventh Congress, through the end of Barack Obama's third Congress, the 113th, in 2014. The figure documents extensive variation in policy productivity, Congress by Congress, across the ninety-four years and forty-seven Congresses. Twenty Congresses produced laws in 20 percent or less of the topical areas the *Digest* covered; we will refer to these as *stalemated* Congresses. Three of these Congresses, we should note, produced laws on only 10 percent or less of the *Digest*'s topical categories, indicating severe stalemate. Twenty-two Congresses produced laws above 20 percent, ranging to 40 percent of the topical categories the *Digest* covered; we will refer to these as our *satisfactory* Congresses, in terms of topical policy productivity. Seven of these Congresses fell above 30 percent, up to 40 percent, indicating highly satisfactory performance. Finally, five Congresses produced laws above 40 percent, indicating *exceptional* productivity.[12]

Figure 9-1 Percentage of Topical Legislation Passed, by Congress, 67th Through 113th

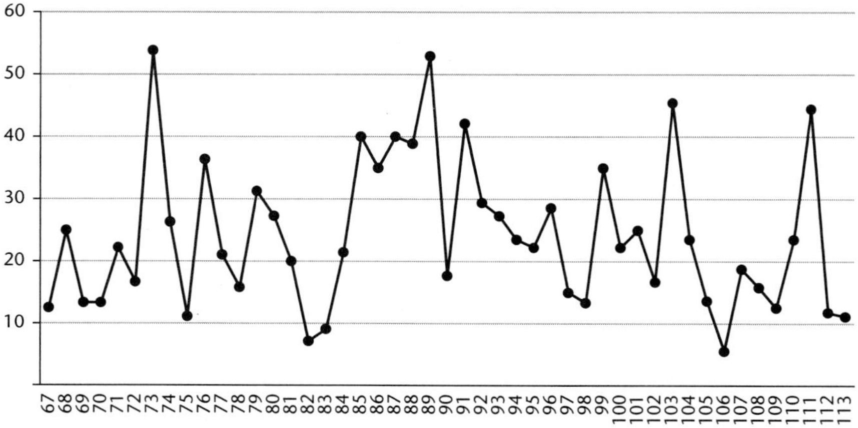

Source: Compiled by authors.

Measuring Party Polarization

To measure party polarization, we turn to an approach developed by John Aldrich, David Rohde, and Michael Tofias.[13] In doing so, we shift away from our own measure of polarization, as detailed in our previous essays in the ninth and tenth editions of *Congress Reconsidered*. We do so to explore how robust our argument is, utilizing an alternative polarization measure. The Aldrich-Rohde-Tofias method uses multiple summaries of the DW-NOMINATE scores created by Keith Poole and Howard Rosenthal to capture interparty difference in roll call behavior of legislators, with greater interparty difference indicating increased party polarization. Consistent with our previous essays in this volume, we use a two-chamber average to estimate overall congressional polarization.[14] Figure 9-2 reports the resulting pattern of party polarization that characterizes Congress from the Sixty-seventh to the 113th Congresses. As the figure indicates, the lowest period of polarization came from the mid-1930s to the mid-1950s, whereas the highest period has come during the two decades following the Republican revolution of 1994.

Comparing the polarization pattern in Figure 9-2 with the pattern in Figure 9-1 on policy productivity, it is clear that productivity does not follow polarization in some easy and consistent fashion. Rather, productivity is more jagged and scattered in its highs and lows across the time period than is polarization. One can find a productive or unproductive Congress amid almost any depolarized or polarized context. This is what one would expect in a multicausal world in which a variety of factors other than moderation can also influence productivity, including major economic crises, presidential honeymoons, and the divided or united nature of government. Our immediate

Figure 9-2 Polarization by Congress: Two-Chamber Average

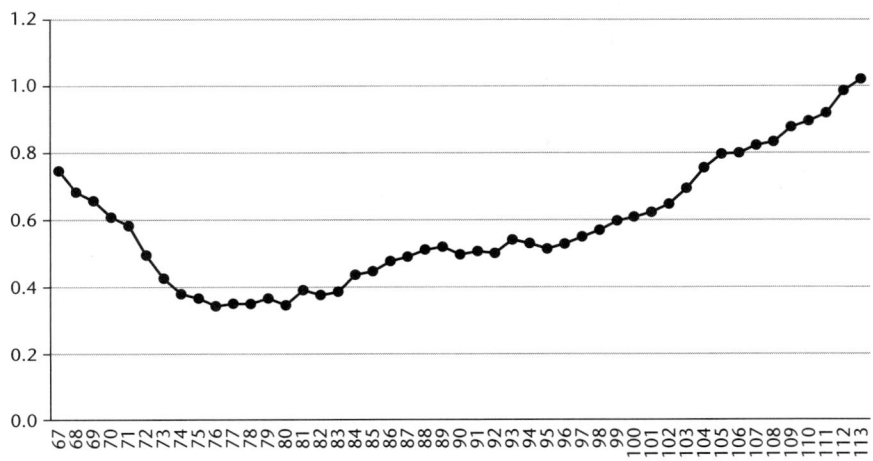

Source: Compiled by authors.

question is whether, amid the scatter, there is a tendency for periods of moderate polarization to produce more productive Congresses while periods of extreme high or low polarization produce less productive Congresses. One way to assess this issue is to look at the bivariate relationship between productivity and polarization.

Exploring the Bivariate Relation

Table 9-1 divides our forty-seven Congresses into those that fall toward the center, moderate positions on polarization and those that fall toward high or low polarization. In dividing the Congresses, we use the median polarization score across the forty-seven Congresses to separate out the depolarized Congresses from the polarized. This gives us twenty-four depolarized Congresses (which includes the median Congress) and twenty-three polarized ones. We then divide both the depolarized Congresses and the polarized Congresses into two groups, using their median scores to do so, so that we can contrast those Congresses that are more extreme in depolarization or polarization with those that are more moderate within the depolarized or polarized categories.[15]

Following these procedures, the table includes twelve extremely *depolarized* Congresses, twelve moderately *depolarized* Congresses, twelve moderately *polarized* Congresses, and eleven extremely *polarized* Congresses. The columns under these four categories indicate the number of Congresses within that category that reached the level of policy productivity listed at the left of the table. We place parentheses around the one score for exceptional productivity in the extremely depolarized category: This Congress is President Franklin Roosevelt's first, the

Table 9-1 The Bivariate Relationship Between Moderate Polarization and Policy Productivity[a]

Productivity	Extremely Depolarized Congresses	Moderately Depolarized Congresses	Moderately Polarized Congresses	Extremely Polarized Congresses	All Congresses
Exceptional (> than 40%)	(1)	2	1	(1)	5
Highly satisfactory (> than 30% to 40%)	2	4	1	0	7
Satisfactory (> than 20% to 30%)	4	4	5	2	15
Stalemated (> than 10% to 20%)	3	2	5	7	17
Highly stalemated (0 to 10%)	2	0	0	1	3
Total	12	12	12	11	47

a. Cells indicate the number of Congresses that fit each category.

Source: Compiled by authors.

Seventy-third New Deal Congress, which took office amid the Great Depression. We also place parentheses around the one score of exceptional productivity in the extremely polarized category: This Congress is President Barack Obama's first 111th Congress, which took office amid the Great Recession. We present these scores in parentheses to alert the reader to the exceptional nature of the time in which these two Congresses occurred.

Based on our moderation thesis, we expect lower levels of productivity among the extremely depolarized and extremely polarized Congresses, whereas higher levels of productivity should occur in moderately depolarized and moderately polarized Congresses. Looking across Table 9-1 we do see this general pattern.

Among the depolarized Congresses, on the left of the table, the twelve Congresses that fall in the moderately depolarized range are more productive than are the twelve that fall in the extremely depolarized range. Looking at low-productivity, the moderately depolarized group has two stalemated Congresses and no severely stalemated ones, whereas the extremely depolarized group has three stalemated Congresses and two that are severely stalemated. Looking at moderate to high productivity, the moderately depolarized Congresses include four satisfactory ones, four highly satisfactory ones, and two exceptional Congresses. In contrast, the extremely depolarized Congresses include four satisfactory ones, two highly satisfactory ones, and the one exceptional Congress, which occurred amid the Great Depression. Overall, as Congresses move from moderate depolarization leftward to extreme depolarization, productivity falls.

Among the polarized Congresses, on the center-right side of the table, the twelve that fall in the moderately polarized range are more productive than are the eleven that fall in the extremely polarized range. The moderately polarized group has five stalemated Congresses, whereas the extremely polarized group has seven stalemated Congresses and one severely stalemated Congress. On the flip side, the moderately polarized settings produce five satisfactory Congresses, one highly satisfactory Congress, and one exceptional Congress. In contrast, extreme polarization yields only two satisfactory Congresses and one exceptional one, in parentheses, which is the Congress that occurred after the onset of the Great Recession (111th Congress). As Congresses move from moderate polarization rightward to extreme polarization, productivity falls.

A general tendency exists for Congresses that fall toward the moderate range of polarization to be more productive than their highly depolarized or highly polarized counterparts. Thus, leaving aside the Seventy-third Congress and the 111th Congress for reasons discussed earlier, the six most productive Congresses in our data set all fall in the moderate terrain. Three of these are exceptional Congresses: President Lyndon B. Johnson's Eighty-ninth Congress (1965–1967), often known as the Great Society Congress; President Richard M. Nixon's Ninety-first Congress (1969–1971); and President William J. Clinton's 103rd Congress (1993–1995). The other three most productive Congresses fell in the very satisfactory range: President Dwight D. Eisenhower's Eighty-fifth Congress (1957–1959); President John F. Kennedy's Eighty-seventh Congress (1961–1963); and the Kennedy/Johnson Eighty-eighth Congress (1963), which witnessed the assassination of President Kennedy midway through its term. These Congresses confronted some of the most divisive policy issues in contemporary history, including civil rights, voting rights, immigration, trade, poverty, and the like, reminding us that Congress is capable of responding to policy controversies in extensive ways, amid moderation.

In addition, there is a distinct tendency for the most stalemated Congresses to arise amid extreme immoderation, both during the depolarized and polarized eras. Three of the six most stalemated Congresses occur amid *extreme depolarization*. These include two of the three severely stalemated Congresses: President Harry S. Truman's Eighty-second Congress (1951–1953) and Eisenhower's Eighty-third Congress (1953–1955). The poor productivity of these two Congresses is consistent with the concerns of Burns and Schattschneider about the deadlocked nature of Congress early in the postwar era. The third Congress in this depolarized group was Franklin D. Roosevelt's Seventy-fifth Congress (1937–1939). The three other most stalemated Congresses then occur amid *extreme polarization*. These include the third most severely stalemated Congress, Clinton's 106th Congress (1999–2001), as well as the 112th Congress (2011–2013) and the 113th Congress (2013–2015) during the presidency of Barack Obama. The poor productivity of these three Congresses is consistent with the concerns of Sarah Binder in *Stalemate* about the detrimental effects high levels of polarization have for policy productivity. More generally, extreme immoderation, either at the depolarized or polarized end of our continuum, appears to create conditions that foster extreme stalemate.

Nevertheless, there are complications for our moderation thesis in the overall patterning of policy productivity in Table 9-1. Thus, moderate depolarization appears more productive than moderate polarization, and extreme depolarization appears more productive than extreme polarization. While a curvilinear pattern remains in the data, with moderate Congresses more productive than immoderate ones, the Congresses on the polarized side of the continuum, as a group, appear to generate weaker-than-expected policy productivity, when contrasted with the Congresses on the depolarized side. This observation points to the need to explore the relationship between moderation and productivity more extensively, through the use of multivariate statistical analysis. Adding control variables to our analysis could strengthen the relationship between moderation and productivity, possibly by identifying special historical factors that account for the lower-than-expected productivity among the moderately and extremely polarized Congresses. Alternatively, it is possible that such controls will undercut or weaken the moderation thesis, with one or more control variables actually explaining most of the variance in productivity.

Assessing the Multivariate Relationships

To assess more fully the capacity of moderate polarization to explain policy productivity, we examine its explanatory power when we control for four other considerations.[16] Our first control variable—and the one most widely discussed among scholars and political observers—is the type of party government that characterizes national institutional politics. It could be that moderation has occurred in Congress in periods when a form of party government existed that was highly favorable to policy productivity, with this overlap unduly magnifying the positive bivariate relationship between moderation and productivity. Alternatively, the predominance of unfavorable forms of party government during periods of moderation could unduly minimize its relationship with productivity. At issue, in testing for these concerns, is determining the *types of government* most likely to foster or hinder policy productivity, *ceteris paribus*, so that we know how to construct our control variables.

Historically, as a predecessor of the responsible-party model of congressional politics, scholars and activists stressed the necessity of united party government—with the same party controlling both chambers of Congress and the presidency—in order for Congress to generate policy productivity. Whatever the level of party polarization, united party government was assumed to be more capable of enacting legislation than divided government, owing to the ability of majority party leaders to call on party loyalty in enacting legislation. In *Divided We Govern*, David

Mayhew challenged the united party government thesis, utilizing extensive data covering the time period 1946 to 2002 (second edition)[17] to demonstrate that, stated in statistical terms, a positive but insignificant association existed between divided government and productivity. In his analysis, it appeared possible for Congress to be reasonably productive under divided partisan control of Congress and the presidency, as well as in periods of united party control, with neither type of government dominant in generating productivity. In explaining this pattern, Mayhew argued that legislators' reelection considerations could offset issues of party loyalty, in divided government periods, fostering productivity even in the absence of united party control.

Subsequently, in her 2003 book *Stalemate*, Sarah Binder challenged Mayhew's position. Examining twenty-seven postwar Congresses and looking at the proportional success of Congresses in passing laws for which substantial demand exists, Binder concluded that divided government undermined proportional policy productivity. She did so, however, with a caveat, differentiating between pure divided government and quasi-divided government.[18] Periods of pure divided government, when one party controls both houses of Congress, and the other party controls the presidency, would be likely to produce policy stalemate, she argued. In this view, the two parties would use control of their separate branch of government to push very different policy agendas, undercutting compromise. Stalemate could be less likely, she proposed, during periods of quasi-divided government, when the president's party also controls one house of Congress, thereby giving the executive special leverage in congressional negotiations over policy.

In our effort to control for the type of government that exists during a Congress, we pursue a two-pronged approach. First, we construct a variable, *divided versus united party government* (referred to in Table 9-2 as *all divided governments*), which examines whether divided or united party government appears to be significant in fostering productivity. Any Congress that fails to reach united-party status is considered a divided-government Congress and is scored a "1." All remaining Congresses, each of which is characterized by united party government, are scored "0." A positive and statistically significant relationship will indicate that divided government is more powerful in fostering policy productivity, whereas a negative and statistically significant relationship will indicate that united government is more powerful in fostering productivity. An insignificant relationship will indicate that neither type of government plays a dominant role in shaping productivity, as argued by David Mayhew, though a positive or negative sign to the statistical coefficient could indicate that one or the other appears somewhat more productive, though not at a statistically significant level.

Second, following Binder, we will separate out our divided-government Congresses into two distinct control variables, in order to consider whether her differentiation between two types of divided party government makes a difference. *Pure divided government* Congresses are those in which one of the two major parties controls the House and Senate, and the other major party controls the presidency. *Quasi-divided government* Congresses are those in which one party controls only one chamber of Congress while the other party controls the presidency and the other chamber.

Our three additional explanatory variables are as follows:

Honeymoon: We follow the lead of others and use a dummy variable coded "1" for each Congress that occurs during the first two years of a presidential administration[19] but with a slight wrinkle. In the cases of Calvin Coolidge and Lyndon Johnson, we code the Congress "1" when the president takes over for a deceased president (the Sixty-eighth and Eighty-eighth Congresses) and also consider the first Congress after their own election as president (the Sixty-ninth and Eighty-ninth Congresses) as a "honeymoon" Congress. All other Congresses are scored "0." We expect to find a positive association between this variable and topical legislative productivity.[20] In this view, productivity may be enhanced in the first Congress to occur after a president has taken office, with Congress and the citizens embracing a period of good will in supporting the leadership of the president.

Severe economic downturn: We control for the two most notable *economic downturn*s that occurred during the time period studied. In this instance, we simply use a dummy variable for the Seventy-third and 111th Congresses to capture the effects that these two periods of macroeconomic collapse had on the behavior of the first presidential administrations and Congresses elected after the collapse. These are the new administration of Franklin D. Roosevelt and his first Congress and the new administration of Barack Obama and his first Congress. Given that the two previous administrations and their parties were widely blamed for the economic downturns, it is difficult to imagine Congress not acting on the topical agenda placed before it after the new presidents were sworn in, particularly since they were joined by large majorities for their parties in Congress. Such circumstances, we suggest, mandated that the new Congresses and presidents, elected to redress severe economic collapse, moved, once in office, to act on their promises.

President's rating: Lastly, we develop a unique measure of presidential prowess so as to take into account the important role the chief executive plays in policy making. In the tables that follow, we refer to this as *president's rating*, with a higher score indicating a president viewed more favorably by observers in terms of personal skill and effectiveness in office.[21] Specifically, we use information from twelve different media outlets and historians that rank the presidents' "success" in office. We use each president's average rank (dividing by the number of available surveys) and obtain a high score of 43 (out of 44 presidents) for Franklin D. Roosevelt and a low score of 3 for Warren G. Harding.[22] We anticipate a positive association with productivity. Our motivation is to assure that our test of moderate party polarization is not simply capturing the aptitude of specific presidents who happened to serve amid moderate polarization.

With these variables in hand, we can determine whether moderate polarization continues to have a positive and significant association with policy productivity when other considerations are accounted for. Before turning to such scrutiny, however, let us detail another aspect of our statistical tests: the use of two distinct strategies for assessing policy productivity.

Two Strategies of Statistical Modeling

Thus far in this essay, we have discussed policy productivity as involving the success of Congress in enacting legislation Congress by Congress—looking at the percentage of contemporary *Congressional Digest* topics that were addressed with new public laws during each individual Congress. Using each Congress as the unit of analysis is the predominant approach that scholars have employed in analyzing productivity. It is also undoubtedly one of the dominant ways that citizens assess a Congress and its members, month by month and at election time: Has this been a "do-nothing Congress" that failed to address the major policy challenges of the day or a productive one that ranks with the best Congresses of a lifetime? Recognizing the salience of such concerns, it is important that we report our findings on a Congress-by-Congress basis, both to allow readers to compare our results with those of other analysts and to inform public debate about the macrolevel factors that facilitate policy performance. In terms of our thesis in this essay, such a perspective is captured by the statement that "the more moderate a Congress, the higher the percentage of topical laws it should pass," taking into account the other macrolevel conditions confronting the Congress.

A macrolevel, Congress-by-Congress comparative analysis, however, does have its drawbacks. When analysts are assessing the relative performance of a limited number of Congresses, looking at the proportion of significant legislation that each Congress has passed, the number of available Congresses to examine is necessarily quite small, so statistical results and resulting generalizations can be influenced by the distinctive behavior of one or two unique Congresses. More data are thus always desirable, as are alternative ways to test empirical arguments. This consideration is then reinforced by a second concern.

Many developments occur within a Congress that can influence the success of specific pieces of topical legislation, so macrolevel factors are not the only variables influencing congressional productivity. Thus, a policy topic can rise to salience early rather than late in a Congress, allowing legislators considerable time to deliberate over it and craft viable legislation. Similarly, legislation may rapidly pass through one chamber or the other, creating momentum for it and encouraging close attention to it by the other house. These intra-Congress developments may be essential to our understanding of policy productivity, and attention to them through statistical controls may be critical to adequately assessing the independent influence that various macrolevel factors also have in fostering productivity.[23]

To address these and other issues, our second strategy for testing our moderation thesis is to take a topic-by-topic, rather than a Congress-by-Congress, approach to testing our thesis. In doing so, we ask, What conditions are likely to produce the enactment of a law on a particular policy topic, at a particular time, given the context in which it is being considered? In terms of our curvilinear thesis, such a perspective is captured by the statement that "a law is more likely to be enacted when the topic is considered by a moderately polarized Congress," controlling for macrolevel context together with specific attributes of the microlevel status of the legislation within Congress when it reaches topical or salient status.

This shift in perspective increases the sample size we analyze from the forty-seven Congresses that the *Digest* included in its coverage of controversial policy topics to the 849 topics that the *Digest* covered across these Congresses.[24] Our primary concern, as we pursue this second way of examining congressional productivity, is to determine whether moderate polarization continues to play a statistically significant role in explaining productivity, as we shift away from a Congress-by-Congress focus and instead examine productivity topic by topic. Is the moderation thesis valuable only in accounting for differences in the proportion of topical legislation enacted by the forty-seven Congresses under study so that moderation's primary value comes in helping to foster a successful Congress? Or does the moderation thesis also explain variation in the enactment of the 849 legislative topics covered by the *Digest* so that we see moderate polarization as a powerful causal phenomenon that fosters the success of an individual piece of legislation, even when we take into account microlevel developments within the Congress that is considering the legislation.

Because the *Digest* publishes its articles on policy topics throughout a Congress so that it covers some topics early in the life of a Congress and some late, we can control for the amount of *time left* (in months) for the enactment of a policy following its discussion by the *Digest*. With more time left in the Congress, we expect a greater probability that legislation will be passed, generating a positive coefficient. This tells us that the earlier legislation reaches *agenda salience* in a Congress, measured here by the date on which it captured the attention of the *Digest*, the more likely it will pass. Additionally, analyzing productivity topic by topic allows us to assess how mature different legislative initiatives are at the time at which the *Digest* determines that they are a controversial topic deserving of attention. The *Digest* (or any source used to determine the demand for legislation) may discuss some policy topics after considerable effort by Congress to address them, whereas other topics the *Digest* discusses may be relatively new concerns. To control for this, we opt for a simple yet practical and reliable strategy. We create two dummy variables (*passed House* and *passed Senate*) that tap whether any legislation dealing with the topic may have passed one or the other chamber in the extant Congress.

Although passing a single chamber does not make a law, we expect a stronger probability of law passage when this has occurred. Of the 849 *Digest* topics we examined across the time period studied, 169 had already seen new legislation passed in the House at the time an article was published on that topic, and 114 had seen new legislation passed in the Senate at the time of article publication. So in the topic-by-topic analysis, we add the three topic-specific control variables—*time left*, *passed House*, and *passed Senate*—and in each instance, we expect a positive association with productivity. In combining these topic-specific controls with our Congress-specific controls, we can get a clearer sense of the power of moderate polarization in shaping policy productivity.

The Multivariate Results

We report our findings *by Congress* in Table 9-2 and *by article* in Table 9-3. In each of these tables, we present a Model A, which reports our multivariate results when using a control for *all divided government*, and a Model B, which reports our results when we divide *all divided government* into its two distinct types, *quasi-divided governments* and *pure divided governments*, and test for their separate effects.

Comparing the results across the four models contained in these two tables, the relationship between moderate polarization and productivity is positive in all four models, as our moderation thesis proposes. Moreover, it is statistically significant in all four models, reaching a strongly significant level of $p < .001$ in three of the four models and an easily significant level of $p < .01$ in Model B of Table 9-2. These findings provide significant support for the moderation thesis. The general positive relationship between moderation and policy productivity presented in Table 9-1 does not appear to be a spurious result that disappears as we introduce a set of contextual variables, including type of government, honeymoon Congresses, severe recessions, or president's rating, into our analysis of the forty-seven Congresses (Table 9-2). It does not appear to rely solely on the comparison of proportional productivity of forty-seven Congresses in order to achieve statistical significance. Moreover, it does not appear to result from subtle biases that may occur in the timing of policy coverage by the *Digest*, as demonstrated by our use of topic-specific controls in Table 9-3 in our analysis of the 849 issues discussed by the *Digest* across the forty-seven Congresses.

Only severe economic downturns rival moderate polarization as an explanation for topical productivity in Congress. Electoral mandates at unique moments of severe economic decline appear to be truly powerful forces predicting productivity. At the same time, our results—after controlling for Roosevelt's New Deal Congress and Obama's Great Recession Congress—underscore how critical moderate polarization can be in fostering productivity outside of such moments of severe crisis. Thus, the New Deal Congress has stood as the historical exemplar of congressional activism, with analysts regularly comparing the performance of all other Congresses to that of the Seventy-third Congress (1933–1935). In the process, united party government, particularly in a honeymoon presidency, has come to be seen as the condition most likely to generate policy activism, based on the example of the first New Deal Congress. The success of the Barack Obama's first Great Recession Congress, also characterized by united party government, has reinforced this expectation. But both of these Congresses came amid extraordinary economic collapse, not the conditions one seeks to generate in order to enhance policy productivity.

The critical issue, we suggest, is to determine the conditions that foster policy productivity outside of moments of extraordinary economic crisis. Controlling for the effects of the Seventy-third and 111th Congresses, moderate polarization appears to be the central factor fostering productivity. But other variables are important as well. *Honeymoons* are linked in a positive and significant way to productivity, as expected, when we look at our analysis by Congress in Table 9-2.

Table 9-2 Variables Associated With Topical Legislation Passed: Congress as the Unit of Analysis, 67th Through 113th Congresses

Model: Prais-Winsten Regression[a]
DV = the proportion of *Congressional Digest* topics that were addressed by a new law

	Model A	Model B
Variables (expected sign)	Coefficient (robust S.E.)	Coefficient (robust S.E.)
Moderate polarization (+)	33.29[b] (9.73)***	29.06 (10.83)**
All divided governments (–)	2.24 (3.39)	
Quasi-divided government (–)		–1.70 (4.73)
Pure divided government (null)		4.55 (3.14)[t]
Honeymoon (+)	7.03 (3.80)*	7.80 (3.67)*
Severe economic downturn (+)	23.79 (4.33)***	22.73 (4.45)***
President's rating (+)	0.17 (.14)	0.19 (.13)[t]
Constant	2.25 (6.23)	3.00 (5.82)
F-statistic	138.07***	101.80***
R²	0.41	0.44
D-statistic (transformed value)	1.98	1.97
N	47	47

Source: Compiled by authors using data obtained from http://www.voteview.com/dwnomin_joint_house_and_senate.html (last accessed September 18, 2016).

*** $p < .001$; ** $p < .01$; * $p < .05$; [t] $p < .10$ (one-tailed tests)

a. Prais-Winsten regression corrects for autocorrelation in the models, and the coefficients can be interpreted the same as ordinary least squares (OLS) regression. It turns out, in both models, autocorrelation of the error terms is somewhat of a problem. Running the models using OLS regression, the Durbin-Watson D-statistics are 1.70 for Model A and 1.80 for Model B. These values suggest evidence that positive autocorrelation of error terms may be present; see Damodar N. Gugarati, *Basic Econometrics*, 3rd ed. (New York: McGraw-Hill, 1995), 422, 820. The transformed values suggest we cannot reject the null hypothesis of no positive autocorrelation. Alternatively, the models can be run using OLS with a lagged dependent variable. These alternative models return ostensibly no change in the results of this analysis and no statistical or substantive change in the value of the moderate polarization variable.
b. The dependent variable is measured as the percentage of *Digest* topics that were addressed by a new law in the contemporaneous Congress, and the measure of moderate polarization has a minimum value of .04 (113th Congress) and a maximum value of .53 (Ninety-fourth Congress). So the coefficients in Model B, representing the average relationship between these two variables, suggest that a move from the most moderate Congress to the most immoderate Congress is associated with little more than a 14 percent increase in productivity, all else being equal ([.53 – .04] × 29.06). In contrast, a presidential-honeymoon Congress is associated with about a 7 percent increase, on average.

This relationship falls to borderline significance, in the analysis by topic in Table 9-3 ($p < .10$). The *president's rating* variable also returns a positive coefficient in all four models but reaches clear statistical significance only in Table 9-3, which assesses the relationship by topic.[25] Honeymoons may aid presidents with their initial success in generating legislative productivity, as captured in Table 9-2, but it may more nearly be their political skills, as captured in *president's rating*, that

Table 9-3 Variables Associated With Topical Legislation Passed: *Congressional Digest* Articles as the Unit of Analysis, 1921–2014

Model: Logit Regression
DV = Scored "1" if *Congressional Digest* topic is addressed by a new law

	Model A	Model B
Variables (expected sign)	Coefficient (robust S.E.)	Coefficient (robust S.E.)
Moderate polarization (+)	3.32 (.57)***	3.32 (.57)***
All divided governments (−)	−0.03 (.17)	
Quasi-divided government (−)		0.003 (.24)
Pure divided government (null)		−0.06 (.18)
Honeymoon (+)	0.27 (.20)^t	0.27 (.21)^t
Severe economic downturn (+)	1.22 (.23)***	1.22 (.23)***
President's rating (+)	0.02 (.007)*	0.02 (.007)*
Topic-Specific Controls		
Time left (months) (+)	0.047 (.012)***	0.048 (.012)***
Passed House (+)	0.751 (.265)**	0.753 (.264)**
Passed Senate (+)	0.601 (.259)**	0.604 (.255)**
Constant	−3.91 (.38)***	−3.90 (.38)***
Chi-squared	231.55***	253.17***
Pseudo R^2	0.07	0.07
N	849	849

Source: Compiled by authors.

*** $p < .001$; ** $p < .01$; * $p < .05$; ^{t} $p < .10$ (one-tailed test)

a. Logit coefficients must be converted back to predicted probabilities in order to be easily understood. When the coefficient for *moderate polarization* is converted using the results from Model B, we learn that as we move from the most immoderate to the most moderate Congress, the likelihood that a *Digest* topic will be addressed by a new law goes from about 6 percent to over 24 percent, on the conditions that the legislation has not passed either chamber, there is no divided government, no honeymoon, no severe economic downturn, there is a president with an average rating, and there is little more than twelve months left in the Congress. In comparison, if some version of the legislation has passed the House of Representatives when the *Digest* discusses the topic, and all other conditions are the same as noted above, the likelihood of a new law passing the most immoderate Congress is about 12 percent, and this grows to over 40 percent for the most moderate Congress.

aids them in topical success across their presidencies, as suggested by the results reported in Table 9-3.

Legislative productivity is also greatly shaped by the conditions that characterize consideration of a topic during the life of a Congress, as demonstrated by the time-specific controls we introduce in the analysis of productivity by topic in Table 9-3. With our time-specific controls, we consider the date on which the *Digest* provides issue-length coverage of a topic as the point at which that topic has reached *agenda salience* during that Congress. We then construct our three time-specific control variables based on this date. The resulting correlations are powerful. *Time left*, *passed House*, and *passed Senate* are all positively and significantly linked to productivity, as anticipated. Topics that reach agenda salience early in a Congress, with considerable time left for consideration, have a strong statistical likelihood of being enacted during that Congress. And topics that have already passed the House and/or the Senate, at the point of reaching agenda salience, are more likely to win enactment, suggesting that the maturity of a legislative initiative also plays an important role in policy productivity. Clearly, there are intra-Congress considerations well beyond macrolevel factors such as honeymoon, president's rating, or moderate levels of conflict that shape productivity and that need close and systematic attention by scholars. On the other hand, such intracongressional factors are not solely determining the fate of our legislative topics.

When we take our intra-Congress factors into account, along with our macrolevel control variables, moderate polarization increases in statistical significance, in the move from Table 9-2, where the intra-Congress controls are not used, to Table 9-3, where they are present.[26] These results strongly suggest that congressional productivity is aided when some degree of distance exists between the two parties and some moderate overlap exists among their members. We propose that such conditions of moderation aid productivity because they help foster serious negotiation and compromise on the controversial issues of the day. Our one remaining question is, What, if anything, can we learn about *government type* as we seek to elucidate opportunities for negotiation, compromise, and productivity?

The Role of Government Type

The debate over the relationship of government type and policy productivity is complicated by the limited number of Congresses scholars have examined in developing and supporting their arguments, the different ways in which they have conceptualized government type, and the ways in which they have measured policy productivity. In the research reported here, we have roughly doubled the number of Congresses used to assess issues of productivity, as compared with the defining books of the leading scholars in the area, David Mayhew and Sarah Binder. Additionally, we focus both on a measure of proportional success by

Congress and on a measure that examines congressional success in enacting topical legislative statutes across Congresses.

Building on Binder, we utilize three measures of government type. Model A, in Tables 9-2 and 9-3, uses a measure of government type that pits *all divided governments* against united party governments. This variable would report a positive sign if all divided governments perform definitively better than united party governments in explaining productivity and a negative sign if united party governments matters more. Model B, in each table, uses two distinct measures of government type. The first measure pits *pure divided governments* against all other forms of government type, with this variable reporting a positive sign if pure divided governments perform better. The second measure pits *quasi-divided governments* against all other forms of government and reports a positive sign if it performs better.

Our findings are intriguing. Table 9-2 presents our results for government type when we examine proportional productivity, Congress by Congress. Looking at the table, Model A reports a positive but insignificant relationship between all divided governments and productivity. This positive sign for all divided governments raises the possibility that divided governments aid productivity more than do united party governments, just the opposite of dominant scholarly expectations, with the caveat that the statistical relationship falls short of significance.

Model B, in Table 9-2, reports a positive and significant relationship (at a $p < .10$ level) between pure divided governments and proportional productivity and a negative, though insignificant, relationship between quasi-divided governments and proportional productivity. Whereas the dominant scholarly literature expects pure divided government to hinder productivity, we find that it may well foster it. And whereas the dominant scholarly literature suggests quasi-divided government may aid proportional productivity, we find that it may hurt it. In contrast, the statistical association between the three forms of government type and topical productivity across Congresses is always weak, as seen in Table 9-3. Government type thus helps explain the variation in proportional success that individual Congresses have in enacting legislation but may be less helpful in accounting for variation that occurs in the enactment of individual pieces of legislation across Congresses.

What is unclear from our multivariate analysis is why pure divided government appears effective in fostering proportional productivity, Congress by Congress, whereas the other forms of government appear less successful. To address this issue, we will break down our data in tabular format, looking to discern additional insight that can help account for these relationships. Specifically, we turn to assess how successful pure divided governments are in fostering policy productivity, at different levels of polarization, when compared to united party and quasi-divided governments. Table 9-4a presents the number of Congresses that fit each government type at each level of productivity when Congresses are depolarized (when the Congress is at or falls below the median polarization score). Table 9-4b presents the number of Congresses that fit each category for polarized Congresses (those falling above the median polarization score). We begin by assessing the difference between pure divided and united party government and then move to further scrutiny of quasi-divided government.

Comparing Pure Divided Versus United Party Governments

The great advantage of pure divided governments, when we look closely at the data in Tables 9-4a and 9-4b, is that they tend to reach a satisfactory level of productivity in a much more consistent manner, avoiding stalemate, than do united party governments. This pattern is seen across depolarized and polarized Congresses. Thus, all seven pure divided governments that occurred within a depolarized setting performed at a satisfactory level or better, whereas only ten of the sixteen united party governments reached this level in depolarized settings. Looking at polarized settings (Table 9-4b), five of the eight pure divided governments reached a satisfactory level, whereas only four of the nine united governments reached this level. When we aggregate our data, 80 percent (twelve of fifteen) of the pure divided governments reached a satisfactory level of productivity, as contrasted with only 56 percent (fourteen of twenty-five) of the united party governments. Why then have scholars and political activists been so enamored with united party governments?

The attraction of united party governments comes in the expectation that they can generate high levels of policy making, perhaps including the great game-changing breakthrough Congresses that enable the nation to address long-neglected policy concerns. In examining this issue, we find that eight of twenty-five united-party-government Congresses (32 percent) reached the level of highly satisfactory performance, with four of these reaching an exceptional level of performance. We include in this count Roosevelt's Seventy-third New Deal Congress and Obama's 111th Great Recession Congress. In contrast, only three of the fifteen pure-divided-government Congresses (20 percent) reached the highly satisfactory level of productivity, and only one of these reached exceptional status. United party governments thus do appear to hold out a greater prospect for highly satisfactory and even exceptional productivity. The dilemma with united party government is that in pursuing high productivity, one risks the emergence of stalemate.

Whereas pure divided government tends to foster sustained, if at times modest, productivity (twelve of fifteen Congresses), united party government appears to generate swings between periods of stalemate (eleven of its twenty-five Congresses) and moments of heightened productivity (eight of its twenty-five Congresses). Seen in this manner, both pure divided government and united party government contribute important features to the overall productivity of Congress. Pure divided governments reliably generate a number of Congresses that reach at least a satisfactory level of productivity and then united party governments add, if sporadically, a series of highly productive Congresses. The reliability

Table 9-4a Polarization, Government Type, and the Proportional Productivity of Depolarized Congresses, 1921–2015

	Highly Depolarized Congresses			Moderately Depolarized Congresses			All Depolarized Congresses		
	DG	QD	UG	DG	QD	UG	DG	QD	UG
Productivity:									
Exceptional (> than 40%)	0	0	1	1	0	1	1	0	2
Highly satisfactory (> than 30% to 40%)	0	0	2	2	0	2	2	0	4
Satisfactory (> than 20% to 30%)	2	0	2	2	0	2	4	0	4
Stalemated (> than 10% to 20%)	0	0	3	0	1	1	0	1	4
Highly stalemated (0% to 10%)	0	0	2	0	0	0	0	0	2
Total	2	0	10	5	1	6	7	1	16

Source: Compiled by authors; cells indicate the number of Congresses that fit each category.

Note: DG = pure divided government; QD = quasi-divided government; UG = united party government

Table 9-4b Polarization, Government Type, and the Proportional Productivity of Polarized Congresses, 1921–2015

	Highly Polarized Congresses			Moderately Polarized Congresses			All Polarized Congresses		
	DG	QD	UG	DG	QD	UG	DG	QD	UG
Productivity:									
Exceptional (> than 40%)	0	0	1	0	0	1	0	0	2
Highly satisfactory (> than 30% to 40%)	0	0	0	0	1	0	0	1	0
Satisfactory (> than 20% to 30%)	2	0	0	3	0	2	5	0	2
Stalemated (> than 10% to 20%)	1	3	3	1	2	2	2	5	5
Highly stalemated (0% to 10%)	1	0	0	0	0	0	1	0	0
Total	4	3	4	4	3	5	8	6	9

Source: Compiled by authors; cells indicate the number of Congresses that fit each category.

Note: DG = pure divided government; QD = quasi-divided government; UG = united party government of pure divided government in avoiding stalemate gives it a statistical edge in our multivariate analysis, but united party government nevertheless makes a meaningful contribution with its periods of heightened productivity.

Most importantly, from the standpoint of our moderation thesis, both pure divided government and united party government appear to perform well amid moderation and more poorly under high or low polarization, thereby demonstrating the power that moderation holds for policy productivity. Looking at pure divided government, eight of its nine Congresses (88.9 percent) that occurred amid moderation reached a satisfactory level of productivity, including one exceptional and two highly satisfactory Congresses. Only one of its moderate Congresses was stalemated. In contrast, four of the six pure divided Congresses that occurred amid immoderation reached a satisfactory level (66.7 percent), with no highly satisfactory or exceptional Congresses and two stalemated Congresses, one of which was severely stalemated.

Looking at united party government, eight of its eleven Congresses (72.7 percent) that occurred amid moderation reached a satisfactory level of performance, including two highly satisfactory and two exceptional Congresses. Only three were stalemated, none severely. In contrast, only six of its fourteen Congresses (42.9 percent) that occurred amid immoderation reached a satisfactory level of productivity. The two exceptional immoderate Congresses, we note, were Roosevelt's Seventy-third and Obama's 111th. Eight of the fourteen Congresses (57.1 percent) that occurred amid immoderation were stalemated, two of which were severely stalemated.

Periods of moderation thus help pure divided government and united party government realize their potential in generating proportional productivity. Immoderation limits the proportional productivity of both forms of government. Moreover, these patterns will hold if one compares moderately depolarized Congresses to highly depolarized Congresses and moderately polarized Congresses to highly polarized Congresses.[27] Against this backdrop, let us turn to examine the productivity of quasi-divided governments—that is, those Congresses in which one party controls the presidency and one chamber of Congress and the second party controls the other chamber.

The Case of Quasi-Divided Governments

In contrast to pure divided governments and united party governments, quasi-divided governments appear to hold out little chance for significant productivity, with our seven quasi-divided governments producing six stalemated Congresses.[28] Our central concern with quasi-divided governments thus lies less with charting and assessing variation in their proportional policy performance and more in understanding why they have such a strong tendency to stalemate and the effects of this stalemate on our moderation thesis.[29]

We propose that two interacting factors foster the strong tendency of quasi-divided governments to generate stalemate. First, the political party holding only one chamber of Congress may believe it has little to gain in cooperating on policy issues with the president and his party. With the president's party controlling both the vast resources of the executive branch as well as the other chamber, voters are likely to attribute policy success to the president's party, to the detriment of the *minor governing party* at the next election. On the flip side, voters also are likely to hold the president's party responsible for policy failure. The incentive for the minor governing party thus can lie in using control of its one chamber to highlight its own policy views while thwarting the policy agenda of the *major governing party*. As it does so, it will likely avoid responsibility for the policy failures of Congress, undermine the credit-claiming abilities of the president's party, and thereby position itself better for the next election cycle.

Second, the likelihood of stalemate may be reinforced by the tendency of quasi-divided government to arise in periods of restructuring in the party attachments of voters, when voters may be seeking to install a new or refashioned partisan regime that can address pressing policy challenges. In such periods of fluidity, the electorate's lack of a definitive partisan tilt can lead it to give control of the House of Representatives and Senate to different parties. There then may be more at stake for these parties in the resulting quasi-divided Congresses than just short-term electoral advantage. Rather, great policy success by the major party in government may enable it to consolidate electoral support and establish long-term control of Congress and the presidency.

With long-term party dominance of national government potentially at stake, the minor party in a quasi-divided government has even greater reason to refuse to work with the president's party, depriving the major party of significant legislative accomplishment that could aid its consolidation of voter support. The resulting stalemate, born of the weaker party's obstruction, may allow pressing policy challenges to fester, to the detriment of the major party, creating bitterness between the parties. Thus, consider the first quasi-divided government in our data set, Herbert Hoover's Seventy-second Congress. This Congress emerged as citizens were in the early stages of reassessing their loyalty to the historically dominant Republican Party, amid the stock market collapse in 1929. Amid this volatility in voter sentiments, together with some untimely deaths among elected Republican legislators, Democrats gained control of the House of Representatives while Republicans, already controlling the presidency, won control of the Senate. The policy stalemate that then characterized the Seventy-second Congress has long been seen as a factor that contributed to the deepening of the Great Depression. Franklin Roosevelt's subsequent policy success during united party government in the New Deal Seventy-third Congress put the Democrats on their way to dominating national governance for the subsequent five decades. This left Republicans angered that the onus of policy failure in the Seventy-second Congress had fallen on Hoover and his congressional party, with the Democrats as the beneficiaries, despite controlling the House of Representatives. It also helped foster the belief within the Republican Party that Hoover's approach to the economic collapse, which was less reliant on expanding the federal bureaucracy, could have worked if given the chance.

Over the past thirty-six years, the nation has experienced another and particularly prolonged period of restructuring in national partisan attachments, starting with the Reagan revolution of 1980.[30] The other six quasi-divided governments in our data set emerged during the eighteen Congresses of this era. Five of these six quasi-divided governments were stalemated, helping to limit the number of productive Congresses during this period. In addition, the timing of these stalemated quasi-divided Congresses—during the two Congresses of Reagan's first term; the first Congress of George W. Bush's first term; and the second and third Congresses of Barack Obama's presidency, following his Great Recession Congress—stymied "historic" opportunities each party had to consolidate public support and majority party status.

The frustration both parties experienced as quasi-divided government thwarted their opportunities to push for electoral consolidation helped fuel an increasingly bitter and extremist form of partisan warfare in Congress. This extremist partisanship emerged most notably in the House of Representatives during the three quasi-divided governments of Ronald Reagan's presidency. During this period, young House Republicans, led by Representative Newt Gingrich, became increasingly outraged that the Democrats, still in control of the House, could thwart Reagan's domestic agenda. As their anger mounted, these young House Republicans embraced a no-holds-barred approach to interparty conflict. This extremist partisanship, spreading to the Senate, subsequently engulfed pure divided governments and united party governments of the era, as seen in the second Congress under President George H. W. Bush, the last two Congresses under President Bill Clinton, and the second and third Congresses under George W. Bush, undercutting their productivity.[31] It also helped foster House Republicans' efforts to repeal or weaken the Affordable Care Act during the two highly stalemated quasi-divided governments during the presidency of Barack Obama.

In our discussion of Table 9-1, early in this essay, we noted the weaker-than-expected productivity that exists among moderately polarized and highly polarized Congresses, when compared to their depolarized counterparts. Unless counteracted in some way, possibly by the existence of unique historical conditions, we expected this would undercut the power of our moderation variable in the multivariate analysis and weaken the credibility of our thesis. In point of fact, the moderation variable held up well, controlling for quasi-divided government and other factors. It held up well, we believe, because quasi-divided government introduced uniquely destructive political calculations, partisan bitterness, and policy deadlock into both the moderately polarized and extremely polarized periods of the past thirty-six years. The extent of this deadlock went well beyond that which would have been expected with pure divided or united party government, under analogous levels of moderate or extreme polarization. Moreover, the deadlock was particularly pernicious because the bitterness it generated infused various pure divided and united party governments of the era, undercutting their productivity. Replace the quasi-divided governments with either of the other two forms of government and policy productivity would likely have been notably higher among the moderately polarized and polarized Congresses.

Looking forward, students of Congress need to pay much closer attention to the conditions under which quasi-divided governments are likely to emerge, their likely role in undermining policy productivity, and strategies for limiting their detrimental effects. For example, perhaps the emergence of quasi-divided government could activate special rules in congressional governance. Such rules could mandate joint governing processes between the two houses in ways somewhat analogous to conference committees at the committee level. Such joint processes could bring the parties' shared governing responsibility more clearly to public attention and thereby provide greater incentive for cooperation and compromise. Periods of moderation might then help quasi-divided governments better realize their productive potential, much as moderation helps productivity during both pure divided government and united party government.[32]

Conclusion

We end our analysis of the relationship between party polarization and policy productivity by concluding that the evidence from the *Congressional Digest* supports the moderation thesis. It points to a strong, positive, and robust effect of moderate party polarization on the enactment of controversial policy proposals. We find this effect both in our examination of the proportional policy-making success of individual Congresses and in the success of individual policy topics in winning passage when we aggregate our Congresses together. Our analysis also highlights positive contributions that pure divided government and united party government can make to proportional policy productivity, in ways enhanced by conditions of moderate polarization. We also note the positive role that the skillfulness of a president (as seen in his historical rating) and presidential honeymoons can play in fostering productivity. And we document negative effects that quasi-divided government, a historically rare phenomenon that has become common in the contemporary period, can have on policy productivity.

Additionally, our analysis documents the great influence that united party government can have in fostering exceptional productivity when it comes in the first national election occurring amid a deep economic crisis. Thus, the united party governments of the Seventy-third Congress (1933–1934) and the 111th Congress (2009–2010) achieved a level of productivity well beyond that experienced by Congresses of a similar polarized status. Yet the significance of these two cases is double-edged: They underscore the extent to which the power of such mandates comes not simply with the election of a new united party government but depends on the existence of deep economic crisis. Outside of such conditions, the case for united party government is more problematic. While party theorists have long stressed the value of united party government, historic moments of productivity amid united party government—absent deep economic crisis—appear to be strongly dependent on the existence of moderate party polarization.

Taking all of these findings into account, we believe the case on behalf of moderate polarization as a path to policy productivity is a strong one, at least for Congresses operating amid the electoral conditions, institutional rules and procedures, and constitutional arrangements dominant over the past ninety-four years. A return to sustained productivity by the contemporary Congress likely depends on a move towards moderated levels of interparty policy conflict combined with conditions that limit the occurrence and temper the disruptive effects of quasi-divided governments.

Notes

The authors would like to acknowledge data collection assistance obtained from Michael Pomante and Martin Claar. In addition, we would like to thank Bradford Bishop for his help obtaining and configuring the measure of party polarization we use throughout the essay.

1. See, in particular, James MacGregor Burns, *Congress on Trial: The Legislative Process and the Administrative State* (New York: Harper, 1949).
2. See, for example, the essays in John R. Bond and Richard Fleisher, eds., *Polarized Politics: Congress and the President in a Partisan Era* (Washington, DC: CQ Press, 2000).
3. Thomas E. Mann and Norman J. Ornstein, *The Broken Branch: How Congress Is Failing America and How to Get It Back on Track* (New York: Oxford University Press, 2008).
4. Barbara Sinclair, *Party Wars: Polarization and the Politics of National Policy Making* (Norman: University of Oklahoma Press, 2006). Sinclair argues that polarization should have its most deleterious effects on legislative productivity when it occurs in the nonmajoritarian Senate. See also Barbara Sinclair, *Unorthodox Lawmaking: New Legislative Processes in the U.S. Congress*, 4th ed. (Washington, DC: CQ Press, 2012), chap. 3.
5. Burns, *Congress on Trial*; E. E. Schattschneider, *The Semi-Sovereign People: A Realist's View of Democracy in America* (New York: Holt, Rinehart, and Winston, 1975).
6. See also the 1993 discussion in Gary W. Cox and Matthew D. McCubbins, *Legislative Leviathan: Party Government in the House* (Berkeley: University of California Press, 1993), 271.
7. Sarah A. Binder, "The Dynamics of Legislative Gridlock, 1947–96," *American Political Science Review* 93 (1999): 519–36; Sarah A. Binder, *Stalemate: Causes and Consequences of Legislative Gridlock* (Washington, DC: Brookings Institution Press, 2003).
8. Joseph Cooper, *The Origins of the Standing Committees and the Development of the Modern House* (Houston: Rice University Press, 1971).
9. Our consideration of moderate polarization should not be confused with the percentage of moderates in Congress. The latter is sometimes used as an indicator of party system polarization. In such an approach, a larger number of moderates suggests polarization is lower, and fewer moderates indicate it is higher. In contrast, we are suggesting that whatever viable measure of polarization is used, a moderate or medium level of party system polarization will be the most productive in policy terms so long as one has a large enough group of Congresses to adequately gauge the full historical range from low to high polarization. It is in this medium or moderate level, between high

and low polarization, that one will likely find parties with relatively clear ideological orientations and members in each party sufficiently heterogeneous and moderate to allow for cross-party persuasion and compromise. For an example of a work that uses the number of moderates as a measure of polarization, see David C. W. Parker and Matthew Dull, "Divided We Quarrel: The Politics of Congressional Investigations, 1947–2004," *Legislative Studies Quarterly* 34 (2009): 319–45.

10. A variety of outstanding data sources exist, providing different approaches to the measurement of policy productivity in Congress, as discussed in Lawrence C. Dodd and Scot Schraufnagel, "Congress and the Polarity Paradox: Party Polarization, Member Incivility and Enactment of Landmark Legislation, 1891–1994," *Congress & the Presidency* 39, no. 2 (2012): 109–32. Regrettably, none of these data sources include postwar and prewar Congresses while also bringing the study of productivity up to the Obama presidency.

11. This issue was raised by Morris Fiorina in his discussion of Mayhew's *Divided We Govern*; see Morris P. Fiorina, *Divided Government*, 2nd ed. (Needham Heights, MA: Allyn and Bacon, 1996), 89. Binder provides the most extensive discussion of the issue and the most widely acknowledged effort to address it. See Binder, *Stalemate*, 35–40, 44.

12. The Congresses that fall into these distinct categories of productivity—listed by number, together with the year the Congress began—are as follows:
    (A) *Severe Stalemate* (0.0% to 10%): Eighty-second (1951), Eighty-third (1953), and 106th (1999)
    (B) *Stalemate* (10.01% to 20%): Sixty-seventh (1921), Sixty-ninth (1925), Seventieth (1927), Seventy-second (1931), Seventy-fifth (1937), Seventy-eighth (1943), Eighty-first (1949), Ninetieth (1967), Ninety-seventh (1981), Ninety-eighth (1983), 102nd (1991), 105th (1997), 107th (2001), 108th (2003), 109th (2005), 112nd (2011), and 113rd (2013)
    (C) *Satisfactory* (20.01% to 30%): Sixty-eighth (1923), Seventy-first (1929), Seventy-fourth (1935), Seventy-seventh (1941), Eightieth (1947), Eighty-fourth (1955), Ninety-second (1971), Ninety-third (1973), Ninety-fourth (1975), Ninety-fifth (1977), Ninety-sixth (1979), One hundredth (1987), 101st (1989), 104th (1995), and 110th (2007)
    (D) *Highly Satisfactory* (30.01% to 40%): Seventy-sixth (1939), Seventy-ninth (1945), Eighty-fifth (1957), Eighty-sixth (1959), Eighty-seventh (1961), Eighty-eighth (1963), and Ninety-ninth (1985)
    (E) *Exceptional* (40.01% and above): Seventy-third (1933), Eighty-ninth (1965), Ninety-first (1969), 103rd (1993), and 111th (2009)

13. John H. Aldrich, David W. Rohde, and Michael W. Tofias, "One D is Not Enough: Measuring Conditional Party Government, 1887–2002," in *Party, Process, and Policy Making, Vol. 2: Further New Perspectives on the History of Congress*, ed. David W. Brady and Mathew D. McCubbins (Stanford, CA: Stanford University Press, 2007), 102–13.

14. House and Senate values for intrachamber polarization, Congress by Congress, correlate very highly ($r = .91$; $p < .001$ for the Sixty-seventh through the 113th Congresses), so it seems reasonable to use the two-chamber average as a general estimate of congressional polarization.

15. Our *extremely depolarized* Congresses include all Congresses starting with the Seventy-third (1933–1935) through the Eighty-fourth (1955–1957). Our *moderately depolarized* Congresses include the Seventy-second (1931–1933), all nine Congresses starting

with the Eighty-fifth (1957–1959) through the Ninety-third (1973–1975), and also the Ninety-fifth (1977–1979) and Ninety-sixth (1979–1981). Our *moderately polarized* Congresses include the four Congresses starting with the Sixty-eighth (1923–1925) through the Seventy-first (1929–1931), the Ninety-fourth Congress (1975–1977), and the seven Congresses starting with the Ninety-seventh (1981–1983) through the 103rd (1993–1995). Our *extremely polarized* Congresses include the Sixty-seventh (1921–1923) and all ten Congresses starting with the 104th (1995–1997) through the 113th (2013–2015).

16. To measure moderate polarization for the multivariate analysis, values for each Congress that fall below the median value stay the same so that higher polarization scores equal more moderation. For polarization scores above the median value, we use the following formula to reverse observation values so that higher values will indicate more moderation: (High Score − 2[High Score − Median Score]). To illustrate considering three numbers—1, 5, and 7—the median value equals 5. The value 1 would stay the same because it is below the median value, and the value 7 would be altered (7 − 2[7 − 5]) so that it now equals 3.

17. David R. Mayhew, *Divided We Govern: Party Control, Lawmaking, and Investigation, 1946–2002*, 2nd ed. (New Haven, CT: Yale University Press, 2005). For Mayhew's more recent effort to address issues of policy productivity by the Congress, taking a comparative and more fully historical perspective, see David R. Mayhew, "Congress as a Handler of Challenges: The Historical Record," *Studies in American Political Development* 29 (2015): 185–212.

18. Binder, *Stalemate*, 74–75.

19. See John J. Coleman, "Unified Government, Divided Government, and Party Responsiveness," *American Political Science Review* 93 (1999): 821–35; George C. Edwards III, Andrew Barrett, and Jeffrey Peake, "The Legislative Impact of Divided Government," *American Journal of Political Science* 41 (1997): 545–63; and Mayhew, *Divided We Govern*.

20. Regardless of the manner in which we operationalize "honeymoon," our findings regarding moderate polarization are unchanged.

21. See Edwards, Barrett, and Peake, "Legislative Impact of Divided Government"; and Charles O. Jones, *The Presidency in a Separated System*, 2nd ed. (Washington, DC: Brookings Institution Press, 2005).

22. For the more recent presidents, we have fewer sources to draw from. Thus, George W. Bush's score of "11" is based on the results of only seven surveys, three conducted before he left office, and Barack Obama's rank of twenty-eighth is based on only two surveys conducted while he is still in office.

23. For instance, in Binder's work that uses *New York Times* editorials to define the issue agenda, it is not clear at what point in the life of a Congress the *New York Times* was discussing the specific topics used in the analysis. Congressional scholars readily recognize that legislation often fails because time simply runs out in a particular Congress, with too many pressing topics for it to deal effectively with them, or because a topic comes to public and media attention later rather than earlier in the life of the Congress, limiting its ability to prepare adequate legislation to address it. Similarly, a Congress-by-Congress analysis does not allow us to gauge how much work has been done to ready legislation for passage by the time an issue reaches salient or topical status. For instance, it might be that the demand for a new law is relatively new, and there has been little previous consideration; in other instances, the demand for action may

occur after considerable behind-the-scenes preparation has already occurred during a Congress. Any systematic occurrence of either scenario might not be picked up when each Congress is the unit of analysis.

24. There were 934 volumes of the *Digest* published between 1921 and 2014, with each volume covering a single topic. Only 849 of the volumes are used in the analysis that follows because fifty-one volumes were dedicated to congressional summaries or presidential or legislative elections. Another thirty-six volumes dealt with a topic after new legislation had already passed the relevant Congress. If an issue was published after a Congress adjourned *sine die* but prior to the next Congress's convening, we count the issue as part of the *demand* quotient for the next Congress. For instance, a February 1923 issue would have been published before the Sixty-eighth Congress was sworn in. Nevertheless, it is coded as being a topic for the Sixty-eighth Congress to address because the Sixty-seventh Congress had already adjourned *sine die*. Calculated in this manner, the number of issues per Congress varies from seventeen for the Sixty-seventh Congress (1921–1922) to twenty-three for the Seventy-sixth Congress (1939–1940), and the modal number of topics addressed by the *Digest* per Congress is nineteen.

25. We try multiple measures of presidential aptitude and always get a positive—and usually significant—association between this variable and topical productivity. Hence, a competent president does not steal explanatory power from our measure of moderate polarization. It is not the case that our findings related to moderation are a product of the president who served when party polarization was neither high, nor low.

26. We make the claim that the statistical relationship is stronger in the *by topic* analysis versus the *by Congress* analysis based on the size of the coefficients relative to their standard errors. The coefficients represent an average relationship between two variables, and the standard errors represent the likelihood that the average relationship is accurate. Hence, when coefficients are larger relative to their standard errors, statistical significance increases, and confidence that the coefficients are an accurate depiction of reality grows.

27. For instance, considering united party government five out of ten (50 percent) of the highly depolarized Congresses are stalemated, whereas only one of six (16.6 percent) of the moderately depolarized Congresses is stalemated. Considering the more polarized context, three of four (75 percent) of united party governments in the *high* category are stalemated, and this drops to two of five (40 percent) for the *moderate* category.

28. Aside from these seven, only two other Congresses have experienced quasi-divided government since the first introduction of the Reed Rules in the House of Representatives during the Fifty-first Congress (1889–1891). The first of these was the Fifty-second Congress (1891–1893), during the presidency of Benjamin Harrison, amid the Populist electoral upheavals of the late 1880s and early 1890s. The second was the Sixty-second Congress (1911–1913), during the presidency of William Howard Taft, amid the electoral transitions associated with the Progressive era. We lack data on the "demand side" for both Congresses and thus cannot compare their productivity directly with the Congresses in the current study. We do note that in our work on landmark legislation, covering the period from the Fifty-second to the 103rd Congresses, the Fifty-second Congress produced two landmark laws, making it one of the six least productive Congresses in terms of landmark laws in our study. The Sixty-second Congress produced four landmark laws, putting it in the bottom 40 percent of Congresses in terms of landmark productivity. See Dodd and Schraufnagel, "Congress and the Polarity Paradox."

29. Our attention to quasi-divided government is based on the effect we believe it has on the electoral calculations and policy actions of House and Senate parties, not its use as a surrogate for the policy distance between the House and Senate. For a discussion of the latter issue, see Fang-Yi Chiou and Lawrence S. Rothenberg, "Comparing Legislators and Legislatures: The Dynamics of Legislative Gridlock Reconsidered," *Political Analysis* 16 (2008): 197–212, and Sarah A. Binder, "Taking the Measure of Congress: Reply to Chiou and Rothenberg," *Political Analysis* 16 (2008): 213–25.
30. For a discussion of the emergence of this period of restructuring with the Reagan revolution and assessments of its longer-term prospects, see Alan I. Abramowitz and Kyle L. Saunders, "Ideological Realignment in the U.S. Electorate," *Journal of Politics* 60 (1998): 634–52.
31. For discussion and documentation of the spread of extreme partisanship from the House to the Senate, see Sean M. Theriault, *The Gingrich Senators* (New York: Oxford University Press, 2013). And on some possible limits to extreme partisanship in the Senate, see Paulina S. Rippere, "Polarization Reconsidered: Bipartisan Cooperation Through Bill Cosponsorship," *Polity* 48 (2016): 243–78.
32. Let us note, in this regard, that the one successful quasi-divided Congress in our dataset, the Ninety-ninth Congress at the beginning of Ronald Reagan's second term, occurred amid moderate polarization. It experienced a highly satisfactory level of productivity. Possibly, Reagan's landslide victory in 1984 gave him special leverage with which to foster compromise during the Ninety-ninth Congress, using his party's control of the Senate to aid such compromise. This possibility is consistent with Sarah Binder's discussion of quasi-divided governments in *Stalemate,* 74–75. Close study of the Ninety-ninth Congress could aid understanding of conditions and political strategies that aid productivity in quasi-divided settings.

10. An Examination of Congressional Efforts to Repeal the Affordable Care Act

Jordan Ragusa

Congressional scholars know little about the politics of repealing legislation. Such a gap is surprising given how much is known about the politics of enacting legislation. My chapter examines repeals in the context of a key case: attempts to repeal the Affordable Care Act (ACA). Needless to say, the GOP's fifty repeal votes in the 112th and 113th Congresses (2011–2015) have elevated the importance of this topic. One of the core questions my chapter addresses is why members of Congress supported or opposed these repeal efforts. Were they the product of ideological disagreements between liberals and conservatives, partisan contests over national policy, a byproduct of the Tea Party's emergence, or a function of constituents' opinions and concerns? In addition to answering these questions, my chapter describes the basic dynamics of the GOP's repeal attempts and situates these efforts within broader explanations of when and why repeals happen.

Introduction

On March 23, 2010, three hundred guests celebrated as President Obama signed into law the Affordable Care Act (ACA). Senator Max Baucus, D-Mont., hailed the law's completion: "Now it is law. Now it is history."[1] Vice President Joe Biden was less diplomatic, caught on camera saying, "This is a big [expletive] deal."[2] Certainly, there was a lot to celebrate. On the one hand, enactment of the ACA was the culmination of more than a year of intense legislative effort. On the other hand, the ACA fulfilled a nearly twenty-year struggle by Democrats to expand national health insurance coverage ever since the failure of Bill Clinton's health care plan in 1994.

Lost in the celebration that day was the fact that the law's future was far from settled. Although textbooks treat enactment as the final step in the legislative process, as a practical matter, the battle over a law's fate continues long after it is signed. Anyone observing American politics in the aftermath of the Affordable Care Act's passage between 2010 and 2016 will appreciate this fact. Among the various efforts to change the ACA after its enactment, none has received more media attention or been the subject of more debate than the GOP's attempts to repeal the law. Although estimates vary, most observers claim that the Republican-controlled House of Representatives held forty to fifty repeal votes in the 112th and 113th Congresses (2011–2015). As just one example, President Obama himself quipped, "You know what they say: 50th time is the charm."[3]

Despite the volume and intensity of the GOP's repeal attempts, American politics scholars know little about this topic. Only a handful of studies have examined when and why Congress revisits prior enactments via statutory amendments, changes in funding levels, program reauthorizations, and so forth.[4] And just two papers have studied repeals in particular.[5] Although the ACA is an extreme case, the fact is that major laws are quite dynamic. So despite the congressional literature's focus on the *passage* of legislation, we know that laws are constantly being *changed* by subsequent coalitions. As Jenkins and Patashnik aptly put it, "A preoccupation on enactment—and *only* enactment—runs the risk of directing attention away from critical features of the lawmaking process."[6]

My chapter's purpose is to examine the basic dynamics of the GOP's efforts to repeal the ACA in the 112th and 113th Congresses. Given how little we know about this topic, the main goals are ecumenical. One of the core questions is whether it is accurate to claim that Republicans held fifty repeal votes from 2011 to 2015. As we will see, answering this question hinges on how repeals are defined and measured. A second key question is *why* members of Congress supported or opposed these repeal efforts. Were they the product of ideological disagreements between liberals and conservatives, partisan contests over national policy, a byproduct of the Tea Party's emergence, or a function of voters' health care concerns? A third issue concerns the lessons we can draw from the postenactment struggle over the ACA, as far as when and why repeals happen. While only a handful of studies exist, the literature on legislative revision emphasizes two overarching explanations: problem-solving motivations versus shifts in lawmaker preferences. Although there is evidence to support both, the postenactment struggle over the ACA clearly fits one explanation. A final issue—addressed in the conclusion section—is what to expect in the 115th Congress (2017–2018) and beyond. Are future repeal attempts likely to succeed, when will the ACA be most "at risk" of repeal, and what are the implications of the 2016 presidential election on the ACA's long-term fate?

A Brief Legislative History of the ACA

Health care reform was a key component of then-senator Obama's platform in 2008 as a presidential candidate.[7] In addition to winning the White House, Democrats picked up eight Senate seats and twenty-one House seats that year. It was the first time the party had unified control of both branches in fifteen years and the first time since 1936 Democrats gained double-digit seats in back-to-back congressional elections.

After enacting a stimulus package in February of 2009, Democrats turned their attention to health care reform. As committees in both chambers drafted legislation, opponents of the burgeoning law organized raucous protests at Democratic town hall events during the 2009 August recess, shouting down lawmakers with concerns about "death panels" and the "government's takeover of health care." Various authors suggest that these protests galvanized the nascent Tea Party movement and signaled a wave election building in the 2010 midterm.[8] Nonetheless, by October of 2009, bills in both chambers had been reported out of committee and were ready for floor action.

With no Republican support and some wavering Democrats, House Speaker Nancy Pelosi and Senate Majority Leader Harry Reid struggled to build coalitions to pass a reform package despite the size of their majorities in both chambers. In the House, the scope of the "public option" (a proposal for a government-run health insurance program) and concerns about federal funds paying for abortion divided Democrats. House leaders eventually conceded to Blue Dog and pro-life Democrats, and on November 7, 2009, the House passed a reform package with a "weak" public option and robust antiabortion language. On the Senate side, the key fault line was whether to include a public option at all. In the end, Harry Reid was forced to advance a package without a public option after Joe Lieberman, D-Conn., threatened to join a Republican filibuster. On December 24, after twenty-five days of debate and thirty-eight roll call votes, the Senate voted 60–39 to pass their version of health care reform.[9]

Resolving House and Senate disagreements was yet another challenge for Democratic leaders. Although most attention focused on the fact that the Senate proposal lacked a public option, key provisions *present* in the Senate bill were the cause of significant disagreement as well (namely, the "Cadillac tax" and the so-called "Cornhusker kickback"). As informal House and Senate negotiations were ongoing, Scott Brown, R-Mass., won a special election on January 19 to fill the vacant seat caused by Edward Kennedy's, D-Mass., death. It is hard to overstate: Brown's victory upended Democrats' efforts to merge the House and Senate bills. Because Brown was opposed to the reform package and because his election broke Democrats' filibuster-proof sixty-vote majority, merging the two bills via traditional routes (a conference committee or by exchanging bills between the chambers) seemed unlikely to succeed.

In the end, Democratic leaders opted for a controversial approach: The House would pass the Senate bill without modifications (to circumvent a Republican filibuster if the bill were sent back to the Senate) and subsequently pass a separate package of changes via reconciliation (a procedural move that only requires a simple majority for passage). Republicans derided the final package as a "legislative Frankenstein."[10] Political scientist Barbara Sinclair (2012) cites the ACA as an example of what she calls *unorthodox lawmaking*.[11] Whatever terminology one prefers, there is no denying that the ACA was one of the most important pieces of social legislation enacted in decades.

A Brief Overview of the ACA's Key Provisions

As Obama signed the ACA, back on Capitol Hill, Republicans were vowing to make the 2010 midterm a referendum on the newly enacted law. Senate Minority Leader Mitch McConnell speculated, "I think the slogan will be 'repeal and replace.'"[12] As we will see in a moment, however, "repealing" legislation is not as straightforward as McConnell's slogan suggests. Because the repeal of specific provisions of a law are much more common than full repeals, it is useful to review a few key elements of the ACA.

One key aspect of the ACA is the goal of lowering the uninsured rate. Among the law's provisions, none has proven to be more contentious than the *individual mandate* (a requirement that all Americans purchase health care). In *National Federation of Independent Business v. Sebelius*, a landmark Supreme Court case in 2012, the Court decided that the individual mandate is a constitutional exercise of Congress's taxing powers. Another way the law seeks to lower the uninsured rate is by expanding the Medicaid program (a social program where low-income individuals can obtain government-run health insurance). Although the ACA survived the 2012 Supreme Court decision, the Court also ruled that the states cannot be forced by the federal government to expand the Medicaid program. At the time this book was published, nineteen states had declined the expansion. A range of additional provisions are designed to lower the uninsured rate as well, including subsidies to help poor Americans buy health insurance and a provision allowing children up to age twenty-six to remain on their parents' health care plans.

A second key aspect of the ACA is the goal of controlling health care costs. According to a Congressional Budget Office (CBO) report, from 1965 to 2005, spending on health care tripled *twice* in inflation-adjusted dollars.[13] Proponents argue that by lowering the uninsured rate, the ACA has the indirect effect of lowering costs. Nonetheless, the law has a range of specific provisions that seek to lower health care costs. One such provision is the Independent Payment Advisory Board (IPAB), a fifteen-member panel empowered to make changes to Medicare payment rates (without explicit congressional approval). Famously, Sarah Palin called the IPAB a "death panel." A second explicit cost control mechanism is the ACA's *80/20 rule*, which requires insurance companies to spend at least 80 percent of premiums on their customers' health care. A third explicit cost control mechanism is the *rate review provision*, a requirement that insurance companies justify any rate increase in premiums greater than 10 percent.

A third key aspect of the ACA is the goal of increasing the quality of health care. One way the law seeks to achieve this goal is by requiring health care plans to provide a set of basic services (called *minimum essential coverage*). The ACA also contains a range of regulations on private health insurance plans. Among the various provisions, the law prevents insurance companies from excluding potential customers with preexisting conditions (for example, those with chronic diseases) and prohibits insurers from placing lifetime limits on an individual's benefits. And finally, the ACA offers financial incentives to hospitals and physicians that use electronic medical records. Proponents of the law argue that electronic medical records reduce the likelihood of medical mistakes (such as harmful drug interactions), thus increasing the overall quality of patient care.

A final key aspect of the ACA is the law's funding mechanisms. Because implementation of some of the policies noted earlier are costly, the ACA has a series of provisions that raise revenue. The first revenue source is the so-called

"Cadillac tax." Under the ACA, health care plans with premiums greater than $10,200 (individuals) and $27,500 (families) are taxed at 40 percent above those limits, beginning in 2018. A second key funding mechanism is an increase in Medicare taxes. In particular, the ACA increases Medicare taxes by 0.9 percent for individuals earning more than $200,000 a year in income. (And notably, this tax includes investment income.) Another revenue-raising provision is the so-called "1099 reporting" requirement. As originally written, the law required businesses to file IRS 1099 tax forms whenever they purchase more than $600 in goods or services. Finally, the ACA raises revenue through the individual mandate. It is important to note, however, that the individual mandate's purpose is not to raise revenue per se but to act as an incentive for Americans to buy health care coverage.

After the ACA's Enactment

Before the Affordable Care Act was even signed, lawmakers in the 111th Congress were hard at work on revisions. While it may seem odd that the enacting Congress would seek to revise their own act, such an occurrence is common for a law with the ACA's size and scope.[14] In fact, a number of these revisions were Democratic initiatives. Recall, for example, that the ACA was amended (via a reconciliation bill) just a week after its enactment. As a whole, the reconciliation package brought the "amended" ACA closer to the House's original proposal. In addition to the reconciliation bill, the 111th Congress passed six laws that made changes to the ACA.

While the Democratic amendments are notable, the postenactment history of the ACA is overshadowed by the GOP's efforts to repeal the law. Like the reconciliation package, Republicans began their repeal efforts before the law was even signed. In the 111th House, three full repeal bills were introduced on March 22, the day *before* the law was enacted.[15] All three were sponsored by Republicans, and two were sponsored by lawmakers who would join the Tea Party Caucus. Although there were fewer repeal bills introduced in the Senate, a full repeal sponsored by Jim DeMint, R-S.C., the day the ACA was signed garnered twenty-two cosponsors. Needless to say, none of these bills passed. Surprisingly, however, one repeal bill had bipartisan support and received votes in both chambers. Among the ACA's funding provisions, the 1099 reporting requirement faced considerable backlash after enactment because of fears that it would pose too onerous a requirement for small businesses. While the 1099 revisions failed over disagreements about the scope of the changes and how to offset the lost revenue, the 1099 revision would reemerge in the 112th Congress after the 2010 midterm election.[16]

In the 2010 midterm, Republicans campaigned on the platform Senate Minority Leader Mitch McConnell suggested the day of the ACA's enactment: "repeal and replace." Riding the wave that emerged during the 2009 August recess, Tea Party–aligned lawmakers were particularly vocal about their goal of dismantling the newly enacted law. Although the Tea Party may have cost Republicans control of the Senate in the 112th and 113th Congresses,[17] there is some evidence that lawmakers who aligned themselves with the Tea Party outperformed non–Tea Party Republicans in the midterm.[18] Another study suggests that Democrats lost about twenty-five seats (enough to have held their majority) because of their support for the ACA.[19] So even though the president's party almost always loses seats in a midterm, the 2010 midterm, in which the GOP picked up six Senate seats and over sixty House seats, seemed to be a referendum on the ACA.

After winning back the House, the GOP followed through on their campaign promise. At the start of the 112th Congress, on January 19, 2011, the House voted on H.R. 2, a bill that sought to repeal the entire ACA and reinstate provisions altered by the law. Titled the "Repealing the Job-Killing Health Care Law Act," H.R. 2 passed the House 245 to 189, with all Republicans and three Democrats supporting the bill. It was one of sixteen repeal bills voted on in the 112th Congress. As we will see in a moment, however, "full" repeals like H.R. 2 are quite rare. In contrast to how the media covered these efforts, the GOP adopted a range of legislative strategies, including repeals targeting specific provisions of the law, defunding efforts, actions to deny federal agencies the power to enforce the ACA, and even a series of amendments. Moreover, of the sixteen repeals passed by the 112th House, two were passed by the Democratic-controlled Senate and signed into law by President Obama. One such repeal was H.R. 4, a bill repealing the 1099 reporting requirement. It passed the House with seventy-six Democratic yes votes in the House and forty Democratic yes votes in the Senate.

Like in the 2010 midterm, the 2012 presidential election had major implications in the ongoing battle over the ACA's fate. Unlike 2010, however, the campaigns did not focus as closely on the two-year-old law. On the one hand, the GOP's presidential candidate, Mitt Romney, was hamstrung by the fact that he signed a similar law as governor of Massachusetts. On the other hand, polls showed that while health care was an important issue in 2012, economic issues were at the forefront of Americans' minds.[20] Nonetheless, the election had major implications for repealing the law, as research shows that control of the White House is a key factor in when and why repeals happen.[21] With Obama winning reelection, the GOP's prospects of repealing the ACA dimmed. One newspaper headline after the presidential election read: "Health Care Reform Lives."[22] Even House Speaker John Boehner, R-Ohio, famously conceded after the 2012 election that "Obamacare is the law of the land."[23]

Despite losing the 2012 presidential election, Republicans maintained control of the House and were undeterred in the 113th Congress in their efforts to repeal the ACA. In fact, many of the bills introduced and voted on in the 112th House were reintroduced and voted on again in the 113th House. Perhaps the biggest change in the battle over ACA is that after losing the 2012 election, the GOP's focus shifted to efforts at the state level. According to the ACA's text, the states were required to tell the federal government by December 14, 2012, whether they would set up their own health care exchanges. In an attempt to cripple the ACA, many Republican-controlled states decided against setting up their own exchanges. One recent study examines the factors that explain why some

Republican governors worked with the ACA (in the context of the Medicaid expansion) and others fought against the law's provisions.[24] Nonetheless, the 113th House would vote on twelve distinct repeal bills.

Research on Legislative Revision

Given the intensity of the GOP's repeal attempts, it is surprising how little American politics scholars know about the topic of legislative revision. On the one hand, there are only a handful of studies on when and why Congress revisits prior enactments[25] and just two on the specific action of repealing legislation.[26] On the other hand, no published work has examined the efforts to revise the ACA in particular. Yet despite the lack of research, we know that repeals are quite common. A recent study of mine with Nate Birkhead estimates that from 1877 to 2012, there was an average of 1.3 major repeals enacted into law per congressional session.[27] Repeals do not occur uniformly throughout congressional history, however. Rather, some Congresses engage in significant repealing activity (passing three to six major repeals) while others enact no major repeals. As far as when repeals happen, we find that the median time from enactment to repeal is about 4.5 Congresses (or about nine years).[28] Notably, multiple studies of legislative revision, each with a different data source, report that there is an increasing risk of legislative revision up until about ten years after a law's enactment.[29] After this ten-year window, the risk of revision declines rapidly as laws become institutionalized.

One of the key topics in the literature is how to best explain when and why these statutory revisions happen. E. Scott Adler and John Wilkerson highlight the often overlooked role of issue attention and Congress's problem-solving motivations.[30] In their view, a significant volume of changes in national policy is solution driven. For example, expiring provisions (when provisions are set to "die" without congressional action) are among the most important factors that compel Congress to revisit statutes in a given policy area. Eric Patashnik takes a similar view, arguing that the durability of major reforms hinges, in part, on policy developments and the timing of exogenous shocks that occur after a law is enacted.[31] In a striking example, given the topic of this chapter, Congress voted to repeal almost an entire bill in 1989 (the Medicare Catastrophic Coverage Act) just a year after its enactment because of a backlash by seniors who were concerned about increases in their health care costs.[32]

An alternative view is that legislative revision is best explained by the preferences of lawmakers and how the distribution of those preferences changes after enactment. For example, my work with Nate Birkhead finds that repeals are most likely to occur in eras when the majority wields strong, positive agenda-setting powers (i.e., is ideologically homogeneous) and wins control of both chambers after a long period out of power.[33] In this respect, we claim that repeals are best understood as "long-term contests between two great 'teams' over the location of the status quo."[34] Related evidence suggests that divided party control—both at the time of enactment and in subsequent Congresses—is a key predictor of when and why legislative revisions happen.[35]

Both perspectives are, of course, correct, as the focus on problem-solving motivations versus shifting preferences is a matter of emphasis rather than a scholarly disagreement. In other words, *both* inform our understanding of when and why Congress revisits past legislative enactments. Although firm conclusions are difficult to draw given the lack of research in this area, the salience of the action is a plausible explanation for these differences in emphasis. As Adler and Wilkerson show, party control and the distribution of legislative preferences seem to matter more when the focus is narrowed to the most significant law revisions.[36] On this point, repeals and amendments may simply have different sets of predictors. As far as the ACA is concerned, however, this chapter emphasizes the role of partisan motivations and changing preferences. When it comes to the ACA, it is hard to ignore these factors. Yet as we will see, even in this extreme case, it is impossible to ignore the key role of problem-solving motivations.

Cataloging ACA Repeal Votes in the 112th and 113th Congresses

Although there have been dozens of attempts to repeal, delay, defund, or amend the ACA, we lack a precise definition of what counts as a *repeal*. It is important to note that *repeal* has both a literal and a substantive definition. In the literal sense, a repeal is an action that strikes statutory text from the U.S. Code. A 2010 study uses this definition to identify statutory repeals to Mayhew's landmark laws.[37] An alternative is to count as a repeal any legislative action that seeks to "undo," "reverse," or "stop" a law. A 2015 study uses this substantive definition to catalog major repeals from 1877 to 2012.[38] Although historians, journalists, and others may use the term *repeal* in reference to actions that are not literal repeals, the policy outcome is substantively the same.

Repeals can further be classified as either full or partial. *Full repeals* are actions to undo an entire law or the law's fundamental elements. For example, H.R. 2 in the 112th Congress sought to repeal the entire ACA and reinstate provisions altered by the law. By comparison, H.R. 2009 in the 113th Congress sought to prevent the IRS from implementing any provisions of the ACA. Both are full repeals because they would have crippled or completely dismantled the law. *Partial repeals*, on the other hand, are those that seek to undo a specific aspect of the law while leaving other major components unaffected. For example, H.R. 5 in the 112th Congress would have repealed the Independent Payment Advisory Board (the infamous "death panel") yet left the major aspects of the law untouched. H.R. 4118 in the 113th Congress counts as a partial repeal as well. It sought to delay the implementation of the individual mandate for five years. Although this delaying action is not a literal repeal, it would have had the same effect for a given period of time.

Table 10-1 lists each bill in the 112th (2011–2013) and 113th (2013–2015) Congresses with a final passage or amendment vote where the proposal would

Table 10-1 Full and Partial ACA Repeal Votes in the 112th and 113th Congresses

		112th Congress					113th Congress		
Type	Bill	Date	Outcome	Yeas/Nays	Type	Bill	Date	Outcome	Yeas/Nays
Full	HR 2	1/19/11	Passed	245–189	Full	HR 45	5/16/13	Passed	229–195
Full	HR 6079	7/11/12	Passed	244–185	Full	HR 2009	8/2/13	Passed	232–185
Partial	HR 4	3/3/11	Became law	314–112	Partial	HR 7	1/28/14	Passed	227–188
Partial	HR 5	3/22/12	Passed	223–181	Partial	HR 2667	7/17/13	Passed	264–161
Partial	HR 8	8/1/12	Became law	257–167	Partial	HR 2668	7/17/13	Passed	251–174
Partial	HR 358	10/13/11	Passed	251–172	Partial	HR 3350	11/15/13	Passed	261–157
Partial	HR 436	6/7/12	Passed	270–146	Partial	HR 3522	9/11/14	Passed	247–167
Partial	HR 1173	2/1/12	Passed	267–159	Partial	HR 4015	3/14/14	Passed	238–181
Partial	HR 1213	5/3/11	Passed	238–183	Partial	HR 4118	3/5/14	Passed	250–160
Partial	HR 1214	5/4/11	Passed	235–191	Partial	HR 4414	4/29/14	Passed	268–150
Partial	HR 1216	5/24/11	Passed	234–185	Partial	HJ RES 59	9/29/13	Passed	248–174
Partial	HR 1217	4/13/11	Passed	236–183	Partial	HJ RES 59	9/29/13	Passed	231–192
Partial	HR 4628	4/27/12	Passed	215–195	Amend	HR 1814	3/12/14	Passed	VV
Partial	HR 5652	5/10/12	Passed	218–199	Amend	HR 2575	4/3/14	Passed	248–179
Partial	HR 6684	12/20/12	Passed	215–209	Amend	HR 2775	9/12/13	Passed	235–191
Partial	HR 1 (Rehberg)	2/18/11	Adopted	239–187	Amend	HR 3362	1/16/14	Passed	259–154
Partial	HR 1 (King)	2/18/11	Adopted	241–187	Amend	HR 3474	3/12/14	Passed	406–1
Partial	HR 1 (King)	2/18/11	Adopted	237–191	Amend	HR 3979	3/11/14	Passed	410–0

(Continued)

Table 10-1 (Continued)

		112th Congress					113th Congress		
Type	Bill	Date	Outcome	Yeas/Nays	Type	Bill	Date	Outcome	Yeas/Nays
Partial	HR 1 (Emerson)	2/18/11	Adopted	246–182	Amend	HR 4302	4/1/14	Became law	VV
Partial	HR 1 (Price)	2/18/11	Adopted	241–185					
Partial	HR 1 (Burgess)	2/18/11	Adopted	239–182					
Partial	HR 1 (Pitts)	2/19/11	Adopted	239–183					
Partial	HR 1 (Gardner)	2/18/11	Adopted	241–184					
Partial	HR 1 (Hayworth)	2/19/11	Adopted	VV					
Amend	HR 674	11/16/11	Became law	422–0					
Amend	HR 3630	12/13/11	Became law	293–132					

Source: Compiled by the author.

have repealed elements of the ACA.[39] Based on an examination of the proposal's key provisions, each bill or amendment is cataloged as either a full or partial repeal. For comparison purposes, I also included votes on bills to amend the ACA.[40]

A few key findings emerge in Table 10-1. First, the GOP held just two full repeal votes in each Congress.[41] Republican leaders scheduled these votes at key dates, highlighting the *symbolic* and *partisan* nature of the full repeals. For example, the vote on H.R. 2 on January 19, 2011, fulfilled the GOP's 2010 midterm campaign promise while the vote on H.R. 6079 on July 11, 2012, occurred just two weeks after the Supreme Court upheld the individual mandate. In the 113th Congress, the vote on H.R. 45 was, by Boehner's account, "for the freshmen" elected in 2012,[42] whereas the vote on H.R. 2009 in the 113th Congress (focusing on the IRS's role in implementing major pillars of the law) occurred as the agency's "targeting" scandal broke. Coupled with the fact that these proposals had little chance of being enacted, it is clear that full repeals fall under the category of what congressional researchers call strategically timed position-taking attempts.[43]

Despite their symbolic and partisan nature, however, it is perhaps surprising that there have been *only* two full repeal votes in each Congress. Ultimately, this contradicts the popular narrative that Republicans have held "dozens" of votes to "repeal the ACA." It is important to be clear: This discrepancy hinges on how one defines repeal attempts. My view, however, is that the larger estimates (thirty, forty, or even fifty repeal attempts) are overstated. As we can see, the bulk of the repeal attempts were partial repeals or even amendments. While some would have undone notable elements of the ACA, others are quite minor in scope and/or attracted bipartisan support. An example from earlier is the 1099 repeal in the 112th Congress that passed with bipartisan support in both chambers and was signed by Obama. Needless to say, the 1099 repeal is a clear example of a problem-solving repeal and likely *strengthened* the law over the long term by reversing an unpopular provision.[44] Moreover, because the number of repeal votes declined from the 112th to the 113th Congress (from twenty-four to just seven) while the number of votes to amend the ACA increased (from two to seven), it seems that there has been some effort among Republicans to fix or adjust problematic elements of the law.

A third and related point is the simple fact that the ACA has been repealed. Almost any law with the ACA's size and scope would require some revision after passage. Few commentators remember H.R. 4 and the repeal of the 1099 reporting provision. As we can see in Table 10-1, other successful repeal and amendment attempts exist as well. Although the attention paid to these revisions is dwarfed by attempts to repeal the entirety of the law's fundamental elements, they represent substantively important changes in the law as originally written. Beyond simply correcting the record, this fact has implications for our conceptual understanding of ACA repeals. Either political commentators must acknowledge that the GOP (with Democratic support) *succeeded* in altering the ACA in both the 112th and 113th Congresses, or they must admit that the scope of the GOP's repeal actions are far more *limited* than most claim.

Explaining Legislative Actions to Repeal the ACA

What explains lawmakers' legislative actions to repeal the ACA? Despite the controversy and attention paid to the GOP's repeal attempts, an examination such as this is absent from the congressional literature. In fact, the only comparable research is a state politics article examining governors' decisions to oppose the ACA's Medicaid expansion.[45] As a theoretical matter, we can classify the predictors of legislative actions to repeal the ACA into four categories: (1) partisan, (2) ideological, (3) reelection seeking, and (4) constituents' health care needs. In the following sections, I test each of these hypotheses on two distinct actions: a lawmaker's decision to *sponsor* an ACA repeal and his or her *vote* on the repeals.

A leading explanation of attempts to repeal the ACA is that they are largely, if not entirely, partisan in nature. On the one hand, media accounts are full with commentary on both sides' unwillingness to compromise. For example, a *New York Times* article in May of 2013 discussed how "partisan gridlock" had hampered the normal process of revising landmark legislation.[46] At the same time, some of the published work cited earlier suggests that repeal actions are typically quite partisan. Factors such as the majority party's cohesion, their time out of power, and whether the law was passed during single-party control are all factors that affect the likelihood of repeal.[47] Furthermore, one study finds that governors' decisions to oppose the Medicaid expansion can be explained—almost entirely—by partisan factors.[48]

At the same time, a number of commentators have claimed that the Tea Party (not the Republican Party per se) was the driving force behind the ACA repeal efforts. For example, a *U.S. News and World Report* article in August of 2013 referred to these efforts as the "Tea Party's unhealthy obsession."[49] Such claims dovetail with research suggesting that the Tea Party's legislative behaviors are distinctly more conservative compared to their GOP brethren not aligned with the Tea Party.[50] As a theoretical matter, there are two ways the Tea Party's effect on repeal efforts could manifest. On the one hand, the Tea Party's effect could have institutional origins stemming from the coordinated actions of the Tea Party Caucus. After all, congressional member organizations conduct the same actions as parties.[51] On the other hand, the Tea Party's effect could have electoral origins. In particular, perhaps Republican lawmakers supported the ACA repeal (in part) because they feared a Tea Party primary challenge. An effect such as this may hinge on the volume of Tea Party supporters in a member's district.[52]

A rival explanation is that legislative actions to repeal the ACA are the product of policy disagreements between liberals and conservatives, not partisan contests over the status quo. In this respect, what appears partisan on the surface is really explained by members' underlying preferences.[53] Indeed, one claim is that the battle over the ACA is really a proxy battle over the government's role in the economy (health care spending constitutes 18 percent of GDP) and individual life (i.e., the individual mandate). A related argument concerns the ACA's cost, with conservatives concerned about the ACA's effect on future budget deficits. And finally, conservatives object to the ACA's redistributive elements. For example, the ACA pays for the Medicaid expansion by increasing Medicare taxes on those earning more than $250,000 in income (including investment income).

A final possible explanation is that legislative actions to repeal the ACA are a function of constituents' preferences. One possibility is that actions to repeal the ACA are explained by members' reelection-seeking motivations. Although the most notable town hall eruptions occurred during the 2009 August recess, in the 112th and 113th Congresses, constituents were quite vocal about their opposition to the ACA during public events. Another possibility is that voters' health care needs explain lawmakers' legislative actions to repeal the ACA. Quite simply, if lawmakers behave as faithful trustees of their constituents' best interests, perhaps those representing districts with a high percentage of voters without insurance are less likely to support a repeal of the ACA while those with a lower percentage without insurance are more likely to support a repeal.

Data and Method

As noted earlier, the above hypotheses are tested with two sets of models: one predicting a lawmaker's vote to repeal the ACA and another predicting a lawmaker's decision to sponsor an ACA repeal bill. In an attempt to assess whether the dynamics of ACA repeal actions have changed over time, separate models are estimated for the 112th and 113th Congresses. In addition, because the hypothesized effects may vary across parties, each factor was interacted with a party indicator. For simplicity, the models below report the marginal effect of each covariate by party.

In the roll call analysis, the full and partial repeals documented in Table 10-1 were combined into a single scale that records the percentage of repeal votes a member voted for.[54] For example, in the 112th Congress, Michele Bachmann, R-Minn., and Jim Sensenbrenner, R-Wis., voted for 100 percent of the ACA repeal bills, whereas John Lewis, D-Ga., and Ed Markey, D-Mass., voted for 0 percent of the repeal bills. In the sponsor analysis, the dependent variable is simply a count of the number of repeal bills a member introduced.[55] In both Congresses, the variable ranges from 0 to 3. Repeal bills were identified by a keyword search and content analysis of bill descriptions using data from the *Congressional Bills Project*.[56] In the 112th Congress, fifty-four repeal bills were identified, and in the 113th Congress, seventy-one repeal bills were identified.[57]

Given the theoretical discussion, in each model, the following variables were included. *GOP* is coded "1" for Republicans and "0" for Democrats and tests for partisan differences in ACA repeal efforts. *Tea Party Caucus* is coded "1" for members who joined the Caucus in the 112th Congress and "0" for non-members.[58] *Tea Party favorability* is the percentage of constituents at the district level saying they have a "very favorable" opinion of the Tea Party. Data for this variable came from the CCES.[59] *Ideology*, which is a lawmaker's first-dimension DW-NOMINATE score, tests the alternative hypothesis that repeal actions are ideological in nature.[60] Higher values indicate more conservative lawmakers and lower values more liberal lawmakers. *Constituents for repeal* tests the effect of voters' opinions on the ACA.[61] It is derived from a CCES question that asks a lawmaker's constituents whether they support or oppose the ACA. And finally, *constituents uninsured* examines the possibility that voters' health care needs explain members' actions on repealing the ACA. Data for this variable came from the Census Bureau.[62]

Findings: ACA Repeal Votes

A key finding emerges when we examine the raw distribution of repeal votes. As one would expect, there is a clear U-shape, with many Republicans voting for every repeal and many Democrats voting against every repeal. However, the data reveal that 45 percent of Democrats voted for at least one ACA repeal in both the 112th and 113th Congresses. Although the mode for Democrats who supported a repeal in both Congresses is just one ACA repeal vote, a surprisingly high number of Democrats supported three repeals or more (15 percent in the 112th and 20 percent in the 113th). On the other side of the aisle, 90 percent of Republicans voted for every repeal in both the 112th Congress and 113th Congress. As a whole, these descriptive statistics reveal that while ACA repeal votes are indeed partisan, there is consequential variation to be explored on the Democratic side.

Looking at Table 10-2, there are a few notable results in the analysis. First, on the Republican side, we can see that the votes are entirely partisan, consistent with the descriptive results above. Other than an incorrectly signed (and small in magnitude) effect of ideology, party affiliation is the only significant factor that explains how Republican lawmakers voted on the ACA repeal bills in both time periods.[63] Highlighting the GOP's unity on repealing the ACA is the fact that the Tea Party variables are insignificant and small in magnitude. Although researchers have documented significant roll call differences between mainstream Republicans and the Tea Party[64] and despite claims that the Tea Party was the driving force behind ACA repeals, at the final passage stage, the GOP was unified in their efforts to undo the ACA.

On the Democratic side of the aisle—where there is much more variation—a few findings emerge. As a whole, the results reveal that there is some nuance to why Democratic lawmakers supported or opposed repealing the ACA. By far the biggest effect on the Democratic side is ideology. According to the results, a standard deviation increase in a Democrat's conservatism increases the number of votes cast in favor of repeal by 2.5 in the 112th Congress and 6.6 in the 113th Congress. Among the Democrats who voted for an ACA repeal, 65 percent in the 112th Congress and 80 percent in the 113th Congress were to the right of the median Democrat. Finally, on the Democratic side, one constituency variable is significant in each Congress. In the 112th Congress, the effect of constituents who said they were "for the repeal" of the ACA is significant while in the 113th Congress, the effect of constituents uninsured is significant. So in addition to being shaped by ideological considerations, Democrats were motivated to support (or oppose) ACA repeals based on electoral considerations. Although there is a risk of overstating the results, one interpretation of the temporal change is that after the GOP landslide in 2010, House Democrats were worried about their electoral future in 2012. After Obama won reelection, however, they were less concerned about winning reelection and behaved as trustees, taking into consideration their constituents' best interests.

Findings: ACA Sponsors

Examining the distribution of ACA repeal sponsorship in Table 10-2, the descriptive statistics reveal a few notable findings. First, unlike the final passage votes, in the distribution of bill sponsorship, there is little variation. In the 112th and 113th Congresses, roughly 88 percent of members sponsored zero ACA

Table 10-2 Predicting ACA Repeal Votes and Bill Sponsorship

	112th Votes	113th Votes	112th Sponsors (GOP Only)	113th Sponsors (GOP Only)
GOP	0.406***	0.411***		
TPC	0.001	−0.002	0.132**	0.192**
Tea Party favorability (D)	−0.001	0.020		
Tea Party favorability (R)	−0.001	0.013	−0.004	−0.001
Ideology (D)	0.120***	0.472***		
Ideology (R)	0.004	−0.024**	0.243**	0.151
Constituents for repeal (D)	0.008**	0.051		
Constituents uninsured (D)	−0.001	−0.002***		
Constituents for repeal (R)	0.001	0.003	−0.005	−0.009
Constituents uninsured (R)	0.011	0.001	0.009	−0.083
R^2	0.95	0.94	0.05	0.04
N	431	429	240	231

*** $p < 0.01$, ** $p < 0.05$, * $p < 0.1$

Source: Compiled by author.

Note: Cell entries are the marginal effects (dy/dx) of a standard deviation change in the variable. Dichotomous variables (GOP and TPC) represent the effect of a 1/0 change.

repeal bills. Like the ACA repeal votes, however, there is a clear partisan pattern in the distribution. Only two Democrats in both Congresses introduced a repeal bill (1 percent of the caucus) compared to roughly 10 percent of Republicans. So while not every Republican sponsored an ACA repeal, almost every Democrat did not. Because of the almost complete lack of variation on the Democratic side, we are unable to include Democrats in the analysis. Yet because of the descriptive statistics, we can once again conclude that party affiliation was a key determinant of ACA repealing activity in the 112th and 113th Congresses.

Looking at Table 10-2, just one variable is a consistent predictor of whether a Republican lawmaker sponsored an ACA repeal bill. According to the results, members of the Tea Party Caucus were significantly more likely to sponsor an ACA repeal compared to non–Tea Party Republicans. It is important to note that this effect exists even with the inclusion of a control for a member's ideology. So the Tea Party's penchant for sponsoring ACA repeal bills is not simply a function of its greater conservatism. Such an effect is consistent with work showing that members of the Tea Party exhibit distinctive legislative behaviors[65] and may be behaving like a distinct party.[66]

Conclusions and Discussion

Passage of the Affordable Care Act was a landmark event. Yet the congressional literature's focus on law creation ignores one of most important aspects of the ACA: the postenactment struggle over the law's future. A systematic examination, such as the one in this chapter, is overdue for a few reasons. First, there is considerable ambiguity about the size and scope of the GOP's repeal attempts. Some commentators claim that House Republicans held upwards of fifty repeal votes in the 112th and 113th Congresses while others put the number at just four. Second, there are unresolved questions concerning why lawmakers supported or opposed these repeal attempts. Were they the product of ideological disagreements, partisan contests over national policy, a byproduct of the Tea Party's rapid emergence, or simply a function of voters' health care concerns? And third, there are broader questions about when and why repeals happen. Because the ACA is one of the most dramatic cases of repeal attempts in recent memory, this examination has implications for our broader understanding of these important legislative actions.

A key claim in this chapter is that there has been a tendency to mischaracterize the size and scope of the GOP's repeal attempts. Simply put, there is much more nuance than most commentators claim. A prime example is the following NBC News quote: "The House has already voted more than 50 times to repeal the law, with zero effect." Although there *have* been fifty votes to *change* the ACA, this figure includes partial repeals that targeted specific elements of the law, others that simply amended the ACA, and yet others that had Democratic support and were enacted into law. By my count, there were only four full repeal votes in the 112th and 113th Congresses. Although these full repeal votes are certainly *symbolic* or *reelection-seeking* actions, the reality is that the GOP's actions reflected a multifaceted legislative strategy to attack the law from various vantage points.

A second set of conclusions emerges from the analysis of legislative actions to repeal the Affordable Care Act. When it came to voting for ACA repeals, the results indicate key differences across parties. On the Republican side, the analysis reveals that the votes were entirely partisan in nature. Virtually every Republican voted in favor of every ACA repeal (no matter their ideology, their constituents' opinions, or their constituents' health care needs). In a larger context, the GOP's unity on this key issue obscures the fact that the party was very divided in both Congresses between "mainstream" Republicans and the Tea Party/Freedom Caucus wing. On the Democratic side, there was considerable variation in support for repeal, with 45 percent of Democrats voting for at least one ACA repeal in both the 112th and 113th Congresses. Why? According to the analysis, Democrats supported ACA repeals largely on the basis of ideological considerations. When it came to sponsoring an ACA repeal bill, these actions, too, are overwhelmingly partisan in nature. Almost all of the sponsored bills were introduced by Republicans. Among Republicans, however, the analysis reveals that members of the Tea Party Caucus were much more likely to introduce an ACA repeal than their brethren not aligned with the Tea Party. Such an effect is consistent with work showing that members of the Tea Party exhibit distinctive legislative behaviors[67] and are behaving like a third party.[68]

Given these findings, a third key claim is that actions to repeal the ACA fit the perspective that these efforts are best explained as long-term contests between the two parties over national policy.[69] Like Barrilleaux and Rainey in their analysis of governors' decisions to oppose the Medicaid expansion, the partisan factors in the model have consistent effects in terms of both sponsorship and roll call behavior.[70] But even in this extreme case, there are unmistakable problem-solving motivations at work. In the end, this is perhaps the most surprising conclusion, given just how contentious actions to revise the ACA have been. When we catalog the attempted revisions, we see there were a range of amendments and a handful of repeals of unpopular provisions that received bipartisan support. By revising these elements of the ACA, the likely consequence is a strengthening of the law.

Looking to the future, there is no doubt that the struggle to repeal the ACA will continue in the 115th Congress (2017–2018) and beyond. Although it is difficult to say what the future holds, there are some intuitive predictions based on this chapter and past research. First, as with the 1099 repeal that was signed into law, there are likely to be some major repeals in the near future. Like the passage of Medicare in 1965, the ACA will undergo a series of inevitable (and necessary) changes in the coming decades. One likely candidate is the so-called Cadillac tax. Indeed, both Hillary Clinton and Donald Trump have advocated repealing the Cadillac tax. Such a repeal would dismantle a major component of the ACA's funding. And like the 1099 repeal, one could argue that this is an example of Congress's problem-solving actions, given how unpopular this provision is on both sides of the aisle. Second, the likelihood of repeal is predicted to increase in magnitude from 2017 to 2020. A number of studies of legislative revision have shown that in the aggregate, major statutory changes are most likely a decade after enactment. In other words, the law will be most "at risk" of repeal in the 115th and 116th Congresses (2017–2020). And third, the results of the 2016 presidential election are important for the fate of the law. Although full repeal remains very unlikely, past work has shown that party control has major effects on the likelihood of repeal. On the one hand, when a party reclaims control of both chambers and the White House after a stint in the minority, repeals are increasingly likely to be enacted.[71] On the other hand, laws enacted during periods of one-party control (like the ACA was) have a greater long-term risk of repeal as well.[72] Simply put, the ACA will be a target for years to come.

Notes

I would like to thank Nate Birkhead, Josh Huder, and Larry Dodd for commenting on this chapter. I would also like to thank Pete Calcagno and the Center for Public Choice and Market Process at the College of Charleston for supporting this research.

1. Sheryl Gay Stolberg and Robert Pear, "A Stroke of a Pen, Make That 20, and It's Official," *New York Times*, March 24, 2010.
2. Ibid.
3. Brian Beutler, "GOP Finally Goes Too Far on Obamacare: Why the 50th Repeal Vote Is Not the Charm," *Salon*, March 3, 2014, http://www.salon.com/2014/03/03/gop_finally_goes_too_far_on_obamacare_why_the_50th_repeal_vote_is_not_the_charm.
4. E. Scott Adler and John D. Wilkerson, *Congress and the Politics of Problem Solving* (New York: Cambridge University Press, 2012); Christopher R. Berry, Barry C. Burden, and William G. Howell, "After Enactment: The Lives and Deaths of Federal Programs," *American Journal of Political Science* 91 (2010): 1–17; J. Kevin Corder, "Are Federal Programs Immortal? Estimating the Hazard of Program Termination," *American Politics Research* 32 (2004): 3–25; Forrest Maltzman and Charles R. Shipan, "Change, Continuity, and the Evolution of the Law," *American Journal of Political Science* 32 (2008): 252–67; Eric M. Patashnik, *Reforms at Risk: What Happens After Major Policy Changes Are Enacted* (Princeton, NJ: Princeton University Press, 2008).
5. Jordan M. Ragusa, "The Lifecycle of Public Policy: An Event History Analysis of Repeals to Landmark Legislative Enactments, 1951–2006," *American Politics Research* 38 (2010): 1015–51; Jordan M. Ragusa and Nathaniel A. Birkhead, "Parties, Preferences, and Congressional Organization: Explaining Repeals in Congress From 1877 to 2012," *Political Research Quarterly* 68 (2015): 745–59.
6. Jeffery A. Jenkins and Eric M. Patashnik, "Living Legislation and American Politics," in *Living Legislation: Durability, Change, and the Politics of American Lawmaking*, ed. Jeffery A. Jenkins and Eric M. Patashnik (Chicago: University of Chicago Press, 2012), 6.
7. Various sources were consulted in the drafting of this legislative history. See, for example, Roger H. Davidson, Walter J. Oleszek, Frances E. Lee, and Eric Schickler, *Congress and Its Members*, 15th ed. (Washington, DC: CQ Press, 2016); Barbara Sinclair, *Unorthodox Lawmaking: New Legislative Processes in the U.S. Congress*, 4th ed. (Washington, DC: CQ Press, 2012); and John Cannan, "A Legislative History of the

Affordable Care Act: How Legislative Procedure Shapes Legislative History," *Law Library Journal* 105 (2013): 131–73.
8. John H. Aldrich, Bradford H. Bishop, Rebecca S. Hatch, Sunshine D. Hillygus, and David W. Rohde, "Blame, Responsibility, and the Tea Party in the 2010 Midterm Elections," *Political Behavior* 36 (2013): 471–91.
9. Sinclair, *Unorthodox Lawmaking*.
10. Stolberg and Pear, "Stroke of a Pen."
11. Sinclair, *Unorthodox Lawmaking*.
12. Jeffrey Young, Eric Zimmermann, and Michael O'Brien, "Jubilant Obama Signs Healthcare Bill," *The Hill*, March 24, 2010, 1.
13. Peter R. Orszag, "Growth in Health Care Costs," statement before the Committee on the Budget, United States Senate, January 31, 2008, https://www.cbo.gov/sites/default/files/cbofiles/ftpdocs/89xx/doc8948/01-31-healthtestimony.pdf.
14. Ragusa, "Lifecycle of Public Policy"; Ragusa and Birkhead, "Parties, Preferences, and Congressional Organization."
15. All data on the repeals sponsored in the 111th Congress were collected by the author from the *Congressional Bills Project*. I would like to thank E. Scott Adler and John Wilkerson for making these data available. E. Scott Adler and John Wilkerson, *Congressional Bills Project: 2016*, NSF 00880066 and 00880061. The views expressed are those of the author and not the National Science Foundation.
16. Carl Hulse, "Senators Cannot Agree on Fix to the Health Law," *New York Times*, November 29, 2010.
17. In two key Senate races, Tea Party–backed lawmakers underperformed by most accounts. In particular, some observers claim that Tea Party–supported candidates Sharron Angle of Nevada and Christine O'Donnell of Delaware cost the GOP control of the Senate in the 112th and 113th Congresses.
18. Christopher F. Karpowitz, J. Quin Monson, Kelly D. Patterson, and Jeremy C. Pope, "Tea Time in America? The Impact of the Tea Party Movement on the 2010 Midterm Elections," *Political Science & Politics* 44 (2011): 303–9.
19. Brendan Nyhan, Eric McGhee, John Sides, Seth Masket, and Steven Greene, "One Vote Out of Step? The Effects of Salient Roll Call Votes in the 2010 Election," *American Politics Research* 40 (2012): 844–79.
20. An October Gallup poll showed that health care ranked as only the fifth-most-important problem. See Lydia Saad, "Economy Is Dominant Issue for Americans as Election Nears," Gallup, October 22, 2012, http://www.gallup.com/poll/158267/economy-dominant-issue-americans-election-nears.aspx.
21. Ragusa, "Lifecycle of Public Policy"; Ragusa and Birkhead, "Parties, Preferences, and Congressional Organization."
22. Jeffrey Young, "Health Care Reform Lives: What Obama Must Do to Ensure It Thrives," *Huffington Post*, November 7, 2012, http://www.huffingtonpost.com/2012/11/07/health-care-reform-obama_n_2088813.html.
23. David Nather, "Boehner: Obamacare Is Law of Land," *Politico*, November 8, 2012, http://www.politico.com/story/2012/11/boehner-obamacare-is-the-law-of-the-land-083605.
24. Charles Barrilleaux and Carlisle Rainey, "The Politics of Need: Examining Governors' Decisions to Oppose the 'Obamacare' Medicaid Expansion," *State Politics & Policy Quarterly* 14 (2014): 437–60.
25. Adler and Wilkerson, *Congress and the Politics of Problem Solving*; Berry, Burden, and Howell, "After Enactment"; Corder, "Are Federal Programs Immortal?"; Maltzman

and Shipan, "Change, Continuity, and the Evolution of the Law"; Patashnik, *Reforms at Risk*.
26. Ragusa, "Lifecycle of Public Policy"; Ragusa and Birkhead, "Parties, Preferences, and Congressional Organization."
27. Ragusa and Birkhead, "Parties, Preferences, and Congressional Organization."
28. Ibid.
29. Berry, Burden, and Howell, "After Enactment"; Corder, "Are Federal Programs Immortal?"; Ragusa, "Lifecycle of Public Policy."
30. Adler and Wilkerson, *Congress and the Politics of Problem Solving*.
31. Patashnik, *Reforms at Risk*, 160–63.
32. Ibid., 85–90.
33. Ragusa and Birkhead, "Parties, Preferences, and Congressional Organization." See also John H. Aldrich, *Why Parties? The Origin and Transformation of Political Parties in America* (Chicago: University of Chicago Press, 1995), and David W. Rohde, *Parties and Leaders in the Postreform House* (Chicago: University of Chicago Press, 1991).
34. Ragusa and Birkhead, "Parties, Preferences, and Congressional Organization," 745.
35. Berry, Burden, and Howell, "After Enactment"; Maltzman and Shipan, "Change, Continuity, and the Evolution of the Law"; Patashnik, *Reforms at Risk*.
36. See a comparison of Maltzman and Shipan's and Adler and Wilkerson's results in Adler and Wilkerson, *Congress and the Politics of Problem Solving*, 176–81.
37. Ragusa, "Lifecycle of Public Policy"; David Mayhew, *Divided We Govern: Party Control, Lawmaking, and Investigations, 1946–1990* (New Haven, CT: Yale University Press, 1991).
38. Ragusa and Birkhead, "Parties, Preferences, and Congressional Organization."
39. Data came from two main sources: a CRS report outlining repeal actions and a *New York Times* database that catalogs repeal votes. See C. Stephen Redhead and Janet Kinzer, *Legislative Actions to Repeal, Defund, or Delay the Affordable Care Act* (Washington, DC: Congressional Research Service, 2016), and "House Votes Repealing or Defunding the Affordable Care Act," *New York Times*, http://politics.nytimes.com/congress/votes/house/aca-repeal-defund (accessed March 3, 2016).
40. Amendments are proposals to alter or adjust aspects of the law without undoing, reversing, or stopping that element. For example, H.R. 674, in the 112th Congress, adjusted how the ACA calculates modified adjusted gross income, used in the determination of Americans' eligibility for health care subsidies. It was passed unanimously by the House and Senate and was signed into law.
41. I do not count each year's budget and a handful of appropriations acts in these estimates, given that these bills contained many extraneous provisions. Some commentators include each year's budget as a full repeal. If these are included, the number of full repeals rises to eight (still far short of the fifty that is often cited).
42. Boehner made this claim in a January interview with Fox News host Bret Baier. See Russell Berman, "Why Republicans Are Voting to Repeal Obamacare—Again," *The Atlantic*, February 3, 2015, http://www.theatlantic.com/politics/archive/2015/02/why-republicans-are-voting-to-repeal-obamacare-again/385105.
43. Janet M. Box-Steffensmeier, Laura W. Arnold, and Christopher J. W. Zorn, "The Strategic Timing of Position Taking in Congress: A Study of the North American Free Trade Agreement," *American Political Science Review* 91 (1997): 324–38. Mayhew, *Divided We Govern*.
44. Adler and Wilkerson, *Congress and the Politics of Problem Solving*.

45. Barrilleaux and Rainey, "Politics of Need."
46. Jonathan Weisman and Robert Pear, "Partisan Gridlock Thwarts Effort to Alter Health Law," *New York Times*, May 26, 2013, http://www.nytimes.com/2013/05/27/us/politics/polarized-congress-thwarts-changes-to-health-care-law.html.
47. Ragusa, "Lifecycle of Public Policy"; Ragusa and Birkhead, "Parties, Preferences, and Congressional Organization."
48. Barrilleaux and Rainey, "Politics of Need."
49. Brad Bannon, "The Tea Party's Unhealthy Obsession," *U.S. News & World Report*, August 1, 2013, http://www.usnews.com/opinion/blogs/brad-bannon/2013/08/01/republicans-unhealthy-obsession-with-repealing-the-affordable-care-act.
50. Jon R. Bond, "'Life Ain't Easy for a President Named Barack': Party, Ideology, and Tea Party Freshman Support for the Nation's First Black President," *Forum* 11 (2013): 243–58; Jordan M. Ragusa and Anthony Gaspar, "Where's the Tea Party? An Examination of the Tea Party's Voting Behavior in the House of Representatives," *Political Research Quarterly* 69 (2016): 361–72; Michael J. Thompson, "Suburban Origins of the Tea Party: Spatial Dimensions of the New Conservative Personality," *Critical Sociology* 38 (2012): 511–28.
51. Matthew E. Glassman and Robert Jay Dilger, *Congressional Member Organizations: Their Purpose and Activities, History, and Formation* (Washington, DC: Congressional Research Service, 2015), https://www.fas.org/sgp/crs/misc/R40683.pdf.
52. Michael A. Bailey, Jonathan Mummolo, and Hans Noel, "Tea Party Influence: A Story of Activists and Elites," *American Politics Research* 40 (2012): 769–804.
53. Keith Krehbiel, *Information and Legislative Organization* (Ann Arbor: University of Michigan Press, 1991).
54. Despite the fact that the response is continuous, it is a percentage bound between 0 and 1. As various authors note, OLS is not an ideal estimation strategy. See, for example, Leslie E. Papke and Jeffrey M. Wooldridge, "Econometric Methods for Fractional Response Variables With an Application to 401(K) Plan Participation Rates," *Journal of Applied Econometrics* 11 (1996): 619–32. For the roll call analysis, I therefore estimated a fractional logit model, which is a generalized linear model with a logit link function.
55. In the sponsor analysis, the model was estimated using Poisson regression. Diagnostics do not indicate a problem with overdispersion.
56. E. Scott Adler and John Wilkerson, *Congressional Bills Project: (2016)*, NSF 00880066 and 00880061. The views expressed are those of the authors and not the National Science Foundation.
57. Using the *Congressional Bills Project*, I searched for bills that contained the term "repeal" and various terms associated with the ACA, such as "Obama," "Obamacare," "Affordable Care," "health care," etc. Each term had to be listed in the bill's description. Although there are certainly repeals contained in laws that don't have these terms in the description (that do not make it into this analysis), this approach restricts the sample to bills that were focused on repeals (and did not contain extraneous provisions).
58. Data on membership in the Tea Party Caucus is explained in Ragusa and Gaspar, "Where's the Tea Party?"
59. In both Congresses, the Tea Party's favorability at the district level came from the Cooperative Congressional Election Study (CCES). The variable catalogs the percentage of respondents who said they had a "very positive" view of the Tea Party. See https://dataverse.harvard.edu/dataverse/cces.

60. Data are available at www.voteview.com.
61. This question was only asked in the 2012 CCES. However, the CCES has a variable that identifies the old (112th Congress) and new (113th Congress) district lines.
62. Data came from the U.S. Census's American Community Survey. See https://www.census.gov/programs-surveys/acs.
63. Subsequent diagnostic examinations reveal that the incorrect effect of ideology is due to problematic collinearity with the party affiliation variable.
64. Bond, "Life Ain't Easy"; Ragusa and Gaspar, "Where's the Tea Party?"; Thompson, "Suburban Origins of the Tea Party."
65. Bailey, Mummolo, and Noel, "Tea Party Influence"; Bond, "Life Ain't Easy"; Thompson, "Suburban Origins of the Tea Party."
66. Ragusa and Gaspar, "Where's the Tea Party?"
67. Bailey, Mummolo, and Noel, "Tea Party Influence"; Bond, "Life Ain't Easy"; Thompson, "Suburban Origins of the Tea Party."
68. Ragusa and Gaspar, "Where's the Tea Party?"
69. Ragusa and Birkhead, "Parties, Preferences, and Congressional Organization."
70. Barrilleaux and Rainey, "Politics of Need."
71. Ragusa and Birkhead, "Parties, Preferences, and Congressional Organization."
72. Ragusa, "Lifecycle of Public Policy."

Part IV
Legislators, Committees, and the Policy Process

11. Legislative Effectiveness and Problem Solving in the U.S. House of Representatives

Craig Volden and Alan E. Wiseman

Volden and Wiseman (2014) argue that the legislative effectiveness of individual members of Congress is important to understanding the workings of Congress and the laws it produces. In contrast, Adler and Wilkerson (2012) argue that individual members' effectiveness is of little importance relative to problem solving around the rise and fall of must-pass legislation. In this chapter, we test competing hypotheses that arise from these two perspectives for the activities of committee and subcommittee chairs from 1973 to 2014. Consistent with Legislative Effectiveness and in contrast to the Problem-Solving Perspective, we establish that the Legislative Effectiveness Scores of committee and subcommittee chairs are positively correlated over time and rise along with their expertise. Illustrative cases question the inevitability of the passage of "must-pass" legislation and instead suggest a central role for the effectiveness (and ineffectiveness) of chairs. These findings highlight how institutional changes over the past twenty years have reduced the effectiveness of committee and subcommittee chairs and limited the lawmaking capacity of Congress.

When and how are new laws created by the U.S. House of Representatives, and how well do they address the country's public policy needs?[1] This relatively simple question has been at the heart of scholarly inquiry on Congress for more than one hundred years. In recent years, vibrant debates have emerged over whether and how political parties might influence the legislative agenda[2] and how party members vote.[3] Alternatively, other scholars have argued that legislation is heavily influenced by the preferences of the chamber's median voter,[4] subject to various constraints like supermajority decision rules[5] and congressional committees.[6]

In our recent book and related research,[7] we advance the argument that the road to legislative success is influenced by the individual lawmakers who advocate for particular legislative measures. That is, bill sponsors vary in their underlying abilities to move their agendas through the legislative process from the time a bill is introduced until it is (perhaps) ultimately signed into law by the president. We denoted this ability as *legislative effectiveness*, and we have argued that the variation in legislative effectiveness can be quantified systematically. To that end, we developed the *Legislative Effectiveness Score* (LES) to measure the relative effectiveness of representatives at moving their bills through the legislative process. We demonstrated how a legislator's effectiveness (as measured by her LES) is correlated with a wide range of expected factors, such as whether a representative is in the majority party, whether she is relatively senior, and whether she holds a committee chair. More intriguingly, Legislative Effectiveness Scores help explain legislators' political career paths, when and why women are more effective lawmakers than men, and how certain "habits" help lawmakers become highly effective. Taken together, our research has presented a compelling picture of the role and relevance of legislative effectiveness in the contemporary lawmaking process.

In contrast, Scott Adler and John Wilkerson advance an alternative and provocative perspective on the drivers of legislative success.[8] They argue that much of legislative activity is a natural consequence of how Congress is organized to solve problems. More specifically, as new problems become particularly salient to the American public and as existing laws expire and are subject to statutory reauthorization, Congress is essentially compelled to engage these pressing concerns in some way. Hence, members of standing committees that have monopoly control over their policy jurisdictions exert an effort to learn about possible solutions to a given problem or about how to modify policies through the statutory reauthorization process and ultimately advance their bills through the legislative process. These bills are given deference by other members of the chamber because they engage compulsory matters and thereby represent "must-pass" legislation that all members of the chamber have an interest in seeing signed into law.

The "Congress as a Problem Solver" Perspective, which hereafter we denote as the *Problem-Solving Perspective*, offers many direct contrasts to the Legislative Effectiveness Perspective on lawmaking. Most notably, the Problem-Solving Perspective puts less emphasis on the relative abilities and efforts of any particular legislator as explanatory factors behind the success that one bill experiences in comparison to another. Indeed, Adler and Wilkerson are quite explicit on this point when they state, "Bill-sponsor success is more a reflection of an institutionalized problem-solving process than it is of a lawmaker's entrepreneurial skills."[9] Hence, bills do not advance further in the legislative process because they are being sponsored by some members who are more skilled at using their institutionally advantageous positions. Rather, bills advance further in the legislative process because they deal with compulsory issues, which, by their very nature, *must* advance in the legislative process, regardless of lawmaker skill, so as to avoid politically unacceptable scenarios.

A consideration of these competing perspectives raises the following question: Is it the sponsor, or is it the bill? Do bills move further in the legislative process because they deal with policy issues that must find their ways into new laws in a given Congress, or do bills advance because they are being advocated by highly skilled lawmakers, who are able to leverage their personal and institutional advantages to forge coalitions, broker policy compromises, and cut through the political clutter to shepherd their bills into law? While engaging this question can be challenging, we believe that the Problem-Solving Perspective and the Legislative Effectiveness Perspective suggest various competing hypotheses, which we explore in this chapter.

Adjudicating between these two perspectives is not just an intellectual exercise. Rather, what is at stake is an understanding of how capable the present Congress is at addressing major problems facing the country. Consider the reforms advanced by Speaker Newt Gingrich, R-Ga., in the mid-1990s to shift power from committees to the majority party leadership. Under a Problem-Solving Perspective, must-pass legislation still passes but now more clearly reflects party interests than those of committee chairs. In contrast, the Legislative Effectiveness Perspective argues that such changes as term limits on committee chairs have more profound effects. No longer as able to fully cultivate their lawmaking skills, chairs diminish in effectiveness, legislation becomes less likely to solve policy problems, and Congress struggles even with "must-pass" legislation.

Perspectives on Legislative Effectiveness and Problem Solving

The belief that some members of Congress are generally *better* at managing the legislative process and making laws is fairly innocuous, on its face. Political biographies, journalistic coverage of Congress, and a wide body of congressional scholarship are rife with examples of representatives being "effective users of inside power."[10] For example, scholars like John Manley have explored how particular chairs, such as Wilbur Mills, D-Ark., who chaired the Committee on Ways and Means from 1958 to 1974, were able to use their positions of influence and their legislative skill to advance their favored policies.[11] Andrée Reeves provides in-depth portraits of the careers and experiences of three chairmen of the House Education and Labor Committee—Graham Barden, D-N.C.; Adam Clayton Powell Jr., D-N.Y.; and Carl Perkins, D-Ky.—identifying how their varying tactics were directly related to their bills moving (or not).[12] Beyond committee chairs, incumbent congressman and political scientist Daniel Lipinski, D-Ill., explains the different tactics that legislators can use to enhance the chances that their bills move further in the legislative process, in the ninth edition of *Congress Reconsidered*.[13]

Individual member effectiveness has been measured based on percentage-of-success "hit rates,"[14] counts of successful bill passages,[15] or reputation-based rankings.[16] Building on these earlier approaches, we embraced a holistic and objective approach to measuring legislative effectiveness as a legislator's "proven ability to advance [his or her] agenda items through the legislative process and into law."[17] To develop our measure, we drew on publicly available data from the THOMAS, the Library of Congress Web site, to identify the sponsor of every public bill (H.R.) introduced from the Ninety-third through 113th Congresses (1973–2014).[18] For each representative in the U.S. House during this time period, we identified how many bills she sponsored in each two-year Congress and how many of those bills received any action in committee (e.g., hearings, markups, and subcommittee votes) or action beyond committee on the floor of the House. For those bills that received any action beyond committee, we identified how many of those bills passed the House and how many ultimately became a public law. We also downgraded commemorative measures and upgraded substantive and significant bills, relative to common substantive proposals.[19] Drawing on these fifteen different bill-level indicators (five lawmaking stages across three significance levels), we calculate each representative's Legislative Effectiveness Score relative to one another in each Congress, with the average score normalized to one.[20]

As expected, on average, majority party members outperform those in the minority party, as do committee and subcommittee chairs and other senior members. Beyond such straightforward results, however, we find tradeoffs between a representative's legislative effectiveness and her electoral security;[21] we show how lawmaker effectiveness overcomes issue-specific policy gridlock in areas such as health policy;[22] and we document how female legislators, particularly those in the minority party, are more effective lawmakers than their male counterparts.[23] Taken together, our results suggest that a bill's prospects for success are directly related to the legislative effectiveness of its sponsor, that legislative effectiveness can be quantified, that our metric of legislative effectiveness comports with many aspects of conventional wisdom, and that analysis of our metric yields new insights regarding the politics of lawmaking in the U.S. Congress.

This picture of the legislator as an agent of change contrasts greatly with an alternative approach to congressional policy making advanced by E. Scott Adler and John Wilkerson. Building on Jack Walker's theory of agenda setting,[24] Adler and Wilkerson argue that "many issue debates begin with the shared premise that Congress must act. For such 'compulsory' issues, lawmakers face considerable pressure to find common ground in timely fashion."[25] In addition, "more often than is generally appreciated, governments have things they must do—crises they must address . . . and policies that require updating."[26] Hence, when a policy matter is deemed to be *compulsory*, Congress has to engage it, ensuring that bills addressing the compulsory policy advance in the legislative process.

What constitutes a compulsory issue? While the relative priority of any piece of legislation might be in the eye of the beholder, Adler and Wilkerson argue that bills that are subject to hardwired time lines (such as those with sunset provisions), as well as those that engage "politically necessary" issues and respond to "salient events," are more likely compulsory.[27] In other words, periodic reauthorizations common in "defense, education, transportation, taxation, law enforcement, and civil rights" would be categorized as being compulsory bills.[28] Likewise, bills that engage discrete crises, such as environmental mishaps or terrorist attacks, are also categorized as compulsory.[29] It is these types of bills that will move furthest in the legislative process, by design, because Congress *must* see them passed. In the Problem-Solving Perspective, the actual identity of the sponsor has little bearing on the likely success of most bills—it is the legislation, not the legislator, that will (essentially) determine whether the bill is signed into law.

Competing Hypotheses

Distinguishing between these competing perspectives can be potentially quite challenging. If, for example, one observes a representative introducing legislation that Adler and Wilkerson categorize as compulsory and that legislation is ultimately signed into law, can we say with certainty that its success was due to the content, rather than the sponsor? Perhaps if a different sponsor had introduced (essentially) the same bill, it would have failed. Alternatively, perhaps highly effective lawmakers seek out bills that engage important problems, knowing that they are best equipped to move those bills furthest in the legislative process. The most direct way to engage many of the implications of these competing perspectives is through counterfactuals that show how the different cases comport with either the Legislative Effectiveness or Problem-Solving Perspective. However, scholars of Congress are observers of real-world politics, and there are relatively few natural experiments that would allow one to assess the consequences of said counterfactuals. Hence, we must turn to less direct methods of empirical analysis to discriminate between these competing perspectives.

Building on Adler and Wilkerson's observation that "successful bills addressing compulsory issues [are] almost exclusively committee sponsored,"[30] we turn our attention to committee and subcommittee chairs in the U.S. House. Consistent with the Problem-Solving Perspective, a committee or subcommittee chair will be highly successful in passing legislation in a given Congress based on addressing compulsory issues. As these newly resolved issues then fade in urgency, that committee (and the committee chair) will be less active in the subsequent Congress and relatively less successful at moving agenda items through the legislative process. This pattern would be reflected in upward bumps in a chair's LES in one Congress, followed by relatively downward bumps in her LES in the next Congress. If pervasive, such oscillating patterns result in negative correlations in LES for such chairs over time, as stated in the following hypothesis.

Temporal Problem-Solving Hypothesis: There will be a negative correlation in the over-time Legislative Effectiveness Scores of committee and subcommittee chairs.

In contrast, the Legislative Effectiveness Perspective predicts different temporal patterns, based on lawmakers' innate abilities and the expertise they cultivate over time. Rather than hopping up and down, the LES of any given lawmaker will be fairly stable, with the most effective lawmakers consistently outperforming the least effective. For chairs, a similar pattern should emerge, coupled with an increase in effectiveness over time due to rising expertise and skills in utilizing their institutional advantages. Hence, two hypotheses follow from the Legislative Effectiveness Perspective regarding the relationships between time and the effectiveness of committee and subcommittee chairs. First, in direct contrast to the Temporal Problem-Solving Hypothesis, the Legislative Effectiveness Perspective would suggest that the effectiveness of a chair in one Congress should be positively correlated with her effectiveness in the next.

Temporal Legislative Effectiveness Hypothesis: There will be a positive correlation in the over-time Legislative Effectiveness Scores of committee and subcommittee chairs.

Moreover, because a committee chair's lawmaking skill and policy expertise is predicted to increase across time, the Legislative Effectiveness Perspective would suggest that a committee or subcommittee chair's LES will likewise rise with experience.

Legislative Effectiveness Expertise Hypothesis: Chairs' Legislative Effectiveness Scores will increase in the number of terms that they serve as chairs.

The null hypothesis to the Legislative Effectiveness Expertise Hypothesis, which is consistent with the Problem-Solving Perspective, is that there is no relationship between how many terms a representative has served as a chair and her lawmaking effectiveness. Instead, any success that a chair experiences is largely attributable to the reauthorization schedule, as well as idiosyncratic events that necessitate various items of must-pass legislation.

These competing theoretical perspectives are illustrated in Figure 11-1. The top panel illustrates the hypothetical relationship between a committee or subcommittee chair's legislative effectiveness and her time in the position, as suggested by the Legislative Effectiveness Perspective. While we see that "highly effective" chairs are expected to have generally higher LESs than "ineffective" chairs, the relative effectiveness of both types of chairs are predicted to rise in a fairly steady manner as they hold their positions for greater numbers of successive Congresses. Hence, capturing the Temporal Legislative Effectiveness Hypothesis, chairs' scores are expected to be positively correlated across time, and capturing the Legislative Effectiveness Expertise Hypothesis, chairs' scores are expected to be higher the longer that they serve as chairs.

In contrast, the bottom panel of Figure 11-1 illustrates the hypothetical relationship between a chair's legislative effectiveness and her time in the position, according to the Problem-Solving Perspective. Here, we see that a chair's Legislative Effectiveness Score might increase starkly in one Congress (most likely corresponding with reauthorization legislation or other compulsory measures), and then, it will go down in the subsequent Congress (after the reauthorization or crisis has passed). These upward spikes, followed by returns to a baseline, are consistent with the Temporal Problem-Solving Hypothesis, which suggests that committee chairs' scores are expected to be negatively correlated across time.

Legislative Effectiveness and Problem Solving 265

Figure 11-1 Theoretical Expectations

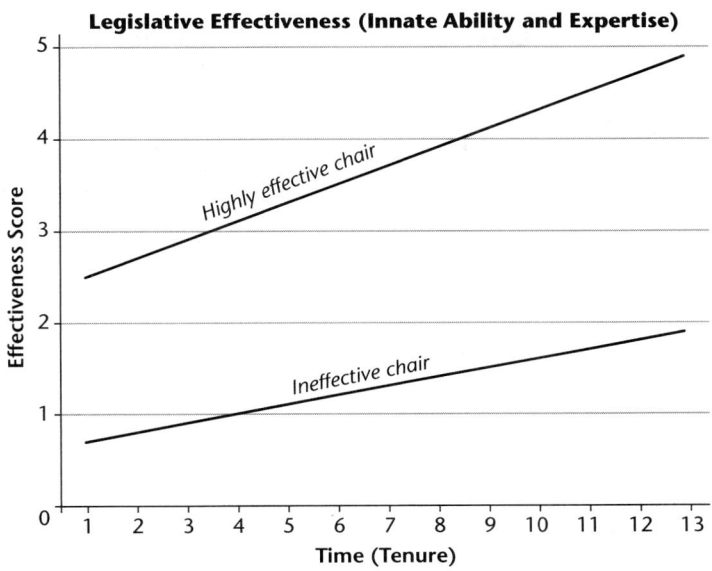

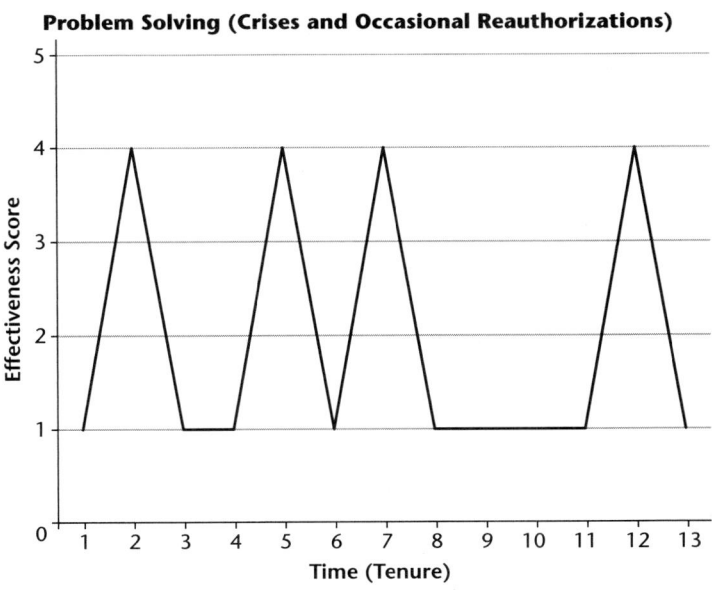

Note: The Legislative Effectiveness Perspective hypothesizes that chairs are consistent over time in their effectiveness, with increases mainly due to expertise gained by longer tenures in their chair positions. In contrast, the Problem-Solving Perspective hypothesizes that effectiveness rises and falls with the arrival and departure of must-pass issues, leading to negative correlations in effectiveness over time and to no increase based on committee chair tenure.

And likewise, there should be no relationship between a chair's LES and how long she has held her chair, as that would have no effect on crisis occurrences or reauthorization timetables.

Data and Analysis

To test these competing hypotheses, we draw on data from Volden and Wiseman's Legislative Effectiveness Project data set. More specifically, for each representative who served as a committee or subcommittee chair during her time in the U.S. House, we identify her Legislative Effectiveness Score to explore patterns in chairs' scores over time and how those patterns comport with the Legislative Effectiveness or Problem-Solving Perspectives.

Preliminary insights can be gleaned from considering Figure 11-2, which plots out the average Legislative Effectiveness Scores from the Ninety-third through 113th Congresses (1973–2014) for members of the minority party, members of the majority party who do not hold chairs, subcommittee chairs, and committee chairs, as their terms of seniority in Congress range from one to thirteen terms.

One obvious point that emerges from a quick glance at Figure 11-2 is that for all categories of legislators, legislative effectiveness is largely increasing with their seniority. Even for minority party representatives, who lack the institutional privileges that might come with holding a committee or subcommittee chair or being part of a majority governing coalition, their Legislative Effectiveness Scores increase as they serve more terms in the House. Second, it

Figure 11-2 Average Legislative Effectiveness Scores, by Seniority and Status

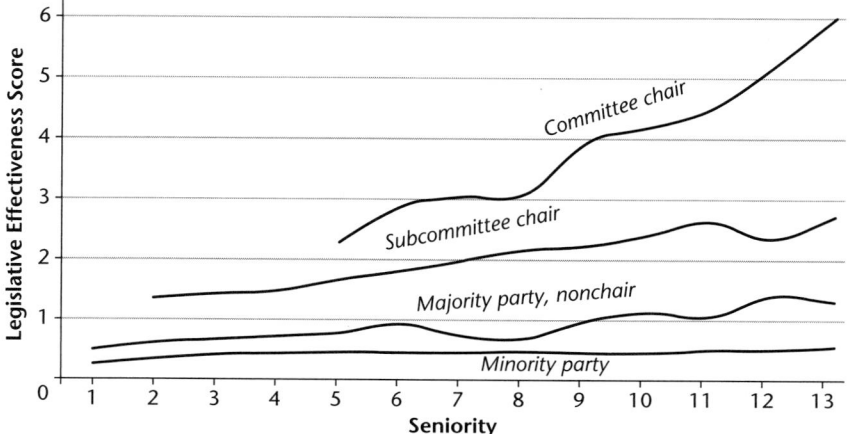

Note: The figure, based on all lawmakers in the House from 1973 to 2014, shows rising effectiveness due to greater seniority, especially for committee and subcommittee chairs.

is also the case that the average Legislative Effectiveness Scores of committee and subcommittee chairs are notably higher than those of rank-and-file majority party members. Likewise, we see that the average Legislative Effectiveness Scores of committee and subcommittee chairs are increasing over their tenure in the House, and the rate of increase is notably larger for chairs than it is for rank-and-file majority party members. (The rate of increase is also greater for committee chairs in comparison to subcommittee chairs.) On its face, Figure 11-2 suggests correlations and positive trends in chairs' LESs over time, but it is quite possible that this presentation of average Legislative Effectiveness Scores masks individual-level variation in representatives' LESs, which might suggest a different pattern.

To explore the determinants of individual-level variation in the Legislative Effectiveness Scores of committee and subcommittee chairs, Table 11-1 presents the results from a series of ordinary least squares regressions where the sample of

Table 11-1 Tests of Temporal-Effects Hypotheses

Dependent Variable: Legislative Effectiveness Score	Model 1: Committee Chairs	Model 2: Committee Chairs	Model 3: Subcommittee Chairs	Model 4: Subcommittee Chairs
Lagged Effectiveness Score	*0.523**** (0.059)	*0.446**** (0.072)	*0.623**** (0.036)	*0.530**** (0.046)
Seniority		0.162*** (0.041)		0.006 (0.012)
State Legislative Experience		−0.512 (0.640)		−0.169 (0.137)
State Legislative Experience × Legislative Professionalism		2.716 (1.915)		0.740* (0.431)
Majority Party Leadership		−1.797*** (0.547)		0.438 (0.294)
Committee Chair				1.420*** (0.222)
Subcommittee Chair		−0.741** (0.349)		
Power Committee		−0.636 (0.387)		0.093 (0.077)
Distance From Median		−0.671 (1.506)		0.364 (0.257)
Female		−0.956 (0.596)		0.068 (0.114)

(Continued)

Table 11-1 (Continued)

Dependent Variable: Legislative Effectiveness Score	Model 1: Committee Chairs	Model 2: Committee Chairs	Model 3: Subcommittee Chairs	Model 4: Subcommittee Chairs
African American		−0.592 (0.604)		−0.568*** (0.122)
Latino		0.486 (0.595)		−0.088 (0.206)
Size of Congressional Delegation		−0.004 (0.013)		−0.004 (0.003)
Vote Share		0.085 (0.106)		−0.005 (0.027)
Vote Share^2		−0.0005 (0.001)		0.00003 (0.0002)
Constant	2.777*** (0.250)	−1.852 (3.884)	1.018*** (0.053)	1.191 (0.986)
N	440	431	2,086	2,052
Adj. R^2	0.26	0.34	0.37	0.42

Results from ordinary least squares regressions, with clustered standard errors (by legislator) in parentheses.

*$p < 0.1$, **$p < 0.05$, ***$p < 0.01$ (two tailed)

Note: The positive and statistically significant coefficient on Lagged Effectiveness Score offers strong support for the Temporal Legislative Effectiveness Hypothesis over the Temporal Problem-Solving Hypothesis.

analysis is either all committee chairs (Models 1 and 2) or all subcommittee chairs (Models 3 and 4). The dependent variable of analysis is representative i's *Legislative Effectiveness Score* in Congress t, where (consistent with Figure 11-2) data are drawn from the Ninety-third through 113th Congresses. Across all specifications, the crucial variable of interest is representative i's Lagged Effectiveness Score, meaning her Legislative Effectiveness Score from the previous Congress. If the Temporal Problem-Solving Hypothesis holds, then we would expect that the coefficient on Lagged Effectiveness Score to be negative due to the rise and fall of compulsory issues, whereas the Temporal Legislative Effectiveness Hypothesis would imply that the coefficient should be positive due to innate ability and cultivated skill.

As we see in Models 1 and 3, the coefficient on Lagged Effectiveness Score is positive and statistically significant, implying that committee chairs' (Model 1) and subcommittee chairs' (Model 3) Legislative Effectiveness Scores are positively correlated across Congresses. The higher a chair's LES was in the previous

Congress, the higher her score is in the current Congress. As demonstrated in Models 2 and 4, these findings are robust to the inclusion of a wide range of variables that would be expected to be correlated with a chair's legislative effectiveness, such as her seniority, previous state legislative experience, and relative electoral security.[31] These large-sample multivariate analyses are consistent with Figure 11-2. Representatives' LESs—and those of committee and subcommittee chairs, in particular—are positively correlated across Congresses in a manner that would be predicted by the Legislative Effectiveness Perspective on policy making.

Turning to consideration of the Legislative Effectiveness Expertise Hypothesis, Figure 11-3 plots out the average Legislative Effectiveness Scores of committee and subcommittee chairs in the House, as a function of their number of terms as chair.

While there are some obvious similarities between the modes of analysis in Figures 11-3 and 11-2, there are some subtle differences that are important to articulate. Whereas Figure 11-2 plots out the average LES of different types of legislators across their careers in Congress (meaning seniority), Figure 11-3 identifies the average LES of a representative who has held a committee (top curve) or subcommittee (bottom curve) chair for a particular number of Congresses, independent of the legislator's seniority. For example, the curves in Figure 11-3 imply that the average LES of a representative who has held a committee or subcommittee chair for three terms is approximately 4.5 and 2.3, respectively, even though those representatives who have held chairs for three terms may vary widely in their congressional seniority. Additionally, the data in Figure 11-3

Figure 11-3 Average Legislative Effectiveness Scores, by Expertise in Role

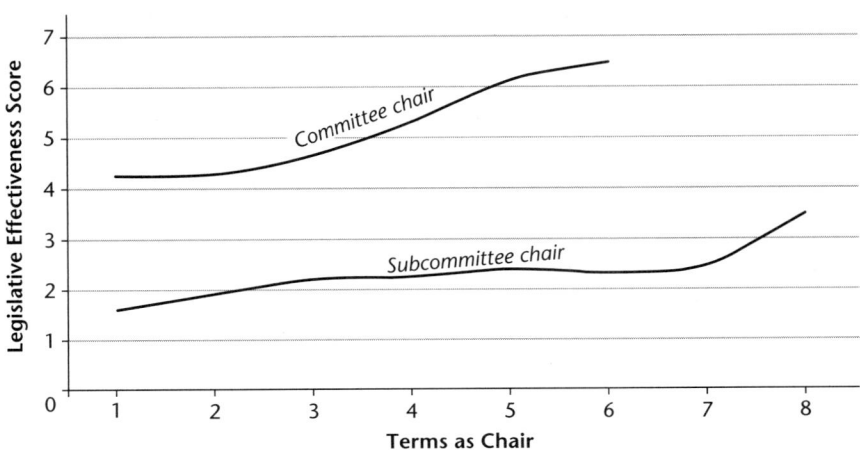

Note: The figure, based on all House chairs from 1973 to 2014, shows rising effectiveness with longer service as a chair.

measure how many terms a representative served as a chair of any committee (or subcommittee), not how many terms she served as chair of the same committee. For example, if a representative (such as Don Young, R-Alaska) served as a chair of the Resources Committee for three terms and then moved to become the chair of the Committee on Transportation and Infrastructure, his first term as chair of Transportation and Infrastructure would be measured as his fourth term as a chair in the House.

As illustrated in Figure 11-3, it is clearly the case that the average LES of committee and subcommittee chairs increases along with longer service in these positions. The average first-term committee chair has an LES of a little over 4.0, whereas a representative in her sixth term as a committee chair averages around 6.5. Similarly, the average first-term subcommittee chair has an LES of approximately 1.75, or about 75 percent greater than the overall congressional average of 1.0. Her score doubles to 3.5 upon eight terms of service as a subcommittee chair. Another interesting finding that emerges from the figure is that the upward slope for legislative effectiveness among committee chairs is particularly pronounced for those representatives who have served as chairs for more than three terms.

Taken together, the data in Figure 11-3 offer support for the Legislative Effectiveness Expertise Hypothesis: As chairs spend more time in their positions, they learn more about the substance of the legislation in their jurisdiction, as well as about the nuance of parliamentary procedure, that can help facilitate their increased legislative success. These findings stand in contrast to what we would expect from the Problem-Solving Perspective, in which chair effectiveness is instead largely the result of must-pass legislation. There is no particular reason to expect such legislation to be clustered in the committees and subcommittees with the most experienced chairs (unless that experience conversely affects what must indeed pass).

Moving from these aggregate summaries to individual-level analysis, Table 11-2 presents the results from a series of ordinary least squares regressions, where the sample of analysis is either all committee chairs (Models 5 and 6) or all subcommittee chairs (Models 7 and 8). Similar to the analysis that is presented in Table 11-1, the dependent variable in all specifications in Table 11-2 is representative i's Legislative Effectiveness Score in Congress t for each of the Ninety-third through 113th Congresses (1973–2014). Across all specifications, the crucial variable of interest is the number of terms that Representative i has served as a committee (Models 5 and 6) or subcommittee (Models 7 and 8) chair, capturing the expertise developed during her tenure in that privileged institutional position. If the Legislative Effectiveness Expertise Hypothesis holds, then the coefficient on *Expertise (Terms as Chair)* should be positive and statistically significant.

As we see in Models 5 and 7, the coefficient on Expertise (Terms as Chair) is positive and statistically significant, implying that committee chairs' (Model 1) and subcommittee chairs' (Model 3) Legislative Effectiveness Scores increase as they hold chairs for more Congresses. This finding is entirely consistent with

Table 11-2 Tests of Expertise Hypotheses

Dependent Variable: Legislative Effectiveness Score	Model 5: Committee Chairs	Model 6: Committee Chairs	Model 7: Subcommittee Chairs	Model 8: Subcommittee Chairs
Expertise (Terms as Chair)	*0.261*** *(0.119)*	*0.324**** *(0.105)*	*0.168**** *(0.034)*	*0.062*** *(0.029)*
State Legislative Experience		−0.887 (0.929)		−0.305 (0.222)
State Legislative Experience × Legislative Professionalism		4.175 (2.752)		1.196* (0.716)
Majority Party Leadership		1.375 (2.403)		1.017** (0.433)
Committee Chair				2.800*** (0.348)
Subcommittee Chair		−0.206 (0.510)		
Power Committee		−0.543 (0.635)		0.101 (0.117)
Distance From Median		−1.532 (2.157)		0.626 (0.423)
Female		−0.410 (1.755)		−0.005 (0.157)
African American		−1.523 (0.976)		−1.092*** (0.198)
Latino		0.401 (0.825)		−0.308 (0.256)
Size of Congressional Delegation		−0.021 (0.020)		−0.005 (0.005)
Vote Share		0.200 (0.136)		0.019 (0.032)
Vote Share^2		−0.001 (0.001)		−0.0001 (0.0002)
Constant	4.154*** (0.325)	−3.634 (5.160)	1.594*** (0.085)	0.860 (1.213)
N	462	452	2,243	2,206
Adj. R^2	0.02	0.07	0.03	0.20

Results from ordinary least squares regressions, with clustered standard errors (by legislator) in parentheses.

*$p < 0.1$, **$p < 0.05$, ***$p < 0.01$ (two tailed)*

Note: The positive and statistically significant coefficient on Expertise (Terms as Chair) offers strong support for the Legislative Effectiveness Expertise Hypothesis, establishing that chairs become more effective as they gain more experience in such roles.

Figure 11-3, displayed earlier, and it speaks to how the acquisition of expertise over time, through repeated Congresses serving as a chair, can enhance a legislator's lawmaking effectiveness. Also consistent with Figure 11-3, we see that the magnitude of the coefficients for committee chairs is greater than that for subcommittee chairs, suggesting that the relationship is even more pronounced for those lawmakers who hold these particularly influential positions in the House.

In Models 6 and 8, we see that these results hold even after we control for the wide range of legislator-specific characteristics from Table 11-1.[32] Once again, the coefficients on Expertise (Terms as Chair) are positive and statistically significant. The effect size is particularly impressive for committee chairs (Model 6). An additional three terms as committee chair increases a lawmaker's LES by almost a full point. This is approximately one more piece of substantive and significant legislation moving from bill introduction to law.[33] Put another way, replacing a fourth-term committee chair with a first-term chair is associated with one less major piece of legislation (perhaps a failed "must-pass" bill).

Illustrations and Implications for Institutional Reforms

Such a replacement of a fourth-term chair with a first-term chair is not just an academic exercise in interpreting regression coefficients. When Newt Gingrich became Speaker of the House in 1995, he instituted institutional reforms designed to concentrate more power with the Speaker and the Republican leadership. Among the reforms were three-term limits on committee and subcommittee chairs. Thus, a chair who would otherwise reach her fourth term would be replaced by a new first-term chair. If our statistical models are correct, such a loss of expertise will result in less legislative activity, even to the point of the failure of otherwise must-pass legislation.

There has, indeed, been more gridlock and dysfunction in Congress in recent decades.[34] But it is difficult to point to a single institutional cause due to simultaneous changes in other factors, such as rising partisan polarization.[35] Nevertheless, we argue that, in support of the Legislative Effectiveness Perspective, the loss of expertise among committee and subcommittee chairs has been an important change in congressional lawmaking in recent decades, even to the point of hobbling must-pass legislation, ranging from the federal budget through major reauthorizations. In turn, Congress may be less able to effectively address crises and major public policy needs than it has been in the past.

To illustrate these arguments and to partially separate them from other competing factors like polarization, we turn to case studies of must-pass legislation in policy areas that tend to be less ideological than many others. Specifically, we concentrate on the policy areas of agriculture and transportation, where legislators across the ideological spectrum have credit-claiming incentives. We explore the role of committee chairs in shepherding their proposals in these areas into law. As quickly becomes apparent, however, even these policy areas have been plagued by high degrees of partisanship in recent years, and few chairs have been sufficiently effective to overcome the resulting gridlock.

To begin our inquiry, it is worth noting that Adler and Wilkerson themselves point to cases in which the House failed to enact must-pass bills, including legislation dealing with Federal Aviation Administration reauthorization[36] and the 1986 highway construction bill.[37] In cases such as these, which Adler and Wilkerson suggest are quite rare, the House ultimately realizes that "not addressing such problems in a timely manner has consequences for real people—and quite possibly personal electoral consequences at the polls,"[38] motivating lawmakers to redouble their efforts. Is it the case, however, that failing to obtain robust reauthorizations are as rare as Adler and Wilkerson suggest? And what is the role of effective (or ineffective) committee chairs in responding to the lapsed authority with new legislation as soon as possible?

We illustrate, in the case studies discussed subsequently, that at least since the early 1990s, contrary to the Problem-Solving Perspective, must-pass legislation appears to be less *must pass* than the term would connote. Simply stated, it is not the case that legislators who sponsor these periodic reauthorizations are essentially guaranteed a legislative victory by design, thereby giving them the appearance of being effective lawmakers (which would correspond to high Legislative Effectiveness Scores). Indeed, in many of the cases that we explore, the sponsors of these reauthorizations were highly effective committee chairs (as measured by their Legislative Effectiveness Scores), but despite being so effective in many aspects of lawmaking, they were unable to secure passage of these ostensibly must-pass bills. High Legislative Effectiveness Scores are not simply proxies for representatives (and chairs, in particular) sponsoring must-pass bills, which are destined to pass. In many cases, even highly effective chairs struggle in advancing such legislation.

Legislative Effectiveness and Problem Solving Down on the Farm

Questions about the must-pass status of reauthorization legislation emerge in an examination of the politics surrounding agriculture policy. Since the passage of the Agricultural Adjustment Act of 1933, the U.S. government has been actively involved with managing the farm sector. Beginning with the Food and Agriculture Act of 1965, federal agriculture policy has come to revolve around the periodic reauthorizations of the *Farm Bill*, which is essentially the guidance document for how the U.S. government engages the agribusiness sector regarding subsidy payments, commodity supports, and nutrition programs. While these periodic reauthorizations could sometimes become the rallying point of partisan disagreements (the 1985 reauthorization was particularly contentious, and the bill was not signed into law until December 23, 1985),[39] the reauthorizations generally occurred "on time," with no gap between the expiration and passage of successive Farm Bills. Consistent with the Problem-Solving Perspective, almost all legislators (especially those from agricultural districts but also those from urban districts, following the coupling of Farm Bills and food stamps) realized that they had a shared interest in seeing the Farm Bill passed.[40] Hence, legislative compromises and solutions were established to ensure its passage.

Business as usual started to break down, however, with the 1995 reauthorization of the Farm Bill (which was being devised to replace the expiring Food, Agriculture, Conservation, and Trade Act of 1990). Recent political circumstances had contributed to an environment whereby the long-standing cross-party coalition that existed between urban liberals (who advocated for nutrition programs that were authorized by the Farm Bill) and rural conservatives (who advocated for commodity subsidies, which were also authorized by the Farm Bill) began to break down. More specifically, a large body of Republicans who were elected into the 104th Congress favored fiscal restraint and the cutting of welfare and food stamp programs, in particular. This change in the political landscape made compromises more difficult to obtain than in previous reauthorization cycles. The Freedom to Farm Act of 1995 was introduced by Chairman Pat Roberts, R-Kans., in August of 1995 and never made it out of the Agriculture Committee; rather, it was incorporated into a broader deficit reduction package (the Balanced Budget Act of 1995), which was vetoed by President Clinton in December of 1995. Hence, several provisions of the 1990 Farm Bill expired, with no new authorization in place.

With no reauthorization, certain aspects of federal agriculture subsidy policy fell under the jurisdiction of the Agricultural Act of 1949 (which had not expired and therefore governed agriculture policy in the absence of new authorizations). In light of broad concerns about the market consequences for wheat and other commodities under the provisions of the Agricultural Act of 1949, the House and Senate passed the Federal Agriculture Improvement and Reform Act of 1996, a seven-year reauthorization of the Farm Bill, in March of 1996, and President Clinton signed the bill into law in early April.

While the subsequent reauthorization was relatively contentious (including a filibuster that prevented the Senate from considering the Farm Bill before Congress adjourned in 2001), the Farm Security and Rural Investment Act of 2002 was ultimately signed into law in May 2002, thereby replacing the expiring provisions of the 1996 act. The 2002 passage of the Farm Bill, however, marks the last time that a Farm Bill reauthorization has occurred on time.

The 2002 Farm Bill was set to expire on September 30, 2007. Yet contrary to the Problem-Solving Perspective, a legislative solution to the problem of the expiring authorization did not seem to be forthcoming. While the House passed its own version of the Farm Bill on July 27, 2007, the Senate Agriculture Committee had not marked up its version of the legislation as of early September. Much of the debate over the Farm Bill dealt with funding sources, as much of the revenue for farm aid was, by policy design, negatively tied to contemporary crop prices, which had been relatively high in recent years. One approach to expand revenue, offered by the sponsor of the House bill, Agriculture chairman Colin Peterson, D-Minn., was to impose a new tax on foreign companies that were conducting business in the United States.[41] Debates also emerged over the scope of subsidy support and the length of the reauthorization, with open disagreement between the relevant House and Senate committee chairmen. They could not hammer out a compromise, and the 2002 bill expired with no replacement, leading to a series of short-term extensions.

The House and Senate finally passed compromise legislation in mid-May of 2008 and sent it to President Bush, who vetoed the measure. The veto was overridden by supermajorities in the House and Senate on May 21 and May 22, respectively, leading to the creation of a new public law—or so lawmakers thought. Further controversy emerged, however, when it became clear that a House enrollment clerk had sent an incomplete bill to the White House when it was passed by both chambers in mid-May. Hence, the president vetoed legislation that was different from what had been passed by both chambers (and the veto override engaged legislation that was substantively different from the bills that had been passed earlier). To deal with this clerical problem, the House and Senate passed bills that were identical to those that were passed in mid-May. In early June, the repassed bill was sent to President Bush, who vetoed the bill on June 18. (And it was subsequently overridden in both chambers.) Hence, after six short-term extensions and two presidential vetoes, the Farm Bill was reauthorized nearly nine months after the previous law had expired.

Moving ahead four years, the Food, Conservation, and Energy Act of 2008 (the title of the 2008 Farm Bill) was set to expire on September 30, 2012, and similar to the previous reauthorization cycle, the must-pass legislation failed. While the Senate passed a bill providing for a five-year reauthorization of agricultural programs, House Agriculture Committee chair Frank Lucas, R-Okla., was less successful at moving his legislation forward. Despite getting a bill reported from his committee that provided for a five-year reauthorization of agriculture programs, Lucas was unable to get a rule assigned to the bill such that it could be considered on the floor of the House.[42] Rather than support his efforts at negotiating a compromise on a five-year bill, Republican leaders pushed for a one-year extension to the expiring 2007 act to help maintain stability in agriculture markets—particularly in light of a devastating drought that was raging in the summer of 2012.[43] In the end, neither approach was successful, and the 2007 act expired with no replacement legislation in place.

Moving into the next Congress, debate continued in the House about the details of various aspects of the reauthorization legislation, particularly the scope of SNAP (Supplemental Nutrition Assistance Program, previously referred to as food stamps) benefits. A Republican-leadership-endorsed bill was defeated on the floor of the House on June 20, 2013, which led Majority Leader Eric Cantor, R-Va., to split the bill into separate parts dealing with agriculture measures and nutrition measures. These measures were passed separately and then recombined in September of 2013, when the legislation was sent to conference with the

Senate. After months of cross-chamber negotiations, the House adopted a conference report on January 29, 2014, and the Senate cleared the report the following week. President Obama signed the Agricultural Act of 2014 on February 7, 2014, more than sixteen months after the expiration of the previous Farm Bill.

The failure of timely Farm Bill reauthorizations may have had many causes. For our purposes, it is sufficient to note that such failures demonstrate problems in classifying certain legislation as must pass and that they show the recent difficulties of key committee chairs. Rather than overcome the difficulties in their paths, such chairs struggled at every lawmaking stage, from guiding their bills out of their own committees to getting a rule assigned to passing the House to coordinating and compromising with the Senate, even to getting the proper bill onto the president's desk. And these issues are not unique to agriculture policy.

Gridlock in Transportation Policy

Beginning with the passage of the 1991 Intermodal Surface Transportation Efficiency Act (ISTEA), which authorized $151 billion in construction projects over six years, Congress has passed four surface transportation reauthorization bills over the past twenty-five years (the most recent in December of 2015). Yet not a single one of these reauthorizations became law by the must-pass deadline established by its predecessor, and in some cases, the gap between reauthorizations has been substantial. Numerous chairs have struggled to overcome policy gridlock.

The first reauthorization, which was initially advanced in the 105th Congress (1997–1998) seemed promising, in that the Transportation and Infrastructure Committee chair Bud Shuster, R-Pa., was proactively developing a bill that would have simultaneously increased transportation funding and moved the Highway Trust Fund "off budget," potentially appealing to liberal and conservative members alike. However, his efforts were defeated in a very narrow floor vote (214–216) in the House in May of 1997. Despite this setback (and, of course, missing the expiration deadline), Shuster redoubled his efforts the following year, leading to the Transportation Equity Act for the 21st Century (TEA 21), which was signed into law in June 1998. The new authorization bill provided for $217.9 billion to be spent over six years, such that a new transportation bill would have to be passed in 2003.

But 2003 came and went with no new law . . . as did 2004. The Safe, Accountable, Flexible and Efficient Transportation Equity Act: A Legacy for Users (SAFETEA-LU) was signed into law on August 10, 2005, two years after the expiration of TEA 21 and after more than ten stopgap extensions had been passed. A fundamental point of controversy in the legislation surrounded the funding sources for new construction projects that would be authorized under the bill. Don Young, R-Alaska, the new chair of the Transportation and Infrastructure Committee,[44] introduced a bill in the 108th Congress (2003–2004) that would have provided for an increase in the federal gas tax to underwrite new transportation expenses. While his bill passed the House, as did a companion bill in the Senate (leading to a conference committee), no further action was taken due to a veto threat from the Bush White House over the proposed tax increase.[45] A compromise was ultimately reached in 2005 that drew on recent changes in the tax status of ethanol-based fuels, such that necessary revenues could be obtained without increasing the federal gas tax. The compromise measure also provided for a substantial amount of spending (nearly 8 percent of the bill's total) to be directed to district-specific projects, a notable increase over prior transportation bills.[46]

In 2009, yet another Transportation and Infrastructure chair, this time James Oberstar, D-Minn., found himself drawn into a similar conflict on funding, now with the Obama administration (similar to President Bush) staunchly opposed to raising the gas tax. The president asked Congress to pass a one-year extension to the expiring SAFETEA-LU until the White House could articulate some governing principles for its transportation priorities. Rather than comply with the White House request, however, Oberstar moved ahead with marking up his favored bill in subcommittee.[47] Despite recent infrastructure failings, such as the Minneapolis bridge collapse, and statements by the American Society of Civil Engineers, which gave the United States a "C+" (or lower) grade across all of its infrastructure categories, Oberstar was unable to move the bill forward.

The 112th Congress (2011–2012) did not begin any easier for surface transportation, which was still sputtering along on short-term extensions, with no clear resolution in sight. After a further year of delay, in 2012, the new chair of the House Transportation and Infrastructure Committee, John Mica, R-Fla., indicated his intention to proceed with a new five-year reauthorization bill. At the same time, the Republican leadership stated its intention to fund the bill with revenue drawn from expanded oil and gas exploration in previously preserved areas, such as the Arctic National Wildlife Refuge, clearly picking a fight with congressional Democrats.[48] Over the next six months, Speaker Boehner effectively took the lead in managing the bill, as the Republican leadership sought to present it as a "jobs bill" and an example of the types of legislative accomplishments that could be expected from a unified Republican government.[49]

Lacking the will or the ability to reach a long-term compromise, Congress and the president decided to kick the can down the road one more time. The Moving Ahead for Progress in the 21st Century Act (MAP-21), signed by President Obama in July of 2012, provided for only a two-year reauthorization of surface transportation (to expire on September 30, 2014). That deadline also came and went without a major reauthorization being passed. It would be more than a year (and only after the passage and expiration of several more short-term stopgap measures) before the Fixing America's Surface Transportation (FAST) Act would be signed into law by President Obama on December 5, 2015. The act ultimately provided for the funding of $305 billion in transportation projects across five years, and it would be funded through a combination of revenue from the Highway Trust Fund and distribution from other extant federal funds.

The surface transportation reauthorizations thus followed the same road of delay and disagreement as we found for the Farm Bills. Rather than rising to the occasion with their years of legislative skill and acquired policy knowledge, one new committee chair after the next failed to meet and overcome the challenges he faced. And rather than patiently cultivating needed expertise in important policy areas, party leaders competed with chairs, pushing their own proposals and even refusing the rules necessary for floor consideration of committee bills. These case studies reveal a Congress with neither a problem-solving view of governance, nor sufficiently effective lawmakers to overcome partisan divides on key reauthorizations.

The Effects of Institutional Reforms, by the Numbers

By limiting chairs to no more than three terms, the Republican leadership set into motion a system by which a set of legislators who held crucial agenda-setting and bill management positions would be removed just at the time when they were beginning to develop valuable expertise that could facilitate the passage of broad-interest legislation, such as the Farm Bills and surface transportation reauthorization bills. To illustrate this point, consider Figure 11-4, which is a refinement of Figure 11-3, now broken down by party.

For committee chairs, the figure shows no obvious substantive differences between the legislative effectiveness of Republicans and Democrats, with slight increases across their first three terms. That said, one clear finding emerges when we consider the full picture of the average effectiveness of Democratic chairs: For those chairs who continue to serve for four or more terms, their LES increases at a greater rate over time in those later terms. Due to term limits, very few Republicans in our sample hold chairs for more than three terms. Their average effectiveness tops out at an LES of approximately 4.5, about one-third lower than more experienced Democratic chairs. Hence, it should not be surprising that the notable increases in reauthorization delays and gridlock correspond to instances when the authorizing committee in question is being chaired by a relatively new chair.

Moreover, one might wonder how the imposition of chair term limits might have influenced representatives' incentives and decisions to acquire policy expertise, with the intention of influencing the substance of legislation. A 1999 *CQ Weekly* profile on Bud Shuster, for example, analyzed how he had cultivated long-term relations with members of the Transportation and Infrastructure Committee (which he chaired) so that he was able to identify their specific needs and structure the surface transportation reauthorization in such a way as to serve their interests. Shuster was considered so effective at navigating the lawmaking process in this regard and cultivating loyalty among his fellow committee members (which consisted of seventy-five members of the House) that he was able to stand up

Figure 11-4 Average Legislative Effectiveness Scores, by Expertise in Role, by Party

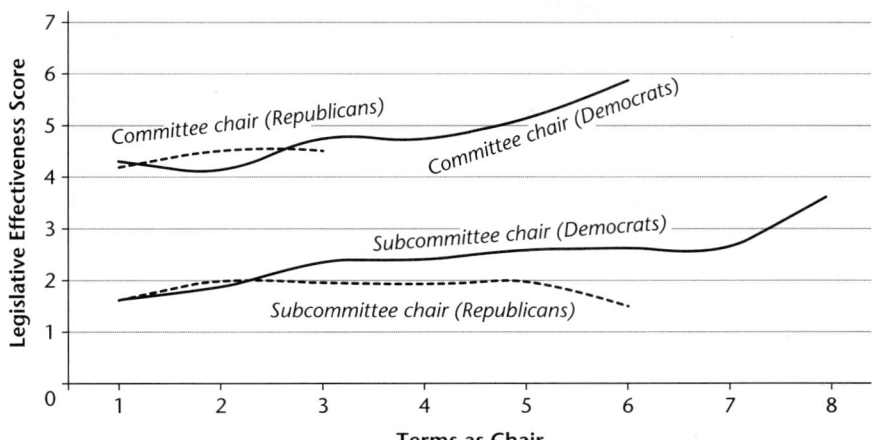

Note: The figure, based on all House chairs from 1973 to 2014, shows rising effectiveness with longer service as a chair among Democrats but shorter terms and thus less overall effectiveness for Republicans.

successfully to then-Speaker Newt Gingrich, who was pushing against Shuster on the highway bill, due to its projected cost.[50]

Even prior to becoming chair of the committee, Shuster had spent many years developing his expertise in this policy area, having joined the Public Works and Transportation Committee in his first term in Congress (1973) and having become the ranking Republican on the Surface Transportation Subcommittee in his second term. Hence, Shuster was essentially drawing on twenty years of experience and expertise when he navigated the legislative landscape surrounding the 1998 transportation reauthorization. He was able to draw on the tools that come with being chair, as well as the ability to disburse earmarks, to put together a bill that passed in a relatively short time frame, following the expiration of the previous authorization. Given the imposition of term limits, one wonders whether Shuster would have had the same incentives to cultivate such rich policy expertise in transportation. If not, one wonders if he could have navigated the reauthorization as successfully as he did, especially with the earmark ban (since 2011) limiting his ability to grease the wheels.

Figure 11-4 also shows the relative effectiveness of subcommittee chairs, those who may be cultivating some of the expertise they would use down the road, upon rising to chair of a full committee. The difference between Democrats and Republicans in the figure, especially in terms four through six, may be further evidence of the effect of institutional reforms. Those Republicans are typically no longer chairing the same subcommittee as during their first three terms as chair, perhaps losing policy- and colleague-specific knowledge. Moreover, with tighter party agenda control and less committee deference, the value of gaining expertise has diminished.

One final comparison of Legislative Effectiveness Scores over time shows the difference in committee chair influence over legislation. Across our data set, the average subcommittee chair scored above 2.0 in every Congress from the Ninety-third through the 106th (1973–2000). That average has been below 2.0 in every Congress thereafter. Moreover, the highest average was 2.65 for the 110 subcommittee chairs in the 103rd Congress (1993–1994), just before the term limit reforms. That average was sliced nearly in half, to 1.41, for the 101 subcommittee chairs in the 112th Congress (2011–2012). For committee chairs, the drop is even more dramatic. At its peak, the twenty-one chairs of the Ninety-third Congress (1973–1974) averaged an LES of 6.65. The twenty chairs in the recent 113th Congress (2013–2014) averaged merely 3.16, less than half of the effectiveness of their predecessors under different institutional rules. Moreover, we fear that these scores themselves may mask the true depth of the ineffectiveness of committee chairs today. Consistent with our case studies, many chairs may receive inflated scores not from responding to crises in a timely manner but instead from repeatedly passing short-term stopgap measures that boost their LES without offering long-term policy solutions. Indeed, it appears that (at least) since the early 1990s, the term "must pass" is not the most substantively accurate way to refer to the periodic reauthorization process. Whether reauthorization politics prior to the early 1990s had more of a must-pass flavor than we have observed in the contemporary Congress is worthy of further attention and study.

Conclusion

In this chapter, we explored competing hypotheses arising from the Problem-Solving Perspective and the Legislative Effectiveness Perspective of policy making in Congress. The former suggests that policy making is best understood as Congress rising to the occasion in passage of compulsory legislation, with the particular bill sponsors being of little consequence. The latter perspective instead suggests that Congress rises to such occasions more easily when bill sponsors are themselves effective lawmakers. The differences between these contrasting views are most profound in their predictions about the effectiveness of committee and subcommittee chairs. The Legislative Effectiveness Perspective expects that effectiveness will rise with experience and that the same lawmakers who were effective in one Congress will be effective in the next. In contrast, under the Problem-Solving Perspective, chairs merely advance must-pass compulsory legislation in response to crises and the need for reauthorizations. Their effectiveness should not increase systematically over time and should perhaps even be negatively correlated over time due to the ups and downs of must-pass legislation arriving and departing from the political scene.

The evidence from our study of every chair across the past four decades strongly supports the Legislative Effectiveness Perspective. Committee and subcommittee chairs differ in their effectiveness from one another, but their effectiveness as individuals is fairly consistent over time. Those who are highly effective in one Congress tend to be highly effective in the next. And that effectiveness rises with their experience in the chair position. It is not merely a reflection of the major issues of the day or the occasional need to reauthorize legislation in a particular area. Moreover, our case studies of major reauthorizations in the agriculture and transportation policy areas show that the "must-pass" label is often inappropriate, with the actual likelihood of passage far from certain.

Despite the evidence presented here, we do not advocate dismissing the Problem-Solving Perspective altogether. There is certainly substantial wisdom in focusing on the problems facing the country and the steps that Congress takes to try to solve them. Yet those solutions come in the form of legislation, and the content and fate of such bills depend significantly on the effectiveness of the lawmakers who advance such proposals. It is in this light that we note with no small concern the apparent decline in the average effectiveness of committee and subcommittee chairs in recent years.

Lawmaking is not easy. At its best, effective lawmaking requires both the policy expertise to match problems and solutions and the political acumen to carry such solutions over complex and often partisan obstacles. Across the first two decades of our study, committee chairs appeared to be such effective lawmakers, increasingly so as they enhanced their skills with additional terms in office. In contrast, the past two decades have seen term limits on committee and subcommittee chairs and other institutional reforms that have substantially limited their effectiveness. Whether perceived benefits of fresh new ideas from rising chairs or of greater partisan coherence in legislative proposals outweighs such declining effectiveness is something observers of Congress will need to consider very carefully.

Notes

1. The authors thank Bruce Oppenheimer for helpful and constructive comments on an earlier draft of this manuscript.
2. See, for example, Gary W. Cox and Mathew D. McCubbins, *Setting the Agenda: Responsible Party Government in the U.S. House of Representatives* (New York: Cambridge University Press, 2005).
3. Examples of theoretical scholarship that engages the role of political parties in influencing roll call votes include John H. Aldrich and David Rohde, "The Logic of Conditional Party Government: Revisiting the Electoral Connection," in *Congress Reconsidered*, 7th ed., ed. Lawrence C. Dodd and Bruce I. Oppenheimer (Washington, DC: CQ Press, 2001); Jeffery A. Jenkins and Nathan W. Monroe, "Buying Negative Agenda Control in the U.S. House," *American Journal of Political Science* 56 (2012): 897–912; and Keith Krehbiel, Adam Meirowitz, and Alan E. Wiseman, "A Theory

of Competitive Partisan Lawmaking," *Political Science Research and Methods* 3 (2015): 423–48.
4. See, for example, Alan E. Wiseman and John R. Wright, "The Legislative Median and Partisan Policy," *Journal of Theoretical Politics* 20 (2008): 5–30.
5. Examples of theories that explore the impact of supermajority decision rules on the lawmaking process include David W. Brady and Craig Volden, *Revolving Gridlock: Politics and Policy From Carter to Clinton* (Boulder, CO: Westview Press, 1998); David W. Brady and Craig Volden, *Revolving Gridlock: Politics and Policy From Jimmy Carter to George W. Bush*, 2nd ed. (Boulder, CO: Westview Press, 2006); Keith Krehbiel, "Institutional and Partisan Sources of Gridlock: A Theory of Divided and Unified Government," *Journal of Theoretical Politics* 8 (1996): 7–40; and Keith Krehbiel, *Pivotal Politics: A Theory of U.S. Lawmaking* (Chicago: University of Chicago Press, 1998).
6. Influential theoretical studies on committees in Congress include Arthur T. Denzau and Robert J. Mackay, "Gate-Keeping and Monopoly Power of Committees: An Analysis of Sincere and Sophisticated Behavior," *American Journal of Political Science* 27 (1983): 740–61; and Keith Krehbiel, *Information and Legislative Organization* (Ann Arbor: University of Michigan Press, 1991).
7. Craig Volden and Alan E. Wiseman, "Legislative Effectiveness and Representation," in *Congress Reconsidered*, 10th ed., Lawrence C. Dodd and Bruce I. Oppenheimer (Washington, DC: CQ Press, 2012); Craig Volden and Alan E. Wiseman, *Legislative Effectiveness in the United States Congress: The Lawmakers* (New York: Cambridge University Press, 2014); and Craig Volden, Alan E. Wiseman, and Dana E. Wittmer, "When Are Women More Effective Lawmakers than Men?" *American Journal of Political Science* 57 (2013): 326–41.
8. E. Scott Adler and John D. Wilkerson, *Congress and the Politics of Problem Solving* (New York: Cambridge University Press, 2012).
9. Ibid., 119.
10. Richard F. Fenno Jr., *Home Style: House Members in Their Districts* (Boston: Little, Brown and Company, 1978), 137.
11. John F. Manley, "Wilbur D. Mills: A Study in Congressional Influence," *American Political Science Review* 63 (1969): 442–64.
12. Andrée E. Reeves, *Congressional Committee Chairmen: Three Who Made an Evolution* (Lexington: University of Kentucky Press, 1993).
13. Daniel Lipinski, "Navigating Congressional Policy Processes: The Inside Perspective on How Laws are Made," in *Congress Reconsidered*, 9th ed., ed. Lawrence C. Dodd and Bruce I. Oppenheimer (Washington, DC: CQ Press, 2009).
14. Much of the "hit rate" scholarship builds on the methodology introduced by Donald Matthews in his influential study of the U.S. Senate. See Donald R. Matthews, *U.S. Senators and Their World* (Chapel Hill: University of North Carolina Press, 1960).
15. A foundational study that employs the bill count methodology is Stephen Frantzich, "Who Makes Our Laws? The Legislative Effectiveness of Members of the U.S. Congress," *Legislative Studies Quarterly* 4 (1979): 409–28.
16. See, for example, Katherine Meyer, "Legislative Influence: Toward Theory Development Through Causal Analysis," *Legislative Studies Quarterly* 5 (1980): 563–85; Carol S. Weissert, "Issue Salience and State Legislative Effectiveness," *Legislative Studies Quarterly* 16 (1991): 509–20; Carol S. Weissert, "Determinants and Outcomes of State Legislative Effectiveness," *Social Science Quarterly* 72 (1991): 797–806;

and Gerard Padro i Miquel and James M. Snyder Jr., "Legislative Effectiveness and Legislative Careers," *Legislative Studies Quarterly* 31 (2006): 347–81.
17. Volden and Wiseman, *Legislative Effectiveness*, 18.
18. Our earlier research drew on data from the Ninety-third through 110th Congresses, but we have expanded our data collection for the analysis presented in this chapter. The current data set (available at www.thelawmakers.org) consists of 158,244 public bills that were introduced into the House.
19. Details and the exact LES formula are found in Volden and Wiseman, *Legislative Effectiveness*, 19–22.
20. Normalization occurs within each Congress to facilitate easy interlegislator comparisons. This normalization scheme, however, complicates intertemporal comparisons of legislators' LESs across different Congresses.
21. Volden and Wiseman, "Legislative Effectiveness."
22. Craig Volden and Alan E. Wiseman, "Breaking Gridlock: The Determinants of Health Policy Change in Congress," *Journal of Health Politics, Policy and Law* 36 (2011): 227–64.
23. Volden, Wiseman, and Wittmer, "More Effective Lawmakers."
24. Jack Walker, "Setting the Agenda in the U.S. Senate: A Theory of Problem Selection," *British Journal of Political Science* 7 (1977): 423–45.
25. Adler and Wilkerson, *Problem Solving*, 8.
26. Ibid., 11.
27. Ibid., 9.
28. Ibid., 67.
29. Compulsory bills do not only address idiosyncratic disasters. Adler and Wilkerson (Adler and Wilkerson, *Problem Solving*, 11) argue, for example, that the Medicare Modernization Act of 2003 was a compulsory bill because of pervasive concerns about rising costs of prescription drugs, which would have implications for the Republican Party's electoral viability if the issue was not resolved as soon as possible.
30. Adler and Wilkerson, *Problem Solving*, 201.
31. All variable codings follow those of Volden and Wiseman, *Legislative Effectiveness*.
32. Unlike in Table 9-1, we do not control here for seniority, which is highly correlated with expertise (as would be expected).
33. See Volden and Wiseman, *Legislative Effectiveness*, 27, for the relevant calculation.
34. See, for example, Thomas E. Mann and Norman J. Ornstein, *It's Even Worse Than It Looks: How the American Constitutional System Collided With the New Politics of Extremism* (New York: Basic Books, 2012).
35. See, for example, Sean M. Theriault, *Party Polarization in Congress* (New York: Cambridge University Press, 2008).
36. Adler and Wilkerson, *Problem Solving*, 200.
37. Ibid., 195.
38. Ibid., 200.
39. Observers described the politics surrounding the passage of the 1985 reauthorization as being a "brutally partisan affair" that ultimately contributed to the defeat of three Republican senators (Mattingly of Georgia, Abdnor of South Dakota, and Andrews of North Dakota), given the Republicans' stance on the bill (David S. Cloud, "Logic Doesn't Always Apply to Multiyear Farm Bills," *CQ Weekly*, February 24, 1990, 576). The defeat of these three senators, in turn, contributed to the Republicans losing control of the Senate following the 1986 elections.

40. See John Ferejohn, "Logrolling in an Institutional Context: A Case Study of Food Stamp Legislation," in *Congress and Policy Change*, ed. Gerald C. Wright, Leroy N. Rieselbach, and Lawrence C. Dodd (New York: Agathon Press, 1986), 223–54, for a logrolling perspective on lawmaking.
41. Catherine Richert, "Fall Agenda: Farm Program Reauthorization," *CQ Weekly*, September 3, 2007, 2541.
42. Serious points of contention emerged between Democrats and Republicans in the House over the scope of Supplemental Nutrition Assistance Program (SNAP) benefits, which Democrats wanted to expand while Republicans wanted to cut. Given that the Republican leadership could not secure enough votes to push their position through, they ensured that a rule was not assigned to the bill. See Ellyn Ferguson, "Key Senate Vote of 2012: Farm Bill Reauthorization," *CQ Weekly*, January 21, 2013, 158.
43. Philip Brasher and Ellyn Ferguson, "Drought Prompts Push on Farm Bill," *CQ Weekly*, July 30, 2012, 1565.
44. As noted above, Young had previously served three terms as chair of the Committee on Resources.
45. Isaiah J. Poole, "Details of Transportation Law," *CQ Weekly*, September 26, 2005, 2578.
46. Ibid.
47. Kathryn A. Wolfe, "Delays Ahead in Needed Roadwork," *CQ Weekly*, June 14, 2010, 1444.
48. Kathryn A. Wolfe, "2011 Legislative Summary: Surface Transportation Authorization," *CQ Weekly*, January 9, 2012, 44.
49. Nathan Hurst and Kathryn A. Wolfe, "Highway Bill: Too Many Drivers, One Big Wreck," *CQ Weekly*, February 27, 2012, 395.
50. Jeff Plungis, "Congressional Affairs: The Driving Force of Bud Shuster," *CQ Weekly*, August 7, 1999, 1914.

12. The Endurance of Nonpartisanship in House Appropriations

Peter C. Hanson

It is common today for scholars to characterize Congress as mired in partisan dysfunction. This chapter strikes a more optimistic note than those accounts—one consistent with Adler and Wilkerson's argument that Congress retains a robust ability to solve problems. Based on the data and staff interviews reported here, recent scholarship on Congress would seem to substantially overstate the degree of partisanship in House appropriations. The writing and consideration of spending bills is notable because it continues to be characterized by strong nonpartisan norms, not because it has grown somewhat more partisan in today's highly polarized environment. The continuance of nonpartisan norms is due to the fact that all members have a variety of interests. They benefit from their party's reputation and also from their ability to claim credit for accomplishments. Today's members place a greater weight on a strong party reputation than past members did, but it is still in their interest to work across party lines to pass spending legislation. The endurance of nonpartisanship in appropriations during a time of high polarization is an encouraging sign about the continuing ability of the House to wield its constitutional power over the purse. It demonstrates that Congress is a multilayered institution capable of serving more than one interest at a time.

Few decisions made by members of Congress are more consequential than those over spending.[1] James Madison observed in *The Federalist* No. 58 that "the power over the purse may, in fact, be regarded as the most complete and effectual weapon with which any constitution can arm the immediate representatives of the people, for obtaining a redress of every grievance, and for carrying into effect every just and salutary measure."[2] Decisions over dollars breathe new programs into life and curtail those that are unpopular. The power of the purse is one of the most potent ways Congress can check the president and make its influence felt in the constitutional system.

Congress exercises its power of the purse through the annual budget and appropriations process. Each year, Congress aims to approve a budget resolution to set a framework for federal spending and to pass a dozen appropriations bills that provide funds for different categories of spending, such as agriculture, defense, and social services. Most federal programs are funded through appropriations bills. Appropriated dollars support scientific research, pay the salaries of soldiers, and subsidize loans for college students. They touch the lives of millions of Americans. If Congress fails to appropriate funds, affected programs shut down, and the lives of those who depend on them are disrupted. Adopting spending legislation is one of the most important tasks Congress faces each year.

The House of Representatives plays the leading role in the writing and management of appropriations bills, acting through the powerful Appropriations Committee. Historically, the Appropriations Committee operated through a norm of nonpartisanship in making appropriations policy. Democrats and Republicans on the committee worked together to write spending bills and secure support for their passage on the House floor. Their cooperation helped appropriations bills to pass by wide, bipartisan margins and boosted the reelection prospects of all members by delivering federal spending on popular programs to their districts. Starting in the 1970s, growing polarization and partisanship in Congress led to concerns that the Appropriations Committee might not be able to maintain this norm and that its operation as an effective committee would collapse. Nevertheless, scholars continued to observe a norm of nonpartisanship in the committee's work into the late 1980s.[3]

Then came the Republican revolution of 1994. Republicans ended four decades of Democratic control in the House with a stunning midterm election victory. Speaker Newt Gingrich and the new Republican majority sought to use their authority to enact long-standing conservative policy priorities, and they enlisted the Appropriations Committee to help them carry out that task.[4] Speaker Gingrich famously packed the normally nonpartisan appropriations bills with controversial spending cuts and policy riders, believing that President Clinton would sign them rather than face a government shutdown. The Speaker's gamble backfired. Clinton vetoed the bills, and the public blamed the resulting shutdown on Republicans. A chastened Gingrich was forced to back down.

What happened to appropriations in the wake of this confrontation? Most scholars find that the Appropriations Committee grew more closely aligned with majority party leadership and that debate over spending became more partisan. This is a reasonable conclusion. Stories of partisan clashes in the House and budgetary dysfunction abound. A more partisan appropriations process is also consistent with popular partisan theories of Congress such as *conditional party government* (CPG). CPG predicts that members of the majority party will centralize power in leadership and use committees like Appropriations to advance their policy goals when parties are highly polarized, like they are today.

I argue that this account misses the mark. Beneath the veneer of partisan conflict, deeply rooted norms of nonpartisanship continue to shape how members of the House make spending decisions. I make this case by looking closely at the writing and consideration of spending bills, drawing from extensive interviews with congressional staff members and new data on appropriations going back to the 1970s. I find strong evidence of continuity with the nonpartisan past. Appropriations bills routinely attract strong bipartisan support, and both parties debate them under open rules that permit amendments by the minority. In interviews, congressional staff members say that bipartisan cooperation is the most reliable way to pass bills that all members believe are essential. Nonpartisanship remains the defining characteristic of House appropriations.

This chapter proceeds in five parts. Part one explains how scholars have understood appropriations in the past. The next three sections present findings from the data to assess whether partisan confrontation has replaced bipartisan consensus building in appropriations. I evaluate whether members of both parties vote for appropriations bills, the rules the majority party adopts for debate on spending bills, and why House leaders sometimes bundle appropriations bills together into omnibus packages. The final section draws on interviews with congressional staff to explore the reasons for the resilience of nonpartisanship. I conclude that members find it in their interest to cooperate so that they can deliver federal spending to their districts and claim credit for accomplishments. The House is not solely characterized by partisanship. It is a multilayered institution that can serve many interests at once.

The Nonpartisan Roots of Appropriations

Richard Fenno's 1966 book *The Power of the Purse* is the classic study of the House Appropriations Committee in the mid-twentieth century.[5] Fenno described the committee as powerful and autonomous, with a norm of "minimal partisanship."[6] Committee members believed that their power rested on their ability to secure the adoption of their bills in the full House.[7] They settled their differences behind closed doors and presented a bipartisan front when appropriations bills were debated on the floor. Fenno quotes a typical comment from a member of the minority during debate observing that a bill represented a "nonpartisan effort" and the "thinking of every member of this subcommittee from both sides of the aisle."[8] These tactics were typically successful. Bipartisanship on the committee generally carried over into broad bipartisan support for appropriations bills on the House floor.

Fenno described the appropriations process at the height of the mid-century "textbook Congress" during a time of strong committees, weak parties, and substantial ideological overlap between Democrats and Republicans. Congress changed rapidly in the 1970s. The House reform movement dethroned powerful committee chairs and set into motion a chain of events that led to the recentralization of power in leadership.[9] Congress adopted the Congressional Budget and Impoundment Control Act of 1974, superimposing new budgetary rules over the older appropriations process.[10] Sunshine laws increased transparency in Congress and brought budgetary trade-offs into sharper public relief.[11] Rising partisan polarization escalated conflict between the two parties.[12]

These changes challenged the nonpartisan norms of the Appropriations Committee and made its yearly effort to manage appropriations bills more difficult. Fifty years after Fenno's study, it has become so difficult to reach agreement on spending that Congress, at times, has failed to provide funding to operate the government, leading to damaging shutdowns that disrupt the lives of the American people and cost the economy billions of dollars. In a substantial break from the past, much federal spending is now appropriated through vehicles like yearlong continuing resolutions or massive omnibus appropriations bills that bundle together some or all of the dozen regular appropriations bills. These unorthodox measures run roughshod over traditional ways of lawmaking and empower party leaders at the expense of the Appropriations Committee. Congress now lurches from budget crisis to budget crisis.

These difficulties raise the question of whether partisan confrontation has replaced bipartisan consensus building in appropriations. This question is important to scholars because it highlights a difference between two competing ways of understanding Congress: partisan and distributive theories of Congress. Both are based in the idea that Congress is best understood as a collection of individual members strategically pursuing a set of interests, the most important of which is the desire to win reelection. Ken Shepsle famously observed that Congress is a *they*, not an *it*.[13] Rules, committee structures, voting patterns, and other observable features of Congress are the result of countless of decisions made by individual members as they seek to maximize their interests. The implication is that the bipartisanship observed by Fenno resulted from how members perceived and pursued their interests. Most observers agree that the electoral incentives of members have changed since the 1960s in ways that reward the greater appearance of partisanship in appropriations. But other interests, such as the desire of members to bring dollars home to their districts, may still create a powerful incentive for cooperation. Understanding the degree to which appropriations is now partisan can shed light on how today's members perceive and pursue their goals and how members balance interests that are in conflict.

The premise of the distributive approach is that members seek funds for their districts to build roads or federal facilities like military bases because it improves their chance at winning reelection.[14] Scholars sought to explain how the 435 members of the House would cooperate to distribute benefits in order to maximize their ability to win reelection. One branch of this work concludes that members' uncertainty about whether they will receive benefits leads them to distribute benefits universally to all members in order to attract a bipartisan supermajority of support for spending bills.[15] This finding fits well with Fenno's description of bipartisanship in appropriations, and it explains why members of both parties might find it in their interest to cooperate to support appropriations bills.

The most recent large-scale study of the House Appropriations Committee is consistent with distributive theories. An unpublished dissertation by Joseph White found the committee in the 1980s was "at the peak of power and influence" and "remained one of the most nonpartisan on the Hill."[16] In White's view, members' collective interest in distributive benefits was the glue holding the committee together. "Both parties want to pass appropriations bills and nonpartisanship is by far the best way to go about that. Neither wants the system to break down in strife that would make distributive benefits an arena of partisan warfare."[17] Other empirical studies, including some published well after the 1995 Republican revolution, offer evidence that leaders distribute benefits widely to build large, bipartisan coalitions to secure the passage of legislation.[18] These studies provide powerful evidence of continuity in appropriations from Fenno's time.

A second account of appropriations emphasizes the degree to which the writing and passage of appropriations bills mirrors the expectations of partisan theories like CPG or the cartel model.[19] CPG outlines a set of conditions under which members of the same party work together. Its premise is that members benefit from the good reputation of their party when they stand for reelection. Members of a party who share a common set of policy preferences are likely to empower their leaders to pursue those policies and strengthen the party's reputation. A standard expectation of CPG is that the majority party will use its control over the agenda to advance its electoral and policy interests when it is unified and ideologically distant from the minority. The cartel model differs in some respects, but its expectations for when the majority can adopt its preferred policies are similar to those of CPG. Today, members in each party have grown more similar to each other and different from members of the opposing party in their preferences. Parties should grow stronger under these conditions, if partisan theories are correct. Consistent with them, scholars have observed a closer alignment between the House Appropriations Committee and leadership, more partisan policy in spending bills, and more sharply partisan debate.[20]

Most accounts mark the Republican takeover of the House in 1995 as a key moment in the transformation of appropriations. Members of the new Republican majority were highly unified in their policy preferences. They delegated new powers to Speaker Newt Gingrich and took steps to ensure that powerful and autonomous committees like Appropriations were brought under the party's control. They ended the tradition of making a committee's most senior majority member its chair in favor of allowing Gingrich to appoint party loyalists. They imposed term limits on committee chairs to prevent them from becoming entrenched and too independent from rank-and-file members. Speaker Newt Gingrich further injected partisanship into appropriations by directing an effort to cut spending and implement conservative policy ideas via the appropriations bills. His immediate effort failed, but the changes he set in motion were consolidated in later years. Aldrich, Perry, and Rohde go as far as to label the period since 1995 as encompassing "The Decline and Fall of Bipartisanship" in appropriations, as the bipartisan Appropriations Committee was permanently transformed into a more partisan body.[21]

The argument that appropriations have become more partisan dominates recent accounts of the House. But it is one thing to observe occasions of partisan wrangling; it is quite another to conclude that partisanship permeates the daily work of the Appropriations Committee and spending debates on the House floor. Political scientists Scott Adler and John Wilkerson have persuasively argued that recent scholars have overemphasized dysfunction and partisanship in Congress and failed to acknowledge bipartisan cooperation that routinely occurs to solve important problems.[22] There is still reason to believe that members retain a strong interest in bipartisan cooperation on spending. For example, members from the same state delegation have an incentive to cooperate to fund important local projects, regardless of party. Members of the majority may also worry that a highly partisan spending bill could be defeated on the House floor and endanger spending for their districts.

Determining whether distributive or partisan theories better describe modern appropriations is a straightforward task. Their expectations differ substantially, and there is a great deal of observable evidence to evaluate since spending legislation must be adopted every year. If members believe their reelection interests in appropriations are better served by securing funds for their districts than passing partisan policies, then a norm of minimal partisanship should be visible in appropriations. If members believe their reelection interests in appropriations are best served by pursuing partisan policy goals in order to enhance their party's reputation, then debate on spending bills should be observably partisan.

In the remainder of this chapter, I test these expectations. First, I examine votes for appropriations bills. Evidence that the minority party routinely supports appropriations bills would be consistent with distributive politics, whereas evidence that it routinely opposes spending bills would be consistent with partisan theories. Second, I evaluate the special rules adopted to debate appropriations bills. Evidence that the majority party routinely adopts rules to restrict minority participation in lawmaking would be consistent with partisan theories, whereas evidence that it permits minority participation would be consistent with distributive politics. Finally, I evaluate patterns in passing appropriations bills in the form of large omnibus packages to assess whether the decision to bundle bills together coincides with the rise of polarization in the House. The weight of the evidence indicates that the theory of distributive politics describes the appropriations process better than partisan theories.

Voting Patterns on Appropriations Bills: Partisan or Nonpartisan?

I first examine whether both parties vote for appropriations bills. Advocates of distributive theories predict that voting coalitions on appropriations bills will be bipartisan supermajorities. By contrast, winning coalitions under partisan theories of Congress are more likely to be narrow, partisan majorities. I gathered data on the initial votes for passage in the House of Representatives for four appropriations bills for every year from 1979 to 2014. The bills are Agriculture, Defense, Energy and Water, and Labor–Health and Human Services (Labor–HHS). I selected these bills because their jurisdictions have remained constant for over three decades. Various reorganizations of the Appropriations Committee have changed the groups of agencies covered by other bills. The four bills selected also

Figure 12-1 Majority and Minority Support for Appropriations Bills: U.S. House of Representatives, 1979–2014

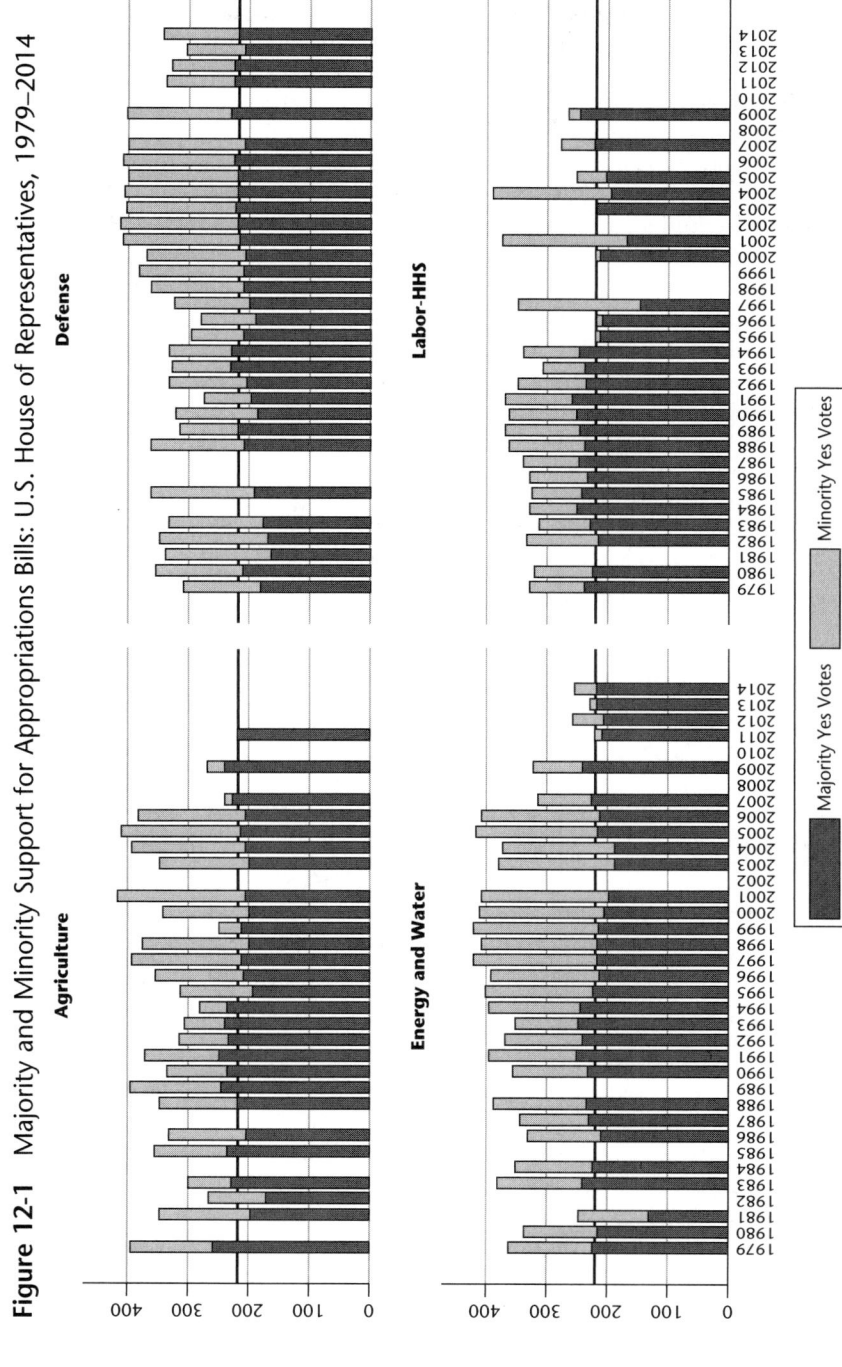

Source: Compiled by author.

represent a range of policy types, including controversial social welfare programs (Labor-HHS) and classic distributive spending (Energy and Water).

Figure 12-1 reports the number of members of the majority and minority voting in favor of appropriations bills between 1979 and 2014, *if the bills received a vote*. (See the discussion on abandoning regular order later in this chapter.) A vote is held on most bills, and most receive the support of a supermajority of members. A simple majority in the House of Representatives requires 218 votes, marked on the chart with horizontal lines. The Agriculture bill receives 333 votes (standard deviation 55) on average; Defense, 348 (standard deviation 40); Energy and Water, 352 (standard deviation 59); and Labor–Health and Human Services, 312 (standard deviation 53). The average winning coalition across all four bills is 341 votes in favor. It is noteworthy that the votes from the majority party alone are not sufficient, in many cases, to pass the bill. Minority support is often required to pass spending legislation.

Figure 12-2 reports the proportion of the minority party voting for each bill. Each dot represents the initial vote to adopt a bill in the House. The lines are smoothed to show patterns over time. On average, the Agriculture bill attracts the support of 64 percent of the minority party; the Defense bill, 78 percent; the Energy and Water bill, 74 percent; and the Labor-HHS bill, 50 percent. The minority party's support varies over time and by bill. Support for the Agriculture bill declines just prior to 1995, rebounds, and declines again starting in 2007. Support for Defense varies over time but is generally strong. Support for Energy-Water

Figure 12-2 Proportion of Minority Party Voting Yes: U.S. House of Representatives, 1979–2014

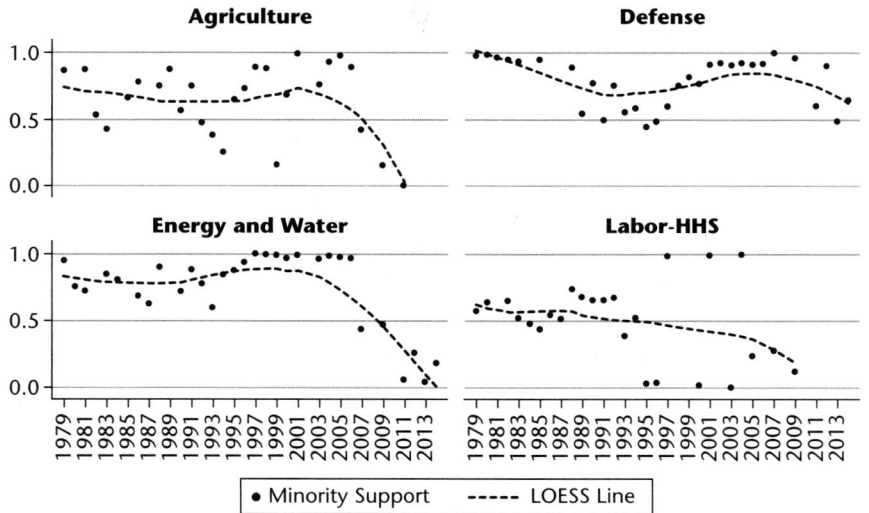

Source: Compiled by author.

is strong through 2007, then declines. Votes for Labor-HHS are highly variable starting in 1995, ranging from nearly unanimous support to unanimous opposition. None of these patterns fit the standard partisan account of appropriations turning steadily more partisan after 1995. Most of the bills receive strong minority party support for much of the time period, consistent with the expectations of distributive politics. The puzzle in the data is the sharp decline in minority support for Agriculture and Energy-Water starting in 2007. The timing of this decline is not well explained by either theory. I offer an explanation for it at the end of the chapter.

Special Rules: Does the Majority Party Allow Open Debate?

One of the most important ways the majority party exercises power is through its control over debate. It can make the minority party a partner in lawmaking by opening debate to all members or block them from influencing a bill. In this section, I show that the House majority party has allowed open debate on appropriations bills even as it has restricted debate on other kinds of legislation. Amendments from members of both parties are routinely debated and adopted on the House floor.

The majority party exercises its power over debate through its control of the House Rules Committee, which assigns a special rule structuring debate for most bills that are brought to the House floor. These rules specify the length of debate, whether amendments will be allowed, when a vote will take place, and other important matters.[23] They must be approved by a majority vote of the House. An open rule allows any member to offer a germane amendment. A closed rule prohibits amendments. Modified rules place some limits on amending. A modified open rule requires amendments to be preprinted in the *Congressional Record* prior to debate. A modified closed (structured) rule requires amendments to be preapproved by the Rules Committee and listed in its report. The use of open rules to debate appropriations bills is consistent with the theory of distributive politics because it allows members of both parties the opportunity to shape legislation. The use of closed rules by a partisan majority is consistent with partisan theories because it allows the majority party to dominate lawmaking.

Appropriations bills are privileged under the standing rules of the House and may be debated without a special rule. In this case, they are open to germane amendments. Previous scholars have found that appropriations bills are generally brought to the floor under open rules if rules are adopted.[24] I gathered data on all House special rules using the annual reports of the House Rules Committee for each Congress from 1995 to 2014 to determine whether that pattern has changed. The reports provide a breakdown of the total number of each type of rule issued during a Congress and the specific rule adopted for every bill debated on the floor of the House during a Congress. I coded rules as *open* if the committee listed them as "open" or "modified open" and *closed* if they were listed as "closed," "modified closed," or "structured" by the committee. Appropriations bills brought to the floor without a special rule were coded as *open*.

Figure 12-3 Open Rules for Legislation: U.S. House of Representatives, 104th–113th Congresses, 1995–2014

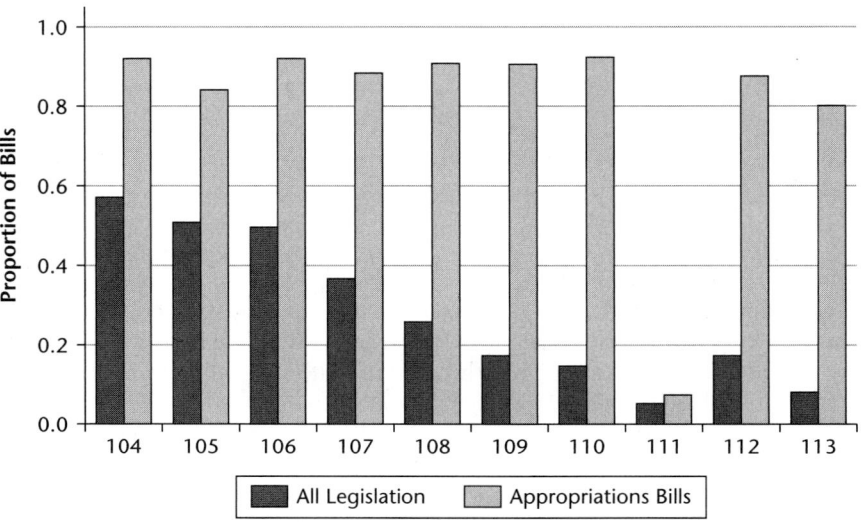

Source: Compiled by author.

Figure 12-3 compares the proportion of appropriations bills debated under an open rule or with no rule (gray bars) with the proportion of open rules on all legislation (black bars). As has widely been reported, the average number of open rules issued by the House Rules Committee has generally declined over time.[25] A total of 57 percent of rules were open in the 104th Congress, falling to 8 percent in the 113th Congress. By contrast, 80 to 90 percent of appropriations bills that are debated are brought to the floor under an open rule or without a rule during a given year. The major exception to this trend is the Legislative Branch Appropriations bill, which is often debated under a structured rule to prevent amendments on congressional salaries. In addition, the Democratic majority in the 111th Congress adopted a structured rule for debate on all but one appropriations bill.

An expectation of partisan theories of Congress is that the proportion of closed rules limiting amendments during debate is likely to rise as the majority party becomes more unified and distant from the minority. By contrast, a relationship between these variables and closed rules would not be expected under distributive theories of Congress. I estimated the correlations among four variables: the proportion of closed rules for all legislation, the proportion of closed rules for appropriations bills, majority party homogeneity, and majority party distance from the minority.[26] Table 12-1 presents the results. The correlation between closed rules on appropriations bill with the two partisan variables is much weaker

Table 12-1 Closed Rule and Party Polarization Correlation Matrix

	Appropriations	All Bills	Majority Homogeneity	Distance
Appropriations	1			
All Bills	0.43	1		
Majority Homogeneity	0.25	0.93	1	
Distance	0.26	0.89	0.78	1
N = 14				

Source: Compiled by author.

than for closed rules on all legislation. The proportion of appropriations bill with a closed rule each year is correlated with majority party homogeneity at 0.25 and with distance at 0.26. By comparison, the two variables are correlated with closed rules on all legislation at 0.93 and 0.89 respectively. The use of special rules in the House, in general, fits the expectations of partisan theories well. The theories do not offer a strong explanation for the use of special rules on appropriations bills, arguably the most important the legislation the House considers and the key to its institutional power.

The data reveal a handful of instances in which more than one rule was adopted in regard to the same appropriations bill. For example, the House adopted an open rule and then a structured rule to debate the fiscal year 2008 Agriculture bill. According to the *CQ Almanac*, the structured rule was a response to strong minority opposition to the bill: "Republicans stalled progress on the measure under an open rule earlier in the week . . . thwarting debate with a barrage of motions to adjourn and similar tactics. Finally, the House voted late in the afternoon to adopt a rule limiting amendments, a rarity for an appropriations bill, but Democrats said it was necessary to get work done."[27] The vast majority of bills in the data set were considered only under a single rule.

Consistent with the majority's practice of permitting open debate, amending appropriations bills is a robust and bipartisan enterprise. I counted the number of roll call votes on amendments to individual appropriations bills and omnibus measures as a rough measure of the amount of legislative activity taking place during the annual appropriations process for the years 1981 to 2012. The number of votes is increasing in absolute number over time, not decreasing, as would be consistent with partisan theories. Members also debate and adopt amendments from both parties. In the 113th Congress, the Democratic minority offered a total of 299 amendments to regular appropriations bills and the Republican majority offered 344.[28] Most amendments were brought to a vote. Roll call votes are generally reserved for controversial amendments. Members of the House cast roll call votes on ninety-four Democratic amendments and adopted seventeen (18 percent). They voted on 120 Republican amendments

Figure 12-4 Roll Call Votes on Amendments to Appropriations Legislation: U.S. House of Representatives, 1981–2012

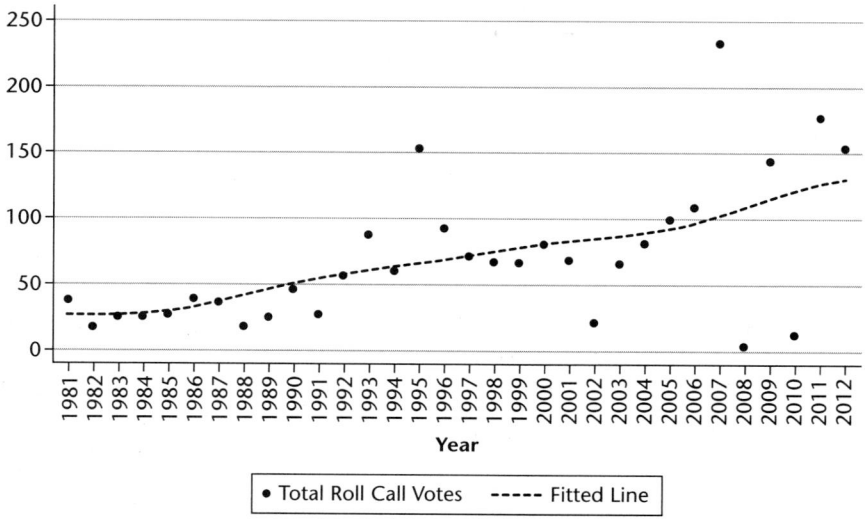

Source: Compiled by author.

and adopted fifty-three (44 percent). Bipartisan support for the amendments was common. Forty-six percent of adopted amendments received the support of at least half of the Democratic minority. Less controversial matters in the House are often considered by voice vote. Members voted by voice on 147 Democratic amendments and 185 Republican amendments, approving 123 (84 percent) and 168 (91 percent) respectively.

What Happens When the Majority Cracks Down?

The House majority party generally allows open debate on appropriations bills, but its tolerance has limits. In 2009, a Democratic majority adopted structured rules to limit debate on every appropriations bill. This section explores the reasons for this decision and its consequences. There are three major findings. First, the Democrats adopted structured rules because they believed Republicans were abusing open debate to delay the passage of the bills. Second, the decision to adopt structured rules generated a sharp backlash from Republicans that further complicated the passage of the bills. Third, the effect of the structured rules was to allow more amendments from ideologically extreme sponsors than from moderate sponsors.

The transition from Republican to Democratic control of the House in 2007 was accompanied by a significant increase in amending activity on appropriations bills. The number of roll call votes on amendments more than doubled from 108 in 2006 to 231 in 2007. Most appropriations bills did not reach the floor in 2008, but Democrats began the appropriations season in 2009 wary they would face a "filibuster by amendment" from the Republican side. The first bill to reach the floor was H.R. 2847, the Commerce-Justice-Science Appropriations bill. Two rules were adopted for debate on the bill. The first, H. Res. 544, required amendments to be preprinted in the *Congressional Record* prior to the beginning of debate. An unpublished case study of the bill's consideration by Anthony Madonna demonstrates that the preprinting requirement sparked an angry reaction from Republicans, who wanted to retain the ability to offer amendments on the fly during debate. A total of 127 amendments were filed in the *Record*. Democrats protested that debating all of the filed amendments would make timely consideration of all the appropriations bills impossible and adopted a second rule (H. Res. 552), selecting a subset of the filed amendments to be eligible for debate.[29] Republicans were further angered by this restriction and employed delaying tactics in response. Madonna reports that the minority tactics added four hours to the debate on the bill and led to a record fifty-three votes being cast during one day.

Each of the eleven remaining appropriations bills was debated under a structured rule in the wake of the cantankerous debate on the Commerce-Justice-Science bill. The Rules Committee required members to file amendments with the committee prior to debate on each bill, and the committee selected which amendments out of those filed would be in order.[30] The rules sharply reduced the number of amendments eligible for debate (Table 12-2). Democrats filed a total of 209 amendments, of which the Rules Committee allowed 13 percent to

Table 12-2 Amendments Filed and Allowed to FY 2010 Appropriations Bills

Bill	Total Filed	Filed (D)	Allowed (D)	Percentage (D)	Filed (R)	Allowed (R)	Percentage (R)
Agriculture	90	17	1	0.06	73	12	0.16
Commerce-Justice-Science	124	23	7	0.30	101	35	0.35
Defense	606	19	2	0.11	587	548	0.93
Energy-Water	103	24	6	0.25	79	14	0.18
Financial Services	97	8	1	0.13	89	16	0.18
Homeland Security	91	27	1	0.04	64	13	0.20
Interior-Environment	105	12	1	0.08	93	12	0.13
Labor-HHS	35	21	1	0.05	14	4	0.29
Legislative Branch	20	4	1	0.25	16	0	0.00
Military Construction-Veterans	32	9	3	0.33	23	5	0.22
State-Foreign Operations	88	26	2	0.08	62	6	0.10
Transportation-Treasury	85	19	2	0.11	66	21	0.32

Source: Compiled by author. Data courtesy of Anthony Madonna.

proceed. Republicans filed 1,267 amendments (including 605 on the Defense bill), of which 54 percent were allowed. Those statistics are somewhat misleading given the large number of amendments proposed and allowed by the Rules Committee to the Defense bill. Setting aside Defense, Republicans filed 680 amendments, and 20 percent were accepted for debate.

Democrats also disproportionately selected amendments for debate from ideologically extreme sponsors on both sides of the aisle. Across all bills except Defense,[31] the average DW-NOMINATE score for Democratic sponsors was –0.35 for amendments that were not allowed compared to –0.38 for those that were. The movement was more significant on the Republican side, where the average DW-NOMINATE of sponsors was 0.77 for amendments that were not allowed and 0.85 for amendments that were allowed. Figure 12-5 illustrates these results by bill. These results are consistent with previous studies showing that structured rules enhance the appearance of partisanship by selecting amendments for debate that are more likely to provoke disagreement between the parties.[32] They may also have increased the likelihood that minority party amendments would be defeated.

Figure 12-5 Permitted Amendments to Appropriations Bills: U.S. House of Representatives, 2009

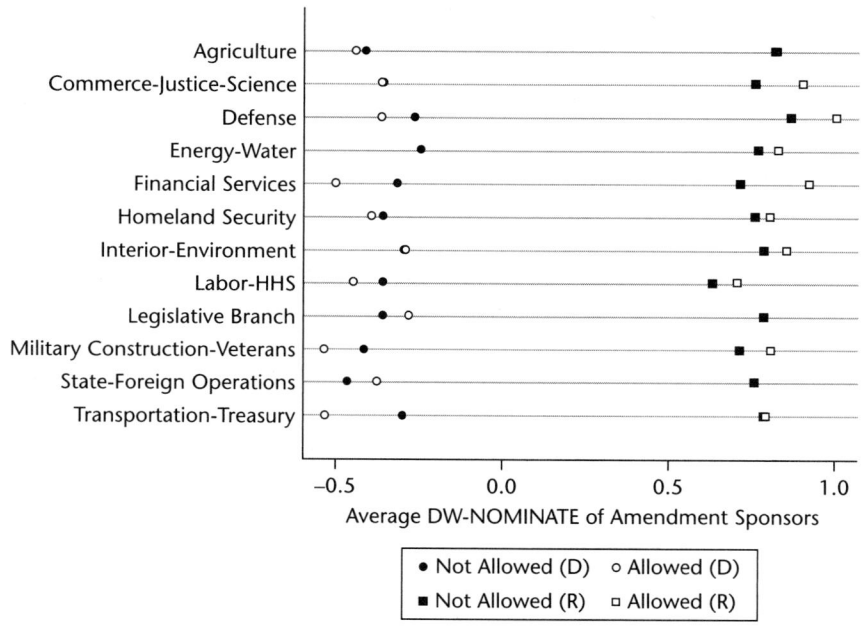

Source: Compiled by author. Data courtesy of Anthony Madonna.

The majority's tactics stirred a hornet's nest of opposition. Reports on the debate on appropriations bills from the *CQ Almanac* from 2009 repeatedly mention Republican protests to the use of structured rules. These criticisms were echoed in the minority views of the annual report of the Rules Committee: "Open rules for appropriations bills have always been considered sacrosanct by Democratic and Republican majorities alike. As long as an amendment was germane, it could always be offered on the floor of the House during debate."[33] Minority resistance to the majority's legislative practices can be significant enough to force it to change tactics,[34] and there is some evidence that it led the majority to avoid bringing all but two appropriations bills to the floor in 2010. Two senior staff members familiar with appropriations observed in interviews in 2012 that House Appropriations chair David Obey opted not to bring individual spending bills to the floor in 2010 because he wanted to avoid a repeat of the Republican delaying tactics.[35] Democrats lost control of the majority in the midterm elections that year. When Republicans assumed control of the chamber in 2011, they returned to the use of open rules on appropriations bills. They continue with that practice today.[36]

Is Partisanship Behind the Breakdown in Regular Order?

Appropriations bills are likely to receive an open debate on the House floor and bipartisan support when they are voted upon, but there may be a *selection effect* present in the data. House members do not debate and vote on every appropriations bill. If they only debate bills that they know will have strong bipartisan support, and they do not debate bills they expect will generate partisan conflict, then vote totals and special rule types may not reflect the true degree of bipartisanship in appropriations. In this section of the paper, I examine bills that did not receive an individual vote in regular order to examine whether they provide evidence of greater partisanship in appropriations. I find no systematic evidence that this is the case.

Regular order in appropriations refers to a textbook legislative process that is regarded by most members as the proper way to adopt spending bills.[37] The House of Representatives acts on the twelve spending bills first. Each subcommittee of the House Appropriations Committee writes and approves a bill covering programs within a set jurisdiction, like defense or agriculture. The full committee approves each bill and sends it to the floor for debate, amendment, and a vote. The Senate takes up the bills after the House and repeats this process. Finally, the two chambers resolve their disagreements and send the final version of the bill to the president.

Since the 1970s, it has been common for leaders to depart from regular order by skipping individual consideration of spending bills and bundling them together into an *omnibus* package.[38] These packages may be thousands of pages long and worth hundreds of billions of dollars. They are often debated under tight time constraints shortly before funding for the government is set to expire, giving members a strong incentive to approve them with little debate. Studies of the Senate show that shifting from regular order to omnibus legislating is an informal way for the majority party to exercise power. Abandoning regular order limits amending and helps leaders to build a broad coalition of support for passage of the budget.[39]

The majority party could decide to abandon regular order for two reasons in response to rising partisanship. First, it might seek to manage partisan conflict by wrapping controversial bills into a package designed to win bipartisan support. Alternatively, the majority party could abandon regular order to suppress the minority and craft a highly partisan package behind closed doors. In either case, it would be reasonable to observe a steady increase in the number of bills failing to receive individual consideration on the House floor after 1995, as partisan polarization rises. Instead, most bills receive an individual vote in the House. Additionally, the majority party appears to abandon regular order and create packages designed to win bipartisan support when it faces opposition from both parties that blocks passage of the regular appropriations bills on the floor.

Figure 12-6 illustrates the legislative history of appropriations bills from 1995 to 2014, showing the proportion of bills debated under an open rule, structured rule, or not debated in regular order. House members voted on most appropriations bills in regular order through 2007—over a decade after the Republican revolution. They abandoned regular order more routinely from 2008 to 2014, but the pattern does not fit an account of rising partisanship. The proportion of bills

Figure 12-6 Debate on Appropriations Bills: U.S. House of Representatives, 1995–2014

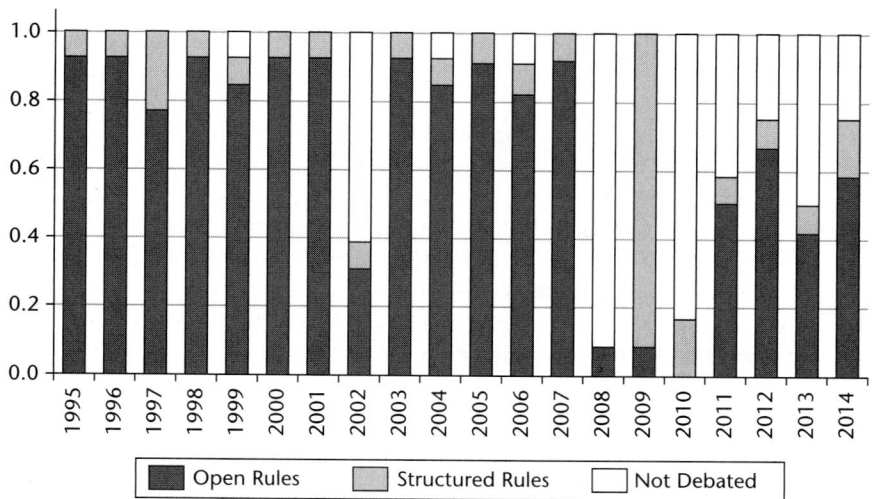

Source: Compiled by author.

that did not receive a vote peaked in 2008 and has declined since then. Other studies show that the Senate bears most of the responsibility for the frequency of omnibus bills in recent years.[40]

Press reports show that the majority party often calls off debate on bills it fears will be defeated on the floor. It instead bundles them together with others that are more popular to build a broad coalition of support. But it is inaccurate to describe this decision solely as a response to partisan conflict. For example, *CQ Weekly* reported that Republican leaders pulled the FY 2014 Transportation-HUD bill (H.R. 2610) from the floor because moderate Republicans and Democrats rebelled against cuts made at the request of conservatives.[41] Opposition to the bill was bipartisan. As I show later in the chapter, the recent breakdown in appropriations stems largely from new divisions among Republicans that have made it harder for the party to assemble a winning coalition. Calling all conflict in the House "partisan" misses this important fact.

The argument that the majority party abandons regular order to write a highly partisan package behind closed doors also finds limited support. Omnibus packages must be negotiated among the House, Senate, and president. Bipartisan packages are likely to result because one-party control of government is uncommon. Staff members from both parties insist that omnibus packages are generally bipartisan—a claim that is reflected in frequent bipartisan votes in favor of them.[42] For example, the Transportation-HUD bill described earlier was included in a package (H.R. 3547) that won the support of 193 Democrats and 166 Republicans.[43] The Democratic minority in the House actually voted for the package in larger numbers than the Republican majority after it was finalized in negotiations with the Senate and President Barack Obama.

The strongest evidence that the majority manipulates the appropriations process for partisan reasons comes from interviews reported earlier. Staff members said that the Democratic majority, in 2010, decided not to bring individual spending bills to the floor in order to avoid Republican amendments. Abandoning regular order functions as an informal closed rule because members cannot amend an appropriations bill that is not debated. The majority party still must pass some form of legislation, such as an omnibus appropriations bill or yearlong continuing resolution, in order to fund the government. In the House, it has been common for omnibus bills and yearlong continuing resolutions to come to the floor under circumstances that prohibit amending.[44] The combination of bypassing floor debate on individual spending bills and limiting amendments on omnibus packages often prevents members from amending any of the vehicles providing funding for affected agencies.

To examine whether abandoning the regular order is associated with a decline in amending in the House, I estimated the correlation between the proportion of bills not receiving a vote in the House during a year and three other variables: the total number of roll call votes on amendments in the House during an appropriations season, the total number of voice votes, and the total number of all votes.[45] I estimated the correlations for the years 1995 to 2014. The proportion of bills without a vote was negatively correlated with the number of roll call votes at –0.43, voice votes at –0.44, and all votes at –0.45. The decline in amending associated with abandoning the regular order can be significant. For example, the number of amendment-related votes declined from 233 in 2007, when all bills were debated in regular order, to four in 2008, when the House failed to debate or vote on eleven bills in regular order. It's clear that abandoning regular order has the practical effect of reducing amending. This decline is more likely the result of the majority party seeking to avoid delaying tactics and protecting its members from politically painful votes on the floor than the result of a concerted effort to adopt highly partisan policies, given evidence that omnibus packages are generally bipartisan.

The Endurance of Nonpartisanship in Appropriations

Contrary to the findings of recent studies, important nonpartisan features of the appropriations process endured in the wake of the 1994 Republican revolution. Open rules remain common for the consideration of appropriations bills on the House floor, amending is frequent, and minority support for appropriations bills remained strong through 2007. Some appropriations bills are passed with strong minority party support even today. Table 12-3 illustrates these patterns, integrating the different types of data presented in this chapter. In 2014, the House approved rules for nine of the twelve regular appropriations bills. Seven rules were open. Two were structured rules that limited amending. The remaining three bills did not receive individual consideration on the floor and were not assigned a rule. Members voted on 130 amendments to appropriations bills from both Republicans and Democrats. Seven of the regular appropriations bills were approved by the full House. Three were approved with the support of over 50 percent of the Democratic caucus while four had sharply partisan votes. All of the bills but one were ultimately adopted in an omnibus package after the Senate failed to vote on them. The package squeaked through the House with 219 votes, including 162 from Republicans and fifty-seven from Democrats.[46]

Partisan theories of Congress cannot easily explain these patterns. They would predict closed rather than open rules and cannot account for the timing in the decline of minority support for appropriations bills starting in 2007. Nor can they account for the timing in the decline of regular order in the House beginning in 2008. In the final section of this chapter, I offer an explanation for these facts, rooted in the distinctive character of the appropriations process and the strategic choices made by House Republicans. This explanation is broadly consistent with the theory of distributive politics. It assumes that most members desire to secure the benefits of appropriations bills for their districts, but it places additional emphasis on the risks to a party's reputation from pursuing partisan policy goals in appropriations.

Table 12-3 Legislative History of FY 2015 Appropriations Bills

Bill	Bill Number	Rule Type	Amdt. Votes	Rep. Support	Dem. Support
Agriculture	H.R. 4800	Modified open	9	n/a	n/a
Commerce, Justice, and Science	H.R. 4660	Open	25	0.92	0.63
Defense	H.R. 4870	Modified open	20	0.97	0.64
Energy and Water	H.R. 4923	Modified open	28	0.95	0.18
Financial Services	H.R. 5016	Modified open	16	0.98	0.03
Homeland Security	H.R. 240	Structured	5	0.96	0.01
Interior-Environment	H.R. 5171	Not debated	0	n/a	n/a
Labor, Health and Human Services	H.R. 5464	Not debated	0	n/a	n/a
Legislative Branch	H.R. 4487	Structured	4	0.96	0.97
Military Construction-Veterans Affairs	H.R. 4486	Open	2	n/a	n/a
State-Foreign Operations	H.R. 5013	Not debated	0	n/a	n/a
Transportation-HUD	H.R. 4745	Open	21	0.95	0.07

Source: Compiled by author.

First, staff members familiar with appropriations say that nonpartisanship endures because members believe it is the best way to ensure the passage of essential spending bills. In 2005, a senior Republican staff member, who had just retired after a decade of working with the House Appropriations Committee, explained that committee members are pragmatic because they believe they must win minority party support to ensure that spending bills are passed.[47] For example, the committee routinely allocated earmarks to vulnerable members in each party and divided money on one bill (Labor-HHS), 60–40, between the majority and minority. In 2012, separate interviews with two senior Democratic and Republican staff members sounded similar themes of nonpartisanship. There is an old saying on Capitol Hill, the Republican noted, "There are Republicans, there are Democrats, and there are appropriators."[48] The Democratic staff member explained that keeping the appropriations process open (such as by adopting open rules) sent a message to all members that their ideas would be heard no matter what side of the aisle they were on. This, in turn, generated bipartisan support for appropriations bills. By contrast, clamping down with a closed rule was likely to spark opposition from the minority.[49]

Second, most members believed that the 1995 to 1996 shutdown was a political disaster for Republicans. The shutdown highlighted the dangers of the single-minded pursuit of partisan policies in appropriations and led Republicans to temper their partisanship to avoid more confrontations. "When we closed the government down under Newt, we got slaughtered," one staff member observed.[50] The staff member compared a government shutdown to Pickett's Charge, the bold but suicidal march toward Union lines during the Battle of Gettysburg. Former Senate majority leader Trent Lott agreed: "Newt . . . thought we could roll Clinton before the shutdown. So, we had a shutdown, we didn't roll Clinton, [and] it burned us very badly. So, Republicans are a little jumpy about that kind of thing."[51] Staff members describe the Appropriations Committee as actively resisting the push for more partisan policy from both leadership and rank-and-file members.[52]

This interview evidence offers an explanation for the endurance of open rules and the quick resumption of minority support for appropriations bills after the shutdown: Republicans limited partisanship in their management of the bills until they lost their majority in 2006. This was a pragmatic decision aimed at protecting the party's reelection interests based on the strategic understanding that limiting partisanship would help the majority to build a bipartisan coalition to ensure the passage of the budget. Democrats, who generally support federal spending, were happy to go along with this approach because it helped them to meet their policy goals, despite being in the minority.

Third, the mixed character of appropriations in the House today is the result of new divisions among Republicans and the erosion of the post-1996 consensus. A key turning point occurred when Republicans lost their majority in 2006 and, with it, the responsibility for adopting a budget. Republicans took advantage of open rules to "filibuster" the bills by amendment and ultimately voted against them. Democrats viewed these tactics as a violation of the rules of fair play. They responded with structured rules and by refusing to bring bills to the floor in regular order. The break with the past deepened when a wave of Tea Party–affiliated conservatives helped Republicans recapture the House in 2010. These new members are deeply opposed to federal spending and appear to reject the premise that distributive spending will help them win reelection. The Republican majority is now divided between seasoned Republicans who have attempted to preserve nonpartisanship and conservative firebrands determined to reduce federal spending however they can.

One sign of change occurred when conservatives spearheaded a successful effort to eliminate the practice of "earmarking" funds for district projects, like museums and bridges.[53] Consistent with distributive theories, both parties had traditionally sought these funds and proudly taken credit for them at reelection time. Conservatives argued that earmarking was wasteful and helped to transform it from a political plus into a political liability. The loss of earmarks is significant because political scientists have found that such spending helps leaders to build coalitions of support for spending bills.[54] Former Senate majority leader Tom Daschle explained, "[Appropriations is] the one thing that used to be fairly bipartisan, and the reason it was bipartisan was because everybody felt invested. They had things in there for their states, and they didn't want to jeopardize those things."[55]

Conservative new members lack the collective memory of the damage inflicted by the 1995 to 1996 shutdown and have demanded that party leaders threaten more government shutdowns to force Democrats to reduce spending. This approach places them at odds with more experienced members, who worry about damaging the party's reputation.[56] "The more senior guys have been saying, 'You're nuts. This is a loser for whoever is held responsible,'" observed a retired staff member.[57] Under pressure from conservative lawmakers, Republicans sparked the first government shutdown in over a decade in a last-ditch effort to derail President Barack Obama's signature health care law in October of 2013. The result was a temporary political disaster. President Obama refused to compromise, and Republican poll ratings fell. The crisis ended when Speaker John Boehner brought funding legislation to the floor that was adopted with the support of almost all Democrats and a minority of Republicans.[58] Conservative unhappiness with Speaker Boehner's willingness to compromise with Democrats ultimately led to the Speaker's resignation in 2015.

The absence of a stable governing majority has left Republicans without a clear strategy to adopt a budget and placed appropriations in disarray. Republicans returned to the use of open rules when they regained control of the chamber in 2011. They now face increasing numbers of amendments each year that complicate their management of the bills, many from zealous conservatives looking for media attention.[59] Republican leaders also face difficult choices on policy. If leaders give into conservative policy demands, they will lose Democratic support and likely provoke a budget crisis. If they resist conservative demands, they may be unable to win support from a majority of Republicans. Republicans have chosen neither course consistently. Some appropriations bills win strong bipartisan support, whereas others are adopted on sharply partisan lines. In other cases, leaders manage their divisions by bundling bills together to attract more votes from both parties. There is little to suggest that the instability among Republicans will end anytime soon. Absent the election of a Republican president in 2016, the incentive structure underlying these patterns is likely to remain intact. Distributive norms in appropriations will likely endure, but the coming years may prove to be an especially challenging time for members to complete their vital work adopting spending bills.

Conclusion

It is common today for scholars to characterize Congress as mired in partisan dysfunction. This chapter strikes a more optimistic note than those accounts—one consistent with Adler and Wilkerson's argument that Congress retains a robust ability to solve problems. Based on the data and staff interviews, recent scholarship would seem to substantially overstate the degree of partisanship in House appropriations. The writing and consideration of spending bills is notable because it continues to be characterized by strong nonpartisan norms, not because it has grown somewhat more partisan in today's highly polarized environment. The endurance of nonpartisanship is due to the fact that all members have a variety of interests. They benefit from their party's reputation and from their ability to claim credit for accomplishments. Today's members place a greater weight on a strong party reputation than past members did, but it is still in their interest to work across party lines to pass spending legislation.

The fact that members are not motivated purely by partisanship is an important reason why the transformation of the House is not as deep as it appears. It is not in members' interest to transform the House into a purely partisan institution. It's also unlikely that a group of reformers could achieve that goal if they desired it. Even the most zealous reformers must adjust rules, procedures, and institutions they inherit from the past. Past periods of rapid change show that reformers are forced to compromise to satisfy members' various interests and that they more often layer new ways of business onto old than replace the old ways altogether. According to congressional scholar Eric Schickler, the result is institutions "based on untidy compromises" and "full of tensions and contradictions."[60]

Such is the case today. Powerful party leaders coexist with a stubbornly independent Appropriations Committee and strong nonpartisan norms in the writing and passage of spending legislation. The endurance of nonpartisanship in appropriations during a time of high polarization is an encouraging sign about the continuing ability of the House to wield its constitutional power over the purse. It demonstrates that Congress is a multilayered institution capable of serving more than one interest at a time. Members benefit both from leaders who engage in high-profile partisan clashes that mobilize voters and from committees that help the parties meet shared goals. This uneasy combination of features may actually serve voters quite well, despite the dismal approval ratings Congress receives from the public and the harsh criticism it receives from scholars. It provides voters with a clear distinction between the two parties while ensuring that cooperation continues on matters important to the lives of the American people. Congress may earn much of the criticism it receives, but it also serves us better than we give it credit for.

Notes

1. I am grateful to Sarah Binder, Frances Lee, Gregory Koger, Jamie Carson, Anthony Madonna, Bruce Oppenheimer, Larry Dodd, and David Karol for their comments on this chapter. I also thank my outstanding undergraduate research assistants, Bryce Anderson-Gregson and Ben Horblitt of the University of Denver, for their work collecting data for this chapter. Earlier versions of this chapter were presented at the 2015 Annual Meeting of the American Political Science Association, San Francisco,

September 3–6, and the Congress and History Conference, Vanderbilt University, May 22–23, 2015.
2. J. R. Pole, ed., *The Federalist* (Indianapolis, IN: Hackett Publishing Company, 2005).
3. Joseph White, "The Functions and Power of the House Appropriations Committee" (PhD dissertation, University of California, Berkeley, 1989).
4. John Aldrich and David W. Rohde, "The Republican Revolution and the House Appropriations Committee," *The Journal of Politics* 61 (2000): 1–33.
5. Richard Fenno, *The Power of the Purse: Appropriations Politics in Congress* (Boston: Little, Brown, 1966).
6. Ibid., 164.
7. Ibid., 416.
8. Ibid., 442.
9. See David W. Rohde, *Parties and Leaders in the Postreform House* (Chicago: University of Chicago Press, 1991); Nelson Polsby, *How Congress Evolves: Social Bases of Institutional Change* (New York: Oxford University Press, 2004); Frances Lee, "How Party Polarization Affects Governance," *Annual Review of Political Science* 18 (2015): 261–82.
10. Aaron Wildavsky and Naomi Caiden, *The New Politics of the Budgetary Process*, 5th ed. (New York: Pearson Longman, 2004).
11. See Leroy N. Rieselbach, *Congressional Reform* (Washington, DC: CQ Press, 1986); Donald R. Wolfensberger, *Congress and the People: Deliberative Democracy on Trial* (Washington, DC: Woodrow Wilson Center Press, 2000).
12. Nolan McCarty, Keith Poole, and Howard Rosenthal, *Polarized America: The Dance of Ideology and Unequal Riches* (Cambridge, MA: MIT Press, 2006).
13. Kenneth Shepsle, "Congress Is a 'They,' Not an 'It': Legislative Intent as an Oxymoron," *International Review of Law and Economics* 12 (1992): 239–56.
14. David Mayhew, *Congress: The Electoral Connection* (New Haven, CT: Yale University Press, 1974).
15. Kenneth Shepsle and Barry Weingast, "Political Preference for the Pork Barrel: A Generalization," *American Journal of Political Science* 26 (1981): 86–111.
16. White, "Functions and Power," 15.
17. Ibid., 225.
18. See Tim Groseclose and James M. Snyder Jr., "Buying Supermajorities," *American Political Science Review* 90 (1996): 303–15; Diana Evans, *Greasing the Wheels: Using Pork Barrel Projects to Build Majority Coalitions in Congress* (New York: Cambridge University Press, 2004); Kenneth A. Shepsle, Robert P. Van Houweling, Samuel J. Abrams, and Peter C. Hanson, "The Senate Electoral Cycle and Bicameral Appropriations Politics," *American Journal of Political Science* 53 (2009): 343–59.
19. John Aldrich, *Why Parties? A Second Look* (Chicago: The University of Chicago Press, 2011); Gary W. Cox and Mathew D. McCubbins, *Setting the Agenda: Responsible Party Government in the U.S. House of Representatives* (New York: Cambridge University Press, 2005).
20. Aldrich and Rohde, "Republican Revolution"; Joshua B. Gordon, "The (Dis)Integration of the House Appropriations Committee: Revisiting *The Power of the Purse* in a Partisan Era," in *Congress Reconsidered*, 7th ed., ed. Lawrence C. Dodd and Bruce I. Oppenheimer (Washington, DC: CQ Press, 2001); Polsby, *How Congress Evolves*; Eric Schickler and Kathryn Pearson, "The House Leadership in an Era of Partisan Warfare," in *Congress Reconsidered*, 8th ed., ed. Lawrence C. Dodd and Bruce I. Oppenheimer (Washington, DC: CQ Press, 2005), 207–26.

21. John H. Aldrich, Brittany N. Perry, and David W. Rohde, "Richard Fenno's Theory of Congressional Committees and the Partisan Polarization of the House," in *Congress Reconsidered*, 10th ed., ed. Lawrence C. Dodd and Bruce I. Oppenheimer (Washington, DC: CQ Press, 2013), 193–220.
22. E. Scott Adler and John D. Wilkerson, *Congress and the Politics of Problem Solving* (New York: Cambridge University Press, 2013).
23. Roger H. Davidson, Walter J. Oleszek, and Frances E. Lee, *Congress and Its Members*, 13th ed. (Washington, DC: CQ Press, 2012).
24. Allen Schick, *The Federal Budget: Politics, Policy and Process*, 3rd ed. (Washington, DC: Brookings Institution Press, 2007).
25. Barbara Sinclair, *Unorthodox Lawmaking: New Legislative Processes in the U.S. Congress* (Washington, DC: CQ Press, 2012). Lee further notes that it has become common for the majority party to restrict opportunities for the minority to participate in lawmaking so that "the minority party enjoys little opportunity to shape outcomes or even to put the majority on record in awkward ways." See Lee, "Party Polarization."
26. Majority party homogeneity is operationalized as the DW-NOMINATE standard deviation of the majority party divided by the standard deviation of the chamber. Majority party distance from the minority is operationalized as the distance between the median DW-NOMINATE scores of the two parties.
27. "Bush Prevails on Cuba, Drug Imports," in *CQ Almanac 2007*, 63rd ed., ed. Jan Austin (Washington, DC: CQ Press, 2008), 2-7-2-9.
28. These data were collected as part of an ongoing study of House appropriations I am conducting with Lee Drutman of New America. I am grateful to him for permitting a preview of the findings to be presented in this chapter and to Bryce Anderson-Gregson for her work coding amendments.
29. Rules Committee chair Louise Slaughter noted at the time, "There was not a single amendment to this bill in fiscal year 2003, but this year we had 127 amendments filed on the bill as of the Tuesday deadline. That suggested to us we were in for what potentially could have been a repetitive chain of deleterious and ill-considered amendments, none of which would have allowed us to get any closer to our goal of getting these bills completed and signed into law by the President. When it became clear this week that the minority was not ready to agree to a clear and firm schedule for finishing the work on appropriations bills, we decided that we had no alternative but to go ahead with a clear and concise plan." See *Congressional Record*, June 17, 2009, H6910.
30. I am grateful to Anthony Madonna for sharing data on structured rules for analysis in this paper.
31. I do not include Defense in the average because of the unusually large number of amendments introduced by Rep. Jeff Flake.
32. Michael S. Lynch, Anthony J. Madonna, and Jason M. Roberts, "The Cost of Majority Party Bias: Amending Activity Under Structured Rules," *Legislative Studies Quarterly* 41 (2016): 633–55.
33. Summary of Activities of the House Committee on Rules, 111th Congress, January 3, 2011, 96.
34. Matthew Green, *Underdog Politics: The Minority Party in the U.S. House of Representatives* (New Haven, CT: Yale University Press, 2015).
35. Staff Interviews A and E, 2012. I conducted two waves of interviews in 2005 and 2012 with current and former members and staff knowledgeable about appropriations.

The 2005 wave of interviews was conducted with colleagues, and some of the findings are reported in earlier work. See Shepsle et al., "Senate Electoral Cycle." Some interview evidence from 2012 also was initially published in my book *Too Weak to Govern: Majority Party Power and Appropriations in the U.S. Senate* (New York: Cambridge University Press, 2014). In both waves, the staff members generally requested confidentiality as a condition for conducting the interview. The paraphrased comments reported here are summaries from notes taken during the interviews. Quotations are verbatim quotes written down during the interview session.

36. Republicans returned to the use of structured rules in the summer of 2016, as this chapter was going to print. Future research should address the reasons for this change.
37. See Schick, *Federal Budget*, and Hanson, *Too Weak to Govern*.
38. See Sinclair, *Unorthodox Lawmaking*; Hanson, *Too Weak to Govern*; Steven S. Smith, *The Senate Syndrome: The Evolution of Procedural Warfare in the Modern U.S. Senate* (Norman: University of Oklahoma Press, 2014).
39. Hanson, *Too Weak to Govern*.
40. Peter C. Hanson, "Restoring Regular Order in Congressional Appropriations," Economic Studies at Brookings, no. 2, November 2015, http://www.brookings.edu/research/papers/2015/11/19-restoring-regular-order-congressional-appropriations-hanson.
41. John Cranford, "2013 Legislative Summary: Transportation-HUD Appropriations," *CQ Weekly*, January 6, 2014, 32.
42. Staff Interviews F and G, 2012. See also Hanson, *Too Weak to Govern*, 33.
43. Roll Call Vote 21, U.S. House of Representatives, January 15, 2014.
44. In some cases, omnibus package or yearlong CR come to the floor under closed rules. At other times, they have been adopted under the suspension of the rules.
45. Vote counts include votes cast related to amendments on regular appropriations bills, omnibus appropriations bills, or yearlong CRs.
46. Roll Call Vote 563, U.S. House of Representatives, December 11, 2014.
47. Staff Interview M, 2005.
48. Staff Interview F, 2012.
49. Staff Interview G, 2012.
50. Staff Interview F, 2012.
51. Interview with author, 2012.
52. Staff Interview M, 2005; Staff Interviews F, G, 2012.
53. Jennifer Steinhauer, "Lawmakers' End of Earmarks Affects Local Programs Large and Small," *New York Times*, February 7, 2011, http://www.nytimes.com/2011/02/08/us/politics/08earmark.html.
54. Evans, *Greasing the Wheels*.
55. Interview with author, 2012.
56. Staff Interview F, 2012.
57. Staff Interview E, 2012.
58. Jonathan Weisman and Ashley Parker, "Republicans Back Down, Ending Crisis Over Shutdown and Debt Limit," *New York Times*, October 16, 2013, http://www.nytimes.com/2013/10/17/us/congress-budget-debate.html.
59. Staff Interview F, 2012. Also see Emma Dumain and Katherine Tully-McManus, "The Unruliness of Open Rules," *CQ Weekly*, June 23, 2014, 888–90.
60. Eric Schickler, *Disjointed Pluralism: Institutional Innovation and the Development of the U.S. Congress* (Princeton, NJ: Princeton University Press, 2001).

13. Filibusters and Majority Rule in the Modern Senate

Gregory Koger

This chapter traces the rise of the modern Senate filibuster and describes how filibustering affects the competition between the majority and minority parties in the Senate. It then explains how a major reform in November 2013 exposed the tenuous nature of the Senate filibuster: It is a very powerful constraint on majority power that is entirely subject to the consent of a majority of the Senate. This overview shows that the Senate has been a rapidly evolving institution, with more change likely in the future.

Filibustering is one of the defining features of the U.S. Senate. Any senator can threaten to delay almost any measure or nomination on the floor of the Senate for strategic gain.[1] Senate Rule 22 states that debate on a measure can only be limited if three-fifths of its membership (sixty senators) vote for *cloture*.[1] This one rule—or more precisely, the absence of a rule—ensures that most major laws that pass the Senate have bipartisan support—or that they don't pass at all. More subtly, the practice of filibustering allows individual senators to have a great deal of influence on issues that they care a great deal about.

For most of the Senate's history, senators had to invest effort and stake their political reputations on a filibuster. As a result, they tended to be intense but rare conflicts waged by individual senators or small bands of senators waging legislative warfare on behalf of their regions, economic industries, or ideology. Over the last six decades, however, filibustering became routinized so that senators found it much easier to filibuster while Senate leaders developed a set of informal routines to accommodate an ever-increasing level of obstruction.[2] The curious element of this narrative is that the Senate did not make a conscious choice to switch from a simple-majority chamber with rare, intense filibusters to a chamber whose daily operations are based on supermajority rule.

However, in November 2013, the Democratic majority in the Senate enacted one of the most significant limitations on filibustering in Senate history by declaring that a simple majority (50 percent plus one) is sufficient to limit debate on nominations to the executive or judicial branch, with the exception of Supreme Court nominations. This event made clear that the Senate filibuster is a powerful but fragile rule.

This chapter does three things: It traces the rise of the modern Senate filibuster, describes how filibustering affects the interaction of the majority and minority parties in the Senate, and then explains how the 2013 reform exposed

311

the tenuous nature of the Senate filibuster—it is a very powerful constraint on majority power that is entirely subject to the consent of a majority of the Senate. This overview shows that the Senate has been a rapidly evolving institution, with more change likely in the future.

The Rise of the "Sixty-Vote Senate"

A critical step in the U.S. lawmaking process is the debate and approval of a measure by the U.S. House and Senate acting as collective chambers. The rules of both chambers allow individual members to make motions, offer amendments, and discuss proposals but also to specify the constraints on these deliberative rights.

Filibustering is the use of delay—or the threat of delay—for strategic gain in a legislative setting. It takes many forms, depending on the rules and practices of each legislature: slow walking to a vote, leaving the chamber to ensure that the legislature lacks enough members to make a decision, or forcing repeated votes on procedural motions.[3] Filibustering in the U.S. Senate is often associated with senators making prolonged speeches, as depicted in the 1939 movie *Mr. Smith Goes to Washington*, but senators have historically used a variety of tactics to filibuster.

During the nineteenth century, there was much more filibustering in the U.S. House of Representatives than occurred in the U.S. Senate. By the end of the nineteenth century, however, the members of the House had adopted new precedents and rules to prohibit the most common forms of obstruction and, perhaps more importantly, ensure that the House Rules Committee can quickly propose new temporary debate rules to suppress any obstruction. Nonetheless, members of the House still occasionally exploit the remaining loopholes in the rules as a form of protest or to force short-term delay.[4]

In the Senate, filibusters were possible but rare into the early twentieth century. After a few major filibusters against President Woodrow Wilson's agenda—particularly legislation to arm merchant ships in March 1917—the Senate adopted its first cloture rule in 1917. The 1917 cloture rule provided for senators to end debate on a measure by a vote of two-thirds of those present, and senators subsequently rejected proposals to lower this threshold to a simple majority. The key reason why senators of this era rejected a simple-majority cloture rule was concern that it would enable the majority party to force through bills that lacked the sincere support of a majority of the chamber.[5]

The 1917 cloture rule had little effect upon the frequency or influence of filibustering. In particular, it did nothing to constrain the end-of-Congress filibusters that had motivated its adoption, which instead were addressed by the Twentieth Amendment to the Constitution, enacted in 1933. The Twentieth Amendment rearranged the congressional schedule to eliminate the three-month *short session*, which had previously occurred after elections for the next Congress.

These short sessions, also known as *lame-duck sessions*, were especially prone to filibusters because there was often a backlog of major bills to consider, including appropriations bills, and the end date of a short session was fixed and known in advance. Since 1933, each two-year Congress consists of two sessions that begin in early January and continue until both chambers declare that the session is finished. The current practice is for each session to last an entire year, with several breaks, or *recesses*, scattered throughout the annual schedule. After the adoption of the Twentieth Amendment, filibusters continued to be rare until the 1950s, and from 1935 to 1960, many of these filibusters were directed at civil rights legislation.[6]

Institutionalizing the Filibuster

The classic view of the U.S. Senate dates from around 1960, when Donald Matthews's *U.S. Senators and Their World* was published.[7] Matthews described a small society dominated by an inner core of elite senators—many of them Southerners—and based upon a system of norms that encouraged senators to begin with an apprenticeship, to treat each other with courtesy and reciprocity, to focus on legislative policy making rather than grandstanding for the media, and to focus on a few substantive issues, particularly issues before their committees. Matthews's classic book barely mentions filibustering.

The classic Senate depended upon consensus to function. While the Senate has formal rules for setting its agenda and daily schedule, in practice, Senate party leaders make these decisions in consultation with the members of their parties. These negotiations yield unanimous consent agreements (UCAs), which are formally adopted on the Senate floor. Senators use UCAs to decide which proposals will come to the Senate floor and how they will be debated. When the Senate is functioning smoothly, noncontroversial bills and nominations are passed quickly by unanimous consent.

The system of social constraints that defined this "textbook" Senate was already fading when Matthews's book was published. A very large class of liberal senators joined the Senate after the election of 1958. These liberals—followed by more in the election of 1964—could not wait a couple of decades for opportunities to lead committees; for both personal and electoral reasons, they sought immediate action on progressive issues. Toward this end, these new senators began to speak and offer proposals on a wide range of issues. These senators tended to support a variety of electoral and institutional changes as well, including cloture reform.[8]

Another transformation under way in the 1960s was the institutionalization of filibustering. This change was set in motion by a subtle decision: When new Democratic majority leader Mike Mansfield, D-Mont., replaced Lyndon Johnson, D-Tex., in 1961, he decided that he would respond to filibusters by trying to use the then-dormant cloture rule. The alternative approach was a *war of attrition*: When a senator or senators began to kill time on the chamber floor, the other senators would keep a quorum (a simple majority of the chamber) present to continue the debate, day and night, until the obstructionists were exhausted, or the majority gave in. Under Lyndon Johnson, the majority attempted to outlast the Southern filibuster against a 1960 civil rights bill. The Southerners won this contest handily, demonstrating that in the modern age, an organized minority had a tremendous advantage over a weakly motivated majority.[9] The lesson Mansfield drew from this embarrassing defeat was that the Senate would be better off responding to filibusters by seeking to develop a supermajority coalition to invoke cloture.

Of course, Mansfield did not make this tactical choice in a vacuum. The switch from attrition to cloture was a response to long-term changes in the agenda of the Senate and the lives of senators. The U.S. Senate's workload grew significantly over time, especially with the expansion of the federal government since the 1930s and the nation's increased military establishment and foreign commitments since the 1940s.[10] Senators' personal lives had changed as well. The availability of railroads and airplanes made it easier for senators to travel back to their home states, to take overseas trips, and to travel the country making speeches and visiting interest groups and party activists.[11] In the modern era, campaign fund-raising is a major share of senators' daily schedules. The average Senate election winner in 2014 spent $10.6 million, and this money must be raised in comparatively small increments.[12] Compared to senators of 1900, by mid-century, senators were likely to spend most of their time off the Senate floor. Senators were aided in their duties by a growing number of personal and committee staffers who freed up senators' time for legislating, travel, or politics. This shift in senators' work habits is evident in their propensity to cluster votes in the middle of the week, as shown in Figure 13-1.

Figure 13-1 displays the percentage of all roll call votes that are held on Tuesday, Wednesday, or Thursday in each session of Congress. If there is no clustering, this statistic would be around 50 percent, as the votes would be spread evenly across a six-day workweek. While there is variation around the trend, there is little clustering until the 1930s, after which there is a steady increase over time in the percentage of votes held during the middle of the week. From 1990 to 2010, the Senate scheduled 80 to 90 percent of all its votes during the middle of the week. These were the historical trends behind the switch from attrition to cloture. The percentage dropped to 76 percent in 2012 and 68 percent in 2013, however, as a frustrated Democratic majority extended the workweek into the weekend to finish work on budgets, spending resolutions, and nominations.

While the cloture-based approach was effective early on, in the long run, it made the Senate more vulnerable to filibustering. Major milestones occurred in 1962, when the Senate invoked cloture on a bill setting up a public satellite corporation, and in 1964, when the Senate invoked cloture on a landmark civil rights bill. However, the switch from *attrition* filibusters to *cloture* filibusters had a major unintended effect: It lowered the *costs* that senators had to pay in order to

Figure 13-1 Percentage of Votes Held Tuesday Through Thursday, 1933–2013

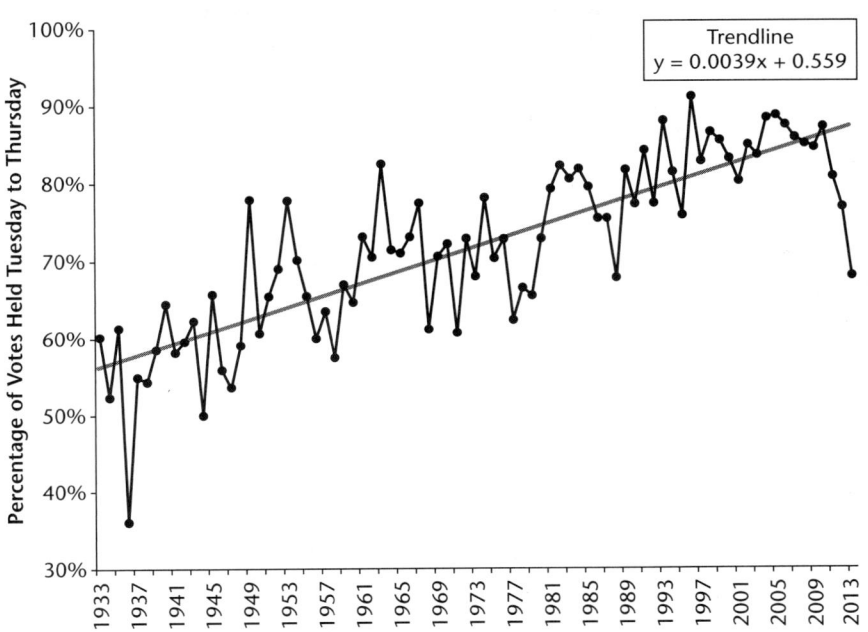

Source: Compiled by author.

filibuster. By *costs*, I mean the physical strain, wasted time, and possible political retaliation for engaging in a very public filibuster in the Senate chamber. These costs were very high when senators had to continually occupy the floor of the Senate around the clock. If, on the other hand, a senator "filibusters" by expressing his *intent* to debate around the clock and objects to unanimous consent requests that would prevent such behavior, the costs for blocking legislation and nominations are quite low.[13]

During the 1960s, senators gradually realized that obstruction was "all gain and no pain" and began to respond to this new system. Figure 13-2 displays this trend. From 1917 to 1970, the number of filibusters—measured by scanning media coverage of the Senate—and cloture votes per two-year Congress was low and relatively constant.[14] There were never more than seven cloture votes per Congress, and the number of filibusters exceeded the number of cloture votes throughout this period, suggesting that senators preferred to settle these disputes through attrition and bargaining, instead of invoking cloture. These patterns reversed during the 1970s. The number of filibusters and cloture votes increased dramatically as senators began to treat obstruction as normal behavior.

Figure 13-2 Filibusters and Cloture Votes in the Senate, 1917–2015

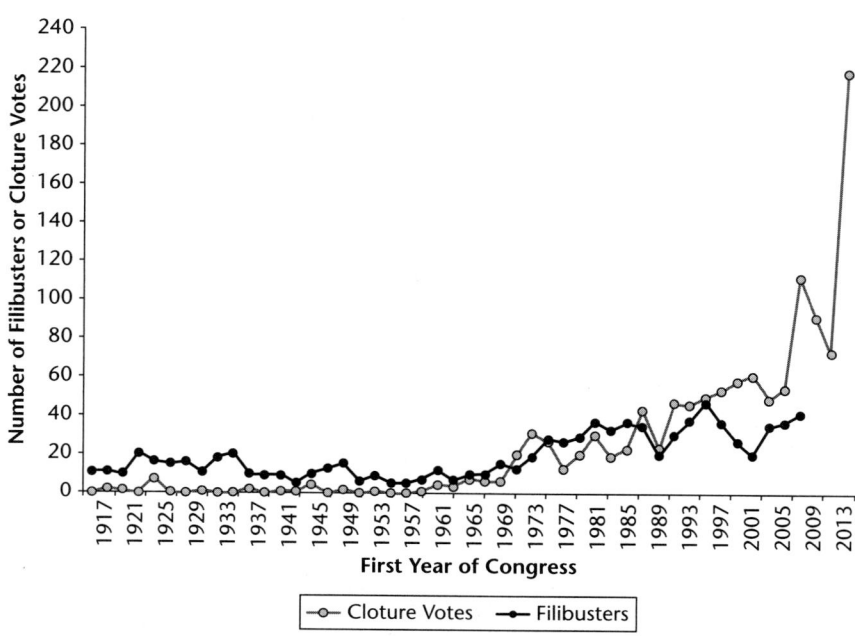

Source: Filibuster counts compiled by author; cloture votes obtained from http://www.senate.gov/pagelayout/reference/cloture_motions/clotureCounts.htm.

As the constraints on filibustering were lifted, senators began to use this power in innovative ways. During the mid-twentieth century, senators' motives tended to be straightforward: They obstructed proposals they did not wish to see pass in the hope of either killing the proposal outright or extracting some amendments to moderate the proposal. As filibustering became more common, senators began using this power for bargaining leverage on other issues, particularly to force the majority party to allow amendments on hot-button issues or to schedule legislation that otherwise might not make it to the Senate floor.[15]

One manifestation of this trend is the increasing use of *holds* by senators. A hold is "a request by a Senator to his or her party leader to delay floor action on a measure or matter."[16] This practice dates back to the 1950s when the Democratic Steering Committee—responsible for agenda setting—received and considered hold requests.[17] These holds may simply ask for a few days of delay to accommodate a senator's travel schedule or allow a senator to read a bill and prepare amendments. However, senators have also used holds to slow or block bills and nominations they oppose. When placing a hold, senators may also express their desire to filibuster the bill or nomination. By doing so, a single senator can signal that it will be costly to pass the targeted proposal, even if the other ninety-nine senators support it. Bills and nominations that are unopposed can pass quickly without a roll call vote. If, on the other hand, it is necessary to schedule hours of debate, file cloture petitions and vote on cloture, and hold a final-passage vote, a single objection can dramatically increase the amount of time required to pass a proposal. For this reason, a hold can act as a unilateral veto on any proposal that is not worth the time to overcome a filibuster.

Senators use the power to hold bills and nominations for a variety of reasons. Walter Oleszek reports that there are

> *informational* holds, where Senators wish to be informed or consulted before a measure or nomination is brought to the floor; *revolving* or *rotating* holds, where one Senator, and then another and so on, will place holds; *Mae West* holds, which suggest that the Senator(s) who employed the hold wants to bargain with the proponents of the legislation or nomination; *retaliatory*, or *tit-for-tat*, holds; and *choke* holds, where the objective is to kill the affected bill or nomination.[18]

In particular, note that senators may hold bills and nominations without any substantive objections to the policies or people involved; senators use holds to maximize their bargaining power or to retaliate against other senators. Also, senators often hold nominations as a means of gaining leverage over the president or executive agencies. In early 2014, for example, Senator Rand Paul, R-Ky., attempted to block nominations for the Federal Reserve Board until the Senate voted on his bill to audit the Federal Reserve System. More recently, senators Pat Roberts, R-Kans., and Kelly Ayotte, R-N.H., have placed holds on nominations for secretary of the army and general counsel of the Department of Defense (respectively) to obtain information and assurances from the Obama administration about the transfer of prisoners from Guantanamo Bay Naval Base in Cuba to the mainland United States.[19] For senators, holds offer low-cost access to real leverage over the Senate's agenda and executive agencies.

However, senators have long realized that the hold system can easily be abused. Since 1985, senators have attempted a series of reforms to ensure that senators cannot make secret holds; they must at least tell other affected senators and should ideally declare their holds to the public. In 2007 and 2011, the Senate adopted reforms to ensure that senators declare their holds on the official records.[20]

While the rampant use of holds may have decreased, the overall pattern is clear: The ability to filibuster has become institutionalized in the modern Senate, so that any senator is now understood to have a legitimate right to block any bill subject to a supermajority vote. The broader effect of this development is historic. In addition to the president, the majority of the U.S. House, and the majority of the U.S. Senate, the Senate has added a fourth veto point to the lawmaking process: consent of the minority party of the U.S. Senate or at least of some of its members.

Parties and Obstruction in the Senate

The institutionalization of filibustering since 1960 has coincided with the partisan polarization of the Senate. Senators are increasingly likely to vote with their parties and against members of the opposing party. This trend is illustrated in Figure 13-3, which displays the average level of party unity across all votes that divide most Democrats from most Republicans.[21] This statistic is calculated by identifying every roll call vote on which most Republicans voted against most Democrats, then averaging the percentage of legislators voting with their respective parties across all of the votes during a two-year Congress.

There are two main patterns in Figure 13-3. First, partisanship was historically low during the 1970s, which is why many scholars from this era emphasized the individualistic nature of the chamber; every senator was a force unto himself. Over the last thirty years, both parties have become more partisan. The second pattern is that the majority party is usually more unified than the minority party. The Republicans were more unified as the majority party during the early 1980s, the late 1990s, and after regaining a clear majority in 2003. The Democrats were more unified during their majority party periods of the 1970s, late 1980s, and from 2007 to 2013. Even when the minority party is cohesive, it will tend to

Figure 13-3 Party Unity in the Senate, 1961–2014

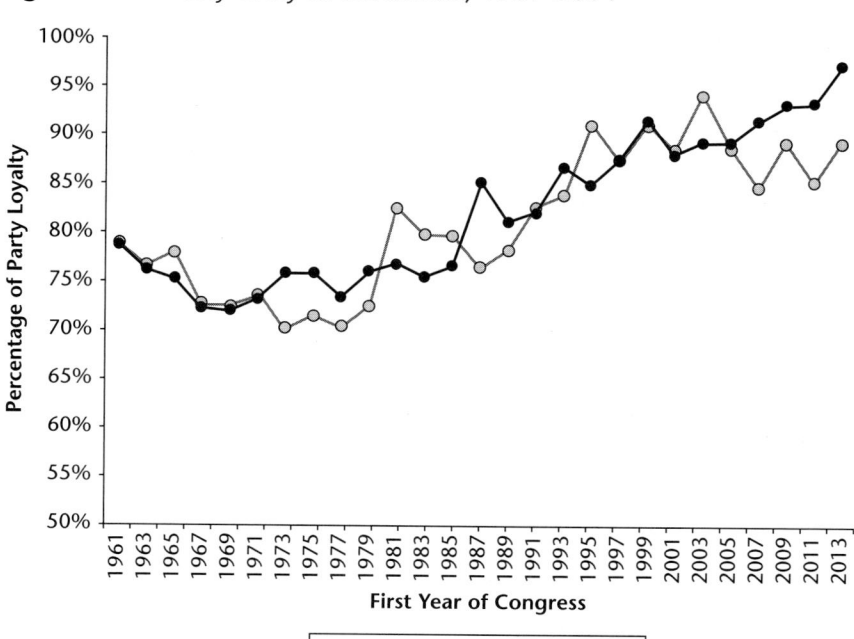

Source: voteview.com/PartyUnity.htm

selectively oppose the majority's agenda. Members of the majority party, on the other hand, are often expected to support the majority party's agenda despite any individual misgivings. This is why the majority party tends to vote together more often.

Since the increase in Senate partisanship since the early 1970s coincides with the recent increase in filibustering, many observers have suggested that partisanship is *causing* this increase in obstruction. However, this correlation disappears if one analyzes a longer time frame. Partisanship is a long cycle in congressional history, so there have been previous highs and lows. The current filibuster-based Senate is a new development, however, and we cannot explain this new trend with a historical cycle.[22]

The combination of partisanship and obstruction has had a tremendous impact on the Senate. As one might expect, the partisanship shown in Figure 13-3 has also affected how senators vote on cloture. The general trend toward increasing partisanship also applies to senators' votes on whether or not filibusters succeed. Voting on cloture has become increasingly partisan, particularly during periods of unified government. When one party holds the White House and majorities in the House and Senate, the Senate filibuster is the minority party's only veto point in the legislative process. The minority party in the House cannot block the majority party's agenda or even ensure that major legislation is thoroughly debated on the House floor, and the president is allied with the majority party in each chamber. Both for political and policy reasons, the supporters of the minority party turn to their party contingent in the Senate, expecting them to block or moderate any proposal on the majority party agenda that (in their view) constitutes unwise or radical change and to advocate for the issues on the minority party's agenda.

How does obstruction help the minority party? I assume that the core goal of a party is to help its members win reelection and gain a majority and that legislation is a means to this end. Toward this end, parties strive to (a) manipulate the set of issues that come up for a roll call vote and hence may be criticized in subsequent elections and (b) frame issues and legislation to affect the overall reputation of the two parties.[23] Filibustering helps the minority party achieve its first goal by taking legislation hostage until the majority agrees to schedule votes on hot-button issues that advance the minority party's electoral themes. In early 2011, for example, the Senate Republicans insisted on holding a vote on repeal of the 2010 Affordable Care Act during the debate to reauthorize the Federal Aviation Administration. While the proposal lost, 47–51, the Republicans successfully put the Democrats on record supporting the controversial law while registering their continued opposition to the landmark law.[24] This sort of *message politics* is common on major issues. In particular, if the majority party brings up a bill that is primarily intended to reinforce their public message and to emphasize an issue distinction between the two parties, the minority party will respond by raising their own message proposals and demanding a vote on their alternative.[25]

Over the last three decades, both parties have filibustered particular bills to prevent a public relations "win" for the opposing party and to raise their own message issues. While in the minority, Senate Republicans, however, engaged in a new strategy. During the 111th Congress, Senate minority leader Mitch McConnell, R-Ky., rallied his party around a strategy of (a) blanket opposition to Democratic initiatives and (b) efforts to drag out debate and slow down the chamber to reduce its output.[26] For example, during the 2009 to 2010 health care reform debate, the Republicans insisted on using all of their allotted postcloture debate time, even though much of this time was spent on quorum calls instead of speaking or voting. The Senate floor debate on the banking-reform bill was also prolonged several weeks by Republican obstruction against the motion to begin debating the bill and then by the slow pace of negotiations between Mr. McConnell and Senate majority leader Harry Reid over the debate and amendment process.[27]

For the Democratic majority, these landmark bills were worth the time consumed by Republican foot-dragging. However, there were opportunity costs for this lost floor time.[28] Early on, President Barack Obama and Senator Reid expected that health care reform would pass the Senate by the end of summer or early fall 2009, after which the Senate would debate climate change legislation. Since health care reform did not pass the Senate until December 2009, and another three months were devoted to finalizing the legislation, climate change was delayed until 2010. Senator Reid also planned to bring up climate change legislation (or a broader energy policy bill) after banking reform, but the long debate on banking pushed the energy policy debate into summer 2010, by which time senators were apparently too exhausted—and wary of tackling any more controversial legislation before the November elections—to debate another major issue.

The Republicans' strategy was especially effective against legislation that was *not* worth the opportunity cost of overcoming a filibuster. As mentioned above, much of the Senate's agenda is actually composed of less salient legislation and nominations. While these agenda items may be important to the functions of government and some senator's state, they typically do not offer enough political payoff for the majority to overcome an obstructionist minority willing to force multiple cloture votes and use all of its postcloture debate time.

Senate Republicans continued to pursue McConnell's strategy after the Republicans won control of the House in the 2010 elections. By limiting the productivity of the U.S. Senate, Republicans helped to focus attention on the legislative agenda of the U.S. House and to limit the Senate's bargaining capacity in a series of crisis negotiations over raising the federal debt limit, finalizing annual spending bills, and extending tax cuts that were due to expire. The Senate Democrats were frustrated by these tactics, but they had little reason to challenge the Republicans' right to filibuster legislation. After all, even if the Democrats could force their legislative-agenda bills through the Senate by narrow majority votes, they would still face a very unenthusiastic reception in the Republican-majority House, especially after many of its new Tea Party members believed they had an electoral mandate to block President Obama's agenda.

Nominations and the Nuclear Option

The frustration that the Senate Democratic majority developed during the 111th Congress would continue to build over the next three years. After a series of small reforms and informal truces, in November 2013, the Senate Democrats made a radical reform to shield nominations from filibusters and, in doing so, left the door wide open for further reforms. This section traces this escalating conflict and the consequences of the November 2013 "nuclear option" approach to filibuster reform. For more detail and a longer perspective, see the chapter later in this volume by Sarah Binder and Forrest Maltzman.

During the 111th Congress, the Senate Rules Committee held a series of hearings on Senate obstruction in 2010, and in January 2011, the Democrats proposed a series of reforms to change the way the Senate works. Apparently lacking the votes for any drastic measures, the Democrats settled for a package of minor changes negotiated with the Republicans: eliminating secret holds (mentioned earlier), reducing the number of executive-branch positions requiring Senate confirmation, eliminating the obligation for amendments to be read aloud if they have been available for seventy-two hours, and a short-lived "gentlemen's agreement" that the Republicans would not obstruct agenda-setting motions if the Democrats would not attempt to limit the right to offer amendments.

The 112th Congress (2011–2012)

In October 2011, there was more sparring over Senate rules, specifically the right to suspend the rules and offer amendments after cloture has been invoked. By a nearly party-line vote of 51–48 (D, 51–1; R, 0–47), senators decided that it would no longer be permissible to suspend the rules and bring up nongermane amendments after cloture is invoked. This was widely interpreted as a sign of Democrats' increasing impatience and willingness to revise Senate procedure.[29]

This action can also be considered foreshadowing. The Democrats demonstrated that they were willing to utilize a rarely used maneuver—establishing new parliamentary precedents—to curtail obstruction. Like statutes or the Constitution, the rules of a legislature are subject to interpretation, and a simple majority of the Senate can decide upon the "right" interpretation of a rule. While it is often difficult to form a large bipartisan coalition to pass a rules change restricting filibustering, a simple majority can redefine what the existing rules mean at any time, with perhaps a large potential impact on the right to filibuster in the Senate.[30] While this tactic is easy to utilize in parliamentary terms, senators have been very reluctant to use it in the past. First, it may provoke retaliation by the minority party, which may use its remaining parliamentary powers to obstruct even more strenuously to protest the majority's actions. For this reason, the use of parliamentary rulings to restrict filibustering has been deemed the "nuclear option" because it would provoke a massive and damaging response. Second, once majorities begin using this tactic, it will be harder for them to resist the temptation to adopt further simple-majority reforms, until eventually the filibuster has been completely abolished.

During the 112th Congress, nominations to executive and judicial positions were a key source of partisan conflict. The Senate voted eleven times on whether to invoke cloture on a nomination, and cloture attempts failed on six of these votes. As a result, four nominations were defeated: three judges and the proposed director of the Consumer Financial Protection Bureau (CFPB). A frustrated President Obama then used his recess appointment power to install the defeated CFPB director, Richard Cordray, and to fill three empty seats (out of five) on the National Labor Relations Board (NLRB) during a short break in congressional action.[31]

The 113th Congress (2013–2014)

The Senate Democrats gained seats in the 2012 elections and returned to Congress with increased interest in restraining minority obstruction. Harry Reid expressed the sentiments of many of his party members when he threatened to "go nuclear" unless the Republicans agreed to change how the Senate operates.[32] Reid then negotiated with Mitch McConnell, and they agreed to a set of incremental reforms:

- Reducing postcloture debate time on executive nominations from thirty hours to eight, except for the most important positions*
- Reducing postcloture debate on district court judges to two hours*
- Streamlining the process for holding a conference committee with the House on a bill, so it requires a single cloture vote (not three), two hours between filing and voting (not two days), and zero postcloture debate
- Two alternative agenda-setting methods: (a) a filibuster-proof, simple-majority motion to proceed to a bill, provided the minority party has the unconstrained ability to offer two amendments,* and (b) a shortened cloture process on a motion to proceed if the cloture petition is signed by the minority party leader and seven minority party members
- *expired at the end of the 113th Congress[33]

A central theme of these reforms is reducing the *time lags* built into the Senate cloture rule instead of trying to reduce the number of votes required to end debate. For many executive and judicial nominations, the critical question is not whether there are enough votes to overcome a filibuster but whether it is worth the required amount of Senate floor time to do so. These reforms altered this equation for nominations and conference committees, making it easier for the Senate to defeat filibusters by individuals and small groups.

Despite these efforts, filibusters against nominations continued. In February 2013, Charles Hagel's nomination for secretary of defense failed one cloture vote, only to survive one twelve days later. In March, Caitlin Halligan's nomination to the D.C. Circuit Court was blocked by a cloture vote of 51–41 and withdrawn by the White House, and Rand Paul, R-Ky., "filibustered" John Brennan's nomination to be director of the Central Intelligence Agency by taking to the floor to speak against the nomination for twelve hours.

In July 2013, Senate Democrats threatened to use the "nuclear option" again unless there were real changes in the nomination process. McConnell agreed to a tactical retreat, allowing votes on Cordray's nomination to director of the CFPB, two new NLRB board members, and nominations for the secretary of labor and director of the Environmental Protection Agency.[34] This truce, however, was purchased with the discomfort of those Republican senators who had to support cloture on controversial nominations in order to stave off Democratic reform. These votes were unpopular with the Republican base, and since multiple incumbent Republicans had been defeated in primaries since 2010, displeasing party activists could be career ending.

The July truce faltered on its shaky foundation. Again, it only takes a single senator to filibuster, so in order for the Republicans to abide by the truce, they needed to unanimously agree not to block a nomination or to provide enough votes to defeat the filibuster. A small core of Republican senators, such as Ted Cruz, R-Tex., were eager to display their conservative bona fides even if it meant embarrassing their colleagues, so they continued to initiate filibusters against nominations. By late October 2013, the nomination process was stalled again. A cloture vote on Mel Watts to be director of the Federal Housing Finance Agency failed, and three nominations for the D.C. Circuit Court were stalled as well.

The revival of Republican obstruction triggered a nuclear option by the Democratic majority. On November 21, 2013, Reid moved to return to the nomination of one of the stalled D.C. judges, Patricia Millett, then made a point of order that a simple majority was required to invoke cloture on all nominations other than for the Supreme Court. The presiding officer, following the rules and precedents of the Senate, rejected this claim, but the presiding officer's ruling was subject to a simple-majority vote. In a pair of 52–48 votes, the Senate supported Reid's bold "interpretation" of the cloture rule's three-fifths cloture threshold. Every Republican and three Democrats voted against this proposal, but the majority succeeded in changing the way the Senate works. While this vote was clearly partisan, it is notable that the Republican reaction was fairly mild. The debate leading up to this vote was brief, with McConnell making a single dilatory motion to adjourn to test the Democrats' resolve; the motion failed 46–54. In contrast, the debate over the 1975 cloture rule stretched for days, with dozens of intricate parliamentary motions, rulings, and votes, all intended to tie up the Senate and stave off major reform. On some level, it appears the Republicans accepted this reform while hinting that it could be very difficult to preserve the remaining right to filibuster legislation and Supreme Court nominations.

The Aftermath: Nominations in the 113th Congress

What happened after the nuclear option? Remember, the reason it is called the "nuclear option" is because the minority party's ability to retaliate with its remaining weaponry is supposed to deter majority power grabs. If the majority party makes major changes by simple-majority ruling, the minority party is supposed to respond with vigorous obstruction. The Republicans played their part in this narrative. While they could no longer block a nomination by mustering forty-one votes against it, they could require the majority party to invoke cloture on any and every nomination passing through the Senate, including many that would have previously gained approval without a roll call vote.

One measure of the Republican response is the sheer number of votes required to process nominations through the Senate. Before 2013, cloture votes on nominations were relatively infrequent; the highest number of cloture votes on nominations in a year was the seventeen votes held in 2003. There were nineteen votes before the Senate "went nuclear" on November 21, 2013, so 2013 was already a record year. From that day to the end of the 114th Congress, there were 131 cloture votes on nominations—more than the 112 votes *total* in the previous ninety-six years. This pattern is displayed in Figure 13-4, which shows the number of cloture votes on nominations per year since 2001.

This surge in nomination-related votes did not reflect a general increase in the number of votes. Including votes on approval of nominations, 254 of the 366 Senate roll call votes in 2014 pertained to nominations. That is, just 30.7 percent of all 2014 votes were related to the other responsibilities of the Senate. Nor did the increased number of votes reflect a more liberal set of nominees proposed by

Figure 13-4 Cloture Votes on Nominations, 2001–2014

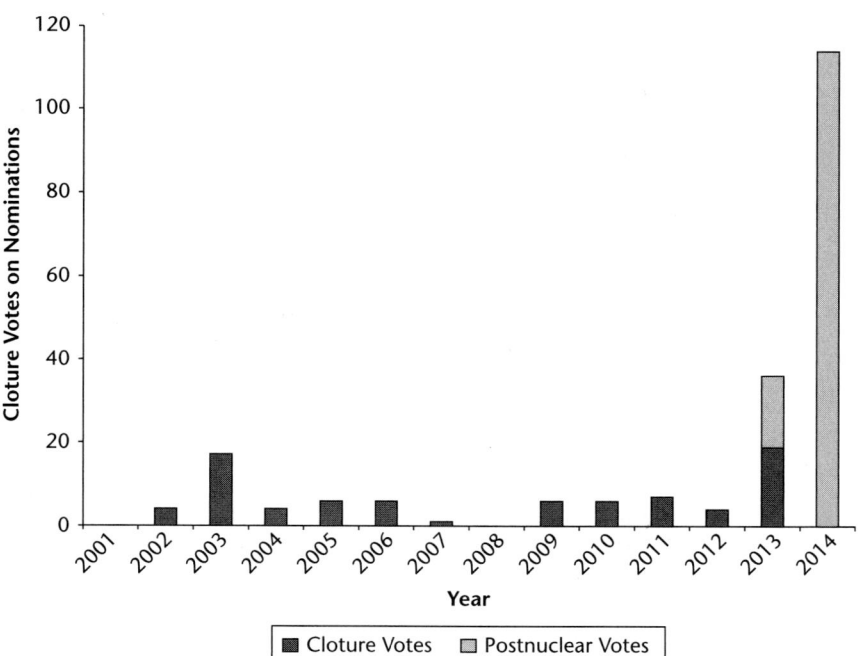

Source: http://www.senate.gov/pagelayout/reference/cloture_motions/clotureCounts.htm

President Obama—one study found that the postnuclear judicial nominees were generally similar to nominees from before November 2013.[35]

To be fair, the Democratic focus on nominations also reflects their electoral strategy of trying to protect their incumbents from a poor national political environment (a midterm election and low presidential approval ratings) by "localizing" the 2014 elections. Part of that strategy was avoiding controversial policy debates on the Senate floor, so it suited the Democrats' interests to focus the floor agenda on processing nominations rather than legislation. As a result, the average time for the Senate to make a decision on a nomination dropped from 185 days to 130 days while the confirmation rate of nominations increased from 62 percent to 80 percent.[36]

Looking Forward

The November 2013 "nuclear option" reform only applied to executive nominations and to judicial appointments other than nominations to the Supreme Court. Treaties, Supreme Court nominations, and most legislation are still susceptible to filibusters.[37] Yet this reform may portend the beginning of the end for the Senate filibuster.

One reason is that a significant number of Senate Democrats are skeptical of the benefits of filibustering. For Democrats elected from 2006 to 2012, their first experience with obstruction has been watching their party's legislative agenda and nominations slowed and blocked by filibustering. Often, Democrats considered the Republicans' justifications for obstruction to be thin excuses for political gamesmanship. While these senators are currently in the minority and experiencing the benefits of obstruction, if these Democrats return to united control of the legislative process, they will be unlikely to accept stalemate again.

Second, the specific method the Democrats used in 2013 lends itself to future reforms. Essentially, Reid argued that the Senate's cloture rule *means* something that is clearly inconsistent with its text. This claim was not explicitly based on any constitutional claims, parliamentary precedents, or nuanced exegesis of the rule. There was no reason given, for example, for exempting Supreme Court nominations. In a recent article with Sergio Campos on the use of parliamentary precedents to limit obstruction, we note that it is definitely *possible* for senators to simply declare that the Senate's cloture rule has some new meaning; this is an especially bold option when compared to the other possible paths to majoritarian reform.[38] The 2013 precedent made clear to senators and observers that the "right" to filibuster will only last until the majority party decides to finish the job, unless there is a bipartisan agreement to restore the balance between action and deliberation.

Conclusion

This chapter has traced the emergence of the modern Senate, in which the informal right of any senator to obstruct, subject to a supermajority vote, is defining the institution of the chamber. Senators did not deliberately choose this system.

It developed as the by-product of a switch in the majority's typical response to a filibuster threat. Instead of forcing senators to follow through on their threat to consume the time of the chamber, Senate majorities began to rely on low-cost cloture votes instead. This switch made sense in the early 1960s but removed the primary impediment to filibustering, so senators began to make an escalating number of filibuster threats, leading to ever more cloture votes. This trend has coincided with increasing partisanship in the Senate, and as these trends intersect, the Senate has become a partisan battleground, as each party competes for public approval by forcing supermajority votes on its public message while treating the legislative process as a zero-sum game. Critically, the minority party in the Senate is able to obstruct legislation to advance its political interests.

The "right" to filibuster was severely limited in November 2013 when the Democratic majority reinterpreted its rules to prohibit obstruction against executive and judicial branch nominations, leaving only Supreme Court nominations vulnerable to a filibuster. The short-term consequences of this action were to allow the Democrats to approve dozens of nominations, albeit at the cost of hours of Senate floor time. The medium-term consequence of the 2013 reform is to make it more likely that senators will use the same tactic to convert the Senate into a simple-majority legislature.

Notes

1. The cloture threshold for resolutions to change the standing rules of the Senate is different: two-thirds of those voting on the question. In addition, some measures are protected from filibusters by laws that impose a time limit on their consideration, such as budget resolutions and budget reconciliation bills.
2. Gregory Koger, *Filibustering: A Political History of Obstruction in the House and Senate* (Chicago: University of Chicago Press, 2010); Bruce I. Oppenheimer, "Changing Time Constraints on Congress: Historical Perspectives on the Use of Cloture," in *Congress Reconsidered*, 3rd ed., ed. Lawrence C. Dodd and Bruce I. Oppenheimer (Washington, DC: CQ Press, 1985); Barbara Sinclair, "The 60-Vote Senate," in *U.S. Senate Exceptionalism*, ed. Bruce I. Oppenheimer (Columbus: Ohio State University Press, 2002).
3. In state legislatures, legislators may even flee the state to avoid being rounded up by state authorities and forcibly returned to the legislature to provide a quorum. This has occurred, for example, in Rhode Island (1924), Texas (2003), and Wisconsin (2011).
4. Koger, *Filibustering*, 39–95.
5. On the 1917 cloture rule, see Gregory Koger, "Filibuster Reform in the Senate, 1913–1917," in *Party, Process, and Political Change in Congress: Further New Perspectives on the History of Congress*, 2nd ed., ed. David W. Brady and Mathew D. McCubbins (Stanford, CA: Stanford University Press, 2007), 205–25. On the Senate's subsequent rejection of majority rule, see Gregory Koger, "Cloture Reform and Party Government in the Senate, 1918–1925," *Journal of Politics* 68 (2006): 708–19.
6. Koger, *Filibustering*, 109–11.
7. Donald Matthews, *U.S. Senators and Their World* (Chapel Hill: University of North Carolina Press, 1960).

8. On the dissolution of Senate norms, see Barbara Sinclair, *The Transformation of the U.S. Senate* (Baltimore: Johns Hopkins University Press, 1989), and Steven S. Smith, *Call to Order: Floor Politics in the House and Senate* (Washington, DC: Brookings Institution Press, 1989). On support for reform, see Julian E. Zelizer, *On Capitol Hill: The Struggle to Reform Congress and Its Consequences, 1948–2000* (New York: Cambridge University Press, 2004). Former senator Fred Harris stresses the importance of a 1975 reform that ensured that support staff would be distributed broadly across all senators, instead of the previous system in which legislative aides tended to work for committees. Fred Harris, *Deadlock or Decision: The U.S. Senate and the Rise of National Politics* (New York: Oxford University Press, 1993).
9. Gregory Koger, "The Filibuster Then and Now: Civil Rights in the 1960s and Health Care, 2009–10," in *The U.S. Senate: From Deliberation to Dysfunction*, ed. Burdett A. Loomis (Washington, DC: CQ Press, 2011).
10. Oppenheimer, "Time Constraints."
11. Koger, *Filibustering*. On visiting activists, see James Q. Wilson, *The Amateur Democrat: Club Politics in Three Cities* (Chicago: University of Chicago Press, 1962).
12. See opensecrets.org. The individual contribution limits for the 2014 election cycle were $2,600 per person per election and $5,000 per election for multicandidate PACs.
13. At the same time, the costs of a single filibuster to the Senate decreased as well. Instead of allowing a single bill to occupy the Senate floor for weeks, Senate party leaders can minimize the amount of time spent on filibustered bills by quickly bringing them up, filing a cloture petition, and then setting them aside while the chamber moves on to bills and nominations that are *not* facing a threatened filibuster.
14. Koger, *Filibustering*. For the filibuster measure, I scanned the *New York Times*, *Congress and the Nation*, *Time* magazine, and *Editorial Research Reports* (1923–1956) for articles using the term "filibuster" or, for the *New York Times*, "Senate" and "filibuster." For each article, I then coded the legislative measure that was the target of the filibuster.
15. C. Lawrence Evans and Walter Oleszek, "Message Politics and Senate Procedure," in *The Contentious Senate: Partisanship, Ideology, and the Myth of Cool Judgment*, ed. Colton C. Campbell and Nicol C. Rae (Lanham, MD: Rowman & Littlefield, 2001), 107–27.
16. Walter J. Oleszek, *"Holds" in the Senate* (Washington, DC: Congressional Research Service, 2008).
17. Koger, *Filibustering*, 173–76.
18. Oleszek, *"Holds"*, 1–2. Emphasis in original.
19. Joseph Lawler, "Rand Paul Threatens to Hold Federal Reserve Nominees Unless His Fed Audit Gets a Vote," *Washington Examiner*, May 12, 2014, http://www.washingtonexaminer.com/rand-paul-threatens-to-hold-up-nominees-unless-his-fed-audit-gets-a-vote/article/2548347; Joe Gould, "McCain Presses Senator to Break Impasse on Fanning Nomination," *Defense News*, April 6, 2016, http://www.defensenews.com/story/defense/2016/04/06/mccain-presses-senator-break-impasse-fanning-nomination/82708948; Joe Gould, "Ayotte Places Hold on DoD Counsel Nominee Over Guantanamo Report," *Defense News*, April 5, 2016, http://www.defensenews.com/story/defense/2016/04/05/ayotte-places-hold-dod-counsel-nominee-over-guantanamo-report/82652268.
20. Walter J. Oleszek, *Proposals to Reform "Holds" in the Senate* (Washington, DC: Congressional Research Service, 2011).

21. On partisan polarization in the Senate, see Sean M. Theriault, *Party Polarization in Congress* (New York: Cambridge University Press, 2008). For the figure, votes that require more than a simple majority are excluded. The polarization of the Senate is often depicted in terms of DW-NOMINATE scores, developed by Keith Poole and Howard Rosenthal. These scores are very useful for some purposes, but they assume a high level of stability in the voting pattern of individual legislators, and this assumption effectively smooths trends in partisanship across time. The statistic used in Figure 13-3 is calculated independently for each Congress.
22. Koger, *Filibustering*.
23. On legislative actions and party reputations, see Gary W. Cox and Mathew D. McCubbins, *Legislative Leviathan: Party Government in the House*, 2nd ed. (New York: Cambridge University Press, 2007); Gregory Koger and Matthew J. Lebo, *Strategic Party Government: Why Winning Trumps Ideology* (Chicago: University of Chicago Press, 2017); and Patrick J. Egan, *Partisan Priorities: How Issue Ownership Drives and Distorts American Politics* (New York: Cambridge University Press, 2013).
24. Anne Kim and Niels Lesniewski, "Democrats Stick Together to Stop Health Care Law Repeal," *CQ Weekly Report*, February 7, 2011, 305.
25. Evans and Oleszek, "Message Politics."
26. Carl Hulse and Adam Nagourney, "Senate G.O.P. Leader Finds Weapon in Unity," *New York Times*, March 17, 2010, A13.
27. Gregory Koger, "The Filibuster Then and Now: Civil Rights in the 1960s and Health Care, 2009–10," in *The U.S. Senate: From Deliberation to Dysfunction* ed. Burdette A. Loomis (Washington, DC: CQ Press, 2011), 159–77.
28. See Chris Den Hartog and Nathan W. Monroe for a broader discussion and analysis of the calculus of Senate agenda setting, including the notion that obstruction imposes an extra "price" on targeted legislation. Chris Den Hartog and Nathan W. Monroe, *Agenda Setting in the U.S. Senate: Costly Consideration and Majority Party Advantage* (New York: Cambridge University Press, 2011).
29. Manu Raju and Scott Wong, "Dems Change Rules; Senate in Chaos," *Politico*, October 6, 2011, http://www.politico.com/news/stories/1011/65383.html.
30. Gregory Koger and Sergio J. Campos, "The Conventional Option," *Washington University Law Review* 91 (2014): 867–909. Another reform effort was launched in May 2012, when Common Cause filed a lawsuit arguing that the filibuster is unconstitutional. This suit was rejected at the district and appellate levels, and the Supreme Court refused to hear it. See David McCabe, "Justices Reject Challenge to Senate Filibuster Rules," *The Hill*, November 3, 2014, http://thehill.com/blogs/blog-briefing-room/news/222633-justices-reject-challenge-to-senate-filibuster-rules.
31. Helene Cooper and Jennifer Steinhauer, "Bucking Senate, Obama Appoints Consumer Chief," *New York Times*, January 4, 2012, A1. The Supreme Court later invalidated the appointments, stating that the Congress was not in a long-term "recess." See National Labor Relations Board v. Noel Canning et al., 573 U.S. ___ (2014).
32. Manu Raju, "Reid Threatens to Nuke Filibuster," *Politico*, January 22, 2013, http://www.politico.com/story/2013/01/reid-mcconnell-meet-on-filibuster-086551.
33. Gregory Koger, "Proposed Senate Reforms: Recap and Discussion," *Mischiefs of Faction* (blog), January 24, 2013, http://www.mischiefsoffaction.com/2013/01/proposed-senate-reforms-recap-and.html.
34. Humberto Sanchez and Niels Lesniewski, "Deal Defuses 'Nuclear Option' in Senate (Updated)," *Roll Call*, July 16, 2013, http://blogs.rollcall.com/wgdb/nuclear-option-may-be-averted-in-the-senate.

35. Christina L. Boyd, Michael S. Lynch, and Anthony J. Madonna, "Nuclear Fallout: Investigating the Effect of Senate Procedural Reform on Judicial Nominations," *The Forum* 13 (2016): 623–41.
36. Ibid., 635–36.
37. Some legislation, such as budget resolutions and budget reconciliation bills, are protected from filibusters by previous statutes. See Molly E. Reynolds, "From Base Closings to the Budget: Exceptions to the Filibuster in the United States Senate," in *Party and Procedure in the United States Congress*, 2nd ed., ed. Jacob R. Straus and Matthew Glassman (Lanham, MD: Rowman and Littlefield, 2017), 235–60.
38. Koger and Campos, "Conventional Option." An example of a less direct approach would be to develop precedents that convert the Senate's motion to suspend the rules from a debatable question requiring a two-thirds majority into a nondebatable simple-majority motion.

14. ANWR and CAFE

Frustrating Energy Production and Conservation Initiatives in Congress Over Three Decades

Bruce I. Oppenheimer

This chapter compares the parallel struggles over whether to enact and increase CAFE standards on motor vehicles and whether to remove the ban on oil exploration in ANWR over three decades. Three overriding conceptual arguments structure the narrative of these two energy issues. First, both issues demonstrate the difficulty Congress has in enacting legislation that has short-term costs and long-term benefits, except under unusual circumstances. Second, the historical analysis of both issues suggests that the move from a committee-centered Congress with weak parties to a far more party-centered institution has made the enactment of legislation more difficult. Third, by examining an issue that proponents of a production approach favored (ANWR), as well as one that proponents of a conservation approach favored (CAFE), I am able to demonstrate the frustration that both sides faced in trying to get Congress to enact legislation and the growing strength of blocking forces in the congressional process.

In this chapter, I examine the struggle over two energy policy issues, CAFE (Corporate Average Fuel Economy) standards and whether to allow exploration and drilling for oil in ANWR (the Arctic National Wildlife Refuge), that played out over an extended part of the period since the initial crisis of the OPEC (Organization of the Petroleum Exporting Countries) embargo in 1973. Much of the chapter will be narrative, detailing the frustration that proponents of policy change had to confront and their lack of success. The purpose of the narrative is to make three major points about the ability of Congress to address major policy concerns and how that has changed over time. First, Congress has great difficulty resolving energy policy issues (and other similar types of issues) and is able to do so only in certain contexts, if at all. Second, the change from relatively weak parties in the Congress of the 1970s to the stronger, more cohesive, and more polarized parties of conditional party government made the resolution of energy issues more difficult, not less so, as many may have anticipated. And third, both sides in the energy policy struggle were frustrated in their efforts to enact legislation. One side has favored conservation and renewable-energy policy approaches, including increasing CAFE standards, and the other has advocated increased exploration for and production of fossil fuels, such as drilling in ANWR, as the way to address the problem of energy dependence. Both had sizable support in the public, in the interest group community, and among government decision makers in Congress and in the executive branch.

In studying congressional energy policy efforts over a more than forty-year time frame, I have been struck with how ironic the struggle has been. On the one hand, decision makers have broadly agreed on an overall policy goal of making the United States less dependent on foreign energy sources. Every president from Nixon through Obama articulated the goal of "energy independence" or the more modest goal of reduced energy dependence. Congressional leaders of both parties in the House and the Senate have consistently favored that policy goal as well. And nearly every national convention platform of both parties throughout the period has included a plank favoring reduced energy dependence. Yet from the time of the OPEC embargo until 2008, except for a few years in the early 1980s, the level of U.S. dependence on imported oil was as high—and often higher—than at the time of the OPEC embargo. Only in recent years has dependence dropped markedly due to a number of factors: the worldwide economic recession, beginning in 2008, that lowered energy demand; recent technological changes, such as fracking; the development of new domestic sources of oil and natural gas; and the inability of OPEC to reduce oil production in response to a decline in demand.[1]

As issues, CAFE standards and ANWR have a number of features that make them appropriate choices for comparison. Their origins date back to the 1970s, although sustained efforts to allow drilling in ANWR did not fully manifest themselves until the late 1980s. Second, both were high-profile energy issues that mobilized both conservation and production forces in the broader energy policy debate. Third, at various times, some members of Congress tried unsuccessfully to merge support for the two issues through a compromise in omnibus energy legislation that would exchange the removal of the ban on drilling in ANWR for the raising of CAFE standards.

One cannot easily blame this failure to achieve a stated policy goal of reducing dependence on foreign energy sources on conditions of party control of government. After all, since 1973, the United States has experienced every combination of party control of government—unified Democratic control, unified Republican control, divided control with Democratic presidents and with Republican presidents, and divided control with the party of the president controlling one house of Congress and neither house. Notably, the one missing contextual condition for much of this period, especially since the parties have become stronger and more cohesive, is that in periods of unified party control, neither party has had large majorities. As I will suggest later, when majorities are narrow, the strategic behavior of cohesive congressional parties may make policy resolutions unusually difficult.

Before I present a detailed analysis of the legislative histories of CAFE and ANWR, first let us consider some of the broader reasons why Congress and a series of presidential administrations have had difficulty resolving energy issues.

Issues That Suit Legislatures

A major problem that Congress has faced in dealing with energy legislation since 1973 has been that energy issues generally are not the types of policies that legislatures and their members are comfortable in addressing.² The literature is filled with sound theorizing and empirical analysis supporting the idea that Congress and its members find it easiest to enact two broad types of legislation. One is pork barrel or distributive in nature because it allows members to concentrate benefits and disperse costs.³ When effectively logrolling with other members on programs that service their constituencies, members take credit for obtaining material benefits for their districts and states without seemingly conferring traceable costs on their constituents. Thus, members receive credit from their constituents when elections occur, without giving potential opponents a visible basis for criticizing them.⁴

The second and related method is one Douglas Arnold explores in his book, *The Logic of Congressional Action*. Arnold asks, How is it that Congress sometimes passes legislation in which costs are not dispersed? He credits congressional leaders with being able to design the legislation in a way that facilitates persuading members that the costs are not traceable. This often involves supplying the benefits of programs in the near term while deferring the costs to some later date. Again, the key is that the leaders persuade their members that a potential electoral opponent cannot use public dissatisfaction with policy costs as a campaign issue.⁵

To these two types, we might also add circumstances where majorities of both parties are willing to support policy changes that exact short-term costs on constituents because broad bipartisan backing inoculates members against either party using the issue in the upcoming campaign. The 1990 Omnibus Budget Reconciliation Act and the 1990 Budget Enforcement Act provide a good example of an effort to avoid electoral damage. As James Thurber observed, "The bipartisan agreements were intended to . . . provide political cover for unpopular election-year decisions."⁶ These three do not exhaust the types of legislation that members of Congress find it relatively easy to support, but they are the methods that political scientists most frequently mention.⁷

Most energy policy proposals do not share any of these qualities, at least not in recent decades.⁸ Instead, they require the public to incur short-term costs to reap long-term benefits. These costs may come in the form of higher energy prices, increased taxes, increased costs of consumer goods (cars, appliances, and heating and cooling systems), higher levels of air and water pollution, more unemployment, and safety concerns. Support for such policies exposes members and their parties to potential electoral vulnerability. This is especially true because competing sides in the energy policy debate are highly critical of the policy proposals of the other side. (Yes, as will be evident in the CAFE and ANWR cases, proponents have, at times, tried to include pork barrel elements that concentrate benefits and disperse costs as a means of attracting additional support and to offset some of the political costs of supporting legislation.) Accordingly, Congress has only passed significant energy legislation when the short-term political costs from maintaining the status quo exceed the short-term political costs of adopting policy changes.⁹

Arnold, in his case example of energy legislation in the mid-1970s, properly credits the skill of party leaders in limiting traceability of policy costs for the success in resolving some energy issues. Congress, however, faced rising energy prices and uncertainties about the supply of gasoline and heating oil in the aftermath of the embargo and also had to weigh the political consequences of maintaining the status quo against the short-term costs of policy change. Even under these circumstances, Congress took until 1980 to resolve all of the key energy issues in a series of separate legislative packages. Once energy prices and supplies stabilized, the incentives for Congress to address energy policy abated. And that is a story that repeats over the forty-year period. For example, if one examines the trends in gasoline prices from 1973 to 2012, Congress passes and the president signs major energy legislation only when there is a sustained period of high prices and/or limited supply. Then, political costs of inaction outweigh the short-term cost of passing new legislation.

Initial Enactment of CAFE Standards and a Ban on Drilling in ANWR

The enactment of the first set of CAFE standards occurred in 1975, in an era when political parties and party leadership in Congress were still weak. Democratic majorities in the House and Senate were large and seemingly permanent. In the aftermath of Watergate, Democrats held sixty Senate seats and a two-to-one advantage in the House after the 1974 election, but it was not a highly cohesive majority. In both chambers, Democrats had an average party unity score of only 75 percent in the Ninety-fourth Congress (1975–1976). The recently adopted Subcommittee Bill of Rights had reduced the power of committee chairs, but it had also further decentralized decision making in the House. Some additional powers were seemingly available to the party leadership. Speaker Carl Albert, D-Okla., however, was reluctant to use them fully.[10] In March 1975, the Senate did change the cloture requirements from two-thirds present and voting to three-fifths of the membership. The number of cloture votes dropped for the remainder of that Congress but then increased, and the success of cloture motions had a modest gain. The rule change did not make Senate party leadership appreciably stronger in its ability to influence the behavior of its members. Moreover, the Ford presidency meant that there was divided party control, with differing preferences for energy policy in Congress and in the White House, although it was not uncommon for constituency preferences to take precedence over party ones when the two conflicted.

The existence of high and unstable oil and gas prices and uncertainty about supplies in the aftermath of the embargo proved critical in reaching an accommodation on CAFE standards and on some other energy issues. Both sides rejected the use of rationing or higher gasoline taxes to reduce consumption. In his 1975 State of the Union address, President Ford argued that "neither would achieve the desired results and both would produce unacceptable inequities."[11] Congressional Democrats concluded that "the cross elasticity between gasoline prices and the fuel economy of new cars is very low, and . . . lifetime fuel costs still have too little effect on consumer automobile purchasing power."[12] With automobiles accounting for 40 percent of domestic petroleum consumption, it was impossible to maintain the status quo. The Ford administration, siding with the domestic automobile companies, opposed imposing fuel economy standards and instead called for voluntary efforts from the auto industry, with a goal of a 40 percent improvement in fuel economy by 1980. The UAW, in contrast, was generally accepting of some required mileage standard.

In the Senate, the energy package was initially considered as four separate pieces of legislation, with the Commerce Committee having jurisdiction over automobile fuel economy. Its hearings in March 1975 built on nine previous days of hearings in the Ninety-third Congress that considered a variety of automobile fuel economy proposals. The end product was one largely developed within the committee, albeit one over which Democrats held sway. The bill called for instituting mileage standards for automobiles beginning with the 1977 model year, with a fuel economy standard reaching 28 mpg by 1985. The committee softened the blow, allowing the secretary of transportation to modify the 1980 and 1985 standards in adopting an amendment from auto state senator Philip Hart, D-Mich. Hart's fellow Michigander, Robert Griffin, R-Mich., provided the major opposition to the CAFE standards in the committee and on the floor. His floor amendment to delay implementation of the standards for a year and his subsequent motion to recommit the bill were handily defeated. At no point did Griffin indicate any intention to filibuster the bill. Even with the Ford administration's opposition to government-imposed mileage standards, the thirty-six Senate Republicans who voted on the bill split evenly, and the bill passed 63–21.

The House also proceeded in a committee-dominated fashion. Unlike the Senate, however, all the nontax aspects of energy legislation were contained in a single piece of legislation, H.R. 7014, over which the Committee on Interstate and Foreign Commerce had jurisdiction. The major focus of debate was on the sections dealing with the continuation and modifications of oil price controls, not the automobile fuel efficiency provisions contained in Title V of the bill. Nevertheless, the committee's Energy and Power Subcommittee held an extended hearing on the mileage issue. Clarence "Bud" Brown Jr., R-Ohio, the subcommittee's ranking minority member, tried to delete the 28 mpg standard for 1985 during floor consideration, arguing that "neither Congress nor anyone else knows how to accomplish the 28-mile-per-gallon standard by 1985."[13] John Dingell, D-Mich., the subcommittee's chair and bill manager and a strong UAW and auto industry ally in the House, led the opposition to the Brown amendment, clearly siding with the UAW's position about the manufacture of more fuel-efficient vehicles. The amendment was defeated handily, but eight of the other eleven auto state Democrats supported Brown's amendment, whereas Republicans only split 72–62 in favor of it. As in the Senate, the competing coalitions engaged a mix of constituency and party forces. The majority party leadership did not use the rule to restrict the amendment process substantially on the House floor, as twenty-four amendments received roll call votes.

Although Republicans opposed the bill on final passage by more than three to one, and Democrats supported it by over five to one, the parties had not moved in lockstep through floor consideration. The conference report scheduled CAFE standards for cars to reach 20 mpg by 1980, in yearly steps, and then increase to 27.5 mpg by 1985 and thereafter. The DOT secretary could make downward adjustments, if necessary, and set lower mileage standards for light trucks. Party loyalty again prevailed in approving the conference report in both chambers. But Majority Leader Tip O'Neill offered a more nuanced and accurate picture of the entire bill when he observed, "This is perhaps the most parochial issue that could ever hit the floor."[14] He then went on to discuss all of the geographic cleavages that affected consideration but did not mention party. Despite the congressional Republicans voting against the bill and little evidence that either chamber was capable of overriding a veto, President Ford signed the bill. He expressed reservations but acknowledged the political and electoral realities: "If I were to veto this bill, the debates of the past year would almost surely continue through the election year and beyond."[15] Bill proponents in a Democratic-controlled Congress had allowed for changes both in the overall legislation and in CAFE standards to produce a bill that President Ford could accept. It also meant that some issues—most notably, a final decision on how to decontrol oil prices—were left unresolved.

The initial set of CAFE standards was enacted largely in a give-and-take context, with a mix of constituency, interest group, and partisan forces in play. Opponents to setting standards and to the legislation more generally, however, were not willing to be veto players, even if they preferred the status quo to the proposed policy changes. The potential electoral costs of blocking action in a period of high energy prices and uncertainty about supply meant that it was better to pass legislation and take the issue off the table before the 1976 campaign began. For much the same reason, those who favored CAFE standards realized that they could support the mileage requirements without suffering electoral consequences. Moreover, with large Democratic majorities in both the House and the Senate and the expectation that they would persist, there was little incentive for Republicans to engage in a strategy of obstruction, making the Democrats appear incapable of governing and using that strategy to win control of Congress in the 1976 election. In addition, failure to produce energy legislation would reflect badly on the Ford administration as well and might hurt the reelection prospects of Republicans. Under these circumstances, Republican members had a strong incentive to resolve some of the energy issues, even if it meant supporting—or, at least, not blocking— a policy position that was farther from their ideal point than was the status quo.

ANWR Ban

The first legislative struggle over ANWR was decidedly less complex than with CAFE. The ban on oil and gas drilling in ANWR was a small issue in a much larger piece of legislation establishing national parks and wilderness areas in Alaska. As an outgrowth of the Alaska Native Claims Settlement Act of 1971,

Congress had to make decisions about lands to be protected from development by 1978. When it appeared that the struggle between environmental and development forces would prevent the deadline from being met, the Carter administration placed certain lands under protection. This decision broke the legislative deadlock, as pro-development forces in Congress preferred a legislative solution to the one that the Carter administration would otherwise implement. With the Reagan landslide in the 1980 election, the lame-duck session produced a bill that moved the resolution of remaining controversies marginally away from those environmentalists' favored. In the case of ANWR, it meant that the ban on drilling would not necessarily be permanent, allowing Congress to remove it after the Interior Department completed a study of the environmental impact and the potential for oil and gas production there. As with CAFE, legislating on ANWR and the broader issue of how much land to protect from development in Alaska involved trying to reach compromises in which a range of cleavages and interests came into play that cut across party lines. Alaska's senators, Mike Gravel (D) and Ted Stevens (R), although of differing parties, threatened to block action at points in the process but largely in response to local issues and interests.[16] Like some of the other energy issues in the immediate post-embargo years, the issue of banning drilling in ANWR and other issues covered in the Alaska National Interest Lands Conservation Act (ANILCA) were not ones Congress easily resolved. Parties played a role, as did the preferences of the Nixon, Ford, and Carter administrations. But they were not tightly cohesive, and at no time did they seem to have an incentive to block the various forces from achieving resolution. Interest group cleavages cut across parties, thus muting their role, instead of reinforcing existing party differences and serving as the basis for building electoral advantage.

With energy prices remaining high and concerns about availability of gasoline and heating oil persisting, Congress eventually resolved a range of energy policy issues between 1975 and 1980. The potential political costs for House members and senators of maintaining the status quo were sufficiently high that they were willing to compromise and support positions that were farther from their "ideal point" in policy terms than was the status quo. And parties and their leaders, not yet strong enough to hold their members' median party positions, instead moved toward median chamber positions to resolve policy differences. Still, resolution of most issues took nearly six years to complete.

Blocking Policy Change

The second period is one during which an increasingly party-dominated Congress enacted few energy policy changes. Most initiatives, including those to increase CAFE standards and to remove the ban on drilling in ANWR, were blocked. Without a sustained crisis for more than two decades, the short-term political costs for members of making nonincremental changes in policy to achieve the longer-term benefits of reduced energy dependence were too great. Even as energy prices again escalated, especially after 2001, energy issues were more difficult to resolve than had been the case in the 1970s. The presence of stronger, more polarized parties in Congress meant that it was easier for the majority party to mobilize its members, but it also meant that the minority was more cohesive in blocking legislation. In addition, after Republicans won control of Congress in the 1994 election, increased electoral competition between the two congressional parties made compromise more difficult, lest the majority party be seen as governing competently. Instead of cooperating in producing long-term policy solutions and insulating each other from electoral damage, blocking majority party and presidential initiatives and reaping electoral gains took precedence. In this environment, it was not until 2007 that Congress passed and President Bush reluctantly signed a bill increasing CAFE standards. But under the most favorable contextual circumstances in the 2001 to 2006 period, Republicans were unable to overcome opposition to ANWR drilling.

The Struggle Over CAFE Standards and the ANWR Drilling Ban, 1985 to 2006

Gasoline prices peaked in 1981 but remained at levels well above those of 1975 until 1985. As the energy crisis abated, GM and Ford successfully lobbied the Department of Transportation through its National Highway Transportation Safety Administration (NHTSA) to roll back the CAFE target from 27.5 to 26 mpg. Congress was unable to block NHTSA from doing so, and the 26-mpg standard for passenger automobiles remained in place until 1989, when it finally rose to 27.5. By that time, the real-dollar cost of gasoline, which had been declining since 1981, had been lower than pre-OPEC-embargo prices for more than three years. As would again be the case in 2015 and 2016, OPEC was seemingly in disarray and unable to enforce cooperation among its members to limit supply in a period of declining demand. The energy crisis had abated, and public and governmental concern in the United States focused on the health of the domestic automobile industry, not increasing fuel efficiency.[17]

Similarly, it was hard for those who favored production approaches to engender much support for removing the ban on drilling in ANWR. The incentives for exploration and drilling in high-cost regions waned during a period of low prices and plentiful supplies. The report on the environmental impact and potential oil and gas reserves in ANWR required years to complete. In 1987, the Reagan administration finally took a stronger posture on ANWR when Interior Secretary Hodel reported back to the Congress and recommended that the ban on leasing and drilling in ANWR be removed. Alaska's House member, Republican Don Young, became the major proponent for opening up ANWR and introduced legislation to do so that garnered 145 cosponsors. House Interior and Insular Affairs Committee chair Mo Udall, D-Ariz., mobilized the opposition and offered legislation (with eighty-eight cosponsors) to close ANWR permanently. Through the remainder of the One Hundredth Congress, a series of hearings on ANWR in four congressional committees and legislative markups demonstrated the jurisdictional stalemate. In the Senate, the Energy Committee reported a bill lifting the ban while the Environment Committee considered legislation naming ANWR a wilderness. And when the House Merchant Marine and Fisheries Committee reported legislation that would phase in areas open to drilling in ANWR, it was sequentially referred to Udall's Interior Committee, which buried the legislation. Committee Democrats did not want to take a tough vote on a bill that was not going to survive, and Senate Energy Committee chair Bennett Johnston, D-La., a proponent of drilling in ANWR, was not going to push his bill to the Senate floor before the House acted.[18]

By the time the 27.5-mpg standard had been reached, and the Reagan administration was recommending removal of the ban on drilling in ANWR, parties in both the House and the Senate had become stronger, more ideologically homogeneous, and more cohesive than they had been in 1975.[19] Especially in the House, the majority party leadership had more resources with which to mobilize its membership to pass legislation. Increasingly, the sides on the energy debate organized along party lines, with those favoring production-oriented solutions and reliance on fossil fuels more concentrated among Republican members and those advocating conservation and alternative fuels more concentrated among the Democrats. Minority positions on energy issues within each party's caucus gradually eroded as Republicans won the House and Senate seats that Democrats from oil- and gas-producing constituencies had held, and the number of moderate Republicans from consuming areas in the Northeast declined.[20] In turn, party positions on energy policy hardened.

Until the 2000s, when another energy crisis emerged, there was little impetus to enact significant energy legislation, such as increasing CAFE standards, because the short-term costs were too much of a political liability when the benefits were all in the future. With the competing sides on energy policy intense and fairly evenly divided, it was likely that floor consideration would be very time consuming, and in the end, no major legislation would be enacted. Opponents to increasing CAFE standards blocked even the potential for such action to occur, just as the opponents of production approaches blocked those as well. Even after energy prices began to increase dramatically, one party or the other prevented major energy policy change until 2007.[21]

This does not mean that there was a total absence of congressional activity on CAFE standards or ANWR. Most of it, however, was futile. In 1989, as the new Bush administration, Republicans in Congress, and remaining energy-producing-state Democrats began to push for oil and gas drilling in ANWR, some congressional Democrats countered with proposals to raise CAFE standards. Shortly after the Iraq invasion of Kuwait set off concerns about a new energy crisis, Senator Richard Bryan, D-Nev., and his Republican cosponsor, Slade Gorton, R-Wash., undertook an unsuccessful attempt to lessen the opposition of domestic auto producers to an increase in CAFE standards by requiring a percentage increase in company mileage standards over their fleetwide averages, thus putting a burden on foreign producers of smaller, more fuel-efficient vehicles and not just on domestic producers. Nevertheless, active opposition of the auto companies and the UAW, in addition to that of the Bush administration, defeated a cloture motion, as several auto state Democrats, Democrats from energy-producing states, and two-thirds of the Republicans coalesced to block a vote on the bill. Had it survived the Senate, it is unlikely that it would have passed the House because the members from strong UAW and auto industry constituencies were proportionately greater there than in the Senate.[22]

Proponents of ANWR exploration made initial headway on removing the drilling ban early in 1989. The new Bush administration included revenues from ANWR leasing in its budget for fiscal year 1990. And Johnston quickly moved a pro-ANWR bill out of the Energy Committee, largely with the support of the committee's Republican members. When the *Exxon Valdez* spill occurred on March 24, 1989, however, Congress "scuttled action" on ANWR for the next eighteen months.[23] Only with the potential of a Mideast war in the fall of 1990 did the administration again renew its efforts to remove the ANWR drilling ban. Interior Department assistant undersecretary Jim Hughes, however, acknowledged the disadvantage his pro-ANWR forces faced, noting that environmentalists had "the home field advantage because all they have to do is block us. Blocking is always easier than doing something affirmative."[24]

In a multiyear effort to pass a major energy bill, Johnston, in his position as Senate Energy Committee chair, tried to couple CAFE with ANWR.[25] He also hoped to take advantage of residual concern over the Gulf War to enact a package that included drilling in ANWR and electric-utility deregulation, among other things, but he recognized the political necessity of a change in CAFE standards if a comprehensive bill were to survive in the Senate. Party leaders, however, were no longer going to allow an autonomous committee chair to bring bills to the floor that were inconsistent with national party and caucus positions. Majority Leader George Mitchell, D-Maine, who opposed lifting the ANWR ban, had already appointed a sixteen-member party task force on energy that would require energy conservation provisions in any bill that reached the floor, including an increase in CAFE standards.[26] President Bush, meanwhile, threatened to veto a bill that mandated CAFE increases, eventually insisting that the administration decide on CAFE standards.

With the Persian Gulf crisis fading, Majority Leader Mitchell delayed bringing the bill to the Senate floor for months, by which time most of the controversial provisions had been stripped from the legislation. Johnston dropped the ANWR provision, and the bill only directed the DOT secretary to study CAFE standards. As in 1989, even if a CAFE increase had been included in the Senate bill, it is unlikely that the House would have agreed to it.

The Gulf War and the resulting energy crisis were relatively brief, even if they again raised concerns about energy dependence. The potential electoral costs of inaction on major energy issues were not as great as the costs of making major policy changes that would yield long-term benefits but impose short-term economic costs on the public. In addition, CAFE standard opponents in 1990 resorted to a filibuster, a tactic which opponents had not employed in 1975.

President Ford accepted some modifications while President Bush threatened a veto. Yet with Democrats in the majority in both chambers, Bush did not have the capacity to pass legislation to allow drilling in ANWR or to control its place on the Senate agenda, even with the support of the key Democratic committee chair. Signs of party and party leadership involvement increased. Johnston and his Energy and Natural Resources Committee did not have autonomy in crafting energy legislation. Majority Leader Mitchell and his energy task force were a significant constraint.

After the enactment of a stripped-down bill, energy policy generally and CAFE standards in particular ceased to be front-burner issues for Congress again until the Clinton presidency, and even then, legislative initiatives were limited, as energy prices remained low and party positions hardened. The Clinton administration's initial energy proposals dealt with energy taxes as a mean of encouraging conservation (and raising revenue) and not efficiency standards. When Republicans took control of Congress in 1995, the political situation flipped from what it had been during the Reagan and Bush presidencies. Instead of congressional Democrats (in the majority) blocking a Republican president on ANWR, Republican majorities in the House and Senate blocked the Clinton administration from exercising authority to raise CAFE standards. And just as Bush would have vetoed any increase in CAFE, Clinton stopped efforts of congressional Republicans to open ANWR.

In 1995, Majority Whip Tom DeLay, R-Tex., added a provision to the DOT appropriations bill prohibiting any increases in CAFE standards for cars or trucks, sending a clear message that it was a party position.[27] For the duration of the Clinton administration, Republicans put this restriction in each DOT appropriations bill.[28] In 1999, Senate Democrats offered an amendment to the bill that would have allowed the DOT to study whether to change CAFE standards. Even that modest step was blocked. The conferees again accepted the ban on spending for updating CAFE standards that was in the House bill, and President Clinton signed the appropriations bill. A year later, with gasoline prices quickly rising in real dollars to the highest price in fifteen years, auto state senators did agree to compromise, allowing for the DOT and the National Academy of Science to conduct a study of CAFE standards and letting the DOT propose an increase if the study supported a change. In exchange, however, any change in CAFE standards would require a vote by Congress, and the House rider continued for another year.[29]

During the eight years of the Clinton presidency, the prospects of opening ANWR significantly diminished. Not surprisingly, Clinton's energy package during the 103rd Congress did not include ANWR, and there was no impetus to add it in either the House or the Senate. In the year of euphoria after winning control of the House in 1994 for the first time in four decades, Republicans made an unsuccessful attempt to force Clinton to remove the ban on ANWR drilling. Republicans made efforts to include income from ANWR in the House and Senate budget resolutions and then in the reconciliation package for fiscal year 1996. ANWR had previously been part of Bush's budgets, but this was the first time it had survived as part of an omnibus reconciliation package and might become law, if a seemingly weakened president accepted Republican budgetary demands. When Clinton vetoed the package, it quickly became clear that the Republicans had overplayed their hand, more critically on their threat of a government shutdown but also on ANWR. In his veto message, Clinton specifically mentioned his opposition to removing the ban on drilling in ANWR as an example of the catchall nature of the omnibus budget package. It was not until 2000 that Republicans again pushed ANWR in the budget resolution as part of a broader effort to increase offshore production. The Senate narrowly included the provision, but the House did not. ANWR again died.

With the election of President George W. Bush in 2000 and continued Republican majorities for six years in the House and for most of that time in the Senate, the prospects for proponents of opening ANWR brightened considerably. But with very narrow House and Senate majorities, unified control of government was not sufficient to enact policy change. As gasoline prices increased markedly, especially after the onset of the Iraq War in 2003, Republican attention focused on increasing domestic energy supplies through tax incentives to encourage fossil fuel production, making ANWR accessible for exploration, and incentives for ethanol production and use.

CAFE, other conservation approaches, and the development of renewable sources were not the focus of the Bush administration or Republicans in Congress. The administration was even reluctant to support ethanol incentives but recognized their necessity in garnering the support of farm state House members and senators. In the 107th Congress (2001–2002), neither the House nor the Senate version of the energy bill included mandatory increases in CAFE standards, although the bills provided guidelines that would likely lead to very modest increases.[30] As I will discuss in greater detail below, that bill died in the Senate, where Democrats briefly returned to majority status after Senator Jim Jeffords, I-Vt., left the Republican party and organized with the Democrats. Again, in the 108th Congress, with Republicans back in majority control of the Senate, their energy bill could not survive a Senate filibuster over liability protection for the MTBE (methyl tertiary butyl ether) additive, a provision on which House Republicans were unwilling to compromise. CAFE standards remained an auxiliary issue.[31]

When Congress finally passed a modest energy bill in 2005, it did not have a provision on CAFE standards, as many controversial elements were purposely kept out of the legislation. Senator Richard Durbin, D-Ill., did offer an amendment on the Senate floor to increase CAFE standards to 40 mpg over eleven years, but it was soundly defeated (28–67), with nearly as many Democrats voting against the amendment as for it, perhaps for strategic reasons.

In 2006, House Republicans did push legislation to allow the secretary of transportation to set car fuel economy standards after weighing a number of factors. By then, gasoline prices had risen to an annual average of $2.637 in real-dollar terms for unleaded regular, over a dollar a gallon higher than at the time of the OPEC embargo.[32] With the 2006 elections approaching, Republicans felt a need to respond in some way to growing public concern over gasoline prices. They did, however, defeat an amendment that Ed Markey, D-Mass., offered to the bill in the Energy and Commerce Committee to increase CAFE standards to 33 mpg by 2015, with auto district Democrats joining with Republicans in opposition. The Bush administration supported the bill. However, when it appeared the bill would face opposition in both chambers, the Republican leadership did not schedule it for floor consideration.[33]

The story of ANWR during the first six years of the Bush administration is far more complicated than that of CAFE. Seemingly, unified Republican control for the first time since 1954 for most of the six years following the 2000 election finally removed most of the obstacles to ANWR drilling. This was especially true as the parties took more uniform production or conservation stances to resolving energy policy issues. Under the most politically favorable conditions to removing the prohibition against drilling in ANWR, opponents were still able to delay, block, or defeat those efforts.

In both the 108th (2003–2004) and the 109th (2005–2006) Congresses, a Republican president who strongly favored drilling in ANWR, Republican majorities in the House and Senate, and high energy prices were not sufficient to open up ANWR. Proponents of ANWR drilling faced repeated frustration. In the preceding Congress, with Democrats briefly in control of the Senate following Jeffords's exit from the Republican ranks, Senate Democrats delayed consideration of the House-passed energy bill that included drilling in ANWR and the committee markup of the Senate's energy bill until the public outcry following 9/11 had subsided. In late 2001, when Senate majority leader Tom Daschle, D-S.Dak., announced that he would schedule debate on energy legislation in mid-February, *Congressional Quarterly* reported, "With gas prices at a yearly low and the California energy crisis at bay, members of both parties say the public is not clamoring for action on energy."[34] Daschle no longer had to fear losing the support of a sufficient number of Democratic senators on a cloture vote on ANWR. When Frank Murkowski's, R-Alaska, cloture motion came to a vote in April 2002, it did not even garner a majority, losing 46–54. One of the five Democrats who voted with Murkowski, John Breaux, D-La., observed, "We're continuing to show that we're good at doing nothing. We did nothing on (automobile fuel economy) standards; they were able to stop ANWR. We're doing very good at stopping things. We're not doing very good at doing things."[35]

Daschle again used his leadership powers to ensure that Daniel Akaka, D-Hawaii, who had supported cloture, was not named to the conference committee after the stripped-down bill passed the Senate. Instead, Daschle appointed Breaux after obtaining an agreement that he would support Daschle's position.[36] In the end, despite numerous efforts in the conference to provide side payments in return for opening drilling in ANWR (including having the House accept the Senate's tripling of ethanol and a set-aside of other wilderness areas), Senate Democrats persisted in making ANWR a deal killer.[37] Daschle could use his powers as majority leader first to delay and then to block the efforts to open ANWR drilling.

But with pro-ANWR Republicans in control of the presidency and both chambers of Congress following the 2002 elections, it did not mean that majority party leaders had the power to remove the ban on drilling. Despite using a range of legislative strategies to pass a pro-ANWR provision in the 108th and 109th Congresses, the end result was the same as in the 107th. The Bush administration and Republicans in Congress focused on a two-pronged strategy. One was to pass an omnibus energy bill similar to the one that failed in the 107th Congress that included a provision opening up ANWR. To succeed, they would need sixty votes for cloture in the Senate, requiring the support of some Democrats. The other prong returned to using the budget process because the legislation that established that process had provided fixed amounts of floor time for debate preceding a vote on passage, thus exempting budget resolutions and reconciliation bills from filibuster threats. The budget resolution would include revenues from ANWR leases and royalty payments and then direct the appropriate House and Senate authorizing committees to lift the ban on drilling in ANWR as part of the reconciliation bill. This was the same strategy that Republicans employed in 1995, but the Clinton veto scuttled that attempt. They considered doing so again in 2000 but removed ANWR when Clinton threatened a veto. Clearly, Bush's pro-ANWR position precluded the veto problem.

In the 108th Congress, neither strategy worked.[38] Putting drilling in ANWR in the budget resolution unraveled on the Senate floor, despite it being part of the president's budget and in the resolution as reported from the Senate Budget Committee. On a floor vote of 52–48, the Senate deleted the ANWR provision from the budget resolution, as eight Republican senators (primarily moderates) voted against the president and more than offset the five Democratic senators who defected from their party's position.[39] Thus, ANWR could not be part of a reconciliation bill. With the stripping of ANWR from the budget resolution, Senate Energy Committee chair Pete Domenici, R-N.Mex., an ANWR supporter, also decided against including ANWR in his formulation of an energy bill, instead depending on its inclusion in the House bill.

In the House, with the House Resources Committee membership heavily skewed with westerners, Ed Markey's, D-Mass., amendment stripping ANWR from the energy bill in markup was easily defeated (17–27), and the omnibus energy legislation that included the Resources Committee bill easily passed the House 247–175, with forty Democrats supporting it and only seventeen moderate Republicans voting against.

After struggling with a number of issues while trying to manage his committee's energy bill on the floor, Domenici aborted his energy bill and instead substituted what was essentially the Democrats' bill from the previous Congress as a vehicle that would allow him to work out a final bill in conference. Domenici indicated that he would support the House's language on ANWR.[40] Republicans, wanting to resolve intraparty differences over provisions in the bill, excluded Democrats from the conference negotiations and produced a report that included ANWR drilling (as well as an ethanol provision designed to attract the support of Midwestern Democratic senators). Domenici remained publicly committed to ANWR drilling because he had promised the Bush administration and House Republicans that he would do so, but he did not expect that the Senate would approve the agreement.[41] Eventually, Majority Leader Frist, Speaker Hastert, Senate Finance Committee chair Grassley, and House Ways and Means Committee chair Thomas brokered a deal that removed ANWR from the bill. Even with that concession, the Senate failed to invoke cloture on the conference report.[42]

Through both the 107th and 108th Congresses, the Senate was the major obstacle that congressional Republicans and the Bush administration faced in removing the prohibition on drilling in ANWR. They were short the sixty votes needed for cloture on an energy bill that included ANWR drilling, even after making a major concession on ethanol to attract the support of Midwestern Democratic senators. And they were just short of a majority when faced with an up-or-down vote on keeping ANWR in the budget resolution. Seemingly, the results of the 2004 election provided the margin needed to get ANWR drilling through the Senate and the ban removed. Eight Senate seats switched party hands, with Republicans winning six that Democrats previously had held and Democrats replacing two Republicans. The gains for ANWR drilling, however, were actually more modest because two of the Republicans replaced Democrats who had previously supported ANWR on the budget resolution vote.[43] The Republicans would still struggle to find the sixty votes needed for cloture on an energy bill that included ANWR, but getting ANWR through the Senate as part of the budget and reconciliation process certainly was feasible. In an ironic twist, however, the House became the new stumbling block for ANWR proponents in the 109th Congress.

Once again, in 2005, the Bush budget included revenues from ANWR leasing, as did the budget resolution that reached the Senate floor. This time, the effort to strip it failed on a 49–51 vote. But in the House, the unified opposition of Democrats to the Republican budget resolution meant that even pro-ANWR House Democrats would not vote for it. With Republicans holding a narrow House majority, moderate Republicans, who opposed drilling in ANWR, among other things in their party's budget resolution, were in a strong bargaining position. They insisted that the leadership produce a budget resolution without an ANWR provision.

Despite the concessions to Republican moderates on the House budget resolution, Republican negotiators were successful in keeping ANWR in the budget resolution conference report. The conference report, however, barely survived on a 214–211 vote in the House, with no Democrats supporting it, as Republican House leaders reduced the number of defections among their own members.

The Senate continued to stymie a separate energy bill in 2005. As in the 107th and 108th Congresses, the House had again comfortably passed an energy bill that included the removal of the ban on drilling in ANWR. The vote on the Markey amendment to strip ANWR from the bill was closer, but the defection of twenty-nine moderate Republicans was offset by the thirty Democrats, largely Blue Dogs, who supported ANWR drilling (but who had remained with their party on budget resolution votes). Senate energy bill managers, knowing that they lacked the votes for cloture on an energy bill if it included ANWR, formulated their bill without it. Instead, Senate Republicans focused on reconciliation as the vehicle for removing the ANWR-drilling ban.[44]

As with the budget resolution, keeping ANWR in the reconciliation bill proved a more formidable task. Twenty-four House Republican moderates, largely from the Northeast, wrote a letter to Speaker Hastert and the chairs of the Budget and House Resources Committees urging ANWR's exclusion from reconciliation.[45] After the Senate kept ANWR in its reconciliation bill, both as reported from its Budget Committee and in defeating a floor amendment to strip it, Republican House leaders dropped it in an early concession to moderates as they struggled to cobble together a majority to pass the broad reconciliation package. Even with ANWR removed and with other compromises, it took until mid-November before House Republicans were able to pass the reconciliation bill on a 217–215 vote, after two members who threatened to vote against it unless ANWR was included cast deciding votes in favor. The leaders hoped to add ANWR back in during conference.

With moderate House Republicans adamant in their unwillingness to support a reconciliation conference report that included ANWR drilling, Republican House leaders initially attempted to use side payments of hurricane relief to lure pro-ANWR House Democrats to vote for a reconciliation conference report.[46] House Democrats, however, remained unified in their opposition to the reconciliation package. To save the reconciliation bill, House Republican leaders had no choice but to insist on removing ANWR in conference after first getting Senator Ted Stevens, R-Alaska, the most adamant ANWR advocate in the Senate, to agree. As chair of the Defense Appropriations Subcommittee, Stevens' alternative strategy was to attach ANWR to the Defense Appropriations bill. Although enough pro-ANWR House Democrats would vote for it so that Republican moderates would not be able to block, the problem for ANWR proponents was again the need to garner sixty votes for cloture in the Senate. But the anti-ANWR side prevailed, 56–44.[47]

In an abbreviated fashion, much the same scenario repeated itself in the second session. The House again passed a bill providing for drilling in ANWR but knowing there weren't enough votes for cloture; the Senate leadership did not even bring it to the floor. The Senate passed a budget resolution that had explicit directions for the Energy and Natural Resources Committee regarding inclusion of a provision for revenue generation from ANWR in the reconciliation bill, but the House did not include ANWR in its budget resolution. In the end, the two chambers never agreed on a budget resolution.

The failure to remove the ban on opening ANWR in the 109th Congress effectively ended the push for it. The Bush administration went through the formality of assuming income from ANWR leasing in its fiscal year 2008 budget, but Interior Secretary Kempthorne admitted that it had no chance of passage in a Congress with Democrats in the majority. During the Obama administration, the Republican push to increase oil production focused on the Keystone XL Pipeline issue rather than ANWR.[48] With Obama's reelection, the prospects for opening ANWR remain bleak, at least until 2017 at the earliest.

More than thirty years after the enactment of the initial CAFE standards (two decades after they were reached) and more than twenty-five years after Congress banned drilling in ANWR as part of the ANILCA, policies on these and a broad range of other energy issues remained unchanged, and the United States was more dependent on oil imports than it had been at the time of the embargo. With increasingly unified and polarized parties in Congress, the capacity to block policy changes, whether the proponents were advocating conservation approaches or production approaches, persisted. Even when one party was in control for an extended period, as Republicans were for most of the 107th through 109th Congresses, the majorities were not large enough to overcome procedural obstacles. The defection or the threats of defection by a small number of Republican House members or senators were enough to block their efforts on ANWR when the minority party was largely united in its opposition. And incentives to compromise on the part of either party were limited when each party could anticipate that party control might shift at the next election. That changed in 2007 when the proponents of increases in CAFE made a significant legislative breakthrough, as the political costs of the status quo forced the opponents of CAFE increases reluctantly to accept a major policy change.

A CAFE Breakthrough in 2007

As noted earlier, most of the efforts to increase CAFE standards from the late 1980s until 2007 had little chance of success. After the 2000 election, Republicans in Congress and the Bush administration were able to block efforts to increase CAFE standards for six years, despite the rise in gasoline prices and projections that they would go higher. CAFE standards—and energy issues more generally—were increasingly partisan. Republicans could pass production-oriented legislation in the House, but fairly united Democratic opposition in a more polarized Senate meant the minority party could prevent cloture if it was perceived that legislation was positioned at the Republican median chamber position.[49] Unlike the initial adoption of CAFE standards in the 1970s, compromises were not readily available, even as the costs of the status quo increased with rising gasoline prices. Moreover, Republicans preferred the status quo to any position that would be acceptable to a sufficient number of Senate Democrats to invoke cloture. That stance, however, became more difficult to defend as gasoline prices and the potential electoral costs of doing nothing increased.

With the return of Democratic majorities in both the House and the Senate for the first time in twelve years after the 2006 election, congressional Democrats resumed control of the policy agenda, giving an increase in CAFE standards higher priority. President Bush had previously opposed a statutory-set increase in CAFE standards, but rising gasoline prices had been one of the issues on which Republicans proved vulnerable in the 2006 elections. Gasoline prices rose to new record highs in 2007, with expectations that they would go even higher (and they did, exceeding $4.11 a gallon by early July 2008 before declining) creating a political context in which status quo on CAFE standards became harder to defend. Both the Bush administration and key congressional Republicans indicated a willingness to support some changes in CAFE standards as part of an overall energy strategy, although they coupled their support with the requirement of also including fossil fuel production provisions. Bush proposed an annual increase in CAFE standards beginning in 2010 but treated it as a goal, not a requirement. Ted Stevens, R-Alaska, the ranking Republican on the Senate Commerce Committee, even introduced a bill calling for a 40-mpg standard as part of a package that included drilling in ANWR.[50] Meanwhile, Democratic congressional leaders designed a strategy to avoid splitting their membership on the CAFE issue and to limit the political costs of supporting an increase. They took advantage of bicameralism in an effort to address three energy issues: CAFE standards, transferring tax subsidies for fossils fuels in the 2005 legislation to alternative energy sources, and requiring utilities to use a certain percentage of renewable energy sources in the production of electricity.

Being in the majority allowed the Democratic leadership in Congress not just agenda control but also strategic advantages. Because support for a CAFE increase was stronger in the Senate than in the House, and the reverse was the case with the other two provisions, Speaker Pelosi used bicameralism to her advantage and did not include CAFE standards in the House bill, instead letting the Senate deal with it. CAFE standards remained a difficult issue for House Democrats, who had ties to two core Democratic interest group constituencies—environmentalists and organized labor, especially the UAW—that were initially on opposite sides on the CAFE standards issue. If they were forced to vote on CAFE standards, many House Democrats would anger one of these groups. The House leadership could hold enough member support to pass a meaningful increase in CAFE standards, but the margin would be narrow. Instead of incurring political costs for her members and herself, Speaker Pelosi persuaded Ed Markey, the CAFE standards' main sponsor, to withdraw his amendment in exchange for Democrats opposed to Markey agreeing to drop their weaker alternative. The energy bill that passed the House contained provisions on subsidies for alternative fuels and on the use of renewables for electric-utility generation but nothing on CAFE standards. By the time that the bill reached the House floor, the Senate had already passed an energy bill that included CAFE increases to 35 mpg by 2020 but without the subsidy or electricity generation provisions. Assuming that the CAFE provision survived a conference or other negotiated House–Senate agreement, Democratic House members might be able to support an increase in CAFE standards without ever having to take a separate vote on a CAFE provision. In this way, Speaker Pelosi's strategy insulated her party's members from potential electoral costs of voting for or against a CAFE increase. In the end, Pelosi held auto district Democrats after negotiating an agreement giving NHTSA greater authority than the EPA in setting standards, as labor opposition to a significant CAFE increase diminished. On the key House vote concurring with the Senate amendment to the bill with an amendment (maintaining all three key provisions), only seven Democrats, all Southern conservatives and/or from oil-producing states, voted against it.

The Senate's resistance to the electric-utility generation provision and the Bush's administration's threat to veto the transfer of the tax break provision from fossil fuels to alternative sources meant that those two provisions were eventually dropped from the bill. The final passage vote of 314–100 in the House and the overwhelming support in the Senate on the cloture vote to concur with the House bill, stripped of the two provisions, understates the levels of controversy and the partisan conflict. Republicans blocked the tax subsidy for renewables and the electricity generation portions of the legislation. Blocking the CAFE change was no longer a viable political option, even for many conservative members who preferred the status quo to an increase in CAFE standards. The political dimension trumped the ideological one.

President Bush, who had wanted his administration to retain the authority over mileage standards and had stated in a White House position paper that "Congress should not legislate a particular numeric fuel economy standard,"[51] signed the bill and tried to share credit with Speaker Pelosi at the ceremony. Between the bill signing and the time Bush left office, neither he nor his Department of Transportation did much to expedite the implementation of the new CAFE standards.[52]

As passed, the Energy Independence and Security Act of 2007 (EISA) was designed to ensure that mileage for passenger and nonpassenger automobiles for sale in the United States would increase to 35 mpg by 2020. It gave authority to the secretary of transportation to "prescribe annual fuel economy standard increases that increase the applicable average fuel economy standard ratably beginning with the model year 2011 and ending with the model year 2020."[53] Congress's intent was that the executive branch would write regulations for auto manufacturers to reach that standard in a steplike fashion. The concern was that the executive would do less. So the law called for the following goal: "beginning with model year 2011 to achieve a combined fuel economy average for model year 2020 of *at least* 35 miles per gallon."[54] In addition, for subsequent years, 2021 to 2030, the legislation set the standard at "the maximum feasible average fuel economy for that model year."[55]

It is fair to say that the parties to the legislation had assumed that as 2020 approached, the DOT would put forth a proposal for additional steps over the following decade or that Congress might then revisit CAFE standards. Shortly after coming into office, the Obama administration unveiled a more far-reaching interpretation of its authority under EISA than anyone involved in its passage in 2007 had or could have anticipated and did so without Congress playing a role. Aware of the growing difficulty of enacting legislation because of Congress's increased use of blocking tactics, the Obama administration acted unilaterally, using existing authority to achieve its policy goals. In a Rose Garden ceremony on May 19, 2009, the president announced an agreement to reach a 35.5 mpg standard by 2016 with the full support of a wide range of affected interests, including environmental groups, auto companies, the UAW, and health organizations. A little more than two years later, he announced that the CAFE standards for model years 2017 through 2025 with a goal of 54.5 mpg by 2025. With gasoline prices having fallen dramatically with the marked economic downturn in the United States and elsewhere that began in 2008, there would have been little incentive for Congress to vote for the acceleration of CAFE increases.[56]

Conclusion

This paper has been largely a narrative in which I summarize and compare the legislative struggle over two energy issues since the OPEC embargo and try to draw conclusions about the inability of the U.S. government to address a national policy goal on which there has been broad agreement for four decades. One issue, CAFE, was in the forefront for proponents of conservation approaches as the means of reducing dependence on foreign energy sources, and the other, ANWR, was the issue that symbolized the efforts of proponents of production approaches to reduce dependence. In many ways, the struggles have been remarkably similar. First, it has been very difficult to enact energy policy change, whether it has been with conservation or a production approach or some compromise with a mix of approaches. Because most of the legislation involved short-term costs to achieve long-term benefits, the bills carried potential electoral liabilities for members of Congress. They could be held electorally accountable for the costs without being able to demonstrate the benefits to their constituents. Only when there were sustained political costs from maintaining the status quo that outweighed the short-term costs of policy change was Congress willing to pass major energy legislation. That was the case during the period from 1975 to 1980 and again in the early 2000s, when there were sustained energy price increases and/or shortages. Of course, those conditions did not mean that energy legislation would automatically be enacted or that Congress would necessarily act quickly. Congress did not remove the ban on drilling in ANWR, even during the 2001 through 2006 period, when Republicans had extended, unified party control. And most of the key energy legislation that did pass took several years of pulling and hauling and the use of considerable skill by party leaders.

The only exception to this pattern occurred when President Obama acted unilaterally to accelerate the timetable on CAFE beyond that which was anticipated when Congress passed EISA in 2007. At the time of both the 2009 and

2011 actions, energy prices were relatively low and had been so since the start of the recession. The same electoral constraints that affected Congress's ability to pass legislation did not limit the behavior of the president. Obama was willing to accept the short-term costs of the policy change to achieve his desired long-term policy benefits. He recognized, however, that he would not be able to make the policy changes in CAFE if he tried to do so legislatively. President Reagan or either of the two presidents Bush might well have taken similar unilateral action in removing the ban on drilling in ANWR had they possessed sufficient existing legislative authority to do so. Despite the enormous growth of legislative authority in the executive branch over recent decades, presidents cannot always find the authority to act unilaterally, even when the costs of passing new legislation are too high or the chances that Congress will respond are minimal.

Second, it does appear, from both the CAFE and ANWR cases, that the move to stronger congressional parties has made it more, not less, difficult to pass legislation. Although it took several years to pass the legislation of which initial CAFE standards and the ban on ANWR drilling were parts, the opponents of those bills did not employ the full range of blocking mechanisms. Instead, they engaged in a bargaining process that produced legislation that was more acceptable. In the case of CAFE, it meant giving the secretary of transportation the power to delay the final steps in the mpg increases. With the ban on drilling in ANWR, the opponents won the inclusion of a study of the environmental effects and of the potential oil reserves, with the chance then of removing the ban rather than placing ANWR in the untouchable-wilderness category. The filibuster was not used, and presidents did not threaten vetoes. In addition, the parties and their leadership did not mobilize to defeat legislation or to block committee-produced bills. By the late 1980s, however, as the parties in Congress became stronger, they and their leaders increasingly engaged in blocking activity. George Mitchell had a task force to counter the Senate Energy Committee bill that included drilling in ANWR and then delayed scheduling the legislation until the Gulf War crisis had receded. Tom DeLay placed a rider on appropriations bills to prevent the Clinton administration from pursuing CAFE increases. And the inability to invoke cloture blocked the lifting of the ANWR-drilling ban when Republicans had unified control in much of the 2001 to 2006 period. Senate Democrats viewed ANWR as a deal killer on any energy package and made good on the threat. And even pro-ANWR House Democrats would not break party lines to vote for a reconciliation bill that included opening up ANWR.

Third and somewhat more speculatively, the narrow majorities in Congress since 1995 have also made the passage of energy legislation more difficult. Most obviously, because of the close divisions, the majority party has not held a large enough number of Senate seats to overcome minority party filibusters that have become commonplace since 1995. Only for a brief period in the 111th Congress has either party had as many as sixty senators since 1979. By contrast, the Democrats had sixty or more seats in seven of the ten Congresses from 1959 to 1978.

Even in the majoritarian House of Representatives, the narrowness of those majorities, especially since 1995, has meant that the majority party leadership has little margin to spare, even with an ideologically more cohesive party than at any point in the past century. From the election of the 104th to the election of the 110th Congress, the majority party never won more than 236 seats in a general election. Under those circumstances, the majority party could not afford many defections without being rolled if the minority party members were unified. Accordingly a small number of majority party members could demand concessions by threatening not to support party positions. In the 109th Congress, two dozen moderate Republicans used that leverage to force their party leaders to remove ANWR and other provisions from the reconciliation bill.

In addition, there may be little incentive for the minority party to seek compromises rather than to block legislation. As mentioned earlier, the minority may believe, accurately or not, that it has a good chance of becoming the majority party after the next election and then achieving a policy result that is closer to its ideal point. Also, the failure of the majority party to produce legislation may be used in an upcoming campaign as evidence that it is incapable of governing effectively.

To the degree that the same patterns are evident in other policy areas, the findings of this research raise questions about the ongoing influence of Congress in the struggle over public policy. When presidents have the option of using unilateral action instead of engaging Congress, they may be more prone to do so. And the public may be more willing to accept an extension of executive authority if the alternative is congressional gridlock.

Notes

1. In 2015, only about 24 percent of U.S. petroleum consumed was from foreign sources, the lowest level since 1970. See U.S. Energy Information Agency, "How Much Oil Consumed by the United States Comes From Foreign Countries?" last updated March 8, 2016, http://www.eia.gov/tools/faqs/faq.cfm?id=32&t=6. For most of the period from 1973 to 2008, net imports exceeded 40 percent of consumption and more than doubled in absolute terms between 1985 and 2005.
2. In this sense, it is useful to think of policy as the independent variable affecting process.
3. Kenneth A. Shepsle and Barry R. Weingast, "Political Preferences for the Pork Barrel: A Generalization," *American Journal of Political Science* 25 (1981): 96–111; Diana Evans, "Policy and Pork: The Use of Pork Barrel Projects to Build Policy Coalitions in the House of Representatives," *American Journal of Political Science* 38 (1994): 894–917; and Diana Evans, "Pork Barrel Politics," in *The Oxford Handbook of the American Congress*, ed. Eric Schickler and Frances E. Lee (New York: Oxford University Press, 2011), 315–39.
4. Of course, this is not always the case, especially in periods of budget constraints, when members with reputations for pork barrel projects sometimes find themselves under attack as "wasteful spenders."
5. R. Douglas Arnold, *The Logic of Congressional Action* (New Haven, CT: Yale University Press, 1990).

ANWR and CAFE   353

6. James A. Thurber, "The Dynamics and Dysfunction of the Congressional Budget Process: From Inception to Deadlock," in *Congress Reconsidered*, 10th ed., ed. Lawrence C. Dodd and Bruce I. Oppenheimer (Washington, DC: CQ Press, 2013), 324.
7. It should be noted that it was easier to reach such an agreement in 1990 because the players did not perceive that partisan control of Congress was likely to be in play in the next election. Importantly, however, House Republicans, influenced by the electoral strategy of Newt Gingrich, refused to support the agreement. And President George H. W. Bush did pay an electoral cost because supporting the agreement violated his 1988 campaign promise not to raise taxes.
8. In the 1950s and 1960s, energy legislative issues were treated according to their separate sources (oil, gas, coal, nuclear, etc.) and fit the concentrated-benefits, dispersed-cost model. Support for ethanol purchase guarantees as part of broader energy packages is a notable exception. It is a more recent example of pork barrel provisions (in these instances, efforts to win support of House members and senators representing corn-producing constituencies).
9. Bruce I. Oppenheimer, "It's Hard to Get Mileage Out of Congress: Struggling Over CAFE Standards, 1973–2013," in *Congress and Policy Making in the 21st Century*, ed. Jeffery A. Jenkins and Eric M. Patashnik (New York: Cambridge University Press, 2016), 272–98.
10. Lawrence C. Dodd and Bruce I. Oppenheimer, "The House in Transition," in *Congress Reconsidered*, 1st ed., ed. Lawrence C. Dodd and Bruce I. Oppenheimer (New York: Praeger, 1977), 21–53.
11. Gerald R. Ford, "Statement on the Energy Policy and Conservation Act," December 22, 1975, in *The American Presidency Project*, ed. Gerhard Peters and John T. Wooley, http://www.presidency.ucsb.edu/ws/?pid=5452.
12. S. Rept. 94-179, 9.
13. *Congressional Record*, September 17, 1975, 28934.
14. *CQ Almanac 1975*, 243.
15. Ford, "Energy Policy."
16. Aside from the conflict between pro-development and environmental groups, the positions of Native Americans, the revenues to the state of Alaska from land use, and hunting and fishing rights came into play.
17. The 1988 Republican platform called for deregulation to bring technological change to transportation as "far preferable to outmoded regulation, such as the current design of Corporate Average Fuel Economy (CAFE) standards, which create substantial advantages for foreign auto manufacturers and actually promote the export of U.S. jobs."
18. In addition, Johnston was in a three-candidate contest for Senate majority leader to replace Robert Byrd, who was stepping down from that position at the end of the One Hundredth Congress and knew ANWR was an issue on which he was at odds with the overwhelming majority of his caucus.
19. David W. Rohde, *Parties and Leaders in the Postreform House* (Chicago: University of Chicago Press, 1991).
20. Neither of these groups has totally disappeared. Republicans continued to struggle for support from their House members and senators from the Northeast when pro-energy-production policies, such as opening offshore and environmentally sensitive areas to drilling, were perceived as having negative environmental consequences. In addition, there remained a few Democratic House members and senators from producing constituencies.

21. Modest energy bills were passed in 1991 and 2005, but both were stripped of controversial provisions.
22. The omnibus energy bill reported by the Subcommittee on Energy and Power of the House Committee on Energy and Commerce did not contain a provision on CAFE standards. If it had, the full committee chair, John Dingell, would have strongly opposed it.
23. Phil Kurtz, "Drilling Fight Continues," *CQ Weekly Report*, January 20, 1990, 161.
24. Phil Kurtz, "ANWR May Be Latest Hostage of Middle East Oil Crisis," *CQ Weekly Report*, September 8, 1990, 2827.
25. Joseph A. Davis, "Arctic-Drilling Plan Clears Committee," *CQ Weekly Report*, March 18, 1989, 598.
26. Holly Idelson, "Energy: Varying Interests Tie Hopes to Fast-Moving Omnibus," *CQ Weekly Report*, March 16, 1991, 669.
27. George Hager, "As They Cut, Appropriators Add a Stiff Dose of Policy," *CQ Weekly Report*, July 29, 1995, 2245.
28. Prior to DeLay's amendment, a Michigan Republican member of the House Appropriations Committee, Joe Knollenberg, placed a provision in the committee report for the Department of Transportation appropriations bill that reduced funding that might be used to implement increased mileage standards on vans and light trucks.
29. Jeff Plungis, "Congress Again Feeling Heat Over Surging Gasoline Prices," *CQ Weekly Report*, June 17, 2000, 1461.
30. In the House bill, H.R. 4, auto producers would have to save about 3.7 percent of gas consumption over six years. The Senate bill, S. 517, required NHTSA to increase mileage standards for cars and light trucks but only after considering costs, economic impact, and safety consequences. And only if NHTSA did not act could Congress decide to raise standards.
31. An amendment Ed Markey, D-Mass., offered during subcommittee consideration in the House requiring cuts in petroleum demand for vehicles over a five-year period, thus forcing an increase in CAFE standards in a circuitous manner, was rejected 6–24. See Samuel Goldreich, "Old Becomes New Again as Senate Passes Energy Bill," *CQ Weekly Report*, August 2, 2003, 1967. In the Senate, advocates of CAFE increases complained that the bill's criteria that DOT had to consider before increasing standards made it more difficult to do so than under existing law. See Samuel Goldreich, "Senate Braces for Floor Battle Over Omnibus Energy Bill," *CQ Weekly*, May 3, 2003, 1042. Thus, had Congress passed an energy bill, it would not have contained any measurable change in CAFE standards.
32. The price data is from U.S. Energy Information Administration, "Total Annual Energy Review," September 27, 2012, http://www.eia.gov/totaltnergy/data/annual/showtext.cfm?t=ptb0524. The price is calculated in chained (2005) dollars.
33. Jeff Tollefson, "New CAFE Standards for Autos Allowed Under House Measure," *CQ Weekly*, May 15, 2006, 1332.
34. Rebecca Adams, "Energy: Murkowski and Allies Fume at Pace of Energy Bill in Senate," *CQ Weekly Report*, December 1, 2001, 2844.
35. Adriel Bettelheim, "Wilderness Drilling Defeat Results in Cropped Energy Bill," *CQ Weekly Report*, April 20, 2002, 1023.
36. Rebecca Adams, "Daschle Must Make Fast Shuffle to Get ANWR Opponents on Panel," *CQ Weekly Report*, May 4, 2002, 1133.
37. Rebecca Adams, "Energy Conferees Optimistic Despite Intractable Issues," *CQ Weekly Report*, September 28, 2002, 2524.

ANWR and CAFE 355

38. The closest Republicans came to opening up ANWR was when Ted Stevens, R-Alaska, successfully removed House language from the fiscal year 2003 omnibus spending bill that would have prevented the Department of the Interior from even using any funds to study drilling in ANWR.
39. The eight Republicans were Chafee, R-R.I.; Coleman, R-Minn.; Collins, R-Maine; DeWine, R-Ohio; Fitzgerald, R-Ill.; McCain, R-Ariz.; Gordon Smith, R-Ore.; and Snowe, R-Maine. The five Democrats were Breaux, D-La.; Landrieu, D-La.; Miller, D-Ga.; Akaka, D-Hawaii; and Inouye, D-Hawaii.
40. Samuel Goldreich, "Old Becomes New Again".
41. Joseph C. Anselmo, "Thicket of Unsettled Issues Delays Energy Conference," *CQ Weekly Report*, October 4, 2003, 2434.
42. In exchange for dropping ANWR, the House and the Bush administration insisted on a provision in the House bill that gave liability protection to the manufacturers of MTBE, a gasoline additive that was found to have negative environmental consequences. Defections primarily of five New England Republican senators were sufficient to defeat cloture, despite the votes that were garnered in favor of cloture from Midwestern Democrats because of the generous ethanol provisions.
43. In addition, one of the Democrats replaced a Republican who had opposed ANWR.
44. Ben Evans, "Energy Bill Is Acronymic, Antagonistic," *CQ Weekly Report*, April 25, 2005, 1084.
45. Jonathan Allen, "Twenty-Four House Republicans Urge Panel to Keep ANWR Out of Reconciliation Bill," *CQ Weekly*, August 15, 2005, 2254.
46. Steven T. Dennis, "Budget Tops Remaining Agenda," *CQ Weekly*, December 5, 2005, 3266.
47. The vote was actually closer because Majority Leader Bill Frist, R-Tenn., voted against cloture to preserve his right to move for reconsideration.
48. House Republicans did pass a bill in 2012 that removed the ban on leasing and drilling in ANWR. It went no further.
49. For a more detailed analysis of the effect of *conditional party government* on efforts to pass energy legislation in the 2001–2006 period, see Bruce I. Oppenheimer and Marc J. Hetherington, "Catch-22: Cloture, Energy Policy, and the Limits of Conditional Party Government," in *Why Not Parties?: Party Effects in the United States Senate*, ed. Nathan W. Monroe, Jason M. Roberts, and David W. Rohde (Chicago: University of Chicago Press, 2008).
50. Manu Raju, "Ted Stevens Gets Ever So Greener," *CQ Weekly*, January 15, 2007, 156.
51. Peter Baker, "Solidarity for Bush, Democrats; Looking Past Disputes, Sides Join Together to Enact Energy Bill," *Washington Post*, December 20, 2007, A18.
52. The administration did propose to increase the target for vans, SUVs, and smaller pickup trucks to 28.6 mpg by 2015 but discouraged states from adopting stricter mileage standards than provided for in the new law. See Adriel Bettelheim, "Regulations Provide Fuel for Federalism," *CQ Weekly*, May 5, 2008, 1154.
53. PL 110-140 (2007), 121 Stat. 1499.
54. Italics added.
55. PL 110-140 (2007), 121 Stat. 1499.
56. For a more extensive analysis of the action of the Obama administration's use of existing authoring to increase CAFE standards more quickly and a more detailed analysis of the CAFE struggle, see Oppenheimer, "It's Hard to Get Mileage."

Part V
Congress and Public Policy in a Separation-of-Powers System

15. The Balance of Power Between the Congress and the President
Issues and Dilemmas
Joseph Cooper

This chapter analyzes and assesses the current state of the balance of power between the president and Congress. It does so by tracing the growth of presidential power from the early twentieth century to today in three prime arenas of national policy making: the electoral system, the legislative system, and the administrative system. It sees such growth as a consequence of the interaction of structural parameters, patterns of motivation, and ideas or doctrines, as well as the contingent effects of the qualities of leaders and unanticipated events. The chapter closes by assessing the case for substantial additions to presidential power. It argues that the viability of our constitutional order rests as much on the needs for consent and the rule of law as on the need for action. Thus, the key to preserving our constitutional order is maintaining a balanced view of our institutional needs, rather than seeing one as so vital that the damage to the others can be disregarded. That is what we have done successfully throughout our history and what we should continue to do to avoid a decline into a plebiscitary democracy ruled by the president.

My work on Congress has been concerned with the role and power of Congress in the American political system. In large part, from the very start, it has been guided by the recognition that Congress is a changing institution and the belief that its relationships to the party system and the presidency are always key to a full understanding of its operation and performance. What I will do in this chapter is present a set of guidelines that have emerged over time in the course of my research on Congress and then illustrate their utility. Abstractly, I could do this in a variety of ways. My choice, because of its advantages in illustrating the utility of my guidelines within a single chapter, is an analysis of the decline in the role and power of Congress relative to the presidency over the past century.

My goal will be to explain and assess the current state of the balance of power between the Congress and the presidency.[1]

Guidelines for Analysis

If Congress is a changing entity, it is not a chaotic one. Neither is the presidency. Hence, a useful way to understand and explain the current state of the balance of power is to place it in historical perspective. In doing so, a primary problem is to account for both stability and change in whatever periods are chosen for analysis. To cope with this problem, I have relied on a number of assumptions that have evolved as I pursued the study of Congress. For me, the key in all periods to explaining change in the role and power of the Congress in relation to the presidency lies in the interaction of fixed and quasi parameters, varying types and combinations of motives and goals, and normative ideas and doctrines. I will also argue that normative analysis and empirical analysis interrelate, that normative assessment of the state of the balance of power is an appropriate and necessary aspect of our task as students of Congress, and that contingencies of various types play an important role in performance and change.

Macrostructure and Micromotives

Despite the preeminence of past and present general theoretical frameworks, such as behaviorism and rational choice, which give primacy to micromotivation and see macrostructures and processes as derivative, a more balanced approach that sees them as interactive is needed.[2] No member of Congress ever enters a Congress that is not to some degree already organized or structured, legitimated by certain normative ideas, and marked by consensus on certain behavioral norms. As a result, the impact of existing macrocontexts on motivation and behavior is significant. Without macrostructures and processes of decision making, the ability of any form of micromotivation to orient decision making would be highly confused, if not blind. Indeed, absent system collapse, members do not have the desire or the courage to redesign the contexts of operation they inherit in any totally comprehensive manner.[3] They are too much invested in an existing context to engage in the challenging task of finding new templates or models to replace those they have previously accepted and too constrained by existing practice and distributions of political power to see even comprehensive change that is limited to a broad aspect of congressional operation as feasible and clearly beneficial, except on rare occasions. Rather, members are highly inclined to accept the existing character of linkages and decision-making arrangements in existence as givens and worthy of challenge only to the degree that some facet of varying but limited overall importance seriously violates their personal goals, shared goals, and normative commitments. As a result, rules change most often is piecemeal and incremental, though at times comprehensive in a broad but particular area.

All this is not to say that micromotives and the shared and personal goals they inspire are the creation of or captive to inherited macrostructures and macroprocesses. They are not. Micromotives and the goals they inspire matter as well as macrolinkages, macrostructures, and macroprocesses. Indeed, the precise character of the existing linkages and decision-making arrangements in any period are themselves the product of past interactions between member goals and existing structures and processes. Member motivation is thus also a fundamental and necessary factor that cannot be ignored in explaining congressional operation and performance in any period. Thus, if I assume that specialization and integration can be treated as general analytical concepts, it is because members see and accept their equivalents, defined less abstractly, as necessities for achieving their personal and collective goals. Member motivations and goals, however, are complex and multifaceted. They include desires for good public policy as well as reelection and personal power in the Congress. They thus can be highly congruent, especially when parties are very cohesive, but also highly conflicting, when members have to choose between their substantive and political preferences. Such motivations and goals nonetheless lead to continuing assessments of the operation and performance of Congress in terms of personal and shared goals as well as normative commitments. As a consequence, as quasi parameters change and prevailing ideas or doctrines about proper practice are challenged, inefficiencies, as well as more substantive problems in performance, lead members to seek to change aspects of the macrocontexts in which they are operating in ways that will relieve their discontent. However, in all cases, the priorities assigned to personal and collective goals vary by member and by the situations in which discontent prompts action for change. Thus, despite the importance of micromotives, which has been amply demonstrated in some of the classic work done in American politics over the past several decades, they cannot provide a primary causal explanation of change in the linkages, structures, and processes of Congress or the relative power of Congress and the president any more than macrostructures can. They do figure in their explanation but only in interaction with structure and ideas.[4]

Structural Parameters

The prime components of macrostructure in the United States at any point in time are the linkages among the electoral system, the legislative system, and the administrative system and the character of their decision-making structures and processes. These three systems of national policy decision making change over time in their linkages and decision-making structures and processes, but change is constrained by both the fixed and quasi parameters the system imposes.[5] Fixed parameters constrain change across time in the linkages that tie the three systems together as well as in the character of their internal decision-making structures and processes. The provisions of the Constitution are the primary source of these parameters. They provide enduring constraints on change and vary in their breadth. Some fixed parameters are quite specific, for example, the requirement for a Senate with two members from each state or the character of the president's veto power. Others are much broader. Nonetheless, the sum total has lasting and important effects on behavior and outcomes within and across systems.

As a legislature, Congress is and must be a nonbureaucratic organization, whose members are subject to election, and in contrast to bureaucracies, all formally have equal status and authority. Congress thus must rely on agreement, not command, in decision making; cannot select or fire its members; and cannot differentiate among them in terms of salary or benefits. As a result, Congress has limited ability to increase in size to cope with expansions in the scope and complexity of policy demands or to rely on vertical organizational elaboration to enhance its specialized expertise in handling its workload. Similarly, it has limited ability to rely on hierarchical divisions of authority and power in integrating the work and views of its members and subunits. It thus has no alternative but to rely on committees to satisfy its organizational need for specialization and on parties to satisfy its organizational need for integration. Similarly, by vesting executive power in the president, decision making in the executive branch is constrained and empowered in very different basic ways. It is, in essence, a bureaucracy characterized by a hierarchical distribution of authority and the appointment of all participants other than the president by persons of higher authority. It thus can rely far more on such authority than Congress in controlling and directing its personnel, who are employees in ways members of Congress are not. The executive branch thus has far greater capacity for expansion in size and division of labor through vertical expansion in its units and specialized task assignments. Yet its linkages to Congress and the electorate remain powerful potential sources of constraint and dependency.[6]

Nonetheless, much is left open regarding the precise character of the linkages among the three systems and the precise character of their decision-making structures and processes. The electoral system is rooted in the requirement for periodic elections; the delineation of different constituencies and tenures for the president, House, and Senate; and the creation of an Electoral College to elect the president. However, the specifics of the electoral process with regard to the formal organization of elections are left largely to the states and the selection of candidates, the conduct of campaigns, and the roles and duties of those elected left largely to politics. In the case of the Congress, the assignment of legislative power to the Congress does involve the designation of specific areas of policy to congressional control, but the only limit on the delegation of policy discretion in any area to the president or bureaucrats is a vague, implicit ban on delegating legislative power to executive officers. Similarly, the delegation of executive power to the president is quite unspecified in its meaning and limits. The exact limits on congressional infringements of executive power are far from entirely clear. The same is true of the limits on what presidents can do on their own authority in implementing laws or exercising other powers granted to them in the Constitution. This is not an accident. The Framers were very hesitant—and rightly so—to assume that the character of legislative or executive power was precisely definable and left the precise dimensions of the authority of each branch to be settled by political dispute, except in those instances in which executive or legislative intrusions were so severe as to justify Court intervention. Indeed, the only standard mentioned in *The Federalist* papers is that one branch not dominate the other. Hence, the Framers' main reliance was not on judicial review but on a set of checks and balances, which themselves mixed legislative and executive power, so as to protect each branch from domination by the other.[7]

Thus, though the fixed parameters set by the Constitution provide a major source of stability, they do not bar change. They only establish boundaries of varying breadth on change. The precise character of linkages among the prime systems of decision making as well as the precise character of their decision-making structures and processes at any point in time result from the manner in which what I call quasi parameters fill in the gaps or spaces that the fixed parameters leave open. These parameters are not fixed in character but variables that have significant parametric effects because their rates of change are constrained to a higher degree than variables that are more fluid and less stable. They can be grouped into five categories: the state of federal roles and responsibilities, the state of technology for political communication and travel, the state of the party system as a coalition and organization, the state of the rules and procedures for decision making, and the state of capacity for decision making. These states have multiple components and are interrelated in their impacts on the character of linkages and decision-making structures and processes. More concretely, what I have in mind as quasi parameters in these categories are variables, such as the volume and complexity of the workload; the advent of new technologies, such as data mining, the Internet, or the jet plane; the forms of agenda and debate control; the levels of party cohesion; modes of choosing candidates and conducting campaigns; and the size and quality of the staff resources the president can rely on to control the bureaucracy. Quasi parameters are therefore important sources of stability in linkages and decision-making structures and processes but also important sources of change. They respond to significant alterations in societal and political conditions, which generate new dissatisfactions with various aspects of existing linkages and decision making that provide new incentives and opportunities for structural and behavioral change.

Normative Ideas and Doctrine

Finally, constructing an unbridgeable wall between the empirical and the normative damages both empirical explanation and normative assessment. In the empirical analysis of institutional change, normative ideas figure significantly in movements for change and their outcomes. Neither policy desires nor career goals are sufficient unto themselves to cause institutional change. Nor can the advocacy and success of important changes in rules or practice rest simply on convenience or efficiency. Rather, they have to be legitimated by claims regarding the needs of representative government, impingements on the balance of power between the branches, and/or the need to bolster the political system's ability to perform.[8] Since these claims are based on ideas that, like the fixed parameters, leave their precise implications open, the empirical explanation of change requires analysis of conflict over the meanings and consequences of these ideas. Moreover, the ideas that underlie successful change often harden into doctrines that have lasting effects in redefining the boundaries of accepted and expected practice. Note the doctrine of presidential leadership of the legislative process as opposed to the original doctrine of noninterference.[9] Thus, it is not only change in quasi parameters or patterns of motivations that underlie institutional change but also changes in prevailing ideas and doctrines.

It is true as well that normative assessment of the need for institutional change is a necessary and appropriate component of the study of Congress and the presidency. The Framers understood that changes in their roles, powers, and internal decision-making arrangements were unavoidable. This is one of the reasons their constitutional design leaves so much open. However, what the Framers also understood is that their approach would require not only continuing assessment of performance based on the goals and standards of the Constitution but also assessment in which the influence of self-serving interests and emotion in distorting judgments of performance and the benefits of proposals for change would be limited.[10] Hence, they wanted assessment here, as elsewhere, to be deliberative—that is, based on rational discussion of the evidence and oriented to what best served the goals of the Constitution. This will strike many as naïve, but it is just as naïve to believe that human beings have no capacity for objectivity. There is thus a deep truth in the Framers' confidence in rational behavior when advantaged by an institutional design that checked self-interest. If our political system is just a subjective preference with little or no claim on our allegiance other than our private interests, it will be highly subject to being undermined by the passions endemic in human nature. In short, to deny the need for and possibility of rational assessment of the goals and aspirations of the Framers is a recipe for their destruction, whereas to affirm them requires bringing rational discussion and evidence to bear on issues of performance, a task we as students of politics have much to contribute.

Performance and Contingency

As important as structural parameters, doctrine, and motivation are in explaining the contours of the balance of power, what is of great importance as well is actual performance. By performance I mean not simply the passage of laws and executive action under the law or the Constitution. Rather, I mean laws and executive action that successfully alleviate societal distress and fears. What is equally critical is that such success preserves a viable balance of power between the Congress and the president. Otherwise, we no longer have a democratic republic but some form of autocracy, whether open or disguised. What is required for Congress to continue to play its designated role is the preservation of a meaningful degree of autonomy from presidential control and retention of a sufficient portion of the whole fund of policy discretion exercised by the federal government to sustain the reality of its role as lawmaker.

If these requirements are met, Congress's ability to play its designated role will be safeguarded, but barriers to its performance will still remain. As suggested, Congress must do more than just legislate. It must legislate in a manner that is wise and effective but at the same time representative. The burdens on performance are thus quite onerous. In legislating, it needs to balance consent and action. Indeed, the Constitution, by requiring that lawmaking involve the agreement of three separate entities, each based on a different constituency principle and different terms of office, seeks to attain these goals by promoting compromise among clashing views and interests and deliberation as well as bargaining to facilitate compromise. The point is to avoid the dangers simple majority rule based on a single principle of representation poses for both representation and wise decision making. However, what can also result is delay in addressing problems that many believe require quick action. As a result, when Congress fails to pass legislation, which is in accord with its responsibilities for action that is both representative and effective, it can damage its own role and power in the political system as well as the performance of the president. Yet the performance of the whole system, not just the Congress, is critical to trust and trust to the maintenance of our constitutional order. The high aspirations of the Constitution thus create a set of conundrums that under modern conditions are far more difficult to solve than a century ago.[11]

Thus, now even more than in the past, much depends on the states of the quasi parameters and their interaction with normative ideas and patterns of motivation. However, contingencies in the results of the interaction within and between these parameters, unanticipated events, and the personal qualities of leaders have significant impacts as well.[12] Note the impacts of divided government, of threats of systemic bank failure in 1933 and 2008, or of Franklin Roosevelt's leadership in peace and war. Our theoretical power at present is such that we can treat these impacts only as random causes. As a consequence, much that happens in politics is unanticipated and highly unpredictable. Even so, reality requires that the impact of contingencies be included, rather than ignored, though we can do so now in only an ad hoc manner. Hence, they will be included in my analysis.

Current State of the Balance of Power

To bring historical perspective to bear in explaining and assessing the present character of the balance of power, I will focus on the decline of congressional power since 1900 in what I have identified as the three prime systems of national policy decision making: the electoral, legislative, and administrative systems. I assume that since the Congress and president are actors in all three systems, gains in presidential or congressional power in one system contribute to gains in power and position in the others and hence shape the contours of the balance of power that exists between them. Thus, the decline of congressional power has been accompanied by the rise of presidential preeminence in all three systems.[13]

The Electoral System

I begin with the electoral system. The parties in the nineteenth century were loose coalitions of state and local parties, headed by party leaders with varying and shifting degrees of centralized control. These parties and party leaders chose the candidates, ran the campaigns, and funded them at all levels of government. As such, candidates were dependent on their party organizations to mobilize party workers to bring voters to the polls, to fund candidate campaigns, and to establish party newspapers to defend and support their candidates. All this hinged on various types of patronage in the form of jobs, special privileges, and contracts granted by party leaders who were central figures in state legislatures and the Congress. This is not to deny the importance of policy differences. Broad but changing policy issues divided the two major parties before and after the Civil War. Nonetheless, if the coalitions that defined the parties varied over time, the basic modes of organizing and conducting politics remained largely the same. Hence, this party system made Congress, given its ties to state and local party organizations, far more powerful in the party system than the president. Presidents, with a few notable exceptions, became the captives of state and local party leaders since these men controlled the nominations process and were vital to winning election campaigns in their states.[14]

Beginning in the late nineteenth century, however, what we may call the traditional party system began to decline. As it declined, the power of state and local party organizations declined, presidents increasingly freed themselves from control by state and local party bosses, and the number of such bosses itself declined so substantially that by the 1960s, few remained. The result over the course of the twentieth century was not simply to free the president from captivity to the party system but to make the president's party his captive and to make electoral politics far different than it had been in 1900. This was due to the increasing prominence over time of two trends that combined to create the current election system in the second half of the century.[15]

The first was the trend toward plebiscitary politics. This trend is characterized by direct appeals by presidential candidates to the people, by issue and personality politics, and by a transcendent relationship between the president and the people. To be sure, elements of this had been present in electoral politics since the Jackson presidency and the start of what may be called the traditional party system in the 1830s. Nonetheless, the presidencies of Harrison, Cleveland, and McKinley in the 1890s began a century of change. These presidents departed substantially from past norms and practice by seeking directly to mold public opinion on important issues and taking leadership in constructing delegate majorities apart from and even against the wishes of the most prominent state party leaders. The presidencies of Theodore Roosevelt and Woodrow Wilson strengthened and legitimized such practices by doing them openly and actively with reliance on mass advertising techniques that had recently been developed to sell commercial products. In so doing, they set new standards for norms and practice in the electoral process.[16]

The next inflection point came with the presidency of Franklin D. Roosevelt. By the end of FDR's terms in office, he had become so powerful in his party that party leaders in the states and the Congress generally deferred to his wishes on policy and political issues. His rise to the position of party chief was accompanied by and dependent on new strides in plebiscitary politics. He further perfected the practices and techniques of plebiscitary politics, and his mastery of them, combined with his leadership in fighting the Depression and winning the Second World War, raised the role and status of the presidency to new heights. For many, the president, not the Congress or party system, became the prime representative of the public interest and the person to be relied on to relieve the nation's fears and dissatisfactions.[17]

Another inflection point occurred in the 1960s. The passage of the civil rights legislation in the mid-1960s vitiated a prime basis of Southern allegiance to the Democratic Party and made the historic role the South had played as an anchor of the Democratic Party coalition unsustainable. The result was to initiate a process of re-sorting the components of the party coalitions along ideological lines in the South and across the nation.[18] The debacle of the 1968 Democratic Convention occurred soon after and demonstrated that severe decay in the strength of the traditional party system was not limited to its coalitional character but extended to the character of party as an organization as well. What occurred almost immediately was a redesign of rules in both parties that made primaries, not jockeying for support among state party leaders, the key to presidential nomination, with the result that our politics became more candidate centered than party centered. Both combined to make our politics more issue oriented and personality oriented, with the result that plebiscitary politics became an increasingly pronounced feature of the electoral system.[19]

The second trend was the emergence, in the last quarter of the twentieth century, of a very different form of party polarization than the type that prevailed in the past. In the traditional party system, party polarization at the electoral level depended more on historic allegiance to party and patronage than on the policy issues that distinguished the parties as sectional alliances. To be sure, an election like the 1896 or 1932 election could result in heightened polarization on issues. But these were rare realignment elections. Within the sectional constraints of the traditional party system, polarization rested on historic patterns of party loyalty as well as the flexibility that separate presidential, congressional, and state elections and control of patronage provided to diminish the importance of the policy disagreement that actually existed. It was thus subject to breakdown in presidential elections when policy differences within the parties reached very high levels, as they did in 1912 and 1924, and even more when they persisted, as they did after 1948. This form of polarization at the electoral level had substantially weakened by the 1950s, and a different basis for polarization based on ideological sorting emerged after the collapse of the traditional party system in the late 1960s.[20] It took several decades to mature, but it has resulted in high degrees of polarization on issues and voting patterns in elections in terms of ideological orientations at the same time that the number of weak party identifiers, leaners, and pure independents substantially increased. However, since weak party identifiers and leaners vote quite like strong party identifiers, declines in the strength of party identification have not canceled out the effects of ideology on voting behavior or polarization.[21]

The results of the trends in both plebiscitary and polarized politics have combined to transform the character of the electoral system. It is an electoral system in which candidate-centered politics and issue politics have become more important, so too have personality and rhetorical skills as media politics has proliferated, as have the techniques of mobilizing support and funds in presidential and congressional elections through the use of data mining, TV ads, and social media. At the same time, party allegiance has weakened as the proportion of the electorate who identify as independents or independent leaners, as opposed to strong or weak partisans, has increased. Nonetheless, polarization has increased and become even more bitter. Organizationally, the national committees have become subsidiaries of the personal campaign organization of presidential candidates and a unit controlled by presidents between elections. Moreover, the parties themselves have become increasingly difficult to differentiate from allied interest groups who play increasingly important roles in mobilizing voters and funding in conjunction with candidate campaigns. All these have redefined the politics of the election system for Congress and the presidency but in a manner that has increased the role and power of the president in electoral politics.

The Legislative System

The current role and power of the president and Congress in the legislative system is also a product of the growth of plebiscitary and polarized politics. These trends have influenced the state of the balance of power between the president and Congress but so too have the results of continuing, substantial delegations of policy discretion to the president and administrative units.

The increases in plebiscitary politics that occurred under Theodore Roosevelt, Woodrow Wilson, and Franklin Roosevelt and continued under Ronald Reagan and Barack Obama have increased the role and power of the president in the legislative process as well as the electoral process. Increasingly frequent and varied use of his office as a "bully pulpit" as well as growth in his ability to define the "party brand" accompanied the decline of the traditional party system and accelerated after its collapse. As a result, plebiscitary politics increased over the course of the twentieth century in the legislative process as well as the electoral process and served to combine political incentives for presidential support with substantive policy incentives, when they did not conflict and even when they did.[22]

As for the growth of party polarization, it is again intertwined with the growth of plebiscitary politics and different in form than in earlier eras. The rise of the president to the position of chief legislator preceded it by decades but was not enough in itself to produce high degrees of polarization. The sectionalism that underlay the traditional party system could only produce highly polarized politics in Congress if their sectional components were sufficiently aligned on salient issues. Even then, on the rare occasions in which it occurred, high degrees of party polarization did not make presidents as powerful in the legislative system as they are today. Thus, when the Congress was highly polarized in the early decades of the twentieth century, the sectional character of the traditional party system gave House members and senators substantial independence in the election system and, as a consequence, in the legislative system. In this era, Theodore Roosevelt was as much a captive of conservative party leaders in Congress as their master, and Woodrow Wilson had to bow to Southern Democratic congressional leaders on major legislation. In both cases, their power in their states and the Congress under the traditional party system was formidable. This is also true, though to a lesser degree, of the only other and far briefer period of relatively high polarization in the mid-1930s. As a result, when Southern defection steadily increased after 1938, it signaled the end of the New Deal and the advent of a Southern–Republican coalition that could control outcomes when it appeared.[23]

This situation persisted though in weakening form into the 1970s, despite the increased but still fragile power of presidents, such as Franklin Roosevelt, John Kennedy, and even Lyndon Johnson, in the legislative system. What was required for a high and stable degree of polarization to emerge in Congress was a drastic resorting of the party coalitions in terms of ideological orientations as well as the collapse of key organizational features of the traditional party system. All of this involved a transition to a new mode of politics and took several decades to mature.

Thus, though the late 1960s and early 1970s were accompanied by low levels of party votes and low levels of party unity on such votes, by the mid-1980s, party votes increased and cross-partisan voting on these votes declined in both the House and Senate. As they did, party polarization in Congress began to mount, strengthened in the 1990s, and climbed to new heights after 2009. As a result, polarization has become a pronounced feature of legislative politics that rivals the degree of polarization that prevailed between 1896 and 1915.[24] This is a distressing anomaly for those who do not see comparable increases in electoral polarization but less so for those who do. The explanations vary and will be explored in the next part of the chapter. Clearly, some mix of external and internal factors are involved, but whatever the character of the mix, increases in plebiscitary and polarized politics have reinforced one another more in the legislative process than in the electoral process due to greater concern among party leaders and their followers to protect the party brand and heightened leadership ability to control what is brought to a vote. In so doing, they have raised the president's leverage in legislative politics to a level that is historically very high.

A third component of long-term developments in congressional relationships to the president has been a decline in the scope or reach of congressional policy power relative to that of the president and administrative units, whether formally inside or outside the executive branch. In domestic policy, sizable increases in the delegation of discretionary policy-making authority have occurred in all the presidencies listed earlier.[25] This has taken place in tandem with an increasing focus on the need to expand federal responsibilities to relieve various sources of societal distress. The growth of plebiscitary politics and partisan politics, both before and after it became polarized, were part and parcel of this broader context of politics and served to enhance the president's ability to lead Congress to delegate huge amounts of discretion to the president and administrative units of all kinds. In foreign and security policy, the president, because of his constitutional powers, has legal authority he does not possess in domestic politics. Plebiscitary politics adds to these advantages because presidents have a bigger megaphone, and the public sees the president as the person to be turned to in times of distress. Thus, the severity of the threats to national security, both before and after the end of the Cold War, have enhanced presidential power. However, once the bipartisan template set during World War II weakened as a consequence of policy failures in the Vietnam War, partisanship again became a divisive factor and increased in importance as polarization grew. At present, policy failures, such as the Second Iraq War, lead to bitter partisan rancor, and partisan conflict over the annual legislation required to authorize and fund military and security programs has escalated.[26]

The growth of plebiscitary and polarized politics has combined with continuing sizable delegations of policy power to the president and administrative units to significantly depress both the autonomy of Congress and the scope of its policy control relative to executive control. In so doing, they have altered the balance of power substantially to the advantage of the presidency. If we turn first to autonomy, plebiscitary and polarized politics have combined in the modern Congress to make the role of the president as leader of the legislative process stronger than in the past, under both unified and divided government. It is true that presidents now give their congressional party leaders more flexibility on substance and strategy, but both are subject to his approval. It is true as well that in divided government, presidential power in domestic policy rests more on his ability to obstruct than to pass legislation. Nonetheless, whether government is unified or divided, voting against the president's desires on important items has become even more akin to treason than in past episodes of polarized politics. This is true because polarized politics that is nationally based, in combination with heightened plebiscitary politics, has made dissent a far greater danger to shared policy goals, the reelection of fellow partisans, and control of the Congress than in the past. For this and other reasons that relate to the preeminence and resources of the president in both the electoral and legislative systems, the role of party leaders of the same party as the president has increasingly become one of agents of the president, not equals or near equals, as it was at the start of the twentieth century, or more than equals, as was typically true in the nineteenth century.[27]

The result has been to transform the internal operation and politics of the Congress in ways that lessen its autonomy. One distinguishing feature of the contemporary Congress is the increase in departures from following the regular order of business. When plebiscitary and polarized politics prevail, the passage or defeat of important legislation the president desires or opposes becomes more important than following traditional procedures that have been time-tested to promote wise legislation. Rather, such procedures are sacrificed to heighten the ability of the parties to win or block action. Hence, for example, in the House, restrictive rules from the Rules Committee that load the dice in favor of the kind of bill the leadership wants to pass have grown substantially. In the Senate, traditional unanimous consent agreements to bring bills to the floor and control debate have largely been abandoned, and reliance on cloture has become an everyday event necessary even to bring bills to the floor. Finally, plebiscitary and polarized politics encourage party leaders to rewrite committee bills and members not to fully read or understand important bills, which can be thousands of pages in length, but simply to vote in accord with their party leaders' wishes.[28]

A related consequence of the strength of plebiscitary and polarized politics has been to make blame game politics a dominant feature of the contemporary Congress. Substantive policy differences still are important, but in both the House and Senate, decision making is determined more by political effects on the public, with an eye to the next election, than by substantive policy goals. For both the president and opposing party leaders, the critical question has increasingly become how much compromise on policy issues serves their political needs and how to take credit or assign blame for the decisions made.[29] However, the president enjoys a number of advantages in blame game politics. He usually has first-mover advantage and, more importantly, has a bigger megaphone in speaking to the public, greater capacity to present a unified message, and the support of a far larger array of skilled staff resources in the White House Office to frame and communicate his message than opposing-party leaders in the Congress. In addition, his negative power is virtually unassailable since overriding his veto requires a two-thirds vote in both houses, which is exceedingly difficult to obtain in a plebiscitary and polarized era. Thus, he can seek to cut his losses for obstructing action rather than compromising by making up some portion of the loss by extending his discretionary policy power under laws already in existence or broad interpretation of what his constitutional authority permits.[30]

As for the relative scope of congressional policy control in important areas of national policy, it also has declined. To be sure, the broad framework for policy is set in congressional legislation, which also includes more specific directions on goals and implementation to varying degrees. Nonetheless, the great bulk of discretionary decision making has been placed in the hands of the president or administrative officials, who have become increasingly subject to his direction, whether inside the executive branch or not. Yet the combination of plebiscitary and polarized politics in the contemporary Congress has seriously undermined Congress's ability to compensate for delegations of authority to the president and administrative officials through oversight of performance that brings Congress's lawmaking, appropriations, and investigatory powers to bear. This is especially true in unified government since the majority party can block all forms of legislative action, and the incentives for corrective action are undermined both in

Congress and the executive branch by the political costs for the president and/or the policy goals of members of Congress and politically appointed executive officials. But it is true in divided government as well. Key appointed administrative officials are quite likely to obstruct providing opposition partisans with the help and information required to make an adequate investigation possible.[31] Past that point, members of the president's party are very unlikely to cooperate in supplying any of the votes needed to overcome a presidential veto or a filibuster in the Senate when corrective legislation is offered in regular legislation or in provisos in appropriation bills. The result is that the proportion of the fund of policy discretion in the hands of Congress as opposed to the executive branch has altered substantially in favor of the latter.

The Administrative System

In the 1880s and for several decades thereafter, Woodrow Wilson saw the president as the "legal head" of the executive branch but so dependent on his cabinet appointees that the administrative process was best characterized as government by commission.[32] This perception was grounded in reality. The president had little or no role in the budget process since departmental estimates were referred to Congress without review, had to share his appointment power with senators, only covertly and irregularly participated in the legislative process, and had only about a dozen staff to assist him, most of whom were involved in moving paper. In contrast, cabinet members ran their departments and looked as much to congressional committees for guidance and support as to the president. This was less so in foreign policy, but even here, cabinet officers were very deferential to the Senate Foreign Relations Committee. In the twentieth century, the situation that prevailed at the end of the nineteenth century drastically reversed.

The changes that expanded presidential power were interrelated and multifaceted. A direct consequence of the reduction in the relative scope of congressional policy control was expansion in the relative scope of executive policy control. This expansion is a necessary backdrop for understanding the growth of presidential power in the administrative system. For more than a century, the overall trend in domestic affairs has been toward an administrative state—that is, a state in which a very large part of the daily lives and activities of individual citizens are governed directly or indirectly by the discretionary decisions of presidents and administrators rather than the concrete provisions of congressional laws. Similarly, in foreign and security policy, the ability Congress had at the turn of the century to influence and constrain presidential decision making has substantially declined. Note, for example, how Congress's power to declare war has become a relic of the past and how the Senate's power to agree to treaties has been bypassed by reliance on executive agreements.

Despite the continuing growth in the discretion vested in the administrative system, Congress did not turn quickly or easily to facilitating presidential control of the administrative system. It was not until 1939 that Congress approved

President Franklin Roosevelt's proposal to create a new layer of units and staff personnel between the president and the regular executive departments that would be subject to his direct control. This new layer, the Executive Office of the President (EOP) initially was composed of six units. Two of these have endured to the present. One was new—a White House Office staffed with six new special assistants to the president for policy advice and coordination in addition to several dozen existing staff personnel, such as a press secretary, speechwriters, and policy advisors, who had been members of the president's staff before the creation of the EOP. The other was the Bureau of the Budget (BB), which had been created in 1921 but was placed in the Treasury Department because Congress believed that such placement would make it amenable to its control, given the historically close relationship it had with Treasury. By 1939, it was clear that the president needed better tools to manage the expanded bureaucracy produced by the New Deal and that in practice the BB was an arm of the president. However, it was also clear that creating an institutionalized presidency would give the president more power to control administrative decision making. That is why it took two years of bitter conflict to pass a stripped-down version of the original bill.[33]

Since 1939, the number and character of the units in the EOP has varied a great deal. So too has the number of staff. The units that have endured once created, though at times under a different name, now number a dozen. The total staff employed in fiscal year 2015 was 1,773 as opposed to about four hundred in 1940. The EOP is a loose collection of units that vary in the character and breadth of their concerns. I want to focus on three of these units because of their importance: the White House Office (WHO), the Office of Management and Budget (OMB), and the National Security Council (NSC).[34]

The WHO had fifty-three employees in 1941, 398 in 2000, and 439 in 2015. It should be noted that the staff of the NSC (eighty-five in 2015) are in reality WHO staff since they are directed by the president's assistant for national security affairs. Organizationally, the WHO has evolved over time. It now has a chief of staff and two deputy chiefs of staff. However, they function primarily as distributors of tasks, overseers, and mediators rather than hierarchical commanders. The subunits of the WHO have varied over time and have expanded to cover all the concerns of the modern presidency, including policy decision making, communication with the public, political strategy, vetting candidates for presidential appointments, and relations with Congress and minority groups.[35]

Similarly, the OMB (before and after it succeeded the BB in the 1970s) has evolved over time. Its staff numbered 305 in 1941, 636 in 1970, and 457 in 2015. More importantly, its orientation changed from what has been characterized as "neutral competence" to serving the policy goals of the president. The turning point came in 1974 after growing presidential dissatisfaction with a budget operation that was more oriented to economy and efficiency than serving their policy goals. In that year, President Nixon convinced Congress to agree to a recommendation to create a layer of political appointees between the director of the BB and the career employees, who headed the five issue areas of annual budget analysis and formulation. In addition, an administrative clearance function for rulemaking was added in 1981 by an executive order of President Reagan that required all proposed departmental and agency rules to be reviewed by a new subunit of the OMB, the Office of Information and Regulatory Affairs (OIRA), in terms of their cost-effectiveness. Such a review system has been adopted by every president, regardless of party, since Reagan and refined to increase its effectiveness.[36]

The development of an institutionalized presidency has contributed greatly to the rise of presidential power in the administrative system. In terms of the units that are specialized in providing control and coordination of administrative decision making, the OMB provides the primary general and regularized mechanisms for such purposes. This flows naturally from its annual review of the funding of all administrative units in order to prepare the levels of funding to be included in the president's annual budget proposal to the Congress. In so doing, the political appointees in the OMB consult with key officials in the WHO on aspects of the budget that are pertinent to major presidential policy goals. In addition, as noted, a unit of the OMB, the OIRA, is vested with reviewing rules proposed by executive-branch units and independent commissions and has the authority to ask for changes or reconsideration if a proposed rule does not meet its cost-effectiveness standards. Such review is now limited to "significant" rules—those that involve $100 million or more of economic costs—due to the heavy burdens of rulemaking review in an administrative state. These rules are less than 3 percent of all final rules, which now number in excess of three thousand annually, and the total annual cost to the economy is close to a trillion dollars. In comparison, the number of congressional bills passed per Congress has averaged 321.[37]

Several WHO subunits provide sources of policy development and coordination as well as control. These include the NSC in foreign and security policy, the Domestic Council in domestic policy, and the National Economic Council in economic policy. The latter two, like the NSC, are interdepartmental councils and led by assistants to the president with staffs of their own. The most powerful one is the NSC. The staff member in charge has greater influence relative to cabinet members on the council than is true of the other councils because of the importance of this area to presidents and because he or she is housed in the West Wing, close to the president. Last but not least, the Office of Personnel provides an essential pillar of presidential policy control. Since the 1950s, the number of political appointments in executive departments and the layering of them between the department or agency head and the career staff have substantially increased. The number of such positions in 2012 was close to three thousand.[38] The rigor of review has also increased, and its focus has changed from accommodating national, state, and local party leaders and important interest groups to regard for presidential policy goals and sustaining the campaign organization of the president. In addition, such vetting now includes the board members of all the independent commissions. Thus, if a president like Barack Obama favors rules and regulations favorable to reduction of reliance on fossil fuels or the imposition of net neutrality to govern the Internet, he can advance these goals in substantial ways by appointing a director of the EPA or a chair of the FCC who will be responsive to presidential policy goals and open to direction by the prime lieutenants of the president in the WHO.[39]

In terms of guarding and promoting the political appeal of administrative decisions in the electoral and legislative processes, as well as public regard for the president, this is the charge of several WHO subunits. They include the Office of Political Affairs, the Office of Communication, the Press Office, and the Office of Legislative Affairs. These subunits contain staff that rank among the highest in their personal interaction with the president. Thus, though conflict between the policy and political subunits of the WHO is endemic in their charges and expertise, the concerns of both must be considered and reconciled to maximize the success of a presidency. The WHO, through its subunits and leaders, thus provides the primary mechanism for taking both policy and politics into account. In doing so, it also enables presidential control of both policy and politics. The president is the one who determines the configuration of WHO units, chooses the leaders and key staff members of the WHO, and decides whom he will consult on particular issues as well as whether he will accept or alter the recommendations brought to him. There are, of course, limits as well to his decision-making power, but their discussion will be postponed until they can be combined with an analysis of a second major source of the growth in presidential power in the administrative system.

That source is the growth in the scope of unilateral action by the president. Such action also requires staff support, but its exercise in recent years has been of even greater significance in enhancing presidential power than the control and coordination of administrative decision making that the institutionalized presidency provides. Though unilateral action by the president in a generic sense is inevitably involved in the exercise of executive power, the critical question is what is the source of authority and does it justify the action in cases in which presidential action exceeds what has been regular and accepted practice? There are two sources of authority. One is authority granted in law, and the other is authority granted in the Constitution. However, what either justifies is now subject to greater dispute than in the past. The words of statutes can be interpreted to legitimize action that substantially extends what has long been understood to be their meaning. An example is the recent executive action on transgender rights in bathrooms and showers. It is argued that such action is justified by Title VII of the Civil Rights Act of 1964 that banned discrimination on the basis of sex, though this is a recent and controversial claim.[40] Similarly, the words of the Constitution include broad grants of authority to the president by vesting executive power in him and by making him commander in chief of the armed forces. These grants in recent years have spawned the theory of a unified executive that claims that executive power is plenary and hence not subject to limitations by Congress that impinge on his inherent executive power under the Constitution. In addition and quite aside from the claims based on the theory of a unified executive, unilateral action can rely on stretching past, accepted notions of executive authority. A case in point is justification of President Obama's decision to exempt 4 to 5 million illegal aliens from deportation as a simple matter of prosecutorial discretion.[41]

The legitimacy of presidential unilateral action that exceeds regular and accepted implementation of the law or the exercise of presidential power under the Constitution is thus now rent by conflict to a greater degree than in the past. The traditional standard was whether the action taken could be reasonably tied to a provision of law or the Constitution, but currently that standard has been seriously challenged. President Bush did so by relying on the theory of a unified executive to legitimize his actions regarding the trial and detention of enemy combatants and rendition, as well as the use of signing statements. Yet the theory of a unified executive is based on a profound misunderstanding of our history, and its claims are unfounded. Thus, the Supreme Court rejected, the George W. Bush administration's reliance on the theory of a unified executive in several cases involving the trial and detention of enemy combatants. President Obama, in contrast, has not based his extensions of his power to act unilaterally on such claims.[42] Even so, President Obama has gone much further than President Bush in reliance on unilateral action in domestic policy. When challenged in federal courts, he has found other grounds than claims of a unitary executive to justify them. Aside from his actions with respect to deferring the deportation of 4 to 5 million illegal aliens and transgender bathrooms and showers, he has suspended a variety of the deadlines and mandates in the Affordable Care Act as a matter of administrative discretion, spent funds that were not appropriated to lower premium costs under Obamacare on the ground that the authorization of the Act alone justified such spending, made recess appointments to vacancies on the National Labor Relations Board (NLRB) based on his right to determine whether the Senate was in recess no matter what the Senate determined, and relied on an executive agreement, not a treaty, to implement an extremely important agreement with Iran on the development of atomic weapons, despite serious disagreement over whether such usage in this case was valid constitutionally.[43] Last but not least, President Obama has invented a new form of unilateral action that merges presidential direction and departmental guidance on the policies and processes to be relied upon in implementing it. Traditionally, unilateral power has been exercised through executive orders, presidential directives, and memoranda, not agency rulemaking. Yet as his recent decisions on immigration and transgender rights demonstrate, he has combined what in effect is agency rulemaking without regard for the legal procedures for rulemaking and unilateral action based simply on the assumption that his generic authority to implement the law justifies such action. If this new form survives Court review, presidential power will be extended substantially.[44]

The consequences of the two sources of the growth of presidential power in the administrative system I have identified are immense. An institutionalized presidency has placed the president far more in command of administrative decision making than at the turn of the nineteenth century by substantially politicizing and centralizing it. Overall, cabinet officers are far less in control of policy in their areas of responsibility, and WHO officials far more powerful, even to the point of co-opting important policy decision making. Nonetheless, overhead control and coordination of administrative decision making is far from perfect. The government is too large, political forces too complex, and the instruments of presidential control and coordination too oriented to policy development to be highly comprehensive rather than highly selective and reactive in instituting presidential control and coordination. Similarly, the expertise, dedication to their professions, and connections to Congress and clienteles of career employees combine with the inexperience and limited tenure of their politically appointed superiors to make career appointees far more than mere pawns. It is no accident that presidents remain dissatisfied with their ability to control and coordinate the administrative process and continually seek new mechanisms, the latest being the appointment of a host of "czars" to control slices of policy across executive agencies and White House units. What is also true, however, is that plebiscitary and polarized politics in united government in combination with the president's veto power in divided government have substantially reduced the ability of Congress to oversee and check presidential power in the administrative process. Despite their importance, few administrative rules or executive orders are ever overturned by congressional laws or provisos in appropriations bills. Rather, the Congress must rely on suits states or citizens bring in the federal courts to prevent agencies, like the EPA, from rulemaking that it believes violates the legal authority granted in their authorizing legislation. That Congress is so dependent on the courts speaks far more to congressional weakness than strength. As for unilateral action by the president, it arguably poses an even greater threat to preserving a viable balance of power. President Obama has proceeded in important policy areas as if he had the expanse of executive power that President Bush claimed.[45] Such actions and claims may well increase since the incentives to use them are substantial. Here too, the Congress must rely on the federal courts to constrain presidential overreach based on claims of plenary or inherent executive power, even when disguised. Yet here too, for a variety of reasons, the federal courts may, as in the case of the Affordable Care Act, sustain executive power, not congressional authority under the Constitution.

Explanation of the Current Balance of Power

Clearly, over the last century, the role and power of the Congress in all three prime national policy decision-making systems has diminished. As noted earlier, I will frame my explanation in terms of how the interaction among changing quasi parameters, ideas and doctrines, and patterns of motivation contributed to the rise of presidential preeminence in each system and how gains in each system reinforced one another. In addition, I will include attention to the role of contingency as a factor that affects the impacts of the interactions my guidelines identify as important.

The Electoral System

The task of explaining the current election system in a few pages can be reduced to explaining the rise of plebiscitary and polarized politics with more attention to plebiscitary politics than polarized politics. From the start of the twentieth century, plebiscitary politics continually increased in strength for decades before polarized politics began in the mid-1980s to climb again to the high levels reached in the early years of the century.[46] To be sure, both contributed to the present character of the election system and the power of the president in it. But polarized politics did so in the context of a politics more defined by issues and personality and less by party loyalty and party organization. As a result, the sorting of voters that occurred was driven more by the increased influence of ideological orientation than changes in the strength of party allegiance, though the two are interrelated. This is strongly suggested by the fact that from 1968 to 2012, the percentage of party identifiers decreased from 71 percent to 62 percent, whereas the percentage of leaners and pure independents increased from 30 percent to 38 percent.[47] Thus, as argued earlier, the polarization that prevails now is a different type of polarization than prevailed at the turn of the nineteenth century. It is a different animal and, as the 2016 primary elections suggest, may be even more open to instability in electoral alignments due to the greater importance of issues and personality.

To explain why the present electoral system arose and the role and power of the president in it expanded, changes in the quasi parameters identified earlier play an important role. The continuing expansion in the role and responsibilities of the federal government since 1900 and its acceleration after 1960 fostered an increasing nationalization of politics.[48] This, in turn, resulted in a politics in which divisions between voters in different regions grew less important and divisions among voters across the nation on the basis of issues and ideology more important. The result was to ease the way for further expansion in the role of plebiscitary politics, especially in presidential elections, and after 1968 for the growth of polarized politics to levels that matched those in the first decade and half of the twentieth century. Equally important, the continuing increase in the power of the technologies that could be applied for purposes of political communication and travel played an important role in providing a platform for the growth of plebiscitary politics and an increase in polarized politics as issue-oriented and candidate-centered politics grew in strength. Indeed, it provided a critical link between the nationalization of politics and the changes in party as a coalition and organization—so much so that without the technological changes that occurred, the current state of the election system is unimaginable.[49] As noted, the alteration of the state of party as a coalition and organization since 1968 has been a critical factor in creating ideologically defined coalitions and party organizations that are the captives of presidents and allied groups rather than vice versa. The other two quasi parameters also had important effects. Changes in election rules and procedures that removed barriers to voting in the South, made the times of voting more flexible, and enhanced the role of primaries helped to expand the electorate and to varying degrees sparked the emergence of candidate-centered politics.[50] Finally, what drove the growth of presidential power in all systems to a significant degree was an expansion in the need for political leadership, which was tied to the challenges posed by an expanding set of governmental responsibilities. Presidents were more able to meet this need because their capacity for decision making was grounded in the hierarchical character of the executive branch and increasingly augmented by the changing states of the quasi parameters.

Similarly, change in ideas and doctrine and patterns of motivation interacted with changes in the quasi parameters to justify and spur presidential power in the electoral system. The heightened inclination of voters to look to the president to solve the problems of the nation was accompanied by a decline in nineteenth-century belief that parties and/or the Congress were the best representatives of the public interest. Involved in this decline was an erosion of belief that there were important differences between a republic and a democracy and thus a growing belief that legitimate government meant power to the "people" and the supremacy of majority rule. Such belief, in turn, substantially contributed to the view that the president was the sole or best delineator of the public interest since he was elected by the nation as a whole. In so doing, it both displaced Madison's belief that the public interest was best found through the accommodation of the clashing views and interests that would result from a House, Senate, and presidency based on different principles of representation and discounted the very need for checks and balances that Madison thought essential as a bulwark against abuse of power by federal officials. Finally, patterns of motivation in voting changed as well. Loyalty to party and regard for character and accomplishment declined, and regard for issues and sheer personal appeal increased.[51]

It is this mix of interactive factors that brought the election system to the point where it was defined by plebiscitary politics and a form of polarized politics that was compatible with it to the great advantage of the presidency and disadvantage of the Congress. However, as always, contingencies that were rooted in complex decision-making processes, unanticipated events, and the personal qualities and skills of political leaders were involved in the results. Now, as in the past, they make elections and their policy effects difficult to predict and, at times when change greatly outpaces stability, can affect the very shape of the electoral system. No one could have predicted the 1929 Depression or its effects on American politics and policy through the election of Franklin Roosevelt in 1932. Indeed, the New Deal evolved in ways Roosevelt himself did not anticipate in the early years of his presidency.[52] We are ourselves now at a point where we sense that something very different is happening in our politics but are uncertain and fearful of what will result. What we will learn is whether 2016 will be a rare election, like 1860, 1896, and 1932, that drastically reshapes our politics or something less.

The Legislative System

To explain the decline in congressional autonomy and the scope of its policy control, I can rely again on the interaction of quasi parameters, normative ideas and doctrines, and patterns of motivation, as bounded by contingencies that randomize their effects. In the case of the quasi parameters, the decline in autonomy was tied to the rise of plebiscitary and polarized politics and hence to the second-order effects of change in the responsibilities of the federal government, the power of political technology, and the state of the party system as a coalition and organization. This is less true of changes in decision-making rules and the capacity for decision making. Though linked to changes in workload that stressed the specialized expertise provided by the committee system and changes in the coherence of party coalitions that in the House promoted centralizing power in the majority party leadership, the character and interaction between the two created a dynamic that made their effects something more than second-order effects of changes in the electoral system. Thus, though there is dispute over the causes of increased polarization, Sean Theriault is correct in arguing that it results from a mix of external and internal causes.[53] The external causes relate to the forces that produced greater electoral polarization, which both enabled and combined with the expanded ability of the party leadership to control the issues voted upon and turn party politics in the Congress into a politics in which protecting the party brand became a far more paramount concern. As for scope, the decline in autonomy was a contributing factor, but equally, if not more, important was the stress that increases in the range and complexities of new proposed legislation placed on the capacity of Congress to fashion legislation that served its policy goals without vesting so much discretion in executive officers as to threaten its ability to control policy in very important regards. Nonetheless, given mounting political and policy pressures for legislative action and its own internal divisions, over time, very broad delegations of discretion were made, even if largely in spurts of activity in particular periods.

In the case of ideas and doctrine, here too, change was essential to legitimize the advance in plebiscitary and polarized politics that change in the quasi parameters produced as well as their effects in depressing congressional autonomy and scope. Several types of doctrinal change were involved. One was change in conceptions of the role of government. The claims and actions of Theodore Roosevelt and Woodrow Wilson challenged traditional notions of limited government that prevailed in the nineteenth century. Still, the triumph of a view that looked favorably on an active role of government awaited the New Deal, which decisively altered the weight of opinion on the proper role and responsibilities of the federal government and thereby completed the process of reframing the context of discussion and debate that began in the Progressive period. The result was not only to legitimize further expansion in the role of government but to confine debate for decades largely to further extensions.[54]

Similarly, the notion that the president, not Congress or one's party, was the sole or best representative of the public interest played an important role in justifying and promoting presidential power in the legislative process as well as in the electoral process. Though not explicit in Theodore Roosevelt's and Woodrow Wilson's open and active advocacy of their legislative policy proposals, it was clearly a premise that justified their sharp departures from nineteenth-century norms and practices. Later, once again, the New Deal extended and anchored such practice to the point where presidential leadership was universally approved and expected in terms of both program initiatives and open and active pressure for their passage.⁵⁵ Last but not least, the emergence of and reliance on the concept of a "party brand" as a substitute for more traditional notions of party discipline and responsible party government served the purposes and reflected the assumptions of plebiscitary politics. It promoted the belief that voter choices in the electoral process, like consumer choices, are made largely in terms of "brand," as defined by a set of ideologically consistent issue positions. As a result, it implicitly justified greater attention to winning elections than achieving substantive policy goals and thus contributed to the rise of blame game politics. To be sure, the differences between the two reflect the more polarized and plebiscitary character of current politics, but they help us to understand the importance of doctrinal change in legislative politics.⁵⁶

The patterns of motivation in the current Congress have also been altered by plebiscitary and polarized politics. Blame game politics requires members of Congress to vote the party line, no matter what their policy preferences or those of their constituents are. Hence, high levels of party voting on roll call votes reflect more than agreement among party members. They also reflect the ability of party leaders to select the issues voted on and to pressure fellow partisans to make their party's ability to win the next election the primary determinant of their votes. As for presidents, they are aware that the motivation of fellow partisans in Congress to support their president is far stronger than in the past, even when they disagree. Still, it remains true that presidents must be cautious in exploiting the advantages their positions as head of their party and command of favors the administrative system can provide. For both presidents and opposing party leaders, the goal is to play blame game politics successfully, which means making decisions that succeed in casting blame on the opposing party for inaction and taking credit for action the public approves.

Finally, once again, various types of contingency play an important role in determining results. Indeed, the current legislative process is rent by contingencies that derive not only from sudden events or differences in the skills of presidents and Senate leaders but also from the effects of plebiscitary and polarized politics in promoting blame game politics. In such a context, contingencies that affect success in playing blame game politics gain added importance. They include whether unified government is present in both houses; whether divided government is present in the Senate, if not the House; and whether the dimensions of majority party size in both houses relative to the levels of defection will be sufficient, given the barriers to bipartisan support, to win the majority support in the House and the sixty votes in the Senate necessary to pass important legislation. The question for the president and opposing party leaders is always how much to compromise since neither side wishes to be tagged as obstructionist from the start. But the need for compromise is affected by whether government is united or divided, and the leeway for compromise is highly restricted in each case by blame game politics and by whether majority party size, relative to the number of majority party dissidents, is sufficient to provide a majority in the House and the sixty votes needed to overcome a filibuster in the Senate. The drivers of contingency in the legislative process have thus been enhanced by the advent of plebiscitary and polarized politics and have made the skills of legislative leaders more important. As a result, legislative politics is now far more like multidimensional chess than a game of checkers and victory far more contingent.

The Administrative System

In the administrative system, as elsewhere, the rise of presidential power can be explained by the interaction of quasi parameters, normative ideas, and patterns of motivation, as bounded by contingency. In the nineteenth century, Congress vied quite successfully with the president for control of the administrative system. However, in the twentieth century, all the quasi parameters altered in ways that elevated presidential control at the expense of congressional control. The expanding responsibilities of the federal government were a key factor. This is true because the executive branch's potential for expanding decision-making capacity is far greater than that of the Congress, and the president's position as its head allows the president to be the prime beneficiary of such expansion. As noted earlier, the executive branch is a bureaucracy, not a collegial organization of formal equals. Its rules and procedures for decision making are thus open to increases in the degree of hierarchical control in decision making as well as increases in the specialization of its operating units. These factors also make it more able to profit from the growth of technology. The executive branch thus has greater capacity for decision making and can extend it as the size and complexity of demands for governmental action increase. In contrast, Congress cannot match it in these regards. It is designed to balance consent with action, not simply to act. As a result, it has always been dependent on administrators to act, and increases in the responsibilities of the federal government have made it even more dependent. Delegation is the price Congress has to pay to realize its policy goals. It is thus no accident that the expansion in the responsibilities of the federal government led to the creation of an institutionalized presidency in which the levers of presidential control continually expanded in number and import. Nor is it an accident, given the impacts of the other systems of decision making on the president's power in the administrative system, that the WHO grew to include units that were designed to extend his control of the electoral and legislative systems as well.

Change in the state of party as a coalition and an organization was a critical factor as well. The long-term decline of the traditional party system that began in the late 1880s, the rise in the stability and power of what Samuel Kernel has called protocoalitions to compensate for party weakness in the early and mid-twentieth century, and their decline after the collapse of the traditional party system all contributed to the power of the president in the administrative system.[57] The initial phase involved the replacement of patronage appointees, most of whom were indebted to congressional benefactors, with merit system appointees. The middle period involved the rise of the president to party chief and the decline of the power of cabinet officers as their political importance in the party system declined. The final period involved the further consolidation of presidential power in all three systems and, ironically enough, the decline of the merit system as political appointments increased—but this time to benefit presidential power, not to sustain party power. As a result, if the role and power of cabinet officers in their own bailiwicks has declined relative to the power of the president and WHO staff, the basic reason is that their influence in a presidentially dominated party system was far less than in a sectional party system dominated by state party leaders in and out of Congress.[58] They became highly dependent on the president and could be treated far more as persons who ran their departments but whose role and power in the administration was subject to the president's wishes and judgment.

As argued previously, the impact of the quasi parameters on presidential power is tied to their interaction with normative ideas and doctrines and patterns of motivation. With respect to ideas and doctrine, the role of the president in the administrative system in the nineteenth century was seen primarily in terms of his responsibility to ensure that congressional laws were faithfully executed. As presidential roles and power grew, a twentieth-century view emerged and became dominant by the 1930s. That view saw the president as a chief executive.[59] This change, in effect, sanctified presidential control of the administrative branch beyond what was acceptable to congressional thinking in the nineteenth century and made seeing the president as responsible for faithful execution secondary and even marginal. Equally important, it was accompanied by and interrelated with the triumph of a theory of presidential power, first fully stated by Theodore Roosevelt after he left office, that the president was the steward of the people and hence entitled by the executive power vested in him to do anything not expressly forbidden by Congress or the Constitution. This view was attacked by ex-president Taft, who restated the consensus view from the start of the republic that the president had no power to do anything that could not clearly be tied to specific provisions of law or the Constitution.[60] This dispute continues to this day, is complicated by the breadth of legal delegations of authority to the president and administrative units, and is highly involved in disputes over the legitimacy of unilateral action by the president. A final and related aspect of doctrine concerns the role of the president as a representative of the public interest. This notion is implicit in Theodore Roosevelt's claim and has become a widely shared view that justifies past increases in presidential power and desires for further increases. It is often combined as well with a dismissal of Congress as nothing more than a representative only or primarily of special interests.[61] A Manichaean distinction of this kind is not only dubious on empirical grounds but conflicts with the Framers' belief that the public interest was something to be found through the interaction of three entities, each of which is based on a different principle of representation. Nonetheless, it contributed powerfully to the broad inclination since the presidency of Franklin Roosevelt to see the president as the savior of the political system and the proper repository of all the hopes and fears of the American people.

With respect to patterns of motivation, their impacts again are tied to their interaction with change in the quasi parameters and ideas and doctrine. As quasi parameters and doctrine changed, presidents came to see themselves as wholly or primarily responsible for identifying and achieving the public interest. This combined with a desire for personal fame, the great and grave responsibilities of the federal government they head, and belief in the correctness of their policies to motivate presidents to subordinate traditional norms of behavior and even the boundaries set by the fixed parameters to political success. Modern presidents, in short, given their and the public's expectations, find it difficult to accept limitations imposed by the Constitution or statutes and seek by various means to escape them. Equally, if not more, important, the motivations of the public and key actors play a role as well. Belief in the president's distinctive responsibilities for the public interest are shared by most of the public and many key actors in government, the press, and academia. The result is to incline both partisan supporters and opponents of the president to take positions they would not take if a president of the opposing party were in office. The subordination of policy to politics is an age-old dilemma in democratic politics, and its negative consequences in hindering the kind of deliberation and compromise required for its success are even greater in an age of heightened plebiscitary and polarized politics.

Finally, here, as elsewhere, contingencies play an important role in the state of presidential power. Whether divided government results from elections matters. It affects how blame game politics is played in administrative and legislative decision making, as well as the feedback effects on the next electoral cycle. Similarly, unanticipated events can provide shocks that alter results in all three processes and have immediate and continuing effects on presidential power depending on how well they are handled. For this and other reasons, the personal qualities and skills of leaders are important. The differences between a Theodore Roosevelt and a William Howard Taft or a Jimmy Carter and a Ronald Reagan impact results at all three stages of decision making.[62] Such impacts, though contingent, have always played a role in outcomes. Yet what the past two presidencies suggest is that the interactive effects of quasi parameters, doctrine, and patterns of motivation have reached a point where presidents can use the power and veneration they now confer to sustain or undermine the fixed parameters set in the Constitution. All this, in turn, makes the contingencies attached to the qualities and skills of the president more important than ever.

Issues and Dilemmas

As argued earlier, performance matters, but performance cannot be judged simply in terms of bills passed or actions taken. It is determined both by the actual outcomes of decision making on people's lives and whether these outcomes are accomplished within the broad bounds of the fixed parameters set in the Constitution. The underlying premise of our constitutional order is that wise and effective action is aided, not impaired, by the limits set in the Constitution.

It is that premise that again has come under heavy attack as performance has increasingly disappointed large groups of voters. Perhaps the simplest and least contestable indicator of performance is the degree of trust in government.[63] When trust declines and reaches very low levels, this signals that at least one of the key prerequisites of performance is not being met and that alienation rather than support of our political system is increasing. There is persuasive evidence that this has been the case over the past two decades. Measures of trust in the federal government have fluctuated somewhat since the late 1950s when trust was very high. However, the overall trend has been down, and in recent years, trust in government has been extremely low, especially in the case of Congress. These findings are supported by the successes of the Donald Trump and Bernie Sanders 2016 primary campaigns. They indicate that large groups of voters are now very angry about the performance of our political system and seriously doubt that our government serves their interests rather than the interests of the wealthy and powerful.

Current high levels of alienation raise a question directly pertinent to this chapter. That is, do current low levels of trust validate the belief of many students of the Congress and presidency that the Madisonian design of our institutions is outmoded and needs to be altered by substantially increasing the system's power to act? This is not a new claim or contention. Opposition to the limitations checks and balances impose on action have been with us since the time of Woodrow Wilson. Modern advocates of this position differ from those in the past in the degree to which they see the solution as greater presidential power, whether accompanied by stronger parties or not.[64] Yet whatever their differences on means, they support further increases in presidential power that has reached new heights historically at the expense of the key entity that limits presidential control of policy. Indeed, many of these advocates see the current levels of congressional power not merely as an encumbrance on performance but as one that has become intolerable, given the pressing need for government action to solve the problems that confront the nation. For these critics, normative concerns, adverse to those of the Founders, are tightly connected to their attack on stalemate in the legislative process. Stalemate is seen not simply as a barrier to action but as the prime enemy of representative government. Thus, decision making that is not founded on simple majority rule is castigated and the sacrifice of deliberation and compromise to the needs of action treated as inconsequential. Reform proposals thus focus on the filibuster, and critics are quite open to increasing the degree to which congressional decision making on key issues is simply a matter of up and down votes on executive proposals.[65] However, there is also a recent strain of objection to the Madisonian design of our political system that is even more adverse to the views of the Founders. Some now argue that in important regards, it has already been largely displaced. They welcome it and believe that fears of presidential power and its further expansion are delusional, if not paranoid.[66]

Most critics, however, are far less sanguine that the game is over and won. They understand that Congress, despite its losses in the relative scope and autonomy of its policy control, is far from a cipher in American politics and believe that further limitations of its power will not be easy to achieve. Yet those who approve of weakening Congress's power to obstruct the president ignore or discount the benefits our constitutional design provides. Indeed, even those students of the Congress and the presidency who are more sensitive to the benefits of a viable balance of power frame the issue by stating that the central question is whether the presidency is imperial or impaired. However, congressional power, though reduced, still makes the presidency less than imperial, and the presidency cannot escape impairment as long as the fixed parameters set in the Constitution continue to prevail. This dichotomy is misleading and, in effect, biases choice in favor of further extensions of presidential power.

There are a number of us who believe that further substantial diminishment of congressional power will entail far greater costs than benefits.[67] We accept Madison's insights about human nature, which caution that limited government is essential to avoid arbitrary and self-serving action by governing officials; his belief that government in the public interest requires the accommodation of conflicting views, which is served by basing action on entities that embody different principles of representation; and his view that the need for action is a need for wise and effective action, which should not be equated either with simply passing legislation or allowing the executive branch to implement it without checks. To be sure, politics being what it is, this means less quick action, but how justifiable is the assumption that the action the president wants is generally so wise and effective that stalemate is an enemy that needs to be reduced if not destroyed and limits on presidential discretion substantially reduced? Certainly, for example, President Bush's decision to invade Iraq as well as President Obama's unwillingness to accept amendments that addressed serious flaws in his health insurance plan testify to the contrary.[68]

Nonetheless, if the advocates of preserving a viable separation of powers have good arguments for preserving the role and power of Congress at a meaningful level, the weight of history creates a dilemma. There has long been a negative dynamic in play against congressional power. As noted, the march of presidential power has been upward since the end of the nineteenth century. Declines are more than made up for by advances. Moreover, when particular presidents fail, the system turns to the next president to do better without any diminishment in the tools of presidential leverage. Rather, they are added to over time since their power to implement their policy goals is always insufficient in the eyes of presidents. All this derives from how dependent the system has increasingly become on the president's decision-making capabilities and on how dependent on his office we have all become both conceptually and emotionally.[69]

However, if those of us who still subscribe to the basic insights and beliefs of Madison have a dilemma in preserving the viability of a balance of power, so too do the advocates of further increasing presidential power relative to the Congress. They need to explain why these insights and beliefs no longer apply. As Congress weakens and presidential power increases, the rule of law is threatened and the ability of the federal courts to protect it impaired since what occurs increasingly is legislation that merges the lawmaking power and the power to implement law. Similarly, if a greater premium is put on action rather than consent, why should we not believe that both action in the public interest and effective action will suffer? The dilemmas that representative government in the United States now face are thus great for both sides of the argument.

The essence of dilemmas is that the conflicts they involve are over matters of such great worth that they resist resolution through compromise or trading. At the institutional level, the barriers to agreement are typically even greater than at the policy level since what is in dispute is the basic framework of decision making. Nonetheless, the conflicts these dilemmas involve cannot be eliminated because they all reflect necessary elements of a viable constitutional order. What we have done over the course of our history is to tolerate and balance conflicting views of the goals and needs of our constitutional order without treating any particular set of goals and needs as so vital that damage to the others can be disregarded.[70] That is what we have to do now as well, with greater attention than in the past to the dangers of expanding presidential power. If we fail, there will be no need to argue about presidential power. It will have triumphed, and all that will remain of our constitutional order will be efforts to maintain appearances until memory of it fades.

Notes

1. This chapter builds on and extends two recent essays of mine. See Joseph Cooper, "From Congressional to Presidential Preeminence," in *Congress Reconsidered*, 9th ed., ed. Lawrence C. Dodd and Bruce I. Oppenheimer (Washington, DC: CQ Press, 2009), chap. 16, and Joseph Cooper, "The Modern Congress," in *Congress Reconsidered*, 10th ed., ed. Lawrence C. Dodd and Bruce I. Oppenheimer (Washington, DC: CQ Press, 2013), chap. 16.
2. Ira Katznelson and Barry Weingast, eds., *Preferences and Situations: Points of Intersection Between Historical and Rational Choice* (New York: Russell Sage, 2005); James Mahoney and Kathleen Thelen, ed., *Explaining Institutional Change: Ambiguity, Agency, and Power* (New York: Cambridge University Press, 2010), chaps. 1 and 7; James G. March and Johan P. Olsen, *Rediscovering Institutions: The Organizational Basis of Politics* (New York: Free Press, 1989); Joseph M. Bessette, *The Mild Voice of Reason: Deliberative Democracy and American National Government* (Chicago: University of Chicago Press, 1994); James E. Alt, Margaret Levi, and Elinor Ostrom, eds., *Competition and Cooperation: Conversations With Nobelists About Economics and Political Science* (New York: Russell Sage, 1999).
3. Kenneth Shepsle, "Institutional Equilibrium and Equilibrium Institutions," in *Political Science: The Science of Politics*, ed. Herbert F. Weisberg (New York: Agathon Press, 1986), chap. 4.
4. Keith T. Poole, *Spatial Models of Parliamentary Voting* (New York: Cambridge University Press, 2005), 6–7, 209.
5. The basic notion of fixed and quasi parameters is adapted from Avner Greif and David D. Laitin, "A Theory of Endogenous Institutional Change," *American Political Science Review* 98 (2004): 633–53. See also Cooper, "Modern Congress," 404–16;

Morton Keller, "Power and Rights: Two Centuries of American Constitutionalism," in *The Constitution and American Life*, ed. David P. Thelen (Ithaca, NY: Cornell University Press, 1988), 15–34; E. Scott Adler and John S. Lapinsky, eds., *The Macropolitics of Congress* (Princeton, NJ: Princeton University Press, 2006); Bryan D. Jones, *Reconceiving Decision-Making in Democratic Politics: Attention, Choice, and Public Policy* (Chicago: University of Chicago Press, 1994); and Lawrence C. Dodd, *Thinking About Congress: Essays on Congressional Change* (New York: Routledge, 2012).

6. On the organization character of the Congress see Joseph Cooper, "Strengthening the Congress: An Organizational Analysis," *Harvard Journal on Legislation* 12 (1975): 307–68; Joseph Cooper, "Organization and Innovation in the U.S. House of Representatives," in *The House at Work*, ed. Joseph Cooper and G. Calvin Mackenzie (Austin: University of Texas Press, 1981), 319–55. For material on the presidency and the executive branch, see Charles O. Jones, *The Presidency in a Separated System*, 2nd ed. (Washington, DC: Brookings Institution Press, 2005), chap. 3, and Daniel Carpenter, "The Evolution of National Bureaucracy in the United States," in *The Executive Branch*, ed. Joel D. Aberbach and Mark A. Peterson (New York: Oxford University Press, 2005), chap. 2. The executive branch, however, is not a classic Weberian bureaucracy since it shares several key powers with the Congress.

7. For material on the Framers' disinclination to adopt an inherent-power view of legislative and executive power, see George Carey, ed., *The Federalist* (Urbana: University of Illinois Press, 1989), 73. See also *Federalist* no. 39.

8. On the need for legitimacy see W. Richard Scott, *Institutions and Organizations*, 3rd ed. (Thousand Oaks, CA: Sage, 2010), chap. 3; Fritz W. Scharpf, *Games Real Actors Play: Actor-Centered Institutionalism in Policy Research* (Boulder, CO: Westview Press, 1994), chaps. 6–9; and Dodd, *Thinking About Congress*, chaps. 3 and 8.

9. See Jeffrey Tulis, *The Rhetorical Presidency* (Princeton, NJ: Princeton University Press, 1987). See also Richard J. Ellis, *The Development of the American Presidency* (New York: Routledge, 2012), chap. 4, and Cooper, "From Congressional to Presidential Preeminence," 368–70.

10. Bessette, *Mild Voice of Reason*, chaps. 1–6. For an informative analysis of the underlying philosophical assumptions of Madison and Hamilton, see Morton White, *Philosophy, The Federalist, and the Constitution* (New York: Oxford University Press, 1987). See also *The Federalist* papers, nos. 42, 55, and 57. On the necessity for and appropriateness of evaluative normative analysis, see also James W. Ceaser, *Liberal Democracy and Political Science* (Baltimore: Johns Hopkins University Press, 1990). Note as well that the founding father of empirical political science, Charles Merriam, subscribed to combining empirical and normative analysis as do a number of the most insightful of rational choice theorists, such as Charles Lindblom. See Charles Merriam and Louise Overacker, *Primary Elections* (Chicago: University of Chicago Press, 1928), 6–7, and Charles Lindblom, *The Intelligence of Democracy: Decision Making Through Mutual Adjustment* (New York: Free Press, 1965), chaps. 15–18.

11. For general analysis of the principles underlying the Framers' design, see Carey, *Federalist*; Samuel Kernell, ed., *James Madison: The Theory and Practice of Republican Government* (Stanford, CA: Stanford University Press, 2003); Jack N. Rakove, *Original Meanings: Politics and Ideas in the Making of the Constitution* (New York: Vintage Books, 1996); Paul A. Rahe, *Republics Ancient and Modern, Vol. 3* (Chapel Hill: University of North Carolina Press), chap. 1 and epilogue; and David F. Epstein, *The Political Theory of* The Federalist (Chicago: University of Chicago Press, 1984).

12. Barry C. Burden, ed., *Uncertainty in American Politics* (Princeton, NJ: Princeton University Press, 2004); Randall Strahan, *Leading Representatives: The Agency of Leaders in the Politics of the U.S. House* (Baltimore: Johns Hopkins University Press, 2007); David Mayhew, *Parties and Politics: How the American Government Works* (New Haven, CT: Yale University Press, 2008), chaps. 12 and 13; Tulia G. Falleti and Julia F. Lynch, "Context and Causal Mechanisms in Political Analysis," *Comparative Political Studies* 42 (2009): 1143–63.
13. See Cooper, "From Congressional to Presidential Preeminence," 361–62.
14. For material on the election system in the nineteenth century, see James Bryce, *The American Commonwealth, Vol. 2* (New York: Macmillan, 1901); Joel H. Silbey, *The American Political Nation, 1838–1893* (Stanford, CA: Stanford University Press, 1991); Mark Wahlgren, *Party Games: Getting, Keeping, and Using Power in Gilded Age Politics* (Chapel Hill: University of North Carolina Press, 2004): and Cooper, "From Congressional to Presidential Preeminence," 361–66. See also Richard Ellis, "Accepting the Nomination: From Martin Van Buren to Franklin Delano Roosevelt," in *Speaking to the People: The Rhetorical Presidency in Historical Perspective*, ed. Richard Ellis (Amherst: University of Massachusetts Press, 1998), 112–33, and Daniel J. Tichenor and Richard A. Harris, "Organized Interests and American Political Development," *Political Science Quarterly* 117 (2002–2003): 587–612.
15. For the decline of the traditional party system during the first half of the twentieth century, see Michael E. McGerr, *The Decline of Popular Politics: The American North, 1865–1928* (New York: Oxford University Press, 1986); Mark Lawrence Kornbluh, *Why America Stopped Voting: The Decline of Participatory Democracy and the Emergence of Modern American Politics* (New York: New York University Press, 2000); Morton Keller, *Affairs of State: Public Life in Late Nineteenth Century America* (Cambridge, MA: Belknap Press of Harvard University Press, 1977); Alan Ware, *The American Direct Primary: Party Institutionalization and Transformation in the North* (New York: Cambridge University Press, 2002). For the decline and collapse of the traditional party system in the second half of the twentieth century, see Everett C. Ladd, *American Political Parties: Social Change and Political Response* (New York: Norton, 1970); John Aldrich, *Why Parties: A Second Look* (Chicago: University of Chicago Press, 2011); Sidney M. Milkis, *The President and the Parties: The Transformation of the American Party System Since the New Deal* (New York: Oxford University Press, 1993); and Theodore J. Lowi, *The Personal President: Power Invested, Promise Unfulfilled* (Ithaca, NY: Cornell University Press, 1985). See also Cooper, "From Congressional to Presidential Preeminence," 362–66, 375–79.
16. On Theodore Roosevelt, see Tulis, *Rhetorical Presidency*. On Woodrow Wilson, see James W. Ceaser, *Presidential Selection: Theory and Development* (Princeton, NJ: Princeton University Press, 1979). For a general history of the growth of plebiscitary politics, see Samuel Kernell, *Going Public: New Strategies of Presidential Leadership*, 3rd ed. (Washington, DC: CQ Press, 1997); Brendan J. Doherty, *The Rise of the President's Permanent Campaign* (Lawrence: University Press of Kansas, 2012); and David Greenberg, *Republic of Spin: An Inside History of the American Presidency* (New York: W. W. Norton, 2016). See also Richard Ellis and Mark Dedrick, "The Rise of the Rhetorical Candidate," in *The Presidency Then and Now*, ed. Phillip G. Henderson (Lanham, MD: Rowman and Littlefield, 2000), chap. 10.
17. On Franklin Roosevelt, see Greenberg, *Republic of Spin*, part III, and Lowi, *Personal President*, chaps. 3–5.

18. See Matthew Levendusky, *The Partisan Sort: How Liberals Became Democrats and Conservatives Became Republicans* (Chicago: University of Chicago Press, 2010).
19. On the rise of candidate-centered politics following the collapse of the traditional party system and its impacts on increasing the importance of issues and personality as well as the conduct of politics, see Aldrich, *Why Parties*, parts 3–4; Lowi, *Personal President*, chaps. 4–5; and Kenneth T. Walsh, *Celebrity in Chief: A History of the Presidents and the Culture of Stardom* (Boulder, CO: Paradigm Publishers, 2015).
20. The traditional basis for party polarization was psychological and emotional allegiance to party based on stable networks of social interaction with persons and families of similar beliefs. Affect and history thus provided the glue. This is the form of party loyalty and identification captured by the Michigan school in the 1950s. However, due to long-term changes in the character of American politics, it was challenged in the 1960s and 1970s by a new approach to party allegiance. In this approach, voters are seen to have standing positions on party identification based on the past policies and achievements of their parties, which are open to revision in subsequent election if assessments of party performance change. This is the view that is now dominant in the field. See Paul R. Abramson, John H. Aldrich, and David W. Rohde, *Change and Continuity in the 2008 and 2010 Elections* (Washington, DC: CQ Press, 2012), 193–97. It should be noted that the original affective basis of party allegiance and polarization was not immune to policy failures, as testified to by the major realignments that occurred. It is true as well that the current consensus on the policy basis of party allegiance and polarization is not immune to the effects of affect. Policy orientations are not free of emotional commitments. This is particularly true of strong party identifiers whose levels of party identification declined somewhat from 1952 to 2012 but then recovered. See American National Election Studies, *Guide to Public Opinion and Electoral Behavior*, Table 2A.1. It is thus not surprising that the Michigan view of the affective basis of party identification has been reasserted and defended, not entirely vanquished. See Donald Green, Bradley Palmquist, and Eric Schickler, *Partisan Hearts and Minds: Political Parties and the Social Identities of Voters* (New Haven, CT: Yale University Press, 2002).
21. Students of electoral behavior differ on whether the transition to a new policy-oriented basis for party loyalty has substantially increased the degree of electoral polarization. See, for example, Alan I. Abramowitz, *The Polarized Public? Why American Government Is so Dysfunctional* (Boston: Pearson Education, 2013), as opposed to Morris P. Fiorina and Samuel Abrams, "Americans Are Not Polarized, Just Better Sorted," in *Political Polarization in American Politics*, ed. Daniel J. Hopkins and John Sides (New York: Bloomsbury Publishing, 2015), chap. 6. This dispute resists resolution since different authors draw different conclusions from pertinent data. See the various chapters in Hopkins and Sides, eds., *Political Polarization in American Politics*. Nonetheless, current data on party identification testify strongly to the importance of ideology in shaping voting behavior. They indicate that though the proportions of weak party identifiers, leaners, and pure independents have increased substantially in recent decades, weak party identifiers and leaners vote largely like strong party identifiers. The data thus testify to a high degree of polarization on the basis of ideology, despite the decline in the strength of party identification. See William H. Flanigan, Nancy H. Zingale, Elizabeth A. Theiss-Morse, and Michael W. Wagner, *Political Behavior of the American Electorate*, 13th ed. (Washington, DC: CQ Press, 2015), chaps. 4 and 8. See also work by Gary Jacobson that shows an increasing concordance between partisan

voting for presidents and House members in elections across different states. See Gary C. Jacobson, "Eroding the Electoral Foundations of Partisan Polarization," in *Solutions to Political Polarization in America*, ed. Nathaniel Persily (New York: Oxford University Press, 2015), chap. 5. My conclusion is that the primary basis for party loyalty and allegiance has altered as policy concerns associated with ideological orientations have trumped affect and history over the past half-century and that the result has been to heighten electoral polarization so that it is higher now than before 1960.

22. Hugh Heclo, "Campaigning and Governing: A Conspectus," in *The Permanent Campaign and Its Future*, ed. Norman Ornstein and Thomas Mann (Washington, DC: American Enterprise Institute Press, 2000), chap. 1; Gary Lee Malecha and Donald J. Reagan, *The Public Congress: Congressional Deliberation in a New Media Age* (New York: Routledge, 2012); C. Lawrence Evans, "Committees, Leaders, and Message Politics," in *Congress Reconsidered*, 7th ed., ed. Lawrence C. Dodd and Bruce I. Oppenheimer (Washington, DC: CQ Press, 2001), chap. 10; and Ron Elving, "The President, Congress, and the Media," in *Rivals for Power: Presidential–Congressional Relations*, 5th ed., ed. James Thurber (Lanham, MD: Rowman and Littlefield, 2013), chap. 8. Note as well that the rise of plebiscitary politics has been accompanied by increasing proficiency in "crafted talk" to gain favor with the public. That indeed is why message politics now figures so largely in the politics of the electoral and legislative politics. See James N. Druckman and Lawrence R. Jacobs, *Who Governs? Presidents, Public Opinion, and Manipulation* (Chicago: University of Chicago Press, 2015).

23. On Theodore Roosevelt's problems with Speaker Cannon and Nelson Aldrich, see Ronald M. Peters Jr., *The American Speakership: The Office in Historical Perspective*, 2nd ed. (Baltimore: Johns Hopkins University Press, 1997), 75–91. On Woodrow Wilson's need to defer to Senate and House party leaders in passing his program, see Daniel Stid, "Rhetorical Leadership and 'Common Counsel' in the Presidency of Woodrow Wilson," in *Speaking to the People*, ed. Ellis, chap. 7. On both, see Stephen Skowronek, *Building a New American State: The Expansion of National Administrative Capacities, 1877–1920* (New York: Cambridge University Press, 1982), chaps. 6 and 8. On the rise and power of the conservative coalition in Congress from the 1940s through the 1970s, see Barbara Sinclair, *The Transformation of the U.S. Senate* (Baltimore: Johns Hopkins University Press, 1989), chaps. 1–5, and Mack C. Shelley, *The Permanent Majority: The Conservative Coalition in the United States Congress* (Tuscaloosa: University of Alabama Press, 1983).

24. The most commonly relied upon measure of party polarization is the DW-NOMINATE score, though more traditional measures continue to be used. See Nolan McCarthy, Keith T. Poole, and Howard Rosenthal, *Polarized America: The Dance of Ideology and Unequal Riches* (Cambridge, MA: MIT Press, 2006). For a more traditional approach, see C. Lawrence Evans, "Parties and Leaders: Polarization and Power in the U.S. House and Senate," *New Directions in Congressional Politics*, ed. Jamie L. Carson (New York: Routledge, 2012), chap. 4. However, the more recent approach, because of its methodological commitment to identifying ideal points, cannot measure cross-partisanship or bipartisanship. They are rather submerged in the polarization score. The more traditional approach has problems measuring partisanship while taking bipartisanship into account. I have, with the assistance of Shangsi Wang, developed a new set of scores that escape these problems. Our scores rely on the percentage of roll call votes in which 50 percent or more of each party opposes one another 75 percent or more of the time or between 50 percent and 74 percent of the

time to identify partisan and cross-partisan votes. Similarly, we distinguish bipartisan and cross-bipartisan partisan votes in terms of the same criteria on votes in which 50 percent or more of each party vote together. These scores can thus more clearly identify voting patterns in periods like the late 1960s and early 1970s, when cross-partisanship was high. The answer to the question of whether polarization is higher in recent years than in the days of Speaker Cannon is no, unless the large proportions, in recent years, of bipartisan votes in which 90 percent or more of both parties voted together are excluded. For data and codebook email me at jcooper@jhu.edu or see my web site at http://politicalscience.jhu.edu/directory/joseph-cooper.

25. See William Novak, "Making the Modern Legislative State," in *Living Legislation: Durability, Change, and the Politics of American Lawmaking*, ed. Jeffrey A. Jenkins and Eric M. Patashnik (Chicago: University of Chicago Press, 2012), chap. 2; Mayhew, *Parties and Politics*, chaps. 6 and 7; and Frank R. Baumgartner and Bryan D. Jones, *The Politics of Information: Problem Definition and the Course of Public Policy in America* (Chicago: University of Chicago Press, 2015), chap. 7.

26. See James L. Sundquist, *The Decline and Resurgence of Congress* (Washington, DC: Brookings Institution, 1981), chaps. 5, 9, and 10, for a review of the growth of presidential power in foreign and national security power preceding and after World War II, including congressional attempts to reclaim its constitutional authority over war making through the War Powers Resolution of 1973. In addition, in 1972 Congress passed a requirement that all executive agreements be submitted to Congress within sixty days, which ostensibly opened them up to negation by law or joint resolution. Nonetheless, the number of executive agreements multiplied, and as the recent executive agreement with Iran illustrates, this provision has serious weaknesses in protecting the Senate's treaty approval power. See Andrew Rudalevige, "Executive Agreements and Senate Disagreements," *Monkey Cage* (blog), March 10, 2015, https://www.washingtonpost.com/blogs/monkey-cage/wp/2015/03/10/executive-agreements-and-senate-disagreements. Nor has the War Powers Resolution had much effect in bolstering congressional power. See James P. Pfiffner, *The Modern Presidency*, 6th ed. (Boston: Wadsworth, 2011), chap. 6.

27. Matthew Green, *The Speaker of the House: A Study in Leadership* (New Haven, CT: Yale University Press, 2010). See also Barbara Sinclair, "The President and the Congressional Party Leadership in a Hyperpartisan Era," in *Rivals for Power*, 5th ed., ed. Thurber, chap. 6.

28. See Barbara Sinclair, *Unorthodox Lawmaking: New Legislative Processes in the U.S. Congress*, 4th ed. (Washington, DC: CQ Press, 2011); Steven S. Smith, *The Senate Syndrome: The Evolution of Procedural Warfare in the Modern U.S. Senate* (Norman: University of Oklahoma Press, 2014); and Peter Hanson, *Too Weak to Govern: Majority Party Power and Appropriations in the U.S. Senate* (New York: Cambridge University Press, 2014).

29. Many incidents of blame game politics in the Bush and Obama administrations can be found in the work of Robert Draper and Bob Woodward. Many concern fights over the debt ceiling and continuing resolutions. See Robert Draper, *Dead Certain: The Presidency of George W. Bush* (New York: Free Press, 2007); Robert Draper, *Do Not Ask What Good We Do: Inside the U.S. House of Representatives* (New York: Free Press, 2012); and Bob Woodward, *The Price of Politics* (New York: Simon and Schuster, 2012). In addition, the demise of Speaker Boehner was largely a result of the difficulties of playing blame game politics. The election of 2014 gave the Republicans over

240 members, but they included forty to fifty members not amenable to subordinating principle to politics. As a consequence, Boehner often had difficulty mobilizing a majority behind positions he felt would not do the party electoral damage and at times had to depend on Democratic support to pass the CRs or debt ceiling measures he had negotiated with Obama and congressional Democratic Party leaders. In the end, his support eroded and so did his patience. Thus, in 2015, we had something quite unusual in American politics: a voluntary departure from the speakership not forced by questionable conduct. See Jennifer Steinhauer, "John Boehner, House Speaker, Will Resign From Congress," *New York Times*, September 25, 2015, http://www.nytimes.com/2015/09/26/us/john-boehner-to-resign-from-congress.html. The need for CRs, especially before 2014, was largely because Majority Leader Reid refused to allow House-passed appropriations bills to come to the floor in order to protect vulnerable Democratic Senators from casting politically difficult votes on amendments. See Smith, *Senate Syndrome*, 233.

30. On presidential bargaining advantages in making veto threats, see Bryan Marshall, "Congress and the Executive: Unilateralism and Legislative Bargaining," in *New Directions in Congressional Politics*, ed. Jamie Carson, chap. 10. On presidential use of executive rules to bypass lack of congressional authorization in a very major policy area, see Bruce I. Oppenheimer, "Energy Legislation From the OPEC Embargo to Obama's Sidestep of Congress," in *Congress Reconsidered*, 10th ed., ed. Dodd and Oppenheimer, chap. 12. The recent flurry of rule changes regarding overtime pay and corporate inversions (transfers of corporate legal status to another country) in President Obama's last spring in office are thus not surprising.

31. An important feature of the impediments to congressional oversight during the Obama administration but also during the George W. Bush administration has been the expansion beyond past practice of the doctrine of executive privilege so that it is claimed to extend to the decisions and behavior of higher administrative officials rather than the behavior and decisions of the president. Equally important, the impediments to oversight posed by executive control of information have been extended in the Obama Administration by deliberate concealment and outright lying by executive officials. Note Justice Department obstruction in the investigation of Operation: Fast and Furious, which planted guns in Mexico; IRS loss of e-mails in the Lois Lerner investigation; and Justice Department admission in May of 2016 that its lawyers lied to a federal judge on whether exemptions had begun under Obama's decision, now before the Supreme Court, to grant exemption from deportation of 4 to 5 million illegal aliens. See post by Lyle Denniston, "Judge in Immigration Case Issues Sweeping New Order," SCOTUSblog, May 20, 2016, http://www.scotusblog.com/2016/05/judge-in-immigration-case-issues-sweeping-new-order. Similarly, it is only because of private suits in the courts that the details of the number and character of e-mails on Secretary of State Hillary Clinton's private server have become known. The ability of the executive branch to control information thus now ranks as one of its most powerful levers of power vis-à-vis the Congress. See Morton Rosenberg "Obstruction of Justice: Does the Justice Department Have to Respond to Lawfully Issued and Valid Congressional Subpoenas?" statement before the House Committee on Oversight and Government Reform, June 13, 2011.

32. Woodrow Wilson, *The State: Elements of Historical and Practical Politics* (Boston: D.C. Heath, 1889), 561, 568, 589. See also Woodrow Wilson, *Constitutional Government in the United States* (New York: Columbia University Press, 1917), 59–81. This book

put in print lectures delivered in 1908 and provided an expanded view of the potential for presidential power in the electoral and legislative processes. But Wilson's view of the role of the president in the administrative process remained largely the same as in 1889.

33. The creation of the Executive Office of the President was based on the work of the Brownlow Commission, appointed by President Roosevelt, that reported in January 1937. For material on the Brownlow Commission, its recommendations, the conflict over their passage, and the recommendations that survived, see B. D. Karl, *Executive Reorganization and Reform in the New Deal: The Genesis of Executive Management, 1900–1939* (Cambridge, MA: Harvard University Press, 1963), and Sidney M. Milkis, "Franklin D. Roosevelt, Progressivism, and the Limits of Popular Leadership," in *Speaking to the People*, ed. Ellis, 200–10.

34. The present units in the Executive Office of the President can be found at https://www.whitehouse.gov. Staffing data for these units in 2015 can be found at same site in *Executive Office, Congressional Budget Submission for Fiscal 2017*. Staffing data for the White House Office, the OMB, and the National Security Council in prior decades can be found in CQ Press, ed., *The Powers of the Presidency*, 2nd ed. (Washington, DC: CQ Press, 1997), 180. See also Michael Nelson, ed., *Guide to the Presidency*, 5th ed. (Washington, DC: CQ Press, 2012).

35. For identification and discussion on the current units in the White House Office, see Bradley H. Patterson, *To Serve the President: Continuity and Innovation in the White House Staff* (Washington, DC: Brookings Institution Press, 2008). See also Thomas J. Weko, *The Politicizing Presidency: The White House Personnel Office, 1948–1994* (Lawrence: University of Kansas Press, 1995); Martha Joynt Kumar, *Managing the President's Message: The White House Communications Operation* (Baltimore: Johns Hopkins University Press, 2007); and Doherty, *Rise of the President's Permanent Campaign*, chap. 5.

36. The change in the title of the BB to OMB reflected a change in the desired character of its operation and was based on the work of the Ash Commission, appointed by President Nixon. See Larry Berman, *The Office of Management and Budget and the Presidency, 1921–1979* (Princeton, NJ: Princeton University Press, 1979), chaps. 4 and 5. The OIRA was created in 1980 and vested with a variety of duties with regard to the control of government information and paperwork. In 1981, when President Reagan's executive order (#12291) was issued that established OMB review of agency administrative rules, the task of review was vested in the OIRA. For material on the exercise of OIRA review since 1981 and changes made in procedures, see Cornelius Kerwin, *Rulemaking: How Government Agencies Write Law and Make Policy*, 1st ed., 3rd ed. (Washington, DC: CQ Press, 1994, 2003). See also William F. West, "The Institutionalization of Regulatory Review: Organizational Stability and Responsive Competence at OIRA," *Presidential Studies Quarterly* 35 (2005): 76–93.

37. Data on agency rules need to be handled with caution. The 2014 Federal Register contained 3,554 final rules and 2,383 proposed rules. See Clyde Wayne Crews Jr., *Ten Thousand Commandments: An Annual Snapshot of the Federal Regulatory State*, (Washington, DC: Competitive Enterprise Institute, 2015). Comparisons with the past are complicated by the fact that the rules reviewed by OIRA were not limited to significant rules—that is, rules with effects of $100 million or more on the economy—until 1993. Still, it seems clear that the volume of rulemaking has expanded

substantially. The number of rules reviewed by OIRA was about 2,750 in 1981 and about 2,250 in 1989. Another indicator that supports expansion in rule-making activity is the number of pages in the *Federal Register*, where final and proposed rules must be published by law. These totaled 40,435 in 1981 and 29,984 in 1989. The number climbed to close to 80,000 in 2010. However, the *Federal Register* includes other material, in addition to the texts of final and proposed rules. See Kerwin, *Rulemaking*, 3rd ed., 16–17, and Harold W. Stanley and Richard G. Niemi, *Vital Statistics on American Politics, 2015–2016* (Washington, DC: CQ Press, 2015), Figure 6-1. In the case of congressional legislation, the average number of bills passed by both houses in the 111th through 113th Congresses (2009–2015) is 321. This average includes two bills vetoed by President Obama. See http://www.archives.gov/federal-register/laws/past.

38. For an analysis of the techniques of layering see David Lewis, *The Politics of Presidential Appointments: Political Control and Bureaucratic Performance* (Princeton, NJ: Princeton University Press, 2008), 30–56. The number of political appointments in the executive branch in 2012 was 2,846. See David Lewis and Terry Moe, "The Presidency and the Bureaucracy: The Levers of Presidential Control," in *The Presidency and the Political System*, 10th ed., ed. Michael Nelson (Washington, DC: CQ Press, 2014), 387. Here again, counting is complex. For a count in excess of 4,000 in the early 1990s, due perhaps to differences in definition, see Judith E. Michaels, *The President's Call: Executive Leadership From FDR to George Bush* (Pittsburg: University of Pittsburg Press, 1997), 113. Indeed, Lewis's count in 2004 in effect is between 3,200 and 3,400. See Lewis, *Politics of Presidential Appointments*, 20–26.

39. Note the recent EPA rules on coal plant emissions and the FCC rule on net neutrality. See Jonathan Adler, "Supreme Court Puts the Breaks on the EPA's Clean Power Plan," *Washington Post*, February 9, 2016, and Ryan Knutson, "FCC Chairman Says Obama's Net Neutrality Statement Influenced Rule," *Wall Street Journal*, March 17, 2015.

40. See Mark Berman, Sarah Larimer and Sari Horowitz, "North Carolina, Justice Dept. File Dueling Lawsuits Over Transgender Rights," *Washington Post*, May 9, 2016. This article contains links to both briefs. It should be noted that neither Title VII of the Civil Rights Act of 1964 nor Title IX of the Education Amendments of 1972 that banned discrimination on the basis of sex were relied upon by the Supreme Court in its recent decision on same-sex marriage. See Louise Radnofsky, "Tricky Questions Posed by Transgender Rules," *Wall Street Journal*, May 27, 2016, A3.

41. On President Obama's announcement regarding his decision to exempt 4 to 5 million illegal aliens from deportation and use of the Department of Homeland Security to implement this decision, see the posts on *United States. v. Texas* at www.scotusblog.com. In particular, see Lyle Denniston, "Longer Argument Set on Immigration Policy," *SCOTUSblog*, April 8, 2016, http://www.scotusblog.com/2016/04/longer-argument-set-on-immigration-policy.

42. On the theory of a unitary executive and its errors and misunderstandings, see Lawrence Lessig and Cass R. Sunstein, "The President and the Administration," *Columbia Law Review* 94 (1994): 1–123. See also Louis Fisher, "The Unitary Executive: Ideology Versus the Constitution," in *The Unitary Executive and the Modern Presidency*, ed. Ryan J. Barilleaux and Christopher S. Kelley (College Station: Texas A&M Press, 2010), 17–40, and Richard M. Pious, "Public Law and the 'Executive' Constitution," in *Executing the Constitution: Putting the President Back Into the Constitution*, ed. Christopher S. Kelley (Albany: State University of New York Press, 2006), 11–36. On

President George W. Bush's reliance on the theory of a unitary executive, its negative reception by the Supreme Court, and President Obama's nonreliance on it, see Jack Goldsmith, *Power and Constraint: The Accountable Presidency After 9/11* (New York: W. W. Norton, 2012).

43. On spending nonappropriated funds, see Richard Wolf, Gregory Korte, and Jayne O'Donnell, "Federal Judge Strikes Down Obamacare Payments," *USA Today*, May 12, 2016. On recess appointments, see Amy Howe, "Court Strikes Down Recess Appointments: In Plain English," *SCOTUSblog*, June 26, 2014, http://www.scotusblog.com/2014/06/court-strikes-down-recess-appointments-in-plain-english. On delays in Obamacare mandates and deadlines, see Andrew C. McCarthy, *Faithless Execution: Building the Political Case for Obama's Impeachment* (New York: Encounter Books, 2014), 96–100. This volume lists other instances of "faithless execution" on the basis of claims of unilateral power (e.g., suspension of the tie between welfare and work and ignoring the law regarding Yucca Mountain). Finally, President Obama's reliance on an executive agreement to implement a nuclear agreement with Iran allowed him to turn past usage to his advantage. Due to the increasing volume of international agreements, since 1940, Congress has tolerated the use of executive agreements in place of treaties, despite the fact that they rest entirely on presidential will. Nonetheless, Congress has sought to preserve congressional control over very important agreements either by insisting they take the form of treaties, which require approval by two-thirds of the Senate, or by requiring approval by majorities in each house, as in the case of NAFTA. Yet over time, political goals and the absence of a clear standard of importance have progressively weakened congressional control. What President Obama has done in this case is to further weaken, if not destroy, the notion that "importance" matters. As in the case of executive orders, executive agreements are a vehicle for expanding presidential power. They bypass the need to secure any form of congressional consent and deter corrective legislation since a two-thirds vote in both the House and Senate is needed to overcome his veto. Nor was this the only way President Obama sought strategic advantage. He secured UN Security Council approval of the agreement in order to make international law a factor that heightened the barriers to congressional legislative action, as well as future unilateral presidential action. See Stephen Collinson, "Iran Deal: A Treaty or Not a Treaty, That Is the Question," *CNN Politics*, March 12, 2015, http://www.cnn.com/2015/03/12/politics/iran-nuclear-deal-treaty-obama-administration, and Michael Dorf, "The Senators' Letter to Iran and Domestic Incorporation of International Law," *Political Science Quarterly* 131 (2016): 45–69.

44. Obama's decisions on immigration are now before the Supreme Court. Note that the issues concern not only standing to sue but also whether the policy guidance he instructs the Department of Homeland Security to provide to implement his decision is rulemaking that violates the Administrative Procedure Act and whether the president violated the "take care" provisions of the Constitution by ignoring existing immigration law and sanctioning its revision on the basis of the policy guidance provided by Homeland Security. See *United States v. Texas*, http://www.scotusblog.com/case-files/cases/united-states-v-texas. See also Richard Samp, "Symposium: The Government's Violation of the APA's Notice-and-Comment Requirements Provides a Simple Solution to a Thorny Case," *SCOTUSblog*, February 10, 2016, http://www.scotusblog.com/2016/02/symposium-the-governments-violation-of-the-apas-notice-and-comment-requirements-provides-a-simple-solution-to-a-thorny-case,

and John Eastman, "Symposium: Barack Obama Is Not King," *SCOTUSblog*, February 11, 2016, http://www.scotusblog.com/2016/02/symposium-barack-obama-is-not-king. The actions on transgender rights raise many of the same issues. In this instance, the policy guidance is provided by the Justice Department, which is now engaged in countersuits with North Carolina, and it is clear that other states will sue Justice as well. See Lyle Denniston, "Federal Judge Urges Prompt Appeal to Court on Transgender Rights," *SCOTUSblog*, June 1, 2016, http://www.scotusblog.com/2016/06/federal-judge-urges-prompt-appeal-to-court-on-transgender-rights.

45. For an instructive and comprehensive empirical analysis of the many facets of presidential unilateral action, including the role of the courts, see William Howell, *Power Without Persuasion: The Politics of Direct Presidential Action* (Princeton, NJ: Princeton University Press, 2003). See also Graham G. Dodds, *Take Up Your Pen: Unilateral Presidential Directives in American Politics* (Philadelphia: University of Pennsylvania Press, 2013), and Andrew Rudalevige, *The New Imperial Presidency: Renewing Presidential Power After Watergate* (Ann Arbor: University of Michigan Press, 2005). On Obama's "czars," note that this is not an official or formal title. In addition, other presidents in the past have, for selected purposes, created czars. However, Obama's use of "czars" has been far larger in number and spanned many more policy areas but has been frustrated by the power of existing units. See Mitchel A. Sollenberger and Marc J. Rozzell, *The President's Czars: Undermining Congress and the Constitution* (Lawrence: University Press of Kansas, 2012).

46. See Cooper, "Modern Congress," 418. See also note 24 *infra*.

47. See American National Election Studies, *Guide to Public Opinion and Electoral Behavior*, Table 2A1. See also note 21 *infra*.

48. On the growth of federal roles and responsibilities, see Ballard C. Campbell, *The Growth of American Politics: Governance From the Cleveland Era to the Present* (Bloomington: Indiana University Press, 1995). Paul C. Light, *The True Size of Government* (Washington, DC: Brookings Institution Press, 1999). See also cites in fn. 25 *infra* and Stanley and Niemi, *Vital Statistics on American Politics*, chaps. 9–11. On the relationship between the growth of government and the nationalization of politics, good evidence is provided by the substantial decline in switch-ticket voting in recent decades. See Jacobson, "Eroding the Electoral Foundations of Partisan Polarization."

49. See Paul S. Herrnson, *Congressional Elections: Campaigning at Home and in Washington*, 7th ed. (Washington, DC: CQ Press, 2016), chaps. 7 and 8; David Axelrod, "Election Overview," in *Electing the President, 2012: The Insiders' View*, ed. Kathleen Hall Jamieson (Philadelphia: University of Pennsylvania Press, 2013), chap. 1; and David Magleby, "How Barack Obama Changed Presidential Campaigns," in *Obama: Year One*, ed. Thomas R. Dye (New York: Longman, 2010), chap. 2. See also Richard J. Ellis, *Presidential Travel: The Journey From George Washington to George W. Bush* (Lawrence: University of Kansas Press, 2008), chap. 7.

50. See Flanigan et al., *Political Behavior of the American Electorate*, 13th ed., chap. 3.

51. See Lowi, *Personal President*, chaps. 4 and 5; Raymond Tatalovich and Steven E. Schier, *The Presidency and Political Science: Paradigms of Presidential Power From the Founding to the Present*, 2nd ed. (Armonk, NY: M.E. Sharpe, 2014), chaps. 1, 4–5; James A. Morone, *The Democratic Wish: Popular Participation and the Limits of American Government* (New York: Basic Books, 1990); and Gary L. Gregg II, *The Presidential Republic: Executive Representation and Deliberative Democracy* (Lanham, MD: Rowman and Littlefield, 1997).

52. Lawrence J. R. Herson, *The Politics of Ideas: Political Theory and American Public Policy* (Homewood, IL: Dorsey Press, 1984), chap. 12.
53. See Sean M. Theriault, *Party Polarization in Congress* (New York: Cambridge University Press, 2008). For a more recent analysis of external and internal causes, see Michael J. Barber and Nolan McCarty, "Causes and Consequences of Polarization," in *Solutions to Political Polarization in America*, ed. Nathaniel Persily (New York: Cambridge University Press, 2015), chap. 2.
54. See Lowi, *Personal President*, chap. 4. See also John Gerring, *Party Ideologies in America, 1828–1996* (New York: Cambridge University Press, 1998).
55. See Ellis, *Development of the American Presidency*, chaps. 3 and 4; Lance Robinson, "Theodore Roosevelt and William Howard Taft: The Constitutional Foundations of the Modern Presidency," in *The Constitutional Presidency*, ed. Joseph M. Bessette and Jeffrey K. Tulis (Baltimore: Johns Hopkins University Press, 2009), chap. 4; and Woodrow Wilson, *Constitutional Government in the United States* (New York: Columbia University Press, 1908), chap. 3–5, 8. See also note 51 *infra*.
56. The importance of protecting the "party brand" as a key factor in explaining legislative voting was developed and relied upon in Gary W. Cox and Mathew D. McCubbins, *Legislative Leviathan: Party Government in the House* (Berkeley: University of California Press, 1993). As such, it represented a new formulation in the literature of the basis of party loyalty in Congress.
57. See the insightful analysis of Thomas Weko, *Politicizing Presidency*, chap. 4.
58. For an informative examination of the distribution of power between White House staff and cabinet officers, see Andrew Rudalevige, "Rivals, or a Team? Staffing and Issue Management in the Obama Administration," in *The Obama Presidency: Appraisals and Prospects*, ed. Bert A. Rockman, Andrew Rudalevige, and Colin Campbell (Washington, DC: CQ Press, 2012), chap. 8.
59. The nineteenth-century view of the president as the legal head of the executive branch or a "chief magistrate" persisted into the twentieth century. See note 32 *supra*. But it eroded and was replaced by the view that that the president was a "chief executive," not merely a "chief magistrate." This expanded conception was a product of the new discipline of public administration that emerged in the first several decades of the twentieth century and particularly of the work of Leonard White and W. W. Willoughby. Its triumph over the traditional view was sealed by the expansion of the bureaucracy during the New Deal and the work of the Brownlow Commission, which recommended the creation of an institutionalized presidency based on the conception that the president was the "chief executive" of the executive branch and needed "help." See Sundquist, *Decline and Resurgence of Congress*, 47–51.
60. See "Theodore Roosevelt's and William Howard Taft's Theories of Presidential Power (1913, 1916)," in *The Evolving Presidency: Addresses, Cases, Essays, Letters, Reports, Resolutions, Transcripts, and Other Landmark Documents, 1787–2004*, 2nd ed., ed. Michael Nelson (Washington, DC: CQ Press, 2004), 108–14. It should be noted that Roosevelt's stewardship theory was much broader than Jackson's conception of presidential power. The latter was focused on the claim that the president was the direct representative of the people and often combined with a strict interpretation of the separation of powers to counter Whig attacks on his actions in removing cabinet officers or discretionary use of the veto power. Note, for example, the following quote: "The President is the direct representative of the American People, but the Secretaries are not. If the Secretary of the Treasury be independent of the President in the execution of the laws,

then—the whole action of Government, (so far as it is exercised by his Department), (will be) in defiance of the Chief Magistrate elected by the People and responsible to them." See Andrew Jackson, "Message to the Senate Protesting Censure Resolution (*)," April 15, 1834, in *The American Presidency Project*, ed. Gerhard Peters and John T. Woolley, http://www.presidency.ucsb.edu/ws/?pid=67039.
61. See Sundquist, *Decline and Resurgence of Congress*, chaps. 13–16. For recent work that questions the notion that the president represents the public interest because he is elected nationally, see B. Dan Wood, *The Myth of Presidential Representation* (New York: Cambridge University Press, 2009), and Douglas L. Kriner and Andrew Reeves, *The Particularistic President: Executive Branch Politics and Political Inequality* (New York: Cambridge University Press, 2015).
62. On the differences that presidents make, see Fred I. Greenstein, *The Presidential Difference: Leadership Style From FDR to George W. Bush*, 2nd ed. (Princeton, NJ: Princeton University Press, 2004).
63. See Joseph Cooper "The Puzzle of Distrust," "Performance and Expectations in American Politics," and "Epilogue," in *Congress and the Decline of Public Trust*, ed. Joseph Cooper (Boulder, CO: Westview Press, 1999), 1–27, 131–85. See also Jeffrey E. Cohen, *Presidential Leadership in Public Opinion: Causes and Consequences* (New York: Cambridge University Press, 2015), chaps. 7–8, and William Flanigan et al., *Political Behavior of the American Electorate*, 13th ed., 28–40. The Gallup Polls indicate that at present, congressional approval in particular is low—up to 17 percent in April 2016 and as low as 9 percent a few months earlier. See www.gallup.com./poll/congressional approval.
64. See G. Calvin MacKenzie, *The Imperiled Presidency: Leadership Challenges in the Twenty-First Century* (Lanham, MD: Rowman and Littlefield, 2017); William G. Howell and Terry M. Moe, *Relic: How Our Constitution Undermines Effective Government and Why We Need a More Powerful Presidency* (New York: Basic Books, 2016); Thomas E. Mann and Norman J. Ornstein, *It's Even Worse Than It Looks: How the American Constitutional System Collided With the New Politics of Extremism* (New York: Basic Books, 2012); and Thomas E. Mann and Norman J. Ornstein, *It's Even Worse Than It Was: How the American Constitutional System Collided With the New Politics of Extremism*, New, exp. ed. (New York: Basic Books, 2016). See also Bert A. Rockman and Richard W. Waterman, "Two Normative Models of Presidential Leadership," in *Presidential Leadership: The Vortex of Power*, ed. Bert A. Rockman and Richard W. Waterman (New York: Oxford University Press, 2007), chap. 14.
65. Mann and Ornstein are particularly critical of congressional obstruction and the need for reform, particularly the elimination of the filibuster. However, they blame obstruction primarily on the Republicans, despite the fact that Senate Democrats use the filibuster like the Republicans when in the minority and that Sen. Harry Reid, in the 113th Senate (2013–2015), used his power as majority leader to keep many bills off the floor to protect party colleagues up for election in 2014 from politically damaging votes. One might thus expect a denunciation of Reid in a sequel to the books cited in fn. 64 *infra*. But none has appeared.
66. Eric A. Posner and Adrian Vermeule, *The Executive Unbound: After the Madisonian Republic* (New York: Oxford University Press, 2010).
67. See Bruce Ackerman, *The Decline and Fall of the American Republic* (Cambridge, MA: Belknap Press of Harvard University Press, 2010); Rudalevige, *New Imperial Presidency*; Charlie Savage, *Takeover: The Return of the Imperial Presidency and the Subversion*

of American Democracy (New York: Little, Brown, 2007); and Cooper, "From Congressional to Presidential Preeminence," 374–89.
68. To refresh one's understanding of the benefits of the Madisonian republic, see the articles on "The Constitutional Order," in *The Public Interest*, winter 1986. See also Bill Press, *Buyer's Remorse: How Obama Let Progressives Down* (New York: Threshold Editions, 2016). This book is by a former chair of the California Democratic Party and leading Washington correspondent. I cite it not to suggest that he is entirely correct in his critique of President Obama but rather to suggest that the Framers were correct in their belief that no president would be smart enough or good enough to be given a free hand in policy making.
69. On the negative dynamic, see Joseph Cooper, "The Twentieth-Century Congress," in *Congress Reconsidered*, 7th ed., 361–63.
70. See Joseph Bessette and Jeffrey Tulis, "On the Constitution, Politics, and the Presidency," in *Constitutional Presidency*, chap. 1; Gregg, *Presidential Republic*, chaps. 5 and 6; and Bert A. Rockman, "When It Comes to Presidential Leadership, Accentuate the Positive, but Don't Forget the Normative," in *Presidential Leadership*, chap. 13. For various articles on various approaches to the growth of presidential power, see Michael A. Genovese, ed., *Contending Approaches to the American Presidency* (Washington, DC: CQ Press, 2012). Not all strike a proper balance between consent and action in my view.

16. Is Advice and Consent Broken?
The Contentious Politics of Confirming Federal Judges and Justices
Sarah Binder and Forrest Maltzman

The Constitution empowers the Senate to offer its advice and consent to the president over the selection of judges and justices for the nation's federal courts. After three decades of partisan and ideological conflict over choosing federal judges, advice and consent for filling lifetime seats on the federal bench is broken. In this chapter, we explore the impact of intensely polarized and competitive parties on confirming federal judges, paying special attention to the Senate's treatment of President Barack Obama's judicial nominations. We put recent trends in confirmation outcomes into historical perspective and pinpoint new battles over the makeup of the federal bench, including conflict over filling Supreme Court vacancies in a presidential election year. We conclude that no corner of Capitol Hill is immune to partisan and ideological conflict waging in Washington in recent years.

> The Senate is surely under no obligation to confirm any particular nominee, but after the necessary time for inquiry, it should vote him up or vote him down.... Vacancies cannot remain at such high levels indefinitely without eroding the quality of justice.
>
> —Chief Justice William Rehnquist, 1997[1]

> Each political party has found it easy to turn on a dime from decrying to defending the blocking of judicial nominations, depending on their changing political fortunes.... There remains ... an urgent need for the political branches to find a long-term solution to this recurring problem.
>
> —Chief Justice John Roberts, 2010[2]

Not even a rebuke by the chief justice of the United States can convince warring parties inside and outside the Senate to lay down their arms in a decades-long conflict over who serves on the federal bench. That battle reached epic proportion in 2016, at the start of the last year of the Obama administration, when the sudden death of Associate Justice Antonin Scalia opened a pivotal vacancy on the U.S. Supreme Court. Within hours of Scalia's passing, Senate Republican leader Mitch McConnell, R-Ky., vowed to shut down advice and consent for any nominee selected by the outgoing Democratic president—knowing that replacing a staunch conservative justice with an Obama nominee would cement the power of liberals on the Court.

Close observers of advice and consent during the Obama years might not have been surprised by Republican escalation of confrontational tactics over the federal bench. When their party lost the White House in 2008, the Senate Republican minority vowed to block any Obama nominee who failed to pass muster with key Republican senators. Advice and consent proved rockier than Republicans had promised, with Senate Republicans launching filibusters against Obama nominees who even had the support of Republican lawmakers from their home states. Democratic tactics also inflamed the conflict, going "nuclear" in 2013 to eliminate filibusters of nominees for the lower federal courts. No surprise that Republicans turned the tables and nearly stopped confirming Obama nominees when the GOP regained control of the Senate in 2014.

After three decades of senatorial foot-dragging by both Democratic and Republican senators, advice and consent for filling lifetime seats on the federal bench remains broken. In this chapter, we explore the contemporary politics of confirming federal judges, focusing in particular on the experiences of the Obama administration. We put recent trends in confirmation politics into historical perspective and pinpoint new flash points in battles over the makeup of the bench. In contrast to scholars who claim that the process of selecting federal judges has always been political, we argue that conflict over judicial appointees has varied significantly over the past several decades and across the various levels of the bench. In many ways, advice and consent has worsened over the Obama years, leading us to conclude that no corner of Capitol Hill is immune to intense partisan and ideological battles being waged in Washington in recent years.

Competing Accounts of Judicial Selection

Federal judges in the United States resolve some of the most important and contentious public policy issues. Some hold onto the notion that the federal judiciary is simply a neutral arbiter of complex legal questions, but the justices and judges who serve on the Supreme Court and the lower federal bench are crafters of public law. We need look no further than the Court's decision to uphold parts of the landmark Affordable Care Act in 2012 and 2015 to recognize the enormous impact of the federal judiciary on the shape of public law. Whether the Court is striking down Washington, D.C.'s ban on handguns or, most famously, determining the outcome of the 2000 presidential election, the judiciary is an active partner in making public policy.

As the breadth and salience of federal court dockets has grown, the process of selecting federal judges has drawn increased attention. Judicial selection has been contentious before in American history, but seldom has it seemed more acrimonious and dysfunctional than in recent years. Fierce battles to confirm Robert Bork and Clarence Thomas to the Supreme Court are now ones for the history books; an even more divisive political climate pervades Washington today. Alongside these high-profile disputes have been scores of less conspicuous confirmation cases held hostage in the Senate, resulting in declining confirmation rates and unprecedented delays in filling federal judgeships. In the summer of 2016, 10 percent of the federal bench was vacant. Even when Senate parties reach periodic agreements to release their hostages, conflict soon recurs.

Political scientists and legal scholars have offered different approaches to understanding conflict over federal judges. Legal scholars have questioned the growing salience of ideology in confirmation hearings while judicial scholars have examined how presidential ambitions shape the selection of judges and how interest groups succeed in derailing nominees they oppose.[3] Such studies provide excellent but partial portraits of the forces shaping the contemporary politics of advice and consent.

Two alternative accounts have been proposed to explain the broader crisis in judicial selection, neither of which fully captures the political and institutional dynamics that underlie contemporary advice and consent. One account—call it the "big bang theory" of judicial selection—points to a breaking point in national politics, after which prevailing norms of deference and restraint in judicial selection fell apart. The result is said to have been a sea change in appointment politics, with a rockier path to confirmation and less certainty about getting there. An alternative account—call it the "nothing new under the sun theory"—suggests that ideological conflict over the makeup of the bench has been an ever-present force in shaping the selection of federal judges and justices. Judicial selection has always been political and ideological, as senators and presidents vie for influence over the bench.

Adherents of the big bang account typically point to a cataclysmic event in Congress or the courts that had an immediate and lasting impact on the process and politics of judicial selection thereafter. Most often, scholars point to the battle over Robert Bork's nomination to the Supreme Court in 1987 that precipitated a new regime in the treatment of presidential appointments by the Senate. Ronald Reagan's willingness to nominate a conservative deemed outside the mainstream by the Democratic majority and Senate Democrats' willingness to challenge a qualified nominee on grounds of how he would rule on the bench—together, these developments are said to have radically altered advice and consent for judicial nominees. Adherents of the big bang have also argued that the Bork debacle spilled over into the politics of lower court nominations, significantly increasing the politicization of selecting judges for the lower federal bench.[4]

Other versions of the big bang theory point to the Supreme Court's 1954 *Brown v. Board of Education* decision. As Benjamin Wittes has argued, "We can reasonably describe the decline of the process as an institutional reaction by the Senate to the growth of judicial power that began with the *Brown* decision in 1954."[5] Still other versions of the big bang point to the transformation of party activists (from seekers of material benefits to seekers of ideological or policy benefits) and the mobilization of political elites outside the Senate seeking to affect the makeup of the bench.[6]

No doubt, the Bork debacle, the changing character of elite activists, and the emergence of the courts as key policy makers—each of these forces has shaped, to some degree, the emergence of conflict over appointments in the postwar period. Still, these explanations do not help us to pinpoint the timing or location of conflict over judges. The increasing role of the Warren Court on a range of controversial issues must have played a role in increasing the salience of judicial nominations to senators. If the Court had avoided controversial social, economic, and political issues, senators would have cared little about the makeup of the bench. But we don't see marked changes in the advice and consent until well after both the 1954 decision and the emergence of more ideological activists in the 1960s. Certainly, the no-holds-barred battle over the Bork nomination showed both parties that all-out opposition to a presidential appointment was within the bounds of acceptable behavior after 1987. Still, the Bork fight leaves us unable to explain significant variation in the Senate's treatment of judicial nominees before and after the One Hundredth Congress. The Senate also began to scrutinize executive-branch appointments in the late 1980s and 1990s. Thus, evidence in favor of the big bang account is incomplete. More likely, episodes like the Bork confirmation battle are symptoms, rather than causes, of a more taxing road to confirmation in recent decades.

In contrast, the "nothing new under the sun" alternative suggests that "the appointments process is and always has been political because federal judges and justices themselves are political."[7] As Lee Epstein and Jeffrey Segal argue, presidents have always wanted to use the appointment power for ideological and partisan purposes, and senators have always treated appointees as a means to "help further their own goals, primarily those that serve to advance their chances of reelection, their political party, or their policy interests."[8] As these scholars argue, we should expect to see legislators and presidents engage in purposeful behavior shaped by their goals. But that is only a starting point in accounting for the dynamics of advice and consent. It is difficult to explain variation in the Senate's treatment of judicial appointments—over time and across circuits—if we maintain that the process has always been politicized. We recognize the political nature of advice and consent but also seek to identify the ways in which politicians exploit Senate rules and practices to target appointees deemed most likely to shift the ideological tenor of the federal bench.

Patterns in Judicial Selection

Figure 16-1 shows confirmation rates for appointees to the U.S. district courts and courts of appeals between 1947 and 2014. One might reasonably conclude from the graph that advice and consent over the postwar period has gone awry. With the recent exception of 2013 to 2014 (which we address later), the bottom has fallen out of the confirmation process in recent decades. Presidents before the 1980s could count on the Senate confirming roughly 90 percent of their nominees. Between 1981 and the end of Obama's first term, the average confirmation rate for appellate nominees fell to 65 percent. District court nominees were largely immune to this conflict over the postwar period. But by the end of George W. Bush's second term, trial court nominees were scrutinized as closely as appellate nominees. In the context of these broader trends, it is notable that Obama nominees in both the 111th (2009–2010) and 112th (2011–2012) Congresses were confirmed at higher rates than were George W. Bush's nominees: The Senate confirmed roughly 60 percent of Obama's appellate court nominees but only 50 percent of Bush's nominees. Overall, Obama's district court nominees also fared slightly better than Bush's nominees but only after Republicans held confirmation rates below 60 percent during Obama's first two years in office.

No doubt, the Senate's slightly better than average record during the first term of the Obama administration led Minority Leader Mitch McConnell, R-Ky., to argue in June of 2013 that "the president's been treated very fairly on judicial [nominees]." Such claims, however, rang hollow to Democrats, who pointed to other metrics for capturing the path to confirmation. Instead of emphasizing confirmation rates, Democrats decried how long it took the Senate to confirm Obama's nominees. Figure 16-2 shows the trend, with the first four years of the Obama administration surpassing previous records set in the late Clinton administration for how long it takes the Senate to confirm nominees. During the Obama administration, Republican senators threw enough curve balls to force nominees to wait more than half a year to be confirmed. If we add in the fates of nominees who the Senate never confirmed, the wait time for a decision extended to nearly eleven months in the 112th Congress. (That said, as of 2014, Democrats held the postwar record for sluggish confirmation of an opposition party's nominees:

Figure 16-1 Confirmation Rates for Judicial Nominations, 1947–2014

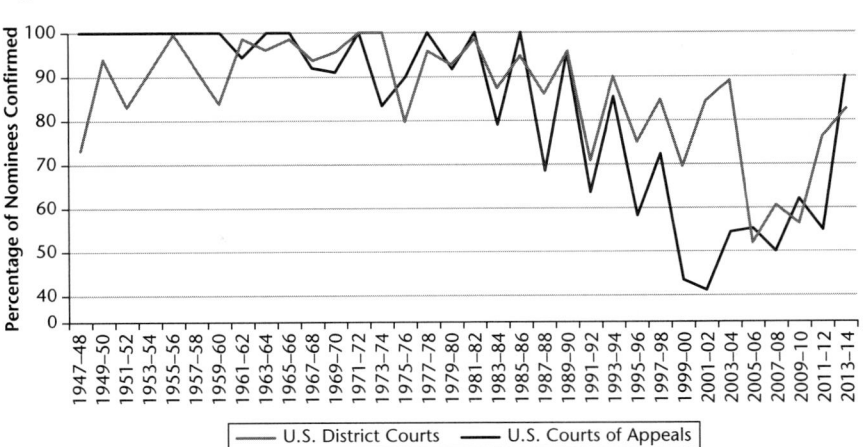

Source: Updated from Sarah Binder and Forrest Maltzman, *Advice and Dissent* (Washington, DC: Brookings Institution Press, 2009).

Confirmation delays hit record delays in 2001–2002 after Republicans lost control of the Senate early in George W. Bush's first term.)

Note, as well, that conflict across the twelve federal circuits is uneven. As seen in Figure 16-3, nominations for some appellate vacancies attract little controversy, such as New York's Second Circuit and the Mountain states' Eighth. Not so for the D.C. Circuit Court of Appeals or for the appeals courts in the Fourth and Sixth Circuits. Since the beginning of the Clinton administration in the early 1990s, more than half of the nominees for these circuits have stalled. The uneven pattern across the circuits reminds us that senators do not care equally about each circuit, meaning that some circuits bear the brunt of conflict over judges while others escape largely unscathed.

Confirmation statistics do not tell the full story of the Senate's treatment of Obama's judicial nominations. Senate Republicans have raised the stakes over nominations by attempting to filibuster some of Obama's appellate and district court nominees. To be sure, Republicans filed cloture some thirty times when Democrats filibustered George W. Bush nominees, filing cloture seven times on one nominee for the D.C. Circuit Court of Appeals. During Obama's first four years in office, Republicans returned the favor: GOP filibusters of Obama nominees led Democrats to attempt cloture on nominations roughly ten times.

Figure 16-2 Length of Confirmation Process for Successful Judicial Nominees, 1947–2014

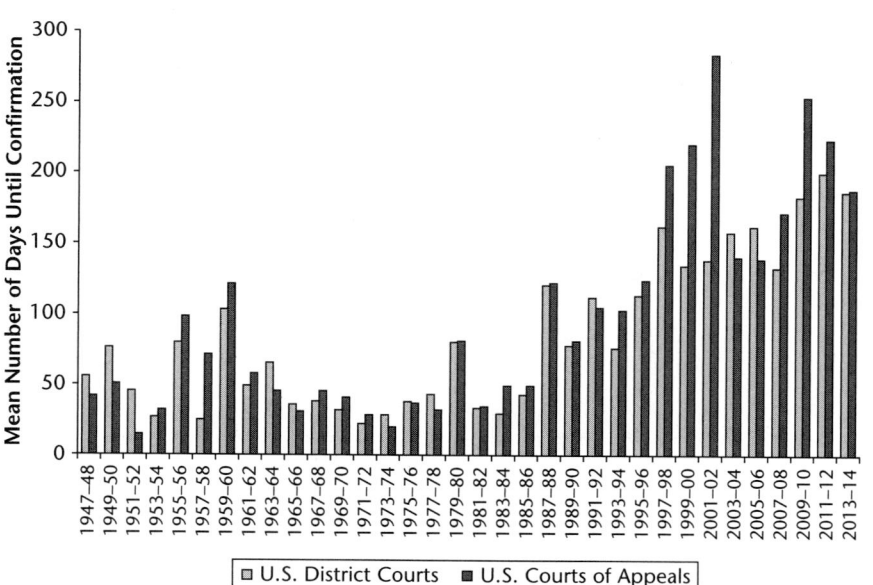

Source: Updated from Binder and Maltzman, *Advice and Dissent*.

Figure 16-3 Confirmation Rates by Circuit, 1993–2012

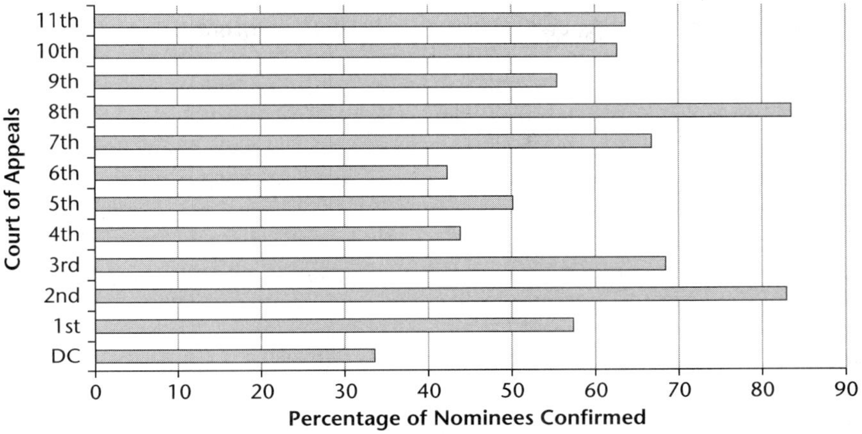

Source: Updated from Binder and Maltzman, *Advice and Dissent.*

Majority Leader Harry Reid, D-Nev., also threatened to move forward with cloture votes on seventeen district court nominees in March of 2012, a tactic that brought the GOP to the bargaining table to resolve the fate of the nominees.

Republican filibusters of Obama nominees are notable for two reasons. First, Republicans filibustered some nominees who had secured the support of Republican home state senators. For example, Republican Richard Lugar of Illinois publicly supported David Hamilton, a candidate for the Seventh Circuit Court of Appeals. But Lugar's GOP colleagues delayed a confirmation vote for eight months on account of Hamilton's ties to the ACLU. As one conservative activist suggested at the time, Hamilton might have been targeted simply because he was Obama's *first* nominee.[9] In contrast, Republican senators offered no reason to justify the six-month delay they imposed on Barbara Keenan's nomination to the Fourth Circuit Court of Appeals. The Senate ultimately confirmed Keenan, 99–0. Such data suggest that Republicans had little interest in blocking some nominees yet felt emboldened to delay confirmation if only to keep the seats vacant for as long as possible.

Second, the GOP also sought to block Senate confirmation votes on district court nominees. Before the GOP launched a filibuster against Rhode Island District Court nominee John McConnell in May 2011, only three district judges since 1968 had ever faced a cloture motion, and all three were ultimately confirmed.[10] The confirmation vote divided the GOP conference. John Cornyn, R-Tex., rallied votes against cloture, arguing that McConnell was unfit to serve on the bench. But other GOP senators drew the line between appellate and trial court nominees, wary of crossing the line into a new era of filibustering district court nominees. "We don't want to establish precedents that will be repeated," warned Senator John McCain, R-Ariz. "Quite often we establish precedents and you find out when you get back in the majority it wasn't that good of an idea."[11] Eleven GOP members heeded McCain's warning and joined the Democrats in voting to cut off debate on the McConnell nomination. Within a year, however, Reid had filed seventeen cloture motions on pending district court nominees in the face of new threats to block the Senate from voting on trial court nominees.

To be sure, there is recent precedent for delaying district court nominations, as the Senate confirmed only about half of President Bush's trial court nominees in the 109th Congress (2005–2006). That trend continued in the following Congresses, leaving the Obama administration unable to fill numerous seats on the lower federal bench. As one Democratic aide noted in 2011, "They [the GOP] have approached district court nominees with the same exacting inquiry standards that used to be reserved for the Supreme Court and for controversial circuit court nominees, not even all circuit court nominees. But now it extends to every lifetime appointment." Republicans that year were not shy about owning up to their new strategy:

> Each nominee is assessed on his or her own merits regardless of the position in the court system to which they are nominated because this is a lifetime appointment. . . . They [district court judges] deal with serious issues. They deal with Proposition 8, they deal with "don't ask, don't tell," they deal with terrorism cases, health care, and that's my boss's view of it. . . . When President Bush was in power and you didn't want to do this and you just rubber stamped District Court nominees, that's your problem.[12]

The GOP strategy of targeting Obama's district court nominees makes plain that every judicial vacancy can have important policy consequences for the political parties.

In some ways, the GOP strategy was just tit for tat—retaliating against Democrats for their foot-dragging over Bush's second-term trial court nominees that began in 2005. One Republican strategist suggested that Obama's relatively moderate courts-of-appeals nominees—and the White House's sluggishness in sending nominations up to the Senate—left relatively few appellate targets for Republicans to oppose. To some degree then, foot-dragging over trial court nominees might be situational. Still, recent developments suggest that advice and consent is on the verge of a breakdown, begging the question why such conflict over judicial selection has taken root and spilled over all three levels of the federal bench.

The Politics of Advice and Consent

How do we account for the Senate's uneven performance in confirming federal judges? Why have confirmation rates slid downward over the past couple of decades, and why does it take so long for the Senate to render its decisions? Four forces shape the fate of nominations sent to the Senate. First and foremost are ideological forces: The array of policy views across the three branches affects the probability and speed of confirmation. Second, partisan forces matter: Electoral competition between the parties has increased each party's unwillingness to easily confirm nominees from the other party. Third, institutional rules and practices in the Senate shape the likelihood of confirmation. Fourth, the electoral context matters. All four of these forces have come into play, especially during the Obama years, fueling conflict over advice and consent and leading the Democrats to ban judicial filibusters.

Partisan and Ideological Forces

Partisan and ideological forces are inextricably linked in the contemporary Senate, as the two parties have diverged ideologically in recent decades. Not surprisingly, Washington pundits assessing the state of judicial selection have often pinpointed poisoned relations between liberal Democrats and President Bush and between conservative Republicans and President Obama as the proximate cause of the slowdown in advice and consent. Democrats' foot-dragging over the course of the Bush administration was often attributed to ideological conflict and partisan pique, as liberal Democrats criticized Bush's tendency to nominate extremely conservative (and presumably Republican) judges. The rise of intense ideological differences between the two parties over the past two decades, in other words, directly affects the pace and rate of confirming new federal judges. Given that polarization of the parties has been rising steadily over the past two decades, no surprise that confirmation rates hover around 60 percent for Obama's nominees.

Partisan politics may affect the process of advice and consent more broadly in the guise of divided party government. Because judges have life tenure on the bench and thus make lasting contributions to the shape of public law, senators have good cause to scrutinize the views of potential judges. Presidents overwhelmingly seek to appoint judges who hail from their own party, so Senate scrutiny of judicial nominees should be particularly intense when different parties control the White House and the Senate. Not a surprise then that nominees considered during a period of divided control take significantly longer to be confirmed than those nominated during a period of unified control. Judicial nominees are also less likely to be confirmed during divided government: Between 1947 and 2012, the Senate confirmed, on average, 83 percent of appellate court nominees considered during periods of unified control but only 70 percent of nominees during divided government.

Partisanship is also likely to affect the fate of nominations to particular circuits when the circuit is balanced between appointees of Democratic and Republican presidents. Because most appellate court cases are heard by randomly generated three-judge panels, nominations to courts that are evenly divided are likely to have a more significant impact on the law's development, as compared to appointments to courts that lean decidedly in one ideological direction or the other. Senate majorities appear especially reluctant to confirm nominees to such courts when the appointment would tip the court balance in the favor of a president from the opposing party. The battle in 2013 over vacancies on the D.C. Court of Appeals is a perfect example. With four Democratic and four GOP appointees sitting on the circuit bench, Senate Republicans resolutely blocked Obama's picks for the court's three vacant seats. In response, Democrats went nuclear that fall, eliminating senators' opportunity to filibuster judicial nominations. In short, partisan dynamics—fueled, in part, by ideological conflict—strongly shape the Senate's conduct of advice and consent, making it difficult for presidents to mold the federal courts to their party's policy advantage.

Institutional Forces

The capacity to derail nominees depends on the rules and practices of advice and consent—a set of institutional tools that distributes power across the Senate. To explain the fate of the president's judicial nominees, we need to know something about institutional venues in which advice and consent take place. Senators seeking to shape the fate of a nominee have several options, including an array of committee and floor rules and practices that can be exploited by individual senators and the two political parties.[13] In theory, nominees only have to secure the consent of a floor majority, as nominations are considered for an up-or-down vote in the Senate's executive session. In practice, nominees must secure the support of several pivotal Senate players—meaning that more than a simple majority may be needed for confirmation.

A nominee's first institutional hurdle is clearing the Senate Judiciary Committee. By tradition, senators from the home state of each judicial nominee take the lead in casting first judgment on potential appointees. The power of home state senators is institutionalized in Judiciary panel procedures. Both of the home state senators are asked their views about judicial nominees from their home state pending before the committee. Senators can return a "blue slip," demarking their support or objection to the nominee, or they can refuse to return the slip altogether—an action that signals their opposition to the nominee. A negative blue slip from a home state senator traditionally sufficed to block further action. As the process has become more polarized in recent years, committee chairs are tempted to ignore objections from minority party senators. Indeed, Senator Pat Leahy's equivocation at the start of the 111th Congress (2009–2010) over how he would treat blue slips from Republican senators led Republican senators, in 2009, to threaten to filibuster nominees from states with Republican senators if their prior consent was not secured. Even today, after floor filibusters of nominees have, in effect, been eliminated, blue slips still weigh heavily in the committee chair's assessment on whether, when, and how to proceed with a nominee.

Historically, greater policy differences between the president and the home state senator for appellate nominees have led to longer confirmation proceedings, suggesting the power of home state senators to affect panel proceedings. Conversely, the strong support of one's home state senator is essential in navigating the committee successfully. Given the often fractured attention of the Senate and the willingness of senators to heed the preferences of the home state senator, having a strong advocate in the Senate with an interest in seeing the nomination proceed is critical in smoothing the way for nominees.

Once approved by committee, a nomination must clear a second hurdle: making it onto the Senate's floor agenda. By rule and precedent, both majority and minority party coalitions can delay nominations after they clear committee. Because the presiding officer of the chamber gives the majority leader priority in being recognized to speak on the Senate floor, the majority leader has the upper hand in setting the chamber's agenda. When the president's party controls the Senate, this means that nominations are usually confirmed more quickly; under divided control, nominations can be kept off the floor by the majority leader—who wields the right to make a nondebatable motion to call the Senate into executive session to consider nominees. With Democrats presiding over the Senate in the 107th (2001–2002) and 109th (2005–2006) Congresses, it was no wonder that the confirmation rates for Bush nominees in those Congresses were nearly fifteen points lower than the rates in the two Congresses in which Republicans controlled the Senate during the Bush years.[14]

Until the fall of 2013, securing a vote on confirmation essentially required the consent of the minority party. If a single senator objected to voting to confirm a nominee, the majority leader either shelved the nomination or pursued a supermajority of sixty senators to end debate and bring the Senate to a confirmation vote. In fact, the chance that a nomination might be filibustered typically motivated the majority leader to seek unanimous consent of the full chamber before bringing a nomination before the Senate. Such consultation meant that nominations were unlikely to clear the Senate without the endorsement of at least some members of the Senate minority party.

The de facto requirement of minority party assent granted the party opposing the president significant power to affect the fate of nominees, even if that party did not control the Senate. As policy differences increase between the president and the opposing party, that party is more likely to exercise its power to delay nominees. Given the high degree of polarization between the two parties and the centrality of federal courts in shaping public law, judicial nominations have become a partisan flash point. Indeed, when Democrats lost control of the Senate after the 2002 elections, they turned to a new tactic to block Bush nominees they disliked: the filibuster. To be sure, some contentious nominations have, in the past, been subject to cloture votes. But all of those lower court nominees were eventually confirmed. In 2003, however, numerous judicial filibusters were successful. Use of such tactics likely flowed from the increased polarization of the two parties and from the rising salience of the federal courts across the interest group community. Much of the variation in the fate of judicial nominees before 2014 was thus likely driven by ideologically motivated players and parties in both the executive and legislative branches exploiting the rules of the game in an effort to shape the makeup of the federal bench.

Temporal Forces

Finally, it is important to consider how secular or cyclical elements of the political calendar may shape the fate of judicial nominees. It is often suggested that delays encountered by judicial nominees may be a natural consequence of an approaching presidential election. Decades ago, the opposition party in the Senate might have wanted to save vacancies as a pure matter of patronage: foot-dragging on nominations would boost the number of positions the party would have to fill if it won the White House. More recently, the opposition might want to save vacancies so that a president of their own party could fill the vacancies with judges more in tune with the party's policy priorities.

Finally, there is ample evidence of vacancy hoarding in presidential-election years in the recent past. For example, with control of both the Senate and the White House up for grabs in November 2012, Senate minority leader Mitch McConnell declared in June of 2012 that he was invoking the *Thurmond rule*, a quadrennial practice (unevenly applied) of preventing Senate action on appellate nominees in the run up to a presidential-election year. Caught in the net of the Thurmond rule that month were several pending appellate court nominees, including four who appeared to have had the support of Republican senators.[15] More generally, over the past sixty-five years, the Senate has treated judicial nominations submitted or pending during a presidential-election year significantly different than other judicial nominations. First, the Senate has historically taken longer to confirm nominees pending in a presidential election than those submitted earlier in a president's term. Second and more notably, these presidential-election-year nominees are significantly less likely to be confirmed. For all judicial nominations submitted between 1947 and 2012, appointees for the courts of appeals pending in the Senate in a presidential-election year were nearly 40 percent less likely to be confirmed than nominees pending in other years.

Explaining Trends in Advice and Consent

How do we account more systematically for variation in the degree of conflict over judicial nominees? The multiple forces outlined before are clearly at play. For social scientists investigating patterns over time, this raises a key question: Taking each of these forces together, how well do the trends noted here hold up? Once subjected to multivariate controls, what can we conclude about the relative impact of partisan, ideological, and institutional forces on the pace and rate of judicial confirmations? Our answers to these questions are consequential, as they help us to evaluate how well the president and the Senate perform their constitutional duties of advice and consent.

To explain variation in conflict over judicial nominees, we tracked the fate of all nominations to the U.S. courts of appeals between 1947 and 2012 and used these data to estimate a model of the likelihood of confirmation.[16] The results help us to disentangle the relative importance of forces shaping the Senate's treatment of presidential appointees to the bench.[17] First, we found that partisan polarization lowers the chances of confirmation. During the least polarized Senate of the postwar period (the Eightieth Congress, 1947–1948), the likelihood of confirmation was 99 percent.[18] During the most polarized Congress in the study (2011–2012), we found a 60 percent chance of confirmation. As the two parties take increasingly different positions on major policy issues, they are less and less likely to give the other party's nominees an easy path to the bench. Second, we found a smaller impact of divided party control on the probability of confirmation. Nominees are about 10 percent less likely to be confirmed in periods of divided government, assuming an average level of polarization over the postwar period.[19] Third, approaching presidential elections matter: Confirmation is roughly 20 percent less likely when control of the White House—and power to nominate judicial candidates—is at stake. Fourth, the partisan balance of the circuit seems to slightly affect the chances of confirmation, dropping 3 percent when senators consider a nomination for a balanced circuit (assuming unified party control outside of a presidential election and average polarization). In a period of much higher polarization, nominations for these critical circuits face a much tougher road to confirmation: The likelihood of success drops twelve percentage points. General disagreement over the policy views of the nominees certainly fuels senators' opposition, but opposition is particularly intense in polarized periods when the ideological balance of a regional bench is at stake.

Finally, we found only weak evidence that nominee quality, as signaled by the American Bar Association (ABA), affects the likelihood of confirmation. Perhaps the ABA is not seen as a neutral evaluator of judicial nominees, and thus, senators systematically ignore the association's recommendations. Alternatively, judicial qualifications might not be terribly important for most nominees. Very few nominees merit an unqualified rating, and senators might not perceive a difference between well-qualified and qualified nominees. Thus, other considerations likely shape senators' decisions about whether to support a nominee.

A New War of Advice and Consent

These analyses suggest that partisan, institutional, and temporal forces mold the fate of presidential appointments to the federal bench. These tensions boiled over late in 2013, when Senate Democrats went "nuclear," reinterpreting Senate rules to ban filibusters of executive and most judicial nominations. The Democrats' nuclear move merits close examination, as does its impact on the fate of judicial nominations during Obama's second term in the White House. Before digging deeper into the Democrats' parliamentary maneuver, we review the political and other forces that brought the Senate parties to this institutional brink.

One the most visible changes to the confirmation process in recent decades is the rising political salience of nominations to the federal bench. Both parties—often fueled by supportive groups outside of the chamber—have made the plight of potential judges central to their campaigns for the White House and Congress.[20] The salience of judicial nominations to the two political parties—inside and outside of the halls of the Senate—is prima facie evidence that there is definitely "something new under the sun" when it comes to the selection of federal judges. Not every nominee experiences intense opposition: Democrats acquiesced to over three hundred of President Bush's judicial nominees, just as Republicans supported scores of Obama nominees. But the public salience of advice and consent increased sharply starting in the early 1980s and continued with full force under the presidencies of Clinton, Bush, and Obama.

The rising salience of federal judgeships is visible on several fronts. First, intense interest in the selection of federal judges is no longer limited to the home state senators for the nomination. Second, negative blue slips from home state senators no longer automatically kill a nomination, as recent Judiciary panel chairs sometimes hesitate to accord such influence to their minority party colleagues. Third, recorded floor votes are now the norm for confirmation of appellate court judges, as nominations are of increased importance to groups outside of the institution. Fourth, nominations now draw the attention of strategists within both political parties.

How do we account for the rising salience of federal judgeships to actors in and out of the Senate? It is tempting to claim that the activities of organized interests after the 1987 Supreme Court confirmation battle over Robert Bork are responsible. But interest groups have kept a close eye on judicial selection for quite some time. Both liberal and conservative groups were involved periodically from the late 1960s into the 1980s. And in 1984, liberal groups, under the umbrella of the Alliance for Justice, commenced systematic monitoring of judicial appointments, as had the conservative Judicial Reform Project of the Free Congress Foundation earlier in the decade. Although interest group tactics may have fanned the fires over judicial selection in recent years, the introduction of new blocking tactics in the Senate developed long after groups had become active in the process of judicial selection.[21] Outside groups may encourage senators to take more aggressive stands against judicial nominees, but by and large, Senate opposition reflects senators' concerns about the policy impact of judges on the federal bench.

Rather than attribute the state of judicial selection to the lobbying of outside groups, our sense is that the politics of judicial selection have been indelibly shaped by two trends. First, the political parties are more ideologically opposed and electorally competitive today than they have been for the past few decades. The analysis earlier suggests that ideological and partisan differences encourage senators to exploit the rules of the game to their party's advantage in filling vacant judgeships or blocking new nominees.

Second, if the courts were of little importance to the two parties, then polarized relations would matter little to senators and presidents in conducting advice and consent. However, the federal courts today are intricately involved in the interpretation and enforcement of federal law. Indeed, pervasive legislative deadlock in recent years (see Chapter 8 in this volume) can make the courts central to the resolution of conflict when legislative disagreements arise. Supreme Court decisions during the Obama years on the constitutionality of the Voting Rights Act, Affordable Care Act, Federal Defense of Marriage Act, and other laws drive home the impact of the federal courts in settling issues that a polarized Congress cannot resolve.

The rising importance of the federal courts makes extremely important the second trend affecting the nature of judicial selection. When Democrats lost control of the Senate after the 2002 elections, the federal courts were nearly evenly balanced between Democratic and Republican appointees: The active judiciary was composed of 380 judges appointed by Republican presidents and 389 judges appointed by Democratic presidents.[22] By the end of the Bush administration, in 2008, Republican-appointed appellate court judges outnumbered Democratic judges, ninety-nine to sixty-five. After nearly six years of Obama appointments to the judiciary, Democratic appointees to the appellate courts outstripped Republicans, ninety-five to seventy-five. Even more dramatic was the partisan turnover of the appellate courts. When Obama came into office in 2009, only one of thirteen federal courts of appeals had a majority of Democratic appointments; six years later, nine of the thirteen featured Democratic majorities.[23]

When federal courts were on the edge of partisan balance, near the outset of the Bush administration, it was no surprise that Democrats, in 2003, made scrutiny of judicial nominees a caucus priority and achieved remarkable unity in blocking nominees they deemed particularly egregious. It was no small wonder then that Republicans responded in kind in 2005, threatening recalcitrant Democrats with the "nuclear option."[24] Republicans envisioned a series of procedural steps that would have led the Senate to a new interpretation of the chamber's Rule 22, the mechanism for ending debate on contentious measures and nominations. The new interpretation would have banned judicial filibusters, requiring only fifty-one votes to end debate and come to a confirmation vote. Republicans backed down when a bipartisan "gang of fourteen" emerged to defuse tensions over the nuclear option, with both sides promising to reserve the filibuster for only the most extraordinary circumstances.

Ten years later, Democrats pulled the fuse and took the chamber nuclear in late November 2013. Repeated GOP filibusters of executive-branch nominees a few months earlier had been resolved with a bipartisan détente.[25] After ninety-eight senators went behind closed doors in the old Senate chamber to air grievances, senators John McCain, R-Ariz., and Charles Schumer, D-N.Y., negotiated what would turn out to be a temporary truce. Republicans ended their filibusters of several long-stalled Obama nominations to labor, consumer, and environmental positions, and Democrats backed away from cracking down on filibusters. The agreement left the Senate's cloture rule unchanged—allowing Republicans to filibuster in the future—and Democrats refused to take the nuclear option to ban filibusters off the table. As Republican senator Lindsey Graham of

South Carolina admitted to reporters, senators were filibustering some nominees because Republicans opposed the law that created their position. "That's not a reason to deny someone their appointment. We were wrong."[26]

Four months later, the truce went up in flames, spectacularly. The immediate spark was a set of GOP filibusters against three Obama nominees to the D.C. Court of Appeals. Some Republicans opposed the nominees on ideological grounds; others admitted that they sought to keep Obama from tilting a perfectly balanced circuit toward the liberal pole—reflecting the dynamic uncovered earlier when senators are called on to approve nominations to critical circuits. More broadly, the battle reflected years of partisan frustrations: Democrats added up the litany of GOP efforts to block Obama's agenda and his picks for prime appointments and collectively lit the fire. After repeated, failed cloture votes and warnings from Majority Leader Harry Reid, D-Nev., that he had the votes to ban filibusters of executive and judicial nominees (save for the Supreme Court), Reid and fifty-one Democratic colleagues detonated their nuclear device.

How did Senate Democrats accomplish this? Senate rules require two-thirds of senators present and voting to cut off debate on a motion to change the rules. Lacking a two-thirds majority for cloture on a resolution to change the Senate's Rule 22 (the cloture rule), Democrats took an easier route (albeit one theoretically easier to reverse). In the Senate, simple majorities can interpret formal rules as they see fit. By mustering a simple majority, senators can set a new *precedent*— a new way of interpreting a chamber rule. In November 2013, Senate Democrats, by a simple-majority vote, set a new precedent that reinterpreted Rule 22. Unless reversed by a future majority vote, the Senate now requires only a simple majority to invoke cloture on all executive and judicial nominations, except for the Supreme Court (rather than sixty votes stipulated in the Senate's formal rules).[27] In other words, the language of Rule 22 was not touched; only the chamber's *interpretation* of the rule changed. That is why Republicans charged that Democrats had changed the rules by breaking the rules. "It's a sad day in the history of the Senate," McConnell told reporters, deeming Reid's move a "power grab."[28] McConnell charged that Reid would be remembered as the "worst majority leader ever," tweeting a drawing of Reid's tombstone with the words "killed the Senate" inscribed.

Three dimensions of the GOP response to the nuclear move bear attention. First, the procedural change markedly increased the prospects for confirmation. Before the Senate went nuclear at the end of 2013, roughly thirty nominees were confirmed to the district and appellate courts. One year later, nearly one hundred nominees who had either been nominated or pending on the floor after the Democrats went nuclear in 2013 were confirmed. Overall, over 90 percent of the president's judicial nominees reached the bench in the 113th Congress—a success rate last reached in the late 1980s.

Second, Republicans did not completely submit to the new parliamentary regime of majority cloture. To be sure, the Senate confirmed Obama nominees more swiftly after the Democrats went nuclear than before.[29] But once a simple majority became sufficient to bring the chamber to a confirmation vote, Republicans retaliated by dragging their feet at all stages of the nomination and confirmation process.[30] The White House found it harder to reach consensus with senators over nominations to vacancies in states with one or more GOP senators, meaning that judgeships remained vacant for longer before nominees could be selected and formally nominated. Republicans also forced recorded votes whenever Democrats sought cloture on a nominee, even though Republican senators did not typically object to most of the nominees.

Figure 16-4 arrays confirmed nominees in 2013 and 2014 in order of the number of votes to confirm. The dark bars show the total number of votes each nominee received for cloture; the light bars record the total number of votes to confirm. Remarkably, Republicans voted against cloture for a large number of nominees, even though they knew that Democrats could invoke cloture on the nomination with just fifty-one votes. Republicans then voted to confirm most of those nominees, nearly unanimously. In fact, GOP senators opposed very few judges on both cloture and confirmation. That is perhaps not surprising. One recent study concluded that after Democrats went nuclear, Obama's judicial nominees were not appreciably more liberal than previous nominees.[31] Still, the opposition party's insistence on running through the time-consuming cloture process—despite strong support for so many of the nominees—highlights the poor condition of advice and consent. Rather than just filling the bench when the parties agree on nominees, the Republican opposition put the chamber through procedural hoops seemingly only to waste the Senate's time. Keep in mind that the White House selected many of these nominees with the consent of Republicans, who were happy to fill vacant judgeships in their home states.

Second, the Republican response to the Democrats' nuclear move was perhaps not as drastic as many predicted beforehand. Republican senators did not in fact "blow up every bridge in sight," as many senators had feared. Some conflict was likely defused because the chair of the Senate Judiciary Committee, Democrat Patrick Leahy of Vermont, retained the panel's blue slip. Leahy's decision allowed Republicans to continue to block nominees to their home states by withholding their blue slips. Nor did Republicans appreciably ramp up obstruction of other Senate business unrelated to nominees. As Gregory Koger noted at the time, we could safely assume that Senate Republicans were probably "already filibustering in every case where the benefits of obstruction outweigh the costs."[32] That is what helped to corral fifty-one Democratic votes to go nuclear in the first place.

Third, despite their dramatic reactions to Reid's move, Republicans kept the new cloture thresholds once they regained control of the Senate in the 2014 elections. Why has the procedural change been so sticky? One reason is that Republicans disagreed about the right course of action. Those GOP divisions were sufficient to derail efforts to reinstate the sixty-vote hurdle for cloture when Republicans began organizing their new majority. Moreover, with a Democrat in the White House, the Republican majority could defeat Obama nominees simply by refusing to call them up for a confirmation vote. Indeed, by spring 2016,

Figure 16-4 Senators' Votes for Confirmed Nominees, 2013–2014

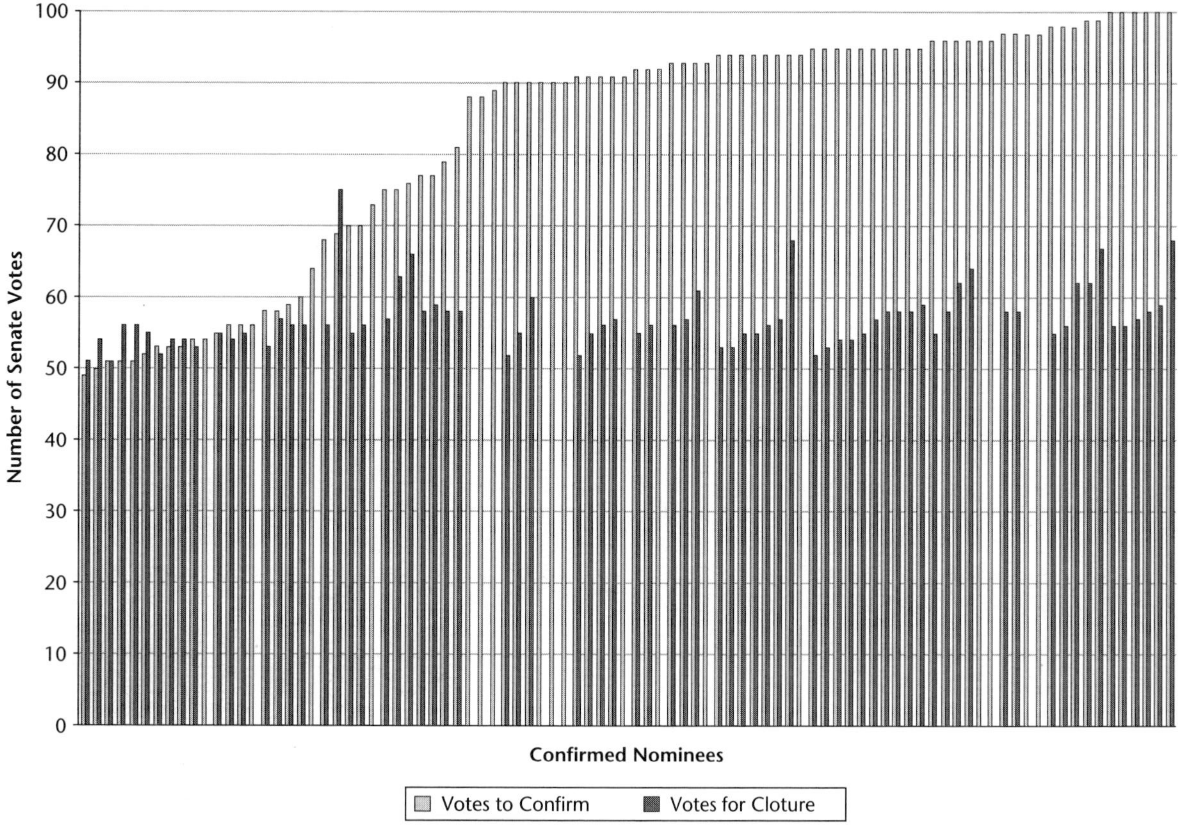

Source: Data from U.S. Senate (www.senate.gov).

confirmation of lower court nominees all but ground to a halt; barely a quarter of lower court nominees had been confirmed by May 2016. Most famously, Republicans blocked the president's pick for the Supreme Court after the sudden death of conservative justice Antonin Scalia earlier that year. Most Republicans running for reelection in 2016 in states won by Obama lined up to support the GOP's strategy of refusing to consider or vote on the nomination of Judge Merrick Garland for the Supreme Court.

The nuclear option also appears to have proven sticky because most senators from both parties quickly adapted to the new parliamentary regime. Sen. Richard Shelby, R-Ala., suggests, in effect, that Republicans have little choice: "It's hard to put the toothpaste back in the tube."[33] Or as Sen. Roy Blunt, R-Mo., put it to *Politico*, the Democrats' change was "long-term and permanent."[34] Because Republicans have thus far kept the Democrats' change, it is fair to call the filibuster ban *institutionalized*—incorporated into the Senate's parliamentary fabric. Remarkably—given how vociferously Republicans objected to the nuclear move—Blunt also argued, "I think it's well within the traditions of the Senate for a majority to decide nominations and a supermajority to decide legislation."[35] Right away, Republicans both rationalized and internalized the nomination filibuster ban as part and parcel of Senate "tradition." Even the most hallowed Senate traditions can be unmasked as no more than the by-product of hard-fought politics.

Conclusions

In the run up to the 2008 presidential election, Senate Democrats opted to close down the confirmation process for nominations to the lower federal courts. Reflecting on the impasse, Texas Republican senator John Cornyn observed that Democrats were playing "a short-sighted game, because around here what goes around comes around. . . . When the shoe is on the other foot, there is going to be a temptation to respond in kind."[36] The senator's point was on the mark: Each party's intolerance of the other party's nominees is reciprocated when the parties swap positions in the Senate. Such behavior by both political parties—and the breach of Senate trust that accompanies it—does not bode well for lifting the Senate out of its confirmation morass.

The breakdown in advice and consent fell to a historic low in 2016 when Republicans refused to consider the president's nomination of Judge Garland to the Supreme Court. Democrats charged Republicans with brazen disregard for advice and consent when they objected to even meeting with Garland. Republicans claimed historical precedent for refusing to consider Supreme Court nominees during a presidential-election year, but most neutral observers refuted their claims as inaccurate.[37] Republican intransigence on Garland was surely propelled by Republican leaders' desire to "respond in kind," as Senator Cornyn had predicted. The GOP strategy—pushing off confirmation at least until after the results of a presidential election were known, if not until a new administration takes office in 2017—raises the possibility that future Supreme Court vacancies will only be filled when a single party controls both the Senate and the White House—potentially after a future majority has gone nuclear to ban filibusters of Supreme Court nominees.

Ultimately, the ease with which Republicans shut down Garland's confirmation process (as of summer 2016) attests to the fragility of constitutional and other norms that senators depend on to keep the Senate's institutional fabric strong. Such norms dictate that the Senate will at least consider the president's nominations to the nation's highest court, even if the opposition would prefer a more ideologically compatible nominee. The Garland affair reminds us that Senate norms are only as strong as both parties want them to be. Unfortunately for the federal bench, there are few signs that wars of advice and consent will abate soon. The stakes of who sits on the federal bench are too high for combatants in partisan battles to lay down arms.

Notes

1. William Rehnquist, *1997 Year-End Report on the Federal Judiciary* (Washington, DC: U.S. Supreme Court, 1997).
2. John Roberts, *2010 Year-End Report on the Federal Judiciary* (Washington, DC: U.S. Supreme Court, 2010).
3. Legal studies addressing judicial selection are surveyed, for example, by Stephen B. Burbank, "Politics, Privilege, & Power: The Senate's Role in the Appointment of Federal Judges," *Judicature* 86, no. 1 (2002): 24–27. On the impact of presidential agendas, see Sheldon Goldman, *Picking Federal Judges: Lower Court Selection From Roosevelt Through Reagan* (New Haven, CT: Yale University Press, 1997), and on the role of interest groups, see Lauren Cohen Bell, *Warring Factions: Interest Groups, Money, and the New Politics of Senate Confirmation* (Columbus: Ohio State University Press, 2002), and Nancy Scherer, *Scoring Points: Politicians, Activists, and the Lower Federal Court Appointment Process* (Stanford, CA: Stanford University Press, 2005).
4. See, for example, Wendy L. Martinek, Mark Kemper, and Steven R. Van Winkle, "To Advise and Consent: The Senate and Lower Federal Court Nominations, 1977–1998," *Journal of Politics* 64 (2002): 337–61.
5. See Benjamin Wittes, *Confirmation Wars: Preserving Independent Courts in Angry Times* (Lanham, MD: Rowman and Littlefield, 2006), 59.
6. See Scherer, *Scoring Points*, and Bell, *Warring Factions*.
7. Lee Epstein and Jeffrey Segal, *Advice and Consent: The Politics of Judicial Appointments* (New York: Oxford University Press, 2005), 4.
8. Epstein and Segal, *Advice and Consent*, 3.
9. Sheldon Goldman, Elliot Slotnick, and Sara Schiavoni, "Obama's Judiciary at Midterm: The Confirmation Drama Continues," *Judicature* 94 (2011): 262–303.
10. The McConnell filibuster is reviewed in Niels Lesniewski and Brian Friel, "Senate Avoids Standoff on Judicial Nominees," CQ Today Online News, May 4, 2011.
11. Ibid.
12. Goldman, Slotnick, and Schiavoni, "Obama's Judiciary," 280.
13. The relative effects of these multiple rules and practices are explored in David M. Primo, Sarah A. Binder, and Forrest Maltzman, "Who Consents? Competing Pivots in Federal Judicial Selection," *American Journal of Political Science* 52 (2008): 471–89.

14. Democrats regained control of the Senate in April 2011 after Vermont Republican Jim Jeffords switched parties and handed control of the chamber midsession to the Democrats.
15. John Gramlich, "Senators Argue Over End-of-Term Nominees, 'Thurmond Rule,'" CQ Today Online News, June 19, 2012, http://public.cq.com/docs/news/news-000004107978.html.
16. Results are available from authors. We compiled data on judicial nominations for the Eightieth through 107th Congresses from the *Final Calendars* printed each Congress by the Senate Committee on the Judiciary. Nominations data for the 108th through 110th Congresses (2003–2008) are drawn from the Department of Justice's Office of Legal Policy Web site: http://www.usdoj.gov/olp. Data for the 111th and 112th Congresses are drawn from the Senate Committee on the Judiciary's Web site. We include the Court of Appeals for the District of Columbia but exclude the appellate court for the federal circuit on account of its limited jurisdiction.
17. The independent variables are measured as follows. We measure polarization as the difference in the mean ideology for each Senate party (as measured by DW-NOMINATE scores available at http://www.voteview.com). The partisan balance of each circuit in each Congress is measured as the proportion of active courts-of-appeals judges appointed by Democratic presidents and serving during the Congress. Nominee quality is rated by the Standing Committee on the Federal Judiciary of the American Bar Association and is available for the 101st through 112th Congresses here: http://www.abanet.org/scfedjud/ratings.html. I thank Sheldon Goldman for ABA ratings for the previous Congresses.
18. We assume a well-qualified nominee pending in a period of unified party control outside of a presidential-election year who is slotted for a circuit that is not balanced between the parties.
19. The impact of polarization on the likelihood of confirmation is resilient across the time period. If we look only at the period before Ronald Reagan came to office (1947–1980), increases in polarization still reduce the chances of confirmation, as does the misfortune of being a nominee pending during a presidential-election year.
20. Involvement of interest groups in lower court judicial selection reaches back decades, but a marked increase in their organized involvement occurred in the early 1980s. See Gregory A. Caldeira and John R. Wright, "Lobbying for Justice: The Rise of Organized Conflict in the Politics of Federal Judgeships," in *Contemplating Courts*, Lee Epstein (Washington, DC: CQ Press, 1995), 44–71. See also Roy B. Flemming, Michael B. MacLeod, and Jeffery Talbert, "Witnesses at the Confirmations? The Appearance of Organized Interests at Senate Hearings of Federal Judicial Appointments, 1945–1992,"*Political Research Quarterly* 51 (1998): 617–31, and Bell, *Warring Factions*.
21. Tactics of two leading interest groups are detailed in Bob Davis and Robert S. Greenberger, "Two Old Foes Plot Tactics in Battle Over Judgeships," *Wall Street Journal*, March 2, 2004.
22. See Alliance for Justice Judicial Selection Project, *2001–2 Biennial Report*, Appendix 3 (2002).
23. Jeremy W. Peters, "Building Legacy, Obama Reshapes Appellate Bench," *New York Times*, September 13, 2014, http://www.nytimes.com/2014/09/14/us/politics/building-legacy-obama-reshapes-appellate-bench.html.
24. The nuclear option conflagration in the Senate in 2005 is detailed in Sarah A. Binder, Anthony J. Madonna, and Steven S. Smith, "Going Nuclear, Senate Style," *Perspectives on Politics* 5 (2007): 729–40.

25. Jonathan Weisman and Jennifer Steinhauer, "Senators Reach Agreement to Avert Fight Over Filibuster," *New York Times*, July 16, 2013, http://www.nytimes.com/2013/07/17/us/politics/senators-near-agreement-to-avert-fight-over-filibuster.html.
26. Ibid.
27. Technically, after Democrats failed to secure sixty votes for cloture on the nomination of Patricia Ann Millett and other nominees in the fall of 2013 for vacancies on the D.C. Circuit Court of Appeals, Reid returned to the nomination on the Senate floor on November 21, 2013. Reid raised a point of order, arguing that only a simple majority was required to invoke cloture on a nomination. The chair—on the advice of the parliamentarian—ruled that according to Rule 22, a three-fifths (sixty-vote) majority was required to invoke cloture and thus the point of order was not sustained. Reid appealed the ruling of the chair. Because cloture-related appeals are nondebatable under Rule 22, Reid's appeal was voted on immediately. Democrats overturned the ruling of the chair with fifty-two votes. That vote set the new precedent, interpreting Rule 22 to require only a simple majority for all executive and judicial nominations below the Supreme Court. Minority leader Mitch McConnell, R-Ky., then made a point of order that cloture requires sixty votes, and the chair—ruling under the newly created precedent—ruled that only a simple majority was (now) required. McConnell appealed the ruling, the chair put the question to the Senate to decide on appeal, and fifty-two Democratic senators voted to sustain the new ruling of the chair. With those parliamentary steps, Democrats went "nuclear."
28. Paul Kane, "Reid, Democrats Trigger 'Nuclear' Option; Eliminate Most Filibusters on Nominees," *Washington Post*, November 21, 2013, https://www.washingtonpost.com/politics/senate-poised-to-limit-filibusters-in-party-line-vote-that-would-alter-centuries-of-precedent/2013/11/21/d065cfe8-52b6-11e3-9fe0-fd2ca728e67c_story.html.
29. Christina L. Boyd, Michael S. Lynch, and Anthony J. Madonna, "Nuclear Fallout: Investigating the Effect of Senate Procedural Reform on Judicial Nominations," *The Forum* 13 (2015): 623–41.
30. Al Kamen and Paul Kane, "Did 'Nuclear Option' Boost Obama's Judicial Appointments?" *Washington Post*, December 17, 2014, https://www.washingtonpost.com/blogs/in-the-loop/wp/2014/12/17/did-nuclear-option-boost-obamas-judicial-appointments.
31. Boyd, Lynch, and Madonna, "Nuclear Fallout," 638.
32. Gregory Koger, "Reid's Tactical Nuke and the Future of the Senate," *Washington Post*, November 21, 2013, https://www.washingtonpost.com/news/monkey-cage/wp/2013/11/21/reids-tactical-nuke-and-the-future-of-the-senate.
33. Sarah Binder, "Why Republicans Are Unlikely to Reverse the 'Nuclear Option,'" *Washington Post*, December 4, 2014, https://www.washingtonpost.com/blogs/monkey-cage/wp/2014/12/04/why-republicans-are-unlikely-to-reverse-the-nuclear-option.
34. Manu Raju, "GOP Unlikely to Reverse 'Nuclear Option,'" *Politico*, December 3, 2014, http://www.politico.com/story/2014/12/gop-senate-filibuster-113308#ixzz45UGzg5a5.
35. Ibid.
36. James Rowley, "Senate Standstill to Let Obama or McCain Tip Balance on Courts," *Bloomberg News*, August 7, 2007, http://www.bloomberg.com/apps/news?pid=washingtonstory&sid=aPaxOvQrYI7k.
37. See, for example, Lauren Carroll, "Mitch McConnell Exaggerates 'Tradition' of Not Confirming Election Year Supreme Court Nominees," *Politifact*, March 22, 2016 http://www.politifact.com/truth-o-meter/statements/2016/mar/22/mitch-mcconnell/mitch-mcconnell-exaggerates-tradition-not-confirmi.

17. Congress, Public Opinion, and the Political Costs of Waging War

Douglas L. Kriner

Since the construction of the modern national security state, the balance of war powers has swung decisively toward the executive branch. Presidents repeatedly dispatch American troops around the globe without prior congressional assent. Moreover, Congress routinely fails to use the legislative levers at its disposal, most notably the power of the purse, to rein in a wayward commander in chief. However, Congress remains relevant in military policy making, but it does so through political rather than legislative or constitutional means. This chapter examines one of the most important mechanisms through which Congress influences military policy: by engaging the debate in the public sphere, turning public opinion against the president, and raising the political costs for the president of pursuing his preferred military course of action. A combination of experimental and observational evidence shows how congressional actors significantly influenced public support for the war in Afghanistan. This capacity and presidents' anticipation of it have produced tangible changes in military policy outcomes. More broadly, the results have important implications for presidents' capacity to rally public support for other items on their policy agendas outside of the military sphere.

The Constitution's ambiguous allocation of war powers across the executive and legislative branches has long served, in the assessment of the great legal scholar Edward Corwin, as an "invitation to struggle" for influence over the conduct of American military affairs.[1] As late as December 6, 1941, President Franklin Roosevelt found himself severely constrained by a Congress unwilling to declare war on Nazi Germany and Imperial Japan. While Roosevelt pushed the scope of his executive authority to its max to make the United States a great arsenal for democracy, until Pearl Harbor, his hands were tied. Roosevelt could not take the United States directly into the fight without a congressional declaration of war.

Since World War II, the pendulum of war power has undoubtedly swung toward the executive.[2] Harry Truman's unilateral commitment of American troops to the Korean conflict marked an important turning point in presidential assertions of executive war powers.[3] Such claims of wartime executive authority reached even greater heights during the "imperial presidencies" of Lyndon Johnson and Richard Nixon.[4] In the immediate aftermath of the Vietnam War and Watergate, Congress endeavored to claw back some of the war power that the presidency had accumulated in the preceding decades, leading some scholars and analysts to proclaim a congressional resurgence in the martial arena.[5] However, recent history—from Reagan's reassertion of an aggressive, presidential-led foreign policy in the 1980s to Clinton's extensive peacekeeping efforts in Haiti and the Balkans in the 1990s to Bush's conduct of the wars in Iraq and Afghanistan to Obama's unilateral military actions in Libya, Iraq, and Syria—makes clear that initiative in the military realm remains firmly with the presidency.

The contemporary Congress has all but ceded its authority to determine when the United States should respond militarily to foreign crises.[6] Similarly, although Congress possesses a range of tools at its disposal to rein in and even terminate military campaigns with which it disagrees—most notably, the power of the purse—in only the rarest of circumstances can it overcome the institutional barriers, such as supermajoritarian requirements and a legislative process riddled with transaction costs, that all but preclude their effective use.[7] Even when Congress does manage to act legislatively, most scholars argue that its influence is often "less than meets the eye."[8] For example, after gaining control of both the House and Senate in the 110th Congress, House Democrats easily passed a supplemental appropriations bill that funded the Iraq War but also set a time line for withdrawing all American combat forces by September 1, 2008. However, Democratic leaders had to make significant compromises to overcome a Republican-led filibuster in the Senate. President Bush then vetoed even the weakened compromise, and his veto was easily sustained by congressional Republicans. Faced with the prospect of cutting off all funding for the troops in the field, Democrats had no choice but to cave and pass a clean appropriations bill.[9]

However, it would be a mistake to conclude that Congress no longer retains *any* influence over the decision making of the commander in chief. Rather, the nature of the contemporary congressional constraint is more *political* than constitutional.[10] Today's Congress routinely exerts influence over military policy not by exercising the formal powers entrusted to it in Article I but by shaping the political calculations of the commander in chief through more informal means. This chapter focuses on perhaps the most important mechanism through which Congress remains relevant in the military policy-making arena: by engaging the policy debate in the public sphere, turning public opinion against the president, and raising the political costs for the president of pursuing his preferred military course of action.

This chapter proceeds in four parts. The following section articulates a theory of why the wartime positions articulated by members of Congress can influence public support for war and which types of congressional cues should be particularly influential with the public. The analysis then begins with a survey experiment examining the capacity of a range of congressional cues to raise or lower support for an expeditious withdrawal from Afghanistan. The experimental design affords important causal leverage and allows us to be certain that the observed shifts in public wartime assessments were produced by congressional cues and not extraneous factors. Moreover, the timing of the experiment, which was conducted in April 2011, affords a critical test of the argument. Even nine years after the initial invasion, congressional elites retained considerable influence over Americans' prospective policy preferences for the war's future conduct. To complement the experimental results, this chapter then turns to an analysis of available polling data and content-coded media coverage of congressional rhetoric over the course of the Afghan War through 2010. While a clear majority of Americans continued to back the Afghan War for its first eight years, public support for the conflict declined precipitously over the first two years of President Obama's administration. During this time, the bipartisan elite consensus behind the war unraveled, a dissolution led by liberals from within the president's own party. This chapter concludes by discussing how Congress's capacity to erode public support for war can produce concrete shifts in military policy outcomes and by reflecting more broadly on how congressional opposition can limit the efficacy of presidential efforts to "go public" and build popular support for their policy initiatives.

Can Congressional Cues Influence Public Support for War?

At first blush, it might seem far-fetched to posit that the positions articulated in Congress can shape Americans' wartime opinions and policy preferences. After all, the contemporary legislature sports a pitiable approval rating that has repeatedly dipped into the single digits. Since 2006, Congress's approval rating has averaged just north of 20 percent.[11] Nevertheless, past scholarship has identified at least two reasons that congressional cues may be particularly influential in shaping many Americans' wartime opinions and policy judgments.

First, most Americans simply lack even basic information on which to evaluate important questions of foreign policy. On many domestic policy issues, citizens posses a number of simple heuristics to guide their choices. Have my personal finances increased or decreased in the last year? How would I rate my own interactions with the American health care system? By contrast, on foreign policy, most Americans begin with a clean slate. They lack basic information needed to form their opinions.[12] Moreover, few Americans are willing to pay the costs to acquire the information about events in far-flung lands needed to form their opinions. Instead, most citizens look to cues from political elites as highly efficient shortcuts. Elite cues provide a cheap and efficient way for many citizens to make judgments concerning complex issues of foreign policy.

Second, elite cues play a critically important role in helping average Americans interpret the limited amount of wartime information that they do receive. As a war unfolds, even relatively inattentive citizens will be exposed to information about events developing on the battlefield through the mass media. Perhaps most importantly, they will receive information about American military casualties.

This information can inform citizens' cost–benefit calculations concerning a war directly.[13] However, political elites may also play a critically important role in providing an interpretive framework to guide Americans' processing of such events. Is a resurgence of violence evidence of a rekindled insurgency that threatens to explode into full civil war? Or is the American mission still on track to succeed? Most citizens are unable to make such sophisticated judgments independently and instead rely on trusted political elites to interpret the evidence.

Citizens may be particularly reliant on elites when forming their prospective policy preferences. For example, how should the United States respond to a spike in American casualties? Is it evidence that the war's costs exceed the benefits of staying the course and therefore constitute a reason to withdraw? Or might a spike in casualties be construed as a reason to stay so that the fallen will not have died in vain? Elite cues provide critically important context about conditions on the ground and help citizens translate new information into policy preferences for the conflict's future conduct.[14]

Past scholarship also suggests that some congressional cues may be more influential in shaping Americans' wartime opinions and policy preferences than others. After all, members of Congress do not strive to shape public assessments of an ongoing war in a vacuum. Rather, they must compete in the public sphere against the president, who possesses the full resources of the presidential bully pulpit.

Past research emphasizes the importance of political cues that are "costly."[15] When presidential copartisans rally around their party leader or opposition party members of Congress attack the policies of the commander in chief, relatively little new information is conveyed. A rational observer could conclude that in such cases, members of Congress are simply playing to type. However, when a congressional elite publicly advances an argument that would appear to harm his or her own partisan interests—for example, when a Republican backs President Obama's calls to stay the course in Afghanistan or when a congressional Democrat breaks with the administration and calls for a more expeditious withdrawal—such a cue is politically costly. These cues convey more information about the state of the world and consequently may be particularly influential in shaping public attitudes toward war. This leads to our first hypothesis:

(H1): War opposition from presidential copartisans should be more influential than identical arguments from the partisan opposition in Congress. By contrast, war support from opposition party members should be more influential than parallel arguments made by congressional copartisans.

Perhaps even more influential than costly elite cues are bipartisan messages about the war and its future conduct transmitted by elites of both political parties. One of the most important findings of decades of scholarship on wartime public opinion is that elite consensus bolsters support for military action while elite dissension undermines it.[16] For example, Zaller's analysis of changing levels of public support for the Vietnam War revealed that during the period of bipartisan consensus before the Tet Offensive, war support remained high in the face of mounting costs. However, after Tet, as elites began to diverge in their assessments of the conflict, war support diminished as the public divided along both partisan and ideological lines, following the cues of trusted elites.[17] In the case of support for war with Nazi Germany, Berinsky observed the opposite pattern. In the early stages of World War II, before America entered the war, elites and the mass public split along partisan and ideological lines into pro-war and antiwar camps. However, this gap disappeared with the emergence of a bipartisan consensus following the Republicans' nomination of the interventionist Wendell Willkie in 1940. This bipartisan consensus was solidified after Pearl Harbor and remained steadfast throughout the war, allowing public support to remain strong, despite the massive number of casualties sustained in the fighting.[18] This suggests our second hypothesis:

(H2): Bipartisan support for and opposition to the war will be more influential on public opinion than identical arguments attributed only to congressional elites from a single political party.

Finally, past research suggests that when congressional elites take competing positions, the net influence of those elite cues on public opinion will be muted. Zaller's receive-accept-sample model suggests that Americans are likely to accept messages from trusted copartisan elites and/or those who accord with their predispositions and incorporate these cues into their opinion formation calculus. However, they will reject cues from untrusted elites or those who contradict any strongly held predispositions. As a result, contrasting cues transmitted by Democratic and Republican elites will likely affect different partisans in the mass public differently, and the net effect should be little opinion change. This produces our final hypothesis:

(H3): When congressional Democrats and Republicans take contrasting positions on the war, they will have no net effect on public support for the conflict.

Assessing the Influence of Congressional Cues: An Experimental Approach

A centerpiece of Barack Obama's 2008 presidential campaign was the argument that the war in Iraq was a war of choice while the war in Afghanistan was a war of necessity. According to Senator Obama, President Bush's fateful decision to pursue the former—which was aided by the authorization votes of Obama's two main rivals for the Democratic nomination, senators Hillary Clinton and John Edwards—misdirected critically needed resources away from Afghanistan, which was the legitimate central front in the war on terrorism. Although many voters perceived Obama to be an antiwar candidate, Obama openly pledged that while he wound down the war in Iraq, he would redouble the nation's efforts to ensure victory in Afghanistan.[19]

Shortly after his inauguration, President Obama took his first steps to reinforce the American troops fighting in Afghanistan, dispatching an additional seventeen thousand soldiers to the region in February 2009. However, military commanders on the ground quickly informed the new president that even more troops would be needed to reverse the tide. In December 2009, Obama announced his decision to send an additional thirty thousand troops to Afghanistan, raising the total to roughly 100,000, almost triple the number that were stationed there when he assumed office. However, wary of becoming mired in Afghanistan indefinitely, even as Obama announced his troop "surge," he simultaneously outlined a timetable for drawing down the American troop level. The first surge troops would begin to return home in July of 2011. Full details of how long or at what pace the drawdown would take place were left ambiguous.

A year later, following the Republicans' massive gains in the 2010 midterm elections, President Obama provided fresh details about how long American forces would remain in Afghanistan. He declared that the troop surge had produced "significant progress" on the ground; however, these gains remained fragile and potentially reversible.[20] As a result, Obama reaffirmed that the first surge troops would begin coming home in July 2011, as promised. Yet Obama declared that he would not withdraw American forces precipitously. Rather, American troops would remain in Afghanistan until security responsibilities could be handed over to Afghan forces, a transition the NATO allies had agreed to complete by the end of 2014.[21]

In sharp contrast to the war in Iraq, the Afghan conflict had long enjoyed significant bipartisan support from other political elites. However, the bipartisan consensus began to crack almost as soon as Obama announced the first batch of reinforcements. Liberal Democrats, tired of war, led the charge against the policies of a president of their own party. President Obama had hoped that his announced time line would sap energy from his critics in Congress. However, Obama's gambit did little to mollify congressional opponents.

Did the public positions articulated by members of Congress for and against the Afghan War sway public attitudes toward the conflict, more than nine full years after its initiation? In important respects, this represents a critical test for the argument that by engaging the policy debate in the public sphere, congressional elites can shape popular attitudes and thereby influence the political calculations of the commander in chief. Indeed, Baum and Groeling have recently challenged prior scholarship asserting elite leadership of wartime opinion to argue that this influence, though significant, is time bound. During a protracted conflict, citizens inevitably accrue information about a war from a variety of sources, and their opinions calcify.[22] As a result, Baum and Groeling argue that the capacity of elites to sway public opinion erodes substantially over time.[23] If Baum and Groeling are right, then congressional-elite cues will have little influence over public attitudes toward the Afghan War so many years after its initiation.

Experimental Design

As a first test of whether or not congressional elites were able to shape public opinion toward the war in Afghanistan, I embedded an experiment within a nationally representative online survey administered by YouGov to two thousand adult Americans between April 1 and 5, 2011. The main advantage of an experimental approach is the causal leverage it affords. By randomly assigning subjects to different treatment groups that vary only in terms of the congressional cue concerning the war or to the control group, we can be sure that any observed change in war support is due to the congressional cue and not to any other factor. By contrast, when analyzing observational data, it is often difficult to disentangle whether any observed change in war support is the result of elite actions—for example, a major debate critical of the war in Congress or high-profile calls for an early withdrawal of American troops by prominent senators on the Sunday morning news shows—or caused by other factors that might be occurring at the same time, such as an increase in casualties or media reports of other setbacks on the ground.

The main disadvantage of an experimental approach is the question of external validity. Admittedly, presenting subjects with a series of elite arguments and then asking them their opinion of the Afghan War does not accurately mirror how news is acquired and processed and opinion formed in the real world. Nevertheless, several features of the experiment were designed to mitigate these concerns as much as possible. First, the experiment began by informing all subjects of President Obama's position. All subjects first read that President Obama believes that "progress is being made in Afghanistan" and that "American troops should stay until Afghan forces are ready to assume security responsibilities," which should happen by 2015. By ensuring that all subjects received Obama's policy position and justification first, the experiment both privileged the president's position and reflected media norms, where the president's position is often accorded disproportionate emphasis.[24]

After receiving Obama's position, subjects were then randomly assigned to one of nine experimental groups. Those in the control group received no further information. Those in the eight treatment groups read an additional prompt informing them of the position of one or more congressional elites. In the first six treatment groups, subjects learned that congressional actors either support or oppose President Obama's plan to keep American troops in Afghanistan through 2014. In the three support treatments, subjects were told that congressional elites "support the President's position" and believe that "American forces are stabilizing many parts of Afghanistan previously controlled by the Taliban." These congressional elites argue that "withdrawing American troops prematurely would jeopardize these gains and undermine America's efforts to combat terrorism." In the first treatment group, these congressional elites were identified as "some Republican members of Congress"; in the second treatment group, they were identified as "some Democratic members of Congress"; and in the third treatment group, the supportive signaling elites were identified as "some Republican and Democratic members of Congress."

In this context, Republican support for staying the course in Afghanistan is a "costly" signal while Democratic support for the policy of a copartisan president is not. If Hypothesis 1 is correct, then the Republican support treatment should have greater influence on public opinion than the Democratic support treatment. Hypothesis 2 predicts that the bipartisan support treatment should also significantly reduce the percentage of subjects favoring an early withdrawal from Afghanistan.

Subjects assigned to Treatments 4, 5, and 6 learned that some congressional elites "oppose the President's position and instead favor an earlier withdrawal of American troops from Afghanistan." These congressional elites argue that "continued attacks by Taliban insurgents and the weakness of the Karzai government show that there is no American military solution to Afghanistan's civil war." Across the three treatments, this opposition was attributed to some congressional Republicans, some congressional Democrats, and some congressional Republicans and Democrats, respectively.

Democratic opposition to President Obama's position and support for an earlier withdrawal is a costly signal. This elite cue conflicts with the signaling elite's narrow partisan self-interests. As a result, Hypothesis 1 predicts that this treatment should significantly increase the percentage of subjects supporting an early withdrawal from Afghanistan versus that observed in the control. By contrast, Republican opposition to Obama is not a costly signal. As a result, it should have little impact on support for withdrawal. Finally, Hypothesis 2 predicts that the bipartisan opposition treatment will also significantly increase support for an early exit from Afghanistan.

The final pair of treatments examined the influence of conflicting partisan congressional cues on public attitudes toward the war in Afghanistan. In Treatment 7, subjects were told that some congressional Republicans support President Obama's position while some congressional Democrats oppose it. The wording for each supportive and opposition cue was identical to that in the treatments described previously. By contrast, in Treatment 8, subjects were told that some congressional Democrats support President Obama's position while some congressional Republicans oppose it. Hypothesis 3 predicts that these treatments, in which congressional cues were evenly balanced for and against the war, will have little influence on support for withdrawal versus that observed in the control group.

All subjects were then asked to select their preferred course for the future conduct of the war in Afghanistan.[25] From the response options, I created a binary dependent variable coded 1 for subjects who said that the United States should withdraw its forces from Afghanistan within one year—well in advance of President Obama's time line—and 0 for those who said that American troops should remain longer than one year.

Experimental Results

Figure 17-1 presents the percentage of subjects supporting an expeditious withdrawal of American troops from Afghanistan within the next year across the nine experimental groups. The horizontal line at 46 percent reports the percentage of subjects backing an early withdrawal in the control group. The bars on the graph present the level of support for a quick withdrawal observed in the eight congressional treatment groups. I-bars illustrate 90 percent confidence intervals around each estimate. Because subjects were randomly assigned to their respective experimental treatment or control group, the resulting differences in means are unbiased.[26] As a result, we can attribute any statistically significant differences in support for withdrawal observed between the control group and a treatment group to the congressional cue received by subjects in that treatment.

Each of the first three treatments presented subjects with a congressional-elite cue supporting the Obama administration's interpretation of events and backing the president's decision to stay the course and not withdraw precipitously from Afghanistan. Although the argument remained identical across all three treatments, consistent with Hypotheses 1 and 2, the effect of the appeal on public opinion critically depended on the partisan identity of the signaling elite. When congressional Republicans backed Obama's position—a costly signal—the

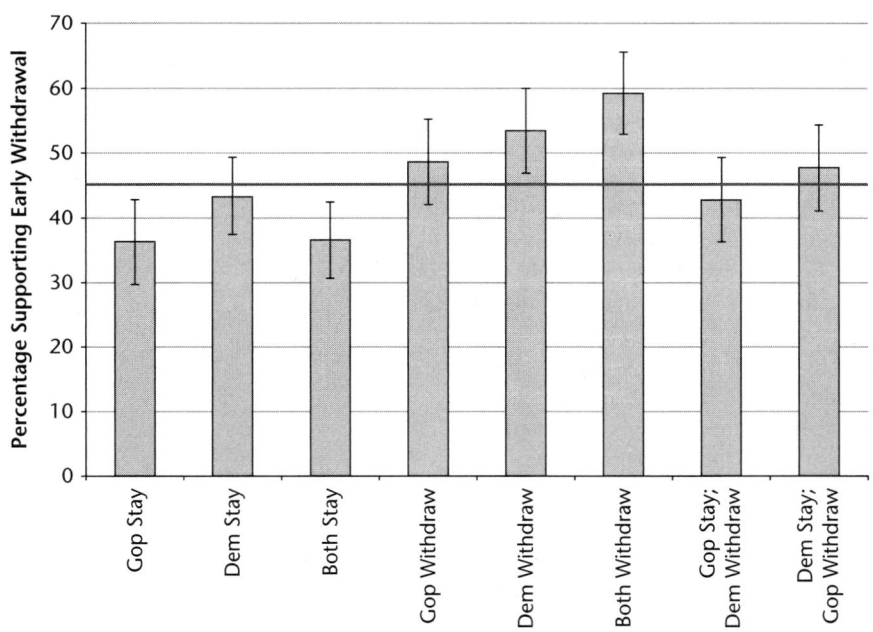

Figure 17-1 Effect of Congressional Position Taking on Support for Withdrawal Within One Year

Source: Compiled by author.

Note: The horizontal line at 46 percent is the percentage of subjects supporting withdrawal in the next year in the control group. I-bars present 90 percent confidence intervals around the percentage supporting withdrawal in each experimental treatment group.

congressional cue significantly muted popular demands for a hasty withdrawal from Afghanistan. The percentage calling for withdrawal within the next year fell from 46 percent in the control group to 36 percent in the Republican stay-the-course treatment. This costly cue, which cut against congressional Republicans' narrow partisan political interests to oppose the policies of an opposition president, resonated with many subjects and significantly reduced support for an early withdrawal.

By contrast, when the same argument was attributed to Democratic members of Congress, it had only a modest influence on the public. Support for an early withdrawal was somewhat lower in this treatment (43 percent) than in the control group (46 percent). However, the difference was not statistically significant and could have been produced by random chance alone. This result was also consistent with Hypothesis 1. When congressional Democrats rally behind a copartisan president, the resulting signal is not costly and does not transmit as much information about the value of staying the course in Afghanistan as when the exact same argument is made by congressional Republicans.

Finally, the bipartisan support treatment reduced support for a quick withdrawal by about 10 percent versus that observed in the control group baseline. This result is consistent with Hypothesis 2, which posited that bipartisan support should also be particularly influential in shaping public support for war.

In Treatments 4, 5, and 6, subjects learned that some members of Congress challenged President Obama's assessment of conditions in Afghanistan. Because these members of Congress believed there was no American military solution to what had effectively become an Afghan civil war, they advocated an early withdrawal of American forces from the country. In each of the three treatment groups, the percentage supporting withdrawal within one year was greater than that observed in the control group. However, the magnitude of the effect again varied considerably depending on who in Congress made the argument.

Republican calls for withdrawal had the weakest influence on public support for the war. Just under 49 percent of subjects in the Republican withdrawal treatment supported withdrawal within the year versus 46 percent in the control group. This difference was small and not statistically significant. This accords with Hypothesis 1. Republican criticism of President Obama and challenges to his policy recommendations are not costly; rather, they accord with what we would expect from the opposition party. As a result, many Americans may judge that they convey little new information and refuse to update their opinions about the war accordingly.

Calls for an early withdrawal by congressional Democrats, by contrast, are politically costly. Most Democrats have strong partisan incentives to rally behind their party leader. According to Hypothesis 1, dissenting Democratic voices therefore should convey more weight and carry more influence over opinion formation. The experimental results are consistent with this hypothesis.[27] Support for an early withdrawal was significantly higher (54 percent versus 46 percent) in the Democratic withdrawal treatment than in the control group.

Consistent with Hypothesis 2, the results suggest that the effect of bipartisan calls for an early withdrawal were stronger still. Just under 60 percent of subjects in this treatment group answered that they supported withdrawing American forces from Afghanistan in the next year, a 14 percent increase from the level observed in the control group. These experimental results powerfully echo prior research emphasizing the importance of bipartisan consensus. Whereas only a small minority of subjects—37 percent—supported a quick withdrawal when Democratic and Republican congressional elites supported President Obama's decision to stay the course, just under 60 percent did so when told that many Democratic and Republican members of Congress disagreed with the president's assessment and favored bringing the troops home.

Finally, consistent with Hypothesis 3, when Democratic and Republican members of Congress took equally balanced competing positions regarding the Afghan War and the proper course for its future conduct, they had no net influence on public support for withdrawal. In both Treatments 7 and 8, the percentage of subjects supporting withdrawal was very close to that observed in the control group, and in both treatments, the 90 percent confidence interval spans the 46 percent support level observed in the control group.[28]

In sum, the experimental results provide strong causal evidence that even after nine years of war, the public positions advanced by members of Congress can shape public opinion. Americans had almost a decade to form their opinions and policy preferences concerning the Afghan War since its inception in October 2001. However, the experiment makes clear that on the critical question of how long American troops should remain in theater, public opinion had not calcified by April 2011. In contrast to recent research arguing that the capacity of elites to shape public support wanes considerably over time, the experiment provides strong evidence that, at least in a laboratory setting, even modest cues advanced by congressional elites that either challenge or reinforce the president's policy positions can have significant influence on the public's willingness to stay the course in wartime. The public still looks to political elites, and members of Congress provide critically important information on which Americans form their opinions and policy assessments.

Congressional Rhetoric and Support for the Afghan War, 2006–2010

The most important advantage of an experimental approach is the causal leverage it affords. The biggest drawback, however, is external validity—that is, how well the experimental setting reflects the opinion formation process in the real world. The experiment establishes the clear potential for certain types of congressional cues—particularly, costly elite cues that conflict with an elite's partisan predispositions—to influence public support for the war in Afghanistan. However, to examine whether shifting patterns of congressional rhetoric can help us understand changing levels of American public support for the Afghan War over time, the analysis now turns to an examination of observational data. Accordingly, this section examines all available polling evidence on public opinion concerning the war and investigates whether changes in aggregate war support correspond to changing patterns in congressional cues reported to the public through the mass media.

In contrast to experimental analysis, a common concern with the analysis of observational data is internal validity. If we observe a correlation between congressional position taking and public opinion, can we infer that the former is driving the latter? Might the relationship instead run in the opposite direction? Or might an alternate factor be driving fluctuations in both congressional rhetoric and public opinion? Grappling with these barriers to inference is difficult in the best of circumstances. It is particularly difficult in the current context for several reasons. The number of opinion polls querying public support for the Afghan conflict pales in comparison to the voluminous body of opinion data concerning the Iraq War exploited by prior scholars.[29] As a result, to construct a time series, it is necessary to rely on a range of polls with different question wordings fielded by different survey organizations. Even then, substantial temporal gaps remain that must be filled through interpolation. Despite these difficulties, marshaling all available polling evidence about Americans' attitudes toward the Afghan War and comparing it to patterns in media coverage of the policy debate in Congress provides strong complementary evidence that the positions articulated in Congress helped inform the public's willingness to support the war.

Figure 17-2 marshals all available polling evidence to illustrate the broad trend in American support for the war in Afghanistan, from the fighting's commencement in 2001 through President Obama's announcement of a timetable for withdrawal in December 2010. Unsurprisingly, in the immediate aftermath of the 9/11 attacks, the vast majority of Americans rallied behind the war against al Qaeda and the Taliban regime in Afghanistan that harbored the terrorists. In the nineteen polls taken during 2001 and 2002, public support for the war averaged over 85 percent. Many factors can explain this strong and stable early support for the war; most importantly, some might argue that it was an inevitable result of a rally-around-the-flag effect following the worst attack against the United States since Pearl Harbor. However, the dynamic is also consistent with elite opinion leadership, given the almost uniform bipartisan support for the war in Afghanistan in these early stages.[30]

From 2003 through 2005, a search of the Roper Center for Public Opinion Research's archive reveals only three relevant polls that query public support for the Afghan War. As the Bush administration quickly pivoted to Iraq, Afghanistan all but disappeared from the public and media agenda. Despite continued fighting and occasional spikes in casualties, the war failed to gain significant media coverage or attention from pollsters. Given the paucity of polling data during this period, the subsequent analyses all focus on the period from 2006 through 2010.

More regular polling resumed in 2006 with the commencement of Operation Mountain Fury. Between 2006 and 2008, American forces routinely sustained casualty totals that dwarfed those suffered in 2001 and 2002, and the cumulative

Figure 17-2 Public Support for the War in Afghanistan, 2001–2010

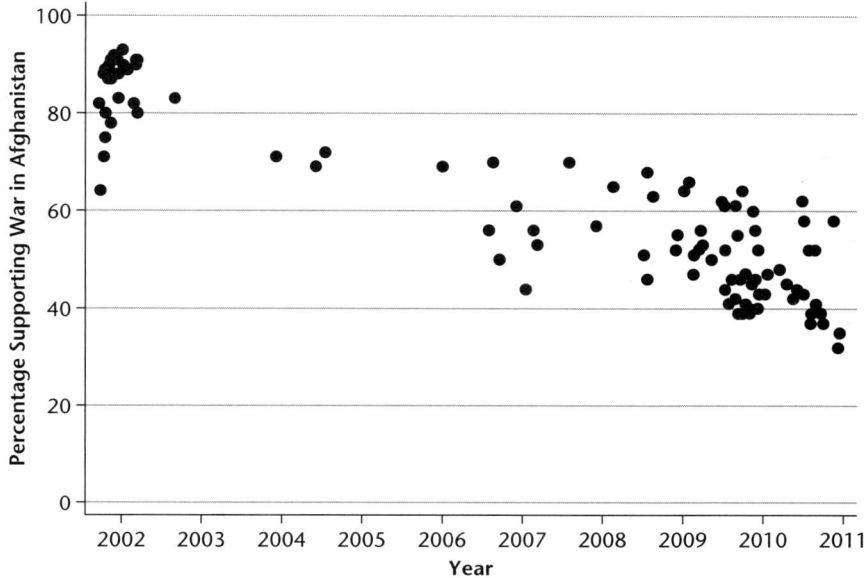

Source: Compiled by author.

casualty tally rose steadily. However, most polls continued to show a strong majority of Americans supporting the war in Afghanistan. This stands in stark contrast to the war in Iraq, which fewer than 40 percent of Americans backed by the end of 2006.[31]

However, the data suggest that public support for the Afghan War began to fall precipitously over the first two years of the Obama presidency. Whereas public support for the war averaged 57 percent across seven polls conducted in 2008, this level fell to just under 50 percent in 2009 (based on thirty-three polls) and to an average of just under 45 percent in 2010 (based on nineteen polls).

Can the elite cues transmitted to the public by members of Congress help explain the two most important features of aggregate level support for the Afghan War—first, the long persistence of majority support for the war through 2008 and then its precipitous decline from 2009 through 2010? To answer this question, we need systematic information on the balance of elite cues for and against the war to which most Americans were exposed through the mass media and how this balance changed over time.

To construct such a measure, I content-coded coverage of the war in Afghanistan in two prominent media outlets: the *NBC Nightly News* television broadcast and the *New York Times*.[32] For the *NBC Nightly News*, which, from 2006 to 2010, was the highest rated of the network evening news programs and reached over 8.5 million viewers nightly, a team of researchers content-coded the transcripts of all 1,327 broadcasts that contained the word "Afghanistan" in a keyword search conducted via LexisNexis. A trained coder read each article and identified any statements made by or attributed to a sitting member of Congress with respect to the war in Afghanistan. Following prior research, statements that, on balance, were supportive of the policy in Afghanistan and the country's and war's future prospects were coded as positive. Statements that, on balance, were critical of the situation on the ground in theater were coded as negative.[33] Each congressional statement was read by two coders. In the rare cases where the two coders disagreed, a third coder broke the tie. Coders also identified all positive statements made by the president concerning the war. Furthermore, they identified each news story that mentioned American casualties in the conflict. Finally, for each article that addressed the Afghan conflict in a substantive way, coders made a summary judgment concerning whether its tone was either positive or negative toward the war.

While *NBC Nightly News* reaches a wider audience than the *New York Times*, its shortened time format necessarily limits the number of elite cues that can be represented in any given broadcast. Although the *Times* has a relatively small direct circulation, its indirect influence on coverage patterns in other media outlets is considerable.[34] Moreover, the *Times* and other elite media may be particularly influential with the attentive public who are most likely to consume political messages and drive opinion change in the aggregate. As a result, to supplement the elite content coding from *NBC Nightly News*, I also coded all 440 articles in the *New York Times* that contained the word "Afghanistan" and either "senator" or "representative" between 2006 and 2010. Each relevant congressional statement was coded according to the same coding scheme described previously.

Figure 17-3 plots the total number of prowar and antiwar congressional cues reported each month on *NBC Nightly News* and in the *New York Times* from 2006 to 2010. Between 2006 and the 2008 presidential election, relatively few congressional cues taking direct positions for or against the war in Afghanistan were reported in major media outlets. When mentioned in media coverage, Afghanistan almost always played second fiddle to the true center of attention: the continuing conflagration in Iraq. Republican members of Congress were all but absent from mainstream media coverage of the Afghan War in these years. In sharp contrast to growing Democratic attacks on President Bush's handling of the war in Iraq, the top panel of Figure 17-3 shows that Democratic cues concerning the Afghan War during this period were almost universally positive.

This pattern changed dramatically following President Obama's election. Throughout 2009 and 2010, Democrats divided over the war. Unsurprisingly, the media gave greater prominence to congressional Democrats who publicly broke with the administration, criticized the surge, and called for a change of course in Afghanistan. Media outlets deem such copartisan criticism inherently more newsworthy.[35] Not only did the media give disproportionate coverage to Democratic critics of the administration in terms of the volume of coverage, but copartisan critics were also given systematically greater prominence within the coverage

Congress, Public Opinion, and the Political Costs of Waging War 435

Figure 17-3 Congressional War Cues Reported on the *NBC Nightly News* or in the *New York Times*

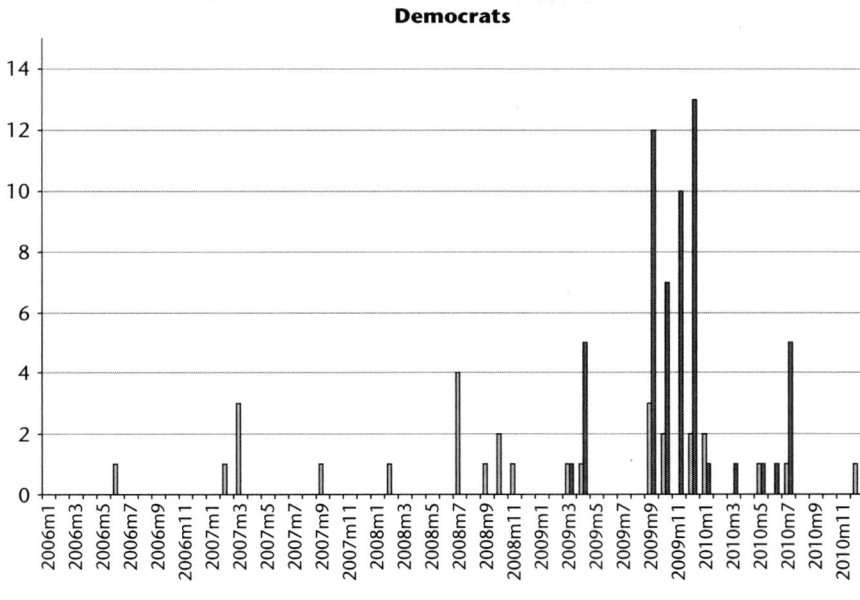

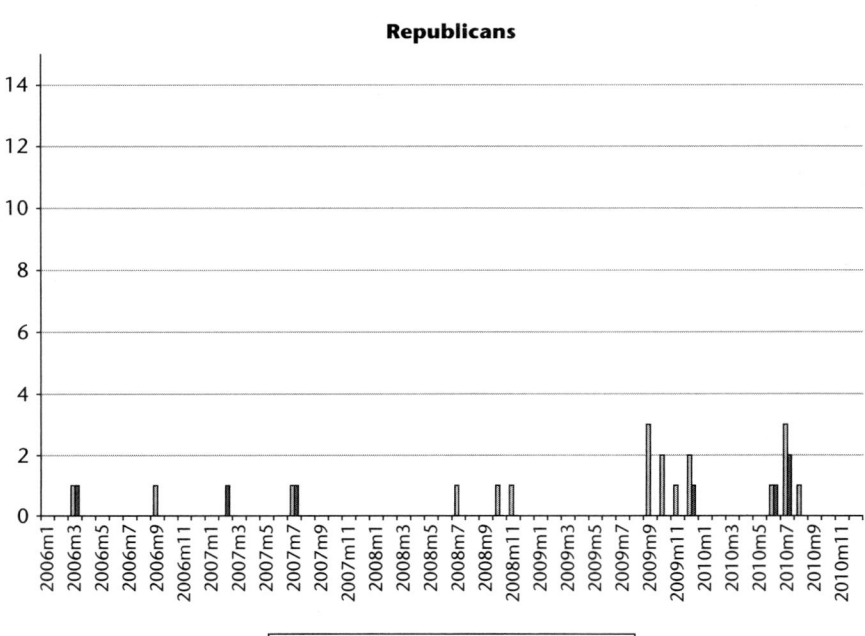

Source: Compiled by author.

itself. When stories reported both Democratic members supporting and opposing the president's handling of the war, the views of opponents were almost always presented first and given greater emphasis. Coverage in both media outlets plainly illustrated the serious challenge President Obama faced within his own party's congressional ranks throughout 2009 and 2010.[36]

The results of the survey experiment suggest that two types of congressional cues are most influential on public wartime opinions: opposition party support for the war and copartisan criticism of it. Accordingly, as an initial, visual examination of whether changing patterns in congressional rhetoric are related to changes in public support for the war in Afghanistan, Figure 17-4 overlays war support and both types of costly elite rhetoric. Each dot represents the average of all polls taken within a given month querying support for the Afghan War. The solid line illustrating the trend was created via LOESS smoothing.[37] The dark gray bars present the number of copartisan elite cues critical of the war in each month (i.e., Republican criticism from 2006 to 2008 and Democratic criticism from 2009 to 2010). The light gray bars present the number of opposition party-elite cues supportive of the war in each month.

From 2006 through the 2008 presidential election, the smoothed trend line decreased slightly but very slowly and steadily. The relative scarcity of polling

Figure 17-4 Congressional Rhetoric and Support for the Afghan War

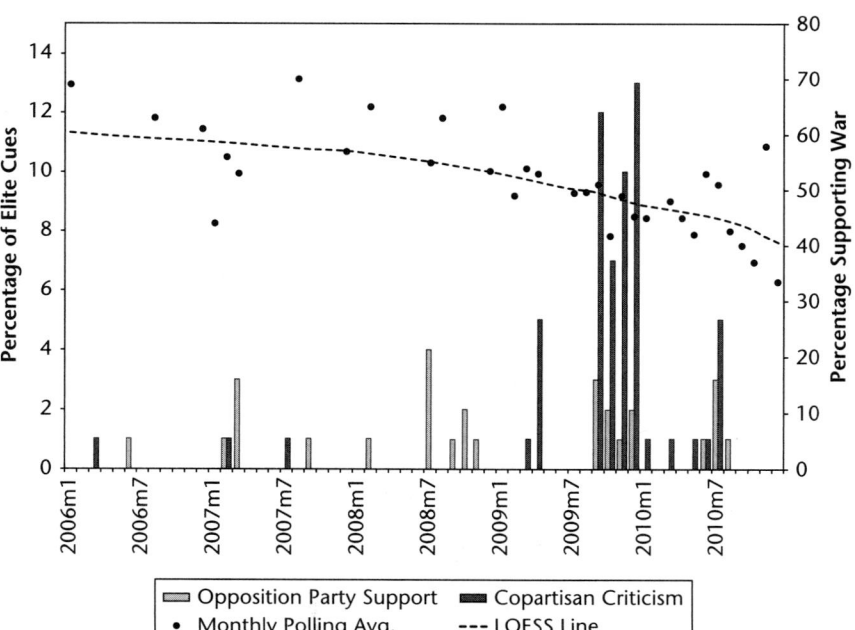

Source: Compiled by author.

data limits the precision of any estimate; however, the trend line decreases from roughly 60 percent to 53 percent over the course of these two years. During this period, the vast majority of the costly congressional-elite cues were supportive of the Afghan War. When the media reported the views of congressional Democrats regarding the war, they were almost universally supportive of it. Illustrative of many Democrats' views during this period was the position staked out by Senator Barack Obama during his quest for the presidency in 2008. Senator Obama sought to distinguish the war of necessity in Afghanistan from the war of choice in Iraq. The latter was draining precious resources from the former and distracting the nation from the legitimate central front in the war on terror.[38] The prevalence of these and similar costly cues supporting the war in Afghanistan may well have played an important role in sustaining strong levels of support for this war, even when public support for the contemporaneous conflict in Iraq had plummeted into the thirties during this period.

However, the combination of the economic collapse, budgetary pressures for economic stimulus and domestic priorities, and the Obama administration's early decisions to escalate the number of American troops on the ground rankled many liberals within the congressional Democratic caucus. The result, as seen in Figure 17-4, was an explosion of media coverage highlighting fissures in the Democratic ranks and open congressional Democratic challenges to President Obama's conduct of the war. The first spikes in Democratic opposition appeared in early 2009, almost immediately after President Obama's initial decision to dispatch seventeen thousand more troops to Afghanistan. Democratic opposition intensified further still as the president considered General Stanley McChrystal's requests for even more troops and a significant escalation of the war. Wisconsin Democrat Russ Feingold warned, "I and the American people cannot tolerate more troops without some commitment about when this perceived occupation will end."[39] House Appropriations chair David Obey, D-Wisc., openly lamented the war's steep financial costs and noted that the Afghan surge could preclude action on other key priorities: "It is obvious to any but the most obtuse that that expenditure is killing our ability to finance a recovery of our own economy."[40] Vietnam veteran Senator John Kerry, D-Mass., openly raised the specter of Vietnam, where the underlying assumptions behind the demands for ever more troops were fundamentally flawed.[41]

During this period of peak copartisan criticism, public support for the war began to decrease at a much more rapid rate. Costly copartisan criticism continued to outweigh costly signals of opposition party support for the war through much of 2010. Between President Obama's inauguration and the end of the time series in December 2010, the time trend estimate for public support for the Afghan War decreased from approximately 53 percent to just over 41 percent.

This surge in congressional criticism of the war—particularly, costly criticism of it from the president's own copartisans on Capitol Hill—may have helped quicken the erosion of popular support for the war in Afghanistan. However, a number of potential confounding factors could also have driven the

Figure 17-5 American Casualties in Afghanistan, 2006–2010

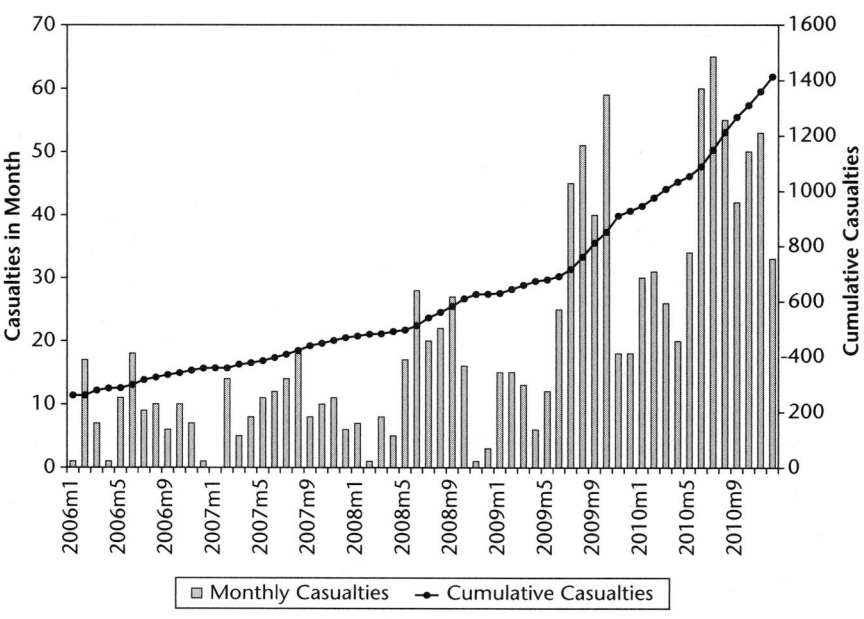

Source: Compiled by author.

observed decrease in public support for the war. Perhaps most importantly, as the United States embraced a more aggressive counterinsurgency strategy early in the Obama presidency, American casualties increased substantially. As shown in Figure 17-5, the spikes in casualties sustained in the summer and fall of 2009 were far greater in magnitude than any suffered in the war to that point.[42] Scholars have long argued that low casualties are among the most important drivers of American support for war.[43] As casualties increase, public support for war wanes.

To examine the relationship between costly congressional cues critical of the war and public support for the conflict while controlling for other factors that may be correlated with both factors, the analysis concludes with a pair of simple time series regressions. The dependent variable for these models is the change in public support for the war in Afghanistan from the preceding to the current month.[44] The main independent variable of interest is the number of costly, copartisan elite cues criticizing the Afghan War reported in the mass media in the previous month. The first model specification simply assesses the bivariate relationship between trends in costly congressional criticism of the war and public support for it. Because Durbin-Watson tests show strong evidence of serial autocorrelation, Prais-Winsten regression was used to model the AR(1) process. Table 17-1 presents the results.

Table 17-1 Costly Congressional Criticism and Change in Support for the Afghan War

	(1)	(2)
Costly opposition cues $_{t-1}$	−0.011*	−0.011*
	(0.005)	(0.005)
Presidential support $_{t-1}$		0.012
		(0.010)
Cumulative casualties $_{t-1}$		−0.063*
		(0.012)
Media coverage of casualties $_{t-1}$		−0.003
		(0.005)
Percentage of negative media coverage $_{t-1}$		−0.023
		(0.050)
Rho	0.945	0.719
Constant	−0.419	0.090
	(0.191)	(0.100)
Observations	59	59
R-squared	0.064	0.392

*$p < 0.05$.

Source: Compiled by author.

Note: Models are Prais-Winsten regressions. The dependent variable is change in support for war over the past month. Cumulative casualties are measured in hundreds. Standard errors are reported in parentheses. All significance tests are two-tailed.

Consistent with the visual interpretation of the patterns in Figure 17-4, in the simple bivariate model presented in Column 1, the coefficient for costly copartisan criticism of the war is negative and statistically significant. As media coverage of copartisan challenges to the Afghan War increased, public support for the war decreased.

The second model examines the relationship between copartisan criticism and changes in public support for the war while controlling for four alternate factors that might also be correlated with changing patterns of war support. First, members of Congress are not the only actors who try to shape public opinion. As recognized in the experimental analysis, presidents also invest considerable effort and enjoy advantages in trying to mobilize popular opinion in the public sphere. As a result, Model 2 also includes the number of presidential cues supporting the war reported in *NBC Nightly News* broadcasts in the preceding month. Conflict events may also drive fluctuations in public opinion. Most importantly, Americans may respond to increasing numbers of American casualties. Accordingly, Model 2 includes two measures of casualties, one objective and one derived from the media. The first is the number of cumulative American casualties in Afghanistan as of the preceding month. The second is the number of stories on

NBC Nightly News that discussed American casualties in the preceding month.[45] Finally, Model 2 controls for the overall tone of recent media coverage of the Afghan War. The final control variable is the percentage of all *NBC Nightly News* stories on the Afghan War that were coded as negative in tone in the preceding month.

Even in this expanded model specification, the coefficient for copartisan congressional criticism of the war is still negative and statistically significant.[46] The coefficient for presidential attempts to rally public support for the war reported in the mass media is positive; however, it fails to reach conventional thresholds of statistical significance. Consistent with a body of opinion scholarship dating back to the wars in Korea and Vietnam, the coefficient for cumulative casualties is negative and statistically significant.[47] Public support for the war decreased as casualties mounted. The coefficient on the measure of recent media coverage of casualties is also negative but not statistically significant. Finally, the coefficient for the negative-media-tone variable is negative but not statistically significant.

Limited data availability, gaps in the time series requiring interpolation, and variations in question wording all necessitate the exercise of considerable caution when interpreting these results. However, the results in Table 17-1 are at least consistent with the theoretical argument that congressional criticism can seriously erode support for war, even after accounting for the influence of increasing casualties.

From Influence Over Opinion to Influence Over Policy

Taken together, the experimental and observational data strongly support the claim that members of Congress retained a strong capacity to shape public attitudes toward the Afghan War and policy preferences for its future conduct, even many years after the war began. Since World War II, Congress has proven itself almost incapable of using the formal constitutional tools at its disposal to assert its influence over the formation and implementation of the nation's military policy. However, individual members of Congress have remained relevant players, in no small part through their capacity to engage the executive in a national policy debate in the public sphere. Such actions represent more than mere position taking designed to pander to existing constituent opinion.[48] Rather, when members of Congress engage the debate over major wars and their future conduct, they can actually *move* public opinion.[49]

However, do members of Congress exert any influence on tangible policy outcomes through nonlegislative means? Recent scholarship has argued that presidents, even when at the height of their unilateral power as commander in chief, are often very responsive to the political costs of pursuing their preferred military course of action.[50] When contemplating the use of force or making decisions concerning the scale, scope, and duration of military actions, presidents know that institutional barriers all but preclude Congress from using the legislative tools at its disposal to compel a change in policy course. However, Congress can influence the political costs of various options for the president. One of the most important mechanisms by which Congress can raise or lower the political costs that presidents stand to incur is by mobilizing public pressure against the president's preferred policy course.

There is some suggestive evidence that such political costs, generated in large part by strident opposition to his plans in Congress, shaped President Obama's strategic calculations over the scope, timing, and duration of the Afghan surge early in his presidency. President Obama was torn by competing imperatives. On the one hand, he had campaigned on the need to be more aggressive in Afghanistan and to give the military the resources needed to finish the job. On the other, he faced considerable pushback from within his own caucus against any effort to escalate the war. The strategy that Obama ultimately chose in December 2009 reflects this underlying tension. The president announced a significant troop surge to Afghanistan, but in the same breath, he made clear that it would be a short-term increase, and he immediately announced a time line for the initial drawdown of the surge forces. It is all but impossible to say how much of this was due to political pressure and how much simply reflected internal conflict within Obama's own preferences and instincts. However, it is undoubtedly true that the political costs generated by congressional opposition greatly complicated his task as commander in chief.

Perhaps an even clearer case in which anticipated congressional reactions—and explicit calculations about Congress's capacity to influence public opinion—shaped Obama's military decision making is his response (or lack thereof) to the Assad regime's use of chemical weapons in Syria. In August of 2012, President Obama warned Syrian President Bashar al-Assad that the use of chemical weapons constituted a "red line" for the United States that the regime must not cross.[51] A year later, the world was confronted with ghastly images of civilian victims of a chemical weapons strike launched by Assad's forces.[52]

Three days after the footage of poison gas victims struggling to breathe spread across the worldwide media, President Obama met with his national security team to consider options for a military response. By all accounts, the president decided at that meeting to order a limited series of retaliatory military strikes against the Assad regime.[53] Bolstering this view, on August 30, the White House released its official assessment concluding that Assad had indeed used chemical weapons in the August 21 attack that killed 1,429 people, including at least 426 children.[54] Secretary of State John Kerry's address that evening, left little doubt concerning what the administration would do. "As previous storms in history have gathered, when unspeakable crimes were within our power to stop them, we have been warned against the temptations of looking the other way," Kerry warned.[55]

However, sometime between the afternoon of August 30 and the following day when President Obama strode into the Rose Garden to address the nation, the president changed his mind.⁵⁶ Obama began by stating what everyone suspected: that he had decided the United States must take action to punish the Assad regime for its use of chemical weapons. What came next, however, was the true surprise. Obama would not order the strikes unilaterally; instead, he would first seek congressional authorization.

> But having made my decision as Commander-in-Chief based on what I am convinced is our national security interests, I'm also mindful that I'm the President of the world's oldest constitutional democracy. I've long believed that our power is rooted not just in our military might, but in our example as a government of the people, by the people, and for the people. And that's why I've made a second decision: I will seek authorization for the use of force from the American people's representatives in Congress.⁵⁷

The reversal stunned most political and legal observers.⁵⁸

President Obama did not reverse course because he believed a unilateral strike would be unconstitutional. Indeed, the Office of Legal Counsel had issued an opinion that because the United States possessed "important national interests" in enforcing international norms against the use of chemical weapons and in bringing stability to Syria, the president had the constitutional authority to act independently of Congress.⁵⁹ In his Rose Garden address, President Obama, like his predecessors, emphasized that he had the independent constitutional authority to order the strikes unilaterally.

Rather, President Obama plainly acknowledged that his reasons for first seeking congressional authorization were political.⁶⁰ The president offered perhaps the clearest window into his thinking four days later at a September 4 press conference where Obama plainly acknowledged how he was anticipating Congress's reaction. If he acted unilaterally, "Congress will sit on the sidelines, snipe. If it works, the sniping will be a little less; if it doesn't, a little more."⁶¹ Legislation constraining his freedom of action was not what Obama feared. Rather, public criticism of his policies, particularly if they should prove to be more costly or less immediately successful than expected, is what Obama hoped to avoid. By compelling members of Congress to vote to authorize military action against Syria, Obama hoped that he could tie members to the mission politically and thereby minimize the political costs downstream.⁶² Thus, in the Syrian case, anticipation of the reactions of congressional actors, corresponding shifts in public opinion, and future political costs produced a dramatic policy reversal.⁶³

Of course, in some cases, presidents may cling to their preferred military policies even in the face of stiff political opposition on Capitol Hill and plummeting levels of public support. So great was the priority President Bush placed on staying the course in Iraq from 2006 through 2008 that he pressed forward undeterred, despite the intense political costs he incurred that all but precluded progress on any of his other political priorities. However, in many other cases, presidents decide that the benefits of their preferred military course of action no longer exceed the heightened political costs it will likely entail, and so, they adjust their course and conduct of military affairs accordingly.

Presidents, Congress, and the Public

The analysis in this chapter has focused on Congress's capacity to influence presidents' strategic calculations as commander in chief by raising or lowering public support for their handling of military operations. However, the findings showing Congress's capacity to significantly influence public support for the conduct of the Afghan War also have implications for the presidents' capacity to rally public support for their policies more generally.

At least since Theodore Roosevelt proclaimed the power of the presidential bully pulpit, scholars and pundits alike have analyzed and debated the presidents' ability to "go public," to rally public opinion to their side, and thereby to gain greater leverage and influence in Washington.[64] Indeed, the transformative power of presidential public appeals—from Franklin Roosevelt's fireside chats to the telegenic John F. Kennedy's mastery of the press conference to Ronald Reagan's command of the media, which earned him the moniker "the Great Communicator"—is deeply embedded in popular political lore. However, decades of empirical research have emphasized the stark limits on presidents' ability to lead public opinion. Presidents can raise the salience of an issue on which the public already agrees with the administration's position; however, presidents are often remarkably unsuccessful at changing public opinion and building popular support for their policies.[65]

Why are presidential public appeals so often futile? One important reason, as the Afghan War case study so vividly illustrated, is that presidents are not the only actors who go public. Rather, members of Congress also routinely engage the policy debate in the public sphere, even in military affairs, where presidents are often believed to enjoy significant advantages as commander in chief. As a result, the reaction of members of Congress to presidential appeals often plays a critically important role in determining whether presidents succeed or fail in rallying public support. In the rare instances when presidential appeals enjoy bipartisan support, they are likely to resonate with the public as well. However, appeals that meet resistance and open opposition from Congress often fall on deaf ears. Media norms emphasizing the importance of institutional conflict lead journalists to amplify congressional critiques of administration policy.[66] By offering a competing narrative to that advanced by the administration, congressional opponents of presidential policies can seriously limit the White House's ability to rally support for its initiatives among the public.

Notes

1. Edward Corwin, *The President: Office and Powers* (London: H. Milford, Oxford University Press, 1940), 200.
2. For an overview, see Stephen M. Griffin, *Long Wars and the Constitution* (Cambridge, MA: Harvard University Press, 2013). For an alternate interpretation of the constitutionality of this shift, see Mariah Zeisberg, *War Powers: The Politics of Constitutional Authority* (Princeton, NJ: Princeton University Press, 2013).
3. Gordon Silverstein, *Imbalance of Powers: Constitutional Interpretation and the Making of American Foreign Policy* (New York: Oxford University Press, 1997).
4. Arthur Schlesinger Jr., *The Imperial Presidency* (Boston: Houghton Mifflin, 1973).
5. James L. Sundquist, *The Decline and Resurgence of Congress* (Washington, DC: Brookings Institution Press, 1981); Randall B. Ripley and James M. Lindsay, eds., *Congress Resurgent: Foreign and Defense Policy on Capitol Hill* (Ann Arbor: University of Michigan Press, 1993).
6. Indeed, critics of the War Powers Resolution of 1973 have argued that it has done (and unconstitutionally) precisely this. See, for example, Louis Fisher and David Gray Adler, "The War Powers Resolution: Time to Say Goodbye," *Presidential Studies Quarterly* 113 (1998): 1–20.
7. On the weaknesses of Congress's formal constraints on presidential war powers, see James Meernik, "Congress, the President, and the Commitment of the U.S. Military," *Legislative Studies Quarterly* 20 (1995): 377–92; Louis Fisher, *Congressional Abdication on War and Spending* (College Station: Texas A&M University Press, 2000).
8. Barbara Hinckley, *Less Than Meets the Eye: Foreign Policy Making and the Myth of the Assertive Congress* (Chicago: University of Chicago Press, 1994).
9. On the limitations of the power of the purse more generally, see Bruce Ackerman and Oona Hathaway, "Limited War and the Constitution: Iraq and the Crisis of Presidential Legality," *Michigan Law Review* 109 (2011): 447–518.
10. For a similar argument in the legal literature, see Eric Posner and Adrian Vermeule, *The Executive Unbound: After the Madisonian Republic* (New York: Oxford University Press, 2011).
11. For congressional approval polling data since 2006, see Real Clear Politics, "Congressional Job Approval," http://www.realclearpolitics.com/epolls/other/congressional_job_approval-903.html#polls (accessed March 1, 2016).
12. Gabriel Almond, *The American People and Foreign Policy* (New York: Praeger, 1960); Walter Lippmann, *Public Opinion* (New York: MacMillan, 1922).
13. A lengthy literature argues that public support for war can be understood as a rational cost–benefit calculation made in response to unmediated combat events. Inter alia, see John Mueller, *War, Presidents, and Public Opinion* (New York: Wiley, 1973); Scott Gartner and Gary Segura, "War, Casualties and Public Opinion," *Journal of Conflict Resolution* 42 (1998): 278–300; Christopher Gelpi, Peter Feaver, and Jason Reifler, *Paying the Human Costs of War: American Public Opinion and Casualties in Military Conflicts* (Princeton, NJ: Princeton University Press, 2009).
14. Recent research argues that elites may be more influential in shaping citizens' prospective policy preferences than in affecting their retrospective war assessments. See Douglas Kriner and Graham Wilson, "The Elasticity of Reality and British Support for the War in Afghanistan," *British Journal of Politics and International Relations* 18 (2016): 559–580.

15. See Randall Calvert, "The Value of Biased Information: A Rational Choice Model of Political Advice," *Journal of Politics* 47 (1985): 530–55; Timothy Groeling and Matthew Baum, "Crossing the Water's Edge: Elite Rhetoric, Media Coverage, and the Rally-Round-the-Flag Phenomenon," *Journal of Politics* 70 (2008): 1065–85; Douglas L. Kriner and William G. Howell, "Congressional Leadership of War Opinion: Backlash Effects and the Polarization of Public Support for War," in *Congress Reconsidered*, 10th ed., ed. Lawrence C. Dodd and Bruce I. Oppenheimer (Thousand Oaks, CA: CQ Press, 2013), 377–400.
16. Richard A. Brody, *Assessing the President: The Media, Elite Opinion, and Public Support* (Stanford, CA: Stanford University Press, 1991); Eric V. Larson, *Casualties and Consensus: The Historical Role of Casualties in Domestic Support for U.S. Military Operations* (Santa Monica, CA: RAND, 1996).
17. John Zaller, *The Nature and Origins of Mass Opinion* (New York: Cambridge University Press, 1992).
18. Adam J. Berinsky, *In Time of War: Understanding American Public Opinion From World War II to Iraq* (Chicago: University of Chicago Press, 2009).
19. Senator Obama clearly articulated this position during both of the first two presidential debates with Senator John McCain. For transcripts, see http://elections.nytimes.com/2008/president/debates/transcripts/first-presidential-debate.html and http://elections.nytimes.com/2008/president/debates/transcripts/second-presidential-debate.html.
20. Barack Obama, "Remarks on United States Military and Diplomatic Strategies for Afghanistan and Pakistan," December 16, 2010, in *The American Presidency Project*, ed. Gerhard Peters and John T. Woolley, http://www.presidency.ucsb.edu/ws/?pid=88847.
21. Lisbon Summit Declaration, November 20, 2010, http://www.nato.int/cps/en/natolive/official_texts_68828.htm.
22. Matthew Baum and Philip Potter, "The Relationship Between Mass Media, Public Opinion, and Foreign Policy," *Annual Review of Political Science* 11 (2008): 39–66; Matthew Baum and Timothy Groeling, "Reality Asserts Itself: Public Opinion on Iraq and the Elasticity of Reality," *International Organization* 64 (2010): 443–79.
23. However, Kriner and Wilson argue that while elites' ability to influence citizens' retrospective wartime assessments may wane over time, they should retain a stronger capacity to shape citizens' prospective policy preferences. See Kriner and Wilson, "Elasticity of Reality."
24. Robert M. Entman, *Projections of Power: Framing News, Public Opinion, and U.S. Foreign Policy* (Chicago: University of Chicago Press, 2004). It is also important to note that the experiment is an example of competitive framing in that it always evaluates the influence of a congressional cue when paired against the president's position. By contrast, in a one-sided framing environment in which public support for war in each congressional-cue treatment is compared to a control group in which subjects received no other information or perspective, the estimated treatment effects for congressional cues would likely be greater. See, for example, Dennis Chong and James Druckman, "A Theory of Framing and Opinion Formation in Competitive Elite Environments," *Journal of Communication* 57 (2007): 99–118.
25. The full list of options was immediate withdrawal; withdrawal within the next twelve months, regardless of conditions on the ground; withdrawal before 2015,

regardless of conditions on the ground; withdrawal by 2015, regardless of conditions on the ground; and withdrawal only when Afghan troops are ready to take over security, even if this happens after 2015.

26. I conducted a series of randomization checks to ensure that the subjects assigned to each treatment or control group looked similar on other demographic dimensions. For example, I estimated a series of logistic regressions modeling assignment to each experimental condition as a function of six demographic variables: whether a subject was a Democrat, whether a subject was a Republican (independents formed the omitted category), age, gender, race, and educational attainment. Only one of the resulting fifty-four logit coefficients was statistically significant, $p < .05$. A few coefficients would have been expected to be statistically significant by random chance alone. Thus, there is little evidence that any of our treatment groups were demographically skewed in comparison to the others.

27. The results are consistent with the hypothesis in that the estimated effect of the Democratic-withdrawal treatment is statistically greater than zero; however, the estimated effect is not statistically greater than that observed for the Republican-withdrawal treatment (which is included in the 90 percent confidence interval).

28. The results presented in Figure 17-1 examine the effect of each elite-cue treatment on support for withdrawal among all subjects. Of course, some groups of Americans may be more responsive to elite cues than others. For example, recent elections have shown that younger Americans have increasingly embraced political preferences distinct from those of older Americans. For example, younger Americans have both trended increasingly Democratic in recent presidential elections and have backed more liberal candidates within Democratic primaries (e.g., Barack Obama in 2008 and Bernie Sanders in 2016). To examine whether age moderated subjects' response to congressional position taking regarding the war in Afghanistan, I disaggregated the sample into two groups: those under forty (roughly a quarter of the sample) and those forty and over. Doing so reveals little evidence of systematic differences between the two age groups. Both older and younger Americans responded most strongly to costly and bipartisan congressional cues supporting or opposing an expeditious withdrawal.

29. For an excellent overview, see Gary C. Jacobson, *A Divider, Not a Uniter: George W. Bush and the American People*, 2nd ed. (New York: Longman, 2011).

30. For example, the Authorization to Use Military Force (AUMF) passed the House 420–1 and the Senate 98–0. Democrats and Republicans were all but unanimous in their support for military action in Afghanistan, in stark contrast to the partisan divides that would quickly emerge as the administration shifted its focus to Iraq.

31. Jacobson, *Divider*, 99.

32. Emily Guskin and Tom Rosenstiel, "Network: By the Numbers," 2012, http://www.stateofthemedia.org/2012/network-news-the-pace-of-change-accelerates/network-by-the-numbers.

33. Sean Aday, "Chasing the Bad News: An Analysis of 2005 Iraq and Afghanistan War Coverage on NBC and Fox News Channel," *Journal of Communication* 60 (2010): 144–64.

34. Guy Golan, "Inter-Media Agenda Setting and Global News Coverage: Assessing the Influence of the *New York Times* on Three Network Television Evening News Programs," *Journalism Studies* 7 (2006): 323–33. On the wider influence of the *New York Times*, see Diana Hicks and Jian Wang, "The *New York Times* as a Resource for Mode 2," *Science, Technology, and Human Values* 38 (2013): 851–77.

35. Timothy Groeling, *When Politicians Attack: Party Cohesion in the Media* (New York: Cambridge University Press, 2010).
36. Monthly counts of Democratic congressional criticism obtained separately from the *NBC Nightly News* and *New York Times* are correlated at $r = .87$ for the entire time period and $r = .85$ for 2009–2010.
37. This approach also accounts for variation in question wording and across survey outlets.
38. "Excerpts from the First Presidential Debate," *New York Times*, September 27, 2008, A14.
39. Helene Cooper, "G.O.P. May Be Vital to Obama in Afghan War Effort," *New York Times*, September 3, 2009, A1.
40. David Herszenhorn, "House Democrats vs. White House," *New York Times*, July 3, 2010, A11.
41. Peter Baker and Elizabeth Bumiller, "Plan to Boost Afghan Forces Splits Advisers," *New York Times*, September 27, 2009, A1.
42. Figure 17-5 follows much of the literature and defines a casualty as a soldier that has died while serving in a foreign theater. The definition is also based, in large part, on necessity, given data limitations concerning nonfatal casualties. Figure 17-5 focuses on the period from 2006 to 2010, given that this is the period for which sufficient public opinion polling data are available. However, extending the figure to include 2001 to 2005 confirms that the spikes in 2009 are far greater than any observed in even the earliest stages of the war.
43. Mueller, *War, Presidents, and Public Opinion*; Gartner and Segura, "War, Casualties, and Public Opinion."
44. The analysis is patterned after Baum and Groeling's analysis of public support for the Iraq War between 2003 and 2007. To construct the monthly time series, all available polling data are used. LOESS smoothing (as shown in Figure 17-4) is then used both to account for inconsistencies in question wording and to interpolate missing data points for months in which no polls were taken. Operationalizing the dependent variable as the change in support for the Afghan War both follows Baum and Groeling's approach and addresses concerns about stationarity in the undifferenced war support time series. See Baum and Groeling, "Reality Asserts Itself."
45. In addition to affording a measure of casualty coverage in the media, the *NBC Nightly News* measure also allows the model to examine fatal as well as nonfatal casualties. This variable was coded 1 for any broadcast story that mentioned soldiers who died or were wounded in the Afghan War.
46. Given the many data limitations discussed previously, it is dangerous to put too much emphasis on any substantive interpretation of the size of the estimated relationship. However, as a rough gauge, the model suggests that a spike in elite criticism of ten costly elite cues produces an estimated half a standard deviation decrease in change in war support.
47. Mueller, *War, Presidents, and Public Opinion*. However, as others have noted, this variable is almost perfectly collinear with time. See Scott Sigmund Gartner, Gary M. Segura, and Michael Wilkening, "All Politics Are Local: Local Losses and Individual Attitudes Toward the Vietnam War," *Journal of Conflict Resolution* 41 (1997): 669–94; Adam J. Berinsky, "Assuming the Costs of War: Events, Elites, and American Public Support for Military Conflict," *Journal of Politics* 69 (2007): 975–97.

48. On position taking, see David R. Mayhew, *Congress: The Electoral Connection* (New Haven, CT: Yale University Press, 1974).
49. On the importance of members' actions in the public sphere more generally, see David R. Mayhew, *America's Congress: Actions in the Public Sphere, James Madison Through Newt Gingrich* (New Haven, CT: Yale University Press, 2000).
50. William G. Howell and Jon C. Pevehouse, *While Dangers Gather: Congressional Checks on Presidential War Powers* (Princeton, NJ: Princeton University Press, 2007); Douglas L. Kriner, *After the Rubicon: Congress, Presidents, and the Politics of Waging War* (Chicago: University of Chicago Press, 2010).
51. Barack Obama, "The President's News Conference," August 20, 2012, in *The American Presidency Project*, ed. Gerhard Peters and John T. Woolley, http://www.presidency.ucsb.edu/ws/?pid=101939.
52. For news coverage, including video footage of the attacks, see Loveday Morris and Karen DeYoung, "Syrian Activists Accuse Government of Deadly Chemical Attack Near Damascus," *Washington Post*, August 22, 2013, http://www.washingtonpost.com/world/syrian-activists-accuse-government-of-deadly-chemical-attack-near-damascus/2013/08/21/aea157e6-0a50-11e3-89fe-abb4a5067014_story.html.
53. See, for example, Adam Entous and Carol Lee, "At the Last Minute, Obama Alone Made Call to Seek Congressional Approval: Change in President's Thinking Confounded White House Insiders," *Wall Street Journal*, September 1, 2013, http://online.wsj.com/articles/SB10001424127887324009304579047542466837078.
54. The White House, Office of the Press Secretary, "Government Assessment of the Syrian Government's Use of Chemical Weapons on August 21, 2013," August 30, 2013, http://www.whitehouse.gov/the-press-office/2013/08/30/government-assessment-syrian-government-s-use-chemical-weapons-august-21.
55. "Full Transcript: Secretary of State John Kerry's Remarks on Syria on August 30," *Washington Post*, August 30, 2013, https://www.washingtonpost.com/world/national-security/running-transcript-secretary-of-state-john-kerrys-remarks-on-syria-on-aug-30/2013/08/30/f3a63a1a-1193-11e3-85b6-d27422650fd5_story.html.
56. Entous and Lee, "Last Minute."
57. Barack Obama, "Statement by the President on Syria," September 1, 2013, http://www.whitehouse.gov/the-press-office/2013/08/31/statement-president-syria.
58. For example, in a *Lawfare* blog post, Jack Goldsmith wrote, "I have been hard on the President—on this blog last week, and today in the NYT—for what just about everyone (except Philip Bobbitt) thought was going to be his strike in Syria without congressional authorization. I was thus surprised, but very happily surprised, when the President announced this afternoon that he would seek congressional authorization for the strike." See Jack Goldsmith, "Congratulations President Obama," *Lawfare* (blog), August 31, 2013, http://www.lawfareblog.com/2013/08/congratulations-president-obama.
59. Charlie Savage, "Obama Tests Limits of Power in Syrian Conflict," *New York Times*, September 9, 2013, http://www.nytimes.com/2013/09/09/world/middleeast/obama-tests-limits-of-power-in-syrian-conflict.html?pagewanted=all#.
60. In the Rose Garden address, Obama argued, "While I believe I have the authority to carry out this military action without specific congressional authorization, I know that the country will be stronger if we take this course, and our actions will be even more effective." See Obama, "Syria."
61. Barack Obama, "The President's News Conference With Prime Minister John Fredrik Reinfeldt of Sweden in Stockholm, Sweden," September 4, 2013, in *The American*

Presidency Project, ed. Gerhard Peters and John T. Woolley, http://www.presidency.ucsb.edu/ws/?pid=104040.
62. At the time of his decision, President Obama also seemed confident that he could secure the necessary votes in Congress. See Chuck Todd, "The White House Walk-and-Talk That Changed Obama's Mind on Syria," *NBC News*, August 31, 2013, http://firstread.nbcnews.com/_news/2013/08/31/20273128-the-white-house-walk-and-talk-that-changed-obamas-mind-on-syria.
63. For an extended discussion of this case, see Douglas L. Kriner, "Obama's Authorization Paradox: Syria and Congress's Continued Relevance in Military Affairs," *Presidential Studies Quarterly* 44 (2014): 309–27.
64. Inter alia, Samuel Kernell, *Going Public: New Strategies of Presidential Leadership*, 3rd ed. (Washington, DC: CQ Press, 1997).
65. George C. Edwards, *On Deaf Ears: The Limits of the Bully Pulpit* (New Haven, CT: Yale University Press, 2003); Brandice Canes-Wrone, *Who Leads Whom? Presidents, Policy, and the Public* (Chicago: University of Chicago Press, 2006).
66. Lawrence Jacobs, "The Presidency and the Press: The Paradox of the White House Communications War," in *The Presidency and the Political System*, 7th ed., ed. Michael Nelson (Washington, DC: CQ Press, 2003), 305–28.

18. Congress in the Age of Trump
The 2016 National Elections and Their Aftermath

Lawrence C. Dodd and Bruce I. Oppenheimer

The 2016 national elections saw one of the most extraordinary partisan contests of modern times produce by a narrow margin a seismic shift of control in the American presidency and yet also generate a remarkable degree of continuity within the U.S. Congress. We write here in the two weeks following the election to assess the implications the results are likely to have for policymaking and governance in Congress. But no such assessment can be realistically made without first highlighting the controversial nature of the 2016 presidential election, its effect on congressional campaigns, and its distinctive outcome, in which Donald Trump emerged as president-elect with an Electoral College victory but a clear popular vote loss. Thus we begin this essay with an overview of the presidential election and the ways it shaped the contest for control of Congress. We then proceed to chart and assess the results of the congressional elections. Finally, we consider how the presidential and congressional outcomes, particularly the victory of Donald Trump, are likely to shape the politics of the new Congress.

The 2016 Race for the Presidency

The race for the presidency saw a former First Lady, U.S. Senator, and Secretary of State, Hillary Clinton, become the first woman to win a major-party nomination for the presidency. She did so by defeating a vigorous Democratic primary challenge from long-term Vermont Senator and Democratic Socialist Bernie Sanders. Sanders mounted a leftist populist campaign that connected with the widespread desire among a segment of American voters for fundamental change in Washington. This desire for change appeared to focus, in particular, on the "establishment" running Washington. Sanders emphasized the need to push that establishment towards a more aggressive effort on behalf of the ideals of democratic socialism, such as ensuring universal access to higher education and government-financed health care. In the face of Sanders's challenge, Secretary Clinton won the nomination by touting her long experience in politics and rallying much of the party establishment and core constituencies to her side. In doing so, she presented herself as a candidate of continuity, seeking to save, improve, and build on the party's social programs but not yet ready to mount an aggressive effort for qualitative expansion.

In contrast, the wealthy businessman and reality TV star Donald Trump, with no experience in elected politics or public office, defeated 17 competitors in the Republican primaries, many with long political résumés and political experience, to win the Republican Party's presidential nomination. He did so by rallying to his side voters disaffected with traditional establishment politics and hostile to ongoing social and cultural shifts in American life. In doing so, as examples, Trump promised to build a wall between Mexico and the United States, in order to stem immigration, and deport 11 million undocumented immigrants; to ban Muslims from entering the United States; to support the overturn of *Roe v. Wade* and its protection of women's abortion rights; and to oppose efforts to address global warming, which he maintained was a hoax. Simultaneously Trump engaged in virulent attacks on both his Republican opponents and various minority groups within American society in ways that broke most norms of public civility. In the process, he dominated media coverage of the campaign, made himself the central topic of most daily news programs, and presented himself as the anti-establishment candidate of change.

As Clinton and Trump won their parties' nominations, two substantial third-party candidates also emerged who had the potential, in the environment of a "change" election, to gain measurable voter support. These two candidates, Gary Johnson of the Libertarian Party and Jill Stein of the Green Party, introduced an element of unpredictability into the election, should it be a close one, particularly should they draw votes more heavily from one major-party candidate or the other.

Policy Agendas and the Surreal Campaign

The general-election campaign for the presidency offered the nation a stark choice in the potential presidents and policy directions that the two major parties offered. In policy terms, Secretary Clinton promised to continue and complete the progressive domestic policies of President Obama; stressed her support for a diverse multicultural society; promised to nominate Supreme Court Justices who would protect and expand citizens' rights to shape their own life choices; and highlighted her extensive foreign-policy experience. She also stressed the extent to which foresighted policy decisions early in Obama's presidency had pulled the nation out of the deepest recession since the Great Depression.

Trump stressed a radical conservative populism designed to appeal to a white working class alienated by the emerging cultural diversity. In doing so, he continued to denigrate a range of minority groups and stake out a range of extremist policy positions. In this, he appeared to be influenced by his closest advisor, Stephen K. Bannon, formerly associated with Breitbart News and its hard-right—or alt-right—nationalist and white-supremacy associations. Additionally, Trump promised tax cuts for wealthy economic interests as a route to stimulating the nation's economy and proposed an "America First" foreign policy that challenged historic alliances and international innovations of the post–World War II era.

Yet as stark and consequential as the policy choices were between Clinton and Trump, in ways reinforced by the presence of Johnson and Stein, the focus on policy and governing agendas was overshadowed by the surreal nature of the presidential campaign. Polls appeared to shift dramatically week by week as media coverage highlighted yet another outrageous set of comments by Trump (focused on racial-ethnic minorities, disabled Americans, and women) or stressed difficulties from the past haunting Clinton.[1]

Such controversies included the discovery of Trump's apparently not paying any income taxes for two decades and his continued refusal to release tax returns; WikiLeaks' release of information about the strategic inner workings of the Clinton campaign, possibly provided by the Russian government; Trump's refusal to promise that he would honor the outcome of the election, if he lost; controversies over Clinton's actions in using a private personal email server as Secretary of State; Trump's assertion that a federal judge of Latino/Mexican heritage could not be trusted to be impartial in adjudicating a lawsuit against Trump; and on the list went.

These and numerous other controversies dominated nightly and weekend news programs, providing a megaphone in particular for Donald Trump. His phone calls to various media outlets during the primaries and into the presidential campaign seemed invariably to lead to televised or recorded interviews, often with additional provocations by him during the interviews sparking yet a new controversy. Nightly political programs thereby took on the character of reality TV, with each week highlighting yet another campaign drama. These ups and downs not only had destabilizing effects on mass voters, who increasingly wished for an end to the presidential campaign,[2] but also on parties and party elites.

The Political Elites Respond

Starting in midsummer, numerous Republican stalwarts and former Republican presidents indicated directly or indirectly their opposition to Trump.[3] Thereafter, as Trump's controversial statements and actions continued, Republican candidates for Congress, including Speaker of the House Paul Ryan, distanced or disassociated themselves from Trump. These responses came both because of candidates' clear disappointment over the content and tone of Trump's campaign but also because of fear that a collapse in Trump's support during the fall presidential campaign, amid continuing controversy, would carry them down with him.

Thereafter came awkward turns and swirls, as candidates moved away from or toward Trump as his indiscretions and fortunes waxed and waned. These exquisite political calculations reached crescendo force as Republicans gathered in Cleveland for their party's national convention. Fearing entanglement in whatever controversy surrounding Trump might engulf the convention, virtually no major-party figures, including former Republican presidents, were in attendance or spoke on his behalf. Simultaneously, Democratic candidates for Congress together with its party elite provided strong support for Clinton, with Sanders endorsing her and speaking on her behalf at the national convention.

The pivotal moment of the election appeared to come in early October with the release of private audio recordings that documented numerous egregious and demeaning comments by Trump about women.[4] The comments were so indisputable and vile, portraying a deeply misogynist candidate, that a stampede appeared underway among Republicans to distance themselves further from Trump and even to remove him as the party nominee. He held on in the face of opposition, with a core constituency of approximately 38 percent of the voters standing by him no matter what. Nevertheless, poll numbers for Trump and his party declined while Clinton's margin in the polls soared, giving her an eight- to ten-point lead.[5]

Simultaneously, support for Democrats in House and Senate seats improved to the point that capture of the Senate seemed virtually certain and capture of the House, which had seemed a near impossibility, was no longer entirely out of the question. Yet, simultaneously, polls continued to report an anti-establishment mood within the electorate and a desire for change in Washington, with disappointment in the presidential campaign fostering ever deeper frustration among citizens. Nevertheless, in light of his poll numbers, it increasingly appeared that Trump was just too extreme as a candidate.

Secretary Clinton won the three presidential debates, by most reckonings, demonstrating her command of policy and tenacity in the face of continuing controversies, and her party continued to provide her strong and unified support.[6] As the end of October approached, Clinton seemed to have sustained momentum with her, as she garnered support in particular from college-educated Republican women alienated by Trump. She appeared to be building to a major and even historic victory in the presidential race. Moreover, polls indicated that her rise was carrying Democratic congressional candidates with her, so that a major-party victory was in the making.[7] At the same time, tensions continued between Trump and congressional establishment figures such as Speaker Ryan, so Trump appeared to attack them as much as if not more than congressional Democrats.[8] A meltdown in the Trump campaign appeared underway, with disastrous results increasingly possible for congressional Republicans. And then, with 12 days to go to Election Day, the surreal campaign took yet another turn.

A Late October Surprise

On October 28th, FBI Director James Comey announced that the bureau had located emails relevant to its investigation into Clinton's use of a private email server while she was Secretary of State, so that he was re-opening the investigation, which he had closed four months earlier.[9] Comey acknowledged that he had no evidence of wrong-doing on her part, but believed the emails should be examined in order to ensure her innocence. In making the announcement, he acted contrary to Justice Department and FBI regulations, which restricted agency officials from making public comments about politically sensitive investigations in the weeks prior to an election. He justified his actions, in informal comments, by noting that he feared that there would be a leak of the discovery of the new emails from within the FBI, given the conservative tilt of many of its agents, which might create the appearance of a cover-up unless he moved first to release the information. These developments and Comey's justifications have raised serious questions about how best to rein in the FBI from interfering with elections and how to restrain officials within it who may seek to do so.

With Comey's actions, the presidential campaign experienced one more massive upheaval. Donald Trump immediately raised the specter of a constitutional crisis, were Clinton elected, in which she would be convicted and jailed following her election for her part in the email controversy, leaving the country without its elected president.[10] Thereafter poll numbers began to tighten.[11] Clinton and the Democrats engaged in a full-scale effort to challenge the FBI director's actions and reassure voters that there was no case against Clinton.

By the Sunday before the election Secretary Clinton appeared to have stanched the slide in her poll numbers, only to have Director Comey go public with the announcement that his investigation had found nothing, thereby bringing the email controversy back to public attention yet again.[12] Polls showed that, prior to Comey's Sunday announcement, Clinton had managed to contain the decline in her support so that she appeared to have a steady lead over Trump of around a 3.5 to 4.0 margin. Democrats' chances in the Senate and House appeared dependent on her maintaining the lead or, preferably, increasing it into the 5 to 6 percent margin. Democrats' fear was that Comey's Sunday comments had reignited public attention to the email controversy and would generate a renewal in her slide downward.

The final week of the campaign witnessed an extraordinary effort by the popular sitting president, Barack Obama, together with his wife, Michelle, to rally support for Clinton in order to ensure the survival of his policy legacies. Trump likewise continued campaigning full-blast, and largely on his own, with party leaders and congressional candidates still distancing themselves from him. In doing so, he became more disciplined, so that he generated no controversies in the last week that would divert attention from Secretary Clinton's struggle with the email scandal. He also began to broaden the states in which he campaigned, including attention to rust-belt states such as Michigan, normally Democratic states that the Clinton campaign had already assumed to be in her column. Clinton likewise campaigned down to the wire, anticipating a narrow but clear win. Late polls likewise predicted a Clinton victory.[13] Election night and the day after had yet another and concluding set of surprises and confusions.

The Republican Victory

Against the odds, Trump emerged victorious in the Electoral College early in the morning of November 9th and thus became the nation's president-elect, but with an asterisk. In the face of Trump's Electoral College victory, Clinton had won the popular vote. She had done so, moreover, with a total that could eventually surpass approximately two and a half million votes. Her percentage vote margin over Trump, exceeding 1 percent, roughly fell within the margin of error of the final polls that predicted that she would win the presidency. Her Electoral

College defeat came with Trump's unexpected and narrow win in the rust-belt states of Michigan, Wisconsin, and Pennsylvania. He did better in these states than expected through his last-minute appeal to white working-class voters,[14] whereas she failed there and elsewhere to garner the substantial support among white educated Republican women that had appeared likely in mid-October.[15] With Clinton as well as Trump carrying baggage into Election Day, many of these Republican women apparently opted in the final days to return to their party. It was also the case that the third-party candidacies of Johnson and Stein drew enough votes that their candidacies may have affected the outcome in close states.

Once the Electoral College results became clear, Hillary Clinton accepted the outcome despite her popular vote lead, conceded to Donald Trump, and Barack Obama called for the public to rally behind Trump. The election outcome and Clinton's bitter-sweet popular vote victory was reminiscent of the 2000 election, when Republican George W. Bush won the Electoral College and thereby the presidency while Democrat Al Gore won the popular vote. With this second tarnished outcome coming within sixteen years of the Bush/Gore election, citizens, the media, and political activists raised pressing questions about the nation's continued reliance on the Electoral College to determine its president.[16]

For their part, congressional Republicans also survived the controversies surrounding Trump during the campaign and again won control of the House and Senate, albeit by slightly smaller margins than they had enjoyed in the 114th Congress.[17] Yet whereas Trump's victory signaled great change in Washington, the Republican victories in the Senate and House showed little sign of citizen concern with renovating Congress. Operating within a surreal campaign environment created by the race for the presidency, both parties in Congress emerged with virtually all incumbents reelected and a stand-pat outcome that appeared to have occurred in an alternative universe. In reality, the final vote tallies for the House and Senate had been an enormously close call, and they almost certainly would have looked different had Director Comey not intervened in the election.

Additionally, we must note that the final results in Congress would also not have been so favorable to the Republican Party had its members not showed such extraordinary dexterity in adjusting their political stances as Trump's fortunes waxed and waned.[18] As this election confirms, politics is as much art as science, with politicians needing to listen closely to their deepest intuitions and personal experience as they seek to maintain their political balance and survive to fight for their ideals some future day. In the end, virtually all Republican incumbents were still standing the day after the election and ready to claim the mantle of majority-party status yet again. They had survived the most surreal election of modern times, and had done so with virtually no loss in their party's incumbents or their majority margins in the House and Senate.

To fully comprehend the stand-pat nature of congressional outcomes, and the sense of continuity they created, we turn now to look in-depth at election results. As we do so, we will look closely inside the election results. In this, we will chart the high level of incumbent success that emerged in 2016 within and across the two parties; highlight the degree of continuity that existed in the support of different social groups for each party; and assess the regional factors that hindered the ability of Democrats to improve their seat margin in the Senate, despite the large number of Republican seats that were in contest in 2016.

Interpreting the 2016 Congressional Election Results

With many academics and pundits discussing the shortcomings of Republican and Democratic party establishments during the presidential nominating process, with the Republican Party organization's inability to control its nominee, with concerns that supporters of Bernie Sanders and a range of Republicans who preferred a candidate other than Trump would defect or not vote, and with a number of Republican officeholders withholding support or waffling on whether they would support Trump, one might have expected the turmoil of the presidential contest to spill over onto Senate and House elections in 2016.

The seemingly constant media reports that there was a populist sentiment in the electorate and an increasing distrust of anything that smacked of the establishment might lead one to assume that congressional challengers would have opportunities to make inroads against incumbents. (Moreover, Gallup's measure of Congress's job approval rating remained low although it rose from 13 percent in July 2016 up to 20 percent in September.) Instead, the congressional elections, as they have been in recent years, demonstrated the continued strength of parties and, in turn, the reelection success of incumbents. The fears among Republicans that the Trump candidacy would switch partisan control to the Democrats in the Senate and, at the least, significantly diminish the party's House majority did not materialize.

In the end, defections of Republican voters from the party's presidential candidate were not abnormally high. Democrats made only marginal seat gains in the House and the Senate despite the fact that Republicans were highly overexposed in the Senate and to a lesser degree in the House. Incumbents were reelected at very high rates, even by contemporary standards. And aggregate analysis suggests that voters stuck with their parties with high levels of party coupling of the presidential voting with the voting for the Senate and the House.

Partisan Underpinnings of Incumbent Success

One reason for the lack of bigger Democratic gains was the success rate of incumbents. In the House of the 392 incumbents who sought reelection, 380 won or are leading. That is a 97 percent reelection rate, the highest rate since 2004. Of the 12 incumbents who were defeated, five lost in primaries (2 Democrats and 3 Republicans), two of whom were facing corruption charges and two others chose to run against other incumbents of their own party after court-ordered redistricting. Of the seven who lost in the general election (2 Democrats and 5 Republicans), two were Florida Republicans, John Mica and David Jolly, and were running in redrawn districts that were less partisan-friendly.[19] And one of the two Democratic incumbents to lose, Mike Honda of California, lost to another Democrat, Ro Khanna, because they were the two leading vote getters in that state's blanket primary. If there was voter dissatisfaction or a populist uprising, it was not in evidence in House races. Moreover, fears of being "primaried" because of ideological splits within parties only led to the defeat of one Republican incumbent, Tim Huelskamp (Kan.), a Freedom Caucus conservative. The main electoral threat to the House Republican majority may be delayed until 2018 when its members have to face a midterm election with Donald Trump as their party's president instead of just a presidential candidate of the out party.

Incumbents fared nearly as well in the Senate as in the House. Of the 29 incumbents who sought reelection, none lost in primaries and only two were defeated in the general election. The 93 percent reelection rate has been exceeded only once since 1990. That result is even more striking because of the exposure level Republicans faced. Of the 34 Senate seats up in 2016, Republicans held 24 of them. They were the result in part of the 2010 election that had a very strong Republican tide. Seven of the Republican incumbents seeking reelection were in states that President Obama carried in the 2012 election. Yet only two, Paul Kirk (Ill.) and Kelly Ayotte (N.H.), lost. This election was a missed opportunity for Democrats to win control of the Senate. More importantly, having failed to make a serious dent in the Republicans' overwhelming advantage in this senatorial class, Democrats may have ensured a continued Republican Senate majority for more than just the next two years. The class's advantage provides the Republicans a base for six years. As we will discuss later the party composition of the class up in 2018 and the geographical make-up of the states having Senate contests in 2020 present significant hurdles for Democrats to regain control of the Senate before the 2022 election.

It is important to realize that the success of incumbents in the House and the Senate is not the result of a growth in incumbency advantage. Incumbency advantage, as measured by congressional elections scholars, has actually been declining since 2000 although the reelection rates of incumbents have remained high. In part this is due to the fact that more House members and senators represent constituencies with favorable enough partisan compositions to win reelection comfortably. Many no longer need to spend time and resources to build incumbency advantage on top of the margin that the partisan edge provides. As other indicators suggest, the strength of party voting in the electorate underpins a good deal of the stable outcomes of House and Senate elections. It is partisan advantage more than incumbency advantage that is at work.

One of the reasons for the survival of so many Republican senators was how closely the Senate elections mirrored the presidential contest. In all 34 races the party of the winning Senate candidate was of the same the party as the presidential candidate who carried the state. In fact, as the data in Table 18-1 show, the margins of victory in the presidential vote and Senate races in selected states

Table 18-1 Victory Margins of Presidential and Senate Candidates by State

State	Presidential Winner	Margin	Senate Winner	Margin	Difference
FL	Trump	1.3	Rubio (R)	7.7	-6.4
IL	Clinton	16.0	Duckworth (D)	14.2	-1.8
IN	Trump	19.3	Young (R)	9.7	-9.6
NV	Clinton	2.4	Masto (D)	2.4	0.0
NH	Clinton	0.3	Hassan (D)	0.1	0.2
NC	Trump	3.8	Burr (R)	5.8	-2.0
PA	Trump	1.2	Toomey (R)	1.7	-0.5
WI	Trump	1.0	Johnson (R)	3.4	-2.4

where Senate contests were seen as competitive were remarkably similar. In only two of eight states was the difference between the margin for the presidential candidate and the Senate candidate greater than 2.5 percent. In Florida, Rubio's margin was 6.4 percent larger than Trump's and in Indiana, former Senator Evan Bayh kept Todd Young's margin far smaller than Trump's. Trump did tend to run behind the Republican Senate candidates, but the differences were generally small. What the data instead suggest is a coupling of the vote for president and the vote for senator.

At this writing, data are not yet available for the presidential vote by congressional district, but some indicators suggest that the coupling extended to House races as well. In 2012, only 26 House districts elected a House member of a different party than that of the presidential candidate who carried the district. That was the lowest level in a presidential-election year since 1920.[20] The 2014 midterm election increased to 31 the number of districts that had a House member of a different party than the 2012 presidential winner, with 26 Republicans representing districts that Obama had carried and five Democrats in districts that Romney had won. When the data on the presidential vote by congressional district are available for 2016, it will likely show a decline in the number of split districts, perhaps to a level even lower than that in 2012. Some preliminary data support that position. In 2016, Democrats won seven of the existing split districts that Republicans had held and Republicans won three of the five districts from Democrats. Even in some of the states that Obama won in 2012 but Trump carried in 2016, Pennsylvania, Ohio, Michigan, and Wisconsin, his victory in those states is not likely to increase the number of split districts. Republican control of redistricting in those states for the current decade packed Democratic voters into a relatively small number of House districts. Accordingly, Democratic House districts in those states are, with a couple exceptions, so safe in partisan terms that Clinton carried them easily. In addition, districts in Nebraska and Maine, where an electoral vote is awarded for carrying each congressional district, all produced the House seat and presidential winners of the same party as the Democratic incumbent House member in Nebraska's 2nd district lost in a district that Trump carried and in Maine's 1st district, the Republican incumbent was reelected in a district that Obama had carried in 2012, but Trump won in 2016.

Another indicator of how party fortunes have impacted the congressional elections in recent years is the outcome of Senate and House races that were rated as "toss-ups." Many analyses of this election year and previous ones assume that the most likely outcome is for "toss-up" House and Senate contests to split evenly. But the data show that one party or the other almost always wins a disproportionate share of the toss-up contests. Tables 18-2 and 18-3 present the results of toss-up Senate and House races, respectively. In the Senate elections since 2004, one party has won an overwhelming majority of the toss-ups, except for 2010. Dominance of one party was the case again in 2016. Similarly, in the House since 2008 one party or the other has won from 62.5 percent to 72.2 percent of toss-up races. With the exception of 2010, the same party has dominated toss-up contests in both houses.[21]

Why is it that the toss-up races in Senate and House produce outcomes that are skewed in favor of one party in most election years? After all, by definition, the term toss-up implies a coin toss, a fifty-fifty event. While much of the discussion during campaign seasons treats these races as if they are individual events, there are likely national partisan trends that influence the outcomes and move these toss-up contests in one direction. Relatively small movements nationally can push the outcome of most of these close contests one way or another. In 2016, whatever late movement there was nationally tended to favor the Republicans, and accordingly they won a larger share of the toss-ups.

Thus, the congressional elections of 2016 are ones that fit with normal trends of recent previous elections. Voters are choosing candidates based strongly on

Table 18-2 Results of Toss-Up Senate Contests, 2004–2016

Year	Toss-Ups	Democratic Wins	Republican Wins
2004	5	1	4
2006	6	5	1
2008	4	4	0
2010*	5	3	2
2012	8	7	1
2014	7	1	6
2016	7	2	5

*Republicans won 4 Senate seats held by Democrats that were not rated as toss-ups.

The data for 2006–2014 are from the *New York Times* ratings of races just prior to the election. The data for 2016 are from *The Cook Political Report*. For 2004, the authors reconstructed the data from an examination of the contests.[22]

Table 18-3 Results of Toss-Up House Contests, 2008–2016

Year	Toss-Ups	Democratic Wins	Republican Wins
2008	26	17	9
2010	42	12	30
2012	25	17	8
2014	24	9	15
2016	18	5	13

The data for 2008–2014 are from the *New York Times* ratings of races just prior to the election. The data for 2016 are from *The Cook Political Report*.

their party preferences. And with fewer states and districts competitive in terms of party, incumbents are faring well. The party balance in the Senate and House does not move a great deal. In a year with a close presidential election in which the popular vote and electoral vote outcome were split (in a country where there is a close competitive divide between the two parties), the results of the congressional elections did not produce a great deal of change.

Differences in Party Diversity in the House and the Senate

If there is one thing that analysts have anticipated that could upset the existing partisan balance in the country, it is the support levels that the two parties are receiving from groups in the electorate. The persistence of a gender gap in which women voters are more likely than men to vote for Democrats and the disproportionate levels of support that Democrats receive from black, Latino, Asian, and younger voters are viewed as a long-term problem for the Republicans.[23]

These cleavages in the electorate are not all new ones, but as the gaps in support levels have increased and as the proportion of some of these groups in the electorate increases, they may be of growing significance. Importantly, many of these cleavages have been even more evident in demographic composition of the Democratic and Republican parties in Congress than in the electorate. But their effect on congressional elections was more muted in 2016 than one might have anticipated.

The 2016 election featured Hillary Clinton, the first woman presidential candidate of a major party in U.S. history. And her opponent, Donald Trump, engaged in extremely inappropriate expression about and behavior toward women. One might have assumed that these two factors would generate support for the candidacies of women seeking Senate and House seats. In addition, Trump's articulated hostility toward various ethnic, religious, and racial minorities and his hard line stand on immigration might have mobilized support for and against minority candidates. So even if 2016 produced little change in the party balance in Congress, it might still have produced changes in the demographic composition of the membership.

Examining the data on women candidates of the major parties for the Senate and the House in 2016, one is struck with how little change occurred and how there appears to have been no apparent impact of a woman being the front-runner for the nomination and subsequently the presidential nominee of a major party. The number of women winning either Democratic or Republican nominations for the House and the Senate was at a similar level as in recent elections. In the House a total of 167 women (120 Democrats and 47 Republicans) won party nominations. That was only one higher than in 2012 and eight higher than in 2014. And only 19 were running in open seats compared to 39 in 2012. In the Senate, the story was similar, with 15 women winning party nominations, the same number as in 2010 and 2014 and down from a high of 18 in 2012.[24] As the data in Figures 18-1 and 18-2 demonstrate, the election of women to the Senate and the House has plateaued over the past three elections. The total number of women elected to Congress in 2016 was the same as in 2014 at 104, increasing one in the Senate from 20 in 2012 and 2014 to 21 and declining one in the House from 84 to 83 (after an increase from 79 in 2012). If there was an expectation that the Clinton candidacy would generate a surge in the number and success of women candidates comparable to that of the 1992 Year of the Woman or that women voters in reaction to the Trump candidacy would be more likely to support women candidates in the general election for the House and Senate, that did not occur.

The longer-term trend that the figures illustrate is the growing magnitude of the gender gap between the parties in Congress that is much larger than the one that exists in the electorate. Until the 1990s there was no marked difference between the two parties in the number of women House members and senators. In both parties the numbers were small. But as more women started to run for and

Figure 18-1 Women House Members, 1982–2016

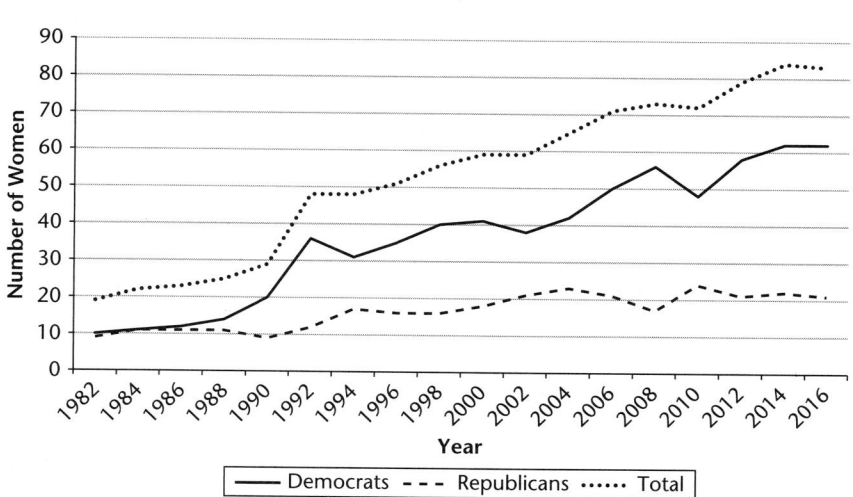

Figure 18-2 Women Senators, 1982–2016

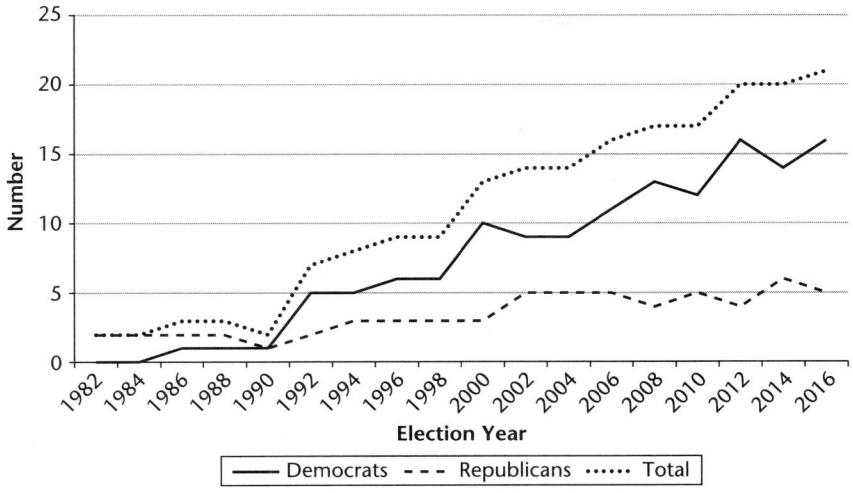

win House and Senate seats, a gender gap larger than in the electorate emerged in Congress. The number of Democratic women in both chambers has increased steadily since 1992, except for years like 1994, 2010, and 2014 when the party has suffered sizable seat losses. By contrast, the number of Republican women has remained fairly flat. The 115th Congress will have the same number of Republican women senators, five, and the same number of women House members, 21, as were present in the 108th Congress in 2002. Meanwhile, the numbers for Democrats will have increased from 9 to 16 in the Senate and 38 to 62 in the House during the same time period. The ratio of Democratic to Republican women in the Senate will be over 3:1 in the Senate and just short of that in the House. With Republicans in the majority in both chambers, the influence of women in Congress is accordingly diminished.

The representational situation for African Americans, Latinos, and Asian Americans in terms of membership in Congress is similar to that of women although the patterns of change differ somewhat. All three groups are overwhelmingly composed of Democratic members, at least in the House of Representatives. The relatively small number of minority members in the Senate is more equally divided between the two parties.

The House in the 115th Congress will have 48 African American members of whom 46 are Democrats while there will be three African American senators, two Democrats and one Republican. The number of African Americans in Congress has increased incrementally since the 1992 election when there was an increase of a third from 26 to 39 (38 in the House and one in the Senate). But it has stayed close to 40 in the House since then as most represent majority minority districts that have not expanded greatly in number. As yet, only few African

American members represent majority white districts. The total number of black House members is not likely to increase until African American candidates have greater success in majority white districts.

After not having a single African American elected to Congress from the 108th to 111th Congresses, two black Republicans were elected to the 112th Congress, one of whom, Tim Scott (S.C.), was reelected to the 113th and subsequently appointed to fill a vacancy in the U.S. Senate. He was then easily elected to fill the remainder of that term and reelected to a full six-year term in 2016. In addition, two new African American Republicans won election to the House in 2014 and reelection in 2016. But as in the electorate, African Americans in Congress remain overwhelmingly Democrats.

Like African Americans in Congress, Latinos and Asian American members are heavily Democratic in composition. What is different is that their numbers, although smaller than African Americans, are growing more rapidly because they are having more success in districts that are less racially homogeneous. The number of Latinos in the House has nearly doubled since the 2000 election from 19 to 37 who were elected in 2016. In 2016, seven new Latinos were elected to the House (the net increase was five), and all of them are Democrats. Perhaps this reflects growing concerns among Latinos with the Republican Party's more uncompromising stand on immigration issues. In the Senate, there are now four Latinos, with two from each party.

Asian Americans who were once considered to lean toward the Republicans in terms of partisan preferences are also now voting more heavily Democratic. And the three senators and ten House members of Asian heritage are all Democrats.

The problem that the Republican Party has with attracting the support of women and minority voters continues to be reflected in the composition of the parties in Congress. The 2016 election extended those advantages that the Democrats in Congress have had among these groups and witnessed a marked growth in the number of Latino Democrats elected to office. Of course, the Democrats have the problem of attracting white male voters, but that is a declining percentage of the electorate. The more diverse base of the Democratic Party in the electorate is magnified in terms of its membership in Congress.

Regional Strength of Parties in the House and the Senate

One of the underpinnings of the ideological polarization of the two parties in the House and the Senate has been the electoral base of their members. Part of this is an urban, suburban, rural split, but that difference resides within a broader regional context with Republicans dominating in the South and Democrats in the East. That division played out in the aftermath of the Voting Rights Act of 1965 and the resulting enfranchisement of southern blacks. In turn, it led to southern Democrats in Congress becoming more moderate and the movement of white southern conservatives into the Republican Party impacting first in presidential elections, then eventually spreading to House and Senate elections (as well as to state legislative elections). The culmination of this transformation took nearly three decades with the Republican Party capturing control of the House and Senate in the 1994 election. As we can see in the data in Tables 18-4 and 18-5, the transformation of the regional bases of the two parties in Congress continued over the six consecutive Congresses in which Republicans remained in control.[25] Although Republicans won a majority of House and Senate seats in the South in the 104th Congress (1995–96), their advantage in that region continued to grow. By the 109th Congress, elected in 2004, in which their overall majorities were quite similar to those they held in the 104th Congress, their majorities among southern House members and senators had increased markedly. A nine-seat South advantage over the Democrats in the House grew to 40 seats and a six-seat advantage in the Senate to 18 seats.

As the Republican Party in Congress became more southern in the House and the Senate, both in terms of numbers and in terms of party leadership, and took on a more uniformly conservative ideological tone, the Democrats made inroads in the East, going from a nine-seat advantage in the House in the 104th Congress to 22 seats in the 109th and increasing their edge by three seats among eastern senators (counting the independent who organized with the Democrats). They also made gains in the West among House members, especially in the coastal states. Excepting the 110th and 111th Congresses (not shown) in which the Democrats held membership majorities and improved their regional numbers in both chambers, the regional composition of both parties has remained remarkably stable since the 109th Congress. The Republican majorities by region in both chambers look very much the same for the new 115th Congress as they did for the 112th and 113th and except for Republican gains in the House, the splits remain close to those of the 109th Congress. If we were to divide the seats into smaller regional groupings, for example, separating out a West Coast state grouping from the West region or removing Florida and Virginia from the South region, the magnitude of the differences would be even more marked.

The regional cleavages, like others in American society, are now reinforcing and strengthening the party and ideological cleavages. Instead of cutting across party cleavages to support regional concerns on some issues and reducing polarization, the regional composition of the parties in Congress may be adding to the level of polarization.

The growing red state–blue state distinction which underpins some of these regional differences plays out in another way when one examines the results of Senate elections. In Figure 18-3, we present data on the number of states that had split-party representation in the U.S. Senate, one Democrat and one Republican, after presidential elections from 1980–2016. Following the election of Ronald Reagan in 1980, half the states had split-party representation in the Senate. That number has declined fairly steadily and is now down to less than a quarter of the states (twelve) in the 115th Congress. This fits neatly with other election phenomena such as the small number of battleground states

Figure 18-3 States With Senators of Opposite Parties after Presidential Elections, 1980–2016

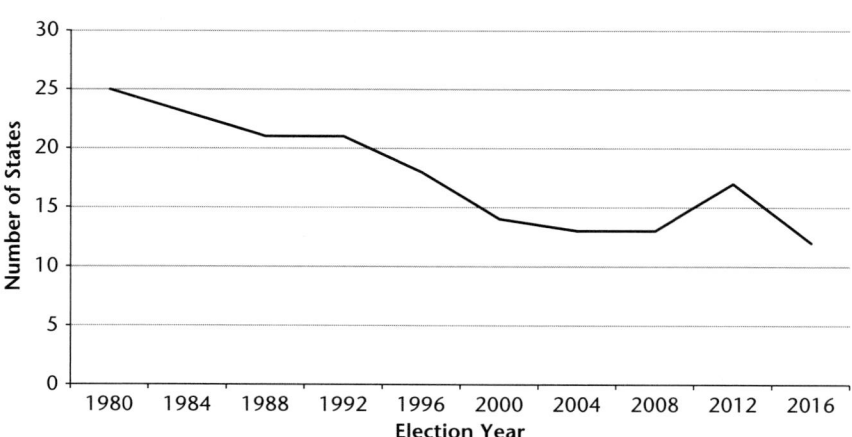

in presidential elections since 2000 and the close correspondence between the results of elections for the Senate and president that occurred in 34 states this year, as we discussed earlier.

But it also has implications for Senate elections more generally and for the skewed party composition of the three Senate classes. Part of the reason that none of the three classes is an accurate reflection of the partisan split in the Senate as a whole is that each class was elected in a year that had a particular partisan tilt. So the class that was up for election in 2016 had previously been elected in 2010, a very good Republican year. The class up for election in 2018 was the one previously elected in 2012 and before that 2006, both excellent years for Democrats, with Obama's reelection and the midterm of George W. Bush's second term. And the heavily Republican class that will face reelection in 2020 won office last in 2014, another election year when the partisan swing favored the Republicans. But part of the skewed composition of each class also reflects the different mix of states holding Senate contests. Of the class that was up for reelection in 2016 in which the Republicans held a 24-10 advantage, 17 of those were in red states, 8 were in blue states, and 9 were in battleground states. The mix of states with Senate contests in 2018 is far more favorable to the Democrats with nearly equal numbers of red, blue, and battleground states (with every state in the Northeast, except New Hampshire, having a Senate election), while the 2020 class has 18 red states with every southern and border state, except Florida and Missouri, having a Senate election. Even without partisan forces of given election years, we would expect these Senate classes to be tilted in favor of one party over the other because of the way Senate seats are distributed in the election cycle and because so many states now have a strong partisan lean.

Table 18-4 Distribution of House Seats by Region and Party

Congress	Party	East	Midwest	South	West	Total
104th	Democrats	54	46	64	40	204
	Republicans	45	59	73	53	230
	Other	1				1
109th	Democrats	58	40	51	53	202
	Republicans	36	60	91	45	232
	Other	1				1
113th	Democrats	62	35	41	63	201
	Republicans	28	59	108	39	234
114th	Democrats	56	33	38	61	188
	Republicans	34	61	111	41	247
115th	Democrats	58	33	40	63	194
	Republicans	32	61	109	39	241

East = Conn., Del., Maine, Md., Mass., N.H., N.J., N.Y., Pa., R.I., Vt., W.Va. Midwest = Ill., Ind., Iowa, Kan., Mich., Minn., Mo., Neb., N.D., Ohio, S.D., Wis. South = Ala., Ark., Fla., Ga., Ky., La., Miss., N.C., Okla., S.C., Tenn., Texas, Va. West = Alaska, Ariz., Calif., Colo., Hawaii, Idaho, Mont., Nev., N.M., Ore., Utah, Wash., Wyo.

Having not taken advantage of an opportunity to make more sizable gains of Senate seats in battleground states in 2016, Democrats now face a 2018 election where they are more exposed. As the data at the bottom of Table 18-5 show, the Democrats (and the two independents who caucus with them) hold 25 of the 33 seats that will be up for reelection. Most of those are either in blue states or in battleground states that Obama carried in 2012. But five of them are in red states. Only a weak economy and/or a low job approval of the Trump presidency provide an avenue for Democrats to avoid significant seat losses in the Senate. Of course, we need to remember that toss-up contests do not split evenly. So truly dire predictions for the Democrats for 2018, just as they were for Republicans in 2016, may be both premature and inaccurate.

Offsetting the potential for Democratic Senate seat losses in 2018 is the chance for significant gains in midterm House elections. With so many seats with seemingly partisan-safe constituencies, however, there may be a limited number of seats in play. But Republicans are likely to still hold more seats which Clinton carried in 2016 than the Democrats hold which Trump carried. Again, much will depend on the priorities and performance of the Trump administration and the new Congress and whether the U.S. economy can continue without a recession.

We have no crystal ball, disclosing to us what the future will look like in these regards. What we can do is to report on the developments that occurred—in

Table 18-5 Distribution of Senate Seats by Region and Party

Congress	Party	East	Midwest	South	West	Total
104th*	Democrats	14	13	10	10	47
	Republicans	10	11	16	16	53
109th	Democrats	16	13	4	11	44
	Republicans	7	11	22	15	55
	Other	1				1
113th	Democrats	19	12	6	16	53
	Republicans	3	12	20	10	45
	Other	2				2
114th	Democrats	18	10	3	13	44
	Republicans	4	14	23	13	54
	Other	2				2
115th	Democrats	19	11	3	13	46
	Republicans	3	13	23	13	52
	Other	2				2
116th (to be contested)	Democrats	9	7	2	5	23
	Republicans	0	1	3	4	8
	Other	2				2

The assignment of states to regions is the same as in Table 18-4.

*For the purpose of this table Richard Shelby, Ala., is counted as a Republican and Ben Nighthorse Campbell is counted as a Democrat at the start of the 104th Congress. Both switched to the Republican Party, but Shelby switched shortly after the election, while Campbell switched after the Congress started.

Washington and with the Trump transition—in the two weeks following the election and offer assessments of what these could mean as Congress now regroups and prepares to operate in a dramatically changed political landscape.

Looking to the Future

In the days following the 2016 elections, the members and leaders of Congress gathered in Washington to assess the election results, determine party leadership for the two chambers, and look to the future. As they did so, Republicans in Congress moved rapidly to embrace Trump's presidency, hopeful that a united Republican government would enable them to move forward on a range of policy priorities, including the repeal of the Affordable Care Act.[26] In contrast, Democrats in Congress challenged the defining nature of Trump's victory.[27] While not disputing his status as president-elect, Democrats pointed to Hillary Clinton's substantial and growing lead over him in the popular vote to argue for Trump's need for caution in rushing to radical change.

Amid these initial reactions, Republicans in the Senate and House of Representatives determined that they would return their leaders from the 114th Congress to these positions in the new Congress. They thus united around Mitch McConnell of Kentucky as Senate Majority Leader and the House Republican Conference unanimously voted to return Paul Ryan of Wisconsin as Speaker, despite threats to oppose him from some House Republicans and from Trump during the campaign. Democrats in the Senate faced an opening in the position of Minority Leader, with the retirement of their long-term leader, Harry Reid of Nevada. His replacement, as had been anticipated, was Chuck Schumer of New York, a senator with long experience in the chamber and broad support in the Democratic conference.

In contrast, confusion and concern existed among Democrats in the House of Representatives. Minority Leader Nancy Pelosi announced her intention to stand again for leader. Yet even long-time supporters indicated a desire to take some time, reassess the leadership structure, and decide Pelosi's fate after Thanksgiving. Pelosi agreed to delay the House Democrats' meeting to select their leader until November 30th. Pelosi was eventually reelected as the Minority Leader, despite a large grouping of Democrats not voting for her.

Despite the delay in the Democrats' vote on the House Minority Leader, the broad sense was that the elections had changed little on Capitol Hill. The pressing question was how this sense of continuity within the parties and chambers of Congress would intersect with the Trump presidency.

The Election Aftermath

As Trump began to announce his personal policy advisers and early nominees for the cabinet and other formal government positions, unease began to mount within the Republican and Democratic establishments with respect to Trump's true intentions as president.[28] Trump's fast move to designate Stephen Bannon as a primary White House adviser intensified concerns that Trump might take a hard right approach to governing, allying with white-supremacy positions on issues of public policy. His subsequent decision to nominate as his Attorney General Senator Jeff Sessions of Alabama, despite the rejection of Sessions's nomination for a federal judgeship by a Republican-controlled Senate Judiciary Committee in the mid-1980s owing to reports of his racist behavior, reinforced such apprehensions. Similarly, the early choice of Congressman Mike Pompeo to be Director of the Central Intelligence Agency and Lt. General Michael Flynn to be National Security Adviser appeared to signal a strong move to an extremist right on issues of foreign policy. The unease created by these nominations may foreshadow controversial confirmation hearings, even if the change the Democrats made in the 113th Congress now means that they can be confirmed without needing 60 votes for cloture.

It is difficult to assess what these early decisions by President-elect Trump actually mean. In truth, he appears to be such a different president-elect from any others in modern history—with limited ties to his own party; a propensity to act in flamboyant, unexpected, and controversial ways that catch partisans on all sides off-guard; and a desire to keep his own counsel without broad consultation—that it is difficult to anticipate precisely how well these earliest and controversial appointments will foreshadow his subsequent choices and actions.

Trump's early moves may be designed to reassure the electoral base of white working-class Americans that he mobilized to win the White House, signaling that he is still one of them,[29] after which he will listen to a broad range of interests and perspectives and make decisions that foster balanced long-term governance. Or they may foreshadow a narrow and militant agenda on both the domestic and international fronts, with Trump hewing closely to the nativist and "America First" positions long identified with Bannon and others on the "alt-right" and pursuing them with aggressive vigor.

Should Trump veer to the alt-right, and aggressively pursue its policy prescriptions, he will surely overreach any minimal "mandate" that the election gave him and create a context that could sorely test Republicans in Congress.

Assessing Trump's Mandate

As our assessment of the congressional elections should make clear, 2016 was not a classic "mandate election."[30] Despite the heated election campaign and moments of seeming break-through, neither party emerged from the election with super-majority dominance in Congress, broad majoritarian voter support for its presidential candidate, and the validation of an activist policy agenda. Rather, the 2016 campaign generated an excessively stable election outcome in Congress, in which the primary change was a slight shrinkage in the margins between the two parties in the two chambers. The two parties are thus closer to parity within the two chambers today than when the election campaign began. Similarly, little alteration has occurred within the parties, whether in gender or racial-ethnic makeup or even the identity of their members. And insofar as change occurred within or across the parties, as in regional distributions of members, it reinforced rather than deviated from partisan trends. Thus the same party controls Congress in the upcoming 115th Congress that controlled the 114th and the leaders of the parties are virtually the same, or come from similar governing perspectives, as in the 114th.

The critical change that did occur with the election, as seen during the first two weeks of post-election maneuvering, is that there now appear to be three competing agendas, rather than two.[31] The Republican majority in Congress has an agenda, well articulated over the past six years, that largely entails repeal of the Obama and Bill Clinton presidencies, as illustrated by the Affordable Care Act and environmental regulation, and replacement by classically conservative Republican strategies for the structuring of social programs and economic innovation.

The long-term agenda then also includes restructuring the financing of Social Security and Medicare. A victory in the presidential election by a classic Republican such as former Florida governor Jeb Bush would have seen the president and Congress avidly pursue this broad agenda, perhaps in ways modified by or perfected by the incoming president. Similarly, the Democratic minority in Congress has a clear, distinctive agenda, as articulated by President Obama, Hillary Clinton, and most Democratic candidates in the closing weeks of the election. It is focused on saving and enhancing the Democratic social programs that Republicans oppose and considering key new ones. An electoral victory by Secretary Clinton, if combined with the Democratic control of the House and Senate, would have seen the party vigorously pursue this agenda.

The third agenda belongs to President-elect Trump. He does appear to have a mandate for change, at least a mandate in the eyes of the 47 percent of voters who elected him to produce change. However, the nature of this agenda is known only to him. His bold and provocative promises were not connected to concrete and consistent language that made clear the parameters that defined his promises. Thus his campaign provided little legislative language that spelled out the content of programs he would seek to enact and his contradictory statements about a range of major and controversial promises left his true intentions in doubt.

In the two weeks following the election, all sides wait to hear what Trump actually intends to propose and do.[32] The hope of congressional Republicans is that he will decide to make their agenda his own, while asserting that it is what he intended all along, and work with them to implement it, to the consternation of congressional Democrats. The hope of congressional Democrats is that he will flounder in articulating his own agenda while refusing to defer to congressional Republicans, leaving Congress in deadlock and the presidential accomplishments of Barack Obama and Bill Clinton in place.

The fear on all sides in Congress is that Trump will engage in provocative moves that challenge the agendas of both parties and seek to impose a hard-right nationalist and white-supremacy agenda, or similarly radical proposals, moving the country back sixty years and engulfing it in divisive controversies that tear apart at the fabric of American society. Among Republicans, such a move would put at risk the golden opportunity that united party government has given them to revise or replace key social and economic programs installed by Democrats and put in place a viable long-term Republican approach to the redesign and funding of such programs. Such a vision, one that promises to ensure the effectiveness and solvency of social programs while limiting the drag they might create on business growth, is particularly associated with Speaker Paul Ryan and his policy leadership during his service as Chair of the House Ways and Means Committee.

Among Democrats, a move by Trump to pursue an alt-right agenda would constitute a direct attack on the party's decades of work in moving itself and the country beyond the eighty-year era of white-only primaries in the American South and southern Democratic dominance of their congressional party. The politics of this earlier era, based on a white-supremacy ethos, proved incredibly harmful to the nation and difficult to overcome. But as the party and nation did so, they set in motion a politics devoted to the valuing of a culturally and socially diverse society and combined this with a commitment to programs that prioritized social justice. Assumedly mainstream Republicans as well as Democrats would be loath to see the loss of these important steps forward toward the ideal of social and political equality that is at the heart of the American creed, even as they disagree on precisely how to proceed further towards that ideal.

Should President Trump attempt to strong-arm Congress as a whole and impose a radical agenda that many or most members in the two parties oppose, particularly one undercutting the nation's hard-won progress towards equal opportunity, the experience and independent electoral mandates enjoyed by the party leaders and most members of the 115th Congress could become major assets in limiting or upending presidential action. In other words, if early appointments such as Bannon and Sessions are indicative of what his broad policy goals and sustained leadership will entail, then President-elect Trump is likely moving down a path that could undo his presidency, with experienced leaders and members of Congress able to draw on a broad array of strategies and mechanisms to constrain him. Should Trump choose continued and massive confrontation with Republicans as well as Democrats, along the lines witnessed at times during his presidential campaign, all bets would be off for the success of his presidency, or even its continuance.

A deft president-elect, confronting the circumstances unfolding before Trump, would hold close to his party in Congress while reaching out to the opposition. Should Trump choose to engage in these more conventional stratagems, pursuing the party's established and well-vetted agenda while nudging it in selective ways, opportunities could then open up—with considerable effort, skillfulness, and cross-party compromise—for a landmark presidency.

Making Congress Work

As the new Congress takes office on January 3rd, 2017, a critical issue will be whether the nation confronts yet another "broken" Congress, unable to address critical policy issues, or whether efforts to foster policymaking success come to the fore. A key challenge for any president is to aid Congress in policymaking, helping to make it work despite the heterogeneity of its members, the difficulties of the policy challenges facing it, and the complex rules, procedures, and partisan conflicts that push it towards stasis. This is a particularly challenging task for a minority president, lacking a popular vote majority, but it is also the kind of challenge that makes being president worthwhile and allows gifted "salesmen" to show their wares.

A great contribution of a Trump presidency could come in "making Congress work," particularly if that goal were accomplished through his efforts at fostering compromise among legislators and parties in pursuit of broader and widely supported national goals. Interestingly, a great lesson in this regard is the presidency of another recent minority president, William Jefferson Clinton. Despite winning only 43 percent of the popular vote, in a three-way presidential race, Bill Clinton worked assiduously with the legislators on Capitol Hill, as did Hillary Clinton, and produced with the 103rd Congress one of the most productive landmark Congresses of the past forty years. Much of the aura surrounding Bill Clinton comes not just from his tenacity in surviving subsequent Republican efforts to convict him of high crimes and misdemeanors, but in this success prior to the Republican Revolution in using his considerable political skills in helping make Congress work.

In order to make the incoming 115th Congress work, strategies must be found that enable it to overcome the close margins that exist between Republicans and Democrats in the House and Senate. Strategies must also be crafted that help the Senate honor its procedural traditions, including the filibuster, while finding ways to foster Senate action on such issues as Supreme Court nominations.[33] As a president with a complex history of policy positioning, who appeared at times to be as much a Democrat and Republican in the decades prior to his presidential campaign, Trump could be well positioned to foster communication, negotiation, and compromise across the parties, were he to focus his considerable energies on that challenge. One place to start in this regard, would be with legislation to rebuild the nation's infrastructure.[34]

Trump could also use his nomination powers, much as Obama did with his nomination of Judge Merrick Garland for the Supreme Court, to choose nominees who are candidates of the center, able to talk and work with all sides. And as part of national healing from the deeply hurtful presidential campaign that his words and actions helped set in motion, Trump could attend closely to the nomination of minority candidates for positions in government. These moves would require the president-elect to distance himself from his early embrace of the altright, as his presidency proceeds. Along the way, the leaders of both parties in both chambers would need to come forward and educate President Trump on the realities of legislative policymaking, given his lack of political experience, and be willing to work with him on policy compromise that fosters national interests. And he would need to listen.

Conclusion

We have focused in this chapter on the Trump phenomenon and its implications for Congress because his election is the most distinctive outcome of the 2016 election, and understanding its implications for Congress, moving forward, is the most challenging issue facing students of Congress. Certainly his election throws a great element of unpredictability into the developments and challenges likely to confront the new Congress. We have tried to acknowledge this unpredictability and lay out some parameters for understanding and assessing it. At the same time, quite distinct from the concerns created by Trump's election, there are internal issues for Congress to resolve, that it would now need to confront somewhat irrespective of the person and the party that held the presidency.

In the House, and to a lesser degree in the Senate, a first question is whether the splits between Freedom Caucus Republicans in the House and their counterparts in the Senate will persist. Will they behave as Republicans did following the 1994 election and put aside ideological differences in favor of pushing a policy agenda? Or will the Republican leadership find that with slightly narrower majorities these rebellious conservatives will make unreasonable demands to obtain their support? And if that occurs, will the Trump administration and the Republican leadership need to attract at least some Democrats to enact parts of a legislative program? The Trump administration is likely to have a good deal of unity from Republicans in Congress initially, but that could erode depending on the agenda he pursues, his support from the public, and as concern of members focuses on the 2018 midterm election. Erosion of Republican support for Trump in Congress could give the Democratic Party, or elements of it, an opportunity to gain critical bargaining leverage with the president, increasing the party's visibility and role in the new Congress.[35]

In addition, as has been the case when there is unified party control of Congress and the president since the 103rd Congress, which was the first Congress of Bill Clinton's presidency, the minority party has relied heavily on the cloture rule to block initiatives of the majority. Initially, Democrats have indicated that they will not block Republican legislation by voting against cloture in a wholesale manner, in this new Congress. And Senator Orrin Hatch (R Utah) has indicated that he opposes changing the cloture rule. The first test of these commitments is likely to come when President Trump nominates a candidate to fill the Supreme Court vacancy. Unlike all the other presidential nominations, Supreme Court justices were an exception to the rule interpretation change the Democrats made in the 113th Congress removing the sixty-vote requirement to end debate on nominations. Will an effort of Democrats to block cloture on a Trump nominee to the Supreme Court serve as a catalyst to a broader consideration of changing the conditions for cloture on Supreme Court nominations and perhaps on legislation as well?

In this regard, we note that the election of a Republican president removes the Obama veto threat from the bargaining situation that Republican majorities in the House and Senate face. But the unpredictability of the Trump presidency, the difficulty Republican leaders in Congress may have in holding together conservatives of various stripes within its membership in Congress, narrowed majorities, and a potentially cohesive Democratic minority in both chambers will test the ability of Republicans to produce policy changes.

Finally, let us close with one last observation. The elections appear to have produced little change in effective control of Congress, or in the apparent partisan loyalties of voters, but they have dramatically altered the chance for change in public policy and in the nation's long-term governing direction.

Depending on whether President-elect Trump is actually willing to work with Congress, and prepared to pursue an agenda it can accept, the nation could be on the verge of an exceptional period of restructuring in its policy programs and national direction, with a substantial shift to the right being possible. Yet this would come despite a reduction in the margin of Republican control of the House and Senate, and the minority status of the president. This fateful moment of choice and direction highlights how critical relatively small shifts in campaign momentum, and in citizens' vote choices, can be in pushing the nation down very different governing paths. The constitutional structure of American government normally requires one side winning a series of elections that establish and sustain a majority for policy change.

With a change in less than two hundred thousand votes across Michigan, Wisconsin, and Pennsylvania, Hillary Clinton would be president-elect, with a compelling popular vote win, and the battle would be underway to save and solidify the Obama legacy. Were Democrats still the minority in Congress, Clinton would be in a position to demonstrate her leadership skills in working with a Republican Congress. They could have incentive to cooperate, given their decline in margins of House and Senate control and the need to shore up public support in the 2018 elections. And were Democrats the victors in Congress, they would be in a position to push forward on new social initiatives, in cooperation with Clinton, refining and even expanding on the Obama legacy.

As the 2016 general elections demonstrate, slight shifts in citizen choice can have major and consequential implications for a nation's future directions. Democracy is indeed a complicated and unpredictable governing endeavor.

Notes

1. We note that political scientists analyzing the poll data argued that there was actually great stability and that the movement largely reflected differences in the samples of respondents, but the variation nevertheless created an appearance of instability in voter preferences that added to the sense of ongoing upheaval in the presidential campaign.
2. Jonathan Martin, Dalia Sussman, and Megan Thee-Brenan, "In Poll, Voters Express Disgust in U.S. Politics," *New York Times*, November 4, 2016: A1.
3. Rachel Chason, "Which Republicans Oppose Trump and Why?" *CNN*, August 10, 2016: online.
4. David A. Fahrenthold, "Trump Recorded Having Extremely Lewd Conversation about Women in 2005," *Washington Post*, October 8, 2016: online; Josh Lederman and Jill Colvin, "Off His Message Again: Trump Vows to Sue All Female Accusers," *Associated Press*, October 22, 2016.
5. Alexander Burns and Amy Chozick, "Hillary Clinton Presses Her Advantage over a Struggling Donald Trump," *New York Times*, October 23, 2016: online.
6. Jason Easley, "A Clean Sweep for Hillary Clinton as Voters Deem Trump the Loser of Final Debate," *Politics USA*, October 20, 2016: online; Alex Daugherty, "Hillary Clinton Won All Three Debates—by Double Digits," *Miami Herald*, October 21, 2016: online.
7. Carl Hulse, "Republicans in Congress Fear Losses, and Then the Hard Part," *New York Times*, October 26, 2016: online; David Leonhardt, "Senate Democrats Surge Ahead," *New York Times*, October 26, 2016: online; Matt Flegenheimer and Jonathan Martin, "Showing Confidence, Hillary Clinton Pushes into Republican Strongholds,"

New York Times, October 17, 2016: online; Emmarie Huetteman, "House Republicans in Close Races Worry Trump's Problems May Hurt Them," *New York Times*, October 14, 2016: online.

8. Emmarie Huetteman, "Tarred by Trump, Paul Ryan Tries to Safeguard Both Party and Job," *New York Times*, October 29, 2016: online; and Jennifer Steinhauer, "Paul Ryan's Twisting, Labored Path from Party's Standard-Bearer," *New York Times*. October 16, 2016: A1.
9. Katie Bo Williams, "October Surprise: FBI Reviewing Emails in Clinton Server Case," *The Hill*, October 28, 2016: online; Julie Pace and Kathleen Hennessey, "Clinton Tries to Quell Resurgent Email Issue Late in Race," *Associated Press*, October 29, 2016; Jonathan Martin, Adam Goldman, and Gardiner Harris, "Obama Faults F.B.I. and Fires Up Clinton Faithful," *New York Times*, November 3, 2016: A1.
10. Melanie Mason, "Donald Trump Warns of a 'Constitutional Crisis' if Hillary Clinton Wins," *LA Times*, October 31, 2016: online.
11. Chris Cillizza and Aaron Blake, "The Electoral Map is Definitely Moving in Donald Trump's Direction," *Washington Post*, November 4, 2016: online.
12. Matt Apuzzo, Michael S. Schmidt, and Adam Goldman, "FBI Says Review Clears Clinton in Email Inquiry," *New York Times*, November 7, 2016: A1.
13. Nate Silver, "Election Update: Clinton Gains, and the Polls Magically Converge," *FiveThirtyEight*, November 7, 2016: online.
14. Thomas B. Edsall, "The Not-So-Silent White Majority," *New York Times*, November 17, 2016.
15. Clare Malone, "Clinton Couldn't Win over White Women," *FiveThirtyEight*, November 9, 2016: online.
16. Jonathan Vankin, "Updated Clinton Lead Growing Fast as Electoral College Faces Challenge," *INQUISITR*, November 16, 2016: A1.
17. Karou Demirjian, "Republicans Keep Control of Congress after Decisive Senate Wins in Missouri, Pennsylvania, Indiana, Wisconsin and N.C.," *Washington Post*, November 9, 2016: online.
18. Bob Christie, "After Rejecting Trump, McCain Navigates Tough GOP Path," *Associated Press*, October 21, 2016: online.
19. Three states, Florida, North Carolina, and Virginia, did various degrees of redistricting.
20. Gary C. Jacobson and Jamie L. Carson, *The Politics of Congressional Elections*, 9th ed. (Lanham, Md.: Rowman & Littlefield, 2016), p. 192.
21. We were only able to obtain ratings on House elections since 2008.
22. Use of the *New York Times* was because the data were easily obtained from archived material. The advantage of *Cook* is that it is updated closer to the day of the election. The *New York Times* listed only five Senate contests as toss-ups in 2016, and those split 3-2 for the Republicans. One of the Senate races it rated as a "Democratic Lean" which Cook rated as a toss-up was the Wisconsin Senate race that the Republicans won.
23. See the Growth and Opportunity Report of the Republican National Committee, March 2013 and Gary C. Jacobson, "The Obama Legacy and the Future of Partisan Conflict: Demographic Change and Generational Imprinting," *Annals of the American Academy of Political and Social Science*, September 2016 (667): 72–91.
24. Data on women nominees are from reports of the Center for American Women and Politics, http://cawp.rutgers.edu/womenrun2016-us-senate-outlook and http://www.cawp.rutgers.edu/womenrun2016-us-house-outlook

25. For part of the 107th Congress, the Democrats were the majority party in the Senate, following Vermont Senator James Jeffords's decision to leave the Republican Party and become independent, but organize with the Democrats.
26. Jennifer Steinhauer, "Republicans in Congress Plan Swift Action on Ambitious Agenda with Trump," *New York Times*, November 10, 2016: P14.
27. Abby Phillip and John Wagner, "Democrats Move to More Aggressive Stance against Trump," *Washington Post*, November 15, 2016: online.
28. Michael D. Shear, Maggie Haberman, and Michael. S. Schmidt, "Critics See Stephen Bannon, Trump's Pick for Strategist, as Voice of Racism," *New York Times*, November 14, 2016: online; Eric Lipton, Charlie Savage, and Michael S. Schmidt, "Donald Trump's Team Shows Few Signs of Post-Election Moderation," *New York Times*, November 18, 2016: online; Editorial Board, "Jeff Sessions as Attorney General: An Insult to Justice," *New York Times*, November 18, 2016; Eric Lichtblau, "Poised to Seek Change as Attorney General," *New York Times*, November 19, 2016: A15; Julie Hirschfeld Davis, "Trump Selects Loyalists on Right Flank to Fill National Security Posts," *New York Times*, November 19, 2016: A1.
29. Jeremy W. Peters, "Trump's Choice of Stephen Bannon Is Nod to Anti-Washington Base," *New York Times*, November 14, 2016: online.
30. Lawrence J. Grossback, David A. M. Peterson, and James A. Stimson, *Mandate Politics* (New York: Cambridge University Press, 2007).
31. Charles Krauthammer, "How the New Republican Majority Can Succeed," *Washington Post*, November 20, 2016.
32. Rachel Martin, Host, "Young Republican Roundtable: Shifting Views after Election of Donald Trump," *NPR*, November 13, 2016; Mike DeBonis and Kelsey Snell, "Trump's Victory Heralds a Golden Age for Republicans on Capitol Hill," *Chicago Tribune*, November 9, 2016: online. For background discussion, see "The Republican Civil War Starts the Day after the Election," *VOX*, November 1, 2016: online; and Nancy Benac, "Conservatives Worry about Direction of Party under Trump," *Associated Press*, May 7, 2016: online.
33. Carl Hulse, "Senate Leader Faces Hard Choices If Democrats Resort to Filibusters," *New York Times*, November 11, 2016: A12.
34. Emma G. Fitzsimmons, "Infrastructure Emerges as a Winner in Elections," *New York Times*, November 10, 2016: A12.
35. See Ginger Gibson and Richard Cowan, "Willing to Oppose Trump, Some Senate Republicans Gain Leverage," *National Memo*, November 22, 2016: online, for a discussion of potential defectors among Senate Republicans.

Suggested Readings

✧ ✧ ✧

Aberbach, Joel D. *Keeping a Watchful Eye: The Politics of Congressional Oversight.* Washington, DC: Brookings, 1990.
Abramowitz, Alan I. "Incumbency, Campaign Spending, and the Decline of Competition in U.S. House Elections." *Journal of Politics* 53 (1991): 34–56.
Abramson, Paul, John H. Aldrich, and David W. Rohde. "Progressive Ambition among United States Senators: 1972–1988." *Journal of Politics* 49 (1987): 3–35.
Adler, E. Scott. Why *Congressional Reforms Fail: Reelection and the House Committee System.* Chicago: University of Chicago Press, 2002.
Adler, E. Scott, and John S. Lapinski. "Demand-Side Theory and Congressional Committee Composition: A Constituency Characteristics Approach." *American Journal of Political Science* 41 (1997): 895–918.
———, eds. *Macropolitics of Congress.* Princeton: Princeton University Press, 2006.
Adler, E. Scott, and John D. Wilkerson. *Congress and the Politics of Problem Solving.* New York: Cambridge University Press, 2012.
Aldrich, John H. *Why Parties? The Origin and Transformation of Political Parties in America.* Chicago: University of Chicago Press, 1995.
Aldrich, John H., and David W. Rohde. "The Republican Revolution and the House Appropriations Committee." *Journal of Politics* 62 (2000): 1–33.
Alesina, Alberto, and Howard Rosenthal. "Partisan Cycles in Congressional Elections and the Macroeconomy." *American Political Science Review* 83 (1989): 373–98.
Anderson, Thorton. *Creating the Constitution: The Convention of 1787 and the First Congress.* University Park: Pennsylvania State University Press, 1993.
Ansolabehere, Stephen, and Alan Gerber. "The Effects of Filing Fees and Petition Requirements in U.S. House Elections." *Legislative Studies Quarterly* 21 (1996): 249–64.
Ansolabehere, Stephen, James M. Snyder Jr., and Charles Stewart III. "Candidate Positioning in U.S. House Elections." *American Journal of Political Science* 45 (2001): 136–59.
Ansolabehere, Stephen, James M. Snyder Jr., and Michael M. Ting. "Bargaining in Bicameral Legislatures: When and Why Does Malapportionment Matter?" *American Political Science Review* 97 (2003): 471–81.
Arnold, Laura W. "The Distribution of Senate Committee Positions: Change or More of the Same?" *Legislative Studies Quarterly* 26 (2001): 227–49.
Arnold, R. Douglas. *Congress and the Bureaucracy: A Theory of Influence.* New Haven, CT: Yale University Press, 1979.
———. *The Logic of Congressional Action.* New Haven, CT: Yale University Press, 1990.

Asher, Herbert B. "The Learning of Legislative Norms." *American Political Science Review* 67 (1973): 499–513.
Bach, Stanley, and Steven S. Smith. *Managing Uncertainty in the House: Adaptation and Innovation in Special Rules*. Washington, DC: Brookings, 1988.
Bafumi, Joseph, and Michael C. Herron. "Leapfrog Representation and Extremism: A Study of American Voters and Their Members in Congress." *American Political Science Review* 104 (2010): 619–22.
Bafumi, Joseph, Robert S. Erikson, and Christopher Wlezien. "Balancing, Generic Polls, and Midterm Congressional Elections." *Journal of Politics* 72 (2010): 705–19.
Baker, Ross K. *House and Senate*. New York: Norton, 1989.
Balla, Steven J., and John R. Wright. "Interest Groups, Advisory Committees, and Congressional Control of the Bureaucracy." *American Journal of Political Science* 45 (2001): 799–812.
Bauer, Raymond A., Ithiel de Sola Pool, and Lewis A. Dexter. *American Business and Public Policy: The Politics of Foreign Trade*. New York: Atherton, 1963.
Baumgartner, Frank R., and Bryan D. Jones. "Agenda Dynamics and Policy Subsystems." *Journal of Politics* 53 (1991): 1044–74.
Baumgartner, Frank R., Bryan D. Jones, and Michael C. MacLeod. "The Evolution of Legislative Jurisdictions." *Journal of Politics* 62 (2000): 321–49.
Bell, Lauren Cohen. *Warring Factions: Interest Groups, Money, and the New Politics of Senate Confirmation*. Columbus: Ohio State University Press, 2002.
Berkman, Michael B. "State Legislators in Congress: Strategic Politicians, Professional Legislatures, and the Party Nexus." *American Journal of Political Science* 38 (1994): 1025–55.
———. *The State Roots of National Politics: Congress and the Tax Agenda, 1978–1986*. Pittsburgh: University of Pittsburgh Press, 1993.
Bianco, William T. *Trust: Representatives and Constituents*. Ann Arbor: University of Michigan Press, 1994.
Bianco, William T., and Itai Sened. "Uncovering Evidence of Conditional Party Government: Reassessing Majority Party Influence in Congress and State Legislatures." *American Political Science Review* 99 (2005): 361–71.
Binder, Sarah A. "The Dynamics of Legislative Gridlock, 1947–96." *American Political Science Review* 93 (1999): 519–34.
———. *Minority Rights, Majority Rule: Partisanship and the Development of Congress*. New York: Cambridge University Press, 1997.
———. "The Partisan Basis of Procedural Choice: Allocating Parliamentary Rights in the House, 1789–1900." *American Political Science Review* 90 (1996): 8–20.
———. *Stalemate: Causes and Consequences of Legislative Gridlock*. Washington, DC: Brookings Institution Press, 2003.
———. *Advice and Dissent: The Struggle to Shape the Federal Judiciary*. Washington, DC: Brookings Institution Press, 2009.

Binder, Sarah A., and Forrest Maltzman. "The Limits of Senatorial Courtesy." *Legislative Studies Quarterly* 24 (2004): 5–22.
Binder, Sarah A., and Steven S. Smith. *Politics or Principle? Filibustering in the United States Senate.* Washington, DC: Brookings Institution Press, 1997.
Black, Earl, and Merle Black. *The Rise of Southern Republicans.* Cambridge, MA: Harvard University Press, 2002.
Bolling, Richard. *House Out of Order.* New York: Dutton, 1965.
Bond, Jon R., and Richard Fleisher. *Polarized Politics: Congress and the President in a Partisan Era.* Washington, DC: CQ Press, 2000.
———. *The President in the Legislative Arena.* Chicago: University of Chicago Press, 1990.
Born, Richard. "Changes in the Competitiveness of House Primary Elections, 1956–1976." *American Politics Quarterly* 8 (1980): 495–506.
Bosso, Christopher. *Pesticides and Politics: The Life Cycle of a Public Issue.* Pittsburgh: University of Pittsburgh Press, 1988.
Brady, David W. *Congressional Voting in a Partisan Era: A Study of the McKinley Houses.* Lawrence: University Press of Kansas, 1973.
———. *Critical Elections and Congressional Policy Making.* Stanford, CA: Stanford University Press, 1988.
Brady, David W., Joseph Cooper, and Patricia A. Hurley. "The Decline of Party in the U.S. House of Representatives, 1887–1968." *Legislative Studies Quarterly* 4 (1979): 381–407.
Brady, David W., and Mathew McCubbins, eds. *Party, Process, and Political Change in Congress: New Perspectives on the History of Congress.* Stanford, CA: Stanford University Press, 2002.
Brady, David W., and Craig Volden. *Revolving Gridlock: Politics and Policy From Carter to Clinton.* Boulder, CO: Westview Press, 1998.
Brunell, Thomas L. *Redistricting and Representation: Why Competitive Elections Are Bad for America.* New York: Routledge, 2008.
Bullock, Charles S., III. "House Committee Assignments." In *The Congressional System: Notes and Readings.* 2nd ed. Edited by Leroy N. Rieselbach, 58–86. North Scituate, MA: Duxbury Press, 1979.
Burden, Barry C. *Personal Roots of Representation.* Princeton, NJ: Princeton University Press, 2007.
Burns, James MacGregor. *Congress on Trial: The Legislative Process and the Administrative State.* New York: Harper, 1949.
Burrell, Barbara C. *A Woman's Place Is in the House: Campaigning for Congress in the Feminist Era.* Ann Arbor: University of Michigan Press, 1994.
Cain, Bruce, John Ferejohn, and Morris Fiorina. *The Personal Vote: Constituency Service and Electoral Independence.* Cambridge, MA: Harvard University Press, 1967.
Campbell, James E. *The Presidential Pulse of Congressional Elections.* Lexington: University Press of Kentucky, 1993.

Canes-Wrone, Brandice, David W. Brady, and John F. Cogan. "Out of Step, Out of Office: Electoral Accountability and House Members' Voting." *American Political Science Review* 96 (2002): 127–40.

Canon, David T. *Actors, Athletes, and Astronauts: Political Amateurs in the United States Congress*. Chicago: University of Chicago Press, 1990.

———. *Race, Redistricting, and Representation: The Unintended Consequences of Black Majority Districts*. Chicago: University of Chicago Press, 1999.

Canon, David T., and Kenneth R. Mayer. *The Dysfunctional Congress? The Individual Roots of an Institutional Dilemma*. Boulder, CO: Westview Press, 1999.

Carnes, Nicholas. *White-Collar Government: The Hidden Role of Class in Economic Policy Making*. Chicago: University of Chicago Press, 2013.

Carson, Jamie L., Erick J. Engstrom, and Jason M. Roberts. "Candidate Quality, the Personal Vote, and the Incumbency Advantage in Congress." *American Political Science Review* 101 (2007): 289–301.

Clausen, Aage R. *How Congressmen Decide: A Policy Focus*. New York: St. Martin's, 1973.

Clem, Alan L., ed. *The Making of Congressmen: Seven Campaigns of 1974*. North Scituate, MA: Duxbury Press, 1976.

Clinton, Joshua D. "Congress, Lawmaking, and the Fair Labor Standards Act, 1971–2000." *American Journal of Political Science* 56 (2012): 355–72.

Clinton, Joshua D., and John Lapinski. "Measuring Legislative Accomplishment, 1877–1994." *American Journal of Political Science* 50 (2006): 232–49.

Clinton, Joshua D., David Lewis, and Jennifer Selin. "Political Influence in the Bureaucracy: The Irony of Congressional Oversight." *American Journal of Political Science* 58 (2014): 387–401.

Collie, Melissa, and Brian E. Roberts. "Trading Places: Choice and Committee Chairs in the U.S. Senate, 1950–1986." *Journal of Politics* 54 (1992): 231–45.

Cook, Elizabeth Adell, Sue Thomas, and Clyde Wilcox, eds. *The Year of the Woman: Myths and Reality*. Boulder, CO: Westview Press, 1994.

Cooper, Joseph. *The Origins of the Standing Committees and the Development of the Modern House*. Houston: Rice University Studies, 1971.

———, ed. *Congress and the Decline of Public Trust*. Boulder, CO: Westview Press, 1999.

Cooper, Joseph, and David W. Brady. "Institutional Context and Leadership Style: The House From Cannon to Rayburn." *American Political Science Review* 75 (1981): 411–25.

———. "Toward a Diachronic Analysis of Congress." *American Political Science Review* 75 (1981): 988–1006.

Cooper, Joseph, and G. Calvin Mackenzie. *The House at Work*. Austin: University of Texas Press, 1981.

Cooper, Joseph, and Garry Young. "Partisanship, Bipartisanship, and Crosspartisanship in Congress Since the New Deal." In *Congress Reconsidered*. 6th ed. Edited by Lawrence C. Dodd and Bruce I. Oppenheimer, 246–73. Washington, DC: CQ Press, 1997.

Cover, Albert D. "Contacting Congressional Constituents: Some Patterns of Perquisite Use." *American Journal of Political Science* 24 (1980): 125–34.

Cox, Gary W., and Jonathan N. Katz. *Elbridge Gerry's Salamander: The Electoral Consequences of the Reapportionment Revolution*. New York: Cambridge University Press, 2002.

———. "Gerrymandering Roll Calls in Congress, 1879–2000." *American Journal of Political Science* 51 (2007): 108–19.

Cox, Gary W., and Mathew D. McCubbins. *Legislative Leviathan: Party Government in the House*. 2nd ed. New York: Cambridge University Press, 2007.

———. *Setting the Agenda: Responsible Party Government in the U.S. House of Representatives*. New York: Cambridge University Press, 2005.

Cox, James, Gregory Hager, and David Lowery. "Regime Change in Presidential and Congressional Budgeting: Role Discontinuity or Role Evolution?" *American Journal of Political Science* 37 (1993): 88–118.

Currinder, Marian. *Money in the House: Campaign Funds and Congressional Party Politics*. Boulder, CO: Westview Press, 2009.

Davidson, Roger H., and Walter J. Oleszek. *Congress Against Itself*. Bloomington: Indiana University Press, 1977.

———. *Congress and Its Members*. 11th ed. Washington, DC: CQ Press, 2008.

De Boef, Suzanna, and James A. Stimson. "The Dynamic Structure of Congressional Elections." *Journal of Politics* 55 (1993): 630–48.

Deering, Christopher J., and Steven S. Smith. *Committees in Congress*. 3rd ed. Washington, DC: CQ Press, 1997.

DeGregorio, Christine, and Kevin Snider. "Leadership Appeal in the U.S. House of Representatives: Comparing Officeholders and Aides." *Legislative Studies Quarterly* 20 (1995): 491–511.

Den Hartog, Chris, and Nathan W. Monroe. *Agenda Setting in the U.S. Senate: Costly Consideration and Majority Party Advantage*. New York: Cambridge University Press, 2011.

Destler, I. M. *Renewing Fast-Track Legislation*. Washington, DC: Institute for International Economics, 1997.

Dexter, Lewis A. *How Organizations Are Represented in Washington*. Indianapolis: Bobbs-Merrill, 1969.

———. *The Sociology and Politics of Congress*. Chicago: Rand McNally, 1969.

Dion, Douglas. *Turning the Legislative Thumbscrew: Minority Rights and Procedural Change in Legislative Politics*. Ann Arbor: University of Michigan Press, 1997.

Dion, Douglas, and John Huber. "Procedural Choice and the House Committee on Rules." *Journal of Politics* 58 (1996): 25–53.

———. "Coalition-Building by Party Leaders: A Case Study of House Democrats." *Congress and the Presidency Journal* 10 (1983): 145–68.

Dodd, Lawrence C. "Congress in a Downsian World: Polarization Cycles and Regime Change." *Journal of Politics* 77 (2015): 311–23.

———. "The Expanding Roles of the House Democratic Whip System." *Congressional Studies* 6 (1979): 27–56.

———. *Thinking About Congress: Essays on Congressional Change.* New York: Routledge, 2012.
Dodd, Lawrence C., and Richard L. Schott. *Congress and the Administrative State.* New York: John Wiley, 1979.
Dodd, Lawrence C., and Scot Schraufnagel. "Congress and the Polarity Paradox: Party Polarization, Member Incivility and Enactment of Landmark Legislation, 1891–1994." *Congress and the Presidency* 39 (2012): 109–32.
Egan, Patrick J. *Partisan Priorities: How Issue Ownership Drives and Distorts American Politics.* New York: Cambridge University Press, 2013.
Endersby, James W., and Karen M. McCurdy. "Committee Assignments in the U.S. Senate." *Legislative Studies Quarterly* 21 (1996): 219–34.
Epstein, David, and Peter Zemsky. "Money Talks: Deterring Quality Challengers in Congressional Elections." *American Political Science Review* 89 (1995): 295–308.
Erikson, Robert S. "The Advantage of Incumbency in Congressional Elections." *Polity* 3 (1971): 395–405.
———. "Is There Such a Thing as a Safe Seat?" *Polity* 8 (1976): 623–32.
———. "The Puzzle of Midterm Loss." *Journal of Politics* 50 (1988): 1011–29.
Eulau, Heinz, and Paul Karps. "The Puzzle of Representation." *Legislative Studies Quarterly* 2 (1977): 233–54.
Evans, C. Lawrence. *Leadership in Committee: A Comparative Analysis of Leadership Behavior in the U.S. Senate.* Ann Arbor: University of Michigan Press, 2001.
Evans, C. Lawrence, and Walter J. Oleszek. *Congress Under Fire: Reform Politics and the Republican Majority.* Boston: Houghton Mifflin, 1997.
Evans, Diana. *Greasing the Wheels: Using Pork Barrel Projects to Build Majority Coalitions in Congress.* New York: Cambridge University Press, 2004.
Fenno, Richard F., Jr. *Congressmen in Committees.* Boston: Little, Brown, 1973.
———. *Going Home: Black Representatives and Their Constituents.* Chicago: University of Chicago Press, 2003.
———. *Home Style: House Members in Their Districts.* Boston: Little, Brown, 1978.
———. *The Power of the Purse: Appropriations Politics in Congress.* Boston: Little, Brown, 1966.
———. *Senators on the Campaign Trail: The Politics of Representation.* Norman: University of Oklahoma Press, 1996.
Ferejohn, John A. *Pork Barrel Politics: Rivers and Harbors Legislation, 1947–1968.* Stanford, CA: Stanford University Press, 1974.
Fiorina, Morris P. *Congress: Keystone of the Washington Establishment.* New Haven, CT: Yale University Press, 1977.
———. *Divided Government.* New York: Allyn and Bacon, 1995.
———. *Representatives, Roll Calls, and Constituencies.* Lexington, MA: Lexington Books, 1974.
Fiorina, Morris P., with Samuel J. Abrams and Jeremy C. Pope. *Culture War? The Myth of a Polarized America.* New York: Pearson/Longman, 2005.

Fiorina, Morris P., David W. Rohde, and Peter Wissel. "Historical Change in House Turnover." In *Congress in Change*. Edited by Norman J. Ornstein. New York: Praeger, 1975.

Fishel, Jeff. *Party and Opposition: Congressional Challengers in American Politics*. New York: David McKay, 1973.

Fisher, Louis. *The Constitution Between Friends: Congress, the President, and the Law*. New York: St. Martin's, 1978.

Fleisher, Richard, and Jon R. Bond. "The Shrinking Middle in the U.S. Congress." *British Journal of Political Science* 34 (2004): 429–51.

Flemming, Gregory N. "Presidential Coattails in Open-Seat Elections." *Legislative Studies Quarterly* 20 (1995): 197–211.

Fowler, Linda L. *Candidates, Congress, and American Democracy*. Ann Arbor: University of Michigan Press, 1993.

———. *Watchdogs on the Hill: The Decline of Congressional Oversight of U.S. Foreign Relations*. Princeton, NJ: Princeton University Press, 2015.

Fowler, Linda L., and Robert D. McClure. *Political Ambition: Who Decides to Run for Congress?* New Haven, CT: Yale University Press, 1989.

Fox, Harrison W., Jr., and Susan Webb Hammond. *Congressional Staffs: The Invisible Force in American Lawmaking*. New York: Free Press, 1977.

Franklin, Daniel P. *Making Ends Meet: Congressional Budgeting in the Age of Deficits*. Washington, DC: CQ Press, 1993.

Freeman, J. Leiper. *The Political Process: Executive Bureau–Legislative Committee Relations*. New York: Random House, 1955.

Friedman, Sally. *Dilemmas of Representation: Local Politics, National Factors, and the Home Styles of Modern U.S. Congress Members*. Albany: State University of New York Press, 2007.

———. "House Committee Assignments of Women and Minority Newcomers, 1965–1994." *Legislative Studies Quarterly* 21 (1996): 73–81.

Frisch, Scott A., and Sean Q. Kelly. *Committee Assignment Politics in the U.S. House of Representatives*. Norman: University of Oklahoma Press, 2006.

Froman, Lewis A., Jr. *The Congressional Process: Strategies, Rules, and Procedures*. Boston: Little, Brown, 1967.

Gamm, Gerald, and Kenneth Shepsle. "The Emergence of Legislative Institutions: Standing Committees in the House and Senate, 1810–1825." *Legislative Studies Quarterly* 14 (1989): 39–66.

Gilmour, John B. *Reconcilable Differences? Congress, the Budget Process, and the Deficit*. Berkeley: University of California Press, 1990.

Gilmour, John B., and Paul Rothstein. "A Dynamic Model of Loss, Retirement, and Tenure in the U.S. House." *Journal of Politics* 58 (1996): 54–68.

Glazer, Amihai, and Bernard Grofman. "Two Plus Two Plus Two Equals Six: Tenure of Office of Senators and Representatives, 1953–1983." *Legislative Studies Quarterly* 12 (1987): 555–63.

Goodwin, George, Jr. *The Little Legislatures: Committees of Congress*. Amherst: University of Massachusetts Press, 1970.

Green, Matthew. *Underdog Politics: The Minority Party in the U.S. House of Representatives*. New Haven, CT: Yale University Press, 2015.
Griffin, John D. "Senate Apportionment as a Source of Political Inequality." *Legislative Studies Quarterly* 31 (2006): 405–32.
Grimmer, Justin. *Representational Style in Congress: What Legislators Say and Why It Matters*. New York: Cambridge University Press, 2013.
Grose, Christian R. *Congress in Black and White: Race and Representation in Washington and at Home*. New York: Cambridge University Press, 2011.
Grose, Christian R., and Bruce I. Oppenheimer. "The Iraq War, Partisanship, and Candidate Attributes: Variation in Partisan Swing in the 2006 U.S. House Elections." *Legislative Studies Quarterly* 32 (2007): 559–95.
Groseclose, Timothy. "The Committee Outlier Debate: A Review and a Reexamination of Some of the Evidence." *Public Choice* 80 (1994): 265–73.
Groseclose, Timothy, and Keith Krehbiel. "Golden Parachutes, Rubber Checks, and Strategic Retirements from the 102nd House." *American Journal of Political Science* 38 (1994): 75–99.
Grossman, Matt. *Artists of the Possible: Governing Networks and American Policy Change Since 1945*. New York: Oxford University Press, 2014.
Hager, Gregory, and Jeffery Talbert. "Look for the Party Label: Party Influences on Voting in the U.S. House." *Legislative Studies Quarterly* 25 (2000): 75–99.
Hall, Richard L. "Participation and Purpose in Committee Decision Making." *American Political Science Review* 81 (1987): 105–27.
———. *Participation in Congress*. New Haven, CT: Yale University Press, 1993.
Hammond, Susan Webb. *Congressional Caucuses in National Policy Making*. Baltimore: Johns Hopkins University Press, 1997.
Hanson, Peter. *Too Weak to Govern: Majority Party Power and Appropriations in the U.S. Senate*. New York: Cambridge University Press, 2014.
Harbridge, Laurel. *Is Bipartisanship Dead? Policy Agreement and Agenda-Setting in the House of Representatives*. New York: Cambridge University Press, 2015.
Harris, Joseph. *Congressional Control of Administration*. Washington, DC: Brookings Institution, 1964.
Hawkesworth, Mary. "Congressional Enactments of Race-Gender: Toward a Theory of Raced-Gendered Institutions." *American Political Science Review* 97 (2003): 529–50.
Heitshusen, Valerie. "The Allocation of Federal Money to House Committee Members: Distributive Theory and Policy Jurisdictions." *American Politics Research* (formerly *American Politics Quarterly*) 29 (2001): 80–98.
———. "Interest Group Lobbying and U.S. House Decentralization: Linking Information Type to Committee Hearing Appearances." *Political Research Quarterly* 53 (2000): 151–76.
Heitshusen, Valerie, and Garry Young. "Macropolitics and Changes in the U.S. Code: Testing Competing Theories of Policy Production, 1874–1946." In *The Macropolitics of Congress*. Edited by E. Scott Adler and John S. Lapinski, 129–50. Princeton, NJ: Princeton University Press, 2006.

Henry, Charles P. "Legitimizing Race in Congressional Politics." *American Politics Quarterly* 5 (1977): 149–76.
Hero, Rodney E., and Robert R. Preuhs. *Black–Latino Relations in U.S. National Politics: Beyond Conflict and Cooperation.* New York: Cambridge University Press, 2013.
Herrnson, Paul S. *Congressional Elections: Campaigning at Home and in Washington.* 5th ed. Washington, DC: CQ Press, 2008.
———. *Party Campaigning in the 1980s.* Cambridge, MA: Harvard University Press, 1988.
Hershey, Marjorie R. *The Making of Campaign Strategy.* Lexington, MA: Lexington Books, 1974.
Hibbing, John R. *Congressional Careers: Contours of Life in the U.S. House of Representatives.* Chapel Hill: University of North Carolina Press, 1991.
Hibbing, John R., and Elizabeth Theiss-Morse. *Congress as Public Enemy: Public Attitudes Toward American Political Institutions.* New York: Cambridge University Press, 1995.
Hill, Kim Quaile, Soren Jordan, and Patricia A. Hurley. *Representation in Congress: A Unified Theory.* New York: Cambridge University Press, 2015.
Hinckley, Barbara. *The Seniority System in Congress.* Bloomington: Indiana University Press, 1971.
Hoadly, John F. "The Emergence of Political Parties in Congress, 1789–1803." *American Political Science Review* 74 (1980): 757–79.
Holtzman, Abraham. *Legislative Liaison: Executive Leadership in Congress.* Chicago: Rand McNally, 1970.
Howell, William, and Douglas L. Kriner. "Congress, the President, and Iraq War's Domestic Political Front." In *Congress Reconsidered.* 9th ed. Edited by Lawrence C. Dodd and Bruce I. Oppenheimer, 311–36. Washington, DC: CQ Press, 2009.
Howell, William G., and Jon C. Pevehouse. *While Dangers Gather: Congressional Checks on Presidential War Powers.* Princeton, NJ: Princeton University Press, 2007.
Huitt, Ralph K., and Robert L. Peabody. *Congress: Two Decades of Analysis.* New York: Harper, 1969.
Huntington, Samuel P. "Congressional Responses to the Twentieth Century." In *The Congress and America's Future.* 2nd ed. Edited by David B. Truman, 6–38. Englewood Cliffs, NJ: Prentice Hall, 1973.
Hurley, Patricia, and Kim Quaile Hill. "Beyond the Demand-Input Model: A Theory of Representational Linkages." *Journal of Politics* 65 (2003): 304–26.
———. "The Prospects for Issue-Voting in Contemporary Congressional Elections." *American Politics Quarterly* 8 (1980): 425–48.
Hurwitz, Mark S., Roger J. Moiles, and David W. Rohde. "Distributive and Partisan Issues in Agriculture Policy in the 104th House." *American Political Science Review* 95 (2001): 911–22.
Jackson, John. *Constituencies and Leaders in Congress: Their Effects on Senate Voting Behavior.* Cambridge, MA: Harvard University Press, 1974.

Jacobson, Gary C. *The Electoral Origins of Divided Government: Competition in U.S. House Elections, 1946–1988.* Boulder, CO: Westview Press, 1990.

———. "The Marginals Never Vanished: Incumbency and Competition in Elections to the U.S. House of Representatives, 1952–81." *American Journal of Political Science* 31 (1987): 126–41.

———. *Money in Congressional Elections.* New Haven, CT: Yale University Press, 1980.

———. *The Politics of Congressional Elections.* 8th ed. Boston: Pearson, 2013.

Jacobson, Gary C., and Samuel Kernell. *Strategy and Choice in Congressional Elections.* New Haven, CT: Yale University Press, 1983.

Jenkins, Jeffery A., and Eric M. Patashnik. *Congress and Policy Making in the 21st Century.* New York: Cambridge University Press, 2016.

Jewell, Malcolm E. *Senatorial Politics and Foreign Policy.* Lexington: University Press of Kentucky, 1962.

Jewell, Malcolm E., and Samuel C. Patterson. *The Legislative Process in the United States.* 3rd ed. New York: Random House, 1977.

Jillson, Calvin, and Rick K. Wilson. *Congressional Dynamics: Structure, Coordination, and Choice in the First American Congress, 1774–1789.* Stanford, CA: Stanford University Press, 1994.

Jochim, Ashley E., and Bryan D. Jones. "Issue Politics in a Polarized Congress." *Political Research Quarterly* 66 (2013): 352–69.

Johnson, Gbemende, Bruce I. Oppenheimer, and Jennifer L. Selin. "The House as a Stepping Stone to the Senate: Why Do So Few African American House Members Run?" *American Journal of Political Science* 56 (2012): 387–99.

Jones, Bryan D., Frank R. Baumgartner, and Jeffrey C. Talbert. "The Destruction of Issue Monopolies in Congress." *American Political Science Review* 87 (1993): 657–71.

Jones, Bryan D., Frank R. Baumgartner, and James L. True. "Policy Punctuations: U.S. Budget Authority, 1947–1995." *Journal of Politics* 60 (1998): 1–33.

Jones, Bryan D., and Walter Williams. *The Politics of Bad Ideas: The Great Tax Cut Delusion and the Decline of Good Government in America.* New York: Pearson Longman, 2008.

Jones, Charles O. *The Minority Party in Congress.* Boston: Little, Brown, 1970.

———. "Will Reform Change Congress?" In *Congress Reconsidered.* 1st ed. Edited by Lawrence C. Dodd and Bruce I. Oppenheimer. New York: Praeger, 1977.

Jones, David R., and Monika L. McDermott. "The Responsible Party Government Model in House and Senate Elections." *American Journal of Political Science* 24 (2004): 1–12.

Joyce, Philip G. *The Congressional Budget Office: Honest Numbers, Power, and Policymaking.* Washington, DC: Georgetown University Press, 2011.

Kahn, Kim Fridkin, and Patrick J. Kenney. *The Spectacle of U.S. Senate Campaigns.* Princeton, NJ: Princeton University Press, 1999.

Katz, Jonathan, and Brian Sala. "Careerism, Committee Assignments, and the Electoral Connection." *American Political Science Review* 90 (1996): 21–33.

Kazee, Thomas, ed. *Who Runs for Congress? Ambition, Context, and Candidate Emergence.* Washington, DC: CQ Press, 1994.

Kelly, Sean Q. "Democratic Leadership in the Modern Senate: The Emerging Roles of the Democratic Policy Committee." *Congress and the Presidency* 22 (1995): 113–40.

Kiewiet, Roderick, and Mathew D. McCubbins. *The Spending Power.* Berkeley: University of California Press, 1991.

King, David C. *Turf Wars: How Congressional Committees Claim Jurisdiction.* Chicago: University of Chicago Press, 1997.

Kingdon, John W. *Candidates for Office: Beliefs and Strategies.* New York: Random House, 1968.

———. *Congressmen's Voting Decisions.* New York: Harper, 1973.

Koger, Gregory. *Filibustering: A Political History of Obstruction in the House and Senate.* Chicago: University of Chicago Press, 2010.

Krasno, Jonathan S. *Challengers, Competition, and Reelection: Comparing Senate and House Elections.* New Haven, CT: Yale University Press, 1994.

Krehbiel, Keith. "Are Congressional Committees Composed of Preference Outliers?" *American Political Science Review* 84 (1990): 149–64.

———. *Information and Legislative Organization.* Ann Arbor: University of Michigan Press, 1990.

———. *Pivotal Politics: A Theory of U.S. Lawmaking.* Chicago: University of Chicago Press, 1998.

Krehbiel, Keith, Kenneth A. Shepsle, and Barry R. Weingast. "Why Are Congressional Committees Powerful?" *American Political Science Review* 81 (1987): 929–45.

Kriner, Douglas L., and Francis X. Shen. "Iraq Casualties and the 2006 Senate Elections." *Legislative Studies Quarterly* 32 (2007): 507–30.

Kriner, Douglas, and Graham Wilson. "The Elasticity of Reality and British Support for the War in Afghanistan." *British Journal of Politics and International Relations* (forthcoming, 2016).

Krutz, Glen S. *Hitching a Ride: Omnibus Legislating in the U.S. Congress.* Columbus: Ohio State University Press, 2001.

Kuklinski, James H. "District Competitiveness and Legislative Roll Call Behavior: A Reassessment of the Marginality Hypothesis." *American Journal of Political Science* 21 (1977): 627–38.

Lapinski, James S. *The Substance of Representation: Congress, American Political Development, and Lawmaking.* Princeton, NJ: Princeton University Press, 2013.

Lau, Richard R., and Gerald M. Pomper. "Effectiveness of Negative Campaigning in U.S. Senate Elections." *American Journal of Political Science* 46 (2002): 47–66.

Lawless, Jennifer, and Richard Fox. *It Takes a Candidate: Why Women Don't Run for Office.* New York: Cambridge University Press, 2005.

Lawrence, Eric D., Forrest Maltzman, and Paul J. Wahlbeck. "The Politics of Speaker Cannon's Committee Assignments." *American Journal of Political Science* 45 (2001): 551–62.

Lebo, Matthew J., Adam J. McGlynn, and Gregory Koger. "Strategic Party Government: Party Influence in Congress, 1789–2000." *American Journal of Political Science* 51 (2007): 464–81.

———. *Beyond Ideology: Politics, Principles, and Partisanship in the U.S. Senate.* Chicago: University of Chicago Press, 2009.

Lee, Frances E. "Senate Representation and Coalition Building in Distributive Politics." *American Political Science Review* 94 (2000): 50–72.

Lee, Frances E., and Bruce I. Oppenheimer. *Sizing Up the Senate: The Unequal Consequences of Equal Representation.* Chicago: University of Chicago Press, 1999.

LeLoup, Lance T., and Steven Shull. "Congress Versus the Executive: The 'Two Presidencies' Reconsidered." *Social Science Quarterly* 59 (1979): 704–19.

Lindsay, James M. *Congress and the Politics of U.S. Foreign Policy.* Baltimore: Johns Hopkins University Press, 1994.

Lipinski, Daniel. *Congressional Communication: Content & Consequences.* Ann Arbor: University of Michigan Press, 2004.

Loewenberg, Gerhard, and Samuel Patterson. *Comparing Legislatures.* Boston: Little, Brown, 1979.

Longley, Lawrence D., and Walter J. Oleszek. *Bicameral Politics: Conference Committees in Congress.* New Haven, CT: Yale University Press, 1989.

Loomis, Burdett A. *The New American Politician: Ambition, Entrepreneurship, and the Changing Face of Political Life.* New York: Basic Books, 1988.

———, ed. *Esteemed Colleagues: Civility and Deliberation in the U.S. Senate.* Washington, DC: Brookings Institution Press, 2000.

———, ed. *The U.S. Senate: From Deliberation to Dysfunction.* Washington, DC: CQ Press, 2012.

Lowi, Theodore J. *The End of Liberalism: Ideology, Policy, and the Crisis of Public Authority.* New York: Norton, 1969.

———. *The End of the Republican Era.* Norman: University of Oklahoma Press, 1995.

Maass, Arthur. *Congress and the Common Good.* New York: Basic Books, 1983.

Maisel, Louis S. *From Obscurity to Oblivion: Running in the Congressional Primary.* Knoxville: University of Tennessee Press, 1982.

Malbin, Michael. *Life After Reform: When the Bipartisan Campaign Reform Act Meets Politics.* Lanham, MD: Rowman and Littlefield, 2003.

Maltzman, Forrest. "Meeting Competing Demands: Committee Performance in the Post-Reform House." *American Journal of Political Science* 39 (1995): 653–82.

Manley, John F. *The Politics of Finance: The House Committee on Ways and Means.* Boston: Little, Brown, 1970.

Mann, Thomas E. *Unsafe at Any Margin: Interpreting Congressional Elections.* Washington, DC: American Enterprise Institute, 1978.

Mann, Thomas E., and Norman J. Ornstein. *The Broken Branch: How Congress Is Failing America and How to Get It Back on Track.* New York: Oxford University Press, 2008.

——. *It's Even Worse Than It Looks: How the American Constitutional System Collided With the New Politics of Extremism.* New York: Basic Books, 2012.

Mann, Thomas E., and Raymond E. Wolfinger. "Candidates and Parties in Congressional Elections." *American Political Science Review* 74 (1980): 616–32.

Matthews, Donald R. *U.S. Senators and Their World.* New York: Vintage Books, 1960.

Mayhew, David R. *America's Congress: Actions in the Public Sphere, James Madison Through Newt Gingrich.* New Haven, CT: Yale University Press, 2000.

——. "Congress as a Handler of Challenges: The Historical Record." *Studies in American Political Development* 29 (2015): 185–212.

——. *Congress: The Electoral Connection.* New Haven, CT: Yale University Press, 1974.

——. *Divided We Govern: Party Control, Lawmaking, and Investigations, 1946–1990.* New Haven, CT: Yale University Press, 1991.

——. *Partisan Balance: Why Political Parties Don't Kill the U.S. Constitutional System.* Princeton, NJ: Princeton University Press, 2011.

——. *Party Loyalty Among Congressmen: The Difference Between Democrats and Republicans, 1947–1962.* Cambridge, MA: Harvard University Press, 1966.

McAdams, John C., and John R. Johannes. "Congressmen, Perquisites, and Elections." *Journal of Politics* 50 (1988): 412–39.

Meernik, James. "Presidential Support in Congress: Conflict and Consensus in Foreign and Defense Policy." *Journal of Politics* 55 (1993): 569–87.

Mezey, Michael L. *Congress, the President, and Public Policy.* Boulder, CO: Westview Press, 1989.

Miller, Warren E., and Donald E. Stokes. "Constituency Influence in Congress." *American Political Science Review* 57 (1963): 45–56.

Minta, Michael D. *Oversight: Representing the Interests of Blacks and Latinos in Congress.* Princeton, NJ: Princeton University Press, 2011.

Moe, Terry M. "An Assessment of the Positive Theory of Congressional Dominance." *Legislative Studies Quarterly* 12 (1987): 475–520.

Mondak, Jeffery. "Competence, Integrity, and the Electoral Success of Congressional Incumbents." *Journal of Politics* 57 (1995): 1043–69.

Mondak, Jeffery, and Dona-Gene Mitchell, eds. *Fault Lines: Why the Republicans Lost Congress.* London: Routledge, 2008.

Monroe, Nathan, Jason M. Roberts, and David W. Rohde, eds. *Why Not Parties? Party Effects in the United States Senate.* Chicago: University of Chicago Press, 2008.

Nelson, Garrison. "Partisan Patterns of House Leadership Change, 1789–1977." *American Political Science Review* 71 (1977): 918–39.

Niemi, Richard, and Laura Winsky. "The Persistence of Partisan Redistricting Effects in Congressional Elections in the 1970s and 1980s." *Journal of Politics* 54 (1992): 563–72.

Norpoth, Helmut. "Explaining Party Cohesion in Congress: The Case of Shared Party Attributes." *American Political Science Review* 70 (1976): 1157–71.

Ogul, Morris S. *Congress Oversees the Bureaucracy: Studies in Legislative Supervision.* Pittsburgh: University of Pittsburgh Press, 1976.

Oldmixon, Elizabeth A. *Making Moral Decisions: God, Sex and the U.S. House of Representatives.* Washington, DC: Georgetown University Press, 2005.

Oleszek, Walter J. *Congressional Procedures and the Policy Process.* 7th ed. Washington, DC: CQ Press, 2007.

Oppenheimer, Bruce I. *Oil and the Congressional Process: The Limits of Symbolic Politics.* Lexington, MA: Lexington Books, 1974.

———. "The Representational Experience: The Effect of State Population on Senator–Constituency Linkages." *American Journal of Political Science* 40 (1996): 1280–99.

———. "The Rules Committee: New Arm of Leadership in a Decentralized House." In *Congress Reconsidered.* 1st ed. Edited by Lawrence C. Dodd and Bruce I. Oppenheimer. New York: Praeger, 1977.

———. "Split-Party Control of Congress, 1981–1986: Exploring Electoral and Apportionment Explanations." *American Journal of Political Science* 33 (1989): 653–69.

———, ed. *U.S. Senate Exceptionalism.* Columbus: Ohio State University Press, 2002.

Orfield, Gary. *Congressional Power: Congress and Social Change.* New York: Harcourt, 1975.

Ornstein, Norman J. *Congress in Change: Evolution and Reform.* New York: Praeger, 1975.

Ornstein, Norman J., and Shirley Elder. *Interest Groups, Lobbying, and Policymaking.* Washington, DC: CQ Press, 1978.

Ornstein, Norman J., Thomas E. Mann, and Michael J. Malbin. *Vital Statistics on Congress, 1995–1996.* Washington, DC: CQ Press, 1995.

Owens, John E. "Curbing the Fiefdoms: Party–Committee Relations in the Contemporary U.S. House of Representatives." In *The Changing Roles of Parliamentary Committees.* Edited by Lawrence D. Longley and Attila Ágh, 183–98. Appleton, WI: Research Committee of Legislative Specialists, 1997.

Parker, Glenn R. *Homeward Bound: Explaining Changes in Congressional Behavior.* Pittsburgh: University of Pittsburgh Press, 1986.

———. *Institutional Change, Discretion, and the Making of the Modern Congress: An Economic Interpretation.* Ann Arbor: University of Michigan Press, 1992.

Parker, Glenn R., and S. L. Parker. "Factions in Committees: The U.S. House of Representatives." *American Political Science Review* 73 (1979): 85–102.

Patterson, James T. *Congressional Conservatism and the New Deal: The Growth of the Conservative Coalition in Congress, 1933–1939.* Lexington: University Press of Kentucky, 1967.

Payne, James L. "The Personal Electoral Advantage of House Incumbents, 1936–1976." *American Politics Quarterly* 8 (1980): 465–82.

Peabody, Robert L. *Leadership in Congress: Stability, Succession, and Change.* Boston: Little, Brown, 1976.

Peabody, Robert L., and Nelson W. Polsby, eds. *New Perspectives on the House of Representatives*. 3rd ed. Chicago: Rand McNally, 1977.
Pearson, Kathyrn. *Party Discipline in the House of Representatives*. Ann Arbor: University of Michigan Press, 2015.
Pearson, Kathryn, and Logan Dancey, "Elevating Women's Voice in Congress: Speech Participation in the House of Representatives." *Political Research Quarterly* 64 (2011): 910–23.
Peters, Ronald M., Jr. *The American Speakership: The Office in Historical Perspective*. Baltimore: Johns Hopkins University Press, 1990.
Peters, Ronald M., Jr., and Cindy Rosenthal. *Nancy Pelosi and the New American Politics*. New York: Oxford University Press, 2010.
Peterson, Mark A. *Legislating Together: The White House and Capitol Hill From Eisenhower to Reagan*. Cambridge, MA: Harvard University Press, 1990.
Polsby, Nelson W. *Congress and the Presidency*. 3rd ed. Englewood Cliffs, NJ: Prentice Hall, 1976.
———. *How Congress Evolves: Social Bases of Institutional Change*. New York: Oxford University Press, 2004.
———. "Institutionalization in the U.S. House of Representatives." *American Political Science Review* 62 (1968): 144–68.
Polsby, Nelson W., Miriam Gallagher, and Barry Rundquist. "The Growth of the Seniority System in the House of Representatives." *American Political Science Review* 63 (1969): 787–807.
Poole, Keith T., and Howard Rosenthal. *Congress: A Political-Economic History of Roll Call Voting*. New York: Oxford University Press, 1997.
Powell, Lynda W. "Issue Representation in Congress." *Journal of Politics* 44 (1982): 658–78.
Price, David E. *The Congressional Experience: A View From the Hill*. Boulder, CO: Westview Press, 2000.
———. *Who Makes the Laws? Creativity and Power in Senate Committees*. Cambridge, MA: Schenkman, 1972.
Price, H. Douglas. "Congress and the Evolution of Legislative 'Professionalism.'" In *Congress in Change: Evolution and Reform*. Edited by Norman J. Ornstein, 2–23. New York: Praeger, 1975.
Primo, David M., Sarah A. Binder, and Forrest Maltzman, "Who Consents? Competing Pivots in Federal Judicial Selection." *American Journal of Political Science* 52 (2008): 471–89.
Ragsdale, Lyn, and Timothy E. Cook. "Representatives' Actions and Challengers' Reactions: Limits to Candidate Connections in the House." *American Journal of Political Science* 31 (1987): 45–81.
Ragsdale, Lyn, and Jerrold G. Rusk. "Candidates, Issues, and Participation in Senate Elections." *Legislative Studies Quarterly* 20 (1995): 305–28.
Ragusa, Jordan. "The Lifecycle of Public Policy: An Event History Analysis of Repeals to Landmark Legislative Enactments, 1951–2006." *American Politics Research* 38 (2010): 1015–51.

Rieselbach, Leroy N. *Congressional Politics: The Evolving Legislative System.* 2nd ed. Boulder, CO: Westview Press, 1995.

———. *Congressional Reform: The Changing Modern Congress.* Washington, DC: CQ Press, 1994.

Ripley, Randall B., and Grace N. Franklin. *Congress, the Bureaucracy, and Public Policy.* 5th ed. Belmont, CA: Wadsworth, 1991.

Ripley, Randall B., and James M. Lindsay, eds. *Congress Resurgent: Foreign and Defense Policy on Capitol Hill.* Ann Arbor: University of Michigan Press, 1993.

Rippere, Paulina S. "Polarization Reconsidered: Bipartisan Cooperation Through Bill Cosponsorship." *Polity* 48 (2016): 243–78.

Roberts, Jason M., and Steven S. Smith. "Procedural Contexts, Party Strategy, and Conditional Party Voting in the U.S. House of Representatives, 1971–2000." *American Journal of Political Science* 47 (2003): 305–17.

Rohde, David W. *Parties and Leaders in the Postreform House.* Chicago: University of Chicago Press, 1991.

Rohde, David W., and Kenneth A. Shepsle. "Democratic Committee Assignments in the U.S. House of Representatives." *American Political Science Review* 67 (1973): 889–905.

Rothman, David J. *Politics and Power: The United States Senate, 1869–1901.* New York: Athenaeum, 1969.

Rudder, Catherine E. "Committee Reform and the Revenue Process." In *Congress Reconsidered.* 1st ed. Edited by Lawrence C. Dodd and Bruce I. Oppenheimer, 117–39. New York: Praeger, 1977.

Schick, Allen. *Making Economic Policy in Congress.* Washington, DC: American Enterprise Institute, 1983.

Schickler, Eric. *Disjointed Pluralism: Institutional Innovation and the Development of the U.S. Congress.* Princeton, NJ: Princeton University Press, 2001.

———. "Institutional Change in the House of Representatives, 1867–1998: A Test of Partisan and Ideological Power Balance Models." *American Political Science Review* 94 (2000): 269–88.

Schickler, Eric, and Kathryn Pearson. "Agenda Control, Majority Party Power, and the House Committee on Rules, 1937–65." *Legislative Studies Quarterly* 34 (2009): 455–91.

Schickler, Eric, and Andrew Rich. "Party Government in the House Reconsidered: A Response to Cox and McCubbins." *American Journal of Political Science* 41 (1997): 1387–94.

Schiller, Wendy J. *Partners and Rivals: Representation in U.S. Senate Delegations.* Princeton, NJ: Princeton University Press, 2000.

———. "Senators as Political Entrepreneurs: Using Bill Sponsorship to Shape Legislative Agendas." *American Journal of Political Science* 39 (1995): 186–203.

Schneider, Jerrold E. *Ideological Coalitions in Congress.* Greenwood, CT: Greenwood Press, 1979.

Schraufnagel, Scot. "Testing the Implications of Incivility in the United States Congress, 1977–2000: The Case of Judicial Confirmation Delay." *Journal of Legislative Studies* 11 (2005): 216–34.

Seidman, Harold. *Politics, Position, and Power: The Dynamics of Federal Organization*. 2nd ed. New York: Oxford University Press, 1975.

Sellers, Patrick J. "Winning Media Coverage in the U.S. Congress." In *U.S. Senate Exceptionalism*. Edited by Bruce I. Oppenheimer, 132–56. Columbus: Ohio State University Press, 2002.

Shepsle, Kenneth A. "The Changing Textbook Congress: Equilibrium in Congressional Institutions and Behavior." In *American Political Institutions and the Problems of Our Time*. Edited by John E. Chubb and Paul E. Peterson, 238–66. Washington, DC: Brookings Institution, 1990.

———. *The Giant Jigsaw Puzzle: Democratic Committee Assignments in the Modern House*. Chicago: University of Chicago Press, 1978.

Shepsle, Kenneth A., Robert P. Van Houweling, Samuel J. Abrams, and Peter C. Hanson. "The Senate Electoral Cycle and Bicameral Appropriations Politics." *American Journal of Political Science* 53 (2009): 343–59.

Shepsle, Kenneth A., and Barry R. Weingast, eds. *Positive Theories of Congressional Institutions*. Ann Arbor: University of Michigan Press, 1995.

Shipan, Charles R. "Regulatory Regimes, Agency Actions, and the Conditional Nature of Congressional Influence." *American Political Science Review* 98 (2003): 467–80.

Sinclair, Barbara. *Legislators, Leaders, and Lawmaking: The U.S. House of Representatives in the Postreform Era*. Baltimore: Johns Hopkins University Press, 1995.

———. *Majority Leadership in the U.S. House*. Baltimore: Johns Hopkins University Press, 1983.

———. *Party Wars: Polarization and the Politics of National Policy Making*. Norman: University of Oklahoma Press, 2006.

———. *The Transformation of the U.S. Senate*. Baltimore: Johns Hopkins University Press, 1989.

———. *Unorthodox Lawmaking: New Legislative Processes in the U.S. Congress*. 5th ed. Washington, DC: CQ Press, 2016.

Skocpol, Theda, and Vanessa Williamson. *The Tea Party and the Remaking of Republican Conservatism*. New York: Oxford University Press, 2012.

Smith, Steven S. *Call to Order: Floor Politics in the House and Senate*. Washington, DC: Brookings Institution, 1989.

———. *Party Influence in Congress*. New York: Cambridge University Press, 2007.

———. *The Senate Syndrome: The Evolution of Procedural Warfare in the Modern U.S. Senate*. Norman, OK: University of Oklahoma Press, 2014.

Smith, Steven S., Jason M. Roberts, and Ryan J. Vander Wielen, eds. *The American Congress*. 9th ed. New York: Cambridge University Press, 2015.

Snyder, James, and Tim Groseclose. "Estimating Party Influence in Congressional Roll-Call Voting." *American Journal of Political Science* 44 (2000): 193–211.

Squire, Peverill. *The Evolution of American Legislatures: Colonies, Territories, and States, 1619–2009*. Ann Arbor: University of Michigan Press, 2012.

Stein, Robert M., and Kenneth N. Bickers. *Perpetuating the Pork: Policy Subsystems and American Democracy*. New York: Cambridge University Press, 1995.

Stewart, Charles, III. *Analyzing Congress*. 2nd ed. New York: W. W. Norton, 2012.
Stimson, James A., Michael B. MacKuen, and Robert S. Erikson. "Dynamic Representation." *American Political Science Review* 89 (1995): 543–65.
Stockman, David Alan. *The Triumph of Politics: How the Reagan Revolution Failed*. New York: Harper and Row, 1986.
Strahan, Randall. *Leading Representatives: The Agency of Leaders in the Politics of the U.S. House*. Baltimore: Johns Hopkins University Press, 2007.
———. *New Ways and Means: Reform and Change in a Congressional Committee*. Chapel Hill: University of North Carolina Press, 1990.
Sulkin, Tracy. *Issue Politics in Congress*. New York: Cambridge University Press, 2005.
Sundquist, James L. *The Decline and Resurgence of Congress*. Washington, DC: Brookings Institution, 1981.
———. *Politics and Policy: The Eisenhower, Kennedy, and Johnson Years*. Washington, DC: Brookings Institution, 1968.
Swain, Carol M. *Black Faces, Black Interests: The Representation of African Americans in Congress*. Cambridge, MA: Harvard University Press, 1993.
Swift, Elaine K. *The Making of an American Senate: Reconstitutive Change in Congress, 1787–1841*. Ann Arbor: University of Michigan Press, 1996.
Talbert, Jeffrey, Bryan D. Jones, and Frank R. Baumgartner. "Nonlegislative Hearings and Policy Change in Congress." *American Journal of Political Science* 39 (1995): 383–405.
Tate, Katherine. *Black Faces in the Mirror: African Americans and Their Representatives in the U.S. Congress*. Princeton, NJ: Princeton University Press, 2003.
Theriault, Sean. *Party Polarization in Congress*. New York: Cambridge University Press, 2008.
———. *The Power of the People: Congressional Competition, Public Attention, and Voter Retribution*. Columbus: Ohio State University Press. 2005.
Theriault, Sean M., and David Rohde. "The Gingrich Senators and Party Polarization in the U.S. Senate." *Journal of Politics* 73 (2011): 1011–24.
Thomas, Sue. *How Women Legislate*. New York: Oxford University Press, 1994.
Thurber, James A., ed. *Rivals for Power: Presidential–Congressional Relations*. Washington, DC: CQ Press, 1996.
Thurber, James A., and Roger H. Davidson. *Remaking Congress: Change and Stability in the 1990s*. Washington, DC: CQ Press, 1995.
Truman, David B. *The Governmental Process: Political Interests and Public Opinion*. New York: Knopf, 1951.
Turner, Julius. *Party and Constituency: Pressures on Congress*. Rev. ed. by Edward V. Schneier Jr. Baltimore: Johns Hopkins University Press, 1970.
Unekis, Joseph, and Leroy N. Rieselbach. *Congressional Committee Politics: Continuity and Change*. New York: Praeger, 1984.
Uslaner, Eric M. *The Decline of Comity in Congress*. Ann Arbor: University of Michigan Press, 1993.
Valelly, Richard M. "The Reed Rules and Republican Party Building: A New Look." *Studies in American Political Development* 23 (2009): 115–42.

Vogler, David J. *The Politics of Congress.* 6th ed. Madison, WI: Brown and Benchmark, 1993.
———. *The Third House: Conference Committees in the United States Congress.* Evanston, IL: Northwestern University Press, 1971.
Volden, Craig, and Alan E. Wiseman. *Legislative Effectiveness in the United States Congress: The Lawmakers.* New York: Cambridge University Press, 2014.
Wahlke, John C., Heinz H. Eulau, W. Buchanan, and L. C. Ferguson. *The Legislative System: Explorations in Legislative Behavior.* New York: Wiley, 1962.
Wawro, Gregory. *Legislative Entrepreneurship in the U.S. House of Representatives.* Ann Arbor: University of Michigan Press, 2000.
Wawro, Gregory J., and Eric Schickler. *Filibuster: Obstruction and Lawmaking in the U.S. Senate.* Princeton, NJ: Princeton University Press, 2006.
Wayne, S. J. *The Legislative Presidency.* New York: Harper, 1978.
Weingast, Barry. "Floor Behavior in the U.S. Congress: Committee Power Under the Open Rule." *American Political Science Review* 83 (1989): 795–815.
Weisberg, Herbert F. "Evaluating Theories of Congressional Roll Call Voting." *American Journal of Political Science* 22 (1978): 554–77.
Weisberg, Herbert F., Eric S. Heberlig, and Lisa M. Campoli. *Classics in Congressional Politics.* New York: Longman, 1999.
Westefield, L. P. "Majority Party Leadership and the Committee System in the House of Representatives." *American Political Science Review* 68 (1974): 1593–1604.
Wildavsky, Aaron. *The Politics of the Budgetary Process.* Boston: Little, Brown, 1964.
Wilson, Rick. "Forward and Backward Agenda Procedures: Committee Experience and Structurally Induced Equilibrium." *Journal of Politics* 48 (1986): 390–409.
Wilson, Woodrow. *Congressional Government: A Study in American Politics.* 1885. Reprint, Gloucester, MA: Peter Smith, 1973.
Wolfensberger, Donald R. *Congress and the People: Deliberative Democracy on Trial.* Baltimore: Johns Hopkins University Press, 2000.
Wolfinger, Raymond E., and Joan Heifetz Hollinger. "Safe Seats, Seniority, and Power in Congress." *American Political Science Review* 59 (1965): 337–49.
Wright, Fiona A. "The Caucus Reelection Requirement and the Transformation of House Committee Chairs, 1959–94." *Legislative Studies Quarterly* 25 (2000): 469–80.
Wright, Gerald C., and Michael B. Berkman. "Candidates and Policy in United States Senate Elections." *American Political Science Review* 80 (1986): 567–88.
Wright, Gerald C., Leroy Rieselbach, and Lawrence C. Dodd, eds. *Congress and Policy Change.* New York: Agathon, 1986.
Wright, John. "PACs, Contributions, and Roll Calls: An Organizational Perspective." *American Political Science Review* 75 (1985): 400–14.
Yoshinaka, Antoine. *Crossing the Aisle: Party Switching by U.S. Legislators in the Postwar Era.* New York: Cambridge University Press, 2015.

Young, Garry. "Committee Gatekeeping and Proposal Power Under Single and Multiple Referral." *Journal of Theoretical Politics* 8 (1996): 65–78.

Young, James S. *The Washington Community, 1800–1828.* New York: Columbia University Press, 1966.

Zelizer, Julian E. *On Capitol Hill: The Struggle to Reform Congress and Its Consequences, 1948–2000.* New York: Cambridge University Press, 2004.

Index

✧ ✧ ✧

501(c) organizations. *See* super PACs
527 organizations. *See* super PACs
2008 economic crisis, 40

Adler, E. Scott, 243, 260, 262, 289
Administrative system, and the balance of power, 370–375, 380–382
Advice and consent
  politics of, 406–410
  tensions, 411–417
  trends in, 410–411
Affordable Care Act (ACA)
  history of, 238–239
  key provisions, 239–241
  postenactment history, 241–243, 468
  repeal votes, 244–249
  research on, 249–252
Afghan War, 425–441
Aggregation of votes, 94 (figure), 94–97, 95 (figure), 96 (figure), 97 (figure)
  forms of, 97 (figure)
Alaska National Interest Lands Conservation Act (ANILCA), 337
Alaska Native Claims Settlement (1971), 336
Albert, Carl, 178, 334
Aldrich, Nelson W., 172–177
Alexander, Lamar, 6
Allison, William Boyd, 172–177
Alt-right, 452, 471
Amendments, Senate floor, 9
American Action Network, 104
American Bar Association (ABA), 411
American Political Science Association, 190, 201
American Society for the Study of Comparative Legislation, 190
ANWR (the Arctic National Wildlife Refuge)
  overview, 331–332
  initial enactment, 334–336
  legislative struggle, 336–337

Appropriations. *See* House appropriations
Arnold, Douglas, 333
Assad, Bashar al-, 441–442
Attrition filibusters, 313–314
Ayotte, Kelly, 317, 458

Bachmann, Michele, 249
Balancing thesis, 67–68
Bannon, Stephen K., 452, 469
Barden, Graham, 261
Baucus, Max, 16
Bayh, Evan, 459
Belief-sharing representation, 120, 124–125
"Big bang theory" of judicial selection, 401
Binder, Sarah, 209
  See also Stalemate (Binder)
Bipartisan Campaign Reform Act (BCRA) (2002), 102–103
Birkhead, Nate, 243
Black–Latino relations
  in the context of federalism, 155–157
  institutional factors, 140–141
Blunt, Roy, 417
Boehner, John, 41–47, 47
  leadership of, 180–181
  passage of the ACA, 242
  resignation, 49–50, 163–164
Bork, Robert, 401–402
Breaux, John, 343
Breitbart News, 452
Brennan, John, 322
Brown, Scott, 239
Brown Jr, Clarence "Bud," 335
Brown v. Board of Education, 31, 401
Bryan, Richard, 339
Budget Act (1974), 166–167
Budget Control Act (2011), 203
Budget Enforcement Act (BEA) (1990), 333

499

Budget process
　See also Balanced Budget and Emergency Deficit Control Act; Budget Control Act; Budget Enforcement Act (BEA); Congressional Budget and Impoundment Control Act (CBICA); Debt ceiling; Deficits; Fiscal cliff; Omnibus Budget; Reconciliation Act
Bureau of the Budget (BB), 371
Burns, James MacGregor, 209
Bush, George W.
　ANWR (the Arctic National Wildlife Refuge), 341
　judicial nominations, 8–9, 403–404
Byrd rule, 21

Cadillac tax, 239, 241, 253
CAFE (Corporate Average Fuel Economy) standards
　overview, 331–332
　initial enactment, 334–336
　legislative struggle, 337–347
　support for, 347–350
Campaign spending, 98 (figure), 98–100, 99 (figure), 103–104
Candidate-centered electoral politics, 108–111, 109t, 110f
Cannon, Joseph, 169–171
Cantor, Eric, 46, 275
Ceteris paribus, 209
Chaffetz, Jason, 49
Chairman's mark, 5
Chamberlain, Lawrence, 191
Citizens United v. Federal Election Commission, 103
Civil Rights Act (1964), Title VII, 373
Cleveland, Grover, 167
Clinton, Bill, judicial selection, 8
Clinton, Hillary
　email controversy, 454–455
　nomination for presidency, 451–452
　presidential campaign, 452–453
Cloture rule
　about, 7, 18–19
　Estrada vote, 9
　filibusters and, 7, 311
　history of, 312
　increases in, 8 (table)
　and the 115th Congress (2017-2019), 474
Coburn, Tom, 14
Comey, James, 454–456
Committee government
　House era, 30–32
　Senate pre-floor process, 5
Competitive campaigns, 106 (figure), 106–108, 107 (figure)
Conditional party government (CPG), 33–35, 52–54, 166, 286, 289
Congressional Digest, 210–211
Congressional elections
　2016 results, 457–461
　and representation, 78–81, 80 (figure)
Congressional ideology, 75, 78 (figure)
Conservative populism, 452–453
Constituencies
　ideological divergence of, 97, 97 (figure)
　polarization of, 96 (figure)
Continuing resolution (CR), 50
Contract With America, 37, 178
Cooper, Joseph, 191, 209
Cooperation
　legislative breakdown without, 24–26
　majority's and minority's need for, 14–15
Cooperative Congressional Election Study (CCES), 79, 81 (table)
Cornyn, John, 405, 417
Corwin, Edward, 421
CR (continuing resolution), 50
Cruz, Ted, 164
"Czars" of the House, 170–171

Daschle, Tom, 182, 343
Deadlock. *See* legislative deadlock, 199–202, 202
Decision-making structure, 359–361
DeLay, Tom, 179, 341
DeMint, Jim, 241
Democratic Study Group (DSG), 31
Depolarization, 207
Depolarized Congresses, 213–214
Dingell, John, 335

District partisanship, 69–70
Diversity of Senate, 5
Divided government, effect on policy productivity, 218, 221
Divided We Govern (Mayhew 1991), 191–193, 216–217
D'mato, Alfonse, 8
Dole, Bob, 183
Domenici, Pete, 344
Durbin, Richard, 342

Economic crisis, effect on policy productivity, 218, 221
Economic crisis (2008), 40
84th Congress (1955-1957), midterm elections, 30
Elections
    midterm elections, 66–68
    national forces in, 61–81
    and policy mood, 65–66
    presidential elections, 66
    results, 81–82, 457–461
Electoral competition, structure of, 203–204
Electoral system, 360, 364–366, 375–377
Electorate, influence, 68
Elite cues, 423–424
Elite-led model, 125
Energy Independence and Security Act (EISA) (2007), 349
Enzi, Mike, 6
Epstein, Lee, 402
Estrada vote, 9
Executive branch, decision making in, 360
Executive Office of the President (EOP), 371
Executive war powers, 421
Exxon Valdez spill, 340

Farm Bill, 273–276
Federal Election Campaign Act (FECA) (1974), 99–100, 102–103
Federal judges. *See* judicial nominations
Fenno, Richard, 287–288
Filibusters
    2013 reform, 321–325
    cloture and, 7. *see also* Cloture rule
    effect of, 318–320
    failure of measures by, 23 (table)
    history of, 312–317
    increases in, 4, 8 (table), 11 (table)
    visible filibusters, 12
"Filling the amendment tree," 19–20
Fiorina, Morris, 204
Fiscal cliff, 42–43, 43–44
501(c) organizations. *See* super PACs
527 organizations. *See* super PACs
Fixing America's Surface Transportation (FAST) Act (2015), 277
Floor schedules in Senate, 12
Flynn, Michael, 469
Foley, Thomas S., 178
Foreign Relations Committee, 370
Framers, intentions of, 360, 362
Franken, Al, 18
Freedom Caucus, 458
Frist, Bill, 6, 183
Full repeals, 244

Garland, Merrick, 417–418
Gay, Claudine, 139
Gelman-King index, 108
Gender gap in Congress, 462–463
Gerrymandering, 106
Gingrich, Newt, 35–38, 178–179, 272, 286, 289
Goodnow, Frank, 190
Gorton, Slade, 339
Government type
    all divided governments, 225
    effect on policy productivity, 224–231
    pure divided governments, 225–228
    quasi-divided governments, 225
Graham, Lindsey, 413–414
Gravel, Mike, 337
Great Recession, 40
Great Society Congress, 31–32
Green Party, 452
Gridlock interval. *See* legislative deadlock
Griffin, Robert, 335

Hagel, Charles, 322
Hale, Eugene, 172
Halligan, Caitlin, 322
Hamilton, David, 405

Hard money, 103
    See also campaign spending
Harkin, Tom, 6
Hart, Philip, 335
Hastert, Dennis, 38–39, 179
Hastert rule, 38–39, 44
Health care reform, 238
    See also Affordable Care Act (ACA)
Hensarling, Jeb, 14
Hold system, 11, 13–14, 316–317
Homeland Security, funding, 48
Honda, Mike, 458
Honeymoons, presidential, effect on policy productivity, 218, 221
House appropriations
    overview, 285–287
    debate, 293–305
    funding, 182
    history of, 287–290
    nonpartisanship in, 302–305
    voting patterns, 290–293
House Freedom Caucus (HFC), 47–52
House of Representatives
    actions, 31
    Appropriations Committee, 39, 286. *see also* House appropriations
    campaign spending, 98 (figure)
    conservative coalition, 32
    "czars" of the House, 170–171
    Democrats' majority, 62–63, 63 (figure)
    elections, 61–81
    ideological representation, 74–78, 77 (table), 78 (figure)
    incumbents, 69–74, 72 (figure)
    legislative effectiveness in, 259–281
    majority party, 166
    postreform House, 178
    problem solving in, 259–281
    reform era, 32–33
    roll call votes, 32
    rules, 30–32
    Rules Committee, 36–37, 297
    special rules, 293
    strategic retirements, 70–71
    See also Speaker of the House
Huelskamp, Tim, 458

Ideological balancing, 67–68
Ideological representation, 74–78, 77 (table), 78 (figure)
Incumbents
    House of Representatives, 69–74, 72 (figure)
    success rate of, 457–461
Independent Payment Advisory Board (IPAB), 240
Independent spending, 103–106, 104 (figure)
Individualism and partisanship, 2–5
Institutional reforms, 272–273, 278–280
Instructed-delegate representation, 120, 124–125
Intermodal Surface Transportation Efficiency Act (ISTEA) (1991), 276–278

Johnson, Gary, 452
Johnson, Lyndon, 31, 313–314
Jolly, David, 458
Jordan, Jim, 48
Jordan, Soren, 130
Judicial nominations
    advice and consent, 406–417
    Bush nominees, 8–9, 403–404
    crisis in, 401–402
    ideological forces, 407–408
    institutional forces, 408–410
    Obama nominees, 9, 405–406
    patterns in, 402–406
    temporal forces, 410
Judiciary, impact of, 400

Keenan, Barbara, 405
Kennedy, Edward, 239
Kennedy, John F., 127, 443
Kernel, Samuel, 380
Kerry, John, 437, 441
Key, V. O., 191
Khanna, Ro, 458
Killer amendments, 10
    See also judicial nominations
Kirk, Paul, 458
Koger, Gregory, 415
Krehbiel, Keith, 192, 201

Labrador, Raul, 48
Lame-duck sessions, 313
Lawmaking, study of, 190–194
Leadership, dynamics of, 163–185
Leadership PACs, 100
Leahy, Patrick, 408, 415
Lee, Frances, 201, 203
Legislative deadlock, 199–202, 202
   gridlock interval, 192
Legislative effectiveness
   in the House of Representatives, 259–261
   perspectives on, 261–263
   research on, 263–280
Legislative performance
   measurement of, 194–199, 203
   See also policy productivity
Legislative power, 360
Legislative revision, research on, 243–244
Legislative system, and the balance of power, 362–363, 366–370, 377–380
Lewis, John, 249
Libertarian Party, 452
Lieberman, Joe, 239
Lodge, Henry Cabot, 172
The Logic of Congressional Action (Arnold), 333
Lott, Trent, 20, 183, 304
Lowi, Theodore, 140
Lugar, Richard, 405

Macropartisanship, 63–68, 64 (figure)
Macropolitics, 191
Macrostructures, and micromotivation, 358–359
Madison, James, 285
Major governing party, 229
Majority leadership of Senate, 7–15
Manley, John, 261
Mann, Thomas, 189
Mansfield, Mike, 313–314
Markey, Ed, 249, 343–344
Matthews, Donald, 313
Mayhew, David, 189, 201
   Divided We Govern (1991), 191–193, 216–217
McCain, John, 10, 406
McCarthy, Kevin, 46

McChrystal, Stanley, 437
McConnell, John, 405
McConnell, Mitch
   and filibusters, 7
   and judicial nominees, 399, 403, 410, 414
   leadership, 164, 184–185
   and partisan opposition, 16, 20
   partisan opposition, 320
   passage of the ACA, 241
   role in 115th Congress, 469
McMillan, James, 172
Meadows, Mark, 49
Message politics, 319
Mica, John, 458
Micromotivation, and macrostructures, 358–359
Micropolitics, 191
Midterm elections, 66–68
Military policy, 421–443
Miller, Warren, 120–121
Millett, Patricia, 322
Mills, Wilbur, 261
Minor governing party, 229
Minority groups, 140–141
Minority intergroup relations. *See* Black–Latino relations
Mitchell, George, 182, 340
Moderation thesis, 208–209
Mulvaney, Mick, 48–49
Murkowski, Frank, 343
Murray, Patty, 6

National Association for the Advancement of Colored People (NAACP), 141–153
National Election Studies, 79
National Federation of Independent Business v. Sebelius, 240
National Highway Transportation Safety Administration (NHTSA), 338
National Hispanic Leadership Agenda (NHLA), 141–153
National Security Council (NSC), 371–372
NBC Nightly News, 433–434, 439–440
New Deal Congress, 209
New York Times, 434

504 Index

Nixon, Richard M., 127
Nominations, presidential
  See also judicial nominations
Nongermane amendments, 9, 20, 24
Normal vote, 64
"Nuclear option" approach to filibuster reform, 321–325

Obama, Barack
  Afghan War, 425–441
  domestic policy, 374
  judicial nominations, 9, 405–406
  support for Clinton campaign, 455
  See also 111th Congress (2009-2010); 112th Congress (2011-2012)
Obamacare, 44–45
Oberstar, James, 277
Obey, David, 299, 437
Obstruction
  strategies, 7–14
  See also Cloture rule; Filibusters
Office of Information and Regulatory Affairs (OIRA), 372
Office of Management and Budget (OMB), 371–372
Oleszek, Walter, 317
Omnibus Budget Reconciliation Act (1990), 333
Omnibus packages, 299–300
108th Congress (2003-2004), 201, 343–345
111th Congress (2009-2010), 198, 209
  actions, 17
  hearings on Senate obstruction, 321
  partisan opposition, 17–18, 320
  passage of the ACA, 241–242
115th Congress (2017-2019)
  challenges, 472–473
  demographic composition of, 461–464
109th Congress (2005-2006), 343, 345
107th Congress (2001-2002), 198
  CAFE (Corporate Average Fuel Economy) standards, 341
106th Congress (1999-2000), 197
113th Congress (2013-2014), 43–47, 197
  2013 reform, 322–323
  efforts to repeal the ACA, 242
  See also Fiscal cliff
112th Congress (2011-2012), 197

  challenges, 41–43
  efforts to repeal the ACA, 242, 249–251
  nuclear option, 321–322
  transportation policy, 277
  See also Boehner, John; Reid, Harry
O'Neill, Thomas P. "Tip," 178, 336
OPEC (Organization of the Petroleum Exporting Countries) embargo, 331–332
Opposition. *See* polarization
Ornstein, Norman, 189

Partial repeals, 244
Participatory management, 183
Partisan opposition, judicial nominations, 407–408
Partisan realignment, 90–91, 91 (figure)
Partisan vote, 69
Partisanship, 64 (figure)
  gridlock from, 8–9, 20
  House elections, 63–68
  Senate developing, 4
Party money, 100–103, 101 (figure), 102 (figure)
Party polarization and issue complexity theory of representation, 122–126
Party size, importance of, 165, 184
Patashnik, Eric, 243
Paul, Rand, 317, 322
Pelosi, Nancy
  passage of the Affordable Care Act (ACA), 239
  role in 115th Congress, 469
  as Speaker of the House, 39–40, 180
Perkins, Carl, 261
Perks, 73
Personal vote, 69
Pivotal Politics (Krehbiel), 192–194
Pivotal politics theory, 192–194
Platt, Orville, 172
Plebiscitary politics, increases in, 366–370
Polarization
  history of, 129 (figure), 129–133, 133 (figure)
  implications for constituency representation, 127–128
  increases in, 366–370
  measurement of, 212–216

moderation thesis, 208–209
negative relationship with olicy productivity, 208
regional context, 464–468
research on, 120
subsiding of, 203
Policy Committee, 182
Policy direction, and the electorate, 68
Policy mood, impact of, 65–66
Policy productivity
  measurement of, 210–212
  moderation thesis, 208–209
  notable Congresses, 215–216
  See also legislative performance
Policy Tracker, 131–132
Political action committees (PACs), 99–103
Political elites, 423–424
Polsby, Nelson, 190–191
Pompeo, Mike, 469
Populism, 452–453
Postreform House, 178
Powell Jr, Adam Clayton, 261
Power
  and the administrative system, 370–375
  balance between Congress and the presidency, 358–385
  current balance of, 377–382
  decision-making structure, 359–361
  dilemmas, 382–385
  distribution of, 165–167
  intentions of Framers, 360, 362
  issues, 382–385
  and the legislative system, 360, 362–363, 366–370, 377–380
The Power of the Purse (Fenno 1966), 287–288
Pre-floor process in Senate, 5–7
Presidential elections, 66
  2016 results, 455–457, 468–472, 475
Presidential honeymoons, effect on policy productivity, 218, 221
Presidential power, 360
President's rating, effect on policy productivity, 218, 223
Problem solving, in the House of Representatives, 259–261
Problem-Solving Perspective
  overview, 260–263

  research on, 263–280
Protocoalitions, 380
Pryor, Mark, 9
Public opinion
  Congress's capacity to influence, 441
  presidential public appeals, 443
  support for war, 423–425

Quasi-divided government, 217, 225, 228–231

Rayburn, Sam, 30
Reagan, Ronald
  and control of Congress, 177
  increases in partisanship, 4
  public appeal, 443
Recesses, 313
Reconciliation bills, 21
Reed, Thomas Brackett, 169–171
Reed rules, 170–171
Reeves, Andrée, 261
Reform era, House of Representatives, 32–33
Regular order, 299–305
Rehnquist, William, 399
Reid, Harry
  "filling the amendment tree,," 19–20
  and judicial nominees, 414
  leadership, 183–184
  negotiations with Boehner, 180
  partisan opposition, 7, 16, 320
  passage of the Affordable Care Act (ACA), 239
Repeals, 244
Representation
  and congressional elections, 78–81, 80 (figure)
  House–Senate differences, 81–84
  models of, 123 (figure)
  party polarization and issue complexity theory of, 122–126
  research on, 120–122
Representation in Congress: A Unified Theory (Hill, Jordan and Hurley 2015), 119
Responsible-party representation, 120, 124
Roberts, John, 399
Roberts, Pat, 317

Roll call votes, 32
Romney, Mitt, 242
Roosevelt, Franklin, 209, 229, 421, 443
Roosevelt, Theodore, 367, 381, 443
Rubio, Marco, 459
Rules Committee, 36–37, 297
Ryan, Paul, 51, 181, 469

Sanders, Bernie, 128, 451
Scalia, Antonin, 399
Schattschneider, E. E., 209
Schickler, Eric, 170
Schumer, Chuck, 14, 15, 469
Segal, Jeffrey, 402
Senate
    chairman's mark, 5
    election results, 81–82
    filibusters, 311–325
    Foreign Relations Committee, 370
    hold system, 11, 13–14, 316–317
    individualism and partisanship, 2–5
    leadership, 2
    majority party, 166
    party unity in, 318 (figure)
    permissive rules of, 1–2
    Policy Committee, 182
    pre-floor process, 5–7
    sixty-vote requirement, 15–23
    six-year term, 83–84
    and state populations, 82–83
Senate Majority Leaders
    Dole, Bob, 183
    Frist, Bill, 183
    Lott, Trent, 183
    McConnell, Mitch, 184–185
    Reid, Harry, 183–184
Senate Rule 22. *See* Cloture rule
Seniority, Senate system, 4
Sensenbrenner, Jim, 249
Sequestration, 42
Sessions, 313
Sessions, Jeff, 469
Shelby, Richard, 9, 417
Shuster, Bud, 276, 278–279
Sinclair, Barbara, 130, 239
Six-year term in the Senate, 83–84
Slurge, 108
Soft-money, 103

See also campaign spending
Southern Democrats, 2, 30–31
Speaker of the House
    Boehner, John, 41–47, 180–181
    Cannon, Joseph, 169–171
    Gingrich, Newt, 35–38, 178–179, 272, 286, 289
    Hastert, Dennis, 38–39, 179
    Pelosi, Nancy, 39–40, 180
    Reed, Thomas Brackett, 169–171
    Ryan, Paul, 51, 181
    Sam Rayburn, 30
    Wright, James, 32–35, 178
    See also House of Representatives
Special rules, 293
Spooner, John, 172
Stalemate. *See* legislative deadlock
Stalemate (Binder), 194–195, 199, 201, 217
State populations, and the Senate, 82–83
Stein, Jill, 452
Stevens, Ted, 337, 346, 348
Stokes, Donald, 120–121
Strategic retirements, 70–71
Structural advantage, 65
Structured rule, 295–296, 297
Sundquist, James, 191
Super PACs, 103–106, 104 (figure)
Supreme Court
    Brown v. Board, 31
    nominations, 474

Tea Party Republicans
    112th Congress (2011-2012), 41
    efforts to repeal the ACA, 242, 249–251
    passage of the ACA, 241–242, 248
Textbook Congress, 29–30
Thurber, James, 333
Thurmond, Strom, 183
Thurmond rule, 410
Ticket splitting, behavioral trends, 92 (figure), 92–93, 93 (figure)
Topical legislation, 211
Transportation and Infrastructure Committee, 276
Transportation policy, deadlock in, 276–278

Treasury Department, 371
Truman, Harry, 421
Trump, Donald
    characteristics of, 470
    election of, 455–457
    mandate of, 470–472
    nomination for presidency, 451–452
    opposition to, 453–454
    presidential campaign, 128, 452–453
    white nationalism, 452, 471–472
    and women voters, 461
Trustee representation, 124
2008 economic crisis, 40
Two-tiered pluralism, 140, 154

Udall, Mo, 338
Unanimous consent agreements (UCAs), 11–12, 313
Unilateral action, 373–374, 442
United party government, 207
    vs. pure divided government Congresses, 225
Unorthodox lawmaking, 239
U.S. Chamber of Commerce, 104
U.S. Senators and Their World (Matthews 1960), 313

Visible filibusters, 12
Visible filibusters
    See also filibusters
Voters
    aggregation of votes, 94 (figure), 94–97, 95 (figure), 96 (figure), 97 (figure)
    behavioral trends, 92 (figure), 92–93, 93 (figure)

Walker, Jack, 262
War. *See* military policy, public support for, 423–425
Washington Post, 175
Watts, Mel, 322
White, Joseph, 288–289
White House Office (WHO), 371–374
White nationalism, 452, 471–472
Wilkerson, John, 243, 260, 262, 289
Willkie, Wendell, 425
Wilson, Woodrow, 176, 190, 312, 367
Withdrawn-coattails argument, 67
Women voters, 461–462
Wright, James, 32–35, 178

Young, Don, 276, 338
Young, Todd, 459